Winner, 2012 Prime Minister's Prize for Australian History

Winner, 2012 Victorian Prize for Literature, and Victorian Premier's Literary Awards (Prize for Non-Fiction)

Winner, 2012 ACT Book of the Year Award

Winner, 2012 Queensland Literary Awards (History Book Award)

Winner, 2012 Canberra Critics' Circle Award

Winner, 2011 Manning Clark House National Cultural Awards (Individual Category)

Shortlisted, 2013 NSW Premier's Literary Awards (Douglas Stewart Prize for Non-Fiction)

Shortlisted, 2012 Australian Book Industry Awards (General Non-Fiction Book of the Year)

Shortlisted, 2012 Australian Historical Association Prizes (Kay Daniels Award)

Praise for *The Biggest Estate on Earth*

'This bold book, with its lucid prose and vivid illustrations, will be discussed for years to come.'

Geoffrey Blainey, *Australian Book Review*

'Australians who care have suspected that Aboriginal land management was far more extensive and more sophisticated than whitefellas were prepared to believe... To read [Gammage's] scrupulous and painstaking account is to feel the scales fall from your eyes. Once you know what to look for, you can see it everywhere.'

Germaine Greer, *Sydney Morning Herald*

'*The Biggest Estate on Earth* is at once new history, new philosophy and detailed new ecology; a master historian's mature work, written with broad sight-lines and far perspectives. Its purpose is moral: in its own calm, cajoling way it may well do much to reshape the nation's intellectual landscape.'

Nicolas Rothwell, *The Australian*

'This is a massive research thesis yet it reads like a detective yarn as it sifts reams of evidence but allows the reader to reach their own revelation. It is never didactic and always entertaining.'

Bruce Pascoe, *Canberra Times*

'This is a beautiful and profound piece of writing, one that has importance for us all.'

Adrian Hyland, *The Age*

'Gammage's controversial thesis that Aboriginals created the biggest estate on Earth is going to be very difficult to dislodge.'

Tim Lloyd, *Adelaide Advertiser*

'*The Biggest Estate on Earth* is unquestionably a landmark in our understanding of how humans lived in Australia when the Europeans arrived.'

Peter Boyer, *Sunday Tasmanian*

'The still common assumption is that Aboriginal Australians in 1788 were simple hunter-gatherers who relied on chance for survival and moulded their lives to the country where they lived. Historian Bill Gammage might have driven the last nail into the coffin of this notion.'

Tony Stephens, *Sydney Morning Herald*

The BIGGEST ESTATE on EARTH

HOW ABORIGINES MADE AUSTRALIA

BILL GAMMAGE

ALLEN&UNWIN

This edition published in 2012
First published in 2011

Copyright © Bill Gammage 2011

All rights reserved. No part of this book may be reproduced or transmitted in any form or by any means, electronic or mechanical, including photocopying, recording or by any information storage and retrieval system, without prior permission in writing from the publisher. The Australian *Copyright Act 1968* (the Act) allows a maximum of one chapter or 10 per cent of this book, whichever is the greater, to be photocopied by any educational institution for its educational purposes provided that the educational institution (or body that administers it) has given a remuneration notice to Copyright Agency Limited (CAL) under the Act.

Allen & Unwin
83 Alexander Street
Crows Nest NSW 2065
Australia
Phone: (61 2) 8425 0100
Email: info@allenandunwin.com
Web: www.allenandunwin.com

Cataloguing-in-Publication details are available
from the National Library of Australia
www.trove.nla.gov.au

ISBN 978 1 74331 132 5

Internal design by Nada Backovic
Set in 11/15.5 pt Caslon Classico Regular by Post Pre-press Group, Australia
Printed in China at Everbest Printing Co.

20 19 18 17 16 15 14

*To the people of 1788,
whose land care is unmatched,
and who showed what it is to be Australian*

Fire, grass, kangaroos, and human inhabitants, seem all dependent on each other for existence in Australia; for any one of these being wanting, the others could no longer continue. Fire is necessary to burn the grass, and form those open forests . . . But for this simple process, the Australian woods had probably continued as thick a jungle as those of New Zealand or America . . .

THOMAS MITCHELL, SYDNEY, JANUARY 1847

. . . observing that the grass had been burnt on portions of the flats the Blacks said that the rain that was coming on would make the young grass spring up and that would bring down the kangaroos and the Blacks would spear them from the scrub.

OSWALD BRIERLY, EVANS BAY, CAPE YORK, 1 DECEMBER 1849

CONTENTS

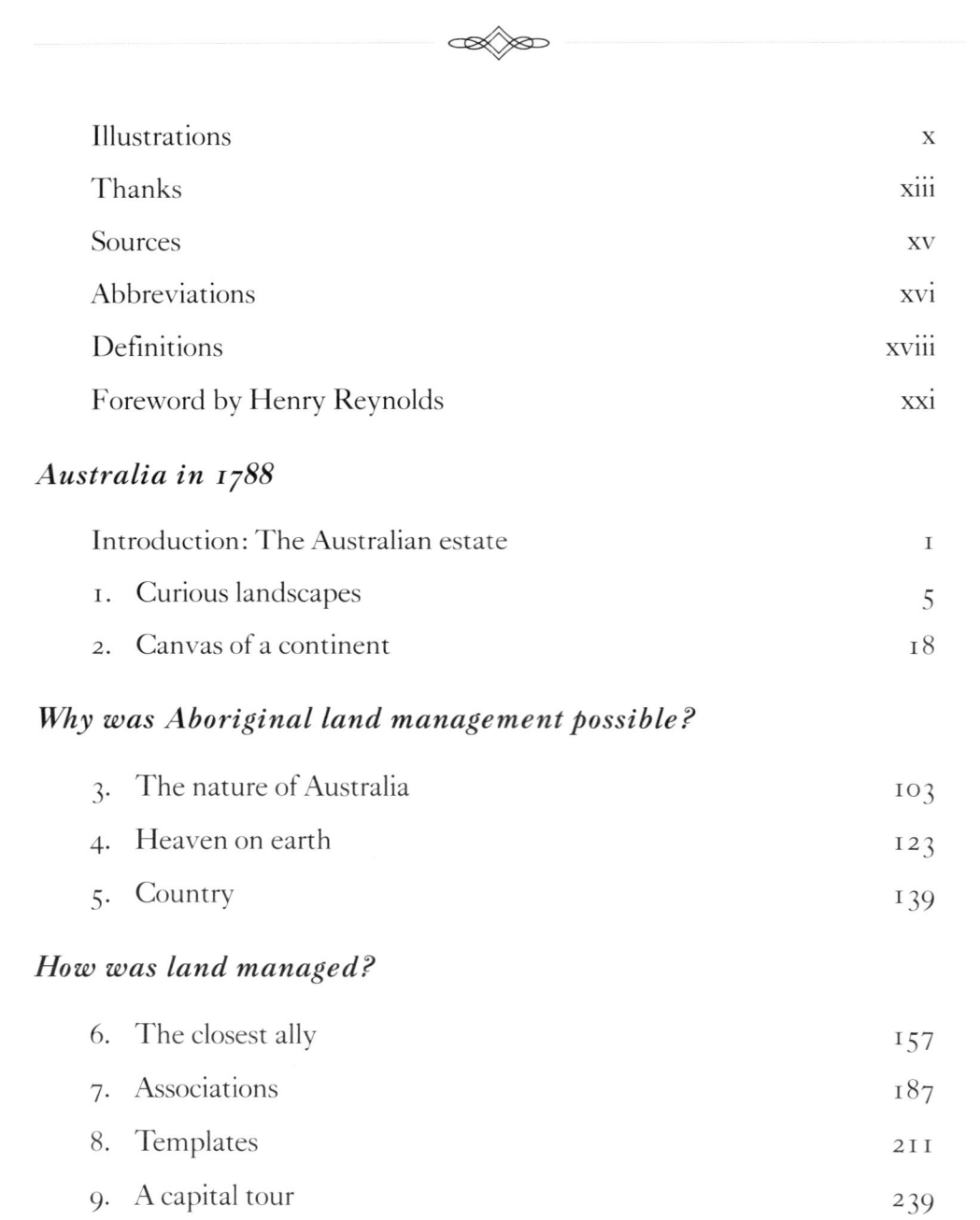

Illustrations	x
Thanks	xiii
Sources	xv
Abbreviations	xvi
Definitions	xviii
Foreword by Henry Reynolds	xxi

Australia in 1788

Introduction: The Australian estate	1
1. Curious landscapes	5
2. Canvas of a continent	18

Why was Aboriginal land management possible?

3. The nature of Australia	103
4. Heaven on earth	123
5. Country	139

How was land managed?

6. The closest ally	157
7. Associations	187
8. Templates	211
9. A capital tour	239
10. Farms without fences	281

Invasion

11. Becoming Australian   307

Appendix 1: Science, history and landscape   325
Appendix 2: Current botanical names for plants named with capitals in the text   343

Notes   347
Bibliography   379
Index   417

ILLUSTRATIONS

All illustrations are in chapter 2.

Pictures 1-4: Light

1. Swamp Gum	21
2. Yellow and Apple Box	23
3. White Gum	24
4. Blakely's Red Gum	25

Pictures 5-12: Fire

5. Snow Gum	26
6. Eucalypts and acacias	28
7. Ribbon Gum	29
8. River Red Gum	30
9. Snappy Gum	31
10-11. Kangaroo Grass	32-3
12. Eaglemont 1889	34

Pictures 13-22: Broad-scale fire

13. Endeavour River 1770	35
14-15. Esk River 1809 and 2008	37
16. Mills' Plains c1832-4	39
17. Onkaparinga 1838	40
18. Adelaide c1840	42
19. Ginninginderry c1832	44
20. Near Melbourne 1847?	46
21-2. Mt Eccles 1858 and 2007	47

Pictures 23-30: Arid-zone fire

23-4. Spencer's Kantju 1894 and 2005	49
25-6. Spencer's Uluru 1894 and 2005	51
27-8. Mountford's Uluru 1938 and 2005	53
29-30. Great Sandy Desert 1953 and 2005	55

Pictures 31-37: 1788 fire patterns—edges

31. Constitution Hill c1821	57
32. Lively's Bog 1998	58
33. Wannon Valley 1858	60
34. Wingecarribee River c1821	63
35. Swan River 1827	64
36. Mt Lindesay c1829	66
37. Milkshake Hills 2002	67

Pictures 38-41: 1788 fire patterns—patches and mosaics

38. Snowy Bluff 1864	68
39. Deadman's Bay c2001	69
40. Bunya Mountains 2003	71
41. Near Mudgeegonga 1963	73

Pictures 42-52: 1788 fire patterns—templates

42. Wineglass Bay c2001	74
43. Branxholm 1853	76
44–5. Cape York 1891	78–9
46–7. Gatcomb 1949 and 1984	81
48. Gatcomb 2002	83
49. Kadina 1874	84
50. Bundaleer 1877–8	86
51–2. Lake George 1821 and 2009	88–9

Pictures 53-58: Templates in use

53. Hunting kangaroos c1820	91
54. Using fire c1820	92
55. Spearing fish c1820	93
56. Barwon Valley 1847	94
57. King George Sound 1832	96
58. Somerset 1872	98

Picture 59: A European mosaic

59. Kangaroo Island 1983	99

THANKS

This book is about achievements of people I never knew. Far too late, I thank them.

Before everyone else I thank my wife Jan. She has always helped my work, but for this book more than any other she gave up much, with extraordinary patience and good humour over many years. She made the book possible.

I next thank three friends, clear-eyed readers: Henry Nix, Henry Reynolds and Denis Tracey, for polishing a draft and for help along the way. I thank Henry Reynolds especially, for years of encouragement, and for his generous foreword.

I thank the Humanities Research Centre at the ANU for hosting my research, and an ARC Fellowship for generously supporting part of it. I thank Pip Deveson, Leena Messina, Mike Powell, Jill Waterhouse and especially Gurol Baba for help with images, and I thank the staff of the archives and libraries listed in the Abbreviations, especially my friends at the National Library of Australia. I thank Elizabeth Weiss at Allen & Unwin for her promptness, courtesy and efficiency.

The following list makes clear how impossible it is to thank as they deserve the many other people who helped me:

ACT: Bryant Allen, Don Baker, John Banks, Tim Bonyhady, Ian Brooker, Phil Cheney, Bill Clarke, Bob Cooper, Jan Cooper, Helen Digan, Mary Eagle, Brian Egloff, Barney Foran, Kevin Frawley, Alison French, Ian Gammage, Jake Gillen, Jack Golson, Janda Gooding, Peter Greenham, Chris Gregory, Niel Gunson, Stuart Hay, Luise Hercus, Robin Hide, Geoff Hope, Iain McCalman, Neal McCracken, Kim McKenzie, George Main, Sally May, John Merritt, Howard Morphy, John Mulvaney, Daphne Nash, Hank and Jan Nelson, Jim Noble, Penny Olsen, David Paterson, Nic Peterson, Tony Vale, Gerry Ward, Elizabeth Williams.

France: Laurent Doussot.

NSW: John Blay, Denis Byrne, Janet and Jim Fingleton, Nic Gellie, David Goldney, Helen Harrison, David Horton, Christine Jones, Ian Lunt, John McPhee, Chris Moon, Eric Rolls and Elaine van Kempen, Yuji and Hiroko Satake, Rob Sellick, Stan Walton, Peter and Bunty Wright.

NT: Dave Bowman, Jim Cameron, David Carment, Stuart Duncan, Ted Egan, Margaret Friedl, Punch and Marilyn Hall, Dick Kimber, Chris Materne, Julia Munster and Sam Spiropoulis, Vern O'Brien, Tom Vigilante, James Warden, Samantha Wells.

NZ: Ian Campbell.

Queensland: John Bradley, Athol Chase, Mac Core, Arch Cruttenden, Russell Fairfax, Rod Fensham, Bill Kitson, Kate Lovett (Steve Parish Publishing), Yuriko Nagata and Terry Martin, Melissa Nursey-Bray, Anna Shnukal, Brian and Jenny Wright.

SA: Carmel and Eric Bogle, Philip Clarke, Rob Foster, Tom Gara, Diana Honey, Rob Linn, Leith MacGillivray, John and Sue McEntee, Jean and Ron Nunn, Bernie O'Neil, Mick Sincock, Peter Sutton.

Tasmania: Jayne Balmer, Mick Brown, Graeme Calder, Sib Corbett, Fred Duncan, Louise Gilfedder, Andrew Gregg, David Hansen, Margaret Harman, Bill Jackson, Jamie Kirkpatrick, Greg Lehman, Jon Marsden-Smedley, Bruce McIntosh, Bill Mollison, Mike Pemberton, Edwina and Mike Powell, Mitchell Rolls, Lindy Scripps, Bill Tewson, Ivor and Sheila Thomas.

Victoria: Corinne Clark, Peter Coutts, Julia Cusack, Beth Gott, Jeanette Hoorn, Lynne Muir, Mathew Phelan, Judy Scurfield, Frances Thiele, Ian Thomas.

WA: Geoff Bolton, Jack Bradshaw, Neil Burrows, Peter Gifford, Ian Rowley, George Seddon, Tom Stannage, Roger Underwood, Dave Ward.

SOURCES

Few sources here come directly from Aboriginal people. Over the years Aboriginal friends and acquaintances in Narrandera, Alice Springs, the Coorong and northern Tasmania have taught me, but this book discusses all Australia, and I had neither the time nor the presumption to interrogate people over so great an area on matters they value so centrally. Instead there are three main source categories:

- writing and art depicting land before Europeans changed it
- anthropological and ecological accounts of Aboriginal societies today, especially in the Centre and north
- what plants tell of their fire history and habitats.

I have tried to exclude sources reflecting such natural determinants as soil or salt rather than human impact. No doubt I have not always succeeded. To compensate for this, and to defuse a charge deniers of Aboriginal impact make—that there is no evidence for it—I have accumulated a wide range of sources. They come from across Australia—not from every corner, but from more than enough corners to join the dots, for no people would apply such detailed skill and knowledge for so long to most parts, yet not manage the rest, or not know how. I hope the sheer volume and detail of the evidence might support the book's central argument: that the 1788 landscape was made, that so many records over so great an area cannot all be wrong.

They are a fraction of what exists. Much lies unread or unnoted in the historical record which might answer important questions about Aboriginal land management. At least some answers are lost, but I believe more is possible than this book offers. It is only a start. It merely offers clues on what to look for on the ground and in the records, so that one day Australians might see more clearly the great story of their country.

ABBREVIATIONS

1. Institutions

AGSA	Art Gallery of South Australia, Adelaide
ANU	Australian National University, Canberra
AOT	Archives Office of Tasmania, Hobart
DENR	Dept of Environment & Natural Resources, Adelaide
ERM	Lands Museum, Dept of Environment & Resource Management, Brisbane
FPB	Forest Practices Board, Hobart
FT	Forestry Tasmania, Hobart
JOL	John Oxley Library, SLQ, Brisbane
LPE	Place Names Unit, Dept Land, Planning and Environment, Darwin
LTO	Lands Titles Office, Adelaide
ML	Mitchell Library, SLNSW, Sydney
MSA	Mortlock Library, SLSA, Adelaide
MV	Museum Victoria, Melbourne
NAA	National Archives of Australia, Canberra
NGA	National Gallery of Australia, Canberra
NLA	National Library of Australia, Canberra
NPWS	National Parks and Wildlife Service
OHU	Oral History Unit, NLA
PALM	Planning and Land Management, Perth
PWS	Parks and Wildlife Service
QSA	Queensland State Archives, Brisbane
SAM	South Australian Museum, Adelaide
SCMC	Supreme Court, Sydney (Miscellaneous Correspondence)
SL	State Library
SR	State Records
TMAG	Tasmanian Museum and Art Gallery, Hobart
UPGS	United Photo and Graphic Services, Blackburn, Victoria
VPRS	Victorian Public Records Service, Melbourne
WCAA	The Wesfarmers Collection of Australian Art, Perth

2. Sources

AAAS	Australian Association for the Advancement of Science
ADB	*Australian Dictionary of Biography*
BG	Bill Gammage
BPP	British Parliamentary Papers
c~	courtesy of
CCL	Commissioner of Crown Lands
ch	chapter
CSC	Colonial Secretary Correspondence
D	Diary
Des	Despatch(es)
FB	(Surveyors') Field Book(s)
HRA	*Historical Records of Australia*
HRNSW	*Historical Records of NSW*
J	Journal(s)
L	Letter(s)
LC	Legislative Council
Mfm	Microfilm
MS, ms	manuscript
N	Narrative
n	note(s)
np	no page numbers
P	Paper(s)
PP	Parliamentary Paper(s)
R	Report(s)
ref	reference
Rem	Reminiscence, Recollection
RSC	Report of Select Committee
SMH	*Sydney Morning Herald*
VDL	Van Diemen's Land
vol	volume

DEFINITIONS

1788
The century or so of first contact between Aborigines and Europeans after white settlement began at Sydney Cove. In that century the contact frontier moved on and out until almost all Australia was known to the newcomers. The great world later found people it did not know of, but they knew of it, and in various ways awaited or avoided its coming. '1788' includes these contacts.

'1788' is also shorthand for the beliefs and actions of Aboriginal people at the time of first contact. Thus "1788 fire" refers to the deliberate use of fire as a land management tool, while "since 1788" indicates a subsequent change to 1788 practice.

English stumbles to find apt words for 1788. Hundreds of pages try to define Aboriginal social units (tribe, horde, clan, mob, language group, family, kin) without achieving clarity or consensus. This book too uses words capable of imprecision:

animals
Usually includes birds, reptiles and insects.

association
Plant communities deliberately connected; a plant mosaic lacking enough evidence to identify as a template.

barren
1) treeless, or 2) useless to settlers.

bushfire
A fire accidentally or naturally lit. Some prefer the US word 'wildfire', but this implies that these fires are difficult or impossible to control, and that what they burn is wilderness. For Australia, and I believe elsewhere, both assumptions are wrong for 1788, and constricting, even defeatist, for today.

estate
Australia including Tasmania. Although comprising many ways of maintaining land, and managers mostly unknown to each other, this vast area was governed by a single religious philosophy, called in English the Dreaming. The Dreaming and its practices made the continent a single estate. In today's terms, it blended a continuum of like-minded managers, mixed farms, and national parks.

people
Aborigines. Europeans are called 'newcomers' or an equivalent. It seems unjust to deprive Aborigines of the most common term for humanity simply because Europeans turned up, especially at a time when they were the only Australians. Similarly I use tribal names very cautiously, especially in the south. As Mike Powell's article shows (see bibliography), these are mostly European inventions, not always sensibly related to 1788 life or land management. Where tribal names are entrenched I do use them; otherwise I use a more general term, such as 'Tasmanians'. For a full list see under 'Aboriginal groups' in the index.

pick
Soft, green, short grass, high in nitrogen, preferred by all grass grazers.

predictable
Capable of being anticipated; certain assuming no adverse influence.

template
Plant communities deliberately associated, distributed, sometimes linked to natural features, and maintained for decades or centuries to prepare country for day-to-day working. Examples are a grassy clearing or plain beside water and ringed by open forest, an alternating grass—forest circuit or sequence designed to rotate where grazing animals fed, and a big open plain with little or no tree cover to deter animals but promote plants. To work well, templates for animals had to be kept suitably apart, but linked into a network ultimately universal (ch 8).

universal
The extent of the Dreaming; the limits of the imagined world; Australia including Tasmania; the Australian estate.

FOREWORD

Henry Reynolds

At the time of Federation there was an upsurge of interest in the Aborigines. Scientists like Baldwin Spencer and enthusiastic amateur ethnographers like FJ Gillen, RH Mathews and AW Howitt carried out research in remote parts of Australia and examined relevant written records which had been accumulating over the previous century. There was a sense of urgency about their work. Ascendant evolutionary theory suggested that the Aborigines were destined to be driven to imminent extinction by the iron laws of evolution. The widely observed decline of the indigenous population appeared to confirm evolution's death sentence. The anthropological information sought by the scholars was endangered. It would soon disappear with the old tribesmen and women and be lost forever. And it was irreplaceable because it was assumed to embody evidence about the pre-historic origins of humankind, about language, religion, art, marriage and other social institutions. This gave these Australian studies international importance. Scientific journals in Europe and North America clamoured to publish their findings, and books on the Aborigines found readers among the intellectual elites, who used the raw ethnological data to weave sophisticated theories about human nature. But the scholars of this time had no interest in the actual Aboriginal communities living among the colonists in fringe camps or on sheep and cattle stations. They were seen as people who had lost both their racial purity and their pristine culture. They were also inclined to be irreverent and un-cooperative.

The twentieth century saw a slow process among settler Australians of re-assessment of Aboriginal society. Many currents came together. Evolutionary theory slowly lost its grip on Western intellectuals. Racial theories, increasingly challenged, were totally discredited by the human disasters in Europe. De-colonisation set up a tidal wave of change, and the adoption of human rights by the fledgling United Nations challenged the whole idea of a white Australia. By the 1920s it had become obvious that Aboriginal communities in settled Australia were growing, giving rise to anxiety about the so-called 'half-caste' problem. Political activists of varying political colours took up the Aboriginal cause. Scholarship slowly and unevenly responded to these swirling currents.

In the 1930s anthropologists began working in many parts of the country. They favoured tribal society in the more remote areas but they also worked with communities that had been in close contact with Europeans for many years. The emphasis was now on the way Aboriginal society functioned rather than a search for ancient roots. Linguists followed in the anthropologists' tracks to record traditional languages. Appreciation of indigenous culture followed. Members of the Jindyworobak Movement of the late 1930s and 1940s sought to incorporate Aboriginal culture into their poetry, painting and music. The emergence of schools of traditional painting in Arnhem Land, the Central Desert and eventually in many regions of the country was one of the most extraordinary cultural developments in late twentieth-century Australia, and one which attracted international interest. From the 1960s there was a brilliant period of archaeology and in a few years the presumed date of human occupation was pushed back from 10,000 years to 40,000 and 50,000. Prehistorians celebrated the Aborigines as the discoverers and explorers of the continent. The 1970s saw historians belatedly recasting the national story and thereby ending what had been called the great Australian silence. Of even greater significance was the revolution in Australian jurisprudence carried through by the High Court in the Mabo judgment of 1992 and the Wik judgment of 1996.

Aboriginal land management was another matter opened up for reconsideration. The common view in the early years of the twentieth century was that, given the uniquely primitive nature of indigenous society, the Aboriginal nations had moulded their way of life to the country in which they lived. This view was fortified, and sentimentalised, by a generation of white Australians who learnt of the intimate relationship which Aboriginal people had with their homelands. It was a view favoured by the emerging environmental movement, which had found a society that lived in harmony with nature and trod lightly on the land. A radically different view of Aboriginal land management began to emerge in the 1970s and 1980s. The prehistorian Rhys Jones and the historian Sylvia Hallam both explored the way that Aborigines used fire to alter patterns of vegetation.

This pioneering work has been vindicated in Bill Gammage's great book *The Biggest Estate on Earth: How Aborigines Made Australia*. It is the result of over ten years of reading in libraries and archives, of investigation of paintings and photographs, and travel across the continent. The amount of research is daunting. His bibliography contains over 1500 books, theses and articles. And this was only a selection of the items read as part of the project. It is the sort of research that will become increasingly rare as scholars are pressured to produce quick results from carefully directed research.

Bill manages to compress his vast amount of research into an entirely engaging narrative which has moments of memorable eloquence. His conclusions will come as a revelation to many readers. He establishes without question the scale of Aboriginal land management, the intelligence, skill and inherited knowledge which informed it. It dramatically changes the way we will in the future see Australian history. It is one of the half dozen or so works which in the last two generations have transformed the way settler Australians understand the world that existed before the European invasion. His achievement is not solely based on literary texts. Reading is only part of the endeavour. This other element is Bill's profound understanding of the Australian environment, which is rare among historians. He is able in a unique way to see the landscape historically; to read it back to what it was like in the past. Anyone who has shared a journey across any part of Australia with Bill will return with intimations about the possibility of seeing the country in a totally new way.

One big question remains. Bill's research is based on hundreds of observers who wrote about the Australian environment. He goes as far back as Abel Tasman in 1642 in his search for evidence. Much had accumulated by the middle of the nineteenth century and yet the synthesis had not been consummated. Why did it take so long to draw the obvious conclusions? The obsession with Aboriginal backwardness was just too useful to be cast aside. Bill's evidence must be the final blow to the comforting colonial conceit that the Aborigines made no use of their land. But his message is not only one of deep regret for what was lost but also a call to his contemporaries to continue the task of 'learning' the continent. His final sentence is both challenge and exhortation: *If we are to survive, let alone feel at home, we must begin to understand our country. If we succeed, one day we might become Australian.*

The BIGGEST ESTATE on EARTH

Australia in 1788

INTRODUCTION

The Australian estate

This book describes how the people of Australia managed their land in 1788. It tells how this was possible, what they did, and why. It argues that collectively they managed an Australian estate they thought of as single and universal (see Definitions).

The Australian estate was remarkable. No estate on earth was on so much earth. Including Tasmania, Australia occupies 7.7 million square kilometres, and straddles great diversity. Its southern neighbour is the Antarctic, its northern third is in the tropics. Cape Byron in the east is 4000 kilometres from Shark Bay in the west, and the land between includes Australia's most productive farmland and its biggest deserts. Southeast Cape in the south is 3700 kilometres from Cape York in the north, yet both support rainforest. Moving inland from the coast, annual rainfall can decline by an inch a mile (15 mm/km), although rain rarely falls predictably anywhere. Over most of the continent highly erratic rainfall is what is predictable. Europeans have yet to get the hang of this. They know that seasons are not always seasonal, and in the north they recognise a Wet and a Dry, but in the south they mark the four seasons their ancestors brought from Europe. This convention recognises temperature but not rainfall, yet rain is central to managing the Australian estate.

The book rests on three facts about 1788.

1. Unlike the Britain of most early observers, about 70 per cent of Australia's plants need or tolerate fire (ch 3). Knowing which plants welcome fire, and when and how much, was critical to managing land. Plants could then be burnt and not burnt in patterns, so that post-fire regeneration could situate and move grazing animals predictably by selectively locating the feed and shelter they prefer.
2. Grazing animals could be shepherded in this way because apart from humans they had no serious predators. Only in Australia was this so.

3. There was no wilderness. The Law—an ecological philosophy enforced by religious sanction—compelled people to care for all their country. People lived and died to ensure this (ch 4).

The Law prescribed that people leave the world as they found it. 1788 practice was therefore conservative, but this did not impose static means. On the contrary, an uncertain climate and nature's restless cycles demanded myriad practices shaped and varied by local conditions. Management was active not passive, alert to season and circumstance, committed to a balance of life.

The chief ally was fire. Today almost everyone accepts that in 1788 people burnt random patches to hunt or lure game. In fact this was no haphazard mosaic making, but a planned, precise, fine-grained local caring. Random fire simply moves people's guesses about game around the country. Effective burning, on the other hand, must be predictable. People needed to burn and not burn, and to plan and space fires appropriately (ch 7). Of course how a pattern was made varied according to terrain and climate: heath, rainforest and Spinifex each require different fire. Yet in each the several purposes of fire remained essentially the same. A plant needs fire to seed, an animal likes a forest edge, a man wants to make a clearing. Means were local, ends were universal. Successfully managing such diverse material was an impressive achievement; making from it a single estate was a breathtaking leap of imagination.

Edward Curr glimpsed this. Born in Hobart in 1820, pioneer squatter on the Murray, he knew people who kept their old customs and values, and he studied them and their country closely in the decades of their dispossession. After 42 years in Victoria he wrote, 'it may perhaps be doubted whether any section of the human race has exercised a greater influence on the physical condition of any large portion of the globe than the wandering savages of Australia'.[1] He knew that linking 'wandering savages' to an unmatched impact on the land startlingly contradicted everything Europeans thought about 'primitive' people. He deliberately defied a European convention that wanderers barely touched the land, and were playthings of nature.

Some researchers still think this (appendix 1). They give ground grudgingly on whether Aborigines altered the land. They argue or assume that nature alone made the 1788 landscape, perhaps via lightning fires.[2] There is no evidence that lightning caused most bushfires in 1788, nor that it could shape plant communities so curiously and invariably as to exclude human fire impacts. Today lightning fire estimates vary from 0.01 per cent in western Tasmania to 30 per cent in Victoria, the latter an overestimate compared to 7–8 per cent for southern Australia and at most 18 per cent in the north. Only for western Queensland (80 per cent) does any researcher think lightning the major cause of fire.[3] Today's 'relatively low frequency of lightning strikes in Australia'[4] was even lower in 1788, because people lit so many fires then, leaving less fuel for lightning to ignite. If lightning fire distributed Australia's plants, outside towns and farms the distribution pattern should be similar now and in 1788. It is not.

Other researchers pioneered a growing awareness that 1788 fire was important to plant distribution, and might explain it. Although early observers like Thomas Mitchell and Ludwig Leichhardt knew that Aborigines fired grass to attract game, not until the 1960s did researchers begin to sense system and purpose in Aboriginal burning. From different perspectives RC Ellis, Sylvia Hallam, Bill Jackson, Rhys Jones, Peter Latz, Duncan Merrilees, Eric Rolls, Ian Thomas and others showed how extensively 1788 fire changed the land.[5]

Where possible people worked with the country, emphasising or mitigating its character. Sometimes this was all they could do. Mountains, rocks, rivers and most swamps were there to stay. Yet even in these places people might change the country. They dammed rivers and swamps. They cut channels through watersheds (ch 10). They used fire to replace one plant community with another.

What plants and animals flourished where related to their management. As in Europe land was managed at a local level. Detailed local knowledge was crucial. Each family cared for its own ground, and knew not merely which species fire or no fire might affect, but which individual plant and animal, and their totem and Dreaming links. They knew every yard intimately, and knew well the ground of neighbours and clansmen, sharing larger scale management or assuming responsibility for nearby ground if circumstance required.

They first managed country for plants. They knew which grew where, and which they must tend or transplant. Then they managed for animals. Knowing which plants animals prefer let them burn to associate the sweetest feed, the best shelter, the safest scrub (ch 8). They established a circuit of such places, activating the next as the last was exhausted or its animals fled. In this way they could predict where animals would be. They travelled to known resources, and made them not merely sustainable, but abundant, convenient and predictable. These are loaded words, the opposite of what Europeans once presumed about hunter-gatherers.

A key difference between how farmers and how Aborigines managed land was the scale of 1788 enterprise. Clans could spread resources over large areas, thereby better providing for adverse seasons, and they had allies, sometimes hundreds of kilometres away, who could trade or give refuge. They were thus ruled less by nature's whims, not more, than farmers. It is unwise to think of 'normal seasons' in Australia, but in seasons which suited farming, 1788 management made resources as predictable as farming, and in times of drought and flood made them more predictable. Mere sustainability was not enough. Abundance was normal.

This was a tremendous advantage. It made plants easier to concentrate, to burn, to let fallow, to make park-like, to share. It made life comfortable. Like landowning gentry, people generally had plenty to eat, few hours of work a day, and much time for religion and recreation. A few Europeans recognised this (ch 11), but for most it was beyond imagining. They thought the landscape natural and they preferred it so.

They did not see, but their own records show how carefully made, how unnatural, was Aboriginal Australia. It is time to look again.

Three rules directed 1788 management:

- Ensure that all life flourishes.
- Make plants and animals abundant, convenient and predictable.
- Think universal, act local.

These rules imposed a strict ecological discipline on every person. A few non-Aborigines have begun to think this worthwhile, but even on a district scale, let alone all Australia, none can do it.

How Aborigines did it is the story of this book.

I

Curious landscapes

In 1770 Lieutenant James Cook, HMS *Endeavour*, saw something remarkable along Australia's east coast: the trees had 'no under wood'. On 1 May he 'made an excursion into the country which we found diversified with woods, lawns and marshes; the woods are free from underwood of every kind and the trees are at such a distance from one another that the whole country or at least a great part of it might be cultivated without being obliged to cut down a single tree'.[1] The land equally surprised Joseph Banks, gentleman on board. 'The country tho in general well enough clothed', he wrote, 'appeared in some places bare. It resembled in my imagination the back of a lean Cow, covered in general with long hair, but nevertheless where her scraggy hip bones have stuck out further than they ought accidental rubs and knocks have entirely bared them of their share of covering.' Hilltops, Banks was saying, were bare. Trees were on lower slopes, but 'were not very large and stood separate from each other without the least under wood'.[2] Sydney Parkinson, Banks' draughtsman, echoed his employer: 'The country looked very pleasant and fertile; and the trees, quite free from underwood, appeared like plantations in a gentleman's park.'[3]

In the Whitsundays further north, Cook saw 'land on both the Main and the Islands . . . diversified with woods and Lawns that looked green and pleasant'.[4] There a century later naval commander GS Nares named Grassy Island, because it was grass-covered with a few trees on its summit. About half the island is tree-covered now. Nares saw other grassy Whitsunday islands, but except where cleared all are wooded today.[5]

On 23 August Cook summed up the east coast. It was 'cloathed with woods, long grass, shrubs, plants &ca. The mountains or hills are chequered with woods and lawns. Some of the hills are wholly covered with flourishing trees; others but thinly, and the few that are on them are small and the spots of lawns or Savannahs are rocky and barren.'[6] This was no shipside impression. Among other landings, Cook spent seven weeks at Cooktown (picture 13).

These remarks are curious. Untended east coast bush today has much underwood and no bare hills, let alone woods chequered with lawns. Yet in the years to come Cook's words were repeated again and again, and Europeans fresh-seeing the land made Parkinson's comparison with a gentleman's park more often than any other.

Across Australia newcomers saw grass where trees are now, and open forest free of undergrowth now dense scrub. South of Hobart, Abel Tasman saw land 'pretty generally covered with trees, standing so far apart that they allow a passage everywhere ... unhindered by dense shrubbery or underwood'.[7] This is dense forest now: why not then? Of course in 1788 there were thick scrubs, impenetrable eucalypts, rainforest walls, but this sharpens the puzzle, for often they gave way abruptly to grass. In 1824 William Hovell reported moving suddenly from grass into tangles of undergrowth and fallen timber piled higher than his horses, almost impossible to walk through, let alone ride.[8] Tasmanian Buttongrass, common in boggy country, also occurs where rainforest should be. How did it get there? Not how does it stay there now, but how did it get there in the first place, despite no change in soil, aspect or elevation from adjacent rainforest? White Grass likes open country, yet can be found under trees. For this to happen, once open country became treed. How? In 1788 Australia had more grass, more open forest, less undergrowth and less rainforest than made sense to Europeans. It was another country.

There is a tandem puzzle. Typically, grass grew on good soil and trees on poor (ch 7). In 1826 Robert Dawson described country behind Port Stephens (NSW) as

> in general heavily timbered, and as usual, without underwood. After crossing a deep, and in some places a dry channel, which in rainy seasons would be called a river, the soil began to improve. The country gradually became less heavily timbered, and the views more extensive. This was in accordance with what I had been previously led to expect, and fully confirmed by my former observations, that the poorest soils contained more than treble the number of trees that are found in the best soil, being also much longer and taller. This, like most other things in this strange country, is, I believe, nearly the reverse of what we find in England.[9]

In South Australia Edward John Eyre, a most competent observer, wrote, 'For the most part we passed through green valleys with rich soil and luxuriant pasturage. The hills adjoining the valley were grassy, and lightly wooded on the slopes facing the valley;

towards the summits they became scrubby, and beyond, the scrub almost invariably made its appearance',[10] and Charles Sturt observed,

> As regards the general appearance of the wooded portion of this province, I would remark, that excepting on the tops of the ranges where the stringy-bark grows; in the pine forests, and where there are belts of scrub on barren or sandy ground, its character is that of open forest without the slightest undergrowth save grass . . . In many places the trees are so sparingly, and I had almost said judiciously distributed as to resemble the park lands attached to a gentleman's residence in England.[11]

Near Gundagai (NSW) in the 1840s two tourists found 'beautiful meadow-land . . . bounded by sloping ranges of hills covered with grass, and thinly timbered. Generally speaking, all fertile lands in Australia appear to be characterized by these beautiful features.'[12] Generally speaking that was so in the 1840s, but not now. Why did the most fertile land grow the fewest trees?[13]

A few travellers puzzled at this. In 1831 William Govett saw summits behind Sydney 'clothed with grass, which circumstance, considering the barrenness and excessive sterility which pervades all the connecting ridges, and that region of the mountains, is certainly very extraordinary . . . In general . . . the ranges are covered with short timber and scrub.'[14] 'The great peculiarity here', RJ Sholl wrote northeast of Broome (WA), 'as well as in the land to the north of the Glenelg, is the total absence of undergrowth bushes; between the widely separated thin and short trees there is nothing but grass and creepers. Let it be thin or thick, good or bad, tall or short, still it is grass.'[15] At Omeo (Vic) about 1843 Henry Haygarth portrayed his perplexity vividly:

> The gloomy forest had opened, and about two miles before, or rather beneath us—for the ground, thinly dotted with trees, sloped gently downwards—lay a plain about seven miles in breadth. Its centre was occupied by a lagoon . . . On either side of this the plain, for some distance, was as level as a bowling-green, until it was met by the forest, which shelved picturesquely down towards it, gradually decreasing in its vast masses until they ended in a single tree. In the vicinity of the forest the ground was varied by gentle undulations, which, as they intersected each other, formed innumerable grassy creeks and open flats, occasionally adorned with native honeysuckles and acacias . . . Two

> remarkable conical hills, perfectly free from timber, rose in the middle of the largest plain . . . The whole, as far as the eye could reach, was clothed with a thick coat of grass, rich and luxuriant, as if the drought, so destructive elsewhere, had never reached this favoured spot.
>
> It was Omio [sic] plain. By what accident, or rather by what freak of nature, came it there? A mighty belt of forest, for the most part destitute of verdure, and forming as uninviting a region as could well be found, closed it on every side for fifty miles; but there, isolated in the midst of a wilderness of desolation, lay this beautiful place, so fair, so smiling.[16]

Omeo's historian wrote,

> When the first white men came to the Omeo Plains all the best country was treeless. On the lower foothills which bordered the plains, there were large gum trees, standing singly, and odd clumps of sally wood . . . northward and almost to the tablelands, about six miles away, the gum timber was dense, and known as The Forest,[17]

and Thomas Walker thought the valley 'the prettiest piece of country I have seen since leaving the Murrimbidgee [sic], very thinly timbered, indeed in many parts clear, with here and there interspersed a few trees or a clump or a belt, the soil sound and good . . . the sward close . . . the whole being intersected by lagoons: it is quite like a gentleman's park in England'.[18]

Other Gippsland travellers saw chains of plains,[19] and in 1834 John Lhotsky confessed of similar chains between Gundaroo and Michelago (NSW):

> It is . . . a most remarkable, but not very easily explicable fact, that they are altogether destitute of trees of any kind, and only on the secondary hills or banks, which divide their plications, are some gum-trees thinly scattered, whereas large timber covers the main ranges . . . it is difficult to understand, how it is, that there is not even a vestige of incipient sylvification in the plains and downs themselves.[20]

Charles von Hugel, a botanist, stated, 'A plain like the Goulburn Plain is certainly an interesting phenomenon . . . as in the case of all the plains mentioned earlier, the soil is good—why is it that no trees occur on it, seeing that they grow splendidly when planted? There is no easy answer to this question.'[21] In the same district Govett observed in 1832,

> The park-like forests of this County are relieved in many parts by plains, or portions of ground altogether destitute of timber. These plains vary in extent and form, some are hilly and undulating, while others appear a mere flat, and the generality of them possess a good soil. It appears as if the seed of the tree has never been, as it were, scattered upon them, for it cannot be disputed, that the trees which surround these plains would also vegetate upon them.[22]

A century later TM Perry investigated these plains. He could find no soil distinctive to them or to the woodland around. Each could be 'on identical soils'. He could not say why.[23] This was land where trees grow now.

Soil can regulate which plants grow where, yet Sturt saw trees vanish without any soil change, and puzzled at 'the sudden manner in which several species are lost at one point, to re-appear at another more distant, without any visible cause for the break'.[24] In the Dorrigo (NSW) brush in 1894 Joseph Maiden reported 'plains which simply consist of grass-land, entirely destitute of trees, or dotted about as in a gentleman's park. Usually the edge of the scrub and of the plain are as sharply defined as it is possible for them to be, as though a Brobdingnagian with mighty sickle, had there finished his reaping.'[25] G Marks investigated in 1911, and found 'open flats that never grew timber in their virgin state, yet they have similar soils to the timber areas that surrounded them, and apparently are identical in their chemical composition and mechanical nature'.[26] By then Leichhardt had discounted soils. At Calvert's Plains on the Dawson (Qld) he noted,

> It was interesting to observe how strictly the scrub kept to the sandstone and to the stiff loam lying upon it, whilst the mild black whinstone [basalt] soil was without trees, but covered with luxuriant herbs and grasses; and this fact struck me as remarkable, because, during my travels in the Bunya country of Moreton Bay, I found it to be exactly the reverse: the sandstone spurs of the range being there covered with an open well grassed forest, whilst a dense vine brush extended over the basaltic rock.

A month later he added, 'It is remarkable that that part of the range which is composed of basalt, is a fine open forest, whereas the basaltic hills of the large valley are covered with a dense scrub.'[27] That stumped him.

In the South Australian mallee in 1839, stumps bewildered Eyre:

> In some parts of the large plains we had crossed in the morning, I had observed traces of the remains of timber, of a larger growth than any now found in the same vicinity, and even in places where none at present exists. Can these plains of such very great extent, and now so open and exposed, have been once clothed with timber? and if so, by what cause, or process, have they been so completely denuded, as not to leave a single tree within a range of many miles? In my various wanderings in Australia, I have frequently met with very similar appearances; and somewhat analogous to these, are the singular little grassy openings, or plains, which are constantly met with in the midst of the densest Eucalyptus scrub . . . Forcing his way through dense, and apparently interminable scrub . . . the traveller suddenly emerges into an open plain, sprinkled over with a fine silky grass, varying from a few acres to many thousands in extent, but surrounded on all sides by the dreary scrub he has left. In these plains I have constantly traced the remains of decayed scrub—generally of a larger growth than that surrounding them—and occasionally appearing to have grown very densely together . . . The plains found interspersed among the dense scrubs may probably have been occasioned by fires, purposely or accidentally lighted by the natives in their wanderings, but I do not think the same explanation would apply to those richer plains where the timber has been of a large growth and the trees in all probability at some distance apart—here fires might burn down a few trees, but would not totally annihilate them over a whole district, extending for many miles in every direction.[28]

Attempts today to explain these puzzles can be unsatisfying. Researchers write of soil boundaries, cracking clay, rain shadows, nutrient supply, frost and aspect. No doubt each applies somewhere, but none where trees grow now but not then. Other explanations—bushfire, salination, overgrazing—may sometimes be cogent, but rarely for sources so soon after newcomers came.

Even particular trees might be curiously placed. Surprisingly often early Europeans crossed rivers and creeks via 'fallen' trees. Records mention twelve in Tasmania, at least seven in Western Australia, four in Victoria, three in New South Wales and one in Queensland, including over rivers like the Murray, Lachlan, Goulburn, Gordon and Tasmania's Emu, 'the widest and deepest river we had seen since leaving Circular

Head'.[29] It is hard to imagine a tree spanning those rivers now, or even a decent creek, yet in southwest Australia JG Bussell crossed several in one journey. Mary Gilmore said Aborigines dropped trees deliberately, by undermining their roots: she saw it done to cross Wollundry Lagoon at Wagga (NSW).[30]

People may also have made straight tree lanes. Some led to initiation grounds. A ground near Mildura (Vic) was approached by a straight line of at least eight marked gums; another on the Macquarie by a 'long straight avenue of trees, extended for about a mile, and these were carved on each side, with various devices'.[31] On the Murray in 1844, a 'natural avenue of gum-trees extends . . . two rows of noble trees growing at almost equal distances; the open grassy space between each row being at least 100 feet in width: so regular are the intervals between them, that it is almost difficult, at first sight, to persuade one's self that they were not planted by the hand of man'.[32] In Tasmania Henry Hellyer 'ascended the most magnificent grass hill I have seen in this country, consisting of several level terraces, as if laid out by art, and crowned with a straight row of stately peppermint trees, beyond which there was not a tree for four miles along the grassy hills'.[33]

Other curious plant stories have emerged since 1788: fire tolerant and fire sensitive plants side by side, plants needing one fire regime beside plants needing another, newcomers driving a carriage or painting a view through country where trees make this impossible now. Clear of settlement, there may be more trees today than in 1788.

Bill Jackson calculated that 47 per cent of Tasmania should have been rainforest in 1788, but wasn't. It was eucalypt forest, scrub, heath or grass, sometimes with burnt rainforest logs beneath. Jackson instanced sites where other plants had displaced rainforest thousands of years ago, and remained ever since. He noted that Tasmania had much less rainforest than New Zealand's south island, a comparable climate, and concluded that deliberate burning best explained the difference.[34] 'The present distribution of floristic units in western Tasmania', Rhys Jones agreed, 'can be explained only in terms of both a high fire regime over a long period during the past, and the lifting of that pressure during the past hundred and fifty years.'[35]

One aspect puzzled Jackson. 'The boundaries between vegetation types at present seem remarkably stable . . . ', he wrote, so it was 'difficult to understand how such extensive areas of disclimax [unnatural] vegetation could arise in even [34,000 years—a 1999 estimate of how long people had been in Tasmania].'[36] If other plant communities had moved so little since they displaced rainforest, Jackson was saying, how did they displace so much, even in so long? He was thinking of random fire. Community boundaries would indeed be unstable if Tasmanians had burnt randomly, but they did not. They burnt with purpose, as the stable boundaries show. In northern Tasmania RC Ellis found that on the same soil the 'boundaries between rainforest, eucalypt forest and grassland were sharp and relatively stable'. Tasmanians selectively burnt rainforest back, then patrolled its edges.[37]

Some boundaries were moved. In Tasmania much rainforest has a curious feature: giant eucalypts overtop it. Hellyer described this south of Emu Bay:

> This is a horrid place [to] be in, neither Sun nor Moon to be seen, no part of the sky, being completely darkened by dripping Evergreens consisting of Myrtle, Sassafras, Ferntrees, immensely tall White Gum and Stringy-bark trees from 200 to 300 feet high and heaps of those which have fallen lying rotting one over the other from 10 to 20 feet high.[38]

Edward Curr, father of Victoria's Edward Curr, echoed Hellyer:

> enormous Stringy Bark Trees many of them three hundred feet high and thirty feet in circumference near the roots exclude the rays of the Sun and in the gloom which their shade creates those trees flourish which affect darkness and humidity . . . sassafras, dogwood, pepper trees, musk trees . . . in some situations blackwood of the best quality . . . fungi, mosses, lichens, ferns.[39]

Others noted the phenomenon,[40] and it can still be seen (pictures 46–8). In Tasmania's Mt Field National Park, opened in 1916 on land reportedly never logged, gullies and lower slopes support giant Swamp Gums, many scarred by fire. Under them is rainforest like Myrtle, Sassafras and Tree Fern, but no eucalypts. This is so too elsewhere in Tasmania: in the Styx, the Tarkine and the Blue Tier; and along the mainland's east coast, for example in the Bunya Mountains (Qld) (picture 40) and the McPherson Range (Qld/NSW). On Cape York Christie Palmerston saw many examples: in the upper Daintree he cut

> through one patch of jungle . . . which has splendid green grass all along the top, but the sides are covered with dense jungle. Kept to this spur to the eastward for about four miles, and cut my road through four patches of dense jungle . . . The timber on the open ridges was principally gum, oak, bloodwood, and honeysuckle, and there was splendid soil on all the mountains.[41]

All this is climax (natural) rainforest country. Eucalypt seedlings can't grow in rainforest: there is no light. How did those giant eucalypts get there? Clearly, when they were young there was no rainforest. Without fire rainforest has returned, so fire once kept it back. No stray marauder can do that. It needs determined burning when conditions are right, and in rainforest that is not often. Eucalypts topping rainforest indicate land people once went to great trouble, working against the country, to clear and keep clear.[42] Ancient eucalypts also stand above dense dry scrub with no young eucalypts. Such places have unnatural fire histories.[43]

Other tree or scrub distributions also signal this. Kurrajongs like open land, which they got in 1788 because the tap root survives fire and the tree re-sprouts from base buds, but on reserves today, fire regenerators like wattle and casuarina are choking the ancient stands, and no seedlings survive. In semi-arid country two fires every five years are needed to clear Hopbush, but it became a major pasture menace after 1788.[44] Fire made Tasmania's dry Buttongrass plains, yet beside them may stand pines which fire kills, some 2000 years old.[45] In Arnhem Land Blue Cypress needs mild fires every 2–8 years. Fires more frequent or intense kill or damage the stand; fires less frequent let it choke with saplings. Lightning or casual burning could neither commence nor maintain such a fire regime, yet the pine stood in vast tracts in 1788, and stopping 1788 fire caused a 'widespread crash' in its population.[46]

Even eucalypts, fire's torchbearers, show that unnatural fire once shaped the land. In 1788 no-one lived on Kangaroo Island (SA) so it was dense forest, but adjacent mainland was open woodland. Without fire Tuart forest develops a very dense undergrowth, but early Europeans reported it 'with plenty of grass'.[47] Spotted Gums near Batemans Bay (NSW) seem pristine, but are not half the size of scattered stumps among them. A century ago this was dairy country, and in 1788 open forest. Without fire it would be rainforest. In north Queensland what looked like primal rainforest was a dairy farm only 40 years before.[48] Other eucalypt forests have either a few giants scattered amid even-aged younger generations showing that once-open forest has thickened, or no old trees or stumps at all, indicating former grassland. Comparing forests in 1788, 1900, and 2000 would show a tree kaleidoscope, never the same.

Bushfire rarely clears eucalypts: they regenerate from lignotubers or beards—branches sprouting from epicormic (sub-bark) buds under stress from drought, fire, poison or axe. Only repeated fire clears them, cool (ch 6) and frequent in dry country, hot and infrequent in wet.[49] To convert eucalypts to grass people had to let fuel build up so fires could run, but burn often enough to kill seedlings, and maintain this over many generations until the old trees died. Burning most eucalypts every 2–4 years would in time make grassland, while burning a little less often would let some saplings survive and create open woodland. Both were common in 1788, some where trees and shrubs grow thickly now, others kept clear for so long that they have lost their seed stock and re-tree only by edge invasion, but re-tree they do.

Burning every 2–4 years promotes perennial grasslands. In 1788 these were common, which means they got with unbroken regularity the fires they needed. They also carried annuals, bulbs and tubers killed by hot fire, but needing ash to thrive, and cool fires every 2–3 years to open the perennial canopy. No random bushfire could strike that balance, or let such unlike partners flourish so widely. All have declined since 1788.[50] Spinifex country supports no food plants until it is burnt, when plants like Desert Raisin appear and fruit prolifically. Fruit production then drops annually until in about 5–8 years, depending on the rain, Spinifex has again smothered the plants.[51] Of twelve food plants in the Centre, five need fire, three tolerate it, and four are killed by it. All twelve flourished in 1788, so people managed them with different but adjacent fire regimes over many centuries. Peter Latz concluded that central Australians 'may have, quite literally, made the country what it is today by their use of fire'.[52] Many other plants need particular and distinct fire at the right time and with the right frequency and intensity (ch 3).

Most curious, these different fires made similar plant patterns across Australia. Crucial as burning was to help plants thrive, something more was going on. Dawson thought the country inland from Port Stephens

> truly beautiful: it was thinly studded with single trees, as if planted for ornament . . . It is impossible therefore to pass through such a country . . . without being perpetually reminded of a gentleman's park and grounds. Almost every variety of scenery presented itself. The banks of the river on the left of us alternated between steep rocky sides and low meadows: sometimes the river was fringed with patches of underwood (or brush, as it is called) . . . in Australia, the traveller's road generally lies through woods, which present a distant view of the country before him . . . The first idea is that of an inhabited and improved country, combined with the pleasurable associations of a civilized society.[53]

Trees planted as if for ornament, alternating wood and grass, a gentleman's park, an inhabited and improved country, a civilised land. Much of Australia was like this in 1788. After 'bush', a word from southern Africa, the most common word newcomers used about Australia was 'park'. This is striking, for three reasons. First, 'park' was not a word Europeans elsewhere associated with nature in 1788. Until 'national park' was coined in the United States much later, a park was man-made. Second, 'park' did not mean a public park as today, for few existed in Europe in 1788. It meant parks of the gentry, tastefully arranged private estates financed by people comfortably untroubled by a need to subsist. Third, few today see parks in Australia's natural landscape. Most use another US word with the opposite meaning: 'wilderness', which they imagine is untouched forest, beyond the pale, inhospitable. Farming people think like that.[54]

Parks chequered Australia. In New South Wales, south of Parramatta in April 1790 John Hunter 'walked through a very pleasant tract of country, which, from the distance the trees grew from each other, and the gentle hills and dales, and rising slopes covered with grass, appeared like a vast park'.[55] At Bong Bong Lachlan Macquarie named Throsby Park for its 'very park-like appearance'.[56] On the lower Talbragar John Oxley remarked, 'Many hills and elevated flats were entirely clear of timber, and the whole had a very picturesque and park-like appearance', and south of Walcha he found 'the finest open country, or rather park, imaginable: the general quality of the soil excellent'.[57] HT Ebsworth stated, 'Brush Wood is seldom to be seen where the soil is good, the land is lightly timbered, resembling a Gentleman's park occasionally, but the traveller is soon obliged to lose this idea by finding no Mansion at the end of the scene: He journeys on, as it were, from Park to Park all day', and near Port Stephens, 'The hills are everywhere clothed with wood, with constant verdure beneath it: unaccompanied by any Brush or Underwood, so that one is often forcibly reminded of Gentlemen's pleasure grounds.'[58] On the Hastings SA Perry noted, 'Most of the country . . . resembled extensive parks, the ground being gently undulated—thinly timbered without underwood—the bottoms rich alluvial land, & the whole covered with grass.'[59] In 1829 JB Wilson observed, 'So much has been said of the scenery in New South Wales resembling noble English domains.'[60]

It was the same in the other colonies. George Haydon recalled southwest Victoria as 'Beautiful plains with nothing on them but a luxuriant herbage, gentle rises with scarcely a tree, and all that park-like country . . . just enough wooded without inconveniencing the settler, whilst there is no lack of good timber for every purpose he may require.'[61] Near Mt Alexander the bush

> was typical of a great portion of the pastoral lands of Victoria. It consisted of undulating open forest-land, which has often been compared, without exaggeration, to the ordinary park-scenery of an English domain; the

only difference which strikes the eye being the dead half-burnt trees lying about. To bring it home to the comprehension of a Londoner, these open forest-lands have very much the appearance of Hyde Park and Kensington Gardens, presenting natural open glades like the east end of the former.[62]

In Tasmania John Hudspeth praised 'the beautiful and rich valley of Jericho... more like a gentleman's park in England, laid out with taste, than land in its natural state',[63] and George Frankland thought the Hampshire Hills afforded 'an instance of the beautiful natural decoration of some of our scenery, for that park like ground is entirely in a state of Nature'.[64] In Queensland Mitchell called the scenery near St George 'park-like and most inviting',[65] and JE Dalrymple admired the Valley of Lagoons 'with its rich grass, lofty gum-trees, and lotus-covered lagoons, till the hills on either side sweeping backwards, the beautiful open forest-ridges opened out in scattered timber, like an English park'.[66]

In South Australia JF Bennett described the Mt Barker district as 'fine undulating country... being partly wooded, partly clear... more the appearance of an immense park than anything that one would naturally expect to find in the wilds of an uncultivated land'.[67] John Morphett wrote, 'The country from Cape Jervis upwards is very picturesque and generally well timbered, but in the disposition of the trees more like an English park than what we could have imagined to be the character of untrodden wilds.'[68] WH Leigh thought the same district 'a wild but beautiful park, which reminded one of the domain of an English noble',[69] and the overlander Alexander Buchanan considered the west side of the Murray below the Big Bend 'really most beautiful, like a gentleman's park all the way. Fine plains and thinly studded with trees. Grass up to the horses' knees; indeed it was like riding through a ryegrass field.'[70]

East of Perth George Moore stated, 'To the distant eye the country has the appearance of being well wooded, but I should not say it was thickly timbered. In some places there are open plains that resemble well ordered parks.'[71] His neighbour William Shaw estimated, 'the trees [do] not exceed more than eight trees to an acre and [are] laid out by nature in the most park-like scenery'.[72] Near Bunbury John Barrow thought 'the whole country wears the appearance of an English park'.[73] In Arnhem Land near the end of a tough journey, Leichhardt could still note that plains 'which had been burnt some time ago, were now covered with delightful verdure. This, with the dark green belt of trees which marked the meanderings of several creeks, gave to this beautiful country the aspect of a large park.'[74]

Parks even dotted arid land. West of the Darling Daniel Brock wrote of Lake

Victoria, 'the banks present nothing but park-like scenery—groups of gum trees most tastefully disposed',[75] and Sturt found 'a beautiful park-like plain covered with grass, having groups of ornamental trees scattered over it . . . I never saw a more beautiful spot. It was, however, limited in extent, being not more than eight miles in circumference . . . encircled by a line of gum-trees.'[76] On Eyre Peninsula Eyre 'passed through a very pretty grassy and park-like country'.[77] North of Glen Helen in the Centre Egerton Warburton observed, 'The country today has been beautiful, with park-like scenery and splendid grass',[78] and in the west Petermanns Ernest Giles noted 'a fine piece of open grassy country—a very park-like piece of scenery . . . natives were burning the country'.[79] In even bleaker country north of Lake Eyre, JW Lewis met 'a plain thickly grassed and studded with fine green gum trees, most park-like in appearance'.[80][81]

Newcomers were often less flattering in describing Australia (harsh, barren, impenetrable, miserable, useless, sterile, waste), but parks were common and widely distributed. It might seem a small jump to think them man-made as in Europe. In fact the leap was so vast that almost no-one made it. Almost all thought no land in Australia private, and parks natural. To think otherwise required them to see Aborigines as gentry, not shiftless wanderers. That seemed preposterous.

The parks have gone. Overgrazing had a transforming impact. Parks were exactly what European land hunters wanted, and how heavily they overgrazed them is notorious.[82] The land cannot have been so heavily grazed in 1788. As well, 1788's controlled fire stopped when Europeans arrived. Today's bushfires devastate, and decimate species which flourished during millennia of Aboriginal burning. In heath near Kiama (NSW), ground parrots needed fire every 3–7 years to balance food and shelter. In 1788 they got this, but after 1788 they got infrequent hot fires, and by 1968 had died out. In the north the same may have happened to the paradise parrot. Since 1788 at least 23 mammal species have become extinct, and since about 1940 almost a third of world mammal extinctions have been in Australia. Recognising how extensive such changes have been, to plants, animals and the land, is crucial to understanding how constant and purposeful 1788 management was.[83]

2

Canvas of a continent

Some critics assume that early colonial artists romanticised their landscapes, making them inaccurate. Certainly artists like John Glover, Eugen von Guerard and Joseph Lycett squeezed scenes horizontally to fit more in, or embellished foregrounds with romantic but transient detail, but this does not make their landscapes inaccurate. Almost all the scenes reproduced here let me or others pinpoint where the artist sat to draw them.[1] A memorable example was when I was edging sideways across a paddock to align features in Lycett's *Lake George* (picture 51). Intent on the painting, I stepped unseeing onto stones of the road Joseph Wild's convicts built in 1820, which Lycett's foreground depicts. Lycett enlarged foreground rocks and mistook distant cloud shadows for land, but key features are easily identified. Von Guerard's accuracy is so well known that since the 1960s his 1855 *View of Moroit or Tower Hill* (Vic) has been used to recreate its vegetation.[2] His *North-east view from the top of Mount Kosciusko* (1866–8) is in fact a northeast view from the top of Mt Townsend, where his rocks are instantly recognisable. I found such accurate depiction so often that if I could not recognise a location I assumed I was in the wrong place.

Artists like Lewin and Glover (pictures 14, 16) took the trouble to say that their scenes were accurate. About 1825 Augustus Earle painted plains and open forest near Cluny (Tas), and commented that it showed 'the general appearance of the country in its natural state, perfect park scenery'.[3] In 1982–3 Dacre Smyth searched for 51 von Guerard locations and readily found almost all. He commented on 'how accurate von Guerard usually was in his delineation of the topography. At times I found that even the rocks in his foregrounds were still unmistakeable today.'[4]

Others had cause to be accurate. Allan Cunningham (picture 36) was a botanist; Robert Hoddle and Edward Bedwell (pictures 19–20, 58) were surveyors. Lycett painted under the patronage first of commandant James Wallis at Newcastle, then of Governor Lachlan Macquarie at Sydney. These officials wanted accuracy, to show people at home what Australia was like.

Tellingly, artists sometimes depict vegetation details we know are correct, but they as newcomers did not. The shoreline tree clumps in Lycett's *Lake George* turn out to be eucalypt stands protected from fire by granite outcrops. The small eucalypts, wattles and casuarinas in Glover's *Mills' Plains* regenerate just so after fire; the post-fire regrowth on the foreground eucalypt in his *The River Derwent and Hobart Town* (1831) is a detail no Englishman could invent. Even later, Fred McCubbin's *Down on his Luck* (1895) shows one big fire-scarred eucalypt amid dense wattle and sheoak regeneration, just as you would expect of southeast land released from fire.

Accuracy is not surprising. Artists were the photographers of their day. Why invent a landscape that viewers might know was false, when the original was so novel? It was safe to embellish a transient foreground, but not the broad span of the land, for along with its people and animals this was a main reason for painting Australia at all.

If a scene was painted before Europeans changed it, as these scenes were, it can be immensely valuable in showing how Aborigines shaped Australia. It can show where to look and what to see. So do early survey plans. The main thing newcomers looked for in Australia was grass (ch 7). Surveyors were ordered to describe and depict pastoral potential, and they speckled their plans with details of grass, open and dense forest, and sterile land, allowing us to compare vegetation then and now. Many plans plot land now under buildings or farms, but others display dramatic differences in vegetation, most commonly grass in 1788 but trees or scrub now. This provokes a useful question: if trees grow there now, why not then? Paintings and plans reveal other odd plant associations, for example good soil/open forest/no undergrowth. Unnatural but common, this can only have been caused by deliberate and repeated fire.

The pictures here sample hundreds of illustrations depicting aspects of 1788 management. Pictures 1–12 present plants as historians, recording their past. They show how eucalypts respond in distinctive ways to light (pictures 1–4), drought (pictures 7–8) and fire (pictures 5–9). These characteristics let people use fire to distribute trees in patterns, and so to regulate where animals lived. They also let historians see an Aboriginal presence in early landscape art and on the ground today. Knowing how Australian plants respond to light, drought and fire is invaluable in detecting unnatural plant patterns, hence the effects of controlled fire as distinct from bushfire, and so the presence of Aboriginal management. Pictures 10–12 illustrate the impact of heavy grazing in European times, implying Aboriginal restraints on grazing in 1788. Pictures 1–12 use as examples plants readily recognisable in colonial art: principally eucalypts, but also acacias and Kangaroo Grass.

Pictures 1–12 help show the firestick in pictures 13–58: paintings, drawings, plans and photographs unconsciously displaying aspects of 1788 management. Most are early colonial, chosen because they show country untouched by Europeans, or a European impact apparent but slight. Some show what plants did when Europeans ended 1788 fire, but pictures of vegetation even possibly changed by Europeans have been excluded. Pictures 13–30 show the broad-scale impact of 1788 fire or its absence; 31–7 illustrate edges; 38–52 show edges used in more complex plant associations; 53–8 show people using templates; 59 shows European tree clearing which illuminates some benefits of 1788 mosaics.

Much can be learnt by studying these examples; much more by comparing them. To see unnatural plant patterns in one picture is persuasive; to see in pictures across Australia the same patterns in different climates and terrain and among different plant species is powerfully convincing; to see those patterns in both mainland Australia and Tasmania is extraordinary. These islands have been separate for 11,000 years, as Ian Thomas observed a 'degree of isolation ... unparalleled in the known history of the world'.[5] Yet in 1788 a Tasmanian would have recognised a Queenslander's care for country, if not how it was done. This comparison alone, seemingly so long sustained, implies universal ends served by myriad local means, and justifies accepting what Aborigines did as managing a continental estate.

Pictures 1–4: Light

1. Swamp Gum southwest of Scottsdale, Tasmania, January 2011
Edwina Powell, Launceston. Compare pictures 2–4, 13–16.

Light shapes eucalypts. In shade they grow straight, on a shade edge they bend and branch to the light, in light they spread. A eucalypt's shape is thus a history of its surrounds (ch 3). Mountain Ash (Swamp Gum in Tasmania) is familiar as tall, straight forest in cool wet regions. Unlike most eucalypts it is fire sensitive. Its wet forests suffer fire rarely, but when fire comes it is a raging furnace, and the trees die. Then in the rich ash thousands of seedlings race straight up, battling their neighbours for light.

This Swamp Gum is about 210 years old. It is this shape because it lives in the open, with plenty of light. Why, if this species usually grows in dense thousands after fire? A bushfire would kill it and replace it with swathes of competing seedlings, whereas in a long absence of fire this land becomes rainforest. Only centuries of controlled fire could burn back adjacent rainforest without ever touching this fire sensitive tree. It is near springs on an old walking track. It tells of Tasmanian management.

Spread indicates spacing (ch 3). Just as trees spread in the open, flagpole stands signal density even after local conditions reverse. This generates useful questions. Does the shape and spacing of one tree generation match earlier or later generations nearby? If not why not, and when was the change? If a generation is missing, for example if there are no really old trees, why? Are there anomalies: the same species in open woodland and adjacent thick forest, clumps in grassland, scrub regenerating in so-called frost hollows, trees invading grass edges? All these raise the possibility of past human intervention.

2. Yellow and Apple Box, Canberra, September 2006
BG. Compare pictures 16, 21–22, 34.

Adjacent eucalypts lean different ways to dodge the shade of neighbours. You can 'see' those neighbours after they're gone: smaller trees lean from the site. If the light moves, for example if a neighbour grows, trees gyrate from the shadow, if necessary reversing 180 degrees, except for balance starving branches which fall into shade and unleashing new branches to the light.

This picture shows such gyrations. At left a Yellow Box leans away from larger trees which once stood between it and the western sun. About 1938 they were cleared to make a view, and the Box pushed into the vacant light. A stump and two branches are shown; other branches are higher up. At right an Apple Box also reached for the vacant light, but turned sharply away as its neighbour's branches took the space. 'Seeing' trees not there can be invaluable.

This land has few big trees: the nearest is about 70 metres away. Yet at rear young eucalypts and wattles, survivors of regular mowing, clutter the ground—off photo at right they are even denser. Why aren't their grandparents as dense? Many seedlings lose the race for light and die, but under similar conditions not in one generation more than another. Some giants may have been felled by axe, fire or age, but if so more should remain as stumps or root depressions.

They were never there. In May 1832, 7–8 years after Europeans first occupied it, Robert Hoddle surveyed this land. The Box is on a ridge he called 'open forest', a category between 'grassy' and 'dense' which he used elsewhere. Along the crest and upper slopes he drew a 150–200 metre wide neck of 'open box, gum and apple' separating 'grassy' plains and lower slopes, carrying few trees or none.[6] The edge between them oscillates over height contours, the same soil and the same aspects, and each side of it now carries post-1788 eucalypts. That was not so in 1832 because this land was controlled by fire.

Hoddle's survey supports other aspects of this picture. Off-picture at left (north) the Box spreads wide: for at least most of its life no trees were there. The tussock grasses prefer open land. Most survive shade for decades, but don't invade it. Here they are dying under the trees but thriving in open patches beyond. This too indicates that this country was once open.

3. White Gum on Ellesmere Station south of Jericho, Tasmania, 1985–6

Fred Duncan, FPB. Compare pictures 1, 4, 6, 18, 21–4, 40, 48.
For help I thank Fred Duncan, Greg Taylor and Charles Burbury.
A similar photo is the front cover of Tasforests 2, Dec 1990.

The big White Gum (Ribbon or Manna Gum on the mainland) was 200–300 years old in 1985–6.[7] Its branches spread, unlike the surrounding saplings which grow straight up, racing for light. Those fast-growing youngsters caught their parent, which first lost lower branches to the shade, then bent its next branches up to compete for light. This Gum began in the open, then adapted to forest.

Open land typified this district in 1788.[8] If trees grow there now, why not then? Soil, salt, climate or aspect do not explain the change. Fire does explain it, but not bushfires. Most big eucalypts survive them, as they prove each summer. Had bushfires kept this land clear,

3

the big Gum would show more fire damage, there would be more big gums, and we would have to explain why bushfires stopped and let the saplings grow. The fires which made this landscape were deliberate, frequent and cool, preserving the big Gum and killing generations of its seedlings.

The saplings were young in 1985–6, showing that trees can grow here, but for most of the big tree's life did not. The land remained open for about a century after the Tasmanians were dispossessed.[9] Perhaps stock kept it so until a grazing break let the saplings take hold.[10] They then shaded the grass. It is White Grass. It needs open land. Its presence among trees shows that once the country was open. Now it struggles, whereas in the open beyond it flourishes.

4. Blakely's Red Gum on Goorooyaroo reserve near Canberra, 7 August 2005

BG. Compare pictures 3, 6, 14–16, 18, 21–4, 40, 48.

The big Blakely's Red Gum died aged about 200. It has no low branches, and its high branches do not spread wide, indicating that it grew with now-gone neighbours not far away. Much later the larger saplings around it got away, perhaps in a grazing break. They began to spread, then were caught by the dense stand of younger saplings, and turned their branches up, chasing the light.

The dead Gum grew in open woodland because the land was burnt, but not by bushfire. A bushfire would either kill the young Gum, or let it and more of its generation survive, like the youngest saplings. Killing all the saplings required fires about every 2–4 years. Kept up long enough, this would destroy all seed stock in the soil, so that except around mature or sheltered trees the country would stay open. No-one now knows how long 'long enough' is. For most eucalypts it is certainly centuries, but non-Aborigines have not been in Australia long enough to know how many.

Pictures 5–12: Fire

**5. Eucalypt recovery from fire or drought:
Thredbo, NSW, 17 February 2006**
  BG. Compare pictures 6, 9.

These Snow Gums are regenerating from lignotubers after the hot January 2003 fire. Mallees too re-sprout like this: near Australia's coldest and hottest extremes eucalypts regrow similarly. In the background are gums twice this size, but really big gums are rare. Why, since the young gums are so dense?

Snow Gum spacing varies with altitude. Near Canberra they grow in dense, tall stands at 1500 metres, are shorter, more branching and wide spaced at 1670 metres, and stunted, wide canopied and scattered at 1840 metres. In general the higher they are the tougher the conditions, the fewer they are, the more light each gets, and the more each spreads.[11] But these gums, crowded young trees visible, older trees at rear, big trees absent, are at the same altitude. The change is between generations. This suggests that fire was once more common than it is now.

Australia's high country meadows are supposedly natural. This may be true above the present tree line (though don't assume it), but here gums have captured meadow. How did it become meadow? Why isn't it still, if it is natural? The obvious answer is a change from regular to sporadic fire.

In 1840 Stewart Ryrie passed near here. He crossed the Thredbo, climbed Rams Head Range, and followed it southwest to Merritt's Spur above Thredbo Village. 'The highest part I reached', he wrote,

> was covered with a short and coarse wiry grass mixed with heath, and a little lower down, long coarse grass and herbage with short scrub at places . . . The only timber growing upon them is the white gum [Snow Gum] and Messmate: the latter only at the foot of them. The white gum scrub extends two thirds of the distance to the summit and is, in most parts, dead. The lower part of the Mountains is covered with long, luxuriant grass.[12]

Six years later surveyor Thomas Townsend saw what converted Snow Gum to grass:

> The summits of the peaks were generally more densely clad than any other part . . . The Blacks had visited the Snowy Mountains, a short time previously to us . . . the consequence was, the country throughout the whole survey was burnt, leaving my bullocks destitute of food. During the time I was on the range the lower parts of the country were burning . . . dense masses of smoke obscuring the horizon in all directions.[13]

In 1788 these slopes averaged big fires every 50 years, but the 2003 fire may have been the hottest the valley ever experienced, because regular cool fires left fewer trees in 1788.[14]

6. Eucalypts and acacias after a December 2001 bushfire, Canberra, 31 August 2008

Peter Greenham, Canberra. Compare pictures 3–4, 16, 18, 24, 28, 35, 40, 48.

Southern Blue Gum and Cootamundra Wattle, exotics in this locality, compete to recover from fire. Southern eucalypts promote fire via highly flammable oil, leaves and bark (ch 3), recovering via beards and lignotubers (ch 1). Already taller than regenerating competition, they take what light they need and block it from competitors, even their own beards. These saplings stand above competing plants, with enough light to branch evenly.

After fire or drought most acacias regenerate from seed, densely and quickly. Before this fire no wattles grew here: for at least 30 years this was a eucalypt plantation. The fire liberated seed in the soil, so wattles crowd the gums, and unless another fire comes might

6

overtop them. But they are short-lived, and in time the gums will outgrow their descendants, take the nutrients, block the light, and kill them. Seed then waits in the soil for another liberating fire.

Early settlers knew this. West of Sydney in 1834 Charles von Hugel noted:

> The woods assume a pleasing aspect here; *Acacia decurrens* and *marginata*, with their bright green foliage and their golden buds just forming, cover every open space in the many clearings, which have partly reverted to forest. It is most extraordinary how, in all those parts of the colony where these trees occur at all, *Acacia decurrens* germinates in every spot which has been cleared of forest and where the felled trees have been burnt, even where not a single tree of that species is to be seen in the vicinity. This led Mr W. Macarthur to conduct an experiment. He covered one half of a bed sown with various varieties of *Acacia* with brushwood and set it alight. This had the expected result. Whereas only a few seeds came up on one side, the other half which had been laid with twigs was covered in seedlings.
>
> This phenomenon appears to demonstrate that the seeds of the acacias of New Holland remain viable for a long time, but always require a high degree

of heat in order to germinate. The same appears to be the case with most of the seeds of plants classed as 'New Holland plants' . . . These scrubs were subjected to regular firing by the Aborigines for so long that it would have been impossible for any plant to grow there without this characteristic.[15]

Various acacia and eucalypt fire histories appear in early colonial art: hot fires (beards, dense wattle), cool fires (trees wide spaced), or no fire (several generations of the same species), while the ratio of eucalypts to acacias can convey how intense and how long ago a fire was. Banksia, casuarina, Mountain Pepper and others also display their fire history, so that artists painting soon after a 1788 fire regime ended often unconsciously depict it.

Eucalypt recovery from fire or drought
7. Orroral Valley, ACT, 1 September 2007
8. Erudina Station, SA, 17 August 2007

BG. Compare picture 9.
For help with picture 8 I thank John and Sue McEntee.

Many eucalypts have a remarkable capacity: their bark heals their wounds and revives trees apparently dead (ch 3). Picture 7 shows a Ribbon Gum at an old hut site. It was lopped, dropped branches when boots and hooves compacted the soil, and seemed to die. The hut was abandoned; the tree revived. At left a lignotuber grows, and bark is re-clothing the old trunk. In time, a long time, bark and branch will conceal the scars as though they never were. Some eucalypts are much older than we imagine.

Picture 8 shows River Red Gums *(erudina)* on Wilpena Creek floodplain on John and Sue McEntee's Erudina Station in northern South Australia. John

8

stands at right. 'Dead' for decades, the centre stump was cut for firewood years ago, but began re-barking after 1968. In the background are 'dead' and re-barking gums. When the creek changed course in 1937, several miles of gums began to die, and by 1955 almost all seemed dead. In 1968 sand choke forced the creek back into its old course, and the trees began re-barking. By 2007 half the forest was back to life.[16]

Harold Cazneaux's famous 1937 photo, *Spirit of Endurance*, shows a River Red Gum bark-regenerating near Wilpena Pound, west of Erudina.

9. Eucalypt recovery from fire: Yelvertoft Station, Qld, 27 August 2007

BG. Compare pictures 5–8, 14–15, 40.

This is pastoral land, patch-burnt as opportunity permits to bring on green pick. A recent fire has not touched background scrub, but foreground Snappy Gums have been burnt too often and are stressed. From their height in this dry country, they survived a fire perhaps 4–5 years before, and have just been burnt again. The contrast between green foreground and prickly background explains why pastoralists burn such land. In 1788 people had more room to rest country.

Many of the ways in which eucalypts treat fire are shown. At left a tree was re-barking and growing a lignotuber before this fire scorched it, at centre a stump seemingly dead is re-barking and growing lignotubers, some with beards, at right lignotubers regenerate. Smaller trunks lean away from larger neighbours, and fire has killed mistletoe on the saplings at right. Of the trees this light soil might carry, only gums have survived the recurrent fires, and even pick vanishes near them.

10–11. **Kangaroo Grass near Berridale (NSW) (10) and in Canberra (11), late summer 2008**
BG. Compare picture 12.

Most introduced grasses are winter or spring flourishing annuals; most natives are summer flourishing perennials. Fire and drought kill annuals readily but native perennials rarely. This made native perennials invaluable: being perennial they re-shoot green when burnt, and being summer flourishing they feed grazing animals when drought is worst and fires most easily lit. Burning thus attracted the animals, and limiting the burn concentrated them. People burnt carefully, for perennial pastures also carried herbs, annuals, tubers and bulbs, each needing different fires.

1788's most widespread grass was Kangaroo Grass (ch 3). Its summer tan was Australia's dominant colour in 1788. Under heavy grazing later it was reduced to refuges, but is now returning to destocked land. Picture 10's dense swathe, 'like an even, sweeping field of oats' as Leichhardt put it in 1844,[17] indicates land not heavily grazed. The lighter vestiges are Wild Oats, an introduced annual dead in summer. Picture 11 shows Kangaroo Grass green, dense and moisture shielding in late summer. Its myriad corkscrew seeds can pincushion kangaroo and bull hides, but Aborigines and early settlers burnt it every 1–3 years to lure and locate grazing animals.

CANVAS OF A CONTINENT

12. Arthur Streeton (1867–1943), *Golden Summer, Eaglemont*, **Victoria, 1889**

95.604, NGA. Compare pictures 10–11, 17, 57.

This land near Melbourne (overleaf) has no stumps, and scattered trees lacking low branches and spreading narrowly, so they grew in forest. They pre-date European occupation, suggesting that settlers cleared the country.

The scene reflects how soon settlers upset Australia's grasses. For over a century Impressionist paintings such as this, Streeton's *Near Heidelberg* (1890) and Tom Roberts' *A break away!* (1891) have declared the colour of Australia. They use glaring whites or creams to conjure up the heat and dry of summer, transforming earlier depictions which mimicked Europe by portraying the land green. They moved the common perception of Australia from other seasons to summer. Thousands of landscapes since have repeated their impression.

They do not depict native grasses. Some do look white or cream in summer, but most look purple to tan. The first Australian grass named by western science, White Grass (Common Tussock), widespread in eastern Tasmania and the southeast mainland, has purple–tan seed heads, as do many other *poa*, while Kangaroo Grass seeds in dense tan plumes. By Streeton's time that Australia had largely vanished. 'Throughout most of the continent', Curr recalled in 1883,

> the most nutritious grasses were originally the most common; but in consequence of constant over-stocking and scourging the pastures, these, where not eradicated, have very much decreased, their places being taken by inferior sorts and weeds introduced from Europe and Africa.[18]

Introduced winter or spring flourishing annuals, dead in summer, replaced summer flourishing perennials. *Golden Summer*'s golden creams are colours of death. Conserving drought-shielding perennials took more skill than newcomers had.

Pictures 13–22: Broad-scale fire

13. Sydney Parkinson (1745?-71), *A view of Endeavour River*, Qld, July 1770

an9193430, NLA. This picture first appeared in Hawkesworth vol 2, pl 19. Ignaz Klauber's almost exact copy, used here because it is coloured, was for the 1795 Dutch translation. Compare pictures 13–31, 39, 42–51, 57–8.

This is Cooktown, where Cook beached *Endeavour* for repairs. It shows a very varied mosaic. On the mountain at right rear a sharp edge separates trees from grass, and the hill below is mostly grass. At right a dense shoreline forest gives way to a mere line of young trees, perhaps broken when Cook's crew cleared a camp and got firewood. At left is an open shore. Hills and slopes carry tree lines or lanes, a feature much more common in colonial art than in the bush today (pictures 19, 20, 27, 38, 58). Careful cool fires made them.

The hills at left carry Blady Grass in different fire recovery stages, some tall, some lawn, some between. It is a rapid coloniser after fire, and useful feed when young. On 19 July Aborigines set fire to it around Cook's camp, and its sudden fury caught his crew by surprise. People were using an ally as a weapon, though July is in the dry season, when grass is still burnt to keep back snakes and to make pick.

The hill at left still has its old name: Grassy Hill. It is tree covered now. A plaque on it states, 'The Guueu Yimithirr often burnt this hill to encourage a "green pick" and bring wallabies to the grass shoots. When the Wangarr (non Aborigines) arrived in 1873 burning was reduced. Tree seeds, carried by birds and the wind, germinated across the slopes. Grassy Hill slowly converted to woodland.'[19] Parkinson shows at least two tree species on the hill, which may have been the seed source.

Cook's journal confirms Parkinson's accuracy. On 19 June he climbed Grassy Hill, got clear views along the coast, and saw other grassy hills. He called them 'barren and stoney': some are stony but none are barren—trees block his views now. On 19 July he wrote, 'I had an extensive view of the inland country which consisted of hills and vallies and large plains agreeably diversified with woods and lawns',[20] and later he recalled how diligently people made them:

> I have observed that when they went from our tents upon the banks of the Endeavour river, we could trace them by the fire which they kindled in their way; and we imagined that these fires were intended in some way for the taking of the kanguroo . . .
>
> They produce fire with great facility, and spread it in a wonderful manner . . . from the smallest spark they increase it with great speed and dexterity. We have often seen one of them run along the shore, to all appearance with nothing in his hand, who stooping down for a moment, at a distance of every fifty or a hundred yards, left fire behind him, as we could see first by the smoke, and then by the flame . . . We had the curiosity to examine one of these planters of fire, when he set off, and we saw him wrap up a small spark in dry grass, which, when he had run a little way, having been fanned by the air that his motion produced, began to blaze; he then laid it down in a place convenient for his purpose, inclosing a spark of it in another quantity of grass, and so continued his course.[21]

Most places now named 'Grassy' or 'Bald' are not, and bush covers old grassland and middens.[22] The well-timed burns which for so long kept 3000 kilometres of coast 'agreeably diversified with woods and lawns' are no more.

14. John William Lewin (1770–1819), *The second Cataract on the North Esk near Launceston*, 1809
15. The second cataract, Launceston, Tasmania, 13 March 2008
   14: PXD 388/6, Mitchell Library, SLNSW. 15: BG. Compare pictures 13, 16–22, 39, 42, 46–7, 50, 57–8.

Painted three years after William Paterson settled Launceston in March 1806, nothing on the North Esk fits the scene shown in picture 14: it is on the South Esk. It is sometimes ascribed to the first cataract from Kings Bridge. That crest does match Lewin better than this, which is less curved than he depicts, but nothing else fits. The line of the river, the small bays at left, the waterline hummock and the conical hill and some rock cracks on it at right, and the mid-stream and gorge-side rocks all match the second cataract seen across First Basin past Alexandra Suspension Bridge. Lewin's foreground rocks were removed to make a recreation area, so picture 15 is from further back than picture 14.

The view can be compared with Lewin's *The Cataract near Launceston Port Dalrymple*, also 1809. That crest too is askew, but the river and gorge-side rocks match the view from Kings Bridge. This makes sensible Lewin's naming the next cataract upstream 'the second Cataract'.

Lewin shows trees sparse on the centre hill, denser but with grass patches on the hill at right, and densest on the gorge-side at left. Three distinct fire regimes made these differences. The centre hill seems too steep to gather plants and too open to trap game even uphill, but safe from killer fires. Possibly it was a wallaby sanctuary (ch 10), whereas at right the tree-ringed grass patch on the waterline may be a wallaby trap. At left the steep, rocky face was burnt less often, and carries Drooping Sheoak, good for spears, sapwood to make a gargle for toothache, and trunks soaked in water to breed grubs. Behind them, Lewin has painted smoke, and people camping.

William Collins wrote of the gorge, 'The beauty of the scene is probably not surpass'd in this world . . . every part of it abounds with Swans, Ducks, and other kinds of Wildfowl.'[23] This beauty and plenty depended on fire. All three hills were burnt, the left perhaps every ten years, the right about every 7–15, the centre about every three. Today's denser trees signal much less burning. Unless Drooping Sheoak is burnt every 7–10 years it crowds out other species, and on all three hills it is now much denser. At left the biggest Sheoaks have gone, but the tendency Lewin shows for the right hill to carry Sheoak on its gorge side and gums on its outer slope is more pronounced.

Here and elsewhere, there was more grass in 1809 than now. *The Cataract near Launceston Port Dalrymple* shows grassy hills with no or few trees. Today dense Sheoak, eucalypts, wattle, scrub and endangered South Esk Pine grow there, but almost no grass. People burnt this part more often than at the second cataract. Fire regimes were local.

16. John Glover (1767–1849), *Mills' Plains, Ben Lomond, Ben Loder and Ben Nevis in the distance*, Tasmania, c1832–4

Pic AG3, TMAG. Compare pictures 1–4, 6, 13–15, 17, 20.

The view is east from the hill shown in Glover's *My Harvest Home* (1835) above his farm near Deddington, northeast Tasmania. Glover's accuracy has been questioned, but contemporaries thought him too accurate: one said his trees had a 'hideous fidelity to Nature'.[24] He has enlarged Ben Lomond, compressed the country horizontally, and replaced the cattle and white stockmen in his sketches with Tasmanians,[25] but the view matches the site.

The curved branches cause debate on what trees Glover depicted,[26] but he stated, 'the taller Trees are Gums, the lesser Whattle'.[27] Spreading White Gums dominate the foreground and dot the plains and hills. 'There is a remarkable peculiarity in the Trees in this Country', Glover wrote, 'however numerous, they rarely prevent your tracing through them the whole distant Country.' He added that this view 'gives a good idea of the thickly [sic] wooded part of the Country; it is possible almost every where, to drive a Carriage as easily as in a Gentleman's Park in England'.[28] Edward Lord did this, declaring on oath in 1812, 'the forest land . . . is very open . . . from Hobart's Town to Launceston, a loaded cart was drawn without the necessity of felling a tree . . . In general a very rich pasturage; it is a fine, beautiful picturesque country as can be.'[29] This country carries the same trees now: sheoak, Blackwood and White Gum, including giants with coolamon (wooden dish) scars. In grazing country naturally the trees are spaced, but are still too dense to photograph the view Glover had.

Glover shows Tasmanians. They were not there in 1832, for in 1828–30 they were shot or rounded up by bounty hunters like Glover's neighbour John Batman.[30] Glover knew this. He captioned his *Batman's Lookout, Benn Lomond* (1835) 'on account of Mr Batman frequenting this spot to entrap the Natives'.[31] Yet he depicts not only their presence, but their absence. His *Mills' Plains* foreground shows young gums, wattles and casuarinas, which all regenerate quickly after fire. They are young because Tasmanians burnt the old; they are there because Tasmanian burning was stopped. They are the first generation for decades not to get burnt, so their height measures the end of Tasmanian dominion.

17. John Michael Skipper (1815–83), *Onkaparinga, South Australia*, 1838

Morgan Thomas Bequest Fund 1942, AGSA.
Compare pictures 16, 18–20, 25, 37, 39, 42, 49–50, 57.

The view is south of Adelaide a year or so after settlement, looking west across the Onkaparinga to the low coast dunes south of Port Noarlunga South. This area is mostly farms or houses now, but in reserves trees grow quite densely.

Skipper depicts no undergrowth, and trees in clumps, implying fire about every three years to make grass. Foreground hills are burnt, but forest fringes distant dunes. It was dominated by Mallee Box and Drooping Sheoak.[32] William Light's nearby *View at Yankalillah* (1836) shows similar sheoak and scrub, very open. Such places were good camping: sheltered, cool in summer, handy to sea and plain. They were burnt less often: Drooping Sheoak needs at least seven fire-free years to seed. So at least two fire regimes, and possibly others for the swamp and the hills, made this land.

Much of the coastal plain was similarly open—'extensive treeless downs, contrasting strikingly in appearance from the woody country around'.[33] At Aldinga it was 'of the richest character . . . covered with so long and thick an herbage that it is quite laborious to walk through it . . . the scenery resembles an English gentleman's park'.[34] Other parts were open forest. 'The scenery about Willunga is the prettiest I have seen in Australia,' Edward Snell wrote. 'There is a fine back ground of hills which at the base slope gently off to the sea, the whole covered with trees through which the roads wind and looking very much like a gentleman's park in England on a very large scale.'[35] George Angas painted a view west to the sea over the Carrickalinga 'river', showing 'the singular manner in which the trees are dotted about in all directions'.[36] His *Entrance to the gorge of Yankalilla* (1850) shows many trees small enough to be post-settlement, but foreground eucalypts and sheoak big and few, while hills are almost bare, as at Rapid Bay further south.[37]

Together these pictures show varied tree spacing, but country always more open than is natural. To make such variety, fire regimes could not be haphazard. Each was distinct, repeated, and integrated with neighbours to maintain a range of plant and animal habitats.

18. Martha Berkeley (1813–99), *Mount Lofty from The Terrace, Adelaide*, c1840

South Australian Government Grant 1935, AGSA. Compare pictures 17, 19–20, 42–3, 50, 56–8.

The view (overleaf) is from East Terrace southeast to Mt Lofty. Berkeley has embellished her foreground with people, a dog, a cart and a pair of blue wrens. The big gum branches narrowly, perhaps to frame the ground. A natural foreground would be dense Grey Box–SA Blue Gum forest,[38] but there is only a dead tree, no stumps, and no undergrowth. To burn land clear of gums like this would take their lifetimes, say 300–500 years.

The middle ground is grassland rapidly being colonised by post-settlement saplings. Beyond them forest sits on the plain and lowest slopes—a few magnificent gums survive there today. Most hill faces are grassy to their crests, where they give way sharply to forest or tree lines. In 1839 Theodore Scott noticed these 'gently undulating hills crowned with trees'.[39] At right tree lines run down grass hills and zigzag across the plain. Mt Lofty Range has grassy slopes below forest.

18

Berkeley could hardly have invented plant patterns so different, and James Backhouse confirmed them:

> After crossing the grassy plains of Adelaide, the first hills . . . are grassy, with a few trees, and a variety of plants. The next hills . . . have trees scattered upon them . . . The next hills are . . . abounding in gay vegetable productions, in forest . . . Some of the hills, like the plains below, are covered with . . . fine Kangaroo-grass, that is green, notwithstanding the temperature has, several times lately, risen to 107 in the shade.[40]

Others painted these patterns. JA Thomas' *View on the Glenelg plains, near the hills* (1837?) shows a grassy, bush (sheoak?)-studded plain meeting dense eucalypt forest at a sharp boundary. The forest rises to tree–grass mosaic hills, some on fire, below a forested Mt Lofty Range. Skipper's *Mount Lofty, Adelaide* (1838) shows the tree-scattered hills approaching it which Backhouse described. Other paintings depict grassy hills with many fewer trees than today.[41] By 1850 at least some were covered 'with young gum trees'.[42]

These patterns went deep into the hills. Dirk Hahn wrote,

> My first glance fell on the beautifully-formed trees, which nature had planted there as if with the hands of a gardener. Every tree stood about 40 feet apart from the others. Some were perhaps an acre apart, so that the land could be cultivated without uprooting a single tree . . . In those spots that seemed to me the most fertile, I found grass 3 feet 4 inches high: they looked like our European cornfields . . . The Onkaparinga, a name borrowed from the savages, also crosses this valley . . . On its surface many fish . . . sported around and certainly had never before been exposed to the fisherman's pursuit.[43]

Sturt remembered the Onkaparinga hills as 'grassy, and clear of trees . . . On the other side of Mount Terrible the country is very scrubby for some miles, until, all at once, you burst upon the narrow, but beautiful valley of Mypunga [sic] . . . covered with Orchideous plants of every colour, amidst a profusion of the richest vegetation.'[44] Many orchids signify recent fire. Jane Franklin wrote that the land between Mt Lofty and Encounter Bay 'was exceedingly pretty; in some parts not unlike an English park, grassy and lightly timbered, and quite free from scrub and underwood', and Sturt remarked that it was 'so open that the labour of felling and clearing is wholly unnecessary'.[45]

Pictures 17–18 illustrate distinct fire regimes, in different seasons, with different timings (ch 6). To burn patterns so complex in terrain so varied needs intricate knowledge of plants and fire, visionary planning, and skill and patience greater than anything modern Australia has imagined.

19. Robert Hoddle (1794–1881), *Ginninginderry Plains, NSW*, c1832

vn3423118, NLA. Compare pictures 16–18, 20, 23–7, 36, 50–1, 57.

Ginninderra Creek runs through Canberra's northwest suburbs. In 1832–5 Hoddle surveyed much of the Canberra district, especially along watercourses (ch 9). About here, along what he called 'Ginninginninderry Chain of Ponds', he plotted 'open plain' and 'open forest', marking their boundary with dotted lines.[46] His foreground is framed with trees perhaps too slender to have grown in the open, but the scene matches his field books. The plains have few trees, and as at Cooktown (picture 13) some are in narrow lines, perhaps wildlife corridors. Except at left and possibly on north facing slopes, hills and ranges are grassy. Hoddle described the ranges west of the Murrumbidgee from Mt Tennant north as 'grassy hills open forest'.⁴⁷ Despite or because of several devastating bushfires, they are dense forest today.

Hoddle painted other district scenes showing open plains with tree lines or clumps in front of sparsely timbered hills.⁴⁸ This template was common (ch 7). Near Peak Hill on the Bogan (NSW) on 15 August 1817, Oxley might have been describing this scene:

> from thirty to forty miles round, the country was broken in irregular low hills thinly studded with small timber, and covered with grass: the whole landscape within the compass of our view was clear and open, resembling diversified pleasure grounds irregularly laid out and planted . . . although the soil and character of the country rendered it fit for all agricultural purposes, yet I think from its general clearness from brush, or underwood of any kind, that such tracts must be peculiarly adapted for sheep-grazing.⁴⁹

20. Robert Hoddle (1794–1881), *View from Melbourne,* **1847?**
PX*D 319, Mitchell Library, SLNSW. Compare pictures 17–19, 25, 27, 36, 50–1, 57.

Hoddle painted views from Batman's Hill in Melbourne, but casuarinas topped it, so this hill is not it. The mountain looks like Mt Macedon from an angle similar to Hoddle's sketches of it from the west side of Port Phillip.[50] I guess that the view is towards Mt Macedon from roughly southeast.

Foreground stumps declare slight European clearing, perhaps by Hoddle's survey gang, but Aborigines made this country. It prompted Hoddle to describe Melbourne as

> prettily situated upon gently undulating hills . . . picturesque and park-like country, which the most fastidious observer of Nature's beauties cannot be insensible to. The soil in the immediate neighbourhood of the town is most excellent, which, with the park-like appearance of the surrounding country, forms a grand contrast to the barren scrub and sandy rocks of Sydney.[51]

20

Much land around Melbourne was similarly 'park-like' (ch 9). Hoddle's *View from Batman's Hill Melbourne Port Phillip* (1840) looks over the country between Station Peak (Flinders Peak) in the You Yangs about 50 kilometres west-southwest, and Mt Macedon about 65 kilometres northwest. Again a few foreground stumps suggest survey clearing, but the vast stretch beyond has no stumps and barely a tree, and those distant few are in lines. Franklin told her husband, 'we drove a few miles out of town towards Mt Macedon on fine open grassy grounds of beautiful verdure in many places and very scantily wooded'. She noted 'fine park-like pasturages, quite green, or more or less so . . . the greenness of the country proceeds from its having been recently burnt & some heavy rains falling since'.[52] This land may have been sheet-burnt regularly to expose Yam Daisy, which grew in millions here (ch 10). Perhaps the yellow streaks in Hoddle's painting depict them.

Von Guerard's *View from the Bald Hills between Ballarat and Creswick Creek* (1858) shows similar grass ('bald') hills, trees regenerating because 1788 fire has ceased, and open forest plains.

21. Eugen von Guerard (1811–1901), *Crater of Mt Eccles*, 1858
22. The crater of Mt Eccles, Victoria, 18 March 2007

21: PIC S1011, NLA [from von Guerard]. 22: BG. Compare pictures 13–15, 20, 31, 38, 56.

Von Guerard's scene is instantly recognisable. Scrub now blocks his shore and slope, but the plateau at left is the picnic ground, and the rocks by the horsemen a photo point. The rim forest at right rear has thinned; most forest has thickened. It was thickening in 1858: most trees in the painting are small and grow straight to compete for light, signalling recent

21

22

capture of grassland. The biggest trees then, Ribbon Gum at left, are the biggest still, but clear of competitors branch widely now.

Von Guerard shows tree lines on crests, and in and above the crater tree belts and grass necks. No soil change dictates their boundaries, and grass then is trees now, mostly Ribbon Gum, Blackwood, Native Cherry or pine, each controlled with different fire. Belts confined and located koalas, now re-introduced here, mosaics put feed near shelter for grass eaters, steep sides advantaged hunters. These are templates (ch 8). Burn the grass in patches for pick, and they become traps. Beyond this scene, the crater's outer slopes hint of former tree belts, suggesting that the inner and outer slopes were similarly patterned.

PICTURES 23–30: ARID-ZONE FIRE

23. Baldwin Spencer (1860–1929), *Ayers Rock northwest aspect,* June 1894
24. Kantju, Uluru, NT, 31 March 2005

23: Gillen Coll AA108, album E-AP 5708, SAM [from Spencer and Gillen 1912, fig 45]. 24: BG. Compare pictures 25–30. I thank Punch Hall, who in one day drove me from Alice Springs and back to take pictures 24, 26 and 28.

Spencer's photo is not the first of Uluru. William Tietkins took several around Mutitjulu in July 1889. Most are unclear, but one shows country like this—an open forest of mature bloodwoods above 'grass flats at the foot of the rock'.[53] Others noted grass there:[54] fire too frequent lets Spinifex take over, too infrequent lets in scrub, as in picture 24.

Erratic rainfall is the arid zone's ace and wild card, spasmodically rearranging its plants. Within days a wilderness of sticks can burst with new growth, then within months shrivel to thirst-stricken survivors. As plants grow their battle for water gets harder, for they need more, and unless they find it drought will kill them. After 1889 Uluru had big Wets in the early 1920s, the mid 1940s, the early 1970s, 2000 and 2009–10, and big Drys in 1890–1, 1896–1906, 1914–15, 1925–34, the late 1950s–1967, the early 1990s and 2005–7.

Desert people knew when a drought was coming, but not how long it would last, so they guarded against it. If rain gave Uluru good feed and water, they left for less permanent water out in the desert; in bad drought they came back. If rain made new growth, they burnt mosaics and fire breaks over miles of country. Pastoralists could not do this so well, and other Europeans not at all, so wet years led to big fires in 1950 and 1976. From 1985 Anungu advice led to patch burning 'every few years' here, to pattern regrowth and break up fuel. Big 1990–91 fires were stopped when they reached mosaics.[55]

Spencer's photo illustrates how local patch-burning was. Uluru sheds water over a narrow strip at its base, providing an extra drought defence. William Murray noted this strip on approaching Uluru during the 1902 drought: 'All poor desert country, spinifex, sagebush, and scanty scrub until nearing the rock, when this gives place to an alluvial flat, with fair-sized bloodwood and dry grass and herbage.'[56] Spencer shows the strip near Kantju, 'a park-like landscape of big old ironwoods and bloodwoods',[57] with grass but almost no scrub. Outside it the foreground has no trees, but scrub appears, and other grasses give way to Spinifex. People have worked with the country, putting trees and grass where they grow best, but also against it, keeping scrub to the drier ground.

23

24

The 2005 photo shows no big trees. A few dead trunks mourn trees possibly standing in 1894. In 1996 elders reported the rest killed by the 1950s drought,[58] which means they survived worse after Spencer's visit. Perhaps they had got too big by the 1950s, but unlike before 1894 and after 1985, no caring management replaced them. On the other hand 'quite dense' young Ironwood, Desert Bloodwood and Plumbush fill the run-off strip, and Spinifex and introduced Buffel Grass have invaded it. Buffel dominates a foreground dotted with sticks and bushes from a controlled burn.

Between 1894 and 2005 water and fire changed this country dramatically, including in stages not shown. While erratic rain regulates Kantju's plant distribution, it does not explain why the strip had big trees and no scrub in 1894, but small trees and dense scrub in 2005. Fire explains this: the same burning repeated for decades, then stopped. Even in arid country 1788's unnatural patterns recur. There was no boundary where people burnt with skill and purpose on one side, and at random on the other.

25. Baldwin Spencer (1860–1929), *Ayers Rock*, June 1894
26. Uluru, NT, 31 March 2005

25: Spencer Collection XP9973, MV [from Spencer and Gillen 1912, fig 44].
26: BG. Compare pictures 23–4, 27–30.

Soil decides which plants dominate where, drought whether they dominate at all. These photos convey the importance of soil type and water, and compare fire regimes. Both were taken near Uluru's sunset car park; Kantju's shade is at left. Both show burnt foreground scrub, but trees and scrub clothe Uluru's run-off strip more densely in 2005 than in 1894, and 1894's tallest trees have gone. In very wet times the middle ground channels Uluru run-off, yet it is bare in 1894 but thick with Spinifex, Cassia and Witchetty Bush in 2005.

Spencer took his photo on the way to Katajuta, noting that the 'sandy plain was dotted over with thin scrub and, away in the distance, it was crossed by dark lines where, mile after mile, the thick mulga scrub stretched across'. At Katajuta he wrote, 'The country between this and Ayers Rock is covered with the usual wiry shrubs of cassia plants and belts of mulga.'[59] William Gosse rode this way from Uluru in August 1873:

> At 2 miles the good country round the rock ends, and spinifex and oak sandhills commence, and continue to eight miles. Here the sandhills end, but the country is still spinifex and sand to twelve miles, with patches of mulga. From here the country is good, with abundance of good grass.

25

26

At Katajuta he reported, 'The country immediately around the rocks is covered with dense mulga' and a 'few native peach trees'.[60] Murray wrote, 'At about one mile [from Uluru] the grassy flat ends, and is succeeded by heavy spinifex, sandhills, patches of mulga. This continues until nearing [Katajuta] . . . These hills are fringed with very dense mulga scrub—a large amount of it dead.'⁶¹ Clear of the rocks Spencer wrote of 'thin scrub' and Gosse of 'spinifex and sand' in country well vegetated in 2005.

Mulga and Desert Oak help to explore these changes. Mulga prefers loam, Oak prefers sand. Both have spread since 1894. In 2005 Mulga covered much more than 1894's 'patches' towards Katajuta. Between 1873 and 1902 only Gosse noted Oak, and only on sand dunes. In 2005 Oak was common, still on sand but not only dunes. Thus in 1894 each species kept to its soil, but not all its soil. Something else influenced their distribution.

Desert Oak accepts all but the fiercest fires, fire promotes its seed, and fires every decade or so help it dominate. All but the coolest fires kill Mulga. Fire opens and rain germinates its seed, but seedlings take 10–20 years to set. Any fire in that time must be very gentle, once a decade at most, on green or wet ground, in light wind. Such a fire promotes grass and thins the stand. A hot burn might be set at most every 50 years or so to kill the Mulga, and the new stand left for another 50 years.⁶² In short, burning Oak about every decade and Mulga about every 50 years kept each flourishing but apart in 1894, whereas in 2005 they grew together.

In October 1873 Gosse saw a hot burn in the Musgrave Ranges. He 'had a most unpleasant ride for about eight miles through burning mulga scrub; the trees were falling in all directions, and quantities of dead wood blazing on the ground . . . Some natives had been seen about here; they have burned the grass all round.'⁶³ Those eight miles were open enough to ride through while ablaze. Cool fires had thinned the stand; now Gosse saw a hotter fire clearing it.

The photos imply fire regimes varying in timing and intensity. On Uluru's run-off they shielded bloodwoods but cleared scrub and grew grass. On Katajuta's run-offs they promoted Mulga. On land between they kept at least one strip bare (as a fire break?), burnt dunes every decade or so for Desert Oak and scrub, but some swales every 50 years or so for Mulga. No wonder managers at Uluru, in the dunes, on the plain and at Katajuta were not the same men. By 2005 they were burning more to tourist taste, promoting plants but limiting fuel. It is incongruous to think, as some do, that they planned in 2005 but not in 1894.

27. Charles Mountford (1890–1976), *The Rock*, c July 1938
28. Mountford's Uluru, NT, 31 March 2005

27: PRG1218/34/1164A, SLSA. [Mountford 1953, at 144].
28: BG. Compare pictures 23–6, 29–30.

Mountford shows his return from Katajuta. 'Stretching out before us', he wrote of this spot, 'was a wide, sandy flat, covered so thickly with spinifex in seed that it resembled a wheat field ready for harvest. Spotted on the flaxen-yellow plain were the graceful,

27

28

dark-foliaged desert oaks.'[64] 1938 was in the cattle times, the 1920s to the 1950s, when this country was a Mt Conner outstation, stocked if rain permitted. Grazing and frequent fire can impact similarly, clearing grass and young scrub, exposing roots, intensifying drought, letting Spinifex dominate. In 1938 Spinifex shrouded dunes and flats much more open than in 1894.

Next day Mountford climbed Uluru and photographed the country back to Katajuta.[65] Most land was bare. Near Uluru were trees but almost no scrub or grass, not even Spinifex. Towards Katajuta there was Spinifex and a few trees, but only hints of Spencer's 'thick mulga scrub'. The land looks drought-stricken; it is cattle-stricken.

In 1950 this area became a national park. For 35 years little was done to manage its plants, and Mountford's track became densely vegetated. 'Perhaps the area hasn't been burnt correctly or often enough,' Johnny Jingo politely suggested in October 1995. 'If it is, it gets green all around after a bushfire.'[66] In 2005 Cassia and Corkwood dunes alternate with acacia and Desert Oak flats. Mature Oaks stand about where a few Oaks dot Mountford's middle ground, and the upright shafts of young Oak scatter widely. There is little Spinifex, though some is just off camera.

Soil type, rain, and patch-burning made this variety. The 2005 scrub is denser than the 'thin scrub' Spencer saw, with less grass, and much denser than in Mountford's time. The land is burnt less often and less precisely than in 1894, but then and now it is made.

29–30. Fire-scarred dunes in the Great Sandy Desert west of Lake Mackay, WA, 24 July 1953 and 25 June 2005

29: Webb run 12, 5092 (detail), PALM, c~ Neil Burrows. 30: Google Earth 2010.

The lighter the scar the more recent the fire. Picture 29 (about 52 km^2) shows people burning small patches in light wind and into old scars. Straight lines mark where a fire lighter walked, choosing what to burn and what not. Directed by wind rather than ground, this was not easy walking. It shows purpose. Picture 30, a slightly bigger area, reflects a critical change after people moved or were moved out: fires became less frequent, bigger and hotter.[67]

From RAAF photos covering 241,000 ha, including picture 29, Neil Burrows and colleagues distinguished scars spanning 'at least 5–6 years'. Local Pintupi people said that fires might be lit at any time to hunt, signal or clean country, and because they were frequent most were small, like the 'several smokes' David Carnegie saw here in 1896.[68]

More exactly, because people wanted them small, most fires were frequent. People used big fires to hunt, but few were lit in order to hunt (ch 6). Small, cool fires hunted best. When they ceased, patch numbers fell from 846 in 1953 to four in 1981, their mean size

CANVAS OF A CONTINENT

29

30

increased from 64 ha to 52,664 ha, and vital habitat edges decreased from 3888 kilometres in 1953 to 392 kilometres in 2000. Along with introduced grazers and predators, notably cats, this huge change caused the extinction or decline of over a third of small desert animal species. Not burning starved them: 'no longer any green shoots', as the Pintupi put it.[69]

In the late 1980s people began returning to the desert. At Amata in 2002 Frank Young found it hard to generalise about fire practices so local and variable, because how and when people burnt depended on what they were burning, and why. In general Spinifex was burnt more often than Cassia or Witchetty Bush, and much more often than Mulga or Desert Oak. Further north big fires might be lit before rain in summer,[70] but Amata people usually burnt in the cold time (June–July) when fires were most easily controlled. The first fires were backburns around places needing protection. Some places were always protected, others varied from year to year. In 2002 elders were concerned for dragon lizards, so burnt cool fires around lizard habitats and Dreaming sites, often the same places. Later fires were generally downwind of protected sites, and lit when the grass was dewy in early morning or late afternoon, depending on how far the fire must travel (ch 6). In the cold time cold air and ground moisture stifle fires soon after dusk, so most were lit about three hours before. Burning stopped when the winds came about late August.[71]

Not everyone at Amata had Frank's concern for country. In 2001–2 kids in cars lit casual fires along roads. Strong northerlies picked them up and drove red lines of flame along widening fronts, stretching white-ash Mulga skeletons on the ground. Yet in 2005 at least four fire generations marked country between Derby (WA) and Alice Springs. Locally they tended to run the same way, but overall might run in any direction, mostly across dunes as in picture 30, although the best controlled fires run along dunes.[72] Most patches were much bigger than in 1953, but near Gosse's Bluff big fires about 2003 were followed by small patches lit in autumn 2005.[73] Over a vast area traditional fire management is being revived.

CANVAS OF A CONTINENT

PICTURES 31–37: 1788 FIRE PATTERNS—EDGES

31. Joseph Lycett (c1775–1828), *View from near the Top of Constitution Hill, Van Diemen's Land*, c1821

PIC U488, NLA [from Lycett 1825]. Compare pictures 13, 18, 34–5, 42, 51, 54–8.

This and pictures 34 and 51 depict places Lycett never saw. As a convict he could not have copied them unless allowed, probably by Macquarie, who visited all three places in 1820–21. This view's original was probably by George Evans or James Taylor, surveyors who came here with Macquarie in April–July 1821.[74] The view is about south from Swans Hill, 2 kilometres south of today's Constitution Hill,[75] over sharp-edged forest–plain belts putting grass near shelter and concealing hunters. This required distinct but adjacent burning regimes, long maintained.

Charles Jeffreys wrote of near here, 'these plains occupy an extent of country of twelve miles in length, and near three in breadth, and are . . . but thinly covered with timber, so that in some places, for upwards of half a mile square, there are scarcely a hundred trees standing; while the grass is in general about three feet long'.[76] Lycett's *View of Tasman's Peak from Macquarie Plains, Van Diemen's Land* (1822?) offers a nearer view of similar forest–plain belts, which Macquarie described (ch 7). They were common not only in Tasmania (ch 7). West of Forbes (NSW) Oxley saw 'considerable spaces of clear ground . . . interspersed amidst the ocean of trees'. His drawing shows plains of varying elevation alternately timbered and clear, much as here.[77]

32. A eucalypt–grass mosaic, northeast Tasmania, 9 February 1998

Colour A113, 1288–167, NE Forestry run 18E (detail). Base image by TASMAP (www.tasmap.tas.gov.au), © State of Tasmania. Compare pictures 14, 21, 31, 37, 41–2, 46–50.

Creeks frame hills: for example the road at left follows a ridge which falls to a creek on each side. Grass is both higher and lower than trees, but most crests are treed. People used different fires to make tree–grass–water edges, and clumps in plains.

Lively's Bog, the land in the road loop at top left centre, typifies the area. East from trees, grassland drops to a swampy creek, then rises past tree clumps to a semicircle of forest. This was a wallaby trap. Prey could reach grass safely through trees, which then let hunters drive it into the swamp.[78] This template fills the country. Grass burnt in sequence rotated wallabies predictably from one patch to the next, harvesting different mobs and never making one mob too spear-shy. The flats are rich but the high ground is poor, so this is a good use of it.

Near Lively's Bog, Patsy Cameron believes, is where George Robinson, the 'great conciliator', met her ancestor Mannalargenna on 1 November 1830. That day Robinson found the area 'tolerably clear, principally peppermint', and the previous day 'found the bush on fire for a considerable distance . . . It had before every appearance of being wet and the rain had now come.'[79] This suggests fire for grass rather than seed or tubers, lit when rain would promote re-greening.

In 1831 Thomas Lewis found the country behind St Helens, not far southeast of Lively's Bog, generally forest alternating between shrubby and grassy understoreys. The west sides of some hills were grassy, and grassy plains about a mile long and half a mile wide alternated with grassy woodland patches of about 500 acres.[80] Without fire most of Tasmania, including here, would be rainforest.

33. Eugen von Guerard (1811–1901), *The Sources of the River Wannon*, Victoria, 1858

PIC S1021, NLA [from von Guerard]. Compare pictures 35–6, 39, 42–3, 55–8.

Von Guerard's vantage point (overleaf) is above the Yarram Gap road near Talbert Point on the Serra Range, looking about south to Mt Abrupt.[81] His painting closely follows his on-site drawing.[82] In the sky two crows (?) strafe an eagle (?), perhaps a detail he saw here.

The slopes, he noted, were 'lightly timbered with gum and she-oak; while the mountains . . . [are] stringybark'.[83] His foreground shows wattle or young gum and sheoak, and in contrast to the mountains it is open. The central plain is not natural: the Wannon escapes from thick forest to thread it, and trees grow on it now. It was burnt for grass. Along its edges sawtooth tongues of forest mimic the mountain rims, and bite into grassland to let hunters ambush prey. CJ Tyers described this pattern:

> the Country for several miles above the Wannon [is] fine, having much the appearance of English Parks. Above Mr Patterson's homestead, the forest is much thicker, and the soil deteriorates although the grass is equally good . . . The Country intersected by the Wannon (Kairairalla of the Natives) is of a very superior description—generally open; some parts lightly covered with . . . Blackwood.[84]

This template was common (ch 8). Von Guerard's *Spring in the Valley of the Mitta Mitta* (1866) depicts an example; in 1839–40 WW Darke surveyed another on the Werribee; in 1840 Townsend surveyed a third on the Moorabool.[85] In 1813 Evans described plains on the Fish River (NSW):

> I came on a fine Plain of rich Land, the handsomest Country I ever saw . . . the Track of clear land occupies about a Mile on each side of the River . . . the Timber around is thinly scattered, I do not suppose there are more than ten Gum Trees on an Acre . . . I stopped at the commencement of a Plain still more pleasing and very Extensive. I cannot see the termination of it North of me; the soil is exceeding rich and produces the finest grass intermixed with variety of herbs; the hills have the look of a park and Grounds laid out . . . there is Game in abundance; if we want a Fish it is caught immediately.[86]

In 1859 William Morton stated of the Mackenzie northwest of Rockhampton (Qld), 'All the open country does not consist of plains, but of thinly timbered and well grassed long narrow strips, running parallel to the river. Behind are patches or belts of scrub. Further back the land generally rises.'[87] On Hooker Creek (NT) Augustus Gregory observed, 'The plain traversed this morning was well grassed . . . [and] extended three to six miles on each side of the track, and was bounded by low wooded country', and next day, 'on the right bank ... wide grassy plains extended from three to five miles back towards a low wooded ridge, but on the left bank the scrubby country came close to the creek'.[88]

The template was flexible but simple to maintain. What fire to use and when varied across Australia (ch 6), but the purpose was the same, to associate water, grass and forest, providing habitats and making the clean, beautiful landscapes dear to Aboriginal feeling.

34. Joseph Lycett (c1775–1828), *View on the Wingeecarrabee River, NSW,* c1821

*PIC U466, NLA [from Lycett 1825]. Compare pictures 35–6, 39, 42–3, 50–1, 55–8.
I thank Peter and Bunty Wright and Bruce Berry of Bowral for
their help and generosity in attempting to locate this site.*

Lycett copied this view, probably from Evans—about 1823 he copied a view of Bathurst's Falls from Oxley's *Journal*, where it is credited to Taylor after an Evans drawing.[89] Like this view, it shows details common in colonial landscapes and unlikely to be systematically invented, such as sharp tree–grass edges. The grassland here may be recent, for it carries tall trees without low branches as though recently freed from forest.

Most cliff country along the Wingecarribee is now forest, and ground and air efforts to locate Lycett's site with certainty failed. It may be Macarthur's Crossing downstream from Berrima, used in Lycett's time, and the only ford now marked on the lower river.[90] There a track drops relatively gently to a riverside basin and the crossing, then climbs steep cliffs beyond. It is much too dense to photograph.

Lycett shows grass–forest edges, even on the narrow flat. This is the precise, fine-scale burning common in colonial art: for example in pictures 35, 51 and 54–5 and in Lycett's *View on Lake Patterson, N.S.Wales* (c1820). In a perceptive passage, Leichhardt described this pattern in central Queensland:

> The natives seemed to have burned the grass systematically along every watercourse, and round every water-hole, in order to have them surrounded with young grass as soon as the rain sets in. These burnings were not connected with camping places, where the fire is liable to spread from the fire-places, and would clear the neighbouring ground. Long strips of lately burnt grass were frequently observed extending for many miles along the creeks. The banks of small isolated water-holes in the forest, were equally attended to, although water had not been in either for a considerable time. It is no doubt connected with a systematic management of their runs, to attract game to particular spots, in the same way that stockholders burn parts of theirs in proper seasons.[91]

Others describing this district reported little dense forest once they cleared the notorious Bargo Brush. Downstream, surveyor James Meehan noted land 'scrubby' in parts, but generally 'all thinly wooded good Forest' or 'all very thinly wooded Forest, good Swathe of Grass'.[92] Upstream, Macquarie hailed the 'grounds' at Bong Bong as 'extremely pretty, gentle hills and dales with an extensive rich valley . . . having a very park-like appearance,

34

being very thinly wooded'.⁹³ Oxley was with Macquarie: his 1822 map, admittedly broadscale, declares all the land back to Mittagong 'Good grazing Country'.⁹⁴

Grass and open forest then is thick bush now. Lycett's open flats and cliff tops have gone, yet few eucalypts are more than 100–200 years old until well back from the cliffs, even though red clay continues. A landscape once carefully maintained has been let run wild.

35. Anon, *Captain Stirling's exploring party 50 miles up the Swan River, WA, March 1827*

PIC T2471, NLA. Compare pictures 34, 36, 39, 42–3, 50–1, 55–8.

Other versions of this painting replace the sailor at right with kangaroos, and slightly change trees, uniforms or swans. Versions are variously attributed to James Stirling (1791–1865), expedition artist Frederick Garling (1806–73), Frederick Clause (1791–1852) or his friend WJ Huggins (1781–1845). This may be Clause's copy of a Garling sketch. The site is sometimes identified as Claisebrook in East Perth, but that is not '50 miles up'. From across the river here Garling's *Encampment at the head of the river, 70 miles up* (1827?) recognisably depicts this same topography at Stirling's highest-up camp on 13 or 14 March.[95] A 1929 plaque at All Saints Anglican Church, upper Swan, is near the site.

The peaks are invented, the ground at right is steeper, the pond is Ellen Brook, running into the Swan beyond, both now shallow. Stirling described the site as 'a Fresh

Water Lagoon and a bieutiful [sic] running brook watering several hundred Acres of natural Meadow, covered even at this Season of the Year with rich green herbaceous grass'. The meadow was not natural, as Stirling implied later that day, 'The Evening was employed by us making a Garden on the Tongue of Land, which intervenes between the River and the Creek; we found there . . . rich soil of great depth; the ground had been cleared by fire a few weeks before and was ready to receive Seed.'[96]

Gardens were already nearby. In 1843 surveyor PLS Chauncey mapped three cultivated yam patches on the Swan at Ellen Brook, each in a 'dog-wood thicket'. Sylvia Hallam noted that on land 'maintained by burning as "open level country thinly wooded with red gums" these "thickets" with their yam vines stand out as areas deliberately protected from fire'.[97] The painting shows similar fine-scale burning. Grass corridors separate water from trees and undergrowth (thickets?). The grass and two healthy Grass Trees suggest burning about every three years; the scrub less often. Trees and weeds smother the site now. It needs a good clean-up fire.

Backhouse called the upper Swan 'poor, and covered with open [eucalypt] forest . . . low scrub of Acacia, Grass-trees, &c. Several species of Banksia and Acacia also form low trees. Along the borders of the Swan, there are narrow alluvial flats, of good land.'[98] The low acacia may have grown following dispossession.

36. John Abbott (1803–75), *Mount Lindesay, from a sketch taken by A Cunningham, Esqr*, Qld, 1829?

PX*D5/34, Mitchell Library, SLNSW. Compare pictures 13, 18, 42–3, 50, 56–8.

This is not Mt Lindesay but nearby Mt Barney, near the Queensland–New South Wales border. Patrick Logan, Allan Cunningham and others explored it in August 1828. Abbott was not with them, but he and Cunningham worked for the New South Wales Survey Office. Cunningham's original is a field book sketch, which shows correctly that the land is not quite as flat as Abbott depicts, and that the trees at left were fewer and, significantly, in lines along rises.[99] Abbott dated his copy 6 May—possibly 1829.

The view is from a camp on the Logan northeast of Mt Barney, with East Peak at left and Logan Ridge at centre. Cunningham climbed the mount partway on 3 August 1828, probably drawing his sketch while resting next day. He described this scene as a 'thinly-timbered flat, recently burnt by the natives, and stretching nearly two miles to the base of the first range of forest hills'.[100] Those hills are dense eucalypt forest with rainforest patches now, so they too were being burnt in 1788, converting rainforest to eucalypts. At right are forest–woodland edges; at left tree lines. Today this is mostly farmland.

36

Cunningham mapped similar templates throughout the Moreton Bay district. North of the Bremer he noted 'Level Country covered in part with dense brushes', and further west, 'Extensive tracts of level country, alternately Plain and Forest'.[101] Charles Fraser, who also climbed partway up Mt Barney on 3 August, wrote from its flank, 'A magnificent district extends to the southward, exhibiting many wide and partially cleared plains, stretching as far as the eye can behold.'[102] Clearly much country was arranged as here, with plains judiciously spaced and, in Fraser's telling phrase, 'partially cleared'.

Further north Fraser generally noted open country, sometimes with scrubby hills or forest belts. Following a grassy valley east of Boonah on 9 August, 'we found ourselves completely surrounded by dense Forests of Araucaria [Bunya Pine], the only outlet being the immediate bank of the Stream'. The outlet was made. Later they met 'an extensive and exceedingly fertile Valley abounding in the most extensive Ponds'.[103] This is climax (natural) rainforest country.

37. Milkshake Hills Forest Reserve, northwest Tasmania, 13 February 2002

BG. Compare pictures 35–6, 39, 57–8.

Buttongrass 'occurs where heath, scrub or forest has been repeatedly burnt, or on poor peaty, acid soils where the water table is high'.[104] There is no high water table here; this Buttongrass was burnt through unknown centuries, most recently late in 2001. Fire made sharp grass–tree edges and left clumps in grassland, duplicating patterns familiar in colonial art. With correct fire, maintaining such a landscape is not difficult. Making it is, for this is climax rainforest country, the plant antipodes of Buttongrass.

A different fire regime made the forest. White eucalypt trunks rise from young rainforest, and though checked by fire, young eucalypts advance. At right the ground drops to a valley dominated by giant eucalypts, notably Messmate. Under them, Myrtle, Sassafras and other rainforest plants are advancing upslope almost to the edge, and on the valley floor are tree ferns in wet forest. Eucalypts advance onto grass; rainforest advances under eucalypts. Similar patterns are at Lawson Plains nearby, and at places like Mt Field, the Styx, the Weld and Blue Tier. Controlled fire and no fire are beacons of history.

PICTURES 38–42: 1788 FIRE PATTERNS—
PATCHES AND MOSAICS

38. Eugen von Guerard (1811–1901), *A view of the Snowy Bluff on the Wonnangatta River, Gippsland Alps, Victoria*, 1864
WCAA c~ Helen Carroll-Fairhall. Compare pictures 36–7, 41, 44–9, 53, 56.

Snowy Bluff is near the Wonnangatta–Moroka confluence. In December 1860 Alfred Howitt was exploring this district, and took von Guerard along.[105]

At centre and right von Guerard shows three sloping clearings split by tree-filled gullies. They face northeast to catch the sun and bring animals to feed and warm. On them patch-burns located animals, and let hunters drive them uphill or headlong into a gully. Two clearings also carry lone trees spared by frequent grass fires, even when young. Perhaps rocks or backburning protected them. Other mountains had clearings 'certainly very extraordinary', as Govett put it in 1831 (ch 1). Von Guerard's *Govett's Leap, Blue Mountains* (1872–3) shows one above the falls; another is in Earle's view of Wentworth Falls (NSW), *Waterfall in Australia* (c1830), which was treed by 1889.[106]

39. Steve Parish, *Deadman's Bay, Tasmania, from the southwest*, c2001

A Steve Parish Souvenir of Tasmania, Brisbane c2001, 31. © Steve Parish Publishing, reproduced c~ Steve Parish and Kate Lovett. Compare pictures 13, 43–9, 51, 54–5, 57–8.

This is near Australia's southern tip. Purrar Point is at right front, Prion Bay at right rear, Precipitous Bluff on the skyline.

Some doubt that Tasmanians lived in the southwest,[107] but fire-promoted Buttongrass covers more than 45 per cent of it, reflecting persistent burning on a scale which lightning strikes cannot explain.[108] Sedgeland 'boasts more edible food than rainforest which probably would have occupied a lot of this area if the resident Aborigines had not persisted in their firings'.[109] There are recent artefact scatters along this coast including here, while at Louisa Bay 6 kilometres west and on the Maatsuyker Islands offshore there is evidence of continuous occupation over the last 3000 years.[110] In March 1772 Marion Dufresne saw numerous fires in the region and judged the coast 'densely populated',[111] a year later Tobias Furneaux' crew saw food scraps at Louisa Bay,[112] and off the Maatsuykers Bass and Flinders

> could not account for the vestiges of fires that appeared upon the two inner large islands; the innermost in particular, which lay at some distance from the nearest point of the main, was burnt in patches upon different parts of it. It must have been effected either by lightning, or by the hand of man; but it was so much unlike the usual effects of the former, that, with all its

difficulties, they chose to attribute it to the latter cause. A great smoke that arose at the back of one of the bights showed the main to be inhabited.[113]

Near here in 1815 James Kelly met 'a large number of natives'.[114]

Water, plain, forest, patch and ridge are associated, with no fire in rainforest but 3–20 year cool fires to promote grass and eucalypts. Inland is Messmate, near the coast Smithton Peppermint. They rim Buttongrass sometimes on wet ground but sometimes not, and at some edges smothered by invading forest.[115] Controlled fire once stopped this invasion. The dark ridges are rainforest 'probably not . . . burnt for several hundred years', yet broken up by grass, especially on ridges and beaches. Rainforest is advancing. If fires like the big 1933 fire recur, it will slow. If not, eucalypts will capture grass, then rainforest the eucalypts, creating a common and memorable landscape: young rainforest topped by old eucalypts (ch 1). The scene is typical of the south and southwest coasts. Even in country now called wilderness, managing hands were there.

Of Precipitous Bluff a botanist wrote,

> The vegetation on the western slope . . . forms a series of altitudinal zones. A great range of species and plant associations, of the wetter forest types, exist in a remarkably compact and undamaged state—there is a complete absence of any intrusion by fire on these slopes for a period of 300–500 years . . . [Nowhere else is there] such a complete set of rainforest vegetation zones adapted to the different altitudes.[116]

40. A Mt Mowbullan bald, Bunya Mountains, Qld, 19 October 2003

BG. Compare pictures 21, 38, 41–2, 44–54, 56–8.

Mowbullan means 'bald head';[117] the head is rainforest now. People cleared forest from a few acres to small plains along water, crests or slopes to camp, lure or hunt. In Tasmania and the southeast most clearings on slopes face north to east; in warmer zones, where they are called balds, south to west. 'Everywhere', Stephen Simpson wrote near here in 1843, 'even on the summit of the mountain, the abundance of grass and the fine timber . . . give the country a pleasing aspect', and on the Mary he noted, 'the country gradually opens out into some beautiful flats of the richest description, nearly clear of timber'.[118]

This bald faces south to the winter sun. Reversing 1788, Forest Red Gum fills its base and rainforest crowds upslope. A few Bunya Pines break the skyline or the grassline. Balds are common in bunya country because the great bunya festivals, held when the pines cropped heavily every three years, brought thousands of people to feast. Their hosts had to feed them

40

on more than nuts. Balds increased and varied plant and animal food. Elders chose which bunyas and balds to reserve for feasts, and each was named. Simpson went through

> a bunya scrub, called Howah . . . [to] a beautiful plain, called Dungale . . . well watered by a fine creek and waterholes. On the borders of the plain fine ridges of open forest land, and behind them scrubs in almost every direction; in fact, this plain seems to be in the very heart of the Bunya country.

He crossed many 'high grassy ridges' to reach 'an extensive flat, called Toon by the natives, which, during [Jack] Davis's 14 years' residence with them, was assigned to him. It appears, in fact, that everywhere to the northward the aborigines lay claim to particular tracts of land, allotting certain portions of it to the individual families composing the tribes.'[119] Early governments knew how important bunyas were: 'To secure the natives in their enjoyment of their triennial banquet, the colonial government has prohibited the felling of the tree; and stations are not allowed to be planted, nor stock run, in the bunya-bunya country.'[120] This did not last: for years bullocks rested here. The foreground whipstick eucalypts show how recently they left.

In 1937 DA Herbert puzzled over balds. Soil or rainfall could not explain them, for some had lone trees 'or sometimes groves', mostly young. 'On the lower slopes', Herbert saw, 'the eucalypts are not aged trees . . . They would thus appear to represent a returned forest rather than a primaeval one.' He concluded that fire made balds: 'great areas in coastal Queensland, formerly savannah, have, following protection from fire, become re-clothed with trees . . . [In] Brisbane, One Tree Hill, which is now heavily forested, was open savannah. That the balds have had trees in the past is shown by the fact that roots can be dug up.'[121]

In 1995 Rod Fensham and Russell Fairfax surveyed 61 bunya balds and assessed 73 others from air photos. Where Herbert had invariably found 'open grassland . . . on the slopes and tops of bald hills backed by a solid wall of rain forest',[122] Fensham and Fairfax found that by 1991 eucalypts and other trees occupied about 26 per cent of what were balds in 1951. They concluded that balds could not be explained by anything but 1788 fire.[123]

Most ecologists accept this here, but perversely declare balds natural elsewhere.[124] Natural fire could not have made and maintained clearings from Tasmania to Cape York which are now reverting to trees. It is not easy to burn rainforest to make grass, or to keep back eucalypts and other fire friendly species while protecting fire sensitive bunyas. To do all these at once evidences expert botanists and fire managers over many generations.

41. A clearing near Mudgeegonga, northeast Victoria, 19 December 1963

Wangaratta run 5, photo 57 (detail), CAD 17, UPGS. Compare pictures 21, 32, 38–40, 43–5. I thank Bill Tewson for showing me this photo.

This air photo shows a grass plain lying in eucalypt forest, drained by a small creek. About 60 by 200 metres, it slopes gently west to where the creek drops over a 5-metre cliff and down a rocky gully into farmland. The landowner says the plain was 'always' there.[125] Sapling stumps ring its rim but not its centre, indicating land kept open first by fire then by axe. The same soil continues into bordering box and stringybark, which cover steep enclosing hills. This is a brilliantly placed trap. Wallabies panicked on the plain would flee downslope and crash over the cliff, and survivors would be ambushed in the narrow gully.

This template recurred across Australia. In the Blue Mountains Evans reported

> spaces of Ground of 3 or 400 Acres with grass growing within them that you can scarce walk through; the ground is strong and good with ponds of water which lead to the River; but when within a 1/4 of a Mile or so of it the course becomes a Rocky gully, and so steep between the hills, that no person would suspect such places were up them,[126]

41

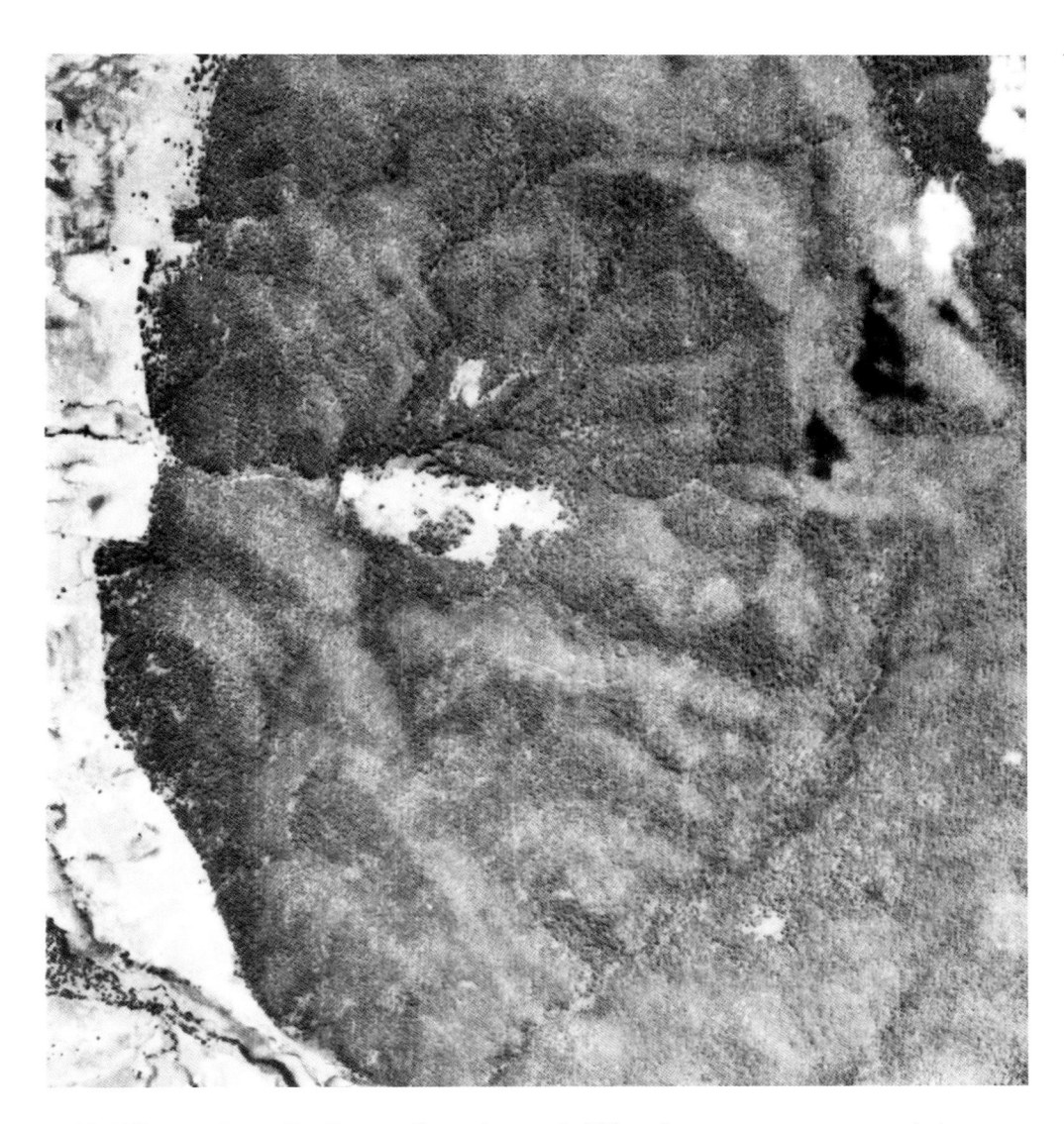

and in Western Australia George Grey observed, 'When kangaroos are surrounded upon a plain, the point generally chosen is an open bottom surrounded by a wood; each native has his position assigned to him by some of the elder ones.'[127]

Middens and shield or coolamon trees dot this locality, and near the creek red, white and yellow paintings lie under granite overhangs. They are faint, mostly of animals, but one might be a map of the template. Rock art is uncommon in northeast Victoria. This site is the largest, with 477 motifs. People used it for at least 3500 years.[128]

Pictures 42–52: 1788 fire patterns—templates

42. Steve Parish, *Wineglass Bay, Tasmania, from the north*, c2001

A Steve Parish Souvenir of Tasmania, Brisbane c2001, 14 (detail). © Steve Parish Publishing, reproduced c~ Steve Parish and Kate Lovett. Compare pictures 37, 43–7, 50–1, 53–8. For help I thank Joyce Dunbabin, Margaret Harman, Jon Marsden-Smedley, PWS Coles Bay and Ian Thomas.

This view down Freycinet Peninsula shows Wineglass Bay at left and Hazards Beach at right. On the isthmus sharp edges divide trees from grass or heath. These have been described as boundaries between wetland and tall open forest,[129] which is so in places, but at centre an edge crosses a hillock and at each end rises to wallaby traps, at the south end on a creek fan. Inland are grass necks, clearings and wetlands. Tasmanian Blue Gum dominates the forest, scattered giants above denser regeneration.

Who made these edges? From 1824 whalers operated from the Bay's south end, but only for about ten years, too briefly to clear generations of tree seedlings. The land has been a reserve since 1906, and was never farmed and reportedly never grazed.[130] Despite a 1980 fire, this scene matches Frank Hurley's February 1939 photo of it, except for a little more scrub then, behind the north end of the beach. JW Beattie's April 1909 photo is the same too, except that more scrub may have rimmed the beach south of the hillock—Beattie's colleague reported there 'a slight rise covered with low shrubs'.[131]

Here Tasmanians associated grass, heath, open forest, slopes, wetlands and two seas, for the more sheltered Hazards Beach at right has coarser sand, mounds of huge oyster and mussel shell, and more middens than Wineglass.[132] In season people camped at Hazards, handy to wetlands but hidden from Wineglass' grass corridor and traps. Habitats and resources were abundant, convenient and predictable.

It is striking that the edges remain so sharp. Trees have germinated in the forest but not much outside it. This suggests that whereas on ground recently cleared by axe or fire trees can grow from seed stock, in grassland kept clear for centuries no seed remains, and trees must generate by edge or wind invasion. Here salt or smothering grass has apparently stopped even that.[133]

43. James Scott (1810–84), Plan of Branxholm, Tasmania, 1853

Margaret Newton, Launceston. Compare pictures 13–14, 39, 42, 44–51, 54–8.
I thank Margaret, Mike Powell and the Queen Victoria Museum for this plan.

James Scott, a relative of novelist Walter Scott, drew this plan, perhaps of land he meant to buy. About 4 x 3 kilometres, it is now farmland north of the town. James' nephew JR Scott bought it in 1864, naming it Branxholm after Walter's seat in Scotland. James' brother Thomas named Deloraine after a Walter Scott character.

The plan illustrates how many resources could be associated. Following the Ringarooma flats downstream from bottom left, Dogwood scrub on the right and fringing forest or scrub then grass ('good land') on the left become Dogwood and Myrtle on the right, then Myrtle on the left, then a grass strip in 'Wattles with ferns & nettles' on the right. Wattles are rapid regenerators after fire, ferns are rainforest survivors, nettles flourish in ash. Together they suggest fire clearing rainforest, and no fire letting wattle capture grass, perhaps to move the template (ch 8). At top, flats continue as 'Open Plains' on the right and forest on the left, then there is a water-locked clearing, and finally forest.

The flats extend between low hills, one at left grass, the rest forest. The plan does not say what forest, but distinguishes it from 'musk and dogwood' and 'myrtles', so it may be eucalypt. At centre, high ground sheds creeks into swamps then 'Open Plains', split into remarkable diversity. At top right a small lagoon sits in grassland; another is across the river at far left, near a ford. The big swamp edges forest and hill before dividing the plains. Grass necks parallel it and edge slopes or push into forest; tree clumps give cover. Diverse plant communities blend beautifully with water and slope to feed and shelter different animals while exposing them to convenient harvest in one part without disturbing them in another. A day or two downriver in August 1831, Robinson

> went through some wooded country, the underwood of which had been burnt off by the natives, and across some extensive heathy plains . . . The country was peculiarly favourable for the boomer and forest kangaroo, consisting of heathy and sword grass plains and open forest . . . The inland natives have their hunting grounds for the different species of game.[134]

Tasmanians told him this. It shows them thinking of country in terms of specific habitats and resources, and making it to suit. The plan shows how neatly and variably they did it.

43

44–5. James Cobon, Cape York survey plans, 24 January 1891

Parish Tribulation surveys C153.301 and C153.302 (detail, redrawn), ERM. Scale 1:3960. Compare pictures 13–14, 18, 21, 39–43, 52–8. For help I thank Bill Kitson and Kaye Nardella of ERM, and Gurol Baba.

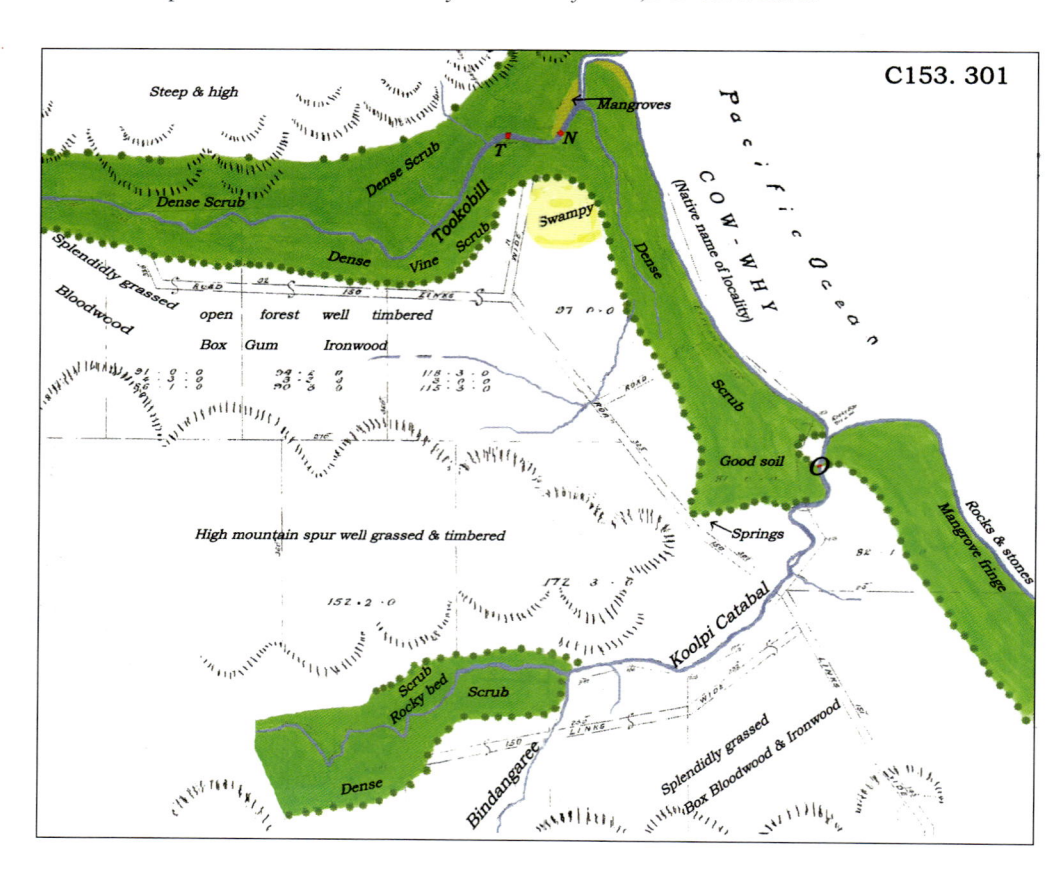

This is north of Cape Tribulation: 301 runs south from Cowie Point, 302 is 3–4 kilometres further south. Cobon had to certify 'on honour' that each plan was accurate. Green denotes rainforest; white open eucalypt forest; N a head of navigation; T a head of tidal water; O a head of navigation and tidal water.

'Vine scrub' fringes creeks, swamps and coast though none entirely, shelters mangroves from fire, and climbs unevenly up slopes. Grassy eucalypt forest covers some but not all crests, and edges some swamps, creeks or coast. Camp clearings, at least one on 'Good soil', lie at a head of tidal water. On 301 springs sit on an edge. The land is pleasant, its resources convenient and predictable.

Without fire this is rainforest country. In 1890 Crown Lands Ranger D Donavon

C153. 302

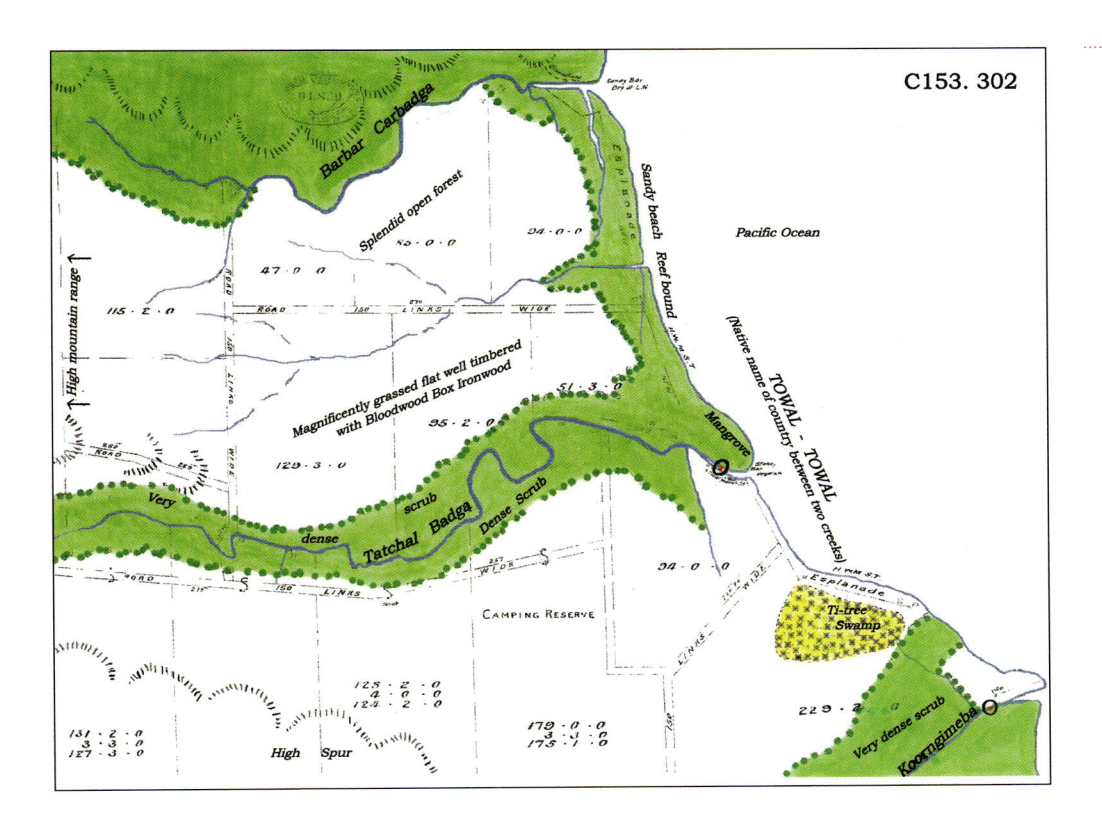

reported of it, 'The Scrub abounds with Scrub Turkeys, Scrub Hens, and a most gorgeous variety of pigeons, and a great variety of nuts, tubers, and wild fruit in luxuriant profusion . . . its waters swarm with a miscellaneous class of fine edible fish.'[135] Yet more plant variety meant more resources, more choice, so rainforest has been cleared. A century later an elder explained, 'You burn a little patch, for wallabies and kangaroos to live on, instead of you hunting them, they'll come to you.'[136] In panic they keep to the open where they move faster, so rainforest shepherds them into water or uphill, depending on the wind chosen. While men hunted, women could get food in screened places without startling animals.

Rainforest burns when dry, but it is rarely dry. Clearing it required watchful opportunism over many generations. Maintaining it was easier (ch 7), but burning it from wet valleys but not drier hills, from one water edge but not another, all while keeping eucalypts and grassland open, demands detailed local knowledge of fuel loads, winds and future resource needs, and skilful, timely burning. Yet there were hundreds of balds on Cape York.[137] Christie Palmerston's description shows how prized they were, and how closely managed:

Its upper part is free of rocks, indeed of everything else, it having been burnt in the early part of this year by an old aborigine named Wallajar, to whom it belongs . . . The S.E. end or horn . . . is 'Care-ing-bah', by some called 'Tachappa' . . . Its N.W. end is named 'Koorka-koorka' [Gourka-Gourka], and is possessed by an old man, whose name I forget . . . four of the young fellows who accompanied me have hunted over [it] often. The other two . . . though born and hunting within its shadow, never were here before.[138]

Newcomers at once thought of agriculture. In 1890 one wrote of the lower Cape, 'The area available for agriculture is cut up into isolated pockets, varying in depth . . . from half a mile to one and a half miles. These pockets comprise rich forest land with belts of dense tropical jungle along the coast.'[139] Donavon reported 'alternate patches of scrub and forest country. The forest land is well grassed . . . [with] a nice friable decomposed vegetable loam well fitted for agricultural purposes.'[140] Cobon thought this land 'highly suitable for an agricultural township and would be readily taken up in small areas for tobacco'.[141]

There is no agriculture. By 1994 301 had no grassland and rainforest was edge-invading eucalypts, though eucalypts still dominated ridges. In 1991 302 had a little grass but was similar.[142] Alma Kerry recalled that Cowie 'used to be open, now its grown back really thick, we can't get wukay [yam] on the beachfront anymore because of the rainforest'.[143]

46. Gatcomb (l and c) and Goderich (r) Plains near Guildford, Tasmania, 12 April 1949
47. Gatcomb and Goderich Plains, 16 November 1984

46: Valentines Run 6/22139, FT, c~ Bill Tewson. 47: Colour M486, 1014–063, NW Forests run 25. Base image by TASMAP (www.tasmap.tas.gov.au). © State of Tasmania. Compare pictures 13–14, 18, 21, 29–30, 39–45, 48–51, 53–8.

These photos illustrate fire and no fire in rainforest. In 1949 this land was part of the VDL Company's 61,000 ha Surrey Hills block. The Company neither made nor allowed any sustained use of it, though the plains may have been grazed, or fired by wallaby snarers.[144] Ridge or valley, damp or dry, in both pictures trees are reclaiming grass and heath. White eucalypt trunks flag pockets once open, especially north of Gatcomb in 1949, and darker patches and edges show rainforest advancing.

In 1788 Tasmanians worked hard on this land. At bottom the Wandle River runs between open eucalypt forest and grass pockets on and off its flats. People protected the river, called *Lare.re.lar*, platypus. Robinson found platypus there,[145] so the banks were less exposed to cool fires which kept open the ridges along Gatcomb's south edge. The ridges,

CANVAS OF A CONTINENT

46

47

thick with snakes, drain boggy creeks alive with frogs to a swamp below Gatcomb's north tip.[146] As their shape conveys, on each plain people used hot northeasterlies to drive fire southwest (ch 8), the fire front expanding and pushing grass neck traps into forest. The trap at Gatcomb's north tip was murderously efficient. Caught in the open and ringed by forest, prey would flee south, hit the swamp, and founder into club and spear. Survivors had to battle upslope over boggy ground into a cordon of hunters, then flee to a similar template judiciously located and primed with pick. People could always find them. At least five distinct fire regimes have conveniently associated rainforest, open forest, grass, swamp, river and ridge.

In 1827 Henry Hellyer, a tireless traveller, followed a Tasmanian track, still clear in 2001, across this country,[147] and wrote that plains just north 'resemble English enclosures in many respects, being bounded by brooks between each, with belts of beautiful shrubs in every vale'.[148] He mapped a sequence of plains large and small in rainforest from Emu Bay (Burnie) south to Surrey Hills.[149] By 1828 he knew that Tasmanians had made them: like Eyre in the dry South Australian mallee (ch 1), he found logs in the grass. Researchers have identified many such rainforest remnants.[150]

Clearing to plant Shining Gum has obliterated these and other beautiful and complex templates in the northwest.

48. An edge of Gatcomb Plain, 14 February 2002
BG. Compare pictures 13, 18, 21, 31, 34–7, 40, 44–7, 49–58.

Gatcomb carried at least three communities: White Grass and open forest on its south ridge and dry slopes, mosses and water plants on creeks and swamps, and elsewhere a wonderland of ferns, orchids, lilies, everlastings and other flowers, and heath.[151] Here heath has captured grass, and in its shelter rainforest advances.

You can see this advance. Edge trees are small, but the skyline shows big pre-1788 Alpine Ash, Messmate or Swamp Peppermint. They can't grow in rainforest: there is no light (ch 1). They are there because rainforest was not. This can happen only if rainforest is burnt back. Not by a bushfire: they are rare in rainforest, and after a lone fire rainforest slowly returns, as it is now. Decades or centuries of judicious fire drove and kept it back. Once grass and herbs were established fire was needed about every 3–5 years to promote them and kill eucalypt seedlings. The big eucalypts mark a boundary of a plain Tasmanians made.

Robinson came to recognise boundaries: '[If] when travelling in these [rain]forests you discover many stringy bark trees—or badger dung—you may always rest assured that you are near to an open country.'[152] Similarly, in the Eungai Creek catchment (NSW), Clement

Hodgkinson's *Halt near a fern tree scrub* (1843?) shows eucalypt forest with no undergrowth almost touching dense rainforest, the narrow space between bridged by tree ferns, which like sunny clearings.[153]

West of Alice Springs in September 1872 Giles wrote, 'The little plain looked bright and green . . . The grass and herbage here were excellent. There were numerous kangaroos and emus upon the plain. [It is] . . . fringed with scrub nearly all round . . . [At] the foot of the hills, I found the natives had recently burnt all the vegetation.'[154] He might have been describing Gatcomb.

49. Wentworth Marmaduke Hardy, Plan in the Hundred of Kadina, Yorke Peninsula, SA, 7 September 1874

Hundred of Kadina diagram 11, LTO. Compare pictures 39, 43–7, 50–1, 53–7. For help I thank Mick Sincock and Leith MacGillivray.

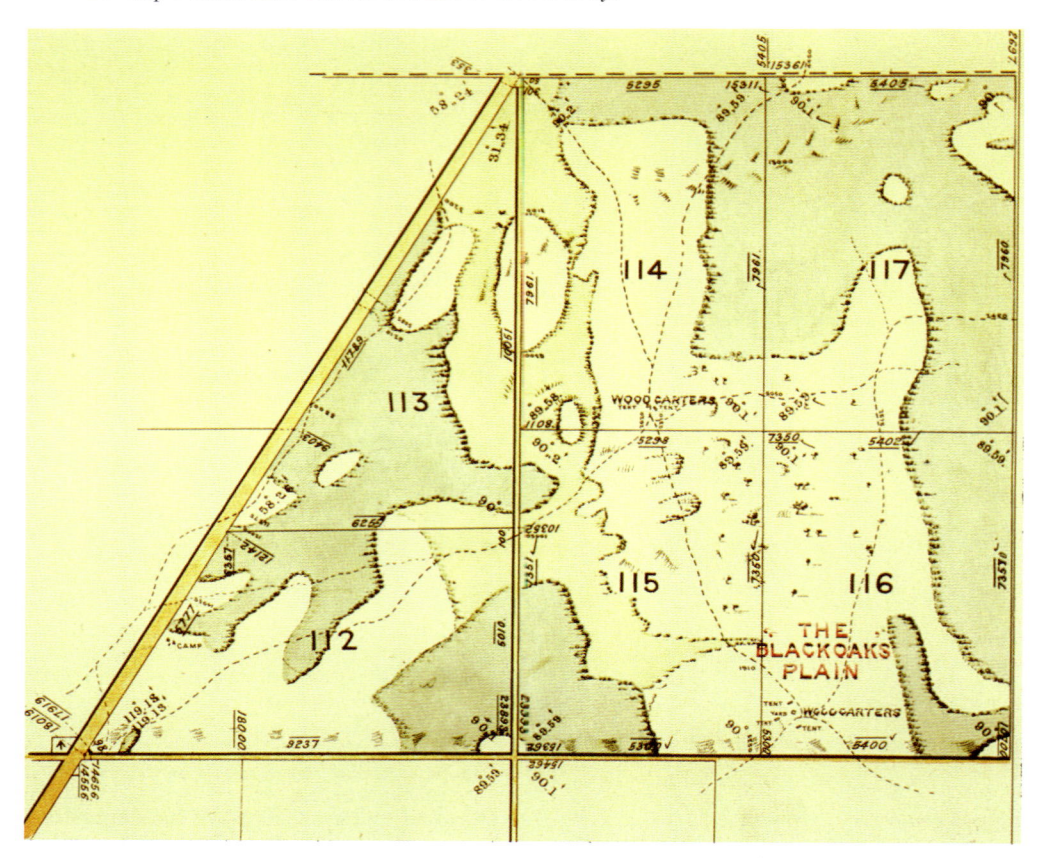

Hardy's plan covers about 3.76 kilometres in width. He coloured mallee scrub green, open forest yellow-green, grass plain pale green. A ground search confirmed that all three communities straddle different heights and soils.[155] Hardy's diagram 10 of the land immediately south is similar.

Before 1874 men cut wood here for copper mines, no doubt extending Blackoaks Plain, but not destroying its 1788 pattern. The country is much drier than at Branxholm or Gatcomb, but is shaped similarly. Small grass clearings sit in scrub and open forest, and grass necks jut into both. Trees sheltered animals; clearings or necks lit in sequence moved them predictably.

In 1839 Eyre noted these patterns further east, reported them common in his 'various wanderings in Australia', but could not explain them. He puzzled at how grassy plains suddenly appeared in scrub or forest, when dead timber showed that trees could grow on them. He thought deliberate fire might explain clearings in thick mallee, but not in open forest where the trees stood too far apart for all to be killed by one fire.[156] He was a most acute observer, sympathetic to Aborigines, but even he could not imagine that the patches were man-made.

In the 1970s Mick Williams used over 1850 plans to build a picture of the mallee north of Adelaide, including here. He considered various natural explanations for its anomalies, but concluded,

> The mallee cover was by no means as complete as is commonly thought ... along the river courses [it] tended to disappear and be replaced by open grassy land with wider spaced trees—the eucalypt savannah woodland ... Of great interest is the evidence of the open, largely treeless 'plains' within the scrub ... [some large], many smaller ones. These 'plains' may have been due to aboriginal clearing by fire.[157]

50. Frederick Montague Rothery (1845–1928), Ups & Downs block, Bundaleer Station, Qld, 1877–8

[Rothery 37]. Compare pictures 39, 43–7, 49, 51, 53–7.

Bundaleer is on the New South Wales border east of the Warrego. In 1858 the country was dry, sandy 'grassy forest, with ridges of dense brigalow scrub'.[158] The run was taken up about 1861, and grew to 1176 square miles, divided into blocks. In 1877–8 Rothery, the manager, drew a plan of each block. Ups & Downs, 100 square miles, Rothery's scale an inch to two miles, got an occupation licence in 1876. Rothery described it as 'Thick belts of Gidyah, Pine, Brigalow and small Scrub with broken plains scattered all through with open Coolibah flats. Cotton and Saltbush more or less all through.'[159] Except that Mulga was common elsewhere, this typified Bundaleer.

Rothery linked each tree species to its soil type. The pine ridge at left in picture 50 (overleaf), coloured orange, is red sand. Along Nebine Creek's left bank grey alluvial carries Coolibah, box, saltbush and grass; the right bank is more open. At bottom left blue denotes Brigalow on red sandy loams; elsewhere blue-green patches mark Gidgee or sometimes Belah on heavier red-brown earths. Yellow denotes Mitchell Grass, Never-fail and Queensland Blue Grass plains.[160]

Yet soil alone cannot explain a distribution so erratic. The map suggests which tree might occupy adjacent grassland, but not why no trees at all are there. Brigalow and Gidgee are in clumps and belts; grass and scrub alternate. At centre left Wilga sits under the pine

50

ridge, with trees shaping a grass vista to Coolibahs on the creek. North is scrub; behind shielding trees south, grass necks fragment Brigalow. Similar patterns are across the creek.

The patterns vanished very quickly. An 1886 report stated, 'brigalow is spreading very much and taking possession of most black soil flats . . . a great portion of the country that is now open, will be dense brigalow scrub in five or six years and . . . the pasture will deteriate [sic] considerably'. Brigalow was also invading Gidgee plains, Mulga had appeared, and False Sandalwood (Budda) was now common. Along Nebine Creek, an inspector lamented in 1910, 'the best grasses, cotton and saltbush have been almost destroyed by drought, heavy stocking and rabbits', yet even in wet times grass and saltbush decreased and scrub increased. After 1886 a century of ringbarking, pulling and burning controlled Gidgee, Mulga and pine, but not Brigalow or False Sandalwood. On the contrary, 'Attempts to clear sandalwood country have invariably resulted in its thick regeneration.' By 1985 a ground survey on Bundaleer, including part of Ups & Downs, found almost all the saltbush gone, much less grass, much more Brigalow and Gidgee, and dense False Sandalwood, even though the station pulled and burnt extensively in the 1960s and 1980s.[161]

Bundaleer's experience typified the back country, although pine was usually the problem (ch 11). If Aborigines could maintain good grass and saltbush, why can't Europeans? Stocking rates are a factor: heavy grazing selectively eliminates fodder plants. 1788 stocking rates not only avoided this but allowed for drought, whereas for decades European stocking rates did not, though some do now. Observers have concluded that firing scrub only makes it thicker (ch 6), yet people burnt clear in 1788. They knew which fire regime worked. We don't.

Kadina and Bundaleer are in country not remotely like Branxholm, Cape York or Gatcomb, yet their plant patterns are similar. I once assumed that different environments would impose different 1788 patterns. Not so. Across Australia the end was the same: to make resources abundant, convenient and predictable. Only the means varied.

51. Joseph Lycett (c1775–1828), *View of Lake George, NSW, from the north east, 1821*
52. Lake George from the northeast, 24 January 2009
   51: PIC U467, NLA [from Lycett 1825]. 52: David Paterson, Canberra. Compare pictures 1, 3–4, 13, 38–9, 43–7, 50, 53–7.

51

Macquarie and Oxley visited Lake George on 27 October 1820, and Oxley's 1822 map shows that they met it near this scene. Macquarie wrote, 'The last 4 miles to the lake was through fine open forest land or rich plains . . . chiefly clear of timber', and next day, 'open forest, plains, and meadows for 7 or 8 miles at least, the soil generally good, fine herbage, and full of fine large ponds & lagoons . . . full of black swans, Native Companions, and ducks'.[162] Joseph Wild, who built the road Macquarie followed, wrote similarly:

> Emu very plentiful and seen in small Flocks—tracks of some large Kangaroos found but none seen in the Neighbourhood—Swans, Geese and Ducks of different kinds in abundance . . . the Grass had been burnt in the neighbourhood of the Lake by the Natives and was springing into nice feed . . . The Plains towards the Eastward are of immense Extent, clear of wood, all beautiful Land, not swampy, though many small Lagoons of fresh Water.[163]

Europeans invariably admired this country. Allan Cunningham, WH Breton, WE Riley and others wrote of 'rich grazing lands' full of emus, brolgas and plains turkeys, and a lake

52

teeming with swans, ducks, eels and crayfish.[164] The lake may have been a sanctuary, its waters safe, its shores fire-cleaned. Govett described it in 1832:

> Its *western* side runs in almost a straight line, and a high steep grassy ridge falls close upon its banks the whole distance . . . The writer himself has seen a cloud of wild ducks, extending for apparently a mile in length, alight upon the waters of Lake George, till they appeared like an island, or an extended sandbank.[165]

In mid-summer 1831 Hoddle thought the lake

> a fine sheet of water. The country around . . . for several miles was on fire, which rendered travelling difficult and dangerous. I felt extremely unwell from inhaling the smoke and dust of burnt embers . . . The immense bodies of fire must be extremely prejudicial to life, from its exhausting oxygen of the atmosphere. I am in constant dread of having my Tents burned by the fires, which have destroyed the herbage for many miles . . . There are immense numbers of Ducks, and some Black Swans.[166]

This seems a summer clean-up fire, unlike the pick fire Wild saw.

Hoddle surveyed around the lake. South were 'grassy hills' well timbered today, and a 'grassy flat' with an 'edge of scrub'. West was an 'open grassy Range', also well timbered now. By May 1833 Hoddle was mapping regenerating 'mimosas' and 'small wattle', signalling the recent end of 1788 fire.[167]

Lycett never saw the lake: he may have copied Evans, who was with Macquarie. His view spans about 240 degrees—picture 52 deletes its left edge. He drew background hills and foreground rocks bigger than they are, across the lake he mistook cloud shadow for a peninsula as can happen today, and he mistook trees for Oondyong Point (named after a district leader), which runs into the 2009 skyline at right. Yet his topography is accurate. Along the shore his three tree copses are on granite outcrops; in picture 52 the site at right is still a copse, that at centre is barely visible through the dead tree, that at left is the bare hillock. The copses indicate fire never hot enough to crest the rocks, yet keeping adjacent grassland clear. At far left in picture 51 a forest–grass edge is where the lake is reached today, and about where Macquarie met it. This was probably an Aboriginal road. At front left a lone Grass Tree confirms regular burning. None are there now, but a few hills southwest of the lake have stands. Remnants of Wild's road in the foreground can be seen today.[168]

Lycett painted a template. The hill is grass, correctly with an emu. Sensibly it would have carried fire-welcoming yams, tubers and bulbs, but today it is improved pasture, and apart from a few grass orchids shows little evidence of plant food. It drops to a grass flat, which on the same soil abruptly becomes dense forest, then another grass flat, then the lake. The lone forest survivor, a Yellow Box perhaps 350 years old, stands at centre in picture 52. Depending on the wind, a flat could be lit for pick, and feeding animals trapped between forest and slope, or forest and lake. Picture 54 depicts hunters using this template type near Newcastle.

Pictures 53–8: Templates in use

53. Joseph Lycett (c1775–1828), *Aborigines hunting kangaroos*, c1820

>PIC R5681, NLA [from Lycett 1830]. Compare pictures 13–14, 21, 32, 36, 38–41, 43–7, 49–51, 54–8.

Lycett never visited Tasmania, and Tasmanians did not use woomeras. Despite his book title this is probably near Newcastle, where Lycett was a prisoner in 1815–17, and commandant James Wallis encouraged him to draw. He was in effect Wallis's photographer. Unlike his Tasmania and Lake George copies, this may be an original, completed in Sydney in 1819–22, and sanitised by his lithographer.[169]

Lycett shows how edges and grass corridors worked. The near trees once grew straight in tall thick forest, then the land under them was made grass, with little undergrowth. A grass lane divides forest from water, and kangaroos laze and feed on it, just as on golf greens today. One might be speared; the rest will flee down the lane to the men hidden in ambush.

54. Joseph Lycett (c1775–1828), *Aborigines using fire to hunt kangaroos,* **c1820**

PIC R5689, NLA [from Lycett 1830]. Compare pictures 13–14, 21, 32, 34, 38–40, 43–7, 49–51, 53, 55–8.

This is probably near Newcastle. It shows a common template and its use. Dense forest rises from low ground between grassy hills. A sharp edge divides trees from grass. Fires drive kangaroos to the spears. Hunters wait. They are not chancing on game, but predicting when and where it will come. They are also protecting the forest, firing its lee edge so that the wind takes the flames into the grass. When the wind lay the other way they would burn the opposite edge. Skilful burning has kept the forest dense, the grass open, the game convenient. If people spread enough templates around, they could always hunt somewhere, and if they planned burning cycles they could shepherd game from one template to the next.

Lycett shows tops clear and bottoms forest. This is sensible: low, wet ground is hard to burn. But in drier country hills inhibit grass, so people left them treed and cleared flats and valleys. Some newcomers puzzled at the difference (ch 1). It was because ends were universal but means adjusted locally.

People usually burnt from eucalypts into grass, but from grass into rainforest (ch 6). In 1910 John Mathew recalled that Moreton Bay people 'used to fire the grass in a line from one projecting point of the scrub to another and force the game away to a corner, formed by the scrub margin', and that when 'the grass was dry enough to burn, one party having been distributed along the margin of a scrub, another party set fire to the grass some distance off; the game, obliged to seek shelter in the scrub, became easy marks for the persons posted along its edge'.[170]

55. Joseph Lycett (c1775–1828), *Aborigines spearing fish, others diving for crayfish, a party seated beside a fire cooking fish,* c1820

PIC R5686, NLA [from Lycett 1830]. Compare pictures 13, 34, 39, 43–5, 51–3.

This is near Newcastle, and is sometimes taken to be Redhead Bluff. It may be. What is now a rocky shore there may have collapsed since Lycett's time, but if so the slope, the far shore, and the short rock shelf lack Lycett's usual accuracy. It may also be Glenrock further north, an important place in 1788.[171]

Lycett depicts a grass corridor like the 'grassy hill' where Newcastle was established.[172] Well-timed fire did this. Clear of houses forest now crowds coastal cliffs, and at Glenrock and elsewhere the edge between it and the older forest Lycett depicts can still be seen. Pictures 34–5 and 50 show similar waterfront corridors, as does Robert Westmacott's *Bulli from the Coal Cliffs* (1840–6).[173] In northern Tasmania in 1823 Charles Hardwicke saw 'the whole distance along the Sea Shore . . . plains extending from 3 to 4 miles inland covered with small heath rather more than ankle deep . . . They . . . are sheltered by clusters of lofty trees growing a little above the Sea beach. They are much frequented by Natives and kangaroo are extremely numerous.'[174] In 1848 William Carron described Tam O'Shanter Point in north Queensland: 'The open ground between the beach and the swamp varied in width from half a mile to three or four miles. It was principally covered with long grass, with a belt of bushy land along the edge of the beach.'[175] It is rainforest now.

The corridors were for travel, hunting and fish lookouts—note the people on the cliff. A similar spot on the New South Wales south coast is still called Black Gins Lookout, and at Milner Point (SA) Snell reported in 1850, 'The children and Lubras remain on the cliffs and by their shouts and yells tell the fellows in the water where the fish are.'[176] Unlike today's wilderness, Lycett shows people enjoying the grassland they have so carefully tended. No wonder Cook saw the east coast 'chequered with woods and lawns'.[177]

56. John Skinner Prout (1805–76), *The River Barwon, Victoria*, January 1847

> BG. A black and white lithograph is in Booth 76.
> Compare pictures 13–14, 33–5, 41, 53–4, 57–8.

Prout sketched this view, now Queen's Park, about a decade after Geelong was surveyed just downstream in 1838. Simpkinson de Wesselow was with him and sketched the same scene: it shows no hut, people or sheep, but almost exactly the same vegetation.[178] If settlers cleared trees here, they have not yet destroyed 1788 patterns.

Without controlled fire the steep slopes would be forested, but though settlers used them least they are almost bare. Trees line the river, and on the flat, colouring has obscured some grass necks pushing into forest then rising to a low central ridge part trees, part grass. Grazing animals have feed and shelter and possums have trees, making both abundant and vulnerable.

Prout thought this land idyllic, and near here in 1841 Anne Drysdale wrote,

> This place is really beautiful. A short distance from the Barwon,
> which is a noble river: all so green & fresh, with trees of the finest
> kinds . . . scattered about, & in clumps, like a Nobleman's Park. The
> clumps are formed by a burning of a large fallen tree; the ashes have
> the property of bringing up a clump of Wattles or gums, &c.[179]

People made the land beautiful, but settlers took it because it was useful. Paddocks in forest gave them water, pasture, timber and security. By shaping land so carefully for grazing animals, people paved the way for pastoral occupation. The more carefully they made the land, the more likely settlers were to take it.

57. Robert Dale (1810–56), *A panoramic view of King George's Sound*, WA, 1832
    PIC NK759/1 (l) and NK759/2 (r), NLA.
    Compare pictures 18, 39, 42–3, 49–51.

This is the north end of Dale's wonderfully detailed 2.74-metre panorama, which Moore called 'a very good representation of the Sound and harbour'.[180] The foreground vegetation is dense, but Grass Trees flower in it. This requires fire. Burn rings on Grass Tree trunks indicate many more fires before 1788 than after,[181] even though people used the fronds to roof huts.[182] In 1788 who could burn, how much, when and why, was intricately regulated (ch 6).

    The view is roughly north from Mt Clarence towards Oyster Harbour and King's River. At centre the government farm at Strawberry Hill sits on ploughed grassland, but in 1832 it was only 4–5 years old, and had cleared less than 6 acres. Beyond it Dale described 'a large plain, interspersed with small lakes, and wooded with clumps of Melaleuca and Banksia'.[183] Where not buildings or a golf course, this is forest today. Dale shows tree–grass belts and clumps associated with slopes and water. The rest of his panorama duplicates these patterns, and they extended beyond. 'Towards the interior', Dale wrote, 'small lakes, thick woods, and open patches, reach to the utmost bound of sight.'[184] The patterns also appear in William Westall's *King George's Sound, view from Peak Head* (1801) and LJ Jacottet's *Vue de Port du Roi Georges* (1833). Controlled fire made them, and Dale shows fires, small and local, nearby and inland.

This is dry, sandy country, not easy to make grass thrive in. On richer soil near the Kalgan River, Joseph Wakefield found 'the Grass soft and high with long thistles, the Trees large and in most parts thinly scattered, and the views extensive, diversified and beautiful'.[185] The richest soil grew the fewest trees, but Charles Darwin's estimate was more generally applicable:

> Everywhere we found the soil sandy, and very poor; it supported
> either a coarse vegetation of thin, low brushwood and wiry grass, or
> a forest of stunted trees . . . In the open parts there were many grass-
> trees . . . The general bright green colour of the brushwood and other
> plants, viewed from a distance, seemed to promise fertility. A single
> walk, however, was enough to dispel such an illusion; and he who thinks
> with me will never wish to walk again in so uninviting a country.[186]

Yet grass thrived well enough for fires to frighten newcomers, and in 1847 Western Australia passed an ordinance to flog or imprison Aborigines for lighting them.[187]

58. Edward Parker Bedwell (1834–1919), *Somerset, Cape York*, 1872

PIC R3929 LOC2121, NLA. Compare pictures 13–14, 21, 32, 55, 57.

Bedwell was surveying this coast for the Royal Navy. His ship, PS *Kate*, lies in the narrow strait between the mainland (front and left) and Albany Island (centre). Somerset is behind the beach at left. Settlers arrived in July 1864 and left in 1877, so Bedwell's scene is late, but it matches written accounts from 1864–5 (ch 8). This is a 1788 landscape.

Somerset lay in coastal rainforest, including plants found nowhere else, some still not identified. People traded and fought with Torres Strait Islanders who were gardeners, but did not copy them, even though they cleared rainforest, tropical gardening's hardest task, and made the ground rich in yams. Most food came from the sea, yet they maintained the land with fire, diversifying it as elsewhere in Australia.

Albany Island is grass with tree-lined shores and ridges part-forest. PP King noted a similar pattern in northwest Australia:

> The trees on the tops and sides of the hills had lately been burned: in the shady parts, however, near the water, the shore was lined with several plants which had escaped destruction . . . and on the top of the hills and shelving places half way down, were observed several coniferous trees . . . at this season in fruit.[188]

The two headland crests flanking Somerset beach have been cleared to enjoy the view, and to see dugong, turtle, fish or canoes. Headland slopes carried rainforest, but slightly inland this pattern changed. 'The ridges are generally clothed with scrub', Surveyor Richardson reported in 1865, 'although on the south-east side of the town the slopes are bald. The land between the ridges slopes down gently to the beach of each bay, being in some instances more openly timbered.'[189] This diverse country is now reverting to rainforest.

PICTURE 59: A EUROPEAN MOSAIC

59. A Kangaroo Island mosaic, 18 April 1983
SVY 2979, photo 63 (DENR) (detail) c~ Jean and Ron Nunn, Adelaide. Compare pictures 13–58.

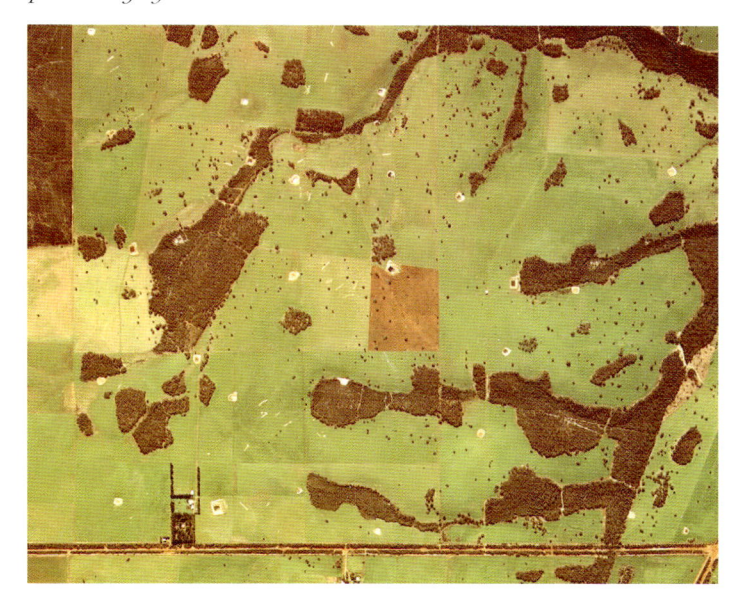

No-one lived on Kangaroo Island in 1788: it was the isle of the dead. From the early 1800s sealers and runaways lived on the coast, but this area west of Parndana was rarely visited.[190] Bushfires periodically swept the island, but it remained dense scrub—an indication that controlled fire made grass elsewhere.

This land was cleared for soldier settlement in the early 1950s. Ron and Jean Nunn moved onto their farm, 'Lyndhurst', Section 14, Hundred of Duncan, in 1954. It has a ploughed paddock inside its east boundary at centre, and a tree block being cleared and burnt outside its west boundary at top left. Out of picture a tree belt along the north boundary sheltered a creek. The soil is sandy and the topsoil shallow. The settlement scheme required at least 5 per cent scrub to be left, and most was bulldozed to about that before settlers took it up.

Ron was a 'dozer driver, but cleared only 240 of Lyndhurst's 1312 acres, and a similar proportion on the farm to the east. He left hill tops, creek lines, run-offs and useful timber like Pink Gum and Swamp Gum for wood and shelter and to slow wind erosion. Cleared land was 'fed and flogged' with super, manure and trace elements, and made good crop and fodder country.

These patterns evoke 1788 fire. So do the results. Ron and Jean saw a big increase in wallabies, possums, bandicoots and many other birds and animals. As expected they found that tree belts saved topsoil and grass. Although their cleared country was less than on most district farms, by the 1960s their production was comparable, and their productivity was going up while that of others was going down.

Progressive farmers today are familiar with such results. Like people in 1788, they know a small area intimately, and apply local remedies to local problems, although too few trees, not too many, is now the more common problem. Landcare encourages tree planting, and Peter Andrews has listed the great benefits of returning pasture to trees or water.[191] Near Gunning (NSW) John Weatherstone ran 50 per cent more stock on 15 per cent less land after he began large scale tree planting.[192] Similar results are sprouting across Australia, especially in the south. Compared to 1788 this is rudimentary, but well ahead of general understanding.

Why was Aboriginal land management possible?

3

The nature of Australia

Australia's plants, animals, insects and bacteria have changed greatly since 1788. Some have vanished, some have prospered, some have arrived. These changes obscure what Australia was like in 1788, and so how people managed it. In this chapter, *Notes 1–7* illustrate how Australia's plants made precise land management possible, while *Changes 1–5* select changes since 1788 which veil this.

Change 1. Since 1788 compacted soil and speeding water have constricted water sources and the foods they nourished.

The earth has changed. Topsoil blows away, hills slip, gullies scour, silt chokes, salt spreads, soil compacts. The last is least noticed. Much of 1788's soil was soft enough to push a finger into—'naturally soft', Thomas Mitchell called it.[1] Hence the Major's Line, the tracks his drays pressed across Victoria in 1836, guiding travellers for decades. Around Clermont (Qld) the soil was 'exceedingly friable and rich; being unstocked and therefore untrodden, it was "ashy", and the horses travelled over their fetlocks in the loose soil'.[2] Some called such soil 'rotten': 'all the country about Lake George', Mark Currie wrote in 1823, 'and between it and Lake Bathurst, is very rotten, making the riding bad'.[3] Such places are rare now, and in a dry continent that matters. In Victoria, Isaac Batey recalled 'the soil becoming hardened with the continuous trampling of the sheep cattle or horses. In proof of that Mr Edward Page said "When we first came here I started a vegetable garden, the soil dug like ashes" . . . Nowadays . . . a common spade would be useless.'[4]

Soft soil let water soak in rather than run off, so less rain sustained more plants. In 1891 the New South Wales Government Botanist lamented,

> There is no gainsaying the fact that ever since pastoral settlement took place there has been a gradual decrease of many valuable salicious

and other forage plants from the central plains of this continent, partly
through the constant trampling of the animals' hoofs, which has also
made the surface soils so hard that seeds with difficulty germinate.[5]

In 1901 James Cotton, a Cobar (NSW) pioneer, recalled,

> before this district was stocked . . . [it] was covered with a heavy growth
> of natural grasses . . . The ground was soft, spongy and very absorbent.
> One inch of rain then, in spring or autumn, produced a luxuriant growth
> of fresh green grass . . . a gradual deterioration of the country caused by
> stock . . . has transformed the land from its original soft, spongy, absorbent
> nature to a hard clayey, smooth surface (more specially on the ridges),
> which instead of absorbing the rain runs it off in a sheet as fast as it falls.[6]

In 1935 an inland pastoralist found that the rain needed to flood his creeks had more than halved since 1900: water 'once absorbed by the surface soil of the slopes now finds its way direct to the creek'.[7]

The water has changed. Once it ran slower and clearer. The Darling below Bourke was 'beautifully transparent, the bottom was visible at great depths, showing large fishes in shoals, floating like birds in mid-air'.[8] Most water ran shallower, on shallower beds:

> A succession of deep depressions is a very common arrangement in the
> structure of the beds of the Australian rivers . . . They act as natural
> tanks or reservoirs, retaining a supply of the vital element long after it
> has disappeared from other parts of the channels, giving to them the
> appearance of a chain of ponds. These depressions . . . belong, more or less,
> to all the Australian rivers, with the exception, perhaps, of the Murray.[9]

Eyre found the Lachlan 'like a deep creek, with water in only for a few hundred yards from its mouth'.[10]

On plains, streams broke bank often. Most were distributaries, not tributaries: they flowed from river to creek to plain. As Australia warmed in recent millennia they slowed and dumped sediment. Beds and banks built up, perching the streams and spreading overflows far. The lower Lachlan 'overflows its banks to a depth of three or four feet', Oxley wrote in 1817, yet 'in dry summers, there is no running water in the bed'. He thought the overflows 'certainly' exceeded 40 miles.[11] Perched beds and silt flanks trace ancient stream courses today. Many have reversed: water flows into rivers, not out.

By 1888 fast water was scouring out so many gullies that erosion was among the first environmental problems Australia recognised.[12] The water did not slow when it reached a stream. It silted then cleared, shiny clay beds showing where it cut deep. Alfred Howitt reported:

> The increase of floods was supposed to be caused by a diminution of timber, but he was inclined to think that they were to be accounted for by the hardening of the country generally ... The water ran off the country far more rapidly than it had previously done, and even assuming that there was no difference in the rainfall, he would expect the floods to come down with far greater rapidity than was formerly the case. The cutting power of the Snowy River for instance, was very great ... In many cases the sides of the valley were completely stripped to the rock, and so far as he knew, there was not a tree standing within the flood marks in that valley.[13]

On big rivers, water was speeded by improvers de-snagging and blasting rock bars for boats or paddle steamers. Clearing the Torrens of scrub and logs let the heavy 1851 rains reach Adelaide fifteen minutes sooner than any earlier flood, with a force that cut deep into the old bed, necessitating bridges. In 1862 an old colonist regretted that the river had 'worn a deeper channel in the soft soil of the plains'.[14]

In 1889 the Deniliquin (NSW) *Pastoral Times* unwittingly indicated how quickly channels could be cut:

> Some time since there seemed to be a doubt in the minds of the Deniliquin civic fathers about the true source of the Edward, and one alderman who had lived as he said, 'for thirty years' in the locality stated that he never could locate the mouth. Well, his powers of observation must have been very limited. The mouth is a well defined channel twenty or thirty feet wide with banks six feet deep and perpendicular. The channel runs for over half a mile from the Murray.[15]

The civic fathers could not have missed that channel. It came after them. When Mitchell saw the Nogoa at 'Lake' Salvator (Qld) in 1846 it was a braided stream: by 1905 the north course was a deep channel, by 1960 the south course was, and the lake was gone.[16] In 1850 Charles Strutt depicted a Murrumbidgee unrecognisable today. At Jugiong it was 'a fine stream, running over pebbles', at Gundagai it had 'clear water', at Bangus there was 'a convenient ford, where the water was about three feet deep, very clear, and flowing over pebbles' and the river was 'here and there shallow, but now and then deep, with great holes'.[17] Most of these holes, so favoured by fish and fishermen, have silted up, and above Gundagai the river is more sandy than pebbly. West of Narrandera it has cut deep into its old bed since Thomas Townsend's 1850 survey of it. With shallow banks and shallow water, his river often ran dry, while at least four fords were so reliable that settlers put head-stations by them. There are no fords now, and the 1850 bed is metres up today's bank.[18] The legendary Clancy's Overflow, on the Cooper, is Channel country now.[19]

Change 2. In 1788 more water softened drought, spread resources, and let people walk easily over more of Australia. Even in arid regions they could expect to care for all their country, and think its plants and animals always sustainable.

Shallow streams and overflows flushed more of Australia, filling billabongs, swamps and holes, and recharging springs and soaks. In 'the middle of an apparently dry forest . . .', Oxley remarked in northern New South Wales, 'the surface gave way but little to the human tread, but the horses were scarcely on it before the water sprang at every step, and the ground sank with them to their girths'.[20] Reed beds which have moved since 1788 flag changing water flows. The Murray pioneer Henry Lewes recalled of near Moama (NSW), 'The low tract between the plains and the Murray . . . was mostly clear swamp, where afterwards it became covered by impenetrable reed beds.'[21] More often, faster water swept beds away, like those on the Murray once so vast and dense that for days overlanders could not get stock to water.[22] Reeds were vital refuges for fish and birds, and bulrush (*cumbungi*) was a staple food for months each year.[23] It still fills backwaters, but fewer, giving little hint of how widespread it was in 1788.

Small water caches were common. Sturt, Eyre, Leichhardt, Giles and others got used to water in unlikely places, and owed their lives to finding it in country now dry. In October 1845 Sturt followed a 'native path' north of the Cooper looking for water. He reached some huts, and

> at length we found a small, narrow, and deep channel of but a few yards in length, hid in long grass . . . The water was about three feet deep, and was so sheltered that I made no doubt it would last for ten days or a fortnight . . . I allowed the horses to rest and feed on the grass for a

> time; but it was of the kind from which the natives collect so much seed, and though beautiful to the eye, was not relished by our animals.[24]

The district was in at least its second year of drought, yet Sturt wrote as though his find was natural. Perhaps it was, but Aborigines sheltered it. They promoted a grass which deterred stock and therefore kangaroos, and its shelter kept open miles of surrounding country.

Over half the water sources in the Murray–Darling catchment, Australia's biggest, have gone since 1788.[25] In arid Australia few remain beyond those people protect, and even on the coast springs and soaks have dried or choked. Water was drained for pasture or crop and diverted from swamps, which dried back. Settlers stripped sheltering scrub, stock trampled protecting edges, wet spots silted up or were ploughed in. Dams and irrigation often replace what was once there anyway.

The changes let drought bite harder. 'Drought' is a subjective notion. What we call a 'drought-adapted' species is adapted to what we think drought is, not what it does. For us drought is the gap between what water comes in, and what goes out. Today we feel this gap sooner than did people in 1788, not least because the gap widens as population increases. Rain which broke a drought then does not now. Fewer overflows and compacted soil let water replenish less country. In 1938 a veteran pastoralist wrote that overstocking forced stock to uproot the grass, which let rain run off the bare ground 'instead of being held up by the rooted pastures as of old, soaking into the ground, finding its own level, and reappearing in the form of springs'.[26] 1788's kind quilt of springs, soaks, caches and wetlands has gone.

Change 3. Grass was widely available during Australia's toughest season, offering management opportunities rare in Europe. Except in the Wet, people could burn grass at almost any time, knowing it would re-shoot green. They could expect to attract grass eaters and their predators, especially in summer when today grass is scarce and animals stressed. This let them manage land not merely to help animals survive, but to make them abundant, convenient and predictable.

Drought has been intensified by the upset of Australia's grasses. In 1788 these were typically drought-hardy, summer flourishing tussock perennials. 'Nothing which I observed', Morton wrote northwest of Rockhampton in 1859,

> caused in me so much astonishment as the greenness of the grass. I had expected to see it all dried up by the heat of the tropical climate. At the beginning of September there had been no rain

for four months, yet everywhere the grass was remarkably green,
and became greener every week till I left in November.[27]

1788's most widespread grass was Kangaroo Grass, caviar to grazers if burnt regularly. It deserves a statue. More than any other it fed Australia's early stock, and settler prosperity. It heads in late summer, its base still green, providing feed when most needed (pictures 10–11). It has disadvantages. Its corkscrew seeds work through the toughest hide, and its tussocks leave bare ground between, which many settlers thought wasteful. Edward Curr noted what others welcomed:

> In the greater portion of Australia, indeed nearly all of it, the grass originally grew in large tussocks, standing from two to twenty feet apart, according to circumstances. It bore no resemblance to a sward, and when one drove over it in a dog-cart, a succession of bumps was experienced from its lumpy way of growing. Gradually, as the tussocks got fed down by sheep and cattle, they stooled out; and the seed got trampled into the ground around them, and in the absence of bush fires grew, so that presently a sward more or less close resulted, such as we see at present.[28]

Squatters speeded the change. They wanted to improve winter pastures when perennials were dormant, and they wanted grasses from home which they knew rotated usefully with crops. North of Armidale (NSW), John Everett was typical of more thoughtful squatters. He admired native grasses, but from 1841 spent heavily on planting clover, lucerne, rye and other familiar pastures.[29]

While squatters improved in this way, their stock ate out native feed. As early as 1820 Gregory Blaxland stated, 'The best is oat [Kangaroo] grass, which I have observed of late years has failed . . . Where much stock has been kept, the oat grass has nearly disappeared, and a new and inferior has appeared.'[30] A west Victorian pioneer blamed fire for the loss,

> In 1846 all the country around here . . . was covered with kangaroo grass—splendid summer feed for stock of all kinds. It was at its best . . . [from] January . . . to May, but it lost its colour after that, and gave place to a finer grass . . . The country was like this for some years after 1846, until destroyed by the indiscreet use of fire.[31]

Kangaroo Grass is promoted by fire, and declines if it doesn't get it. For generations discreet fire let it flourish while conserving herbs, yams, orchids, lilies, winter annuals and other grassland plants. Inept burning and overgrazing put this assemblage under stress.[32] Fodder grasses yielded to unpalatable grasses and woody weeds. The loss led graziers to introduce more exotics, then superphosphate, essential for exotics in Australia's phosphate-poor soils but lethal to natives. Wherever settlers made grassland pasture, native perennials faded. By the 1940s Kangaroo and similar grasses were refugees in fenced-off reserves and parks where stock and improvers could not get at them, although they are coming back now as stock numbers fall.

The change was revolutionary. Tall summer flourishing perennials resist drought by shielding soil moisture or holding it in dense roots. Roots are typically half their bulk, whereas in annuals roots vary from half when mature to almost none when dead or sprouting. Summer feed is priceless in Australia. In summer most native annuals seed; exotic annuals die; native perennials thrive. Equally important, most perennials tolerate fire. Burn them in summer and they re-shoot green. Burn annuals and they die. This fact is critical to understanding 1788 management.

Few newcomers realised this, though they saw its effects. On the Macintyre (NSW) during the 1827 drought Allan Cunningham was 'surprised to observe how wonderfully the native grasses had resisted the dry weather on the upper banks of this dried watercourse. They appeared fresh and nutritive, affording abundance of provision to the many kangaroos that were bounding around us.'[33] Near Adelaide in mid-summer Dirk Hahn saw shepherds 'grazing their flocks on meadows made green by Nature'.[34] On the Macquarie and Narran in the 1845–6 summer, Mitchell wrote often that it was hot, but as often of the many 'verdant grasses'.[35] On Flood's Creek north of Broken Hill (NSW) in November 1844, Sturt wrote,

> the heat was very great, [but] the cereal grasses had not yet ripened their seed, and several kinds had not even developed the flower. Everything in the neighbourhood looked fresh, vigorous, and green, and on its banks (not, I would observe, on the plains, because on them there was a grass peculiar to such localities) the animals were up to their knees in luxuriant vegetation.[36]

In 1788 Australia's summer tan proclaimed life; by 1888 dead creams and whites were fast becoming proof of unyielding drought (picture 12).[37]

Change 4. In 1788 trees, saltbush and perennial grasses mitigated salinity; now it is spreading.

Salt infuses most of Australia. This was so in 1788. The Centre's vast lakes are salt, and Salt, Saltwater and Saltpan rivers and creeks speckle maps. Victoria's Maribyrnong was once Saltwater River; WA's Mortlock was once Salt River. In April 1839 Jane Franklin reported 'a dried lagoon whitened with salt' near Mt Macedon (Vic),[38] and on Darling backblocks in August 1875 George Fortey found several lakes 'even more salt than the Ocean. All this part of the country appears to be a mass of salt as you may see it on the ground as you ride along.' The salt was up to eighteen inches thick.[39]

Salt has spread menacingly since 1788. This is commonly attributed to tree clearing, which erodes soil and lets scalds emerge, water tables rise, and salt surface.[40] Yet along southeast inland rivers salt now kills forests denser than in 1788, veterans and flood-borne youngsters alike. Faster water has cut into a salt basin below, or into subsurface salt in nearby land.

Dryland salinity is extensive, and can occur in quite small seepages. Tree clearing poorly explains its spread: in 1788 the plains may have carried fewer trees, not more, than now (appendix 1). Overgrazing saltbush has been blamed. Saltbush sweats salt to its leaves, whence water or fire recycles it. In the 1830s squatters seeping over the inland stopped at those dry, salty leaves, thinking them useless, but they are palatable and nutritious. John Peter, the squatter who claimed to discover this, made so much from the discovery that even after accumulating over a million acres in Australia, a castle in Scotland and a mansion in London he complained that he could not spend all his money.[41] Much of his land had few trees, and he grazed his saltbush so heavily that it is still recovering, yet little of his land is salted now. On Moira on the Murray, Lewes recalled,

> The small strips of plain near the swamp were covered with *mesembryanthemum* and salt-bush. The higher plains were entirely bare of any vegetation whatever but occasional salt-bushes. The box forests skirting the plains had here and there a few tufts of dry grass . . . the same appearance of intense drought and sterility pervaded the whole.[42]

Little saltbush or grass, yet no mention of surface salt. Elsewhere too land almost bare of trees in 1788 was not saline. In short, forests have salted up but open places have not. Why?

Rain and soil are factors. Over centuries rain on soft red-brown earths filtered finer particles down, leaving loam topsoil over almost solid clay. Fresh water sat on that clay, screened from salt beneath. In the eastern Riverina this precious barrier was only 25–50 centimetres down and farmers tried not to break it when ploughing, although now erosion and compaction have destroyed much of it. At Moira the clay was 4–6 metres down; elsewhere up to 20 metres down. 'More than 70 per cent of Australia's landmass', Peter Andrews says, 'has a layer of clay beneath it'. This keeps salt down, and is why deepening rivers which cut that clay layer become saline drains.[43]

Even so, places above the clay, lightly wooded but not salt in 1788, are saline now. Perhaps those places grew too many trees after 1788, not too few, for trees break the clay barrier where grass does not. As well, fresh water, being lighter, sits above salt water. Trees drink it, letting salt water rise. The more and bigger the trees the more fresh water they drink, and the more readily salt rises to kill them. This argues that tree clearing does not necessarily cause salinity, and that trees do not necessarily prevent it. But perennial grasses mitigate it. In 1788 their dense roots trapped what rain fell, keeping barriers of fresh water and dry earth between the salt below and the plants above. Especially inland where salinity is so far most severe, agronomists now recommend deep-rooted grasses like phalaris and lucerne to avert it, replicating what native perennials did for millennia.[44] Burning can increase salinity,[45] but in 1788 people could burn perennials without salting the land.

Change 5. In 1788 people used almost every plant in some way. Losses since 1788 mask how widespread and connected resources were.
Most plants survived 1788's calamities, and some thrived, but some valued species became extinct or rare. Local extinctions were continuous—Red Cedar, Cabbage Palm and New Zealand Spinach on the coast, Pituri, Native Truffle and Native Gooseberry inland. Orchids, lilies, herbs and the winter annuals essential for small animals vanished from familiar ground. Any species loss dislocates its ecosystem, no doubt often in unseen ways, but some losses were so extensive that they changed the face and colour of Australia. Daisy Yam's bright yellow, for example, followed Kangaroo Grass into refuge pockets (ch 10).

Note 1. Climate, soil and local moderators regulate plant growth and distribution, but almost all Australia supports plants, so people could use it all, including its deserts.
Australia has 25,000 native plant species, 10 per cent of the world's total, in myriad associations.[46] Some straddle the continent; others defend a few square metres. Few are deciduous: Deciduous Beech and Red Cedar in rainforest, Red Bauhinia, Poplar Gum and bloodwoods in the north. A broad impression is that over millennia drought

sensitive species have retreated before drought tolerant neighbours into higher rainfall zones and sheltered pockets.

Climate, soil type and depth, and local moderators (altitude, aspect, shelter, predators and competition for moisture, light and nutrients) limit where plants grow, and engender both consistency and variety. Mulga grows in dry country but is denser in hollows than on hilltops and shallow soils, and denser on cooler south than north facing slopes. In the Adelaide hills gums prefer deep soils facing north, while Messmate tolerates shallow soils but for moisture likes to face south. Hills east of Hobart carry Risdon Peppermint on north or northwest facing slopes, but Black Peppermint on south facing slopes, with a sharp boundary on crests between.[47] In 1788 William Bligh noted that Tasmanian vegetation was more luxuriant on south slopes than on north.[48] On Mt Macedon and in Gippsland species vary according to whether a slope faces north or south, and how high or exposed it is.[49] On coasts, wind shears scrub height. High country has a line above which trees don't grow. Shelter lets rainforest species survive in arid gorges, and a few such as Weeping Pittosporum and Ooline have adapted to aridity.[50]

Aridity is a significant regulator. Its long dominance is evident in the many plants which reflect heat and conserve water with hard, waxy leaves; in the rapid growth of others if rain falls; and in how well both recover from stress. WH Breton wrote of New South Wales after the 1826–9 drought,

> A circumstance respecting this colony, which must excite astonishment in every one, is the truly wonderful way in which the vegetation will recover itself after a drought. Land so completely burnt up that not a blade of grass is visible, will, within a few days after rain, become covered with a verdure most refreshing to the eye.[51]

Floods trigger similar miracles. In 1885 a surveyor described the Cooper as 'beautifully grassed country, the grass in some instances being as high as the camels'.[52] With water the Cooper grows the best feed in Australia. Arid land is not necessarily inhospitable. In 1788 very few places grew no plants, and no climate or region was so harsh people stopped using it.

Similarly, while soil limits particular species, some plant uses almost every soil, nutrient-poor though 90 per cent are.[53] Cracking clay belts from northwest Victoria to Queensland and the Northern Territory supported no trees in 1788 and few now. As the clays wet and dry they swell and shrink, snapping all but the smallest roots.[54] Yet they grow good feed, including Mitchell Grass, Bluegrass and sometimes saltbush, and on their creeks and rises scrub like Brigalow can grow densely.[55]

Many plants, including such trees as Kurrajong, Bottle Tree, callistemons, many wattles and some eucalypts, use a variety of soils. Mugga Ironbark, tough and beautiful, is native to inland soils from Victoria to Queensland, and to the New South Wales coast. Ghost Gum grows in central Australia and Papua. On Sydney sandstone *gummifera* is a mallee with lignotubers up to 75 metres square; on better soils it is a bloodwood with no lignotubers.[56] Other plants need a specific soil: volcanic or sedimentary, sand or loam or clay, rich or poor in humus or phosphorus or lime.[57] Near Barellan (NSW) two eucalypts, Bimble Box on sandy loam and White Mallee on lime, grow within a metre of each other:[58] lime can be a nutrient or a poison. On the Cooper, Sturt reported, 'I stood more than once with one foot on salsolaceous plants growing in pure sand, with the other on luxuriant grass, springing up from rich alluvial soil.'[59] Sturt knew how important soil–plant associations were. He cited River Red Gum on flood land beside box off it, 'though the branches of these trees might be interwoven together, the one never left its wet and reedy bed, the other never descended from its more elevated position'. He pointed to the

> open grassy and park-like tracts . . . The trees most usual on these tracts, were the box, an unnamed species of eucalyptus, and the grass chiefly of that kind, called the oat or forest grass, which grows in tufts at considerable distances from each other, and which generally affords good pasturage.

So important did he think such associations that he risked asserting, 'The light ferruginous dust . . . to the eastward of the Blue Mountains, is as different from the coarse gravelly soil on the secondary ranges to the westward of them, as the barren scrubs and thickly wooded tracts of the former district are to the grassy and open forests of the latter.'[60]

Note 2. Plants form communities, so people could group them, predict their whereabouts, and link them to totems in ecologically consistent ways.
Climate, soil and local conditions shepherd plants into communities—plants sharing common ground under similar conditions. A community might be named for a dominant species (Karri, Brigalow, saltbush, Spinifex), or a climate or terrain (wet or dry rainforest, alpine scrub), or both (pine–box woodland, Mitchell Grass plain, tea-tree swamp). Some species keep to one community, others are comfortable in several. Each

community locates animals, which in turn alter communities: birds spread seed, grazers suppress scrub. Jim Noble and his colleagues found that burrowing bettongs, now extinct over most of their 1788 range, were crucial 'landscape engineers'. Their digging made Mulga soils friable, fertile and absorbent, which with bettong seed storing increased the number and diversity of palatable perennials, attracting kangaroos and other grass eaters onto their warrens.[61] Plant–animal communities might blend at boundaries, but locally each was distinct enough for people to see that maintaining the habitat each plant and animal preferred let them predict where each would be.

Note 3. Two dominant Australians, acacias and eucalypts, illustrate challenges and opportunities people faced in 1788.

Australians like wattle. They call golden, not merely yellow, its flowers splashing bush and park. Golden Wattle is the national flower, green and gold the national colours. Wattle decorates cards, crests, coats-of-arms. People even admire tough, dusty inland species without bright flowers or perfume, seeing them as battlers, typically Australian, heroic because they survive. Australia has a wattle for every sentiment.

Acacias may have originated in Australia. Counts vary and species are still being found (ten in the Pilbara alone in the last few years), but Australia has roughly 1000 of the world's 1300 species, more than any other Australian genus, and they range more widely, almost as widely as all other genera combined. They are sparse in rainforest but nearly reach the continent's extremes of cold and heat, and they rule the inland. Mulga dominates 20 per cent of Australia; Brigalow, Gidgee and other acacias typify large areas.

One acacia, Mimosa Bush, arrived before Europeans. Native to south and central America, it was named *farnesiana* in 1611, from a plant in Italy's Farnesi Palace gardens. Perhaps the Spanish took it to Europe, and to the Philippines where it is now common, then sailors brought it south. It has thorns and leaves, uncommon in Australian acacias, and has adapted so well that it is now a weed. Other wattles are rare and reclusive: *gordonii* keeps to Blue Mountains sandstone, *quornensis* to hills near Quorn (SA), *pataczekii* to the southeast high country. The tallest wattle, Blackwood, common from north Queensland to Tasmania, prefers wet country; the next tallest, Silver Wattle, cool mountains; the next, Ironwood, desert. Other species are shrubs or ground covers. Variety can occur even within a species. Georgina Gidgee poisons stock in some places and feeds it in others. Mulga has different forms, and its spacing can vary widely.

Wattles expect drought. They use little nutrient, but in seeking moisture a seedling's root can be four or five times its height, and it goes straight down: try transplanting one. Most seedlings and some adults have leaves; others mature as phyllodes—sun-dodging, moisture-shielding needles or stem stubs. They point up or down to channel rain down branches and trunk to roots concentrated below. Mulga points up, begging the sky. The drier the season the straighter it points, the harder it begs. When drought kills it, sometimes over hundreds of miles, its seed waits decades, perhaps centuries, for rain. Across Australia acacia seed waits (picture 6).[62]

Acacias share Australia with eucalypts. Familiar but distinctive, no other plant so dominates any continent, nor so strongly calls exiled Australians. Sun through canopies, grey-green leaves shining, oil scent on hot days, distant blue ranges—this is the bush, as Australian as gum trees, white Australia's bush legend: tough, adaptable, battlers in hard times, opportunists in good, conquerors of a continent. Eucalypts could almost teach newcomers how to be Australian.

Almost. Most newcomers fear drought, suppress fire and dislike poor soils. Most eucalypts tolerate drought, ally with fire and welcome poor soils. They leave to Spinifex and acacias truly dry regions—perhaps half Australia—but for 350,000 years their tuning to Australia's long drying and swings of cold and heat has entrenched their dominance, and made them so adaptable that they defy rules: one species or another is always an exception. Their responses to drought, light, soil and fire demonstrate their extraordinary flexibility.

Drought made eucalypts. Even in cool wet habitats their leaves are drought-ready, paper-thin and waxy to reflect heat and hold moisture. As seedlings most have broad horizontal leaves to catch light, but clear of cover the leaves narrow and face down, dodging light and aiming water at their roots. Some have three leaf stages, some one, in the north some are deciduous and put out green or red leaves during the build-up to the Wet. Most prize leaves as drought defences and nutrient stores, and shed them reluctantly.

Drought, fire or insect predation, except when long sustained, trigger a tree to put on new growth. Mallee trunks stay underground and send only branches above. Three tropical eucalypts sprout from their roots,[63] all but Mountain Ash and some northern species sprout beards (ch 1) from trunk and branch, and all but about fifteen species sprout lignotubers—the more marginal the environment the more likely lignotubers are.[64] Many a clearing axeman has been broken by a red sea shooting from stumps behind him. If we see that rapid flush as merely a stress response we may not be Australian enough: it reflects opportunity as much as challenge. Other Australian genera deploy beards, but it is rare outside Australia.

Most eucalypts have another trick. Their bark not only heals wounds, but revives trees seemingly dead. It snakes from the ground up a dead trunk, then sprouts buds. In time branches hold and the dead trunk is covered anew (pictures 7–8). Many eucalypts may be much older than we assume.

Buds and bark depend on a remarkable capacity. No trees in the world grow so big and so quickly on such poor soils. The size and splendour of eucalypts commonly deceives newcomers about soil quality. Many early settlers attacked the biggest trees, the densest stands, assuming that the best soils lay under them, until years of sweat taught them to link species and soil: don't clear stringybark, clearing mallee sends topsoil to New Zealand, Yellow Box means good cropland, River Red means heavy ploughing, and so on. On every soil one species or another flourishes.

Eucalypts grow a lot with little by storing nutrients, some of which they harvest. Roots release chemicals to extract nutrients like phosphorus from iron and aluminium compounds in the soil, and organic acids to generate electric currents which reach beyond the roots to draw in distant nutrients. Leaves drip leaching chemicals, and before dropping a leaf the tree withdraws phosphorus and adds calcium to help cycle polyphenols (chemical compounds) to poison competitors. Bark is similarly treated, and dropped mostly in summer, letting chemicals work by keeping soil moist. If fire or improvident Europeans clear such litter, a tree might reduce its nutrient need by dropping branches, having first re-absorbed their nutrients, or it might burst into flower and seed. It is hard to think of ways to scavenge food and water eucalypts don't use. That bare patch so common under them signals how well they do it.[65]

Most nutrients are ready for instant use, stored in lignotubers or in sapwood cradling epicormic buds. This gives eucalypts an astonishing resilience. In 1990 I planted a Mugga Ironbark on our nature strip. By 1998 it was 4 metres high. One night a neighbour drilled two holes into the trunk and filled them with poison. The tree seemed to die. Three years later it sprouted, and by 2002 was half a metre high. Our boundary was changed and neighbours chopped the tree down, ran a bobcat over the stem, buried it under heavy clay, and dug and filled a 2-metre deep trench beside it. On New Year's Day 2004 it sprouted again, tiny red leaves breaking through the clay. Within a fortnight it was 10 centimetres high. The neighbour bulldozed it and covered it with bitumen. It hasn't reappeared, but I'm hopeful.

As with acacias, Italy named a eucalypt, in 1832—*camaldulensis*, River Red Gum, from a mature tree in the Count of Camalduli's Naples garden.[66] It is the most widespread eucalypt, flanking water across Australia. About 1928 a log dug from under the Yarra, wood and bark perfectly preserved, was estimated at 250,000 years old.[67] Other eucalypts are rare, in tiny enclaves, often on soils poor even by Australian standards.

Imlay Mallee was not described until 1980, when about 70 plants were found in a single location on the New South Wales south coast. In the Blue Mountains two *copulans* were found in 1957 and described in 1991: it may be extinct now. Only two Mongarlowe Mallees are known; Silver-leaved Gum is found in two Blue Mountains locations and two south of Canberra; Risdon Peppermint occupies a few spots in southern Tasmania; Morrisby's Gum two small areas near Hobart. At Mt Bryan are South Australia's only known Southern Blue Gums: one might be 2000 years old. Ramel's Mallee was collected in the Western Australian desert in the 1890s, then not for another 100 years. Thirteen southwest eucalypts are known in only one location. The oldest and rarest eucalypt found, Meelup Mallee, is a single plant probably over 6000 years old, its lignotubers covering 40 metres.[68]

How many species there are will never be fixed since some cross-pollinate,[69] but let's say 700, five not native to Australia. They range from low shrubs and stumpy trees to Mountain Ash, the world's tallest flowering plant. The tallest Mountain Ash known is 101 m, in southern Tasmania, yet in the Snowy Range not far north are mature Varnished Gums less than 50 cm high. Such variability makes eucalypts more a spectrum than a family. They merge species, change form, appear at widely separate locations. River Red Gum has at least three recognised varieties. In the Adelaide hills it and SA Blue Gum are distinct species, but the blue looks like a red which has climbed off the flats, and both look like Blakely's Red Gum, a hill tree. Grey Box shades into 'a chain of related species'. The same species can have different coloured flowers: Mugga Ironbark in New South Wales and several West Australian species can have cream, pink or red flowers. Near Bulli Pass (NSW) two mature trees stood side by side, one smooth barked like Sydney Blue Gum, the other rough barked like Bangalay. Both rose from the same root.[70]

How to classify a plant which does that? A Gippsland bushman did it by tasting the leaves, blindfolded.[71] Others classify the bark. As a boy I learnt four bark groups: gum (smooth), box (trunk rough, branches smooth), stringybark (fibrous) and ironbark (hard, corrugated). Other barks include Blackbutt, Minni-ritchi, bloodwoods and mallees. The bark of the first eucalypt Europeans described, Messmate Stringybark, found on Bruny Island in 1777, is more ash than stringybark. The bark of two majestic species, Yellow Box and River Red Gum, seem equally between box and gum. Most puzzling, if its bark lets a species choose how to counter drought—smooth reflecting heat, rough shielding it—why do both smooth and rough barks grow near Australia's hottest and coldest extremes? In other ways too eucalypts defy botanists, who now identify three genera, *Eucalyptus, Angophora* and *Corymbia*.

Another eucalypt trait is handy for historians. It chases light, even though Australia has plenty (pictures 1–6). Most plants seek light, but no tree so dramatically. In shade it grows straight, on a shade edge it bends and branches to the light, in light it sprints up to outpace neighbours, then spreads wide. From twigs to trunk its shape declares how much light it had in the past, where light came from, and if and when the light changed. Its shape thus reflects the conditions it grew up in. A history of its surrounds emerges, showing whether a locality was once open or forest, or first one then the other. As a rule, the wider the canopy, the more open the country was.

This history can be extended from locality to landscape by noting the spacing of each eucalypt generation. It is hard to decide a standing tree's age. Growth rates vary, but locally this smoothes to an average, so trees growing under similar conditions can be sorted by size into generations. In alpine forest or mallee usually only one generation is apparent, but elsewhere several readily emerge. Even in dense forest they can be distinguished as easily as gums on the Murrumbidgee from the 1870, 1916, 1956 and 1974 floods. Each generation's size and spacing announces its age and history, and so the history of the land around. Where scattered and wide-canopied giants tower over their straight, slim, crowded children, the country was open once but forest later. Where big trees stand straight and alone, branches hugging trunks, forest has been cleared.

Why isn't a generation like its parents? Why are straight-limbed trees topped by wide-canopied elders? How could land be open in 1788 but forest later? Why within a few metres does one tree lean into the prevailing wind, another away, a third across? In open country why does one tree twist its branches in one direction but another doesn't (picture 2)? To cause such things the landscape itself must have changed. Eucalypt shape and spacing are valuable guides to the nature of Australia. They convey what landscapes were like in 1788 and how they have changed since, provoking a central question: were they natural or made?[72]

Note 4. People could manage plants with fire.
Climate, soil and local moderators are compounded by a notoriously random constraint: fire. Fire is drought with legs. Many plants deal with both in the same way: they re-shoot or seed. Yet whereas drought is rarely a friend, fire often is. Plants relate to it so closely that it can group them. Species are fire dependent (needing fire to survive), fire promoting (encouraging fire with oil, resin or flammable material, often because they are fire dependent), fire tolerant (accepting fire), fire sensitive (killed by fire but seeding after it) or fire intolerant (killed by fire).

Fire dependent species include some near the hottest (Mitchell Grass, Spinifex) and coldest (Buttongrass) parts of Australia. Near both extremes Grass Tree trunks resist fire but rot without it, and fire generated the wonderful arrays of bulbs, tubers and flowers early Europeans saw. In settled districts this is uncommon now, but a year after the big 2003 fire Kosciuszko National Park had its best flower show for decades on ash and cleared ground. Without fire, shrubs and grasses smother these species before themselves becoming moribund, and even with fire, stock might eat or trample them out. But suitably timed fires can trigger species to regenerate (Yam Daisy, Bracken), or sprout from lignotubers (banksia, waratah, tea-tree, heath), or flower (Christmas Bell, Gymea Lily, grasstree, waratah, daisies, lilies, orchids), or germinate (Indigofera, banksia, hakea, heath and others with hard seeds or pods), or die but set seed (Mountain Ash, Mulga, many central Australian shrubs), while fire ash provides nutrients (Blady Grass, Bracken, heath) or activates soil bacteria to increase nutrient supply (Zamia). At the other extreme a few species, most in cold or wet areas where fire is uncommon, are killed outright by any fire (rainforest), and some which welcome cool fire die in hot fire (Budda, Yarran, Tasmanian pines, tropical open forest trees). Knowing how plants treat fire let people in 1788 manage them suitably.[73]

Note 5. Most wattles regenerate densely after fire.
Acacias have a range of fire responses, but most meet it with their drought defences. Some use lignotubers; most die or die back after releasing copious seed. Seedlings soon crowd the land. Mention in early records of dense young wattle may well mark country recently burnt, while sapling height can suggest how recent the fire was.

How much fire kills an acacia, and how hot it must be, varies greatly. A mild fire kills Mulga, Gidgee and Brigalow, though it rarely takes hold in Brigalow—its dense stands smother competition, it drops no bark, and it sheds leaves mostly during rain, so it offers little to burn. Some central Australian acacias tolerate fire, yet if the season permits, seed within six months. Others die but hold seed for years, waiting for rain. Such diverse responses often co-exist. In 1788 people fired acacias judiciously, conserving stands in different fire recovery stages.[74]

Note 6. Eucalypts and fire formed an ancient alliance, which people joined.
In one of Australia's great alliances, eucalypts greet fire with astonishing ingenuity and diversity, encouraging, tolerating, resisting, deflecting, re-greening, seeding. Tropical eucalypts welcome fire far less than their southern cousins. They don't drop flammable bark, their leaves carry less oil, they don't hold seed for post-fire recovery, and few use

buds or lignotubers, and those rarely. Yet they use fire, seeming to expect what they usually get, frequent cool fires which suppress competitors without damaging crowns. They dominate northern savannah.

Most southern eucalypts promote fire. From alps to desert they use their drought defences to help fire kill insects, mistletoe, fungi, soil bacteria and any plant in range. They don't like competition. If understorey Blackwood, Black Sheoak, Sweet Pittosporum or the like becomes dense, even a hot fire, which most are in thick scrub, may not eliminate it, because the seedlings surge from the ash and capture nutrients. So most southern eucalypts encourage frequent fire. Normally this would mean cool fire because fuel can't accumulate, but this might not destroy competition, so eucalypts make fires hotter. Their trunks resist fire, their open crowns fan it, their bark, leaves and oil intensify and channel it.

Barks vary, letting each species manage fire in its own way. On the tree most undamaged barks do not catch fire. They contain kino (gum) which resists burning. Ironbarks are tightly packed. A careless axe bounces off, and an average fire, finding no hold and no oxygen, merely licks the surface. Stringybarks offer a few loose strands to help fire up to the crown, then defend their trunks like ironbark. Mallees offer curling bark; Spotted Gum, Karri, Sugar Gum and others shed flakes. Desert trees like Ghost Gum and Lemon-flowered Gum have smooth white powdered bark which deflects heat and offers fire no hold. Mountain Ash has thin bark and almost any fire kills it, yet its leaves are the most flammable of all eucalypts, and it drops more litter than most. It recovers from seed, so needs fire to clear the ground and lay ash. If a fire comes it makes sure the fire is big and hot, for if no fire comes in 400 years or so it dies, and scrub chokes its seedlings. Most southern gum barks, Ribbon Gum for example, burn poorly when tight on the tree, well when loose, and explosively when dried, packed with toxins, and shed. Barks shed mostly in summer, when fire is most likely, and they become fuses, among the world's most flammable forest fuel. Colonial cooks used the sudden flare to bake cakes, and in the right conditions the bark flies on the wind, starting spot fires 30 kilometres and more away. The bigger the tree the more bark it drops, so the tree both promotes fire and regulates how big it will be.

Leaves release volatile oil on hot days when fire is most likely, the scent flooding the bush. Leaves are evergreen, moulting all year. The tree dries and drops them, then waits. A spark catches. Leaves become candles, bark becomes fire bombs, crowns catch and fan updrafts, terrifying infernos race, oil-laden trees explode. Leaves and bark are torches for their own destruction, but the fire is hurried on, not boiling the sap and clearing earth and air. Competing plants are destroyed, trunk and branch sprout, the refreshed tree stands metres above any competition, capturing the food and the light (picture 5). In a nutrient-poor continent, this is a tremendous advantage. Allying with fire let eucalypts conquer Australia.

The alliance amazed Europeans. Breton wrote of

> fires which prevail every year, for the grass being ignited, scorches the bark of the tree . . . It has often excited my surprise that even a single tree should escape from the tremendous fires which so frequently occur! The fire very frequently runs up the bark to the topmost branch, making the tree as black as charcoal; yet it goes on flourishing, although every succeeding year brings a recurrence of the same scorching, and, occasionally, twice in the same season: sometimes, indeed, the tree is destroyed, and nothing remains but a black and hollow stump. It often happens that a shrub, or young tree, is so effectually charred externally, that a person naturally infers it must have perished, but in the course of a few weeks it will throw out leaves.[75]

Or seeds. In some species seeds are the last resort, in others the first, but no eucalypt discounts seeds and almost all protect them in hard nuts. The seeds are tiny, often like powder, and seem impossibly vulnerable, but the nuts resist fire as efficiently as bark and oil promote it. They heat and cool quickly, then in 'a miracle of timing' shower millions of seeds into the rich ash below.[76]

Note 7. Erratic fire is the least, controlled fire the most, manageable of the variables constraining Australia's plants. In 1788 fire-diverse communities grew comfortably together. This argues that most fires were managed. Understanding fire locally made management possible.

In 1788 plants with unlike fire responses were neighbours. Grass burnt every 1–4 years edged rainforest never burnt, open eucalypt forest cleared of undergrowth every 3–5 years gave way to dense eucalypt forest burnt at most every fifteen years. Tranquility Mintbush, a shrub of eucalypt–rainforest boundaries, germinates best after low intensity fire and neighbouring grass after high intensity fire, but neighbouring rainforest is killed by almost any fire.[77] Kangaroo Grass shared land with tubers. Fire every 2–3 years lets the grass flourish, and over much of Australia in 1788 it was so dominant that fires must normally have burnt this often (too often for fuel to build up for raging bushfires). Yet if fires burn every year the tubers die out in time, and if fires burn less than every three years the grass chokes them out, then itself becomes moribund.[78] Central

Australia's most important plant food, Desert Raisin, dies without fire, but adjacent plant foods can be either fire tolerant (Bush Banana, Bush Plum) or intolerant (Fig, Quandong). Mulga and Gidgee die even in mild fires, and fires more than once a decade or so eradicate entire stands because no tree can flower in time. Yet both species grow among Spinifex, which needs fire every five years or so to flourish. In heathland too much fire creates sedgeland, too little creates woodland,[79] yet Heath Banksia needs fire to germinate but is discouraged if burnt more than every 8–10 years and killed if burnt every 3–4 years.[80] Across Australia, tuning to so erratic a constraint should sooner or later have made most communities vulnerable, yet in 1788 they flourished in intricate diversity. Clearly, erratic fire was rare and controlled fire normal (ch 6). This was no fluke.[81]

After 1788, some newcomers imitated 1788 burning, or thought they did, but most banned fire, which meant abandoning land to erratic fire. What happened speaks volumes for the precision of 1788 burning. Either bushfires increased in number, severity and extent, or fire sensitive species were favoured. Both transformed plant communities. By the 1810s John Macarthur's land near Sydney 'had become crowded—choked up in many places by thickets of saplings and large thorn bushes (*bursaria spinosa*) and the sweet natural herbage had for the most part been replaced by coarse wiry grasses which grew uncropped'.[82] Across the mountains a mere two decades of grazing and fire suppression let unpalatable fire sensitive species like cassia, Budda, Yarran and White Cypress smother 1788 grassland.[83] After 1860 the Cypress captured so much country that it became a major pest (ch 11). Had 1788's fire regimes been natural, this change would have been at least less dramatic.

Fire let people select where plants grew. They knew which plants to burn, when, how often and how hot. This demanded not one fire regime but many, differing in timing, intensity and duration. No natural regime could sustain such intricate balances. We may wonder how people in 1788 managed this, but clearly they did. The nature of Australia made fire a management tool. No doubt some plants suffered during the learning centuries, and there are hints that there was more to learn in 1788 (ch 11). But with fire as an ally people worked the land as intimately as humans can.

4

Heaven on earth

All religions attempt two things: to explain existence, and to regulate behaviour. Aboriginal religion integrated these by assuming the spiritual parity of all life, and by subjecting every aspect of it to overwhelming religious sanction. This pivoted on the Dreaming, a word tolerably conveying the sense of timelessness central to Aboriginal belief. 'The great and specifically Australian contribution to religious thought', Ted Strehlow declared, 'has been the unquestioning Aboriginal conviction that there was no division between Time and Eternity.'[1] The Dreaming conceives an unchangeable universe, hence free of time. This can be so because the universe is not natural: it was made from darkness by God. Who made God and darkness no-one knows. They are as much puzzles as chance and death. No religion has solved them, but denying time makes them easier to pass over, and people accept that although it is worthy to strive to understand, they are not meant to know.

Across Australia the creation story is essentially the same: God made light, brought into being spirits and creator ancestors, and set down eternal Law for all creation. The creator ancestors accepted the Law or suffered if they didn't, and made epic journeys across a formless space, giving land and sea substance and shape before settling to rest in a place important to them. They are there still, and where they went still bears marks of their trials and adventures. All things derive from their presence or deeds, and are ruled by the Law they passed on.

Since universe and Law never change, time is irrelevant, as in a dream. Change and time exist only as cycles: birth and death, the passage of stars and seasons, journeys, encounters, and after 1788 the appearance of plants and animals seeming new but always there. Cycles are eddies, ending where they begin or eclipsed by larger cycles: travel by death for example, or seasons by life spans. Eddies exist not on a river of life, for a river has a beginning and end, but on bigger eddies, in a boundless pool. Time is an eddy; the pool is timeless. Pool, eddies and Law are the Dreaming.

The Dreaming has two rules: obey the Law, and leave the world as you found it—not better or worse, for God judges that, but the same. The first rule enforces and exists for the second. Together they let place dominate time, and translate well understood ecological associations into social relations—kin, marriage, diplomacy, trade and so on. They apply the same relations and obligations to all creation, guarding the universe by outlawing fundamental change, so making all creatures conservationist and conservative. In most other societies an urge for change is so entrenched as to be thought natural, nor is it clear that people entirely succeeded in leaving the world as they found it (ch 11), but they dedicated their lives to conserving what they inherited, and within the perception of living generations generally they succeeded.

The Dreaming is comprehensive, as you would expect of people with much spare time. It gives and explains a role to every part of creation, and decrees how each must act. This does not stifle human curiosity, but innovation and creativity become means not ends, eddies not the pool, and do not disturb a sense that the fundamentals of existence are beyond challenge or improvement. About 1838 Adelaide missionaries

> took two Natives lately tattooed to their home, and spoke of the rite they had undergone (the origin of which is ascribed to a species of Red Kangaroo) endeavouring to shew them the foolishness of the practice and observing of Jehovah that he alone was to be feared and not the Red Kangaroo, for they believe the Red Kangaroos will kill them if they do not thus cut themselves.[2] One of them growing angry said, why do you charge us with a lie, i.e. reject our opinion, we do not charge you with lies; what you believe and speak of Jehovah is good, and what we believe is good. We replied that only on one side the truth could be, and that was on our side. Very well, he answered, then I am a liar, and you speak truth, I shall not speak another word, you may now speak.[3]

A fatalist theology is hard to undermine. Christians generally manage it by aggressive missionising and the plenty of western goods. This rarely impressed Aborigines. Few if any troubled over the question others ask westerners: 'Why do you have more than us?' They knew why—the Dreaming made it so (ch 11).

All Australia obeyed the Dreaming.[4] By world standards this is a vast area for a single belief system to hold sway, and in itself cause for thinking Australia a single estate, albeit with many managers. Australia included Tasmania, which some say did not have the Dreaming, but when the last full-blood person in Tasmania died in May 1876, outsiders had no notion of a Dreaming on the mainland either. Tasmanians managed land as mainlanders did (ch 6–8), and with similar mindsets. Oyster Bay people called gum trees 'countrymen', other groups claimed other trees, and people told Robinson, 'Moinee was hurled from heaven and dwelt on the earth, and died and was turned into a stone and is at Coxes Bight, which was his own country . . . Laller a small ant first made the natives.'[5] In what records survive of Tasmanian practice, in their links and duties of care with named animals and places, in their taking plant and animal names, in their belief in the transmigration of souls, in their kangaroo, emu, fire, wind and horse dances, and in their ancestral paths apparently like the songlines which mesh the mainland, Tasmanians thought like mainlanders.[6]

A songline or storyline is the path or corridor along which a creator ancestor moved to bring country into being. It is also the way of the ancestor's totem, the geographical expression of the songs, dances and paintings animating its country, and ecological proof of the unity of things. Strehlow quoted many central Australian songs illustrating this. A verse for winnowing nut grass bulbs is:

> With lowered heads, those yonder are holding aloft;
> With heads tilted sideways, those yonder are holding aloft.

This evokes winnowing ancestors, and living women holding coolamons high to shield their eyes from dust, and nut grass ready for harvest when its seed heads droop and tilt sideways.[7] Part of a native cat ancestor song is:

> The ringneck parrots, in scattered flocks —
> The ringneck parrots are screaming in their upward flight.
>
> The ringneck parrots are a cloud of wings;
> The shell parrots are a cloud of wings.
>
> Let the shell parrots come down to rest —
> Let them come down to rest on the ground!
>
> Let the caps fly off the scented blossoms!
> Let the blooms descend to the ground in a shower!

> The clustering bloodwood blooms are falling down —
> The clustering bloodwood blossoms, nipped by birds.
>
> The clustering bloodwood blooms are falling down —
> The clustering bloodwood blossoms, one by one.

When bloodwoods blossom, clouds of ringnecks nip them, and shell parrots take advantage of this on the ground. The song ensures that the cycle continues, reflecting the truth that the universe is made and needs ritual to maintain it.[8]

Every particle of land, sea and sky must lie on a songline, otherwise an ancestor can't have created it and it could not exist. Songlines threaded Australia, linking 'people of many local groups . . . separated by great distances',[9] sometimes thousands of kilometres. The native cat song went across language boundaries through the Centre at least to Port Augusta (SA). Another song ran from the Kimberley to the Centre, south to Port Augusta, then west to Albany and beyond. A third went from the Kimberley to Uluru to Cairns, though it may have lengthened recently. In 1882 Carl Lumholtz heard the same song in different languages on the Herbert (Qld) and 800 kilometres south at Rockhampton.[10] Without knowing the language people still recognised their song and its dances, because each had independent 'embedded characteristics': painting design, colour or symbol, and song melody, rhythm or pitch. To survive its continental journey each song must in theory be exactly repeated in at least most of these ways, because it came from the Dreaming, and its creator ancestor is listening.

Being born on or near a songline decides a person's most important totem, and being taught part of a song or dance legitimates being on the country it describes. People learn their songs, dances and country in minute detail. From far away they can discuss a tree or soak and who is responsible for it. Senior people who learn more song expand their geographical and spiritual knowledge and acquire more rights to responsibilities, including the duty of singing country into life, sometimes beyond their boundaries. In turn a properly sung song's plains, hills, rocks and waters care for its people and animals. Songlines are places of refuge, of comfort, of communion. They affirm a powerful message: the universe is one; all creation has a duty to maintain it; at the risk of your soul, keep things as they are.[11]

All things have a soul. Overlanding on the Murray in 1838, Joseph Hawdon

> was much amused in the course of the day with the simplicity of four
> or five Blacks who were standing together whilst a number of the cattle

were walking towards the spot they occupied—snorting as they drew nearer to their black observers. It was quite evident that the Natives looked upon the oxen as rational beings, for they gravely saluted them with their usual friendly salutation of 'Bo-Bo-marurood' (go! go! we are friendly) and waved green boughs at them in token of peace. The cattle not at all appreciating these marks of respect continued to move onwards, when the poor fellows were obliged to run off, not daring to wait the nearer approach of visitors so rude and unceremonious.[12]

People know three truths about the soul. First, it confers shape. Human, animal or plant, something unseen passes recognisable features and personality from parent to child. This is the soul. Thus everything with shape has a soul: plants, animals, rocks, wind, fire. If the soul leaves, the body dies and loses shape, but the soul remains in living offspring. In this way it continues forever, taking shape in later generations as in earlier, though since time is irrelevant not necessarily in that order. In some languages, especially in the south, the word for 'soul' and 'flesh' is the same, a reminder that flesh is a temporary chariot of a soul eternal.[13]

Second, since in death things lose shape, shape signifies life, so all things with shape must be living, and all life must have a soul. How otherwise could things get and lose shape? If a thing exists it has a soul, so it can choose to help or hinder. This is why ritual matters. Correct ritual persuades a soul or spirit to help.[14]

Third, since souls transcend time and death, and since like creator ancestors their number can't be infinite, there is no reason why a soul which confers one shape might not confer several, no reason why a soul leaving a fire need pass only to another fire, or a soul from one human pass only to another. On the contrary, a soul's ability to move from one chariot to another gives creation order and cohesion. It moves through the particular community of natural and supernatural things created by the same ancestor in the Dreaming. It makes each part dependent on it and each other for their existence. It makes them a congregation.

A congregation forms a totem. Souls deny time; totems assert place. In English 'totem' can mean just a badge, but for Aborigines it is a life force stemming from and part of a creator ancestor. An emu man does not have emu as a mere symbol: he is emu, of the same soul and the same flesh. He must care for emu and its habitat, and it must care for him. He is of its totem, not the reverse, and normally he can no more kill it than murder his grandson or grandmother—and since time is irrelevant he risks both if he does. A man 'born along the track of . . . the wallaby, might say, when seeing a wallaby, "that is me, that wallaby, that is me"',[15] or 'that is my father'.[16] Ted Egan's brilliant song 'Poor feller my country' begins,

> Once when I'm young boy
> Old man tell me
> 'Always look after
> This you country.
> You are a river
> You are the sea
> You are the rocks, boy,
> This you country.'[17]

In March 1854 William Thomas

> was out with a celebrated Western Port black tracking five other blacks. The tracks had been lost some days at a part of the country where we expected they must pass. We ran down a creek; after going some miles a bear made a noise as we passed. The black stopped, and a parley commenced. I stood gazing alternately at the black and the bear. At length my black came to me and said, 'Me big one stupid; bear tell me no go you that way.' We immediately crossed the creek, and took a different track. Strange as it may appear, we had not altered our course above one and a half miles before we came upon the tracks of the five blacks, and never lost them after.[18]

Everything has a totem: people, animals, stars, flu, lice, dust, frost, wind. Fire is an important totem, which people must consult before unleashing. Dogs have totems, and like humans 'are expected to conform to the rules on incest, adultery, and choice of partner generally, as laid down in the Dreamtime. The indiscriminate sexual behaviour displayed by dogs is a source of frequent embarrassment and annoyance to their owners.'[19]

Totem members are responsible for each other more than for the rest of creation. Wenten Rubuntja explained,

> My *Altyerre* Dreaming comes from Mpweringke [Burt Well, north of Alice Springs] because I was 'found' there. I am boss for *Mpwere* [Maggot] Dreaming. My worship is maggots and witchetties and flies . . . and itchy

grubs—those hairy caterpillars that line up—and those *angente* [sawfly] grubs that attach themselves in a mass to the river red gum trees. Those trees can't be cut down or there will be lots of maggots—maggots everywhere.[20]

At Sydney after 1788 the most determined resister of the English was Pemulwuy. He was not from Sydney Cove, but an inland group near Georges River. Why should he take on the strangers? Because his totem, like his name, was *bhimul*, earth. That was what he was defending. Again, the longest war any people fought against settlers was on the Hawkesbury. There in 1788 people now called Dharug received Governor Phillip hospitably, but in the 1790s his successors began concentrating farms on the flats. 'Dharug' may mean yam. The Hawkesbury's yams were a major totem and a staple famous among distant people. Governor Hunter may have glimpsed this when he wrote in 1793 that the Dharug

> appeared to live chiefly on the roots which they dig from the ground; for these low banks appear to have been ploughed up, as if a vast herd of swine had been living on them. We . . . found the wild yam in considerable quantities, but in general very small, not larger than a walnut; they appear to be in the greatest plenty on the banks of the river; a little way back they are scarce.

The farmers took land, yam, totem and trade. The clans fought back for 22 years, until all were dead or hiding. Few Europeans understood why they fought so hard, but the yams say.[21]

They say not only, perhaps not mainly, because they were food. They were totem allies needing help. Central Australian women recently demonstrated the power of this affinity when shown a model cash crop:

> seeing bush tomatoes growing in neat horticultural rows was disturbing. Bush tomatoes, as with everything else in the world, are supposed to be *made* through ceremony, not grown by people . . . these captive plants may have seemed to the women to challenge the proper order of the world; in short, to be sacrilegious . . . these are not just foods: they are bound up in stories of creation, in kinship, and in multiple layers of personal and collective memory . . . bushfoods are an inseparable part of themselves.[22]

Beyond particular totem bonds is a duty to all creation. On the Hawkesbury yam men may have decided whether to fight, but others fought with them. Totems share the Dreaming, so all are responsible for all. Totems of disease, rain and fire obviously affect everyone, but all totems do in some way. By singing their totem songs, people play their part in maintaining creation for all. Everyone thus venerates and depends on the totem idea, and is blended into an inter-dependent universe.[23]

Totems are a central organising principle. Kin are recognised, marriage usually restricted, and population controlled by totem rules; messengers state their totem not their name; strangers recognise soulmates if their totems are the same or allied; in hard times people can find refuge with totem kin outside their country; even among enemies a person tries to save the life of a totem brother or sister; when people meet the most important answer to that universal question, who are you?, is the totem. Totems still regulate behaviour, openly in the north, coded as surnames in the south. That they retain such power conveys how life shaping they were in 1788.

They are more complex than outlined here. Details vary regionally, for example on whether people may kill or eat their totem. People and places have more than one totem, and all totems have allied totems, as they must if people are to represent all creation. West of Kununurra (WA), Mandi told Bruce Shaw,

> My other, blackfeller, name was Munnai (Munniim). My father put that, from the Dream now. He saw the water bubbling, moving all the time while the sun shone on it. In language you called it *munniim-munniim*: light on quiet water . . . And you know Grant's wife . . . ? Her father's name, Budbirr, was given to me by my father because I was his ghost, his spirit come back . . . Flying fox is one of my Dreams, and . . . a bird like an owl . . . and *Yiralalam* the Dream for that tree belonged to my father . . . When the father passes away the son takes over his Dreaming.[24]

All these totems must survive, and be in balance.[25]

Since creator ancestors made all the land, no land can be wilderness. It is made and has a Dreaming, or it does not exist. People see in land, sea and sky proofs of the Dreaming and their own past and future. Every hill, plain, rock and tree is alive with story and imagery, and filled with presences. The land is a spiritual endowment far more important than any economic value it might have. Travelling with two senior men near Lake Eyre, Isabel McBryde 'was constantly impressed by how different were the landscapes . . . [we] were observing. Theirs were numinous landscapes of the mind, peopled by beings from an ever-present Dreaming whose actions were marked by the features of the created landscape . . . a landscape "mapped by stories".'[26] Strehlow described

> the overwhelming affection felt by a native for his ancestral territory. Mountains and creeks and springs and water-holes are, to him, not merely interesting or beautiful . . . [but] the handiwork of ancestors from whom he himself has descended. He sees recorded in the surrounding landscape the ancient story of the lives and the deeds of the immortal beings whom he reveres . . . The whole countryside is his living, age-old family tree. The story of his own totemic ancestor is to the native the account of his own doings at the beginning of time, at the dim dawn of life, when the world as he knows it now was being shaped and moulded by all-powerful hands. He himself has played a part in that first glorious adventure, a part smaller or greater according to the original rank of the ancestor of whom he is the present reincarnated form . . . Gurra said to me: 'The Ilbalintja soak has been defiled by the hands of the white men . . . No longer do men pluck up the grass and the weeds and sweep the ground clean around it; no longer do they care for the resting place of Karora . . . [but] It still holds me fast; and I shall tend it while I can; while I live, I shall love to gaze on this ancient soil.[27]

Such love helps immeasurably in meeting the Law's demand to leave the world as found, but as Gurra said, this does not mean leaving things untouched. On the contrary, the cycles of life and season change constantly, and a manager's duty is to shepherd land and creatures safely through these changes. Eddies they may be, but they are part of the Dreaming and must be cared for. This might require dramatic or spasmodic change (burning forests, culling eels, banning or restricting a food), and it certainly demands active intervention in the landscape. Ancestors do this still, obeying the Law and seeking balance and continuity. Humans should do no less. Land care is the main purpose of life.[28]

Law protected land and property. Stone tools are common today because people rarely carried them, instead leaving a kit at each halt. Until 1788 they were safe. In 1882 Augustus Gregory said, 'A native discovering a Zamia fruit unripe will put his mark upon it and no other native will touch this; the original finder of the fruit may rest perfectly certain that when it becomes ripe he has only to go and fetch it.'[29] Near Brisbane in 1828 Fraser saw

> three sticks fixed in the ground forming a triangle, and fixed at the top by a cord, and on which was placed a sheet of bark, and on seeing something suspended under cover of the bark, Capt Logan pointed it out to us as being a place where they deposit their Kangaroo Nets (Dilly Bag) and superfluous Elemans [shields], Chisels, etc. etc. until they return to that district again, it being considered the greatest breach of Faith in this District to touch any of them . . . On examining the contents of this depot, I found it to consist of a Kangaroo Net fifty feet long, and five and a half in width, made of as good twine as any European net but much stronger, and put together in a manner which would do credit to any professed networker, a Fishing Net of the finest material stained black, forming when in the water, an inverted cone seven feet long, a Dilly, a Luggage Bag, which the females carry, this is formed of the leaves of a species of Santhorhea [Xanthorrhoea] strong enough to hold anything.[30]

Sturt thought it 'a remarkable fact that we seldom or never saw weapons in the hands of any of the natives of the interior'.[31] Mervyn Meggitt found 'little reason for all-out warfare between communities. Slavery was unknown; portable goods were few; and the territory seized in a battle was virtually an embarrassment to the victors, whose spiritual ties were with other localities.'[32]

Religious sanction makes sense. Nothing is more powerful, but as explanation it misled observers into thinking that people subordinated or lacked ecological understanding. On the New South Wales south coast in 1836 Alexander Berry told a visitor,

> the natives . . . believe in transmutation, after death. This first claimed his notice, when he had wounded a Porpoise, which some Blacks, who were with him in the boat, tried to dissuade him from firing at. On landing, the men told the women what had been done, at which they made great lamentation; and he learned from them, that they regarded the Porpoises, as having been the ancient chiefs of the neighbourhood, who, when they died, had changed into these animals; and who, they said, drove fish on shore for them, sometimes whales, when the people were very hungry![33]

Porpoises did do that (ch 5); it was the explanation Berry baulked at, leading him to miss Aboriginal knowledge of the practical benefits of porpoise conservation.

This broaches a key truth about the Dreaming. In its notions of time and soul, its demand to leave the world as found, and its blanketing of land and sea with totem responsibilities, it is ecological. Aboriginal landscape awareness is rightly seen as drenched in religious sensibility, but equally the Dreaming is saturated with environmental consciousness. Theology and ecology are fused.

The Dreaming seems dominant because people tend to describe the world in its terms. In explaining why certain plants or animals have gone, they say that the relevant ceremonies were not done or not done properly. They know well the link between extinctions and wrong fire, overstocking, feral predation and so on, and often they know a remedy, but these are not sufficient explanations, for none would have happened had the proper ceremonies been done. Again, they are famously expert trackers, but see these skills as stemming from knowing the rituals. In the north people know that fire kills rainforest: they take great care not to burn jungle thickets, but explain this by saying that if one did burn, its spirits would blind them.[34] On Bathurst Island (NT) women harvesting a yam always leave the top and cover it with earth. They know this grows more tubers, but explain it by saying, 'if dig it all out, then that food spirit will get real angry and won't let any more yam grow in that place'.[35] Queensland people kept open with fire a grass pocket in thick scrub, but said it was carved out by the moon throwing his boomerang around it.[36] People know their environment well, but equally know that they are not only maintaining a habitat or invigorating an eddy, but working in tandem with creator ancestors. The more Law a person knows, the more certain he or she is to undertake and succeed in any activity.

Ecology explains what happens, the Dreaming why it happens. Striving to learn how the world works is fundamental to life, for knowing is safety, comfort and power. People prize knowledge as Europeans prize wealth. Teaching and testing begin in childhood. 'Listen, I'll only tell you this once', a teacher might say. This signals a test. If months later you can repeat what you were told, you are told more. If not, you have reached your limit. The more you learn the more you are told. The most senior learning is always theological, and only the able and committed progress to its more complex realms. Those who learn most become clever people, with immense sacred and secular power. The cleverest can be telepathic or fly through the air or point the bone, in these ways coming nearer to unveiling the Dreaming, though they will never reach that distant grail.[37]

The Dreaming explains, but in terms of the real world. The rituals and management it ordains work. They can be repeated and their effects predicted, and they maintain biodiversity and affirm life's balance and continuity. Social groupings too are enforced theologically but expressed ecologically. A person has totem names, but might use a name from a natural event—stung by bees, heaps up grass, watches water. Some mobs were known by their country's geography (coast, forest, grass) or its dominant ecology (mangrove, heath, Spinifex). At big gatherings visitors camped in the direction of their country, so that camp layouts imitated a region's ecology. For marriage or totem or trade, social divisions might reflect those between sun and rain, fire and water, predator and prey. On the Darling, one division was between light and shade:

> The shadow thrown by the butt and lower portion of a tree is called 'nhurrai'; that cast by the middle portion of the tree is 'wau-gue'; whilst the shade of the top of the tree, or outer margin of the shadow, is 'winggu'. Again, the men, women and children, whose prescribed sitting places are in the butt or middle shades of the tree are called 'guai'mundhan', or sluggish blood, whilst those who sit in the top or outside shade are designated 'guai'gulir', or active blood . . . [They] are supposed to keep a strict watch for any game . . . friends or enemies, or anything which may require vigilance.

The shade divisions helped regulate marriage.[38] The Dreaming enforces hard-learnt ecological practice.

An ecological cradle is exposed where theology and society clash, and theology defers. Three examples:

1. In theory the Dreaming gives and asks equally of all things. In practice human freedoms and duties are more visible and varied than those of other species. It is not that animals or fire or water do not have duties: they do, and they perform them—shortening grass, scavenging, making food or habitat, performing ceremony. But only people take shapes unlike their totem, or light fires, or eat so many other species, or trade, or bury or burn their dead.
2. Humans and their totem animals and plants do not always decline or increase at the same rate, but when a human totem population declines its species is at risk, and other totems lack marriage and trade partners. Totem allegiances are therefore adjusted from time to time.[39] Similarly, even where a creation myth explains why a certain food or place is taboo, under intense pressure this might be lifted.
3. Sometimes all a country's carers died out. Someone must then move in, and elders went to great lengths to decide who, and to induct them, for if you

knew neither the songs nor the country it was dangerous to be there. Often neither exterminating tribal wars[40] nor the many catastrophes after 1788 led to enemy occupation, but if necessary even enemies might learn the songs and slowly move in. No land or sea could be vacant, all must have its care and ceremonies or it would vanish, fragmenting the world. Peter Sutton comments of western Cape York that re-allocating land in this way, changing the Law, is 'further support for the claim that Aboriginal land tenure—at least in this area—is primarily based on secular premises rather than sacred ones'.[41] This was generally so. The change met the Law's demand that every inch of land be cared for, but the demand stemmed from an immutable ecological imperative. If the Dreaming were truly free of the environment, human intervention need not occur. Instead, theology served ecology.[42]

Songlines show the Dreaming's grounding in the land and its creatures. In depicting the country it passes through and naming the creatures in it, a songline states its ecological associations. Allan Newsome demonstrated this memorably west of Alice Springs. He studied in detail the major totem sites along a red kangaroo songline, and found that each coincided 'with the most favourable habitat for the species', notably where range washouts grew the best grass. Further, whenever the red kangaroo ancestor flew through the sky or went underground, it avoided an unfavourable habitat. No-one told Newsome this—his informants invariably spoke in spiritual terms. But they knew: they were describing the land from a red kangaroo viewpoint, and they banned hunting at its major sites. The songline decreed a clear conservation imperative: in bad seasons roos have refuges, but when in good seasons their numbers build up and some move out, they can be hunted.[43]

A songline is also a map, compass and calendar. It follows paths ecologically suited to its creator ancestor, and teaches how to exploit resources en route. If you can sing a song you can follow it, even into country you have never been. If you can't, unless someone with you knows it you are lost. If you stray too far off line you might be trespassing. People learn their local sector first, or only, but learning beyond it licenses travel further along it. Songlines also recite countless ecological signals to people and animals: when coral trees flower it is time to dig crabs, when a bird sings a grub lays eggs, when the west wind blows blue-tongue lizards emerge and women dig for honey ants, when march flies appear crocodiles lay eggs, when the blackwoods flower northwest Tasmanians hunted muttonbirds.[44] Such specific associations are necessarily local and seasonal, varying each year. It is easy to see how ancestral hands might regulate these mobile marvels of timing, but each states and obeys an ecological reality.

Totems are ecological. The well-known Eaglehawk and Crow division separates hunters from gatherers, and most totem names combine place, creature and totem: Tarnda (Adelaide) red kangaroo, Wurundjeri (Melbourne) Ribbon Gum, Narrandera (NSW) jew lizard and so on. People studied first their own totem and its allies and habitat, to everyone's benefit. Jew lizard people studied the plants and animals around *narrung*'s sandy habitat, the insects in the sand and the bark, the birds visiting, the winds, the water, the fire needs. To keep each in balance required repeating spiritually the same ancestral ceremonies, and ecologically the same management practices. Both are work, a dance as much as a fire regime, both protect the Dreaming and biodiversity, from long repetition both can be fine-tuned for success. Yet if the ecology changed, for example when rabbits or camels arrived, totems were adjusted to fit. 'Those totems were always there', people say, 'it's just that we didn't know about them before.'

Totems work as ecological alliances. John McEntee sees Europeans as splitters, looking inwards, classifying more and more precisely, but Aborigines as lumpers, looking outwards, seeking ever wider associations. He illustrates with an Adnamatana (SA) grouping: goanna and western quoll are the same 'skin' because both eat meat and have white chests, five toes and spots on the back. Adnamatana explain this in spiritual terms: for example the spots are spear wounds, got when the two ancestors were killed for having an illicit affair.[45] The myth has a moral lesson (the Law punishes offenders), and an ecological teaching (goanna and quoll scavenge similarly).

Totem alliances are local. Although both are birds, cockatoo and grebe might or might not be allied, depending on their local links. In Arnhem Land brown goshawk and red-bellied barramundi live along the same stretch of the Roper so have the same skin, and in the Centre, Mulga country is honey ant country so people of these totems share responsibility for it, but neither link is universally so.[46] Wagga Wagga is Wiradjuri for 'many crows'. To say this is also to name open country with many lizards and few small birds, one a cause and the other a consequence of many crows, but not all open country is crow country. In Canberra yellow-tailed black cockatoos once fed on pine and river oak kernels, so caring for them meant caring for these trees. This required stable river banks, which are platypus habitat. Platypus eat worms and shrimps, which need reeds to breed, which is waterbird habitat, which attracts snakes, and so on. Such lumping makes a cycle or eddy too big for one totem to manage, so the Dreaming assigns each a part, and commands them to negotiate to balance the whole. The tone is theological, the teaching ecological.

When totem interests conflict, for example when firing pine threatens cockatoo habitat, some negotiations must be difficult, but they are done, emphasising the totem system's central ecological role in maintaining biodiversity. Although a Ngarrindjeri (SA) man, David Unaipon told a beautiful Darling River myth of how the land became too crowded, so the animal, bird, reptile and insect families met in the Blue Mountains to negotiate a solution. Frilled lizard grew impatient, and caused a huge storm which killed almost all the platypus. Grieving, the other creatures gathered to help platypus. This led to very long debate on who platypus was related to and who it could marry.[47] The myth continues, but this fragment shows creator ancestors negotiating, a concern for the welfare of every totem, and a Dreaming answer to an ecological puzzle which stumped Europeans after 1788: what exactly a platypus was.

Totems make clear how basic to the unity of creation an ecological perspective is. All must care for the land and its creatures, all must be regenerated by care and ceremony, no soul must be extinguished, no totem put at risk, no habitat too much reduced. That mandate, not the theology, made land care purposeful, universal and predictable. This is true of every part, even what might seem untouched wilderness, and even where ecologists today can't see why. The parks and puzzles Europeans saw in 1788 were no accident.[48]

Especially in the face of local omnipotence, a universal Dreaming was a great intellectual achievement. By so thoroughly implanting means and incentives to shackle body and soul to the survival of all things in heaven and earth, it made environmental management obligatory. Its reach and power were evidenced late in 1830, when eight Tasmanians and two white men were seeking northeast Tasmanians still free. One white, George Robinson, hoped to persuade free people to leave their land for Swan Island, just off the coast. His party saw a lot of burnt land and a few tracks but no Tasmanians, until on 31 October they 'descried a smoke inland... from its appearance the natives was burning off'. The party hurried forward, and late that day found tracks and 'the bush on fire for a considerable distance'. Next day they came up to the Tasmanians.

Four men and a woman were in camp. In all 69 people lived in the northeast, the hunted remnant of perhaps 700 people two decades before. The camp was led by Mannalargenna. He knew whites killed men and children and stole women, he knew Robinson's party was seeking his though not why, and he knew soldiers were hunting, for the Black Line, the military cordon bent on capturing every surviving Tasmanian, was under way. He knew too that smoke would betray his small band, yet still they fired the land, in the face of death toiling to do what perhaps ten times as many would once have done. Nothing shows so powerfully how crucial land care was. This was no casual burning. It was a mortal duty, a levy on the souls of brave men and women.[49]

This was repeated across Australia after 1788. Defying catastrophe, people tried above all to continue a spiritual and ecological life. Before 1788 they did this easily. In most seasons they had plenty of spare time, and spent it nourishing the mind more than the body. Art was voluminous and intricate: imagine a dot painting on sand several metres square, composed of different coloured feathers, most of them tiny, stuck down with blood. Songs were long, corroborees might last months, initiations years. Not only in their parks did people think and act like gentry.

This hardly reflects people constantly on the edge of want. They cannot have been the scavenging, chance-dominated savages Europeans thought them. A rich and time-eating spiritual life builds on abundance, not poverty. In the driest and most fire-prone continent on earth, abundance was not natural. It was made by skilled, detailed and provident management of country.

5

Country

The Dreaming taught why the world must be maintained; the land taught how. One made land care compulsory, the other made it rewarding. One was spiritual and universal, the other practical and local. Songlines distributed land spiritually; 'country' distributed it geographically. Everyone had a country: narrowly defined, land, water and their sites and knowledge in the care of a family under its head. A family was a man, perhaps his brothers, and their wives, relatives and descendants, though some moved out on marriage and others moved in or out as suited. 'The inhabitants of these wilds must be very few . . .', Oxley decided, 'their deserted fires and camps which we occasionally saw, never appeared to have been occupied by more than six or eight persons.'[1] In their country a family saw an environment shaped in the Dreaming and thronged with sites and stories, witnessed the familiarity plants, creatures and elements had with particular localities, and thought itself part of these intimacies. Not only obvious features which Europeans name, but every pebble and ripple disclosed both the ecological logic of its existence and the Dreaming's presence. Here wallaby and wallaby ancestor live, there *nardoo* and *nardoo* ancestor, there avenging fire killed lawbreakers, here a punishing flood reached. Totem site and ecological niche alike proved the need and reward in caring for country. Some places might not be touched for years, but not for a moment did carers forget them.

Each country was

> surrounded by other countries, so that across the continent and on into the sea, there is a network of countries. No country is ruled by any other, and no country can live without others. It follows that no country is the centre toward which other countries must orient themselves, and, equally, that each is its own centre.[2]

Countries formed a national continuum. To ensure this, qualified others might mediate to adjust a country if human populations fluctuated too much, at least in the north specialist managers advised on fire, and neighbouring elders had a working knowledge of a country and its stories, and dropped hints if they felt it needed care.

The literate habit of fixing boundaries imposes an illusory rigidity on 1788. Spirits or totems limited where someone could go, but generally the boundaries of country were permeable. Almost everyone had rights and interests in other countries. At New Norcia (WA) 'each family regards one particular district as belonging exclusively to itself, though the use of it is freely shared by nearby friendly families'.[3] Core territory lay amid zones open according to kin, totem, clan, neighbour, trading partner or occasion. Within a family one member might have access rights denied another, yet neighbours came 'to each other's assistance. The tribal boundary may not be crossed over without permission. But if conditions become dry within one tribal area it is customary to offer one's tribal neighbours a section of country for hunting or a lake on which to fish.'[4] People helped neighbours or kin fleeing war, initiating children, or tackling big projects like fish and game drives or clean-up fires, and came hundreds of kilometres for seasonal harvests of bogong, bunya, cycad, eel and their associated ceremonies. In these ways rights to country were spread but like the magic pudding never reduced.[5]

The right to say who could enter country was the decisive expression of legitimate possession. 'No individual of any neighbouring tribe or family can hunt or walk over the property of another without permission of the head of the family owning the land. A stranger found trespassing can legally be put to death', James Dawson wrote of western Victoria in 1881.[6] In northwest Australia no tribe used another's land except by invitation. Each 'has its own district in which it reigns supreme; such district is again sub-divided into portions belonging to the individuals of that tribe, the children inherit and females share equally with the males in the distribution of landed property'.[7] John Browne stated of Albany people,

> it is difficult to say in what the rights of ownership consist . . . members of the tribe hunt indiscriminately over each other's ground . . . [Yet] should an enemy, or one of another tribe wilfully trespass on these grounds, such a liberty would be immediately noticed, and would in all probability lead to acts of violence and retaliation on both sides.[8]

Around Bunbury (WA) in 1841–3, each family had

a more or less defined area of country belonging to it—a kind of heritage; its rights over such track were respected, and any infringements regarded in the light of trespass. Even if an individual of the same tribe, yet of a different family, had occasion to traverse it, he would only, if obliged at all, take just enough to appease his hunger—e.g., one bird, or one egg, from a nest, leaving the remainder for its rightful owners. And it was wonderful to note how each knew exactly what was on their piece of land; they were never selfish about its products, but during the superabundance of any food plants, game, fish etc., at any particular season would send round for neighbouring families to come and make common property of what Nature had so plentifully supplied them.[9]

Eyre wrote,

> particular districts . . . are considered generally as being the property and hunting-grounds of the tribes who frequent them. These districts are again parcelled out among the individual members of the tribe. Every male has some portion of land, of which he can always point out the exact boundaries. These properties are subdivided by a father among his sons during his own lifetime, and descend in almost hereditary succession . . . Tribes can only come into each other's districts by permission, or invitation, in which case, strangers or visitors are well treated.[10]

Especially in the southeast, neighbours named groups by their word for 'yes' or 'no', the word they used to permit or deny access to country. Eora (Sydney), possibly from *eor*, 'yes', is a post-1788 invention,[11] but at least fifteen groups in western New South Wales and northwest Victoria, at least six in New England, and some in southern Queensland were named, presumably by neighbours, from their word for 'no'. 'Always ask' was and is the rule, strict and universal, even for kin confident of the answer. This was closely guarded. 'Their wars generally originate . . . in their hunting beyond their limits', a New South Wales squatter remarked in 1841,[12] and east of Perth George Moore observed,

> among themselves the ground is parcelled out to individuals, and passes by inheritance. The country formerly of Midgegoroo, then of his son Yagan, belongs now of right to two young lads (brothers), and a son of

Yagan. Some trespassers went upon this ground, lighted their fires, and chased the wallabies. This was resented by the young lads, and, as it happened, there was a large meeting of natives at the time, a general row commenced, and no less than fifteen were wounded with spears.[13 14]

People felt intensely for their country. It was alive. It could talk, listen, suffer, be refreshed, rejoice. They were on it and others were not because they knew it and it knew them. There their spirit stayed, there they expected to die. No other country could ever be that. Even as he was dispossessing them Robinson confessed, 'The natives of VDL are patriots, staunch lovers of their country.'[15] When an elder could no longer travel easily and death might come, he stayed at a favoured place, teaching the country to two or three attending wives and warriors.[16] 'Within the boundaries of their *own country*, as they proudly speak', James Dredge remarked in 1837, 'they feel a degree of security and pleasure they can find nowhere else—here their forefathers lived and roamed and hunted, and here also their ashes rest.'[17] Puntutjarpa rock shelter, in very tough desert south of Warburton (WA), was occupied for most of the last 10,000 years, and Richard Gould paid 'tribute to the aborigines whose resourcefulness led to the establishment and maintenance of this dignified and rewarding way of life under what were perhaps the most rigorous environmental conditions ever encountered by any historic or prehistoric hunters and gatherers'.[18] Country was heart, mind and soul.[19]

Country was not property. If anything it owned. 'The above families belong to this Ground', John Wedge observed near St Leonards (Vic) in 1835.[20] A family head might speak of a country as his, but only because he had a right and duty to manage it. He did not own it, for he could not dispose of it: the Law decreed who inherited. When Bundal was ordered off government land at the Cowpastures near Sydney, he exclaimed, 'The government land, well, that's a good joke. It's my land, and was my father's, and father's father's, before me.'[21] At Adelaide Clamor Schurmann found that 'every adult native possesses a district of land, which he calls his country, and which he inherited from his father'.[22]

Some newcomers thought families owned land. In southwest Australia Henry Chapman stated, 'the land is allotted, in comparatively small portions, to different families, as their hunting and provision grounds. The boundaries of these tracts are very distinctly defined, and scrupulously observed amongst themselves. This fact implies the existence of personal property in the soil.'[23] Others judged that a clan owned land, since in necessity it could re-apportion it among families, or that a tribe did, since in necessity it could re-distribute groups, but in Victoria Robert Smyth neatly captured the progressive devolution of country:

> Each of these tribes had its own district of country—its extent at least, and in some cases its distinct boundaries, being well known to the neighbouring tribes. The sub-division of the territory even went further than that; each family had its own locality. And to this day the older men can clearly point out the land which their fathers left them, and which they once called their own.[24]

'No English words', Bill Stanner concluded in 1969,

> are good enough to give a sense of the links between an aboriginal group and its homeland. Our word 'home', warm and suggestive though it be, does not match the aboriginal word that may mean 'camp', 'hearth', 'country', 'everlasting home', 'totem place', 'life source', 'spirit centre' and much else all in one. Our word 'land' is too spare and meagre . . . The aboriginal would speak of 'earth' and use the word in a richly symbolic way to mean his 'shoulder' or his 'side' . . . When we took what we call 'land' we took what to them meant hearth, home, the source and locus of life, and everlastingness of spirit. At the same time it left each local band bereft of an essential constant that made their plan and code of living intelligible. Particular pieces of territory, each a homeland, formed part of a set of constants without which no affiliation of any person to any other person, no link in the whole network of relationships, no part of the complex structure of social groups any longer had all its co-ordinates . . . the aborigines faced a kind of vertigo in living. They had no stable base of life; every personal affiliation was lamed; every group structure was put out of kilter; no social network had a point of fixture left.[25]

People cared for and took life from country. Possession was duty, making them life curators in two senses: bound for life to keep country alive (ch 8).[26]
    They were bound to all their country, not just its best parts. Eyre observed,

> no part of the country is so utterly worthless, as not to have attractions sufficient occasionally to tempt the wandering savage

into its recesses. In the arid, barren, naked plains of the north, with not a shrub to shelter him from the heat, not a stick to burn for his fire (except what he carried with him), the native is found.[27]

He added,

there are no localities on [Australia's] coast, no recesses in its interior, however sterile and inhospitable they may appear to the traveller, that do not hold out some inducements to the bordering savage to visit them, or at the proper seasons of the year provide him with the means of sustenance.[28]

In Victoria, 'rather than forego the pleasures of a change of scene, the horde will break up its encampment among an abundance of game, and remove to a site where all their address in hunting can scarcely satisfy their wants'.[29] Between Berrima and Albury (NSW), 'whatever place we have been in, whether on the top of the highest mountain, or in any of the deepest ravines, we always find evident marks that the natives occasionally resort to them, although there does not appear to be any inducement to visit these secluded places'.[30] Sooner or later people patrolled every corner, burning, balancing, refreshing.[31]

The chances of a family's travel led newcomers to find empty land, and some to assume that this was permanent. That was unthinkable. Country was always in mind. Eyre pointed out,

although a tribe may be dispersed all over their own district in single groups, or some even visiting neighbouring tribes, yet if you meet with any one family they can at once tell you where you will find any other, though the parties may not have met for weeks. Some one or other is always moving about, and thus the news of each other's locality gets rapidly spread among the rest.[32]

Land without Law, the notion that any country could run wild, denied the Dreaming. Ecology permeated society. In Arnhem Land Frank Gurrmanamana

marked out two parallel sets of small holes. One set, he said, were vegetable foods which grew *gu-djel* (in the clay), namely roots and tubers. The other set were the vegetables *gu-man-nga* (in the jungle/vine thicket), namely fruits. These two sets were linked, a pair, one from each set, appearing together at the same time of the year to be successively replaced by another pair, and so on. He then listed the names of both sets of plants in their predicted order of appearance in nature. They were likened according to Gurrmanamana to plants walking side by side through the seasons.[33]

Arnhem Landers classified country

> as accurately as any ecologist, and they are able to state without hesitation what food supply, animal and vegetable, each association will yield . . . The accuracy with which an Arnhem Land hunter could name and give an association according to its botanical composition, and the food supply, woods for spears and other purposes, as well as resins and fibre plants that it would yield at any season of the year, was astonishing. It showed that these natives are far from the shiftless and improvident people of popular report.[34]

Walking and in camp, before birth and at play, teaching never ceased. As with totem links (ch 4), it lumped rather than split:

> The child is taught from a holistic point of view, and the example used is a tree. He/she is taught everything there is to know about the existence of that tree. When it blooms, the insects that live in its branches and bark, the birds and animals that use that type of tree only for food and shelter, what certain parts of the tree can be used (food or healing). Then he or she is taught about the surrounding vegetation, landscape, geology and climate. This method teaches the child about symbiosis, and how significant the relationship of one thing is to another, so as to gain a complete understanding of each of the organisms within the whole picture.[35]

Ecological knowledge was unavoidably local. Season and circumstance compelled local adjustments, while plants and animals changed over their life cycles, eddies in place as well as time. People expected help from ancestors and totems, but help hinged on knowing country. What they knew decided how well they lived, sometimes whether they lived. 'The main technology for the organization of country', Debbie Rose wrote, is and was knowledge. Knowledge is country-specific, and virtually the whole body of knowledge for any given country is related to the generation of life in and around that country. Countries are interdependent, so it is not the case that one person's knowledge is restricted only to one country, or that countries are self-sufficient in their knowledge, but it is the case that each country has its own specificities, the knowledge of which belongs to some people and not to others.[36]

Eyre illustrated this:

> Another very great advantage on the part of the natives is, the intimate knowledge they have of every nook and corner of the country they inhabit; does a shower of rain fall, they know the very rock where a little water is most likely to be collected, the very hole where it is the longest retained . . . Are there heavy dews at night, they know where the longest grass grows, from which they may collect the spangles, and water is sometimes procured thus in very great abundance. Should there be neither rains nor dews, their experience at once points out to them the lowest levels where the gum scrub grows, and where they are sure of getting water from its roots, with the least possible amount of labour that the method admits of, and with the surest prospect of success.[37]

Strehlow reported,

> my guide Lilitjukurba, when taking me across the southern Pintubi area where most of the waters were either deep holes in the ground or clefts in sunken boulders scattered in the mulga thickets, located these difficult sites with astounding precision. We would often travel 'blind' through thick mulga scrub for several hours, and then halt suddenly before a soak or a rock-plate invisible even from a distance of fifty yards.[38]

Local supremacy allied with wide geographical knowledge, continental connections, and a universal theology. These levied the soul, but were the means and measures of a proud contribution to eternity. 'Think global, act local' is an apt maxim for 1788. It made an entire continent structured and committed to making resources abundant, convenient and predictable.

Local detail let people predict what animals would do, and when. They forged alliances, most obviously with dogs, most famously with killer whales or porpoises on the east coast. In Moreton Bay (Qld) Roger Therry watched as men

> crowded to the beach, all armed with spears, and watched with intense interest a shoal of porpoises tumbling and rolling from the Pacific towards the bay. The sight of these porpoises is always an occasion of joy to these poor people. They regard the porpoises as their best friends, and never allow them to be caught or injured. They even know and recognise some of them by name.[39]

Foster Fyans saw people

> fishing in consort with the porpoises along the shore. It was . . . amusingly agreeable to see the natives working, spearing the fish driven towards the shore, and the porpoise devouring what escaped the natives or [was] driven back by them. The very best of terms existed. The porpoise appeared in no fear by the approach of a native so close as four or five yards; neither did their yelling and shouting in the least alarm them.[40]

Tinker Campbell was more precise:

> Here, for the first time, I saw the blacks fishing. There were many hundreds along the beach with their towrows (nets) in hand. As soon as the shoal of fish appeared in the offing some two or three of the blacks would advance to the water's edge, and, striking the water with their spears as a signal to the porpoises to drive the fish into the bank—which signal the porpoises would instantly obey—the main body of blacks, some hundreds in number, would rush in with their towrows and dip up the fish . . . The blacks even pretend to own particular porpoises, and nothing will offend them more than to attempt to injure one of their porpoises.[41]

On land people in their country grabbed what they chanced on, totem permitting, but typically found what they expected. From miles away they could discuss with ease a nesting bird or a termite mound. They left plants to grow, and by watching sun and rain knew when a harvest was ready. Jenny Isaacs reported, 'Women know where to go to get food, and discuss where to go before leaving camp',[42] and during a Kimberley drought Phyllis Kaberry asked a friend if she had any magic for goanna or honey. 'She answered in a matter-of-fact tone "me find em that one sugar-bag (wild-honey), me can't lose em". When I pressed her further with "suppose you no bin find em", she looked contemptuous and said, "me find em alright; me savvy".'[43] This was harvesting, not random gathering. People were ruled not by chance and hope, but by knowledge and policy.[44]

Knowledge so intricate could hardly terminate anywhere. It was inextricably continent-wide, and cradled in knowing the continent. Since people could neither deny nor deflect creation, they depended on understanding it as fully as possible—the more they knew the better they could manage their lives and their country. They strove to know what lay beyond. They travelled to harvest, initiate, marry, celebrate, sit in council.[45] Coast and inland they exchanged long-distance visits, there to learn of far lands and skills. In 1820 Shoalhaven coast men were familiar with Lake George, and north of Albury in 1825 a man in a yellow jacket addressed Hume and Hovell in English and had been at the lake. It was thus known in most of southeast New South Wales, and probably more widely, since south coast people travelled to Tumut, and in August 1844 Robinson saw Monaro people at Twofold Bay watching a dance composed by an Omeo man who may also have been there.[46] At the lake, men 'described' the Murrumbidgee 'to communicate with the sea, at a great distance, pointing southerly' and named tides and marine fish there. No white man knew that then. Upper Shoalhaven men said that limestone abounded west of the river mouth. No white man knew that either. In 1840 Fowler's Bay (SA) men assured Eyre that there was no inland sea, and told him of big trees with strange animals far to the west which Eyre identified as koalas.[47] In 1844 Toonda surprised Sturt

> by drawing in the sand a plan of the Darling for 300 miles of its course, also of the Murray a good distance both above and below its junction. He drew all the Lagoons on the Western side and gave the name of each; by comparing afterwards the bends he drew with Major Mitchell's chart, they both agreed. The part he drew was from the junction of the Bogan to the junction of the Murray.[48]

Murray men walked at least to the lower Barwon, linking it to the Darling,[49] and Daly men at least to the Cooper.[50] In 1835 Moore stated, 'the natives are all aware that [Australia] is an island, and that the sea which Tomghin spoke of is the sea which bounds the north coast. I had no idea that their knowledge of geography had been so extensive and accurate.'[51] [52]

Trade webs meshed thousands of kilometres, 'among the world's most extensive systems of human communication recorded in hunter-gatherer societies'.[53] Dieri people east of Lake Eyre (SA) visited places at least 800 kilometres apart, desert people walked for months for Parachilna (SA) ochre. On the Finke in 1870 Christopher Giles found in a rainmaker's bag 'a curious example of extremes meeting. Here was a boy's marble from Adelaide, handed on and bartered from tribe to tribe . . . and side by side with it a pearl shell from the extreme north coast, obtained originally most likely from the Malays.'[54] Kimberley and Torres Strait shell and Daly River (NT) goods went through the Great Sandy Desert to the Nullarbor coast, and Papuan shell reached western New South Wales. Any item might go anywhere.[55]

Songs and ceremonies were traded, sometimes travelling 'a thousand miles in a very short period'.[56] 'Picked men may be sent to a distant tribe just for the sake of learning [a dance] . . .', Walter Roth wrote,

> It may thus come to pass, and almost invariably does, that a tribe
> will learn and sing by rote whole corrobborees [sic] in a language
> absolutely remote from its own, and not one word of which the
> audience or performers can understand . . . That the words are very
> carefully committed to memory, I have obtained ample proof by taking
> down phonetically the same corrobborees as performed by different-
> speaking people living at distances upwards of 100 miles apart.[57]

Eyre noted that new dances and songs went constantly 'to distant parts . . . where a different dialect was spoken, and which consequently could not be understood where I heard them . . . the measures or quantities of the syllables appear to be more attended to than the sense'.[58] From the 1890s the Molonga ceremony went round Australia, and Robinson reported that on the Lachlan,

> Italian melodies had been introduced and were sung by the native youth
> with considerable ability. These new corroborees had been passed with
> amazing celerity to distant tribes. The rapid communication of the natives
> in this respect is astonishing. At King George's Sound the news of the Swan
> River Settlement was obtained from the natives long before it reached
> them [the settlers] through the ordinary channel and songs and dances

of the natives even from the Hunter have been brought to Port Phillip and for aught to the contrary may have passed around the continent.[59]

These continental systems let people everywhere use similar tools, techniques and protocols. Nic Peterson concluded, 'one can speak of a common indigenous way of life, created in part by the systems of exchange that linked people indirectly with others, right across the continent'.[60] Over wide areas people knew the land's geographic, ecological and spiritual fabric. They knew that the Dreaming was universal, that how they managed country mattered to creation, that they were contributors to a greater whole.[61]

Yet of all creatures they were most likely to unbalance creation, by increasing their population, so they limited their numbers. Long-term equitable resource use depended on this, otherwise sooner or later it would disintegrate, and in inevitable bad times people would confront catastrophe. Many laws and customs restricted family size, among them mobility, old marrying young, totem prohibitions and restrictions especially for women, abortion, dislike of twins, in extreme cases infanticide, and other 'powerful regulatory mechanisms'.[62] Local populations remained stable enough to stay within country. There were no population-driven conquests, and almost no territorial expansion: desert Walpiri and food rich Wiradjuri were rare exceptions.[63] Naturally more people congregated on rich land, and some districts carried more people then than now,[64] but they spread much more evenly over Australia, and nowhere were they crowded.

This was deliberate. Even allowing for killing diseases which raced ahead of Europeans (ch 11), Australia had fewer people in 1788 than it could carry. Murray valley and Arnhem Land pioneers thought their districts could have supported twice the people they did, while Geoffrey Blainey estimated Tasmania's 1788 population at about 4000 but its resources able to support about 70–80,000.[65] In arid regions people could afford to leave permanent water and good feed for bad seasons.[66] Everywhere population levels seem tuned not to 'normal' times but to harsh and erratic uncertainty, and not merely to bad times but to the worst times, such as giant floods or 100 year droughts, shorthand for the severest droughts of a drought-ridden continent. People apparently anticipated them, building up resources and limiting population. On the Darling

> there is no evidence of drastic reductions in population during droughts. More than likely the Bagundji had adapted themselves and their own population density to a situation where strenuous

efforts could support most people during bad seasons and very little
effort would support everyone during normal and good seasons.[67]

Even in plenty people reserved sanctuaries and imposed bans to counter scarcity (ch 10). This is strikingly provident: most societies today, including people who call Aborigines improvident, can't do it. Supporting fewer people than possible is a key feature of 1788. It made resources abundant.

Abundance was thus a precaution, but normal. People usually satisfied their material wants quickly, with less toil than all but privileged Europeans in 1788. It helped that they ate almost everything, many more foods than Europeans ate, perhaps a greater variety than any society on earth in 1788. Yet they ate nothing to scarcity or even short of plenty, and they could afford to prohibit food to host ceremonies for hundreds of guests, sometimes for months. Newcomers commented endlessly on plains rich with life, skies dark with birds, seas black with fish. In Tasmania Hardwicke reported places where 'Kangaroo are very numerous and easily caught' and 'in great abundance'.[68] From St Valentine's Peak, Hellyer 'saw kangaroos in abundance, and tracks of them in all directions'.[69] Throughout a bush walk near Goulburn (NSW) one night in 1832, Govett heard possums grunting and saw glider possums flying.[70] EPS Sturt thought the Murrumbidgee in 1837 'most beautiful . . . Every creek abounded with wild fowl, and the quail sprung from the long kangaroo grass which waved to the very flaps of the saddle',[71] and in the 1870s station hands could tickle fish from the river by hand, and shoot possums without leaving camp.[72] 'It is no wonder that the blacks were well-conditioned', Alexander Le Souef wrote near Swan Hill (Vic) in the late 1840s, 'for no native tribes could gain their living more easily, as their river was full of fish, and the country abounded in game, while quantities of small yams were obtained on the river flats, and the root of one of the large rushes was edible'.[73] Near Bairnsdale (Vic) Angus McMillan saw a lake 'alive with swans, ducks and pelicans . . . On the north side of the lake the country consists of open forest, and the grass was up to our stirrup-irons as we rode along. The country was absolutely swarming with kangaroos and emus.'[74] 'I have always found the greatest abundance in their huts . . .', Grey concluded. 'In all ordinary seasons . . . they can obtain, in two or three hours, a sufficient supply of food for the day.'[75] Even desert people got their food, medicine and shelter in 4–5 hours a day, and seemed to handicap themselves by performing ceremonies taking months to complete in places accessible only after heavy rain. In richer areas people needed even less time: for example Tiwi Islanders spent only about 20 per cent of their waking hours getting food. These were not people worried at where their next meal might come from.

It is true that many accounts, notably of Sydney during the 1788 winter, report starving people. Newcomers assumed that this happened every winter, and was evidence that hunter-gatherers depend for food on the whims of nature, as Thomas Malthus was to claim (ch 10). Yet had the Sydney people indeed starved every winter, they would have gone somewhere else. That was one point of being mobile. Mobility saved the colonists too, when in their hunger they sent ships to South Africa, China, Batavia and anywhere they could think of for food, including 700 kilometres to Lord Howe Island to catch turtles. For months they had hauled fish every day, feeding over a thousand mouths. Not surprisingly, by winter they noticed that fish were becoming scarce. The starving Aborigines were people whose food they had taken.

Abundance showed in physique, especially men's. Sydney people were reported to be shorter and slighter than newcomers,[76] and sometimes this was repeated of thin and 'shrivelled' people elsewhere, but Europeans often thought people well built. In 1829 Allan Cunningham described three men near Brisbane as 'of the ordinary stature of the Aborigines of Moreton Bay (viz about six feet), appeared very athletic active persons, of unusually muscular limb, and with bodies (much scarified) in exceeding good case'.[77] In 1884 Rolf Boldrewood recalled southwest Victorians as a fine race physically and otherwise, the men tall and muscular, the women well-shaped and fairly good-looking.[78]

Similar descriptions come from arid Australia. For centuries people there weathered terrible droughts, albeit at times with real distress, but lived comfortably where today others cannot. In the Great Sandy Desert, Carnegie met two well-built men with 'well-fed frames'.[79] Deep in the 1895–1902 drought, the worst on record, Richard Maurice led two expeditions through the southern and central deserts. He saw few people, but those few were well fed and apparently under no stress. At Mt Gosse (NT) his companion William Murray remarked, 'These blacks were fairly well nurtured and apparently do not lack food. With the exception of one, who was rather weedy, all were well developed and muscular.'[80] Eyre wrote that men were

> well built and muscular, averaging from five to six feet in height, with proportionate upper and lower extremities . . . fine broad and deep chests, indicating great bodily strength, and are remarkably erect and upright in their carriage, with much natural grace and dignity of demeanour.[81]

On the Cooper in 1845, where sixteen years later Burke and Wills became famous by starving to death, Sturt wrote,

> The men of this tribe were, without exception . . . a well-made race, with a sufficiency of muscular development . . . Of sixty-nine who I counted round me at one time, I do not think there was one under my own height, 5 feet 10¾ inches, but there were several upwards of 6 feet . . . I am sorry to say I observed but little improvement in the fairer sex. They were the same half-starved unhappy looking creatures whose condition I have so often pitied elsewhere.[82]

In thinking much less well of the women he was not alone, but few Australians today think the Cooper plenteous, nor the southwest Tasmanian coast, where Kelly was 'accosted by Six Large Men, Black Natives, Each of them above Six feet high and Verry Stout', and two days later by 'a Stout good Looking Man about Six feet High 30 years of age . . . [and] an old Man about Six feet Seven Inches High'.[83] Newcomers similarly described men and sometimes women near Melbourne, Brisbane and Darwin, in western Victoria, western New South Wales, southern South Australia, the Centre and north, and on Cape York. Big, well-fed people were typical.[84]

Abundance, knowledge and mobility reinforced each other. In discussing human societies, some writers take mobility to reflect uncertainty about food, and sedentism to show its predictability, but in 1788 people were so mobile and so confident of getting food that only in harsh places did they bother to store it (ch 10). In better country they could live by their staples permanently, or nearly, yet they walked. After 32 years with Victorian people, William Buckley said that plenty was usual, scarcity rare, and most travel not from necessity but 'as it suited our purposes, either for hunting, or for mere pleasure'.[85] How often people travelled varied: Tasmanians moved more often in the east than in the west for example,[86] and desert families more often than both. Everywhere people normally had more food than they needed.

Soon after 1788 smallpox ravaged much of Australia, killing perhaps half the people it met,[87] especially the very young and the very old, the future and the past. Some researchers think the disease came from the north, but Watkin Tench's denial may be deliberately ironic: 'It is true, that our surgeons had brought out variolous matter in bottles; but to infer that it was produced from this cause were a supposition so wild as to be unworthy of consideration.'[88] The plague spread far, and came again in 1828–30. It hit hard. Knowledge was lost, families amalgamated, totems re-assigned, boundaries re-located. More women than men died, so men may have taken over women's places and rituals.[89] Survivors suddenly had more resources but more work, since the Dreaming still required every inch of country to be cared for. Newcomers may have seen mere relics of more precise land management, but so sacred a gift, so intricate a weaving of country and soul, could never be given up. Instead survivors toiled harder to keep Law and country alive. In their terrible predicament they may have turned even more to their closest ally: fire.

How was land managed?

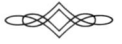

6

※

The closest ally

For countless generations people have stared into safe fire. The dancing flames mesmerise, the warm glow is a friend. Not so that other fire, heralded by haze, smoke, red lines in the scrub. That fire is implacable, alive. It roars, races, leaps, kills, devours. On 17 January 2003 a fire burnt over 70 per cent of the ACT. It killed four people and destroyed over 500 houses and many public buildings, including ACT Forests HQ and Kambah Fire Brigade Station. It ripped trees 70 cm across into the air, and dumped into a back yard a garden shed complete with tools and shelving from so far away that no-one could find where it came from. It killed 95 per cent of wildlife in southwest ACT parks, including over 500 kangaroos and wallabies. It was stopped only by a fire scar left on 24 December 2001.[1]

People could not have survived such fires in 1788. Had they faced the Black Saturdays and Ash Wednesdays white Australia has suffered, most must have died. Any uncontrolled fire menaced: a day's fire might eat a year's food. Latz observed of central Australia,

> After several very good seasons the amount of flammable material can build up to such an extent that a single wildfire, initiated in the height of summer, can sweep over huge areas of the desert destroying everything in its path. When good rains do not follow these fires, the effect on the flora and fauna (and even the soils) can be devastating. If this situation had arisen in the past it is hard to imagine how Aboriginal people could have survived.[2]

This situation rarely arose. People had to prevent it, or die. They worked hard to make fire malleable, and to confine killer fires to legends and cautionary tales. But a great challenge was a great opportunity. Fire could kill, but fire or no fire could distribute plant communities with the precision of a flame edge (ch 3). Fire could be an ally.

Most Europeans never saw a bushfire until they reached Australia. They thought any they saw horrific. A few were. Augustus Gregory recalled 'a party of three natives were destroyed by a fire of their own lighting—the fire closed round behind them in the scrub, and their only means of escape lay in their going through the flames the consequences of which act cost them their lives'.[3] Lightning or enemies could start conflagrations, and periodically people lit hot clean-up fires. Mitchell saw 'All the country beyond the [Namoi] . . . in flames . . . from the time of our arrival in these parts, the atmosphere had been so obscured by smoke, that I could never obtain a distinct view of the horizon. The smoke darkened the air at night, so as to hide the stars.'[4] On the Murray, Sturt saw where fire had scorched trees 'to their very summits and the trunks of those which had fallen were smoking on the ground'.[5][6]

Most fires blackened ground and charred trunks, but few scorched canopies. In Tasmania in 1823 James Ross found the Shannon's banks 'completely burned but a few days before by the natives. All the underwood was destroyed . . . and the whole surface of the ground was without a leaf . . . To this practice of burning the bush . . . may be attributed the general openness of the forest land in the island, and its usefulness for pasture', but he added that the flames were 'checked by the fresh and green parts of the upper branches'.[7] In the Blue Mountains Jean Quoy found

> vast forests where you walk beneath very pleasant domes of verdure. We noticed that all of these were blackened right up, a circumstance due to the fact, the natives liking to set alight the grasses and brushwood obstructing their way, the fire often catches the fibrous bark of the largest trees, which then burn without their trunk being in any way damaged by it and without injuring the vegetation of their tops.[8]

Off southwest Australia in December 1792 Claude Riche described a blazing field, but it went out overnight.[9] Near Hobart in January 1802 Francois Peron saw

> on all sides the forests . . . on fire. Their savage inhabitants . . . had withdrawn to a lofty mountain, which itself looked like a huge pyramid of flame and smoke . . . the fire had destroyed all the grass, and most of the bushes and small trees had met with the same fate; the largest trees were blackened almost to their summits, and in some places had fallen under the violence of the flames and huge blazing heaps had been formed of their remains,

yet he walked behind the fire up to unburnt huts on the summit, and next day the fire was out.[10] It was nowhere near the ferocity of Hobart's 1967 fires, though lit in summer. Ian Thomas notes that all Peron's fires were in cool north-easterly conditions, and none lasted more than a day.[11]

These men were fleeting visitors. James Kelly was thought a good bushman. Off Macquarie Harbour (Tas) in December 1815 he wrote,

> The Whole Face of the Coast Was, on fire and Lucky it Was for us it Was on fire, for the Smoke was so thick We Could not See a Hundred yards a Head of the Boat, on pulling into the Narrows at the Small Entrance Island We Heard a Large Number of Natives Shouting and Making a Great Noise as if they Were Hunting Kangaroos.

Next day this fire too was out.[12] In New South Wales in 1814 Evans wrote that the Blue Mountains 'have been fired; had we been on them we could not have escaped; the Flames rage with violence through thick underwood, which they are covered with'. He recorded more fires next day, but walked close behind the flames.[13] He could not have done so behind any of Australia's recent big fires. West of the Bogan Mitchell saw 'that much pains had been taken by the natives to spread the fire, from its burning in separate places. Huge trees fell now and then with a crashing sound, loud as thunder, while others hung just ready to fall . . . We travelled five miles through this fire and smoke.'[14] The fire was hot enough to burn trees, but not to link 'separate places', or to prevent riding among them.

Settlers described fearsome fires in the Adelaide hills,[15] but all or most were out next day. Angas wrote that hills trees had their

> massive trunks blackened, in many places as high as fifteen or twenty feet from the ground, by the tremendous fires that sweep through these forests, and continue to blaze and roll along, day and night for many miles, in one continuous chain of fire. These conflagrations usually take place during the dry heats of summer, and frequently at night; the hills, when viewed from Adelaide, present a singular and almost terrific appearance; being covered with long streaks of flame, so that one might fancy them a range of volcanoes.[16]

At any time, let alone in the dry heat of summer, forest fires rising a mere 15–20 feet to blacken trunks but not canopies are not big. The *South Australian Register* thought hills fires less fierce than those on the plains: 'though the fire has evidently raged fiercely in many places, yet it never seems to attack anything but the grass and the leaves of the lower bushes, leaving the trees unscathed, the larger ones being seldom found hollow and blackened as are those on the plains below'.[17] Not even new chums thought plains fires fierce.

Hallam points out that in southwest Australia settlers stood downwind of fires, so they were hardly intense.[18] In Victoria in 1824 Hovell met fires he thought hot, but which left big unburnt patches, indicating cool burns. 'All the country from where we started this morning is all burned', he reported, 'and in every direction the bush is all on fire . . . a little to the westward of our course, we can see the blaze some feet above the ground. At noon we rested for a few hours beside some waterholes, where there are a few acres of grass which had escaped the fire', and a week later, 'the grass for miles around was burnt . . . we at length came to a spot of about two acres where grass had escaped the fire . . . beside some waterholes'.[19] Breton wrote of 'tremendous fires' which scorched trees annually, even bi-annually (ch 3):[20] annual fires could not find the big fuel loads typically fed to today's infernos.[21]

These were summer fires, yet Europeans could travel near them, and most were out in a day. A Pitjantjatjara elder explained, 'before the arrival of white people Anungu did not know about really large bushfires, but now they do . . . the country had been properly looked after and it was not possible for such things as large scale bushfires to occur'.[22] A Darling and Paroo pioneer noted

> another remarkable characteristic of the aborigine . . . the care taken by them to prevent bushfires. In my long experience I have never known any serious bushfire caused by the blacks, and the condition of the country, the growth of the trees and bushes, such as sheoaks, pines, and acacias and a score of other kinds of trees that bushfires always destroy were, when the white man arrived, flourishing in the perfection of beauty and health . . . Australia in its natural state undoubtedly was liable to the ravages of extensive bushfire, and with so many hostile tribes it seems as if they would be a frequent occurrence, yet they evidently were not.[23]

Controlled fire and its ceremony was 1788's main management tool (digging sticks were second, dams and canals third). To burn improperly was sinful. Even innocent mistakes might be punished severely, and unleashing uncontrolled fire was a most serious offence. Fire was a totem. Whoever lit it answered to the ancestors for what it did. Understandably, fire was work for senior people, usually men. They were responsible for any fire, even a campfire, lit on land in their care. They decided which land would be burnt, when, and how, but in deciding obeyed strict protocols with ancestors, neighbours and specialist managers. On the Gulf of Carpentaria a Tiger Shark Ancestor put Australia's biggest cycad stand on the Wearyann. He requires it to be burnt annually, so people can feast on abundant nuts ripening at the same time. Generations of elders obeyed, but today the stands are in decline because ceremonies are fewer and the land burnt less often.[24] 'What must be made absolutely clear,' a West Australian researcher concluded, 'is that the rules for fire and fire use are many and varied, and are dependent upon an intimate knowledge of the physical and spiritual nature of each portion of the land. Without this knowledge, it is impossible to care for country in the appropriate way.'[25] An Arnhem man explained, 'you sing the country before you burn it. In your mind you see the fire, you know where it is going, and you know where it will stop. Only then do you light the fire.'[26] Burning was purposeful—as Leichhardt put it, part of the 'systematic management of their runs'.[27][28]

The first reason to burn was to control fuel. This meant neither today's 'No fuel no fire', nor yesterday's 'Prevent bush fire'. Fuel was a resource. It was managed, not eliminated. People wanted to choose, to plan, to make most fires cool, some hot, and some between, for each had its time and use. In a fire friendly continent this was not easy. Fuel accumulates quickly even in grassland. In 1841–2 Robert Murray wrote that grass fires in Victoria were

> common during the summer . . . The flames came on at a slow pace . . . as the grass happened to be short, the fiery line seldom rose above the fuel on which it fed; and it would have been no difficult matter to have leapt across it . . . The frequency of these fires is the principal cause of the absence of underwood, that renders the forest so pervious in all directions, and gives to Australia the park-like appearance which all agree in considering its characteristic feature. All the trees were scarred black, and any shrubs which sprouted were cut down by the next fire.[29]

In the next decade settlers regularly lit fires, but let them burn. This was a mistake. On Black Thursday, 6 February 1851, in conditions very like 7 February 2009, a fire burnt almost half Victoria. On a suffocating day in a drought summer, hot northerlies linked up small fires in remote bush which had been let burn for months. William Howitt reported, '300 miles in extent, and at least 150 in breadth, was reduced to a desert. It was one blackened and burning waste . . . the country was actually one blaze for thousands of square miles.'[30] The inferno fed on crops and hay as well as forest and scrub, but its speed and extent only a decade or so after European occupation shows how readily the bush leaps into deadly flame.

This alone was cause to manage every corner of the continent. There was no remote bush in 1788. To the furthest places, sooner or later, the firestick came. People burnt the most useful land most and the most sterile or sensitive land perhaps not for generations, but sooner or later they burnt everywhere, in 'every part of the country, though the most inaccessible and rocky'; on 'the highest mountains, and in places the most remote and desolate . . . [in] every place'; in 'every portion of their territories'.[31] In the Centre one hot day Giles found himself in 'such frightful and rocky places, that it appeared useless to search further in such a region, as it seemed utterly impossible for water to exist at all. Nevertheless, the natives were about, burning, burning, ever burning . . . The fires were starting up here and there around us in fresh and narrowing circles.'[32] If fuel built up, it was burnt.

This sparked a learning curve in fire management.

1. The more fuel is reduced, the more easily fire is controlled, and up to a point the more useful it is.
2. Even hot fires leave unburnt patches, but the cooler the fire the bigger the patches.
3. Burnt and unburnt patches benefit animals by balancing burnt (feed) and unburnt (shelter) country.
4. Patches form mosaics, which can be adjusted in size by varying fire intensity.
5. Intensity can be regulated by fire frequency and timing.
6. Frequency and timing are local. They depend on local flora and local moderators like rain, wind, temperature and aspect.
7. The better people understand these variables, the more they can burn with purpose. They can move from limiting fuel to shaping country.
8. This lets them selectively locate fire tolerant and fire sensitive plants, situate and shape mosaics and resources conveniently and predictably, and arrange them in sequence so one supplies what another does not.
9. Australia becomes a single estate, varied in means but not ends.
10. Maintaining the estate is enforced by universal Law (ch 4).

In 1788 most fires were cool. Cool fires burnt most land, and patches were common from rainforest to desert. In mid-summer 1802 a valley south of Port Lincoln (SA) was 'recently burnd, the old Casuarinas remaining. Besides the general fire there seemd to have been others more partial & more recent.'[33] In southeast Queensland 'natives had very recently fired the grass of the plain, but as its herbage was generally very young and verdant, only small patches of it had become ignited'.[34] In central Australia,

> although fires were lit wherever sufficient fuel was available the fires rarely extended over large areas. The effect of traditional burning regimes was to produce a series of small patches of country at different stages of recovery from fire with associated different plant and animal communities. This almost completely eliminated the risk of large scale wildfires which would have been disastrous for any group attempting to survive in a completely burnt-out area.[35]

In east Arnhem Land,

> As soon as the grass begins to dry in a normal season—often as early as April—the people start to burn it systematically in conjunction with organized hunting drives. The grass is not fired at random but in limited areas always held under control... The burning of the grass, although it yields much animal food, has the disadvantage of destroying the vines of food plants and so is carried out with great care until the vegetable harvest is well advanced.[36]

People burnt some patches every year, balancing each burn against those past and future. In September 1891 Lawrence Wells met at least three fire recovery stages in mallee 'burnt in vast patches a year or two ago. The fires must have been enormous... entered the unburnt giant mallee country... [then] found burnt country with young mallee 3 ft to 6 ft high.'[37] As the Wet ended, north Queenslanders burnt a succession of fires to make a mosaic of recovery stages, stopping in the hot months of the late Dry, when 'fire climb up over the mountains... it might kill some yam and all that you know, kill the trees, too hot'.[38] It might take 4–5 years to build a good Spinifex mosaic, but with fuel stifled and neighbours consulted, central Australians could let patch fires run over big tracts of country. On plains west of the MacDonnell Ranges in 1872, Giles commented,

the country seemed to have been more recently visited by the
natives than any other part, as burnt patches could be distinguished
as far as the vision could be carried . . . probably forty miles away,
we saw the ascending smoke of grass fires still attended to by the
natives . . . We camped in a grove of casuarinas, where the old
grass had been burnt, and some young stuff was springing.[39]

Latz explained:

In a simplistic sense, all that is required to obtain this mosaic is to burn
over as wide an area as possible as often as possible. To see how this
system works one must take the end of a drought as the starting point.
The first good rains will produce little fuel and most fires will only cover
small areas. If good seasons continue, fires lit in the second year will
extend over greater distances but will be either halted by the previous
year's burnt areas or by natural features such as sandy riverbeds or rocky
hills. The third year is the dangerous period. By this time there is enough
accumulated fuel to enable intense fires to spread over large areas and
even to enter fire-sensitive communities such as mulga stands. This, of
course, will not occur as the fires initiated previously will have reduced
the fuel load and provided natural firebreaks. (Even so, it does appear
that Aboriginal people rarely burn during the summer months at this
critical period.) This system of burning, with minor adjustments in relation
to the particular type of country and the time of the year, produces a
mosaic of plant communities in different stages of fire recovery. Once
this mosaic has been initiated it would be relatively easy to maintain and
could be used to protect certain areas from fire for a considerable time.[40]

Fire was a life study. Seasons vary, rain is erratic, plants have life cycles, fire has long and short term effects, people differ on what to favour. How each species responded to fire had to be set against deciding which to locate where. In the Centre old-growth fire sensitive plants are rare and in poor country, because in good country fuel builds up and fire kills them.[41] Here was a dilemma (fire kills sensitive species but no fire lets fuel build up) and a solution (locate such species on poor land where less fuel means fewer fires). Many such dilemmas demanded detailed local knowledge, yet in 1788 people shepherded fire around their country, caging, invigorating, locating, smoothing the immense complexity of Australia's plants and animals into such harmony that few newcomers saw any hint of a momentous achievement.

Fire managers burnt precisely. They did not light in the wrong conditions or with the wrong fuel. 'They pick the grass up, and scrunch it up in their hand, and if it gets too powdery well it's no more lighting grass.'[42] They aimed fires at breaks or patches. At Albany Isaac Nind reported, 'The violence of the fire is frequently very great, and extends over many miles of country; but this is generally guarded against by their burning it in consecutive portions.'[43] If necessary they put fires out. In the 1870s people complained to a station manager near Narrandera about his carelessness with fire. When a fire menaced the station while its men were away, an elder studied the flames, then organised women and children to light spot fires in five staggered rows across the advancing front. This broke up the fire, and it was put out.[44]

Above all, managers kept control. Near Westernport (Vic), 'About 6pm [they] doused their fire at once, although it must have covered near an acre of ground.'[45] In Cambridge Gulf (WA) King saw

> four natives seated on the sand, watching the progress of a fire
> they had just kindled; which was rapidly spreading through, and
> consuming the dry and parched up grass that grew scantily upon
> the face of the island ... The fires ... rapidly spread over the
> summit of the hills, and at night, the whole island was illuminated,
> and presented a most grand and imposing appearance.[46]

Yet the men who lit it simply sat down. In the central desert where fires so often seemed big and random, in years of research Gould 'never encountered an occasion when a fire actually invaded an area that was already producing wild food crops',[47] and Dick Kimber concludes, 'large Aboriginal fires were not accidental, random or otherwise uncontrolled'.[48]

How quickly fuel built up, or what balance people wanted, could be decisive, for quite small differences in frequency and intensity might re-set the ratio of ground, midstorey and canopy plants and the animals in them. Broadly, the faster growing and more fire welcoming the dominant plant, the more frequent the fire. In fire prone communities 'a fire a day kept bushfires away', while protective burns ringed fire sensitive places. Northern grassland was burnt annually, Kangaroo Grass every 2–3 years, Mulga at most once a decade, dry ridges perhaps every 15–25 years, Tuart every 2–4 years and Jarrah every 3–4 in early summer, Karri about every five years in late summer. Mountain

Ash needs fire every 400 years or so, yet is the most flammable eucalypt. Whole forests rage with a ferocity none can fight and few survive. Almost certainly people managed Mountain Ash in winter: they lived on the coast in summer (ch 9). Perhaps for generations they winter burnt to keep edges back and clearings open, sensibly beginning when a forest was young. Yet a winter cool-burn could not ensure enough heat for those wet forests to kill and replace themselves. That needs a dry summer, yet it was done. It must have been a time for brave men, their families safely on the coast.[49]

Burning whenever possible is too often for many plants and animals. Max Lines learnt near Alice Springs, 'Sometimes you burn at the wrong time and it's too bloody hot; it scalds everything and it takes a couple of years to come back.'[50] Fuel rationing and timing kept most fires cool. Cool fires could burn one species without much harming another, speed regrowth, let people hunt close up, and stop or cage random fire. Sometimes people had to work to keep the fires going, but they were precise and malleable. North of Cairns rainforest people combined timing and precision (pictures 44–5): 'You burn . . . in the *bulur* [cold] time, inside the old scrub is still damp, wet, it won't go into the scrub, you just sort of burn on the edge with the dry, that's how we save the scrub . . . [fire] only follow the kangaroo grass right on the edge, doesn't go far into the scrub.' Precision burning exposed animal tracks, protected yams on forest margins, and shielded forest from dry season hot fires. When the wind was right, people burnt inside the forest, gently to reduce surface litter, more intensely to make clearings and tracks.[51]

In early summer John Lort Stokes

> met a party of natives engaged in burning the bush, which they do in sections every year. The dexterity with which they manage so proverbially a dangerous agent as fire is indeed astonishing. Those to whom this duty is especially entrusted, and who guide or stop the running flame, are armed with large green boughs, with which, if it moves in the wrong direction, they beat it out . . . I can conceive no finer subject for a picture than a party of these swarthy beings engaged in kindling, moderating, and directing the destructive element, which under their care seems almost to change its nature, acquiring, as it were, complete docility, instead of the ungovernable fury we are accustomed to ascribe to it.[52]

In southwest Australia Lew Scott recalled 1920s graziers burning docile summer fires:

> native grass in those days, you don't see it now . . . Because it's not burnt, you have to burn to get native grass . . . you would light it up at about ten o'clock in the morning and three or four o'clock it would all go out, the next day you would light it up again. The bush was alive with possums and wallabies and kangaroo rats . . . it was only a little fire, it never used to get up in the trees and burn the possums . . . the real oldies followed the burning patterns of the natives in keeping the place green . . . learnt to burn little patches, that they wanted for their existence the same as the blackfellow—of course not winter and not spring—because you kill all the little birds and animals—and so summer burning.[53]

Scott makes clear how crucial timing was. Whereas fuel control was a fire plan's baseline, timing was its end point, considering both fuel and purpose. Particular animal and plant communities needed and got very precise fire timings and intensity.[54] Trickling cool fires and clearing hot fires were timed to keep species in balance. On dry Sydney sandstone people burnt cool fires in spring, but hot fires in early summer to open hard seeds and pods or germinate legumes.[55] In north Queensland early Dry fires promote some shrubs and grasses, late Dry fires promote others and herbs.[56] When to burn grass might hinge on its varying growth from year to year, or on associated tubers or annuals, some killed by fire, others needing it to flower, seed or compete. These needs are easily unbalanced. For example badly timed fire promotes unpalatable perennials like Blady Grass or Bunch Spear Grass at the expense of fodder grasses,[57] and has let Spinifex expand its range to become 'the most common organism in the dry three-fifths of Australia'.[58] Yet plant communities embracing different fire responses thrived in 1788. Multiply this by Australia's 25,000 species, and a management regime of breathtaking complexity emerges.

Situating plants located grazing animals and their predators as precisely as a farmer with paddocks. 'The burning of country was not at all random', Kimber observed,

> there was greater attention to areas favoured by certain nutritious or otherwise useful plants and to areas favoured by certain animals . . . Knowledge of the locality of previously burnt areas clearly aided men in their hunting—and also resulted in greater focussing of animals than if lightning-induced fires spread fiercely, wildly and unpredictably.[59]

Many animals depend on specific and unnatural fire:

> The Tjukurpa [Dreaming] shows Anungu how animals will be with fire and burnt country. For example, some dragon lizards and other small animals don't like the ground after it's been burnt. They go away for a while, and then come back when the spinifex has grown again. Some animals, such as the spinifex hopping-mouse, like it both ways. They move into the burned areas to feed and then return to safety in the large unburnt spinifex hummocks where they have their burrows. *Kalaya* and *malu* (emu and kangaroo) do not like freshly burnt country but come back to it after rain has put on the green feed. Most animals and birds love the green feed near water.[60]

Mallee fowl survive only small, patchy fires, frequency depending on terrain,[61] so people burnt often enough to limit fuel, but carefully enough to let the birds flourish. Gliders and possums like frequent fire,[62] but rat kangaroos need casuarinas burnt about every seven years, a native mouse needs heath burnt every 8–10, mainland tammar wallabies need dense melaleuca burnt very hot every 25–30.[63] In the Centre, 'When the little emus are on the ground [about August] you do not burn.'[64] Small desert marsupials need mature Spinifex for shelter beside young Spinifex to eat, which cool fire makes, but in West Australian heath cool fire is associated with an alarming decline of both the lowland grass wren, apparently by depleting its food, and Caley's Grevillea, because patches attract small mammals which eat out its seed.[65] All these plants and animals thrived in 1788, making clear that people timed a great variety of local and specific fires over many centuries.

Most of Australia was burnt about every 1–5 years depending on local conditions and purposes, and on most days people probably burnt somewhere. Winter fires were common, especially in the inland and north. On the Lachlan Oxley saw frequent winter fires,[66] and on the Maranoa (Qld) Mitchell explained that in winter 'the natives availed themselves of a hot wind to burn as much as they could of the old grass, and a prickly weed which, being removed, would admit the growth of a green crop, on which the kangaroos come to feed, and are then more easily got at'.[67] In South Australia's winter Johannes Menge saw plains 'exactly like the Parks I saw in London . . . the old grass having been burnt by the natives & the new grass having grown a foot high an emerald colour out of the black gave the eyes a delightful impression . . . The grass is everywhere 5ft when not burned [and] bears a corn like barley.'[68] Northwest of Ooldea (SA) William Murray saw winter fires promote both scrub and grass: 'sandhills to the west, which are very high, have had large areas burnt, and there is very plentiful young bush feed and some fair grassy patches. The fires bring up a lot of young acacia, and the patches which have been burnt are always much better for feed than the older scrub.'[69] Only cool winter fires make the feed–shelter mosaics essential for Western Hare Wallabies, now close to extinction,[70] while McDouall Stuart, Giles and David Lindsay all saw grass springing from autumn to spring fires apparently where Spinifex is now, suggesting that fires today may be too hot.[71]

Except in the Wet, most fires were lit in summer, when this is now a criminal offence. 'The Natives . . . fire . . . the thick brushes and old grass every summer,' James Atkinson wrote, 'the young herbage that springs up in these places, is sure to attract the kangaroos and other game.'[72] On desert dunes Wells saw extensive areas blackened 'apparently last summer',[73] and Francis Singleton commented on a West Australian government proposal to ban summer burning by Aborigines:

> It appears to be about one half of the sandy land is burnt over by the fires annually . . . The herbage, unless it has been burnt in the previous summer becomes exceedingly hard, and is usually refused by the stock . . . To frame a statute forbidding the Natives to fire the bush would I fancy prove abortive; and could such a law be carried out in practice I should conceive it to be an unjust one. The Aborigines look forward to the summer season with the same feelings as Europeans. To both it is the time of harvest. It is then they gather in by means of these fires their great harvests of game.[74]

When in summer fires were lit varied with how damp the country was, how big people wanted patches to be, which food plants were ready, which seed had germinated, whether game was to be attracted or moved, and so on. Grass-seed eaters burnt after harvest, usually in late summer, relying on timing and damp plant bases to fetter the flames; tuber eaters mostly in early summer once tubers matured. Wet country was lit whenever fuel was dry enough, which meant mostly in summer.[75]

In any season, people timed most (not all) fires to go out at night: overnight fires could confess loss of control. To decide what day, even what hour, to burn, managers took account of wind, humidity, aspect, target plants and animals, and fuel loads. They burnt on hot, windy days if it suited,[76] but wind was commonly an autumn or winter ally. It aimed fire; dew, rain, frost or snow restrained it. In southwest Tasmania, William Sharland

> suddenly . . . opened into ground recently burnt . . . apparently
> immediately before the late snow, and, I conclude, by the natives. The

> valley had all the appearance, at a distance, of undergoing all the various processes of agriculture,—some parts (the most recently burnt) looking like freshly ploughed fields; and again, other parts possessing the most beautiful verdure from the sprouting of the young grasses and rushes.[77]

North of Port Hedland (WA) Frank Gregory passed 'several miles over a plain . . . covered with a short sward of bright green grass, the native fires having swept off the dry grass a few weeks previously; and although there had been no rain since, the heavy dews that fell during the night in these latitudes had been sufficient to produce a rapid growth'.[78]

Although few noticed the connection, many newcomers saw fire before rain. Wedge reported this in Tasmania.[79] On the Lachlan, Allan Cunningham met hills 'lately fired by the natives'—for the next two days it rained heavily.[80] Country southeast of Clermont

> had evidently been burnt before this late rain by the blacks, and the undulating plains . . . were clothed with a carpet of burnt feed, forming a vivid green dotted with a variety of wild flowers, also many kinds of wild peas and vetches, wild cucumbers, and other trailing plants . . . Never after, during my long experience of the district, did I see it in such splendid condition—I might, indeed, say glory.[81]

On Cape York, Robert Logan Jack recorded a big fire on 25 August 1879, a thunderstorm the next night, and next day a fire which left 'grassy patches'.[82] In December 1831 Mitchell wrote that for three days 'the woods were burning before us . . . This evening . . . the country seemed on fire all round us', but next day rain put the fires out.[83] In the Centre fire was commonly timed before rain.[84] Walter Smith Purula, a southern Arrernte elder, made clear to Kimber how important rain was, and how much else must be considered:

> They watch the white ants—when they start carrying their eggs out of the creek and put them on a high place, then they know it's going to rain. They start burning again. They generally burn a little patch first . . . close to the rockhole or soakage . . . they make for that burnt patch if the main fire gets out of control. If it's hilly country, they only burn . . . along the hill, perhaps to promote feed for wallabies or kangaroos or something. If flat

country they got to wait for the wind . . . When it is blowing hard enough, they light it, watch it, stand right around, and put it out if need be. They burn in little patches first, and then they put them out. They start on this [bigger] . . . fire then. Some fallen trees might be burning. They got to bury that. Might be ironwood, might be corkwood, and if the wind gets hold of that, it chucks that coal a long way. Instead of that, they bury it. They burn him early, before that weather gets too hot . . . in the middle of the day a fire is dangerous. That whirlwind comes too, and carries the fire along. No good. That's the whirliwind time then. You got to wait till nearly sundown, and then you can start burning again. Certain time of the year though, they got to do that. You can't burn wrong time, like, summer time it's got to be burnt, but no good winter time. They die. All them tucker trees . . . But if they burn them summer time and a storm comes, it grows lovely.[85] [86]

The centrality of timing is seen in what happened to southeast eucalypt forests after 1788. Some scientists think that firing scrub promotes not grass but more scrub, and that the more it is burnt the scrubbier it gets. A sensible example is Norman Wakefield's account of the Rogers family's experience in northeast Gippsland between 1902 and 1969. When JC Rogers arrived in 1902 old hands told him of

the open, clean-bottomed, park-like state of the forests . . . it had been the accepted thing to burn the bush, to provide a new growth of shorter sweet feed for the cattle . . . The practice was to burn the country as often as possible, which would be every three or four years according to conditions. One went burning in the hottest and driest weather in January and February, so that the fire would be as fierce as possible, and thus make a clean burn . . . the long-followed practice of regularly burning the bush in the hot part of the year has resulted in a great increase of scrub in all timbered areas except the box country. The fires forced the trees and scrub to seed and coppice, and in time an almost impenetrable forest arose.[87]

Yet in Gippsland no fire also results in dense scrub. At Venus Bay, Robinson noted, 'This tribe once powerful are defunct and the country in consequence is unburnt having no native inhabitants. This is the reason the country is so scrubby.'[88] To make Gippsland 'park-like' and 'clean-bottomed', it must be burnt correctly, not 'as fierce as possible'. In Arnhem Land David Bowman found that frequent and timely fire opened the vegetation and stunted woody species.[89] South of Canberra John Banks found that frequent hot fires promoted scrub, but fires too cool to germinate scrub replaced it with a grass dominated understorey. By dating eucalypt scars he found that high country fire frequency increased after Europeans came, even in the early period when settlers attempted to imitate 1788 fire. From about a fire a decade from the 1750s to the 1830s, numbers rose to almost one a year by 1950, then under better control fell almost to 1788 frequency. In Aboriginal times hot 'widespread fires were rare, even in dry periods', whereas in European times they became common. As a result, whereas 'the original forest consisted largely of uneven-aged stands of older, widely spaced trees . . . Today this picture has been reversed, with dense even-aged stands—typically dating from major fires in the 1880s, early 1900s, 1926 or 1939—dominating the forest.'[90] In short, because of more and hotter fires per decade, scrub fuel built up in European times. Gippsland cattlemen used the wrong fire.[91] Timing is crucial.

People lit clean-up fires last in a burn sequence. The fires tidied what was left, cleared mosaics needing rejuvenating, and gave managers clean ground. Cleaning country 'dominates all other reasons . . . If everything is clean the dreaming will be quiet.'[92] In May 1838 Eyre wrote,

> The country which had been so burned up and bare as we passed thro'
> it in March was . . . beautifully green and verdant . . . all nature's aspect
> was so lovely and smiling that we could hardly persuade ourselves
> that it really was the same region . . . Had my experience not taught
> me this lesson before I might now have learnt how great a difference a
> trifling change of time or season makes in the aspect of the country.[93]

Remarkably, frequency, intensity, timing and scale made similar plant patterns across Australia, whatever the local flora. Comparing fire programs in unlike regions demonstrates this.

On Top End floodplains fire programs began as the Wet ended and continued just into the next Wet. Forest people started later because they needed hotter fires, while dry or stone country programs began in the cold time about the mid-Dry and ended when the grass got too flammable. People began by burning breaks round camps, cemeteries and sensitive places like jungle thickets, pine forests and Paperbark swamps. Fires were careful, cool and small, perhaps burning only a few metres, with respectful ritual, on damp ground, near water, and when dew or rain would put them out, but they protected the places and their spirits, who would blind anyone who burnt too close.

People next began burning grass, then wood. They burnt every day, at first patchy fires near water to make pick, or around fruit trees before they flowered, or on plains to isolate unburnt grass for later hunting fires. They followed the drying country, lighting last the country last to dry. They lit bigger and less patchy fires in the cold time after wind had flattened the grass, allowing more control. By then they might burn over many miles and in the middle of the day, but still with fires which rarely scorched canopies and usually went out at night. On Cape York, Jack so often saw fires in the late Dry that he remarked, 'The blacks had neglected to burn the country passed over to-day.'[94] In all perhaps half the country would be burnt, some more than once, depending on local conditions and purposes.[95]

In the Centre fuel took longer to build up and plants longer to recover, so most land was burnt less often. People burnt hill bases where water soaked in perhaps every 3–4 years; dune country, especially swales, every 4–10 years depending on regrowth; stone or ridge country perhaps two or three times a lifetime. With fewer people, managers had more but less diverse country to care for than further north. Reaching a desert fire in September 1891, Lindsay 'found only one native track . . . Reached the second fire in four miles, and found it had been made by the same native. Then sped on hurriedly to another fire, and found it also had been made by the same man.' Later he found other individuals burning in the same way.[96] This was typical desert burning (picture 29).

Since more fuel was dry than further north, fires were more often bigger, but as fully controlled. People began with day fires using damp and wind to protect important places, deter snakes, insects and bad spirits near camps, and promote or preserve feed as drought insurance near water. Explorers came to assume that a lot of burnt ground meant water. Leichhardt noted, 'we were sure that a greater supply of water was near, as many patches of burnt grass shewed that the natives had been here very lately',[97] and west of Mt Kintore Tietkins remarked, 'There is a large area of burnt ground here, leading me to infer that a good water will be found.' He found it soon after, a claypan sheltering ducks and cranes.[98]

Hot fires were lit when the tail of the Wet was furthest south in late summer, but not until after the seed harvest, not on dangerous days, preferably not scorching tree canopies, and aimed at stone, sand or earlier breaks. A good fire was slow enough to let animals escape and people keep up, sometimes for weeks, helping it along until rain or burnt ground or a neighbour's decree put it out. If there was no rain people still burnt in season, though not near sensitive places.[99]

With unmatched insight, Hallam used historical records to describe southwest Australian fire programs. People adjusted frequency and intensity to how quickly fuel built up, and to plant and animal needs. In late spring or early summer, earlier inland than near the coast, they burnt cool fires around camps, sensitive sites and water. David Ward described a

> technique of burning with a fresh breeze in light fuel, so that the back and flank fires are blown out, and the headfire cuts a narrow strip, which can be deliberately aimed at some natural fire break, such as rocks, a lake or swamp, or recently burnt country... Coastal Aborigines were (and some further north probably still are) very proud of their ability to anticipate diurnal wind changes from land to sea breeze, so that a strip fire would swing around in a hooked or loop shape, extinguishing itself before nightfall.[100]

These early fires gave people control when they burnt most ground in late summer. They might burn grass valleys or the Darling Scarp twice a year, but dry ridges only every 15–25 years. Summer fires got into crops, angering settlers, yet some saw their value:

> it has always been the custom of the Natives to fire the country during the summer season for a variety of purposes, first to assist them in hunting, it also clears the country of underwood, which if not occasionally burnt, would become an impenetrable jungle, infested with snakes and reptiles... I consider it an advantage that portions of the country should be burnt every year, provided it is not done till late in the summer, the feed is always better where the dead grass has been previously burnt off.[101] [102]

In half of Tasmania fire replaced rainforest with other plant communities. To do this Tasmanians probably burnt against the country more than anywhere in mainland Australia. They burnt grass every 1–3 years, open forest every 3–5 years, wet forest rarely. They needed hot fire to burn back wet forests and cut roads and clearings through them, which may be why Buttongrass is common. Cool fire maintained grass and heath patches and plains (pictures 46–8), which even in the wet southwest, between Mt King William and Frenchman's Cap, commanded 'an extensive prospect, the large expanse of bare hills to the right, left and front, affording by the absence of wood a great relief to eyes so much habituated to seemingly interminable forests', and further southwest, 'charming plains... Broken into countless varieties of hill and dale, of floral mead and grassy knoll, of verdant copse or sunny bank . . . description fails me.'[103] Grass patches were probably smaller in the southwest, even on the coast (picture 39). The east had less rainforest: typically, grass or woodland valleys and low hills ran between eucalypt ranges (picture 16).[104]

A rain loop governed 1788 fire programs, high and seasonal in the north, falling to low and uncertain in the Centre, rising in the south to high and seasonal in western Tasmania. Local adjustment was normal, but everywhere fire was a constant duty. Managers regulated fuel, burnt somewhere every season, burnt mostly in summer, burnt early cool fires to protect places and plants, ran later fires into controls, and calibrated fire frequency, timing and intensity to plant and animal cycles. What Dean Yibarbuk says of north-central Arnhem Land was generally true: most fires were small, local and cool, shielding sensitive species but promoting plant foods and perennials, and greatly reducing the risk and impact of uncontrolled fires.[105] This preserved a complex biodiversity, and made and maintained similar landscape patterns in vastly different terrains and climates from the Top to Tasmania.

Controlled fire gave people almost limitless burn options. They could burn freely for transient purposes—to smoke out possums, hollow out trees to camp in, fragment bushfires, keep warm on the march, pick up tracks in ash and so on.[106] Europeans believed, sometimes correctly, that warriors lit fires to cover retreats or target crops or huts,[107] and Eyre stated that people

> appear to dread evil spirits . . . They fly about at nights through the air, break down branches of trees, pass simultaneously from one place to another, and attack all natives that come in their way, dragging such as they can after them. Fire appears to have considerable effect in keeping these monsters away, and a native will rarely stir a yard by night, except in moonlight, without carrying a fire-stick.[108]

Most fire was to make grass. Grassland is pleasant and bountiful, and visibility matters to hunters and gatherers, so people cleared trees and scrub, and burnt old grass to make new (ch 1). In Victoria Hovell reported, 'The general appearance of the country, together with that of the soil, is rich and beautiful. The grass having apparently been burnt early in the [summer] season, and being now in full seed, is fresh and luxuriant, frequently as high as their heads, and seldom lower than their waists.'[109] On Cooper's Creek in a drought year, Sturt noted, people 'had fired the grass, and it was now springing up in a bed of the most beautiful green'.[110] In New England,

> The great heat is sometimes increased by the burning grass, which is generally lighted by the aborigines carrying fire about with them; these fires, when there is a wind, will sometimes burn for days, but if there is no wind, there is almost always a dew at night, which often puts them out. The sight of fires at night is sometimes magnificent, as whole ranges are lighted up by them. They have a great effect on the character of the country, as they burn many of the young trees, and thus prevent the forest from being too thick. All the country, except when very heavily stocked with sheep, is sure to be burnt every two or three years . . . young acacias spring up luxuriantly where the fires have been under the old trees.[111] [112]

People burnt grass mainly to promote, protect or restrict plants, or to lure game. Correct fire was 'a horticultural tool'.[113] Latz observed,

> the judicious use of fire was, in the past, the single most important aspect of the desert economy. Not only can burning increase the total quantity of plant foods, but it can also reduce the effort required to harvest their products. Fire can also be used to influence the distribution of the food plants and it certainly increases the chance of finding them . . . Although many of the important food plants are encouraged by fire others are not, and the Aborigines' burning system results in optimum food production from both these plant groups by producing a mosaic of vegetation in different stages of fire recovery.[114]

Fire or no fire protected flowers and fruit, refreshed and flavoured reed rhizomes, cleared land for ground-feeding birds, and stimulated or exposed grassland plants (ch 10). At Sydney in the winter of 1788, Hunter saw

> not less than three or four acres of ground all in a blaze; we then conjectured that these were made for the purpose of clearing the ground of the shrubs and underwood, by which means they might with greater ease get at those roots which appear to be a great part of their subsistence during winter. We had observed that they generally took advantage of windy weather for making such fires, which would of course occasion their spreading over a greater extent of ground.[115] [116]

All grazers chase pick. Mitchell recognised that grass to lure game was 'worked from infancy'.[117] West of the Macquarie Sturt found 'the grass, which had been burnt down, was then springing up most beautifully green, and was relished exceedingly by [our] animals'.[118] Kangaroos, George Bennett advised in 1832, 'like the cattle, frequent those places where the grass, having been recently burnt, they meet with the sweet young herbage'.[119] Allan Cunningham found it

> a common practice of the Aborigines to fire the country in Dry Seasons particularly where it is wooded & bushy, in order to oblige such Game of the Kang'o Kind to quit their Couch & subject themselves to be spear'd, and the object these people have in View in firing the herbage of clear open tracts is, that as the young Grass grows immediately after such an Ignition, especially should rain succeed these Conflagrations, which often times are very extensive, Kangaroos & Emus are tempted to leave the forest brushes to feed on the undershoots, and thus are likewise exposed to their missile weapons.[120]

So obvious was the value of burning grass for grazers that settlers imitated it. In Western Australia one wrote, 'I consider it an advantage that portions of the country should be burnt every year, provided it is not done till late in the summer [because of crops], the feed is always better where the dead grass has been previously burnt off.'[121] In New South Wales,

> The old withered grasses are usually burnt off in the spring, and often at other periods of the year if you have an extensive run for your stock; and it is astonishing to see how quickly and how luxuriantly the new grasses will push up after these burnings, if a shower of rain should happen to follow them. When judiciously accomplished, they certainly produce most beneficial effects, by destroying all the old grass which the sheep and cattle refuse to eat . . . while they destroy, too, the various broods of insects that nestle about the roots of the grasses.[122]

Northern graziers still burn off annually, though more for cattle than diversity as in 1788.[123]

Burning to drive game, rather than lure it, was much less common. People hunted because they were burning, not the reverse (picture 29). JD Lang, Grey, Eyre and

Collett Barker all agreed that a hunting fire was organised only when an owner wanted to burn anyway.[124] It let loose a dangerous ally; it had to be timed properly. A Pintupi man said, 'We would burn areas and hunt while the fire was burning; then we would move on and return to these areas later to collect food from plants that had regenerated and to hunt animals that had moved in to feed.'[125] Near Albany (WA) at the end of summer,

> the natives burned great tracts to make sure the grass would come up green and sweet with the first rains and to drive out the game for hunting purposes. All the young of the birds that build their nests on the ground were hatched and the young ground rats old enough to run about before these fires were made. When the time was held ripe for the bush fires (*man carl*) the *man carl* ceremony was held. This dance was done at night.[126]

The 'ripe' time was the fire season. A Bunbury (WA) settler wrote:

> In December, but more particularly in January and February, the natives burn large tracts of country to catch wallabee, or bush kangaroo. For this purpose they generally go in considerable numbers and select a fine and warm day, and ... fire a portion of thick scrub or grass where they know the animals to live ... The fires when thus lighted generally proceed spreading and consuming every thing in their progress, and before the coldness and dew of the night repress their fury or intervening barren spots stop their rage, overrun some square miles of surface, and exhibit a splendidly bright spectacle amid the gloom and darkness of the night.[127]

On the Kimberley coast JRB Love reported:

> A month or so after the end of the wet season, which lasts from December till April, the country is smothered beneath a rank growth of grass, up to eight feet high, which dries fast. It is very difficult to walk through it, almost impossible in dense parts. So the men welcome the time when the grass is dry enough to burn. They will decide, from May till July, indeed as long as there is any country left with grass to burn, what spot they will choose for the next burning party. These are exciting expeditions, in which all the men take part. Early on the morning of the burning the men will be seen

> rubbing and painting their bodies with white clay. Soon after sunrise they will muster, carrying their weapons, and go through a performance that might be called a dance. Then they went off, some to burn, some to hunt.[128]

In east Arnhem Land in 1946–7, Donald Thomson observed, 'As soon as the grass begins to dry, the people start to burn it systematically in conjunction with organized hunting drives. The grass is not fired at random but in limited areas always held under control.'[129] In March 1788 Hunter stated, 'they also, when in considerable numbers, set the country on fire for several miles extent; this, we have generally understood, is for the purpose of disturbing such animals as may be within reach of the conflagration; and thereby they have an opportunity of killing many'.[130] For all these fires people gathered and danced, so they were planned. Weeks before, people enclosed a chosen location with cool fires, burnt refuges for vulnerable species, set pick fires to bring game into the target area, then kept away to quieten game. While waiting they watched for bushfires, for if one took hold guests and neighbours might ridicule them, and ancestors would take offence.

Francis Barrallier's description of a hunt in November 1802 conveys how much preparation preceded it:

> When the natives assemble together to hunt the kangaroo, they form a circle which contains an area of 1 or 2 miles . . . They usually stand about 30 paces apart . . . holding a handful of lighted bark, they at a given signal set fire to the grass and brush in front of them . . . as the fire progresses they advance forward with their spears in readiness, narrowing the circle and making as much noise as possible . . . The kangaroos, which are thus shut into that circle, burn their feet in jumping on every side to get away, and are compelled to retire within the circle until the fire attacks them.[131]

In open country fire circles might initially enclose 40–50 kilometres. In 1932 people purposely avoided burning a large area, waited for the right wind, then two lines slowly walked apart, firing Spinifex until they had a wide horseshoe of flame burning into the wind. The flames closed in slowly, allowing plenty of time to capture fleeing animals and reptiles.[132] That timing the fire rather than hunting was central is also evidenced by the great efforts people across Australia made to hunt in the off-fire season with nets of hundreds of metres and brush fences kilometres long.[133][134]

People also burnt to make walking easier (pictures 34–5, 42, 55). This ranged from clearing grass ahead to making roads or tracks through forest, scrub, mangroves or reeds.[135] Especially in wet country, clearways took sustained skill to make and maintain, yet they braided the land, criss-crossing rainforest, following ridges and water, marking boundaries. In southern Australia, around most of Tasmania, and probably elsewhere, was 'a belt of open country without large timber, running parallel with the coast and varying in width from a quarter to one, or one and a half, miles'.[136] Hunter saw fires 'intended to clear that part of the country through which they have frequent occasion to travel, of the brush or underwood, from which they, being naked, suffer very great inconvenience'.[137] Tasmanians reached their ochre mines by well-defined roads and chains of plains.[138] Charles Hall recalled miles of roads he saw through the Grampians to the Wannon and on to the Glenelg (Vic).[139] In north Queensland tracks 'on the coastal side of the main range are lit from the bottom and move up the slope, undoubtedly burning the rainforest margins; on the inland side of the coastal range they are lit from the top of the hill and move down'.[140] John Blay has mapped in detail a road from the coast south of Twofold Bay (NSW) to the Snowy Mountains, with branches to Gippsland and the western plains.[141] Mountain people often went to the coast in winter and coastal people to the mountains in summer (ch 5), except perhaps in Mountain Ash country.

Newcomers commonly 'discovered' by following roads, but rarely noted them. Oxley wrote of dense mallee south of the Lachlan,

> these scrubs we avoided, by keeping close along the base of Peel's range, where the country had been lately burnt. It is somewhat singular that those scrubs and brushes seldom if ever extend to the immediate base of the hills: [even though] the washings from them rendered the soil somewhat better for two or three hundred yards.[142]

In the vast, flammable Murray reedbeds Mitchell puzzled at 'one remarkable difference between this river and the Murrumbidgee . . . in the latter, even where reeds most prevailed, a certain space near the bank remained tolerably clear: whereas, on this river, the reeds grew most thickly and closely on its immediate banks'.[143] He missed the precision burning Sturt saw on the Murray: 'narrow lanes, or openings which the Natives had burnt, the reeds forming an arch over our heads and growing to the heighth of eighteen or twenty feet', and 'reeds, through which we could not have pushed but for the narrow lanes made in them by the Natives'.[144] On the Gordon (Tas) Sharland

> entered a very thick scrub . . . cut through this to an open point, which had been burnt; and then followed a small marsh [Painters Plain], where there was only low scrub; but on each side the same impervious scrub continued . . . We followed the said Marsh and some burnt ground until it brought us out to a bare hill where a fire had been made by the blacks; and I am inclined to suppose that the track I have followed is that which they pursue.[145]

Scrub has now locked up this country, and fit walkers take days longer than early Europeans to walk it. How much grass and how little undergrowth there was in 1788 manifests persistent and purposeful burning. The spread of scrub since is among Australia's most visible but least recognised landscape changes.[146]

Fire could signal. In open country it could alert watchers 100 miles away.[147] People lit fires to announce something of interest or to declare their lawful intrusion. Sometimes they burnt large areas, but ideally they lit small, carefully placed patches.[148] A line of smokes showed their direction and so their destination, purpose and identity. Less or more precise fires and light or dark smoke sent different messages. Smoke was like a party phone: everyone knew what the neighbours were doing. Barrallier wrote in 1802, 'I perceived fires in several places, and Bungin told me that it was a chief called Canambaigle with his tribe, who were hunting, and had on that very day set the country on fire', and a month later, 'I saw the country a mass of flames towards the north-east, at about 5 miles from us, near the mountains. Gogy told me it was Goondel, who with his party was hunting bandicoots, lizards, snakes, kangaroo rats etc.'[149] In the 1940s three desert men

> held urgent conferences and pointed excitedly to the smokes . . . 'That one—might belong to half-caste feller—maybe—go out with one camella to get puppy-dawg scalp. 'Nother one—thataway.' He pointed directly south. 'Maybe Ernabella men go back across desert, and walkabout little while in rocky country, spear kangaroo-euro.' He then indicated a line of smokes extending for several miles. 'Maybe someone come up tonight from Petermann country—maybe we see 'em.'[150]

Fire killed insects. In 1802 Peron thought it worth remark if he met insects in number, and several times went into forests at Parramatta into which the English had not yet gone with either implement or fire, and we observed that the insects are much less common there than in the areas already cleared by Europeans. This odd situation seemed to us to arise from the natives' practice of setting fire to the forests, thereby destroying a vast number of insect eggs and larvae and even fully developed insects.[151]

In Jervis Bay (NSW) Dumont D'Urville concluded, 'the plants and insects hardly came up to the expectations raised by the first sight of these beautiful places. I would say that the scarcity of both must be due in great part to the frequent burning off carried out by the natives.'[152] At Albany (WA) Quoy noted regretfully, 'Either the season was not sufficiently advanced for insects, or this place contains very few; we added almost none to our collections.'[153] 'The annual burnings by the natives for their hunting purposes have destroyed not merely the impeding brushwood, but also every kind of annoying insects and injurious reptiles,' Menge observed near Adelaide.[154] 'Reptiles and insects . . . are scarce, on account of the continual fires the natives use in their perpetual hunt for food,' Giles stated in the west MacDonnells.[155] Curr noted that few locusts, caterpillars, ants and moths meant a 'comparative scarcity of insectivorous birds and birds of prey'.[156]

Even flies were restricted. In 1827 Peter Cunningham discussed ants, fleas, ticks, mosquitoes, caterpillars and blowflies, but not bush flies.[157] Until 1788 the only suitable fly-breeding dung came from emus, marsupials, dingos, possibly wombats, and people who usually buried it. Travellers went weeks without mentioning flies, then for a day or two bewailed their ceaseless harassment, then again fell silent about them. On the Bogan (NSW) in January 1829 Sturt complained,

> Our camp was infested by the kangaroo fly, which settled upon us in thousands. They appeared to rise from the ground, and as fast as they were swept off were succeeded by fresh numbers. It was utterly impossible to avoid their persecution, penetrating as they did into the very tents. The men were obliged to put handkerchiefs over their faces, and stockings upon their hands; but they bit through every thing . . . the animals were driven almost to madness, and galloped to and fro in so furious a manner that I feared some of them would have been lost. I never experienced such a day of torment; and only when the sun set did these little creatures cease from their attacks.

At first light the party fled, and Sturt wrote, 'I did not expect that we should have got rid of them so completely as we did. None of them were seen during the day; a proof that they were entirely local.'[158] He wrote similarly at Depot Glen in January 1845.[159] Mosquitoes too were penned, 'clear interior country being quite destitute of such annoyances... They have always been common at Parramatta, but never made their appearance in Sydney till within these last three years.'[160]

How restricted insects were in 1788 is conveyed by their increase since. Around Sydney caterpillar plagues began about 1810, and for decades 'millions and millions' devastated crops and pastures and were swept in heaps from houses.[161] In Gippsland they ate out pastures in 48 hours,[162] as did locusts. In '[WA] districts where the vegetation has not been burned for some years, [locusts] increase so much, as to threaten serious mischief to the pastures'.[163] Near Adelaide after 1836 locusts advanced as fire retreated. They

> were first observed close to the town, and for two years were confined to some two or three miles around Adelaide; but now they have extended their march, and bid fair to ravage the whole country... annual burnings... had the effect of destroying countless multitudes of insects that now are allowed to live and increase. The grass is eaten at present as soon as it appears, and during the hot weather is much too scarce to enable the fire to make a continuous line, without which very many insects must escape the flame.[164]

Forest insects became equally devastating. Most eucalypts use fire to cycle nutrients and toxins. Without fire this defence is weakened, exposing the tree to disease, insects and predators like possums and koalas. In Tasmania Ronald Gunn wrote,

> I have never been able to trace the cause of this universal death of old and young trees in whole tracts of land, and many individuals over here remember when these trees in some of these spots were flourishing. I can only account for it by supposing it the ravages of an insect that marches through a tract of land destroying all the Eucalpti [sic] but find the Banksia & Acacia too little to their Taste. These dead forests are not peculiar to any one District in the Colony, neither do they always occur on the same soil.[165]

West Australian leafminers did not begin to attack Jarrah until 50 years after Europeans arrived,[166] and in Victoria Neil Black, Edward Curr, Alfred Howitt (ch 11) and others blamed the death of whole forests on leaf insect plagues which began after 1788. The fires that once curbed them were precise, not scorching canopies but roasting the ground, and favouring birds which eat leaf insects over birds which don't.[167]

Fire to regulate fuel, make mosaics, control animals and insects, and clean country gave the land a certain look. Not only Europeans admired Australia's parks. Correct burning was deeply satisfying, announcing managers who respected the land and the Dreaming. 'Smoke from country that is burning tells the observer that everything is good. The people on that land are well and doing what is required of them. Country that is not burning, especially where it is known that people are present, is not good. It means that something may be wrong and people should go and visit.'[168] Dirty country was a reproach. On west Cape York the 'commonest response of those returning to country in which they had formerly lived was that it had "gone wild" . . . the scrubs are thicker, the grass is long and unburnt, the footroads have closed up, the open ridge tops have grown over'.[169] In the Kimberley,

> The old woman leading the group was quite distressed by the country not being 'looked after', and clearly felt hemmed in. This was 'dirty country'. The obstacles it put before her are exactly the reasons other people maintain they burn: fear of snakes (children were exhorted to stay in the vehicle); the vehicle might end up in a hole; you can't see where the goannas and other tucker are and you can't get access to special places.[170]

Even at the wrong time, country needing fire must be burnt. 'You gotta burn', an elder declared, 'you don't burn then country will get poor, it will shut itself up . . . no good for anybody then.'[171] A bad fire was better than no fire, for no fire let fuel build up, making a bad fire worse.[172]

Good things came from fire. It made the land comfortable, comforting, bountiful and beautiful. Yibarbuk declared, 'The secret of fire in our traditional knowledge is that it is a thing that brings the land alive again. When we do burning the whole land comes alive again—it is reborn.'[173] Ida Ninganga recalled, 'Oh, all of the islands, they would once be burning, from north, south and east and west, they would be burning, the smoke would be rising upwards for days, oh it was good . . . you knew where all the families were, it was really good, in the times when the old people were alive.' Dinah Marrngawi agreed: 'Look! All of you, look to the distance, look north, look east, look west, the islands are burning, this is how it should be, this is how it was when the old people were alive, look this country is burning it has been lifted up, we have embraced it again.'[174]

Words embraced fire. Darling people used the same word for 'flame', 'open country', and 'flame, whereby open country is made'.[175] Yanyuwa say *ngarrki* 'badly burnt country', *warrman* 'well burnt country, good to hunt on', and *rumalumarrinjarra* 'lighting small fires in a row, to burn a beach front or a large plain'.[176] West Arnhem Landers say *anbirlu yahwurd* for 'low, creeping fires', *arri wurlhge* 'cleaning the country', *wurga* 'burnt ground' and *angolde* 'green pick'.[177] Martu speak of *nyurnma* 'freshly burnt area', *waru-waru* 'green shoot stage', *mukura* 'mid stage', *mangul* 'mature spinifex' and *kunarka* 'old spinifex, dying in the centre. Burn in winter with the right wind, and use it to hunt or track on the burnt ground'.[178] Walpiri say *wajirrki* 'vegetation which grows following rain' and *yukuri* 'green vegetation, new growth; time of the year immediately following rains'.[179] Perth people said *boykt* 'ground clothed with vegetation which has not yet been burned', *narrik* 'unburned ground, but ready for burning. Land of which the vegetation is abundant and dry, fit to be set on fire', *yanbart* 'ground where vegetation has been burnt', *nappal* 'burned ground; ground over which fire has passed . . . free from all scrub and grass', and *kundyl* 'young grass springing up after the country has been burned . . . the seed of any plant'.[180] None of these words have an English equivalent, none describe random fire. All reflect ingrained familiarity with fire–plant cycles. Near Perth *kalla* meant 'fire; a fire; (figuratively) an individual's district; a property in land'.[181] *Kalla* took fire into the intimate centre of how people lived, blending heart and soul with country.[182]

Five features marked 1788 fire. It was planned; it was precise; it could be repeated hence predicted; it was organised locally; and it was universal—like songlines it united Australia. People accepted its price. They must be mobile, constantly attendant, and have few fixed assets. In return they could ration its feed, unleash but never free it, and move it about, sustaining more diversity than any natural fire regime could conceivably maintain. It was scalpel more than sword, taming the most fire-prone country on earth to welcome its periodic refreshing, its kiss of life. Far from today's safe and unsafe fires, campfire and bushfire were one; far from a feared enemy, fire was the closest ally.

A few observers glimpsed this. In 'many important particulars', Curr realised, Aborigines were responsible for the state of Australia's flora, fauna, soil and water in 1788:

> there was another instrument in the hands of these savages which must be credited with results which it would be difficult to over-estimate. I refer to the *fire-stick*; for the blackfellow was constantly setting fire to the grass and trees . . . he tilled his land and cultivated his pastures with fire,[183]

and Mitchell concluded,

> Fire, grass, kangaroos, and human inhabitants all seem dependent on each other for existence in Australia; for any one of these being wanting, the others could no longer continue . . . But for this simple process, the Australian woods had probably contained as thick a jungle as those of New Zealand or America, instead of . . . open forests.[184]

These were sympathetic men, yet neither touched the shattering loss the people of 1788 felt at the land's subsequent mismanagement and destruction, for their alliance with fire was a means, not an end, and only the beginning of their achievement.

7

Associations

Watching the shores of King George Sound (WA) burn in October 1791, George Vancouver mused, 'Fire is frequently resorted to by rude nations, either for the purpose of encouraging a sweeter growth of herbage in their hunting grounds, or as tools for taking the wild animals, of which they are in pursuit.'[1] He may have been first in Australia to make this thoughtful remark. Perhaps he was also thinking of people in America or Africa, whose pre-contact use of fire could be studied with benefit.[2] In Australia some newcomers knew that people burnt to hunt or to lure, and in the 1960s researchers revived this understanding (Introduction). As Vancouver saw, these fires were alternatives, a different purpose fuelling a different nature and effect. Plants were burnt selectively.

Grass was the most closely managed community. It grows best in the open. Some land is naturally treeless (ch 1), so you might expect people to prefer this for grass. They did the opposite. Grass was a crop, deliberately grown on soil 'of the richest description',[3] 'a rich black mould', a mix of ash and compost now mostly gone. Even resilient perennials were put there. Where no soil was rich, the best available still carried grass. Arthur Phillip walked west from Sydney 'over a vast Extent of fine Meadow Ground, where, the Trees were at a greater Distance from each other, than they are in the Country round about the Settlement. The Soil, they found was far superior.'[4] Northeast of Emerald (Qld) Henry Turnbull

> passed through a most splendid, open country, consisting of plains and downs—plains stretching as far as the eye could reach on one side, and beautiful grassy slopes running down from a long and high range of mountains on the other. With only a tree to be seen every 500 or 600 yards, the whole face of the country was covered with the finest grasses and richest herbage, with wildflowers of every tint

and colour... Kangaroos would bound by us in scores at a time, and frequently ten or a dozen emus would march up to within 30 yards.[5]

Settlers sought grass above all. Moored to an export economy, they saw Australia as pasture. Botany Bay's 'meadows' helped Britain select it to settle, expeditions were told to report good grass, and from 1788 travellers wrote pages about it. They did not find gold for another 63 years. 'The country itself is superb', Thomas Walker wrote of the Campaspe (Vic) in 1837, 'the soil very rich, and well clothed with grass, with very few trees... a great portion, is totally devoid of trees... We were indeed enchanted with this country, and well we might, for no art could improve it, either for use or ornament.'[6] Evans was moderately impressed in the Blue Mountains. It had 'a fine appearance, the Trees being thin and the hills covered... with pasture to their tops; This Range is rather overrun with underwood and larger Timber growing thereon, but the sides are as green as possible'. Then near Bathurst he enthused over real plains 'pasture':

> came on a fine Plain of rich Land, the handsomest Country I ever saw... worth speaking of as good and beautiful; the Track of clear land occupies about a Mile on each side of the River... the Timber around is thinly scattered, I do not suppose there are more than ten Gum Trees on an Acre... At 3 o'clock I stopped at the commencement of a Plain still more pleasing... the soil is exceeding rich and produces the finest grass intermixed with a variety of herbs; the hills have the look of a park and Grounds laid out... there is Game in abundance; if we want a Fish it is caught immediately,

and three days later,

> The Grass here might be mowed it is so thick and long, particularly on the flat lands... the whole excellent good land, and the best Grass I have seen in any part of New South Wales; the hills are also covered with fine pasture, the Trees being so far apart must be an acquisition to its Growth; it is in general the sweetest in an open Country.[7]

John Howe cast a pastoral eye on the Hunter above Jerry's Plains (NSW),

> a country thinly timbered, and for the last hour many acres without
> a tree on it. One spot, I think, exceeds 50 acres with not 20 trees
> on it, and very fine ground . . . It is the finest sheep land I have
> seen since I left England . . . Caught a few perch. A great number
> in the river. The land on both sides very fine, and a great part of
> it may be cultivated without felling a tree. Even the high land
> is well clothed with grass and lightly timbered, though mostly
> thicker than the low ground. The grass on the low ground equals
> a meadow in England, and will throw as good a swathe.[8]

East of Boort (Vic) Mitchell too saw profit in pasture:

> crossed a low ridge of forest land . . . entered a fine valley, backed on
> the west by romantic, forest hills, and watered by some purling brooks,
> which united in the woods to the east. The flat itself had a few stately
> trees upon it, and seemed quite ready to receive the plough; while some
> round hillocks, on the north, were so smooth and grassy, that the men
> said they looked, as if they had already been depastured by sheep.[9]

At the other extreme, dense forest or brush comprised big, close trees over undergrowth and debris, often locked up by vines. In 1842 Hodgkinson, generally cheerful, found Bellingen (NSW) rainforest 'toilsome . . . in addition to forcing our way through entangled briars and creepers, we were incessantly compelled to clamber over huge fallen trees, and other obstructions'.[10] Dense scrub might be coastal heath or tea-tree, inland acacia, alpine shrubland or young rainforest, all hard walking for people and too thick for horses. In southwest Australia, Grey met cool-burnt scrub under thick eucalypt forest kept from destructive fire for a very long time:

> On this table land there was little or no herbage; the lower vegetation
> consisted principally of a short prickly scrub, in some places completely
> destroyed by native fires; but the whole country was thickly clothed
> with mahogany trees, so that, in many parts, it might be called a
> dense forest. These mahogany trees ascended, without a bend or
> without throwing off a branch, to the height of from forty to fifty
> feet, occasionally much more, and the ground was so encumbered by
> the fallen trunks of these forest trees, that it was sometimes difficult

> to pick a passage between them... I have never, in any part of the world, seen so great a want of animal life as in these mountains.[11]

Dense timber apart, tree distribution had two striking features. First, often trees were few, scattered, and without undergrowth (ch 1). Second, while some like mangroves chose their own ground, remarkably often forests were on poor or stony soil, like ridges and steep slopes. Grass on good soil and trees on poor was almost invariable (ch 1). Oxley commented, 'It is a matter for regret, that in proportion as the land improves the timber degenerates.'[12] Atkinson stated,

> With the exception of alluvial land, good timber is very seldom found upon good land. The fertile plains in the interior are wholly destitute of it... [around Sydney] the best forest lands are invariably thinnest of trees; and in general it will be found that the best lands are least encumbered with timber.[13]

Gunn saw how grass west of Deloraine (Tas) kept to valley soils, or more oddly how trees kept off them:

> Here the Country breaks into long plains one and two miles long containing from 500 to 1500 acres each—these plains are in general almost clear of timber, with an average of not one tree per acre... The intermediate Hills... are in general very poor & stoney, yielding comparatively little grass, and very thickly timbered with fine large Eucalpti [sic] growing to an astonishing height, frequently 100 feet clear in the Stem before they begin to branch out. I have found some from 30 to 40 feet in circumference.[14]

On the Goulburn (NSW),

> rich grazing tracts meet the eye, consisting of clear open levels or small plains, and grassy hills of the most easy acclivity... bounded by ridges of forest land, thickly clothed with timber. The level tracts, immediately bounded by the river, occasionally break into small plains, whose areas comprise from 100 to 150 acres, clear of tree or shrub.[15]

Liverpool Plains (NSW) were

all fine rich grassy soil without a tree, excepting where a small woody hill
occasionally rises from the bosom of the plain to vary and beautify the
prospect . . . the country appears to be spread out like a green ocean, of
unbounded extent, with clusters of woody islands bespangling its surface.[16]

South of the Lachlan, Oxley noticed something 'singular' in how dense mallee was distributed: 'those scrubs and brushes seldom if ever extend to the immediate base of the hills: the washings from them rendered the soil somewhat better for two or three hundred yards' yet it bore grass.[17] In the Centre better watered hill run-offs carried most grass and fewest trees,[18] and on the Barcoo (Qld) Gidgee ridges were 'thickly wooded', but on 'the flats, where the old grass had been burned, good grass had grown up'.[19]

Trees can grow densely in these places now. Why not then? Charles Darwin implied an answer:

> The woodland is so open that a person on horseback can gallop through
> it. It is traversed by a few flat-bottomed valleys, which are green and
> free from trees: in such spots the scenery was pretty like that of a park.
> In the whole country I scarcely saw a place without the marks of a fire;
> whether these had been more or less recent—whether the stumps were
> more or less black, was the greatest change which varied the uniformity.[20]

West of Bathurst (NSW) Allan Cunningham crossed 'a fine, rich, grassy tract of country, which, however, has at this period rather a bare and naked aspect, having been fired by the natives . . . The soil throughout this day's journey is good and rich . . . and abounds with emu and kangaroo', and approaching the Macquarie, 'having passed the grassy forest land near the creek', he

> arrived at the margin of an open plain . . . Stretching over the plain about a
> mile we passed through a very sterile scrubby district, somewhat elevated,
> thickly wooded . . . This brush continues for . . . 12 miles, and we pitched our
> tent near some holes of water, where there was burnt grass for the horses.[21]

North of Camperdown (Vic) George Russell discovered a

> great extent of deep rich soil, many hundreds of acres being almost
> without a tree . . . covered with a rich sward of kangaroo-grass. The

> country around had all been burnt by bush-fires during the previous summer, and the grass that was now growing on the ground was as green and luxuriant as if it had been a field of grain. The kangaroos here were very numerous . . . They came down from the wooded hills near Mount Leura in the afternoons to feed on the green grass . . . It was a striking sight to see them bounding along in hundreds.[22]

In central Tasmania Robinson found that the Brady's Sugarloaf district was 'frequently burnt by the natives and is fine hunting ground for them . . . open plains of good land free from timber bounded by grassy hills. It is a delightful country . . . arrived at a plain which the natives had set on fire and the trees round the plain was still burning',[23] and Hellyer found climax rainforest country

> grassy . . . The timber found on these hills is in general of fine growth, very tall and straight; some of it would measure more than 100 feet to the lowest branch. The trees are, in many places, 100 yards apart. They . . . will not in general average ten trees to an acre. There are many square miles without a single tree.[24]

To describe open country he used agricultural language: it had 'a cultivated & diversified appearance from its having been lately burnt in several extensive tracts, looking fresh & green in those places, & in others so completely covered with fields of blooming heath, that it resembled vast fields of clover divided by shrubs'. In a brilliant insight, he suspected their purpose: 'It is possible that the natives by burning only one set of plains are enabled to keep the kangaroos more concentrated for their use, and I can in no way account for their burning only in this place, unless it is to serve them as a hunting place.'[25] In 1788 people judged that grass needed rich soil more than trees, and moved forest to suit. Being able to do that made almost any plant distribution possible.[26]

People moved plant communities to associate their resources. Much grass and few trees was a valuable and extensive association. Batman found Bellarine Peninsula (Vic)

> excellent, and very rich—and light black soil, covered with kangaroo grass two feet high, and as thick as it could stand . . . The trees not more than six to the acre, and those small sheoak and wattle . . . Most of the high hills were covered with grass to the summit, and not a tree, although the land was as good as can be. The whole appeared

like land laid out in farms for some hundred years back, and every
tree transplanted. I was never so astonished in my life.[27]

A tourist in Victoria noted,

> Everywhere but on these fertile spots the trees straggle away from each
> other, or form themselves into picturesque clumps: sometimes leaving
> wide plains untenanted by a solitary shrub, at other times capriciously
> dotting the expanse, as if planted by the hand of art. Rarely do they
> stand so close as to prevent a free passage between their trunks; so that
> you may gallop for miles under their shade, over hill and dale, without
> meeting any other obstacle than that caused by fallen timber. In truth,
> as has often been remarked, an English park, with its lawn and scattered
> trees, gives a better idea of the prevailing scenery than anything else.[28]

Persuading fire to do that took finesse and persistence.

Grass and woodland often alternated along water. This can occur naturally, when streams bend into forest on one bank and leave grass on the other, as perhaps east of Darwin, where the Adelaide was flanked by 'rich grassy plains, but each alternate reach wooded on the opposite side'.[29] In 1788 it also occurred unnaturally, where no bends were. Upper Lachlan plains ran 'alternately on each [bank], and nearly the same size; opposite to the Plains are Woodlands'.[30] On the Macquarie 'park-like' country was 'alternately plain and brush, the soil on both of which was good'.[31] Upper Hunter plains were on

> alternate sides, the whole distance, varying in breadth from one
> half to two miles. Some parts are without timber, and others
> have no more than enhances, rather than detracts from, their
> value, with an inexhaustible soil, and a natural herbage, but
> little inferior to the most improved English meadows.[32]

On good water both banks might be grass (pictures 33–4). In Queensland in 1829, Lockyer Creek's banks were 'a succession of grassy meadows, singularly level and occasionally so thinly and lightly wooded, as scarcely to furnish two or three trees in the area of an acre; indeed in some parts, patches of plain broke upon us, without a tree or a shrub for half a mile'.[33] In the 1840s Murrumbidgee flats were 'impossible . . . to be finer... extensive rich grassed meadows, with a few clumps of trees... a succession of ornamental parks that would vie with the finest forest-lands in the world'.[34] In the mallee east of Angaston (SA) Sturt met a 'dark and gloomy sea of scrub... but it may be said, that there is an open space varying in breadth from half-a-mile to three miles between the Murray belt and the river'.[35] In Ayers Range (NT) Giles 'came to a number of native huts... of large dimensions and two storied' in scrub by a creek:

> On each bank of the creek was a strip of green and open ground, so richly grassed and so beautifully bedecked with flowers that it seemed like suddenly escaping from purgatory into paradise when emerging from the recesses of the scrubs on to the banks of this beautiful, I might wish to call it, stream... Natives had been here very recently, and the scrubs were burning, not far off to the northwards, in the neighbourhood of the creek channel.[36] [37]

Off water too, one forest type might give way within metres to another, or to grass. 'It is a singular character of this remarkable country', Leichhardt observed, 'that extremes so often meet; the most miserable scrub, with the open plain and fine forest land; and the most paralysing dryness, with the finest supply of water'.[38] In Queensland Karl Domin found 'Most interesting... the contrast between the open forests and vine scrubs... *The line of demarcation between them is most distinct*, a phenomenon which is unique in the whole world.' He saw similar edges in Lancewood scrub between Jericho and Alpha 'with a most decided line of demarcation'. Very different forests had parallel sharp-edged associations. He decided that 'the open forests in all parts of Queensland are not a natural association, but a *secondary* one, changed through the influence of their aboriginal inhabitants, mostly by means of bushfires'.[39] Sturt nominated three inland landscapes:

> first, plains of considerable extent wholly destitute of timber; secondly, open undulating woodlands; and, thirdly, barren unprofitable tracts. The first almost invariably occur in the immediate neighbourhood of some river... The open forests, through which a horseman may gallop in perfect safety, seem to prevail over the whole secondary ranges of granite, and are generally considered as excellent grazing tracts... The barren tracts... may be said to occupy the central spaces between all the principal streams.[40]

While generally true of the first two in 1788, though not now, this was only partly true of the third. Explorers found both grass and dense timber off rivers. Hume and Hovell met frequent vegetation changes in northern Victoria. Hills north of the Ovens had 'brushwood', no trees on their north sides, and thick timber on top. North of the Goulburn was 4–5 miles of 'burnt grass... On one side of the creek is a sort of meadow, but the... soil, being good, produces an abundance of fine grass and the whole, both hills and lowlands, are thinly covered with timber.' On King Parrot Creek, after three days' solid scrub-bashing, sometimes having to walk hundreds of yards on logs, Hovell wrote in exasperation:

> To describe this brush or scrub is almost impossible, as it cannot be compared with any that is known in the Colony. Suffice to say that it is worse than any that is known in it, or worse than any jungle in any other country... we could not see either over or under, nor two yards before.

They battled on to 'a small plain... The farther we get from the mountains the more open we find the country, till at last we find the hills almost destitute of trees and the lowlands but thinly covered also.'[41] Hovell's lowlands are now farms, but where untended his high country is unbroken forest. He and Hume crossed a patterned landscape.

In very different country, 'dense' Mulga near Newcastle Waters (NT), Stuart met similar patterns. From grass on a cracking clay plain, he crossed a soil boundary into 'wooded country... in some places very thick, but in most open... At the end of eighteen miles I again got into the grass country.' Next day he met 'a dense forest of tall mulga, with an immense quantity of dead wood' very difficult to move through. It became more open, then so thick that he turned back to a plain where fire had 'burned every blade of grass, and scorched all the trees to their very tops'. In 2001 Peter Sutton found very dense scrub where Stuart mapped 'open' country in 1862.[42] Southwest of Bourke (NSW) in 1875, George Fortey reported:

> The country being fine and open up to this and about two miles further on when I got into pretty thick scrub for about Four miles it then opened into Plains interspersed with Giddia which appeared to be the general character of the country as far as the eye could reach... I passed into some Mulga Scrub for about three miles and then into [a] very soft plain with a little Scrub and which had evidently been

cleared by fire, so I could judge by the dead Timber lying about which extended for about 4 miles then into scrub for about 3 miles.[43]

Europeans tend to quarantine 'good' country from 'bad', condemning dense forests, scrub and heath. Yet these split up grass and open forest, and had Dreamings and value. Heath was home to berries, tubers, animals and birds.[44] In northeast Tasmania Robinson came on country 'sterile and consists of heathy hills and undulating and open forest. Opossums were in abundance . . . The whole of this country is much resorted to by natives. Forest kangaroo were to be seen all the journey.'[45] Eyre pointed out:

> the very regions, which, in the eyes of the European, are most barren and worthless, are to the native the most valuable and productive. Such are dense brushes, or sandy tracts of country, covered with shrubs, for here the wallabie, the opossum, the kangaroo rat, the bandicoot, the leipoa [mallee fowl], snakes, lizards, iguanas, and many other animals, reptiles, birds, &c., abound; whilst the kangaroo, the emu, and the native dog, are found upon their borders, or in the vicinity of those small, grassy plains, which are occasionally met with amidst the closest brushes.[46]

Rainforest carried scrub wallabies, cuscus, flying foxes, gliders, brush turkeys and their eggs, pythons and their eggs, black bean, cunjevoi, yam, fig and fern root—a food and medicine bonanza.[47] It too was split up. On the Hastings (NSW) Oxley saw it alternating with 'open forest with good grass, casuarina or beefwood, and large timber', and next day remarked, 'the brush land is of the richest description . . . the forest ridges between the brushes were well clothed with grass'.[48] In the Nambucca (NSW) back country Hodgkinson had to cut through miles of thick brush, but on emerging 'crossed alternately low forest ranges clothed with thick succulent herbage and brushy hollows containing limpid pebbly creeks, until we began ascending a long narrow brushy slope which led us to the summit of a high range' timbered with 'gigantic' Blackbutt, forest oak and 'rich grass'. Many mountains were 'covered with one universal brush similar to that on alluvial land', but next day he climbed a ridge through brush and gigantic ferns and palms to a razor-back crest where 'grass was of the greatest luxuriance'. For weeks he passed through country 'either very lightly wooded and grassy, or else covered over with brush timber and entangled vegetation. Most of the park-like hills rose in round conical summits.'[49] Using early portion plans, WK Birrell found the same associations in the Manning Valley, and concluded, 'It is likely that this was a disturbed forest community brought about as a result of the repeated firing of the original vegetation cover, over many centuries, by Aborigines hunting small animals.'[50] East of Circular Head (Tas) in 1829, the 'first eight miles of the coast ran through a thick forest, after which comes a succession of small plains, which lie in the midst of the forest... From the last of these plains... the road passes through four miles more of forest.'[51] Northwest of Innisfail (Qld) Palmerston saw 'alternate scrubby and open spurs steeply narrow down and connect with alternate scrubby and grassy plots below, and near the river's border',[52] and in southeast Queensland Allan Cunningham reached an 'extensive patch of plain... flanked on its west and north-western sides by densely brushed rocky ridges... abundantly watered by a chain of ponds... The soil... exceedingly rich... the rocky barrier to the westward... clothed with so thick a jungle of twining plants.'[53]

Two expeditions showed the value of dense eucalypt forest. In 1792 John Wilson, a First Fleet emancipist, quit Sydney and became a tribal man. In May 1797 he was proclaimed an outlaw, but in November returned, and in January 1798 led Governor Hunter's servant John Price, who kept a diary, and a man named Roe southwest. They reached the Wingecarribee–Wollondilly junction northwest of Berrima. In what is now mostly dense forest, they crossed 'fine open country, but very mountainous', grass meadows, thinly timbered plains, and scrub and vine brushes, including Bargo Brush, soon notorious for poor soil, stringybark, and tangles of scrub and fallen timber. In one memorable week, Price noted the first koala, the first lyrebird, the first gang-gang cockatoo and the first mainland wombat recorded by a European. The gang-gang was new to Wilson, but he knew the wombat and the koala, giving their Aboriginal names, *wombat* and *cullawine*, from which no doubt 'koala' derives (pronounce it). He knew the lyrebird but called it a pheasant, which perhaps is why today it has no familiar Aboriginal name. It is telling that no-one in a settlement thirsty to discover new fauna had reported these animals. Their country was wilderness, bad, formidable, seeming untouched. Wilson knew them because Aborigines valued them, and made or left habitats for their benefit.

In March 1798 Wilson led another party to Mt Towrang east of Goulburn, well past those Blue Mountains so famously crossed in 1813. He found 'a most beautifull country, being nothing but fine large meadows with ponds of water in them; fine green hills, but very thin of timber'. They are very thick of timber now. The party also met 'barren' scrub. Wilson's unknown diarist saw that kangaroos and sometimes emu swarmed on grass and left 'no signs' in scrub, but not that those 'fine green hills' would be 'barren' too, without fire.⁵⁴ Both had value: as Robinson remarked in Tasmania, 'in mountainous country I live on badger, porcupine, rats, grubs and opossum; in clear country on kangaroo'.⁵⁵

Hamilton Hume knew that pastures were paddocks. He was native born, a better bushman than any migrant. In 1821 he explored the upper Shoalhaven with Nullanan from the Cowpastures and Udaaduck from Lake Bathurst. On 28 November they met people and stopped with them for the day to 'gain from them what information I could respecting the Country'. They assured Hume of an easy track east to the coast. He 'caught them several Kangaroos with which they were much pleased', and they told him where there were plenty. South, they said, you come to a scrubby hill called Coorook [Currockbilly] abounding in 'Roombat & Coolers'. Beyond was 'a very fine country with extensive plains': kangaroo country. They were describing dense forest alternating with grass, and what lived where.

Hume saw such country. He described 'extensive meadows of rich land thinly wooded; Kangaroos are here in great plenty', the Shoalhaven shallow with a pebbly bottom and 'well Stocked with Water Fowls as Ducks, Black Swans &c, on the Banks and adjacent thereto are numbers of What we call in this country Wild Turkey . . . several good meadows along this Stream'. He 'passed over some Bushy hills . . . came on good Forest Land Fine Grass . . . ascended a Forest Hill . . . crossed a pretty Rivulet' abounding in eels, wound through some 'fine meadows', 'entered a thick brush which continued for 3 miles . . . passed over some clear barren Hills'. He was just west of the Pigeon House, probably on the Sugarloaf—dense forest now, but he named it Mt Barren, stating 'This Hill commands a very extensive view of the Country in every direction particularly to the N.W. & N. as far as the eye can reach it is without Timber or Grass of any Kind, on account of its being so barren'. Most of the country from Lake Bathurst to the Pigeon House, he concluded, 'is well adapted for Grazing and in many parts for Cultivation . . . and quite easy of access'. This is not the thick forest of today's Shoalhaven back country, but Hume proved his accuracy by walking in one day from three miles south of the Pigeon House to 30 miles north of it through parts now almost impenetrable, and swimming a flooded river. He stopped 'in a thick Barren Brush quite destitute of Grass'.⁵⁶ As early as 1851 WB Clarke unwittingly reported Shoalhaven trees regenerating. From Oranmeir he described 'a series of "bald hills" . . . running southward on each side of the Shoalhaven . . . These "bald hills" [are] . . . clothed with a scrub of *Casuarina*, seldom more than two feet in height, and mostly not more than one.'⁵⁷ ⁵⁸

Edges

The richest associations were at edges, where 'three or more plant communities occur in close proximity'.[59] In southeast South Australia, Angas crossed at least two edges:

> The country for some distance was now a vile scrub, full of dangerous holes half hid by the brushwood . . . This scrub terminated as suddenly as it commenced, and we next entered upon an extensive and beautiful country, covered with luxuriant grass, and studded with . . . trees like a nobleman's park . . . Here was a country fresh from the hand of Nature and complete in its native loveliness, with green pastures, shady trees, and wells of pure and limpid water.[60]

Edges made good camps, and many plants and animals prefer them, finding there the right balance of sun, shade and nutrient. For animals which feed in the open but shelter in cover, an edge is a centre, so edges were made and varied to suit and locate each animal. Kangaroos, crows and magpies prefer grass–open forest edges; scrub wallabies and potoroos prefer to tunnel to grass through dense cover; forest wombats like slopes of rock, scrub and debris above grassy creeks; galahs prefer mature open forest with nest hollows and short seed-grass nearby. Variously shaping edges created other opportunities. Scrub turkeys and small animals use scrub wallaby tunnels, open forest suits possums, denser forest suits koalas and lyrebirds, echidnas like wombat or possum country. Prey is channelled, country is diversified.[61]

Belts

People increased the number and convenience of edges by making belts—grass lanes in timber or timber lanes in grass, width varying from a few metres to several kilometres (pictures 31–2, 43, 49–50). Northwest of Fowler's Bay,

> The scrub between Wanganyah and Eyre's Flat, though not of great extent, was most perplexing . . . on account of the numerous openings which tempted the travellers to enter, but which after a while were closed in by impenetrable masses of thicket, proving to be perfect culs de sac. Frequently the travellers entered these delusive avenues only to find themselves compelled at last to turn back and try another, which often proved as bad.[62]

'Scrub is one of the characteristic features of the Australian scene', Angas wrote, 'belts of it frequently intersect the good country, and many miles are covered with it.'[63] Most evident in flat or undulating country, but also occurring on slopes (pictures 13, 21), belts were habitats, wildlife corridors, sanctuaries and nurseries. Big plains reduced edges and let game see people; belts split plains up. East of Perth,

> several parallel veins or belts of land . . . extend for a considerable distance, nearly in a north and south direction. These veins are much superior in fertility to the adjacent lands, and composed of rich, dark vegetable mould. Being generally clear of trees, and covered with rich grass alone, they are locally called 'clear streaks'. No probable cause has yet been assigned for this appearance.[64]

North of Fowler's Bay Eyre battled for ten miles 'through a dense heavy scrub . . . [to] an open pretty looking country, consisting of grassy plains of great extent, divided by belts of shrubs and bush'.[65] Northwest of Mt Kintore (NT) Herbert Basedow saw how useful belts were:

> triodia [Spinifex], with belts of casuarina, kurrajong, few quandong, thick mallee, and patches of mulga. The triodia has recently been burnt by natives hunting . . . game that live under the tussocks. The leaves of the mallee are covered with lerp manna . . . The taste is sweet and honey-like. Rats are very plentiful in the mallee scrub; they build large dome shaped nests with twigs and leaves.[66]

A good belt site was a rise or low hill between plains, giving prey and predator the view they preferred. In South Australia John Bulmer described

> a tract of country which with very little variations in its features extends to the Great Bight . . . a succession of grassy downs, divided from each other by belts of timber growing upon either very sandy or very rocky soil but principally the former. These vary in extent from a few yards to that of the Wallanippie scrub with a breadth of about 60 miles . . . The ground on which the belts of scrub grow usually takes the form of ridges of no great elevation, these running in irregular directions surround the grassy flats in serpentine sweeps and divide them from each other.[67]

In Tasmania Macquarie entered

> Maclaine Plains and travel through them for 2 miles to a rising ground covered with wood, which separate them from the next plains... which are beautifully interspersed with trees... travelled for 7 miles across Macquarie Plains... very extensive and beautifully interspersed with trees and... in most places a good soil.[68]

Further west Hellyer thought the Surrey Hills 'resemble English enclosures in many respects, being bounded by brooks between each, with belts of beautiful shrubs in every vale... the Hampshire Hills... appear even more park like... and are handsomely clumped with trees'.[69]

In New South Wales the country from Bathurst to the head of the Hunter was 'clear pastoral downs and open forest land extending in stripes nearly all the way'.[70] West of Forbes were 'extensive plains divided by lines of small trees',[71] and off the lower Castlereagh 'rich and extensive plains, divided by plantations' of trees.[72] South of Manilla 'the whole territory bore a remarkable resemblance to an enclosed and cultivated country... Trees grew in rows, as if connected with field enclosures, and parts, where bushes or grass had been recently burnt, looked red or black, thus contributing to the appearance of cultivation.' On the Gwydir,

> open forest... growing gradually thinner, at length left intervals of open-plain... next through a narrow strip of casuarinae scrub... we crossed a beautiful plain; covered with shining verdure, and ornamented with trees, which, although 'dropt in nature's careless haste', gave the country the appearance of an extensive park,

while country near Lake Waljeers 'was wooded in long stripes of trees'.[73]

In Victoria 'forest land' near Natimuk 'opened into grassy and level plains, variegated with belts and clumps of lofty trees, giving to the whole the appearance of a park'.[74] Near Echuca Hawdon crossed 'a succession of plains, here and there intersected with a narrow belt of pine trees',[75] further northwest BL Beilby looked from a burnt mallee ridge over a grassy plain 'fringed with lofty pines and small grassed ridges, interspersed with narrow belts of mallay [mallee]', and near Lake Hindmarsh a 'black... gave me a clear account of all the belts of mallay to be passed through, and the wells to be found... westward and northwest'.[76] On the Loddon Eyre 'found a most beautiful country, open undulating forest and extensive and rich plains intersected with narrow belts of trees in every direction . . . The plains were full of native yams indicating the richness of its soil.'[77] South of Wallan Hovell crossed 'a very extensive plain, extending from west to S.E. for several miles with patches of forest which appear to separate one plain from another . . . all the soil of the best quality'.[78] Near Mt Alexander Robinson described a beautiful valley, 'undulating with grassy hills and open forest trees . . . A belt of forest bounds each side of the road . . . When leaving this forest belt, and opening out upon the plain, the change of scene was delightfully pleasant.'[79] North of Maffra McMillan 'travelled over a beautiful country, consisting of fine, open plains, intersected by occasional narrow belts of open forest',[80] and north of the La Trobe William Brodribb crossed 'beautiful plains of fine rich land . . . intersected with belts of forest, not thickly timbered, and we saw numerous emus from day to day, on the plains'.[81]

Beside Lake Clarendon in southeast Queensland, Allan Cunningham found

> a fine patch of plain . . . the soil . . . remarkably rich . . . Onward, the forest ground bounded the view for about a mile and a half, when we reached the margin of a second plain, about a mile in length, by half a mile in breadth . . . Passing this, and on penetrating the wooded lands, we immediately came to a third plain . . . of circular form and about a mile in diameter.[82]

On the Darling Downs Leichhardt met plains 'covered with the most luxuriant grass and herbage . . . Belts of open forest land . . . separate the different plains; and patches of scrub.' Further north a 'belt of scrub at the foot of the slopes runs out in narrow strips towards the river, and these are separated by box-tree thickets, and open box-tree flats', then 'fine plains . . . well grassed, separated from each other by belts of forest', later 'a succession of plains separated by belts of forest', and on the Staaten in the far north,

> After passing several miles of tea-tree forest, intermixed with box, and alternating with belts of grassy forest land, with bloodwood and Nonda, we entered upon a series of plains increasing in size, and extending to the westward as far as the eye could reach, and separated from each other by narrow strips of forest; they were well-grassed, but the grasses were stiff.[83]

Turnbull thought country east of Clermont 'as fine as any we had hitherto travelled over, only there were occasionally belts of thick scrub running through it and through which it was difficult to force our way. But in all these scrubs we invariably found plenty of water',[84] and near Blackall William Landsborough 'passed through several narrow belts of land, thickly wooded with westernwood acacia [Gidgee]. The country we saw between these belts was [rich and well-grassed].'[85] [86]

Clumps

Clumps or copses of trees or scrub stood in grass, heath or open forest. They made edges, gave shade and shelter, and protected springs, nests, plants and special places. Near rocks or water they were easily maintained by cool burning, but they also occurred with no change of soil or elevation, where people backburnt to make and maintain them. This needed fire controlled in intensity, direction and extent, decade after decade.

Clumps were in every climate and terrain, but may have been a Tasmanian specialty. Bruny Islanders showed Robinson that they were deliberate:

> Traversed a vast extent of clear country interspersed with clumps or copses intended as a cover for the kangaroo, the whole range for miles forming a beautiful picturesque scenery. This has been done by the natives: when burning the underwood they have beat out the fire in order to form these clumps.[87]

About ten miles west of Mt William he crossed 'very picturesque, grassy plains interspersed with Copse . . . Kangaroo is very plentiful. Passed over a large tract of ground where the bush had been burnt by the natives', and west of Derby he

> came to a large plain of tolerable good feed; it was of great extent and abounded with kangaroo. I had seen no place like it on this side of the island, and the clumps of trees of various sorts gave it a delightful park-like appearance. I named it kangaroo park. This country had been well burnt off.[88]

East of Launceston Matthew Flinders saw coastal hills 'well covered with wood . . . There are also some grassy tracts of open ground, that are prettily varied by clumps of wood and large single trees.'[89] On plains below Frenchman's Cap were 'two emerald banks, the headlands, if I may so term them, of a land bay of transcendant loveliness, being magnificently studded, by the hand of nature, with small clumps of elegant trees and coppice, displayed in the most park-like style'.[90] In the midlands,

> The contrast is very striking when, after riding through the 'bush', the traveller comes unexpectedly upon a plain, sprinkled only here and there with small clusters of trees, and on crossing it again finds himself in an extensive forest . . . the transition is not at all gradual, as a person may ride many miles without meeting a single open spot, while on the plains it often occurs that scarcely a tree is visible,[91]

and a 'recently arrived emigrant' wrote,

> There are some extensive and very fertile plains, with scarcely a tree on them, in their natural state; generally, however, you find a thinly wooded country, adorned here and there with clumps of trees like a gentleman's park, seldom so close but you may ride at a canter with the utmost safety. In other districts the underwood is so dense as to be quite impenetrable.[92]

In Victoria Hume and Hovell crossed 'a beautiful plain' near Tallarook, 'Ornamented with clumps of that beautiful tree, the native Willow'.[93] Near Beaufort Robinson camped on a 'plain interspersed with clumps of honey suckle trees, gum and stringy bark. Saw plenty of quail. The grass was immensely thick and rich, good soil. It had the appearance of a park . . . A beautiful place.'[94] In New South Wales the Gwydir country 'was chiefly open, being beautifully variegated with clumps of picturesque trees',[95] and the lower Darling was flanked by 'flat after flat of the most vivid green, ornamented by clumps of trees, sufficiently apart to give a most picturesque finish to the landscape . . . the banks of the river, grassed to the water, had the appearance of having been made so by art'.[96]

Climbing a ridge to Cunningham's Gap (Qld), Allan Cunningham saw 'Patches of brush' on its slopes and in 'the gullies falling from it, leaving its back clear of wood, open and grassy'.[97] Leichhardt praised country as 'most beautiful, presenting detached Bricklow groves, with the Myal, and with the Vitex in full bloom, surrounded by lawns of the richest grass and herbage',[98] and in the Dawson Valley John Gilbert wrote,

> One of the most beautifully picturesque and extensive scenes met our anxious gaze. The immediate vicinity of the hills was like park scenery—clear undulating grassy hills, with here and there small clumps of Brigalo, while the sides of many of the hills were dotted with single scrubs, as if picked out by hand.[99]

North of Mt Bryan (SA), James Henderson camped by 'a small wood of [fire sensitive] pines in a grassy plain . . . The country had a very pretty appearance, studded with numerous clumps of pines and sheoaks.'[100] Northeast of Northam (WA) Robert Austin's eyes 'ranged over a broad expanse of undulating sand plains, studded with clumps of gum forest and thicket',[101] and Robert Sholl found on the McRae 'kangaroo grass up to the horses' bellies . . . on a small flat containing about 100 acres of this feed . . . our camp is fixed in a clump of young trees about 60 or 70 yards from the river's bank'. Across the river sandstone hills rose steeply, so the feed was rich but confined.[102] Stokes saw this on the Fitzroy: 'the country was open; the trees were small, and in clumps, with green grassy patches between; but in other directions it was densely wooded, and on the eastern bank the trees were large'.[103] On the Barnett Frank Hann wrote, 'Right opposite my camp was a magnificent clump of immense pine trees, and behind the pines a beautiful little plain—an ideal place for a homestead . . . Above us all the country was on fire.'[104] [105]

Clearings

Grass clearings (patches, pockets, corners, grasses or balds) lay in forest, scrub, heath or Spinifex (pictures 32, 38–50). When a clearing becomes a plain is a matter of opinion, but each varied habitats and multiplied edges. Many can still be 'seen', notably where eucalypts are recapturing grassland. Sometimes newcomers learnt a clearing's purpose. On Bellenden Ker (Qld),

> a small level zone was reached. These zones, Merrewah explained, were . . . used as camping grounds by the natives when making their flying hunting trips to these mountains, and were swept clean for spaces of ten to twenty feet. They were known as 'plarriah' and denoted by numbers. Each plarriah had certain tribal responsibilities and laws attached to it.[106]

East of Herberton (Qld) Palmerston found 'a pocket—that is a piece of open country about a quarter of an acre in size, circular-shaped, used by the aborigines for war dances and fighting. They take particular care to keep the place free from jungle, which would creep over it in a few seasons if allowed.'[107] Further south Dalrymple saw the 'whole of the open ground of this portion of the floor of the valley . . . dotted with old and recent "bora" [dance] grounds . . . the soil was beaten down hard and bare over a space of a quarter of an acre'.[108] On a creek off the Macquarie (NSW), Robert Mathews surveyed a dance ground, a 'dry level' patch 150 x 20 metres surrounded by open forest enclosing a 'thick scrub of belah, [False] sandalwood and other brush timber'. Alfred Howitt told Mathews of a similarly secluded ground in southeast Victoria.[109]

South of Tasmania's Great Lake, Wedge found 'Rocky rises, with patches of good land free from timber varying in size from 10 to 100 acres, and a long Valley . . . free from Timber', and in the Ouse forest 'many spots of land free from timber and of considerable extent . . . to the Southward—I found an open space on the top of the Hill which continued for about two Miles to the edge of the tier; from this I beheld an extensive Valley . . . there appeared to be open spaces in it'.[110] Curr remarked of twelve 'patches of grass' in dense eucalypt-topped rainforest inland from Burnie,

> These plains are of varying sizes six of them I saw wh I judged to be of the following dimensions viz 5, 30, 80, 120, 120, and 600 although Mr Hellyer estimates this last wh he measured at 1000 ac[res]. They are all of one character, sound, light and dry soil . . . well watered with springs and Creeks, and surrounded by the best timber; the grass coarse but plentiful.[111]

In 1829 Robinson was on Bruny Island, not yet imagining such a thing as 1788 land management. He walked 'through an extensive swamp covered with lofty shrubs. Passages about two feet wide are formed in a serpentine direction and at short distances are open clear spaces, supposed to have been burnt out by the natives so that they might be better able to pursue the kangaroo with the dogs.' In central Tasmania in 1834, more knowing, he described

> low hills and open forest and small grassy plains of from ten, fifteen, twenty and thirty acres each. Passed through a forest overgrown with underwood, the indigo was very thick. All this country had been burnt and the fallen timber was very thick. After travelling a few miles came to . . . wombat [edge] country . . . The natives had been here recently and burnt the grass.[112]

In 1838 John McArthur similarly recounted walking from burnt ground

> through a thick scrub which the fire had not destroyed, I suddenly emerged from this, and found myself unexpectedly in a beautiful meadow, to all appearances very extensive . . . a line of trees running through the middle . . . passed the remainder of the flat when I entered thickly wooded land.[113]

He might have been in Tasmania; he was at Port Essington in Arnhem Land.

In central west New South Wales, Oxley halted 'on a small patch of burnt grass... our view was confined to the scrubby brush around us'.[114] Similar clearings pocked Blue Mountains forest. Above Grose Valley in 1804 was 'a small piece of ground, which was destitute of trees, and no herbaceous brush', north of Katoomba in 1813 'about two thousand acres of land Clear of trees', and further west 'spaces of Ground of 3 or 400 Acres with grass growing within them that you can scarce walk through'.[115] On the Macleay, 'All the distance of twenty miles from the mouth of the river, and from thence to the point where the river ceases to be navigable, the brush land is interspersed with small alluvial plains, clear of trees, and varying in extent from fifty to a hundred acres. These clear patches of ground possess all the exuberant fertility of the brush land', and were no lower.[116] On the Illawarra coast, 'Lofty cedars, graceful tree ferns, and stately palms, raise their heads over a thick undergrowth of wild vines, creeping plants, and shrubs... Grassy meadows are interspersed throughout, destitute of timber, and enclosed with a border of palms.'[117] On the range behind Wollongong

> was a small grassy forest on the hill side; and everywhere around it... was thick tangled brush growing amidst lofty trees, so thick set that beneath them was perpetual shadow... a little patch of grassy forest would assert a place for itself on the shoulder of a hill, and partly down the side; but generally the entire surface of this mountain, for many miles up and down the coast every way, was clothed with this thick brush.[118]

A grassy slope in dense forest was ideal for food vines and brush wallabies (pictures 38–41, 44–5).

In June 1822, though later he claimed it was earlier, Berry sailed south from Sydney seeking land. At the Shoalhaven he met Wagin, who courteously told him of 'a piece of clear meadow ground... I asked him who cleared it. He replied that all he knew about it was—that it was in the same state in the days of his grandfather.' It was one of several clearings in rainforest fringing the river. Berry put his head-station on one nearby, naming it Coolangatta after the name Wagin gave him of a dominant mountain, a 'well grassed eminence' now forest. Later he gave a ship the name, and when it was wrecked on a Gold Coast beach, the beach took the name north.[119]

In western Victoria 'a long extent of indifferently heathy country, extend[ed] eastward nearly to the valley of the Glenelg, but interspersed with patches here and there of grassy land'.[120] Northeast, Curr found a narrow opening in the reeds into what proved to be a charming little savannah of perhaps half a square mile in extent. The grass in it was about a foot high, and so thick that the tread of our horses was as noiseless as that of the camel . . . The reeds were by [sic] patches and strips of different hues and growth, in accordance with their ages and the periods at which they had last been burnt . . . we also noticed several patches of good open country.[121]

In 'a thick part of the scrub' near Mt Serle (SA), Henderson 'crossed a small patch of luxuriant grass, certainly the richest herbage since we left the depot', and below Mt Bryan 'the scrub . . . was intersected by several small grassy plains'.[122] Near Mannum (SA) Eyre had

to force our way thro' a very dense pine scrub for some distance; then came an open plain for three or four miles, followed by scrub again and heavy sand . . . On the tableland there was also a good deal of open land at intervals, grassy and suitable for sheep . . . the country back from the river sandy but very grassy, lightly wooded and well adapted for grazing. Kangaroo, emus and wild turkies abounded.[123]

East of Perth Moore described the plain behind his house:

perhaps two hundred acres, upon which large trees are not numerous, or more than sufficient for ornament. There is one spot looking like a cleared field, of eight or nine acres, not encumbered with a single tree or shrub . . . This large plain is skirted by a thick border of red gum trees, intermixed with banksias, black wattles, and other shrubs.[124]

The same pattern yarded desert kangaroos.[125] East of Ooldea 'Wynbring was certainly a most agreeable little oasis, an excellent spot for an explorer to come to in such a frightful region . . . there being splendid green feed and herbage on the few thousand acres of open ground around the rock.'[126] At Warman Rocks west of Kintore (NT) an Erldunda man 'pointed out' to Tietkins 'a particular burnt patch, it was not the only one by any means, there were dozens, but Billy seemed convinced that water was there'. They found 'a grassy glade dotted over with mulgas . . . a native well, and after that a rock waterhole', and at the same spot next day, 'some few hundred acres of excellent grass land . . . which in this region is almost as scarce as water'.[127] At the head of the Bight, Warburton rode 'through scrub, in the midst of which were occasional oases of green herbage, singularly clear and defined, and contrasting strangely with the surrounding scrub. There was, however, no water in these verdant spots.'[128] Not far inland John Forrest rode

> through dense mallee thickets, destitute of grass or water, for eighteen miles. We came upon a small patch of open grassy land . . . continuing, chiefly through dense mallee thickets, with a few grassy flats intervening, for twenty-two miles, found another rock water-hole . . . after travelling one mile from it, camped on a large grassy flat, without water for the horses.[129]

Water was often handy but hidden (ch 8)—Eyre met people in Murray mallee clearings, where artifacts are still found.[130] [131]

In rainforest especially, hills might be cleared (pictures 44–5). In Queensland's brushy Cardwell Range, Dalrymple saw 'a line of perfectly open, bald, grassy summits for about two miles . . . [and to] the west a shallow valley full of scrub, bounded by a second line of low bald hills'.[132] These clearings were named and valued. Augustus Leycester walked through

> a glade in the brush, we saw at a distance 'Bald Hill' . . . an old camping ground of mine (called by the blacks 'Byangully') and replete with every comfort a bush camp in Australia can afford, that of grass, water, and game, in abundance of the best kind. It was a small prairie on a bald hill, surrounded by a dense brush twenty miles distant from the open country we had left behind.

Southwest of Mt Warning (NSW), 'Mt Tanning' had

> a table-top covered with fine grass, and studded over with a beautiful species of palm-tree called by the aborigines 'Tanning', its sides were covered with a dense brush, containing cedars and pines of gigantic size. What a lovely spot, all Nature seemed to be indulging in repose. The birds and animals seemed to know no danger, and looked on us with curiosity more than fear, they knew not that we were their most dangerous enemies. The pigeons and turkeys would sit to be shot at in the trees, and appeared only to wonder when their feathered companions

fell from the deadly effects of our weapons of war . . . This was the one of the grandest spots for a naturalist, or an artist, I ever met with, for it was surrounded with Nature's charms—all in their primitive beauty.[133]

District table-tops are forest now, with few animals. In Queensland, Tooalla

> was not insignificant in size, being over a mile in length east and west, and a little less in breadth, its uppermost level small, and almost bald hills, connected by low saddles, all its outer boundary falling steeply away in radiating spurs, its centre dished by a miniature swamp that was drained by a puny but never ceasing stream . . . In this swamp there are rushes, and round about plenty of good grass; timber scant and stunted—oak and ti-tree.[134]

Grass-forest associations varied by belts, clumps and clearings marked out a continent deliberately and usefully arranged. But people did not stop there. They integrated these associations into a brilliantly efficient land use system. They made templates.

8

Templates

People today think of what animals need. In 1788 people thought of what animals prefer. This is a crucial difference. What animals prefer always attracts them. Kangaroos crowd onto golf greens. They don't need to, they prefer to. For short grass they defy flying golf balls and angry greenkeepers even when safer grass is metres away. Possums prefer fresh tips, so move readily from unburnt urban parks and fringes into green-laden backyards. In the Centre native bees prefer Desert Bloodwood, so people take care not to let flames or smoke damage its flowers.[1] Most animals prefer particular shelter: euros rocky hills, koalas tall eucalypts, scrub wallabies thick growth. Even scavengers have preferences. Emus eat grain, tips, flowers, insects, mice and small lizards but prefer fruit, so such adaptable opportunists can still be attracted.

People catered to preferences. They coupled preferred feed and shelter by refining grass, forests, belts, clumps and clearings into templates: unlike plant communities associated, distributed and maintained for decades or centuries to prepare country for day-to-day working. Templates set land and life patterns for generations of people. They were the land's finishing touches, offering abundance, predictability, continuity and choice. Typically people chose a feature like water, hill or rock, and laid out a template on or beside it. Grass might separate forest from water, tree belts channel a plain, grass and heath alternate, clearings line a rainforest ridge, and so on. Templates for a plant were put where best suited plant and people; templates for an animal were kept suitably apart but linked into mosaics ultimately continent wide. Each template might have multiple uses or overlap, but together they rotated growth in planned sequences, some to harvest, some to lure and locate. They were thus of many kinds, some still detectable, others now gone forever in resurgent forest or dried-out wetlands.

All demanded controlled fire. It was not the only shepherd: bans, sanctuaries and totems reinforced abundance; open seasons and culling limited excess; planting improved crop yields (ch 10). But fire was the closest ally. Random fire defied the logic of templates. It could damage a template but not repair it. It could leave clumps and patches but not sustain them over generations. It made animals disperse, not concentrate. It could not distinguish fire to hunt from fire to lure. It was never welcome. System and precision were its enemies.

Controlled fire could govern where animals would and would not go because Australia, alone of continents, had few big predators. Crocodile, dingo, goanna, snake, eagle, quoll and Tasmanian tiger and devil exhaust the list, and some of these scavenge more than hunt. Few threatened people or deterred grazers, so templates activated in rotation could be as close and apart as suited their animals, and alternated with country meant to deter—an unlike template or a natural feature. Robinson noted, 'The inland natives have their hunting grounds for the different species of game, i.e. boomer, forester, wallaby, kangaroo, wombat, porcupine &c, the same as the coast natives have for their fish, such as particular rocks for mutton fish, crawfish, oysters, mussles, chitons &c.'[2] These are very precise distinctions. Speckling land and sea in this way secured diversity, predictability and convenience. Few Europeans recognised this deliberate variety. Almost all thought the landscape natural. The great gift Australia's plants gave, to let people shape the land with fire, had few British parallels.

Tasmania and the mainland can each be seen as one template system, island-wide, for given the Law a system could not terminate. It was inescapably co-operative. Like templates had to be not too many or too few, too close or too far. They had to reconcile sometimes delicate and conflicting interests: predator vs prey, fireweed vs seed eater, annual herb vs perennial feed. Was a template for hunting, harvesting, camping or sanctuary? Was a ceremony planned or completed? How normal was the weather, how experienced the fire managers? What should be done if it was time to burn grass for kangaroos or yams, but its lizards or bees had had a bad year? Neighbours and totems must negotiate. The very existence of totems evokes the centrality and flexibility of fire in Aboriginal thinking, because totems assume that people and animals have power to make pivotal decisions about the environment, and that ritual plus burning or not burning implements those decisions. This sensibly assumes country laid out to empower totems and enforce the template system, for in every place the Law decreed which template and totem had priority.

Siting templates was not simple. Templates for plants might divert and disperse animals; templates for animals must be away from crops (ch 10): there was no point in having a crop eaten, or in luring animals to places people regularly disturbed. Patches to clear tracks or margins or protect cultural sites might still make pick, so had to be blended in. Even then a patch alone rarely supports any animal. Some use it, some its edges, some move from patch to patch, some stay between. Patches too many or too few let game scatter, too small made it flighty, too big put feed too far from shelter or spear. What was not burnt mattered as much as what was. These problems were met by connecting unlike templates, and by leaving some templates dormant while others were active, so that none detracted from another's working. Mobility made this possible: people walked not only to care for country, but to leave it alone. A plain left after a hunt or a harvest soon became too rank for grazers, allowing its use, as distinct from its existence, to be rotated in concert with others suitably spaced.

Coasts were carefully made. Recall Cook's 'lawns' (ch 1). A similar pattern circled most of Tasmania, edged inland by forest with clearings up to the highlands, where grass, heath, eucalypts and rainforest alternated (picture 37). On the Vasse near Busselton (WA) Nicholas Baudin described a coast common in 1788. Inside coastal dunes the land was

> completely covered with scrub and stubby trees of various kinds. Next, one finds a plain, about a short quarter-league [1 km] in extent, ending at the edge of an immense forest that offers a most pleasant view ... The plain just mentioned is scattered throughout with full-grown trees ... There were so many traces of fire everywhere and the paths were so well-worn, that it looked to me as if this place were much frequented ... As we crossed the plain, we encountered a fairly large number of quail.[3]

At Rockingham Bay (Qld) the doomed explorer Edmund Kennedy saw 'open ground between the beach and the swamp var[ying] in width from half a mile to three or four miles; it was principally covered with long grass, with a belt of bushy land along the edge of the beach ... There were a great many wallabies near the beach.'[4]

In 1846 GD Smythe and in 1847 Robert Hoddle surveyed the Cape Otway (Vic) coast. It is climax rainforest country, but Smythe's plan showed 'Undulating Grassy Hills Timbered with She-Oak' backed inland by 'Undulating Heathy Hills', then by 'Red & Blue Gum, Iron Bark, Stringy Bark & Lightwood'. Hoddle's plan showed coastal 'Open Plains' 'Good Grass' 'Good Grass She Oak Timber', and inland 'Heath' then 'Thick Forest'. From the coast inland, the surveyors mapped a fire sequence of diminishing frequency. Two hot fires within seven years eradicates Drooping Sheoak, the Cape Otway species. Seeds grow, but need 5–7 years to seed in turn, and 10–12 years to seed well. Cool fire kills seedlings and spares mature trees but won't provoke seed release. No fire lets seedlings become dense whipstick forest. The Otway sheoaks were neither too dense to impede good grass nor too sparse to warrant mention. The land was managed by finely balanced fires, yet was on a coast where for half the year people lived on fish and shellfish. By 1849 it was reverting to scrub. In April 1846 Charles La Trobe took three days to walk 75 kilometres or so from Cape Otway to Gellibrand River. In March 1849 he took five days, and needed 'a good deal of exertion, a great deal more indeed than on my first excursion, for it was found quite impossible to follow my old track'. Within three years a complex landscape was vanishing.[5]

Elsewhere people refined country without much changing its character. On western Victoria's 'very extensive plains, with here and there a tree upon them', William Buckley, veteran clansman, recalled, 'we remained many months, there being plenty of animal food and a great deal of fish in the water holes',[6] and Hoddle 'travelled 16 miles upon Plains destitute of Wood & Water . . . and encamped upon a bleak Plain, a few Banksias about a mile distant . . . not a single Tree for the last 12 miles. Abundance of Bustard, the native Turkey of Australia . . . Abundance of Ducks on the Lakes.'[7] People may have used big plains to deny kangaroos shelter and farm *murnong*, Yam Daisy, the flavoursome yellow-flowered tuber once common in southeast Australia (ch 10). Roos eat yam tops, so were not welcome on the fields, and yams were on big plains. On 'large plains' near Crystal Brook (SA), Eyre 'came suddenly upon a small party of natives engaged in digging yams of which the plains were full'.[8] North of the Hutt (WA) in 1839, Grey followed unlike templates keeping animals and food plants apart. He took a path through alternating scrub and plain to a well 'surrounded by shrubs and graceful wattle trees', then over 'sandy downs, abounding in kangaroos', and past 'springs of water at every few hundred yards, generally situated at the edge of a large clump of trees'. This was kangaroo country, but soon it ended. Quitting the path, Grey met 'an almost impenetrable belt of scrub . . . in two hours and a half I had forced my way throw [sic] it . . . we were all totally exhausted, as well as dreadfully torn and bruised'. He rejoined the path, and

> my wonder augmented; the path increased in breadth and in its beaten appearance, whilst along the side of it we found frequent wells . . . We now crossed the dry bed of a stream, and from that emerged upon a tract of light fertile soil, quite overrun with *warran* [yam] . . . After crossing a low limestone-range, we came down upon another equally fertile *warran* ground . . . about two miles further on . . . we found

> ourselves in a grassy valley . . . Along its centre lay a chain of reedy fresh water swamps, and native paths ran in from all quarters . . . In these swamps we first found the *yun-jid*, or flag (a species of *typha*).[9]

Neither Grey nor Eyre or Mitchell in *murnong* country[10] mentioned kangaroos with yams, even though yams and grass both grow best on rich soil.

In some places roos could be kept off even small paddocks. Near Daylesford (Vic) in 1840 John Hepburn showed Robinson

> a small plain with some open forest upon it . . . where he said the natives usually encamped. Said it was a favourite place for the natives. He has seen 30 women on the plains at the time, digging murnong whilst the men went into the forest to hunt kangaroos, opossums &c which are abundant . . . The trees . . . stood at a distance of from 20 to 40 to 50 yards, and the whole, which was about half a mile square, had a park-like appearance . . . The banks on the opposite side [of a creek] was thickly wooded. A small table land, grassy, was directly opposite.[11]

In other places separating roos and yams was not possible or not preferable. In Tasmania,

> kangaroo bounded before us in every direction. The country in this part is delightfully pleasant, with little grassy hills and extensive plains where the young kangaroo grass was shooting up on the burnt ground, forming a beautiful carpet of green pasture, and the plain was studded with a yellow flower.[12]

Possibly the grass was burnt at harvest time, deterring the roos and exposing the yams.

The most obvious templates were for kangaroos, the biggest and fastest grazers. These illustrate how precise templates must be, but how possible this was. Red (plains) and grey (forest) kangaroos prefer to graze in the open. They eat herbs, grass and tips, but as a professional hunter put it in 1860, are 'very partial' to Kangaroo Grass.[13] They prefer, and when young need, grass golf-green high and fresh, when it is softest to eat and most nutritious, with high nitrogen content—except in drought it is 75–95 per cent of their diet. Usually only young males travel far, but reds can see and smell rain up to 20 kilometres away, and will move up to 30 kilometres to green pick. Searchers spread, one finds feed, the mob smells its breath and follows it back. In forests with more water and grass, greys will travel 5–7 kilometres for pick. Reds have favourite places but are opportunist in finding feed; greys have a beat between feed and camps. Both drink little, dew often sufficing, but prefer water nearby. For shelter reds seek shade, not too dense, with a view and in open country, preferably in long grass in summer and short grass in winter. Tree clumps on tussock plains are ideal. Greys prefer cool gully scrub on hot days, dry rises out of the wind on cold days, and timbered rises at night, all without enough undergrowth to slow them down. Both prefer edges. Both fear recent killing ground, so places to lure them must be changed frequently, and the roos left to forget the spears, locate on another template, stand 'gazing at us like fawns, and in some instances came bounding towards us',[14] and breed. In the north pick has most nutrient in the late Dry so grass for breeding was burnt then, but in general roos are opportunist breeders, holding a foetus until conditions are right.

To meet such complexities, simply patch-burning here and there—the management level Europeans have so far detected—is haphazard and awkward. The work of decades was not to be frittered away like that. Instead, 'Only a small fire was lit so that it would not get out of control and burn neighbours out. Marsupials would, of course, be attracted by the new shoot of grass after a burn, and if the area were restricted the game would be more easily taken.'[15] People chose and patch-burnt templates in sequence to give a mob a good beat and to schedule which edge it would use, so from which to hunt. A mob fleeing one template to seek another made ready might cross several with no burnt patches or appeal. These would be worked later. All this must be varied as seasons, species balance, and ceremonies or gatherings dictated. Hard work and planning were constant, but so vital that after 1788 survivors risked their lives to do it. In Tasmania Mannalargenna's people took this risk (ch 4), and Backhouse saw Tasmanians still working templates after most of their kin were 'removed'. 'This forest . . .', he wrote in November 1832, 'is interrupted by a very few, small, grassy plains. One of these had recently been burnt by a few Aborigines still remaining in the neighbourhood. They burn off the old grass, in order that the Kangaroos may resort to that which springs up green and tender.'[16]

On the other hand, many smaller marsupials prefer the safety of long grass. There were templates for them too. Whereas a clearing might be patch-burnt to bait a kangaroo trap, for scrub wallabies grass might be left long until a hunt was ready. On the Herbert, Lumholtz watched a hunt on

> a large plain, surrounded on all sides by scrub and overgrown with high dense grass . . . [Men] spread themselves out, set fire to the grass simultaneously at different points, and then quickly joined the rest. The

dry grass rapidly blazed up, tongues of fire licked the air, dense clouds of smoke arose, and the whole landscape was enveloped as in fog.[17]

Templates were highly effective. Grey glimpsed their efficiency:

[people] always regulate the visits to their grounds so as to be at any part which plentifully produces a certain sort of food, at the time this article is in full season: this roving habit produces a similar character in the kangaroos, emus, and other sorts of game, which are never driven more from one part than from another—in fact, they are kept in a constant state of movement from place to place.[18]

From patch to patch, he might have said. North of Swan Bay (Vic) Batman crossed

land a little sandy in places, but of the finest description for grazing purposes; nearly all parts of its surface covered with Kangaroo and other grasses of the most nutritive character, intermixed with herbs of various kinds; the Kangaroo grass, and other species from ten to twelve inches high, of a dense growth, and green as a field of wheat . . . As a relief to the landscape, the rising eminences were adorned with wattle, banksia, native honeysuckle and the she-oak . . . we passed over another thinly-timbered and richly-grassed plain, of not less than two to three hundred acres, on whose rich surface a large number of kangaroos were feeding.[19]

Batman described a sequence of fire sensitive herbs and grass 'of the finest description' too tall for kangaroos, belts of fire tolerant trees on rises, and kangaroos concentrated on a 'richly-grassed plain'. Understandably, he missed the significance of these changes. Southeast of Tambo (Qld), Mitchell saw a little more:

we traversed fine open grassy plains. The air was fragrant from the many flowers then springing up, especially where the natives had burnt the grass . . . The extensive burning by the natives, a work of considerable labour, and performed in dry warm weather, left tracts in the open forest, which had become green as an emerald with the young crop of grass. These plains were thickly imprinted with the feet of kangaroos, and the work is undertaken by the natives to attract these animals to such places.[20]

The work made animals predictable. Allan Cunningham realised that the 'marks of kangaroo and emu among the fine brown grass and forest land in the vicinity of the creek are proofs of the abundance of these animals in these fine grassy grounds',[21] and Mary Bundock recalled,

> a man came to an uncle of mine and asked him for matches, as he had lost his firestick while following a big old man kangaroo. My uncle asked him 'What do you want matches for?' The black man replied, 'To cook my kangaroo.' 'Have you killed him then?' asked my uncle. 'No' was the answer 'he is up there' pointing to a mountain about two miles away, 'very tired and I go back there and kill and eat him.' Which he accordingly did![22]

He found what he expected. Predictability is an advantage farmers claim over hunters, but a template system spread and programmed was more drought and flood evading, more certain, than a farm.[23]

Templates explain 1788 plant patterns otherwise puzzling. From the 1880s until the 1967 fires, the McDermott family had a small farm on Hobart's Pipeline Track, where their cattle kept open a skilfully placed clearing. *Poa* grassland covered a saddle and ran up slopes at each end to meet forest edges. Depending on the wind, people could drive game uphill either way, slowing it for spears or nets in the timber. Today wattle and peppermint are reclaiming these edges.[24] In the southern alps in 1840, amid

> the apparent sameness of the forest, may be often found spots teeming with gigantic and luxuriant vegetation, sometimes laid out in stately groves, free from thicket or underwood, sometimes opening on glades or slopes [picture 38] . . . Sometimes, again, the forest skirts an open country of hill and plain, gracefully sprinkled with isolated clumps of trees, covered with the richest tufted herbage.[25]

On the Gwydir west of Moree (NSW), Mitchell

> crossed a small plain, then some forest land, and beyond that entered on an open plain still more extensive, but bounded by a scrub, at which we arrived after travelling seven miles. The soil of this last plain was very fine, trees grew upon it, in beautiful groups—the

acacia pendula again appearing. The grass, of a delicate green colour, resembled a field of young wheat. The scrub beyond was close,

and four days later:

The country consisted of open forest, which, growing gradually thinner, at length left intervals of open-plain . . . Penetrating next through a narrow strip of casuarinae scrub, we found the remains of native huts; and beyond this scrub, we crossed a beautiful plain; covered with shining verdure, and ornamented with trees, which, although 'dropt in nature's careless haste', gave the country the appearance of an extensive park. We next entered a brush of the acacia pendula, which grew higher and more abundant than I had seen it elsewhere.[26]

Walker thought the country around Mt Alexander (Vic)

good undulating forest, very open, with here and there, spaces devoid of trees altogether . . . for a couple of miles we passed through scrubby ranges; but just where we halted, the country . . . looked beautiful, *and we all exclaimed*—'There is Australia Felix!' The country was not a flat or level one, but consisted of fine ridges, ranges of very open forest, with many apparently open tracts entirely devoid of timber: these are what are called 'plains' or 'downs'.[27]

Mitchell found this country a sequence of dense and open forest, and grass. He approached Mt Alexander over rich 'downs' full of emu and kangaroo, crossed a eucalypt wood to its base, climbed the north face through giant eucalypts open enough to ride through, and on top met dense timber, the south edge thick with tree ferns, wombat holes and fallen trunks. Some researchers argue that this area carried grass on basalt and trees on granite,[28] but the changes were too local for that. People were working both with and against the country. They linked forest hills to grass and scrub belts on plains, and left dense timber on colder south slopes but north slopes open enough to ride horses up. Mitchell continued southeast to Mt Macedon, crossing from granite to basalt. The forest was denser, but again north slopes were more open than south, and both were more open than now. South of the mount Hawdon found both thick forest and downs of 'park-like scenery'.[29]

In Tasmania and probably on the mainland, people moved grass templates. 'Grass is a fertility debtor; trees aren't,' Peter Andrews has noted.[30] Despite careful fire and stock rotation, sooner or later the best grasses are eaten out and give way to less palatable species, or accumulate silica, or acidify and sour. Pick becomes less alluring and herbs and tubers thin as soils break down and lose nitrogen, fire ash and other nutrients. As on cropland, such signs show that the soil needs rest and revival.[31]

The simplest way to move a template was to drive successive grass fires downwind into forest, and let forest recapture grass on the trailing edge. This cycled each community, yet kept plains a useful hunting size, and over centuries steadily moved grass—forest templates across country. In northwest Tasmania in the 1950s Bill Mollison noted 1788 plains moved progressively north to south by firing rainforest. At south edges grass gave way abruptly to mature rainforest; in the north eucalypts were advancing onto grassland. There was no soil change. Every few years hot summer northerlies sweep down from the mainland, bringing shrivelling heat. Tasmanians waited for it, moved clear of the young eucalypts north, and drove grass fires south into the rainforest. Slowly, sometimes no doubt by mere metres, they pushed the rainforest south, regulating the eucalypts north to match.[32]

In this way Gatcomb Plain looks to have moved south (picture 46), and in a valuable chapter in 1988 RC Ellis and Ian Thomas concluded of Paradise Plains near Mathinna (Tas):

> The present area of grassland on Paradise Plains was formed during the last 200 years or so by the burning of rainforest. To the east of the Plains is primaeval rainforest; but to the west of the Plains is closed eucalypt forest of recent origin, as is shown by the presence of old open-grown trees and occasional remains of rainforest trees, amongst the tall forest-grown younger eucalypts. As one progresses further west across the plateau, the eucalypt forest appears to have been established for longer, since it contains forest-grown veterans and fallen trees and older secondary rainforest. At the western extremity of the plateau, the remains of eucalypt logs were found on a ridge top beneath secondary rainforest more than 200 years old. It may be that, as existing grassland became impoverished or overgrown with fire-resistant vegetation, the Aborigines abandoned it and generated new grassland by burning adjacent rainforest.[33]

Fire drove rainforest east, grass and rainforest survivors like tree fern took charge of the burnt ground, eucalypts reclaimed the trailing edge, rainforest returned under shielding eucalypts. This was no random pattern. It required varied fire regimes and more skill than today's firemen have. Tasmanians did it consistently for centuries. Ellis and Thomas noted similarly transformed landscapes nearby, at Diddleum Plain and near Mt Maurice, and Thomas thought grassland at Big Heathy Swamp may have been moved 5500 years ago.

Robinson unwittingly crossed a template being moved. On the Ringarooma he met 'immense gum and stringy bark trees, some of which was forty and fifty feet round, and the intermediate space filled up with lesser trees of the dogwood, stinkwood, sassafras and musk, as also the stately ferntree'. Four miles west he

> passed through an extensive forest of mimosa . . . trees . . . and numerous ferntrees . . . After travelling in this route for about ten miles came to an open and extensive plain covered with grass and fern . . . I was much gratified at meeting with this country after being immured in a forest for four days . . . kangaroo . . . were plentiful . . . The fern and trees had been fresh burnt.[34]

'Mimosa' regenerates quickly and thickly after fire (picture 6). It is among the first colonisers of burnt land. Without fire, in time other species top it and it dies. Here this had not yet happened, so the burning was quite recent. Tree fern prefers rainforest. It resists fire and survives in grass, but under repeated burning does not generate there.[35] Its presence indicates former rainforest. So walking east to west, Robinson described eucalypts over rainforest indicating no fire for centuries, then recently fired land carrying wattles and tree fern, then a grass and fern plain made by fires repeated for enough decades to clear the trees. Like Ellis and Thomas, he reported colonising fires moving from west to east.

Curr 'saw' templates being moved in the Hampshire Hills. 'It has always been a matter of some doubt to me', he wrote,

> whether the forests in this Island are encroaching on the clear grounds, or the clear grounds on the forests. An attentive examination of the Hampshire Hills establishes the very important fact that the forest by the agency of fire is undergoing gradual destruction & that useful grass is taking its place.

> I am of the opinion that, compared with the old settlements, these plains are of very recent date & almost every season is adding something to their extent. The middle of the clear ground near the banks of the river, seems the oldest formation; towards the outskirts the burnt forest in some parts thickly strews the ground as yet undecayed & in one place the destruction of the Forest has been so recent that the ferntree still survives . . . added to the above circumstances I observed that the tops of the forest trees immediately surrounding the clear ground were in most parts dead & lifeless—indicating that they will soon be in a state to burn & that the process of destruction of forest and the spread of grass is going on gradually but surely.[36] [37]

On the other hand, water might anchor a template. It was a valuable component, varying and extending resources, most obviously in dry country. On the Balonne (Qld) Mitchell passed

> through woods partly of open forest trees, and partly composed of scrub . . . [to] land covered with good grass, and having only large trees on it, so thinly strewed as to be of the character of the most open kind of forest land. Saw thereon some very large kangaroos, and throughout the day we found their tracks numerous . . . [Camped] on a grassy spot surrounded by scrub.[38]

North of Julia Creek (Qld) John McKinlay

> crossed a couple of small creeks flowing northward (the natives burning a short distance on our left); then over a variety of fair open country, and a small portion of very thick and scrubby myall forest; then over a spinifex ridge; then over well grassed table lands for several miles; then over a pretty thickly timbered spinifex rise of considerable length; and lastly, for the last five miles over plains, light belts of timber here and there.[39]

On the Flinders a mile east of Hughenden (Qld) Ernest Henry found

> a lovely valley of undulating downs, studded here and there with groups and belts of graceful myall trees . . . the grass had evidently been burnt off a few weeks previously, but now clothed the rising and falling ground with

the very richest pasture, trackless and undisturbed by a single hoof. A small creek, whose winding course is indicated by the trees that grow on either bank, trends northward through the centre of the valley . . . to the north [it] widens out and joins the extensive valley of the river, along whose course open downs stretch far away, unbroken save by narrow belts of timber.[40]

He put his head-station there. Allan Cunningham came

to an exceedingly pretty patch of plain . . . Its soils proved to be exceedingly rich, and well clothed with grass and other esculent vegetables . . . [It] is watered on its western side by the Logan . . . In the forest ground on the south side of the plain we reached a lagoon . . . [then] through an open forest, having the river, overshadowed by a density of viney thicket immediately on our right, we traversed flats of good ground, liable, however, to occasional inundation.[41]

East of Rylstone (NSW) he sketched a more open template:

a timbered grassy country about four miles, when we entered the open bare lands of Daby, through which the Cugeegong winds . . . well covered with an abundance of grazing herbage, thinly wooded, having patches perfectly bare of tree or shrub, and of an exceedingly rich, black, moist, loamy soil, adapted to all the purposes of agriculture . . . [Northwest is] a rising forest land, tolerably well watered, lightly timbered, and occasionally interspersed with confined brushes.[42]

On the upper Hunter Lang found a complex and beautiful template:

a peninsula, which the natives call Narragan . . . without exception the finest piece of land, both for quality of soil and for beauty of scenery and situation I have ever seen . . . over its whole extent patches of rich grassy plain, of thirty or forty acres each, alternate with clumps of trees or narrow beltings of forest, as if the whole had been tastefully laid out for a nobleman's park.[43]

On Mowle (Molle?) Plains in northwest Tasmania, Hellyer

> entered a green forest belt which encircles its Westn end. This green forest is very free from underwood and the trees are wide apart . . . the soil being excellent & nearly level, exactly similar to the adjacent plain . . . [It] does not extend a mile through. Just beyond it was a marshy patch . . . [then] a fine tract of dry open forest which I regretted to find did not extend far . . . There is much good grass in it . . . Entered upon a large tract of heathy country . . . it appeared to have been burnt last summer, it is about a mile wide from E to West & more than double that extent in length . . . [crossed a creek into green forest with possums] leaping from tree to tree in all directions.[44]

Hodgkinson wrote of the upper Macleay (NSW),

> The alluvial brushes on its banks are now frequently superseded by park-like forest ground . . . and luxuriant grassy flats of the greatest richness, lightly timbered . . . on the south side is Dongai Creek. In the narrow valley of this stream, the land is of the richest quality possible, consisting of a narrow border of alluvial flats, covered with broad-bladed grass, growing breast high [Blady Grass, which flourishes after fire], and with a few large blue gum trees scattered so far apart as to offer no impediment to immediate tillage . . . [It] is hemmed in on both sides by fertile ranges, well clothed with grass, and lightly wooded . . . their sloping sides, covered with bright green verdure, contrast strongly with the dark glistening green of the brush vegetation which occasionally invades some of the hills.[45]

Off-farm these hills carry rainforest now.

Jack encountered a template sequence about 65 kilometres south of Cape York. From 'a narrow belt' of dense vine scrub, he went over heath for 400 yards to a scrub-fringed creek, crossed a mile of open country split by two boggy pandanus gullies, entered dense scrub he had to cut through, then a mile of forest with brush undergrowth, more scrub to cut through, 800 yards of heath and brush to a creek, and two miles to 'a belt' of scrub (pictures 44–5). Next day he followed the 'edge of the scrub' then cut through it for a mile, partly on 'a TRACK CUT one or two seasons ago BY THE NATIVES'. He emerged into half forest, half scrub to a creek, then scrub, then dense scrub to 'a sort of pocket', where he camped.[46] All this is climax rainforest country.

TEMPLATES

Exploring with Mitchell, Granville Stapylton conveyed how templates varied the land. On the Glenelg near Casterton (Vic) he exclaimed

> By Jupiter this is a paradise of a country An Eldorado The Cowpastures are positively inferior to it in excellence Here we have undulating ground clear of timber except occasional picturesque clumps of Trees Mould of the finest and richest black soil of great depth, and grass and herbage so verdant and thick that the ground is literally matted with it,

but a few miles south he met 'a barren sandy Heath . . . Encamped near a swamp great vicissitudes attend exploring From a Paradise in the morning we are led into a desert at night . . . Alas Alas how vain sometimes are the hopes and projects of weak mortals.'[47] He was in Australia Felix, which Haydon described as

> Beautiful plains with nothing on them but a luxuriant herbage, gentle rises with scarcely a tree, and all that park-like country . . . The greater part of the country has that happy medium of being just enough wooded without inconveniencing the settler, whilst there is no lack of good timber for every purpose he may require. It has been my lot to travel for many days through a country, the only hindrances being an occasional scrub, or belt of thickly wooded forest, a large lagoon, or a deep flowing river where the ground was spread with eternal verdure.[48]

In 1839 William Russell detailed a template north of Shelford (Vic),

> a valley extending from half to three quarters of a mile in breadth, stretching as far as the eye can reach, and on each side are sloping banks—one of them thinly wooded, the other with very little wood upon it at all. At the back of the huts is another gentle rising hill, well wooded, which almost unites the two hills on each side . . . the river Leigh . . . is marked by a row of White Gum trees on each side . . . The valley is . . . of rich alluvial soil and without either bush or tree and all ready for the plough.[49]

Northeast of Derby in northwest Australia, James Martin came on a 'Happy Valley' of fire sensitive pines and palms in burnt grassland, of no great breadth (say an eighth of a mile at the widest), clothed with a very carpet of green grasses. The first pines we had seen here fringed our track and formed . . . picturesque clumps of eights and tens intermingled with palms, acacia, eucalypti, and melaleuca, of great variety and beauty. A deliciously cool and clear stream of water flowed everywhere copiously along the valley . . . [which] terminated in a happier circular plain of about half a mile diameter, covered with the most luxuriant grass, not less than three feet high and perfectly level; this plain was bounded by timber of different kinds . . . the neighbourhood had been lately burnt, was easy to travel over, well watered and grassed, and had an abundance of fine timber.[50]

He depicts pleasant campsites with palm foods and water comfortably near a small enclosed plain to lure and trap.

Off the coast, and perhaps on it, swamps were 1788's richest resource. They supplied fish, shellfish, birds, eggs, frogs, snakes, bulrush, reeds and *nardoo*, a staple harvested from wet alluvial soils for flour. 'Large lagoons full of fish or mussels form a greater attraction to the natives than a stream too shallow for large fish', Leichhardt noted.[51] In summer and autumn Murrumbidgee people frequented swamps rather than the river, and the rest of their country in winter and spring.[52] In the eastern Riverina and South Gippsland, people blocked water to extend swamps,[53] and on the Roper (NT),

> Being so shallow and wide-spreading, the lagoons would dry up early in the Dry were it not that the blacks are able to refill them at will from the river, for here the Roper indulges in a third 'duck-under', so curious that with a few logs and sheets of bark the blacks can block the way of its waters and overflow them into the lagoons, thereby ensuring a plentiful larder to hosts of wild fowl, and, incidentally, to themselves.[54]

Roper people also built stake, bark and mud dams to stop lagoons and vine-forests drying out, attracting birds and nourishing plants 'so that we can get plenty of food easily'.[55]

Naturally people made swamp surrounds to suit. Near Narrandera plains adjoined every known swamp,[56] and in northwest Victoria Beilby met

> hills fringed with dense mallay [mallee] . . . [Then] sandy desert which had been covered with heath, but was lately burnt . . . a small grassy knoll . . . having a native well, and near it a small

swamp in which wells had recently been dug to retain the surface water . . . dense mallay . . . a pretty plain fringed with lofty pines and he-oaks, with clumps of mallay studding it here and there . . . a tract of mallay which had been burnt two or three years ago.[57]

At a big swamp near Dunkeld (Vic) Robinson wrote,

The whole face of the country had been burnt and the rushes of the swamp and the young grass . . . had attained a growth of seven or eight inches and a most verdant appearance. The land round the swamp is elevated and undulating, of good quality and lightly timbered. It is a very fine country and the scenery beautiful . . . Turkey frequent this country.[58]

On Carmichael's (now Deering) Creek in the west MacDonnells (NT), Giles found 'an open grassy swamp or plain':

The little plain looked bright and green . . . The grass and herbage here were excellent. There were numerous kangaroos and emus . . . [and] many evidences of native camping places about here; and no doubt the natives look upon this little circle as their happy hunting grounds. Our little plain is bounded on the north by peculiar mountains; it is also fringed with scrub nearly all round . . . thick, indeed very dense, scrub, which continued to the foot of the hills; in it the grass was long, dry, and tangled with dead and dry burnt sticks and timber, making it exceedingly difficult to walk through. Reaching the foot of the hills, I found the natives had recently burnt all the vegetation from their sides, leaving the stones, of which it was composed, perfectly bare . . . [South is] scrub . . . recently burnt near the edge of the plain; but the further we got into it, the worse it became.[59]

He might have been in Tasmania.[60]

Westernport east of Melbourne illustrates how carefully swamp templates were made. Behind the bay sat the big Kooweerup Swamp, with smaller swamps nearer the shore. In 1798 George Bass described the land as

low but hilly . . . the soil almost uniformly the same all round—a light brown mould free from sand . . . grass and ferns grow luxuriantly, and yet the country is but thinly and lightly timbered . . . Little patches of brush are to be met with everywhere, but there are upon the east side several thick brushes of some miles in extent, whose soil is a rich vegetable mould. In front of these brushes are salt marshes.[61]

In 1826, a decade before Melbourne was occupied, Westernport had a tourist boom. At least four parties visited, and around those 'salt marshes' found a varied landscape. D'Urville thought it 'rather like our royal forests round Paris', yet took it to be natural. 'The open terrain', he wrote,

> is delightfully undulating. Here there are fine stands of trees easy to penetrate, elsewhere vast grass-covered clearings, with well-defined paths and linked one with the other by other tracks [tracts] so regular and well defined that it is hard to conceive how these could have happened without the help of man.[62]

FA Wetherall reported swamps 'interspersed with a few elevated patches of rich meadow and occasional rows of Tea tree', the rising ground nearby 'most beautiful . . . Trees are dispersed in clumps over an extensive plain of rich meadows . . . at least 10,000 acres . . . unencumbered with brushwood.' The meadows carried 'luxuriant grass' which 'the frequent fires of the Natives keep free from brambles, or obstacles of that sort. Behind this, clumps of jungle begin to appear, and, becoming gradually closer and more prolonged, at length intermix with reeds, and prevent all progress in that direction.'[63]

Hovell may have ventured into that 'jungle'. He met an 'impassable Tea Tree brush', then 'a barren tract of Country of an heathy description, in parts it was covered with low brush, in other places it was swampy, and in consequence of its having been burned previously the stumps of brush were sharp and made it very unpleasant walking'. Then

> after crossing a fine Meadow of 1/2 or 3/4 Mile in width entered into a Tea Tree brush which after going a short distance into it, I had every reason to repent—it became so very thick and in other parts it had been burned, and the young wood growing up between the old pallid trees, which hid them from our sight, this occasioned us many a fall.[64]

A Tasmanian paper reported Westernport as made, valuable and beautiful:

> In parts it resembles the park of a country seat in England, the trees standing in picturesque groups to ornament the landscape . . . In other parts the eye roams over tracts of meadow land, waving with a heavy crop of grass, which, being annually burned by the natives, is reproduced every season,[65]

and in 1839 Stokes thought the area had 'in many places a most inviting rich park-like appearance, swelling on all sides into grassy downs, with patches of open woodland interspersed'.[66] Even in the 1950s the tea-tree was broken by curious grassy 'avenues . . . completely devoid' of trees.[67] [68]

In dry country people made dams for animals and caches for themselves, and managed nearby land more intimately than far places. In northwest Victoria dams were

> made to hold storm-water, which was led into them by surface drains. They were sunk in hard clay . . . and were from 4 to 8 feet deep, perfectly circular, and most accurately sunk, the bottoms made concave, so that the last drop of water might be more easily baled out. The bushes around the edges of these 'wells' twined, apparently by art, to dome-shaped arbore over them.[69]

A clay dam on the Bulloo east of Tibooburra (NSW) was 120 metres long, up to 2 metres high and up to 6 metres wide at the base. People camped by it, but made a track to a stone arrangement 3 kilometres west, edging parts with parallel stone lines.[70] Perhaps this led them off the dam when game was wanted, a supposition propped by a template dam Giles lyrically described at Pylebung southeast of Ooldea:

> The moon had now risen above the high sandhills that surrounded us, and we soon emerged upon a piece of open ground where there was a large white clay-pan, or bare patch of white clay soil, glistening in the moon's rays, and upon this there appeared an astonishing object—something like the wall of an old house or a ruined chimney. On arriving, we saw that it was a circular wall or dam of clay, nearly five feet high, with a segment open to the south to admit and retain the rain-water that occasionally flows over the flat . . . [It] was two feet thick at the top of the wall, twenty yards in the length of its sweep, and at the bottom, where the water lodged, the embankment was nearly five feet thick. The clay of which this dam was composed had been dug out of the hole in which the water lay, with small wooden native shovels, and piled up to its present dimensions.

> Immediately around this singular monument of native industry, there are a few hundred acres of very pretty country, beautifully grassed and ornamented with a few mulga (acacia) trees, standing picturesquely apart. The spot lies in a basin or hollow, and is surrounded in all directions by scrubs and rolling sandhills . . . there was a sandhill with a few black oaks (casuarinas) growing upon it, about a quarter of a mile away. A number of stones of a calcareous nature were scattered about on it . . . I was surprised to find a broad path had been cleared amongst the stones for some dozens of yards, an oak-tree at each end being the terminal points. At the foot of each tree at the end of the path the largest stones were heaped; the path was indented with the tramplings of many natives' feet.[71]

Mulga stood 'picturesquely apart' here, yet unburnt Mulga clumps densely. People had dug a dam, burnt a grass-shelter template around it, and moved away to let it work. Desert dams were 'fairly frequent' around Ooldea.[72] In 'probably the worst desert upon the face of the earth', Giles found Boundary Dam, an earth wall in mallee on the South Australian–West Australian border:

> This would be considered a pretty spot anywhere, but coming suddenly on it from the dull and sombre scrubs, the contrast makes it additionally striking. All around the lake is a green and open space with scrubs standing back, and the white lake-bed in the centre. The little dam was situated on a piece of clay ground where rain-water from the foot of some of the sandhills could run into the lake.[73]

Three weeks later he found a dam 'lying in a small hollow, in the centre of a small grassy flat . . . Further up the slopes, native wells had been sunk in all directions, in each and all of which was water.'[74] The dams and grass were for animals, the wells for people.[75]

People therefore dug wells where water was not scarce, for example in the Blue Mountains, and near swamps between the Murchison and the Hutt (WA).[76] They dug more in desert, making them too deep for animals or covering the openings. In the bed of a Diamantina (SA) tributary Sturt found a well 7 metres deep, and paths 'to almost every point of the compass'. One led to 'a village consisting of nineteen huts'.[77] West of Lake Torrens (SA) Tom Worsnop chanced on a template based on a well in 'dense mallee scrub',

> an open space of about sixty or seventy acres, almost circular in form. On the fringe of the mallee, and well in the shade around the whole place, were mounds of bones of animals and shells of native fruits, particularly the quondong or native peach, all of which had been broken or bruised by large stones still left there . . . this place must have been for ages the favourite resort of native tribes . . . The most remarkable feature . . . was a hard limestone crust which was raised like a small mound about the middle of this open space. Through the highest point . . . the natives had sunk a well 12ft deep, had then in a westerly direction cut a drive 10ft long, and tapped a most delicious spring of cool water . . . Down the sides of the well holes for the hands and feet had been cut in the hard limestone rock.[78]

In 'dreadful' scrub near Streaky Bay (SA) which required 'keeping the axes constantly at work', Eyre

> succeeded in slowly forcing a passage . . . emerging in about seventeen miles at an open plain behind Point Brown, and in the midst of which was a well of water. The entrance to this well was by a circular opening, through a solid sheet of limestone, about fifteen inches in diameter, but enlarging a little about a foot below the surface. The water was at a depth of about ten feet.[79]

In northeast South Australia Sturt saw how wells extended access to dry plains:

> we noticed some natives, seven in number, collecting grass seeds on them, on which alone, it appears to me, they subsist at this season of the year . . . Their presence . . . assured us that there must be water somewhere about, and as on entering the plain . . . we struck on a track, I directed Mr. Browne to run it down, who, at about half a mile, came to a large well . . . nine feet deep,[80]

and at Inkadunna Soak south of Katajuta (NT), Giles

> was fortunate to discover a small piece of flat rock, which was hardly perceptible amongst the grass; on it I saw a few dead sticks, and an old native fireplace, which excited my curiosity, and on riding up to it, I found to my astonishment under the dead sticks

two splendid little rock-holes or basins in the solid rock, with
ample water in them for the requirements of all my horses.[81]

Wells and caches drove game onto free water including dams, reduced evaporation, and extended templates into dry country.[82]

Three template systems convey how universal the Australian estate was. Kangaroo Valley (NSW), both pivoted on water and blended into rough country above, showing distinct templates in continuum. Somerset on Cape York (picture 58) details what was done; Albany in southwest Australia (picture 57) when it was done, and by whom.

Kangaroo Valley

Hoddle surveyed Kangaroo Valley in August 1831. Kangaroo River's south bank was 'fine open forest' and 'open forest good soil brushy' but no grassland, yet from the north bank the ground rose from grassy alluvial flats to sandstone cliffs with 'grassy' lower slopes and upper slopes of 'very thick brush and rocks'. Barrengarry Creek, flanked by 'undulating, grassy' slopes, cut deep into cliffs. The plateau above was 'rocky brushy range the soil of good quality', 'barren rocky range thick scrub' and 'barren scrub swampy'. Above Fitzroy Falls a 'large reedy swamp' edged a 'very thick brushy range' leading to another 'large swamp'.[83] Charles Throsby confirmed Hoddle's survey: from 'barren' ridges the land fell to 'a beautiful piece of Meadow, by the side of a considerable stream of water . . . land and grass very good', but across the stream were trees and no meadows.[84] Others, including Westmacott's *View in the Kangaroo Valley* (c1840–6), also depict grass flats and lower slopes north, open forest but no grassland south, and dense scrub alternating with swamps on the plateau.[85] Without fire this is climax rainforest country; some is rainforest now, including under giant eucalypts. The valley required at least four distinct fire regimes, but confined and located the plants and animals of almost every conceivable local habitat.

Somerset, July 1864

In 1864–5 surveyor WCB Wilson plotted Somerset and its hinterland. Somerset Bay 'is formed by Points', he wrote, 'headlands rising abruptly from the extremities of a low sandy shelving Beach' called *Kai'hibi*. About 400 metres long, half shut in by mangroves, it was backed first by grass, then by 'Fig, the Coral Tree, the Cotton Tree [Red Kapok?], and . . . many new kinds of Tea Tree some of which measure six feet in diameter'. Behind rose sandy hills covered with 'dense scrub'. On one, half open, half vine scrub, the Government Resident, John Jardine, put his house. Along the coast rainforest covered the lower slopes, but partway up the northwest headland Jardine's barracks stood in a clearing, while open ground occupied the southeast headland's upper slopes and crest, then fell to follow the coast south. Settlers put a 'Pioneers Garden' on this open coast, yet the slopes and ridges behind were 'dense scrub'.

About 5 kilometres southwest were two lakes, Baronta (Bronto) and Weechoura (Wicheura), 'beautiful sheets of deep and excellent water'. Except where swampy land linked them, both were ringed by grass, then 'dense Tea-tree Scrub'. An open neck 200–800 metres wide extended 2 kilometres into the tea-tree, then split, one arm pushing a kilometre northwest into tea-tree, the other northeast up Polo Creek and onto a 'barren swampy flat'. This was soon blocked by a joining creek and a narrow belt of dense scrub. Polo Creek was fringed by alternate dense scrub and open flats or slopes, backed by hills 'more open' to summits mostly dense scrub but sometimes open. Downstream, open land split by narrow necks of dense scrub ran up the hills behind the bay.[86]

Climax rainforest had been made an intricate mosaic of rainforest, open forest, swamp, creek, coast, tea-tree and grass. There were 'many fruit bearing trees—the nonda [Nonda Plum]—and a tree bearing fruit as large as an apple [Lady Apple] many edible berries & a species of black grape'. Open runs channelled game onto water, up steep slopes, or into scrub-edged traps. Grass allowed camps on the beach and around the lakes with easy access to plant and animal foods in rainforest and scrub. Grass also carried bulbs: in December 1864 Wilson remarked,

> heavy showers fell which had a wonderful effect upon the hitherto parched up ground innumerable bulbous roots shooting up their long green stems in every direction and clothing the earth with a profusion of flowers [Cape York Lily?] . . . It is very delightful to contemplate Nature in her holiday garbs, but unfortunately both the flowers and the coarse green grass are intrinsically worthless.

Wilson didn't value anything much. He cursed the scrub, 'composed of a sort of bastard tea tree—so dense that it is almost easier to walk over it than through it'. He thought the country south 'the most totally barren spot in the whole district . . . It only required the absence of water to render it a complete Sahara . . . patches of coarse bladygrass interlaced with interminable worthless scrubs.' He missed seeing that the country had been made, even though across the water the face of Albany Island was a plant mosaic (picture 58), and at Somerset the 'weeds and grass have all been burnt round the camp and every thing hopelessly covered with sand charcoal & ashes'.[87] People burnt camp surrounds carefully to avoid damaging fruit and shade trees.[88]

Others described this country. It was

> wooded in every direction, but with constantly recurring open patches covered with scattered acacias, gum trees, and Proteaceae with grass only growing beneath. In the dense woods, with their tall forest trees and tangled masses of creepers, one might for a moment imagine oneself back in Fiji or Api [Vanuatu], but the characteristic opens, with scattered Eucalypti, remind one at once that one is in Australia.[89]

Swamps were sometimes in brush, sometimes not, while high ridges southwest of the town were 'tolerably well grassed, and crowded with dense vine-scrubs', a striking contrast.[90] Jardine described ridges

> covered with a thick scrub, laced and woven together with a variety of vines and climbers; while the small valleys intervening bear a strong growth of tall grass, through which numerous creeping plants twine in all directions, some of them bearing beautiful flowers . . . The scrubs are formed with an immense variety of trees and shrubs . . . [some with tasty fruit, including a] wild banana, with small but good fruit.

Banana, yam, taro and several fruits and nuts cultivated in Malaysia and New Guinea are 'wild' on Cape York.[91] People had freed them.

They were also sea people. The sea floor and its reefs, cays and sandbars were named, enriched with myth, portioned into 'countries', managed and inherited. Jardine listed green turtle as the 'principal food' during the Wet, also naming fish, shellfish, birds, roots and fruit.[92] Understandably, even he did not fully grasp the rich diversity around him. He missed naming dugong, reptiles, pandanus, mangrove shoots, marsupials and more. Grass, forest and scrub each carried dozens of useful plants. In the sandy scrub behind his house grew the main food yam. People planted them in lots, poles marking boundaries, and harvested them without disturbing their tops. Some lots were reserved for guests. On the beach and at camps people planted coconuts and shade trees, sometimes fencing or clearing round them.[93]

By 1992 almost all the land open in 1865 was forest or scrub, and trees were edge-invading the 'barren swampy flat' and the open high ground on the coast.[94] People visiting said, 'Poor old country, come wild now. No-one look after him.'[95] [96]

Somerset Bay had little water. Ships called, then moved northwest to Evans Bay, which had wells behind the beach. In 1844–5 and 1848–9 officers on HMS *Fly* and HMS *Rattlesnake* wrote similar accounts of the land there. A narrow rainforest belt backing the beach gave way to grassy eucalypt woodland, then rocky hills 'covered by an almost impenetrable thicket, forming a natural fence' or 'pleasant grassy flats', 'a likely place for kangaroo'. In October 1848 a 'bush fire' 'passed over', and flats which reached to a mangrove swamp full of fish were 'covered with a stubble of coarse grass'. Seasonal freshwater pools dotted the plains, ringed by pandanus, tea-tree or rainforest, in November 1849 laden with Lady Apples, like an 'orchard'—which it was. The plains ended in a jungle 'cul-de-sac' which ran up flanking hills. Across open flats south, luxuriant rainforest and 'beautiful palms' rich in pigeons and scrub turkeys edged a river. East, the Mew River's upper reaches carried luxuriant rainforest and 'beautiful palms', but lower down 'grassy sloping meadows' rose to 'flanking ridges' 'covered with dense scrub occasionally extending in struggling patches down to the water, and forming a kind of imperfect natural fence'. Downriver lay 'open forest land, or nearly level and thinly wooded country covered with tall coarse grass'. West to Cape York were 'low wooded hills alternating with small valleys and plains of greater extent', and behind the coast, 'where the country is flat, there is usually a narrow belt of dense brush or jungle'.[97]

These templates ran right along Cape York's east coast (pictures 44–5). Their managers knew what they were doing. Behind Evans Bay on 1 December 1849, 'observing that the grass had been burnt on portions of the flats the Blacks said that the rain that was coming on would make the young grass spring up and that would bring down the kangaroos and the Blacks would spear them from the scrub'.[98]

Albany, 25 December 1826

At Somerset newcomers killed people;[99] at Albany officials got to know an independent people better than anywhere in Australia, learning who could burn, and when.

The land was 'low and beautifull covered with woods & frequent natural meadows'.[100] South from King River was 'a pretty extensive wood in wh I observd the largest trees I had seen . . . we enterd on an extensive plain . . . Having crossed this we again enterd a wood & crossing several swampy meadows we arrived . . . on the banks of a little lagoon or Pond [Lake Seppings?].'[101] The Kalgan's banks were 'here and there bordered with extensive plains and meadows . . . a little way off . . . [was] a thick wood . . . without any underwood . . . We seldom met with these trees or the other gum plants anywhere about the Sound without observing their stems burnt or scorshed [sic] with fire.'[102]

Fire was universal: 'we did not see a spot which had not ... felt its effects', but cool: 'the largest of the trees had been burnt, though slightly',[103] and burnt 'in consecutive portions'.[104] People used fire to make grass, to ambush wallaby plunging from the smoke and, like central desert people, to 'walk over the ashes in search of lizards and snakes'.[105] They burnt mostly in summer (ch 6), 'the fishing season', when inland friends came to stay. In winter they went inland, implying that inlanders burnt then.[106] This let both peoples exploit and rest their country in turn. In mid-winter 1828 people were

> anxious we shd go to see a part of the Country by them called Mordellawa, lying N.N.W. about fifty Miles from us. They say that, after the third day's march, we shall come to abundance of grass, the trees very large, great quantities of Kangaroo, Emu and Birds that, from their description, I take to be Bustards; we shall pass a river running to the Westward and also a lake ... in the Summer time, 'when water becomes scarse [sic]' they [the inlanders] retire [there].[107] [108]

Country was allocated (ch 5). 'Each tribe occupies a large and determinate tract, which is subdivided into smaller portions as hunting-grounds for individuals, who jealously watch over, and instantly retaliate encroachment upon their shares.'[109] Backhouse was told,

> in the Swan River Country, as well as at King Georges Sound, the Natives have their private property, clearly distinguished into hunting-grounds, the boundaries of which are definite, trees being often recognized by them as landmarks ... possession rests in the head of a family. Several of these families residing in a district, form what the white people call a Tribe; but these tribes are not subject to any recognized chief, though a man of prowess will often gain great ascendancy among them.[110]

Nind observed,

> the natives who live together have the exclusive right of fishing or hunting upon ... [their] grounds, which are, in fact, divided into

individual properties; the quantity of land owned by each individual being very considerable. Yet it is not so exclusively his, but others of his family have certain rights over it; so that it may be considered as partly belonging to the tribe. Thus all of them have a right to break down grass trees, kill bandicoots, lizards, and other animals, and dig up roots; but the presence of the owner of the ground is considered necessary when they fire the country for game.[111]

Barker reported,

> Nakinah & several others asked for a boat to put them across to burn for Wallabi at Bald Head. He did not know the exact day as it depended on Coolbun's arrival, whose ground it was, & their starting there without him would be considered stealing . . . They also required his presence or permission now to burn at King George, as since Dr Uredale's death it had become his property. They might kill Wallabi but not burn for them. They were joking with each other on the consequences of having burnt for Wallabi yesterday on some of Maragnan's Ground & talked laughingly of his spearing some of them for it. Females never possess ground . . . If a man dies without leaving sons, or males of his family, his next neighbours have his ground. Certain parts are often portioned out to sons as soon as they are born, but they do not enjoy possession until they are grown up & able to use it.[112]

The English settled in Nakinah's country, an extensive estate, 6000 square kilometres by one estimate, which on his death passed by Law to Mokare. 'Mokare and his brothers were often troubled by poachers', WC Ferguson found,

> Not that hunting wallaby was generally considered a violation of the owners' rights. Other Aborigines, close neighbours and those linked by kinship, had some acknowledged rights on the estate, one of which was hunting wallaby. Problems arose, however, because wallaby hid in the dense thickets. This made them difficult to spear unless fire was used to drive them towards the hunters, and it was strictly forbidden to set fire to the bush without the participation or the express permission of the owner. When exuberant groups of hunters overlooked this restriction,

heated exchanges of words or blows could follow. The family was very precise about what of the estate it wanted burned, and when.[113] [114]

At Albany and across Australia, Sylvia Hallam neatly reflects the importance of templates:

> Aboriginal Australian people, through a long prehistory, used fire as a tool to create, conserve and exploit *fine-grained habitat mosaics*; thus increasing bio-diversity and developing a raised carrying capacity; allowing increased human numbers; leading to further diversified and intensified usage, in a positive feedback spiral; and/or to mechanisms of demographic restraint.[115]

This was not all, and not central in 1788. The land was no passive space, but the Dreaming's timeless gift, wondrous bounty, and ageless duty. It was alive, giving, receiving, teaching, correcting, balancing. People loved its beauty, generosity and wisdom. Dalrymple wrote lyrically of country inland of Cardwell:

> Passing through rather dense and lofty forest for about 6 miles, we entered a very beautiful tract of rich country, of limited extent, openly timbered ridges descending from the range into small rich plains and forest glades, intersected with many clear running stony streams, all joining a small rapid river (which I have named the Marlow), its banks clothed with dense lofty jungle, a mass of creeping vines, palms, &c. At the head of the valley, where it was surrounded by almost an amphitheatre of precipitous mountains, the river fell from the crest of the range in a fine cascade into the woodlands below. A broad, hard-beaten path of the blacks led us into this retreat, where small verdant plains, bounded and broken by clumps of vine, jungle, and fig-trees, varied by the fresh, bright green of groves or single trees of the wild banana, and the tall, graceful stems of the Seaforthia elegans [Solitaire] palm, half completed the delusion that we were entering one of the beautiful mountain villages of Ceylon or of the islands of the Pacific.[116]

No chance of Nature, no careless hand, no random fire, could make so rich a paradise.[117]

9

A capital tour

Until 1788 almost no-one in Australia imagined attack from the sea. Sea and shore belonged to the Dreaming, eternal eddies. Only in Sydney and Adelaide did any invader attempt to understand this or any aspect of 1788 life, but the land that newcomers took tells much about the people who made it, while fire and no fire patterned country in ways which influenced where newcomers settled. In this way, sometimes slightly, sometimes clearly, the people of 1788 shaped the layout of Australia's capital cities.

Capital sites had two primary needs: a port, and fresh water. It was an elusive combination. The need for water pushed all but Darwin onto streams slightly inland, like the great British ports. All these streams were shallow, some of them mere chains of ponds. They served not because their supply was good, but because it was worse elsewhere. This obliged all but Perth to reject earlier sites, and Brisbane, Perth, Adelaide and Melbourne to separate port and capital. Even so, every capital was soon pressed by want of water, and still is. All had swamps, springs, soaks and wetlands, but by 'fresh' newcomers meant 'running', for them and for their mills, tanneries, breweries and other improving enterprises. Few liked swamps, many despised them, none knew how to care for them. What people until 1788 prized most, the newcomers prized least. Sometimes deliberately, sometimes not, as soon as they landed they began to destroy.

Sydney, 26 January 1788
Below the Archibald Fountain in Hyde Park a spring percolated through sandstone into a small marsh, then trickled west and north down a gully to a cove west of Bridge and Pitt streets. In flood it sprayed mud flats there, but usually it had only a small flow, and in drought it dried up. Newcomers called it the Tank Stream, because they

cut a water tank in it. Fresh water was precious in this porous sandstone, and until 1788 people sheltered the creek with tiers of foliage, many with edible leaves, berries or fruit. Banksias and acacias below giant Scribbly Gum, Red Bloodwood or Sydney Red Gum gave an outer shield. Inside, orchids, lilies, herbs and a 'fairy dell of wild flowers and ferns' flourished beneath Cabbage and other palms and a damp-loving scrub of melaleuca, kunzea and leptospermum. Fire welcoming and fire sensitive plants grew together. Few fires came, but perhaps every 4–5 years careful cool burns, probably in winter, kept these unlikely companions side by side.

About 350 metres from the cove, just where it was easiest to maintain such lush vegetation, it gave way to a gum grove and a camp. Newcomers recorded the cove's name as Warrang, from *ngurrung*, camp, and found scatters of stone tools and chips at Angel Place, off Pitt Street.[1] 'Along shore was all bushes', Jacob Nagle wrote, 'but a small distance at the head of the cove was level, and large trees but scattering, and no under wood worth mentioning, and a run of fresh water.' The grove was burnt more often than up the creek, perhaps in late winter for it was a summer camp, close to fish when the harbour water was warm.[2]

From the head of the cove, mud flats grew mangroves until rocks blocked their advance, then gave way east to saltpans and thin sand beaches until more rocks at Bennelong Point, and west to sand beaches, rocks, and a small creek. The sea bed shelved steeply, letting ships close inshore. As well as 'Wild Spinage, Samphire & other leaves of Bushes which we used as Vegetables', the cove sheltered fish, prawns, mangrove crabs, lobsters, mussels and rock oysters. In the clean water the rock oysters were famed before and after 1788. 'All the rocks near the water are thick cover'd with oysters...', Arthur Bowes Smyth wrote two days after arriving, 'very small but very finely flavour'd; they also adhere to the branches of the mangrove trees'.[3] William Bradley thought the oysters 'very large'.[4]

Sydney is often described as thickly timbered in 1788, and superficially it was: a 'very thick wood', 'very considerable in size, and grows to a great height before it puts out any branches', a sure sign of close growth. But this description misses the subtleties of its management. At Sydney 'the trees stood more apart, and were less incumbered with underwood than in many other places'.[5] This was most obvious east of the creek, where the ground rose with no or little undergrowth and big fire-scarred trees to a crest along Macquarie Street. On this slope the senior officers settled themselves and the women convicts, and it remains a government centre. West of the creek was land steep and scrubby, burnt less often but more intensely, probably in summer. The marines, male convicts and at a distance the hospital were put on its lower slopes. It became the

Rocks, Sydney's sea-trade hub, and remains a commercial centre. Thus the Sydney families broadly shaped the city that displaced them.

Among the trees were clearings with fire ash: 'here & there a small space of Clear Ground where the soil in General is a Black Mould Mixd with sand'. Phillip described

> the close and perplexed growing of the trees, interrupted now and then by barren spots, bare rocks, or spaces overgrown with weeds, flowers, flowering shrubs, or underwood, scattered and intermingled in the most promiscuous manner . . . tents . . . are pitched, or huts . . . erected . . . wherever chance presents a spot tolerably free from obstacles, or more easily cleared than the rest.[6]

Maps locating those tents and huts imply where 'tolerably free' spots were, even though the newcomers began clearing as soon as they landed. The land at the creek mouth included clearings, and the newcomers at once took them over, including for gardens. At Bennelong Point the tree 'scattering' was enough to make a 'little pasturage', and three days after the newcomers swarmed ashore they put their stock there, and named it Cattle Point.[7]

Dense unbroken forest would have kept kangaroos away, but they were there. 'A herd of 11 Kangaroos were this day started near the Camp', Smyth wrote on 15 February, and in May Phillip reported, 'Kangaroos were frequently seen, but very shy, and it is a little extraordinary that more of these animals are seen near the camp than in any other part of the country, notwithstanding they are fired at almost daily.'[8] They had few places to go: grass kept most of them by the Kangaroo Ground, 'a narrow strip' from Leichhardt–Petersham across the watershed between Port Jackson and Botany Bay near Sydney University. David Collins thought its soil 'much better for agriculture' than at Sydney; Tench thought it better than anywhere between Broken Bay and Botany Bay. Good soil meant grass, and grass meant fire.[9]

Fire did more. Ralph Clark found not 'one tree out of fifty but what is burnt'—'with the lightning' he added, forgivably.[10] Phillip reported in 1790, 'My intentions of turning the swine into the woods to breed have been prevented by the natives so frequently setting fire to the country.'[11] Others reported many fires, but almost none were big, almost all burnt patches, none threatened. On North Head in early winter George Worgan saw

> a great Fire; we found it to be the burning of a Heathy brush-wood, which we supposed the Natives had set on Fire for some Purpose, but what,

> we could not Conjecture. We observed likewise, Fires of this Nature, in several other Parts of the Country ... whenever the Wind blows strong, there are a Number of these kinds of Fires about the Country.[12]

Heath needs 6–8 years to recover, so was burnt no more than once a decade. Fires to clear undergrowth were lit every 2–4 years on good soil, less often on sandstone. Fires to promote undergrowth were lit perhaps once a decade plus rare clean-up fires, depending on the soil and the plants. On Brickfield Hill, for example, where 'trees of an immense size' with 'lofty and wide spreading Branches' (flagging that fire had opened them) stood over 'underwood ... mostly of flowering shrubs'.[13] People managed very locally, even burning single trees.[14] No newcomer reported the big killer fires typifying Sydney's margins today.[15]

East, in Farm Cove, trees stood 'at a considerable distance from each other'.[16] Phillip began a farm there: the Botanic Gardens displays the site. Below it, about today's ponds, people held Kangaroo and Dog dances.[17] Was Sydney Cove a rest camp for Farm Cove ceremonies? Towards the Heads the land was burnt much as at Sydney. The first impression was of big trees. 'The necks of land that form the coves are mostly covered with timber, yet so rocky that it is not easy to comprehend how the trees could have found sufficient nourishment to bring them to so considerable a magnitude.'[18] Yet there were many clearings, 'many spots of tolerably good land, but they are in general of but small extent'.[19] On 26 January Smyth rejoiced,

> To describe the beautiful and novel appearance of the different coves and islands as we sail'd up is a task I shall not undertake ... Suffice it to say that the finest terras's, lawns, and grottos, with distinct plantations of the tallest and most stately trees I ever saw in any nobleman's grounds in England, cannot excel in beauty those w'h nature now presented to our view.[20]

Worgan thought Port Jackson

> suggests to the Imagination Ideas of luxuriant Vegetation and rural Scenery, consisting of gentle risings & Depressions, beautifully clothed with [a] variety of Verdures of Evergreens, forming dense Thickets, & lofty Trees appearing above these again, and now & then a pleasant checquered Glade opens to your View ... [or] a soft vivid-green, shady Lawn attracts your Eye.[21]

In 1790 Daniel Southwell wrote that the 'ground for a good space' about Watson's Bay 'is unusually clear, with here and there a shrub, and at a dist. in passing looks like a pleasant lawn'.[22] Lycett's *View of the Heads* (c1821) shows 'lawns' on the harbour side at Watson's Bay and the coast side near The Gap, split by dense forest or scrub. Above Parsley Bay, von Guerard's *Sydney Heads* (1859–66) depicts a steep grass slope and a grass neck ringed by scrub—a kangaroo trap. Seaward, Camp Cove carried grass trees. They need fire to flower.

'Between Sydney Cove and Botany Bay, the first space is occupied by a wood, in some parts a mile and a half, in others three miles across; beyond that, is a kind of heath, poor, sandy, and full of swamps.'[23] '[S]ome parts appear'd barren, others pleasant Downes . . . [one had] a remarkable clump of trees on it; The land over the sandy bays is in general woody, as is a very considerable part of the higher lands.'[24] Perhaps Worgan had this district in mind when he told his brother,

> Though we meet with, in many parts, a fine Black Soil, luxuriantly covered with Grass & the Trees have 30 or 40 Yards distance from each other, so as to resemble Meadow Land, yet these Spots are frequently interrupted in their extent by either a rocky, or a sandy, or a Swampy Surface, crowded with large Trees, and almost impenetrable from Brushwood which, being the Case, it will necessarily require much Time and Labour to cultivate any considerable Space of Land together.[25]

At Botany Bay the 'Shore all round is like a thick Wood & the Soil very Sandy, the Grass in most places is about 2 feet high but not thick here & There is spots of underwood The Trees are in General about 20 Yards Distance from each other.'[26]

West from Sydney Cove, the scrubby nature of the Rocks continued past Balmain, which was 'covered with a dense tea-tree scrub, through which some gum-trees straggled . . . The shores were rough and rocky, and the rocks were covered with brambles and native currants.'[27] About Drummoyne the land opened: 'the sides of this Arm are formed by gentle Slopes, which are green to the Water's edge. The Trees are small and grow almost in regular Rows, so that, together with the Evenness of the Land for a considerable Extent, it resembles a Beautiful Park . . . the Soil was extremely rich, & produced luxuriant grass.'[28]

Further west and along the coast north were more parks. Phillip followed a 'much frequented' path from Manly to Pittwater, and 'found many hundreds of acres of land, free from timber, and very fit for cultivation'.[29] Hunter found

> a very considerable extent of tolerable land, and which may be cultivated without waiting for its being cleared of wood; for the trees stand very wide of each other, and have no underwood: in short, the woods on the spot I am speaking of resemble a deer park, as much as if they had been intended for such a purpose.

Which they had, though dormant when Hunter passed: 'The grass upon it is about three feet high, very close and thick.'[30]

At the head of the harbour was Rose Hill, later Parramatta. Its parrots were called 'Rose Hillers', hence rosellas. They kept to Rose Hill's seed grasses, so were not at Sydney, habitat for scrub or heath birds like cockatoos and Turquoise and Ground Parrots.[31] Peron mentioned Rose Hill's 'large spaces between the trees, which is covered by a very fine and sweet-scented grass, that forms a beautiful verdant carpet',[32] and Bradley wrote,

> Towards the upper part of Port Jackson the Country opens & is covered with long grass growing under the trees, there are some spots of clear ground round P Jackson but none of considerable extent until near the head of it, from which, along by the flats & creeks it improves & near the fresh water at the top of the creek it is a fine open Country & good soil.

These were templates, 'open ground where the Kanguroo frequent',[33] with good soil and grass, water, spaced trees and little undergrowth.[34]

Open country continued west 'about twenty miles ... but in a north and south direction it does not extend more than three or four miles, when you come again into barren, rocky land'.[35] Phillip probed west in April 1788, strayed offline into thick scrub, went back and started again. He followed a scrub-fringed creek, then broke into grass with many paths, 'in general entirely free from underwood, which was confined to the stony and barren spots'—grass on good soil, scrub on bad. He followed this 'beautiful' country to Prospect Hill, which 'might be cultivated with ease'. It already was, for yams and grass: it was Cannemegal ('fire people') country.[36] 'In all the country thro' which I have passed', Phillip noted, 'I have seldom gone a quarter of a mile without seeing trees which appear to have been destroyed by fire.'[37] Worgan noticed:

> in our Excursions Inland ... we have met with a great Extent of Park-like Country and the Trees of a moderate Size at a moderate Distance from each other, the Soil, apparently, fitted to produce any kind of Grain,

and clothed with extraordinarily luxuriant Grass ... It is something singular, that all, of this kind of Trees, and many others, appear to have been partly burnt, the Bark of them being like Charcoal.[38]

A road soon ran from Sydney past Parramatta to Prospect Hill and north to the Hawkesbury. Elizabeth Macarthur took it in 1795,

through an uninterrupted wood, with the exception of the village of Toongabie ... which we distinguish by the name of Greenlands, on account of the fine grass and there being few trees compared with the other parts of the country, which is occasionally brushy and more or less covered with underwood. The greater part of the country is like an English park, and the trees give to it the appearance of a wilderness, or shrubbery commonly attached to the houses of people of fortune, filled with a variety of native plants, placed in a wild, irregular manner.[39]

The Hawkesbury had rich swamps, and 'abounded' in swans, ducks, quail, small birds[40] and yams. Yams signalled open, tilled ground. Colonists took it for small farms (ch 4).[41]

Port Jackson had many resources. Of food alone, settlers named kangaroo, emu, possum, glider, echidna, goanna, swan, duck, parrot, fruit, berries and 'fern and another root', 'all of which are in abundance'.[42] This missed much of what harbour families ate, even on land, yet they were water people. They 'depend for food on the few fruits they gather; the roots they dig up in the swamps; and the fish they pick up along the shore, or contrive to strike from their canoes with spears', Tench observed. 'Fishing, indeed, seems to engross nearly the whole of their time, probably from its forming the chief part of [their] subsistence.'[43] The harbour was

Tolerably well stocked with fish some of them Very Good. The Natives ... do not seem to live in Community, but by separate familys in Caves & Hollows of the Rocks & As far as we know live only on fish & the Root of the Fern which Grows here in Plenty—they dive for fish & Oysters with Great Dexterity.[44]

Each family, perhaps one or two to a cove, shared its land and water, with clan help for big works and ceremonies.

Coves seem designed to offer a seafood specialty each. Some families or clans took their name from this (*burramatta* eel, *wallumede* snapper, *cadi* reed spear), together mapping a connected complex of resources. East, the head of Farm Cove had mangroves, Woolloomooloo and Elizabeth Bays deep water for fish, rays and sharks, Rushcutter's Bay reeds for fish, crabs, prawns, shellfish, waterbirds and eggs. West, Cockle Bay's shell heaps were so big that the newcomers burnt them for lime. Balmain's bays were home to the Balmain Bug, still a delicacy. West to Homebush and Parramatta tidal mangrove flats gave way to clear, spear-fishing water. The north shore was similarly diverse: oysters in Middle Harbour, crabs at The Spit, water clear to the bottom.[45]

Across this clear water the strangers came. On 22 January 1788, while their ships waited in Botany Bay, the first of them rowed in, sea birds seeking to settle. They chose Warrang, the cove with the best water.

> We got into Port Jackson early in the afternoon, and had the satisfaction of finding the finest harbour in the world, in which a thousand sail of the line may ride in the most perfect security ... The different coves were examined with all possible expedition. I fixed on the one that had the best spring of water, and in which the ships can anchor so close to the shore that at a very small expence quays may be made at which the largest ships may unload. This cove ... I honoured with the name Sydney.[46]

They reported no people, but at Manly a 'party of natives' had appeared. Cautious but fearless, and 'very vociferous', they accepted the offerings every visitor should make.[47] They had not yet heard from Botany Bay, where these same intruders had begun plundering as soon as they landed, and were already unwelcome. There the 'Natives were well pleas'd with our People until they began clearing the Ground at which they were displeased & wanted them to be gone', Bradley wrote, and Worgan remarked that they 'expressed a little Anger at seeing us cut down the Trees, but it was only by jabbering very fast & loud'.[48] His contempt was ominous.

The First Fleet was a great achievement. In 257 days six convict transports, three store ships and two warships carried 1057 people, 44 sheep, 32 pigs, seven horses, six cattle, dogs, cats, poultry and Australia's first houseflies, all unwanted, across half the globe. No other nation could have done it. Few had the ships, none the stores. The Royal Navy victualled the Fleet not only for the voyage, but for a year after. This matched landing a man on the moon, and it seemed something like it to the people of

1788. Some of them stored, but their mobility meant that none depended on it. Now came people who combined mobility and storing. It was a lethal combination.

Hobart, 20 February 1804

Even from the sea, the land approaching Hobart advertised how carefully it was made. To Abel Tasman in 1642, it was 'widely provided with trees, which stand so, that men may pass through everywhere, and see far from them . . . unimpeded from thick dense forest or thicket'.[49] In the Derwent estuary David Collins noted,

> All the hills are very thinly set with light timber, chiefly short she oaks; but are admirably covered with thick nutritious grass, in general free from brush or patches of shrubs. The soil in which it grows is a black vegetable mould, deep only in the valleys, frequently very shallow, with occasionally a small mixture of sand or small stones. The shore on the east side of the river, proceeding up, is covered with a good but shallow soil, and lightly wooded.[50]

Around Mt Rumney Flinders marked 'Pasturage' in 1799, and in 1836 Darwin described the mountains as 'covered with a light wood'.[51] Hobart's forests today are not 'thinly set'.

Bligh saw how the woods were made. 'The country looked in all parts pleasant and covered with wood. We saw numerous fires as if the country was fuller of inhabitants than has hitherto been supposed, and particularly about the shore of the Table Mountain [Mt Wellington] . . . certainly the finest part of the country.'[52] This was February, high summer and the month of Hobart's most terrible fires in 1967, yet Bligh saw no conflagration but 'numerous fires'. Peron watched astonished a

> multiplicity of fires . . . In every direction immense columns of flame and smoke arose; all the opposite sides of the mountains . . . were burning for an extent of several leagues. Thus were destroyed these ancient and venerable forests, which the scythe of time had respected throughout the course of so many centuries, only to fall a sacrifice to the destructive instinct of their ferocious inhabitants.[53]

We know too well now that hot fires link up, yet Peron reported not one fire but many, and of course the forests were not destroyed. People burnt into March, until valley and hill were 'much burnt',[54] but they did not fear the flames, as we do.

Storm Bay guards the Derwent, and storms pushed port-seekers to its head. On 12 September 1803 they came to Risdon Cove. Collins wrote,

> The land at the head of Risdon creek, on the east side, seems preferable to any other on the banks of the Derwent. The creek runs winding between two steep hills, and ends in a chain of ponds that extends into a fertile valley of great beauty. For half a mile above the head of the creek, the valley is contracted and narrow; but the soil is extremely rich, and the fields are well covered with grass. Beyond this it suddenly expands, and becomes broad and flat at the bottom, whence arise long grassy slopes, that by a gentle but increasing ascent continue to mount the hills on each side, until they are hidden from the view by the woods of large timber which overhang their summits. With this handsome disposition of the ground, the valley extends several miles to the SE in the figure of a small segment of a circle. The tops of its hills, though stony, produce abundance of tall timber, which, as it descends the slopes, diminishes in size, and thins off to a few scattered she oaks and gum trees, interspersed with small coppices of the beautiful flowering fern. The soil along the bottom, and to some distance up the slopes, is a rich vegetable mould, apparently hardened by a small mixture of clay, which grows a large quantity of thick, juicy grass, and some few patches of close underwood.[55]

Grass on good valley soil, timber on crests younger as it descends, ferns and flowers amid fire-prone trees. This was a template. The creek mouth was a swamp in a grassy flat, sheltering birds, eggs, reeds, roots, tubers and wallaby. A steep slope edged it, mostly timbered, but towards the creek a narrow grass strip led up to a flattish plateau. On the creek side the plateau fell to a half-basin of about 30 acres which sat like a giant armchair above a steep cliff. People could trap wallaby against the cliff, or spear them from the plateau's timber edge, or drive them down into the armchair and over the cliff to hunters below, then run round to join the kill. Perhaps they were doing this on that day in May 1804 when the British saw them running down, and shot many. Edward White, the most reliable witness to the killings, was on the plateau when he saw '300 natives, men, women and children, coming down the valley in a circular, or, rather, a semi-circular form, with a flock of kangaroo between them. They had no spears, but were armed with waddies only, and were driving the kangaroo.'[56] [57]

In February 1804 the British moved down to Sullivan's Cove, for fresh water, a port, and a secure convict camp on Hunter Island.[58] From Mt Wellington a creek ran into the cove, in 'many places . . . dammed back, and spread out into marshes covered with rushes and water', and reaching the cove through 'a dense tangle of tea-tree scrub and fallen logs, surmounted by huge gum trees'.[59] The dams may have been deliberate. The scrub was denser than along the Tank Stream, but off the creek soon met grassy forest.

Behind a sandy beach south of the creek, samphire flats rose slightly to a 'plain extensive' with grassy forest and little or no undergrowth,[60] the land 'good and the trees very excellent . . . well calculated in every degree for a settlement'.[61] Convicts were put on the flats and Hunter Island, soon Hobart's commercial district. As at Sydney the officers chose the commanding slope southwest, still a government and cultural centre. Open forest rose to Mt Wellington. 'The Land here is good in some patches of no great extent', Meehan stated, 'Is Gently rising to a ridge of hills . . . There is a good Quantity of good pasturage on the sides of these hills.'[62] Near the 'high Platform Mountain', Peron remarked, the 'forests . . . are much less dense than in the Channel itself, and moreover they appeared to have been devastated by fire'.[63] The forest thickened higher up: amid dense underwood, giant eucalypts were 'all streight [sic] and not branched out till near the top'.[64] George Harris noted the change:

> The Shores rise gradually into hills covered with fine Grass & noble Trees . . . The Town is built on a fine gently rising plain, on the back of which are a succession of hills rising until they are terminated by Table Mountain . . . The hills & sides of Table Mountain are covered with immense Trees . . . some . . . of an incredible size.[65]

One was 44 feet round breast high, another 70 feet. They had welcomed centuries of fire, yet amid them were rainforest patches and wet gullies of Sassafras, tree fern and vine. No conflagrations sheet-burnt Mt Wellington.[66]

Upriver, grass plains lay in open forest, as at Sydney. King George's Plains at Glenorchy, 'very fine', the nearest to the Mount about 300 acres, tracked the Derwent north.[67] Near New Norfolk 'the country formed a series of downs, in general so thinly sprinkled with trees, that it resembled a noble park, in which one would hardly wish to fell a tree, save an occasional unsightly Eucalyptus: the Acacias, too, were in full flower, and the fragrance exhaled by them was delicious'.[68] Then came 'Gentle hills almost bare of Trees & the Vallies narrow & Covered with Trees'.[69] Macquarie Plains were extensive with abundant kangaroos, emus and pigeons, and 'not more Timber than would adorn a Park anywhere'.[70] Lycett's *The Table Mountain from the end of Jericho Plains* (c1820) shows a plain scattered with trees and ringed by forest, just as James Ross described it.[71] 'In the borders of all these Plains', Lycett remarked, 'Kangaroos and Emus are numerous... The Bush abounds with Parrots, Paroquets, Cockatoos, and Pigeons and Wild Ducks frequent the Ponds and Rivulets.'[72]

The estuary's east side was similarly patterned. Near its head were 'extensive plains interspersed with Gentle Grassy Hills... Very good pasturage', and '*fifty thousand* Swans in a flock'.[73] At Herdsman's Cove, aptly named, the 'Banks are more like a Nobleman's Park in England than an uncultivated country; every part is beautifully Green and very little trouble might clear every Valley I have seen in a Month... in many places the plough might be used immediately.'[74] Edging this cove, Green Point was grass, possibly a kangaroo trap. Towards Risdon the land was 'unusually thin of timber', with 'grassy hills'.[75] East, near Buckland, the hills were 'mostly of a Beautiful verdure with some patches nearly clear of Timber'.[76] On Kangaroo Point at Bellerive, grass–forest edges on good soil near the water lay below denser timber on higher ground sometimes open, sometimes scrubby. Middens and shell piles fringed the estuary.

Eleven thousand years of water separated Sydney from Hobart, but their patterns were alike. At Hobart as at Sydney much land was unnaturally open, the 'most beautiful & romantic Country I ever beheld...', Harris told his mother,

> plenty of fresh water & immense forests of astonishing large trees fit for every purpose... The Woods abound with Kangaroos and Emus... Duck & Teal are in great plenty and Swans in such astonishing Numbers, that a Boat has taken 150 in a Day by running them down.[77]

'We no sooner doubled the point formed by the great hill', Peron wrote off Sandy Bay, 'than we observed a prodigious number of black swans—the river was in fact covered with them.'[78] Had it not been so, had it not been so well managed, had there been no templates, the invaders might not have come.

Brisbane, May 1825

Like most 1788 rivers, the Brisbane was fordable in places, letting people manage both sides as one. It paraded a profusion of plants. From its mouth in Moreton Bay, the south bank was 'covered with thick Vine and Mangrove scrubs, the banks steep and muddy of alluvial soil, the land a little distance from the river is an open undulating well watered, and good country, with timber of all varietys'.[79] Along the first reach this was broadly true of the north bank, until about the golf course small salt creeks ran through a kilometre of scrub into tidal flats. Three small clearings lay in the scrub, which gave way east to a swamp, and north at the airport to part swampy, part open land, probably flood prone, but with three small tree clumps.[80]

West, the scrub abruptly became 'open forest' of ironbark and gum extending north to where Kedron Brook spread into swamp, and west towards Breakfast Creek. About Albion Park Racecourse the forest stopped at a 'lagoon' flanked by 'vine brush' enclosing a grassy clearing, perhaps a place of significance. Allan Cunningham chanced on the spot: 'Numerous were the beaten paths of the wild aborigine. His several fireplaces showed me that this part of the River was numerously inhabited.'[81] Brush and lagoon then met a narrow eucalypt strip edging Breakfast Creek: Sandgate Road roughly follows its edge. Distinct fires associated these unlike neighbours. Breakfast Creek's south bank was open forest of 'tolerable pasturage', broken by a small brush patch a kilometre or so upstream. Open forest then ringed a tea-tree and mangrove swamp filling the creek's loop at Mayne. About Burrows Street a fish trap bridged the creek, and there and upstream the land was 'fine open forest good pasture'. About where the creek becomes Enoggera Creek, alternate swamp, eucalypt forest, grass and brush patches flanked both banks. 'Rich pasture', Henry Wade wrote in 1844 of grass pockets in brush and swamp in now-gone meanders between Bowen and Normanby bridges.[82]

From Enoggera Creek northeast to Nundah Creek and north to Kedron Brook the 'ranges' were not yet surveyed, but Nundah Creek was 'in some parts very open & in others rather brushy. Near to the creek the soil is very superior.' The brook threaded swamps and 'good open forest land until the ridge at the back is met where it is a stoney grass tree country. The timber is various—Oak Gum and Stringy and Iron Bark with a good quantity of apple Tree and some honeysuckle. The bed of the creek is stoney and fish are found in it.'[83]

Upriver from Breakfast Creek, 'open undulating forest' was varied by swamps, small creeks, grass patches and at Teneriffe a 'barren stoney ridge'. Above it dense brush fringed the river, Hoop Pine topping a cascade of vines, Red Cedar, Silky Oak, Tulipwood, fig and other dry rainforest trees. The fringe continued past Story Bridge, while inland from Teneriffe a 'timber' belt with 'good pasturage' stretched to the bridge. Upstream, two long reaches circled a ridge 15–30 metres high, from which ran two small, reedy creeks or chains of ponds. Oxley remarked that the vicinity was 'low land gradually rising'.[84] 'On the banks, Pine trees on both sides', Edmund Lockyer noted in 1825, 'The Indian Fig tree—blue gum, swamp oak, Iron bark, and occasionally thick brush.' There were also edible yams.[85] This ridge, with its mix of fire tolerant and fire sensitive plants and a swamp on the Botanic Gardens site, became Brisbane.

From Milton up to Toowong was 'a magnificent crescent' of 'principally open forest, not reaching far, beyond which it is clothed with pine brushes'.[86] Next the banks became brush-lined with fine Hoop Pine, then right up to Goodna 'alternately brushy or densely overhung with a matted or tressed mass of vegetation and the open Forest land, abundance of pine existing in the former'. Inland, from Brisbane to Mt Coot-tha, the land was

> hilly, sterile, and devoid of interest. On ascending the high ground, the soil and grass improve, and continue to do so till the very summit of the range, which is clothed with [trees] . . . The view from south-east to north-west was extensive and very grand, presenting an immense, thinly wooded plain, whose surface was gently undulated, and clothed with luxuriant grass.[87]

Along the south bank opposite New Farm, brush traced the river and Norman's Creek up to the Grammar School. Off-river west between hills, a 'poor flat country' of 'open woodland' ran to a 'bold rocky ridge' on the river above Kangaroo Point. 'Poor stoney ranges' dominated South Brisbane, but at Victoria Bridge the river could be waded, and newcomers caught bagfuls of fish by hand. Nearby were several ceremonial grounds: then as now South Bank was a cultural centre. Along Montague Road a creek parallel to the river was enclosed by a narrow strip of 'rich scrubby land' as far as Hill End, much like the Tank Stream and Hobart Rivulet. It

> was a tangled mass of trees, vines, flowering creepers, staghorns, elkhorns, towering scrub palms, giant ferns, and hundreds of other varieties of the fern family, beautiful and rare orchids, and the wild passion-flower, while along the river bank were the waterlily in thousands, and the convolvulus of gorgeous hue.

It covered hill and flat, but was pocked by small clearings and, along a sharp boundary 300–500 metres from the river, gave way to country part open and part 'rather heavily timbered' with eucalypts and casuarinas.[88]

Similarly varied country lay around Oxley Creek:

> a tract of land formed of alternate strips of Tea Tree . . . Swamp and Sandy Forest Land covered with Banksias . . . Forest Oak . . . and

stunted Gums. The Creek having taken a sudden turn to the Eastward we were obliged to ascend a low range of Hills, having on our left, some beautiful flats of rich land. This range is formed of light sandy Soil but is covered with a good sward of grass. On it I observed an extensive Native encampment.[89]

Upriver, Chelmer was 'Rich Land', Fig Tree Pocket 'Rich Flats & Fine Timber', Kenmore 'GOOD open Grazing'.[90] At Westlake Oxley climbed Green Hill and saw southwest 'immense extended *Plains*, of low undulating hills and vales, well but not heavily wooded'.[91] At Wacol–Moggill open plains backed the flats.

Further up the land opened even more, as fire made grass king:

> The wood on the banks—fig-tree, blue gum, swamp oak, and ironbark, for the last half distance no pines, but here and there a solitary cedar. On landing, found spinach in great abundance, mint, parsley and the wild poppy . . . the country . . . delightful, thinly wooded, to a great extent fine pasturage . . . and only occasionally thick brush . . . very high grass of the oat species [Kangaroo Grass]; very few pines.

Then came 'hills beautifully covered with pine trees of a large size, the banks as before with swamp oak, honey-suckle, blue gum and ironbark . . . quite a park-like appearance . . . kangaroos in abundance'.[92] At Bremer Creek,

> the change in the character of the Country is very apparent, the country on each side is of the richest description, thinly timbered, and abundantly watered, that on the left is formed of gentle declining flats . . . of the richest Black Loam, covered with an extraordinary Species of Angofera, and an unpublished species of Zanthorfea [Xanthorrhoea] which obtains the height of Twenty Feet, averaging not more than 15 trees to an acre.[93]

Along the creek lay

> a large open country with scarcely any wood of consequence to impede cultivation upon it. The trees, chiefly blue gum, being at least an acre or more apart, and more ornamental than otherwise. The natives had lately set fire to the long grass, and the new grass was just above

ground, making this plain appear like a bowling green; the soil rich beyond any idea . . . plenty of kangaroos and wild turkeys.[94]

These were early summer fires to make grass, but rainforest ('brush') patches survived. Oxley mapped Bremer Creek up to Limestone Station (Ipswich) then north back to the river, noting alternate brush, open forest, dense forest and grass.[95] Similar country lay upriver. At Fairneyview the land was 'very good on both sides, soil good; walked up the hills, the country behind them having quite a park-like appearance . . . Kangaroos in abundance, but they were extremely shy'.[96] Opposite Lockyer's Creek an 'extensive level forest country' held 'patches of brush' and two plains by a swamp, with a belt of forest between.[97]

Without fire most of Brisbane is naturally rainforest. 'It looked as though some race of men had been here before us, and planted this veritable garden of Eden,' one of the first convicts to see it recalled. 'Skirting the water for miles on each side was dense vine-clad jungle, festooned with the blue and purple convolvulus, while on the tidal brink grew the beautiful salt-water lily—its flowers white as alabaster, its glorious perfume filling the air with fragrance.'[98] Brush was especially dense along water, but not only there, and not always there.

People changed the country precisely and locally. Their sharp-edged fires put an immense diversity of plants and animals within easy reach of every family. They accepted brush on banks and alluvials, but threaded it with open forest and clearings. They accepted stony hills but made them grass or 'barren' forest. They welcomed swamps but alternated their edges with eucalypts, grass, and brush. They put grass patches in forest and tree clumps in open country. 'The face of the country is very beautiful, consisting of green hills thinly wooded, interspersed with a flat country; also, thinly but fairly wooded; also, occasionally hills, with thick brush and pine trees,' Lockyer reported.[99] 'The country in the vicinity of the Brisbane River . . . is variegated by brush land of exuberant richness, clear alluvial plains of the greatest fertility, and good grassy park-like forest land,' Hodgkinson stated in 1841.[100] The land was minutely made, integrated from family to family, planned to ensure abundance and maintain the Dreaming, patterned for beauty and variety.

Oxley thought it so. He came on the river on 2 December 1823, followed it up, and along the first reach found scenery 'peculiarly beautiful . . . the Soil of the finest description of Brush woodland, on which grew Timber of great magnitude . . . The Timber on the hills was also good.' At Hamilton he noted 'Rich Flats and Fine Timber', and at Breakfast Creek 'Fine open Grazing Country'. He named the river the Brisbane, and concluded,

'I think a permanent Settlement would be more advantageously formed on the West Side of the River at the Termination of Sea Reach [Breakfast Creek]. The River here is not fresh, but there is plenty of water, the Country open.'[101] The British were not seeking beauty and variety. They wanted a gaol, fresh water, and a port. They preferred the coast. They tested Amity Point on North Stradbroke, but in September 1824 chose Red Cliff Point. It was barely a port, it had little fresh water, and it was near two ceremonial grounds where intruders were resented. In May 1825 the newcomers moved up to Brisbane.[102]

Perth, 12 August 1829

In December 1696 Willem Vlamingh's ships stood off the Perth coast, and he saw a sight soon familiar to sailors. Smoke from many fires came like thick fog from the land. Vlamingh realised that people had lit them, and decided to catch someone to take home. A party walked inland; others rowed up a river they named the Swan, for as at Sydney and Hobart the birds were common. A ford stopped the boats at the Causeway. The water was 'a little brackish', but fresh in nearby wells. Today it is salt: the Avon and the Helena upstream flow less, and a rocky bar at the Swan mouth was removed in 1895–7, letting in the sea. The river had many fish and birds, the land was pleasant, 'open land mixed with forest', with 'millions of flies'.[103] Vlamingh caught no-one.

James Stirling established Fremantle on 1 June 1829, and Perth on 12 August, where the Causeway ford stopped him. He argued:

> a Town at the mouth of the Estuary would be requisite for landing goods and as a Port Town, while another sufficiently high on the River to afford easy communication between the Agriculturalists on the Upper Swan and the Commercial Interest at the Port would tend much to the speedy occupation of that useful District. In selecting a site for this purpose, the present position of Perth seemed to be so decidedly preferable in building materials, streams of water and facility of communication, that I was induced on these grounds to establish the Town there.[104]

His decision followed a quick trip upriver on 10–14 March 1827.[105] At Point Heathcote he found good soil and 'Many Fresh springs of water', and later put a garden there.[106] His first camp was

> a landing-place on the left shore, and in a few Minutes a blazing fire, with roasting Swans before it, shed chearfulness on our resting place;

> our dominion here however was not undisputed for [of] all places I have ever visited I think it contained the greatest number of Musquitoes. This phenomenon was easily accounted for when daylight shewed us that we had taken up our Quarters on a narrow ridge between the River and a Swamp.[107]

Probably this was Perth. Understandably they moved early, to 'a level Country 15 or 20 feet above the water, covered with bronze grass and studded by a few green trees... Swans and Ducks, which at Frazer's Point were numerous, now became still more so, and of the first kind we killed with ease as many as we wanted. Fish we saw in abundance.'[108] Upriver, beautiful grass–forest templates seemed suited to agriculture:

> On the Flats the Blue Gum Tree flourishes, but in a ratio of not more than 10 to an Acre, and they are generally unaccompanied by any other Tree or Shrub except a long leaved and beautiful Species of Acacia... [an] open forest-like character... the lowlands resemble fields of grain, for the high grass had been turned yellow by the Sun.[109]

Grass–forest belts continued to Ellen Brook (picture 35), as far as Stirling's men could row. Charles Fraser, Stirling's botanist, wrote that the country varied

> alternately, on each bank, from hilly promontories of the finest red loam and covered with stupendous Angoferas, to extensive flats of the finest description, studded with magnificent Blue and Water Gums and occasional stripes of Acacias... Plains were seen to extend to the base of the Mountains, interspersed with stripes of good forest Land.[110]

Fraser was supporting Stirling's colonial venture, so their superlatives may exaggerate, but their account of the Swan's alternating grass-forest 'stripes' is accurate enough. When James Turner went upriver to Perth in 1830, he was 'quite astonished at the splendid scenery on both sides of the river, although the soil is nothing but white sand. The foliage of the trees was exquisite and together with the many beautiful turnings in the river one might fancy themselves in fairyland.'[111] In 1838 Backhouse was more prosaic, although his comments may reflect the rapid impact of stock on sandy soil. The land below Perth was

> marked on maps 'gently undulating grassy country, thinly timbered', it is difficult to find grass upon many parts of it, but there is an abundance of

rigid herbage, chiefly of a stemless *Xanthorrhoea*, called here the Ground Blackboy, and a profusion of rigid shrubs, unfit for pasturage . . . as in other instances, the soil with the gayest productions, is the worst in quality.[112]

Above Perth the land 'improved'. The

> scenery was frequently of a beautiful description, and the banks, in many places, were composed of a rich alluvial soil, covered with excellent grass. Unfortunately, the good soil was rarely found to extend more than half a mile from the river, and often not more than fifty or a hundred yards . . . In some parts, the country was thickly clothed with forest; in others it had the appearance of a fine park, in which scarcely a tree was to be seen that one would think it necessary to destroy . . . not more than two trees to the acre . . . the country being more commonly what is denominated 'open forest', with spots where the trees are very close together.[113]

This was also true of the Canning,[114] and such was the skill of its managers that as late as 1841 the 'whole country of the middle and upper Swan resembles a vast English park'.[115]

'Perth, the intended capital, stands on a rising spot covered . . . with trees . . . The river, at this part, is about half a mile wide, or rather more, but is so shallow that it may sometimes be forded.'[116] The 'rising spot' ran down from Mt Eliza along Hay Street. Here Stirling put his camp beside a spring feeding a small creek. North lay swamps, including at Perth Station and Hyde Park. South to the river was marshy, west the timbered ridge carried springs and a camp, then rose to tree-studded land burnt for grass. Now King's Park, it was a kangaroo trap. As at Risdon, fresh pick lured mobs into a cul-de-sac, where hunters drove them down a steep drop beside the river along Mounts Bay Road to ambushers below. The Perth survivors Daisy Bates knew in 1907 were kangaroo totem people.[117] Traders as well as pastoralists, they mined high-quality ochre and sent it thousands of miles over tough country into South Australia and the Northern Territory. One pit was at Success Hill, near a spring, swamps and a ceremonial ground.[118]

Perth illustrates the value of swamps in 1788. Dozens surrounded the lower Swan, some big, some small, with tubers, roots, crayfish, mussels, birds, eggs, tortoises, snakes and goannas. Fish and eel traps threaded the water, and templates improved the land. On better alluvial soils huts stood by yam grounds,[119] and eucalypts or acacias split Kangaroo and similar grasses into plains. In late summer the grass stood tall, dense and 'bronze', looking to newcomers like a crop.[120] Yet swamps and dry, sandy soil are unlikely places for farmers. People looking inland might not have occupied them, but these settlers looked to the sea, obliging them to strike an awkward balance between a port and fresh water. This was also so of the next capital newcomers founded.[121]

Melbourne, 20 August 1835

At Queens Bridge, 8 kilometres up the Yarra, an odd feature lay in 1788: a row of basalt stones along the top of shallow falls, where people crossed the river. Newcomers assumed they were natural, and perhaps they were. Above them the river was fresh except in king tides; below was brackish. The river was deep whereas nearby creeks were at best chains of ponds, and the falls fell into a broad basin where small ships could turn. The place was literally pivotal.

It was not a port. The Yarra emptied into Port Phillip, which in 1802 Flinders thought might suit to settle. 'The country around Port Phillip has a pleasing, and in many parts a fertile appearance', he wrote, 'It is in great measure a grassy country, and capable of supporting much cattle, though better calculated for sheep.'[122] Peter Good saw why: the west side 'was an extensive plane which is chiefly rich Meadow land . . . which if it were not frequently cleared by burning would soon become impenetrable as was the case which had escaped the last conflagration . . . a few months before'.[123] This warned that perhaps the land was not so 'fertile', but in October 1803 David Collins arrived to found a settlement, and James Tuckey enthused,

> The face of the country is the most beautifully picturesque that can be imagined, swelling into gentle elevations of the brightest verdure, and dotted with trees as if planted by the hand of taste, while the ground is covered with a profusion of flowers of every colour; in short on entering the port, we looked on it as a perfect paradise and flattered ourselves into the most illusive dreams of fruitfulness and plenty.[124]

'The timber within two miles of the beach', he added, 'is generally small. In the more sandy spots, they are close, and, where the best Soil is found, they are very thinly scattered.'[125] William Crook thought the Port

> beautifully diversified with hills and dales. It is nearly covered with . . . trees . . . with grass between, and no underwood scarcely, so that some parts look like a park, others orchards, &c.; but the soil is universally

> light and sandy . . . One can scarcely walk 10 yards without meeting traces of the natives . . . Perhaps a tenth part of the trees are burnt.[126]

Later arrivals described 'a beautiful carpet, covered with grasses, herbs and flowers of various sorts—the scenery was that of an extensive park'. The head of the bay was 'enchantingly beautiful—extensive rich plains all around with gently sloping hills in the distance, all thinly wooded and having the appearance of an immense park. The grasses, flowers and herbs that cover the plains are of every variety that can be imagined.'[127] The praise paid unknowing tribute to the port's managers, for it described land carefully burnt. But there was little fresh water, and soon fires skirted the bay. On 30 January 1804 Collins left to settle Tasmania.

From Tasmania in June 1835 the next settlers came. They admired the port, but beauty would not catch them again. They wanted water and grass. At the head of the bay they went up a salt river guarded by mangroves, samphire flats and tall tea-tree banks. Three kilometres up it branched, north to the Saltwater (Maribyrnong), east to the Freshwater (Yarra). They took the Yarra, clogged with debris. Scrub lined both banks except where 'Contiguous to the river, there are some beautiful pieces of land, clear of trees', and 'vistas of grassy land . . . here and there'.[128] The land further back had few trees and good grass, mostly Kangaroo Grass, the most 'beautiful sheep pasturage I ever saw in my life . . .', Batman claimed.[129] James Flemming concluded, 'In several places there are small tracts of good land, but they are without wood or water . . . The country in general is excellent pasture and thin of timber . . . newly burnt.'[130] The land south was more swampy, but 'varied . . . by open clear land and . . . clumps of trees'.[131] Batman rowed on to the falls and noted the city site, then moved off to find grass.

On 20 August 1835 more settlers came from Tasmania, finding

> a continuation of good land with plenty of good grass and herbage, but thinly timbered with she-oak and honeysuckle; but we found no fresh water till we came to the east branch of the river at the head of the bay, where we found a good stream of fresh water, and beautiful hills and plains of good soil and excellent grass. Here we made up our minds to settle.[132]

In 1853 John Fawkner claimed that his men

> reached with great joy the basin at Melbourne, and were delighted, in fact, half wild with exultation, at the beauty of the country. The velvet-like grass

carpet, decked with flowers of the most lively hues, most liberally spread over the land, the fresh water, the fine lowlands, and lovely knolls around the lagoons on the flat or swamps, the flocks, almost innumerable, of teal, ducks, geese, and swans, and minor fowls, filled them with joy. They all with one voice agreed that they had arrived at the site of the new Settlement.[133]

South, hills and rises interrupted swampy and often scrubby flats, 'an immense wilderness',[134] but carefully arranged. Tea-tree belts edged grass, grass and scrub alternated along swamps, tree clumps stood in open land, clearings broke up scrub. Near the falls clans met in a large clearing hidden in tea-tree to talk, dance and, some newcomers said, fight.[135] West were 'grassy hills forest land'. South was swamp, then 'Sandy forest land the timber indifferent', swamp at Albert Park, 'Barren heath' to the coast and 'Open forest land' at St Kilda. Near Albert Park rose 'a strikingly green grassy hill' where kangaroos grazed—Emerald Hill, burnt every 2–3 years.[136] Towards Arthur's Seat, country on fire in January 1804,[137] grass dominated, 'fertile and beautiful . . . one extensive surface of green . . . very lightly wooded with mimosa, shea oak, gum and lightwood', which 'teems with life. The large Kangaroo . . . may be seen in flocks of 3 or 400 . . . The Koala, petaurus or flying opossum, Bandicoot, Wombat, Native Cat, Dasyurus Opossums, both kinds, Phalangers are very numerous.'[138] The valleys around Arthur's Seat, especially on the Melbourne side, 'had a very pleasant appearance, in some places being thickly clothd with wood, in others nearly bare of wood but coverd with a bright green verdure & in others bare spots of a brownish colour' marking recently burnt ground.[139] The district had 'a very pleasing appearance, having much resemblance to a Gentlemans Park in England, being covered with a fine Green grass and Numerous Trees and Bushes in pleasing irregularity, and so far apart as to admit the whole surface to be covered with Grass . . . much of the herbage had been burnt a few months ago'.[140]

The land north of Yarra falls appealed most to newcomers. It was 'park-like', 'beautifully situated', 'open, grassy forest, rising into low hills'.[141] Tea-tree patches stood on the river below Spencer and King streets and round a small swamp below Russell and Exhibition streets. Wallaby and other grasses, herbs and *murnong* swathed the riverbank, and grass and scattered trees cloaked hill and valley over the city's southwest third from Swanston Street to Flagstaff Hill, which 'being covered with a beautiful grassy surface . . . had the appearance of a large lawn'.[142] Northwest was Blue Lake (North Melbourne Swamp), a real lake, intensely blue, nearly oval, and full of the clearest salt water; but this, by no means deep. Fringed gaily all round by ... pigs-face in full bloom, it seemed in the broad sunshine as though girdled about with a belt of magenta fire. The ground gradually sloping down towards the lake was also empurpled, but patchily, in the same manner, though perhaps not quite so brilliantly, while the whole air was heavy with the mingled odours of the golden myrnong flowers and purple-fringed lilies.[143]

In the city's east a dance ground lay in or near dense forest east of Swanston Street and south of Bourke Street.[144] Just west a small creek, often dry, ran down Elizabeth Street, 'a jungly chasm—an irregular broken-up ravine, through which the winter flood-waters thundered'. It split two hills, 'rising and picturesque eminences ... on the verge of a beautiful park',[145] one cresting east at Spring Street, the other west at William Street, each burnt differently. 'The Eastern Hill was a gum and wattle tree forest, and the Western Hill was so clothed with sheoaks as to give it the appearance of a primeval park.'[146] Both were 'lightly wooded', the west topped with mushrooms,[147] the east with grass between the Museum and Parliament House. It may have been a family camp. In most directions it commanded ground burnt often, as in March 1836, when the area 'looked very pretty. The grass had been all burnt off by bush-fires and the autumn rains had caused it to spring up again.'[148] At Fitzroy and Treasury Gardens to the east, open forest gave way to 'dense gum forest', mostly Manna Gum, where in the 1840s boys would 'gather and devour the manna fallen from the milk-white boughs ... it was perfectly delicious'.[149] Fire had promoted grass and reeds but suppressed tea-tree, secluded clearings in dense timber, burnt sharp tree–grass edges across hill and valley, and put grass on one hill, sheoak on another, and eucalypts and grass on a third. It made Melbourne abundant and beautiful, yet at most a few families patterned and seamlessly integrated its diversity.

On 4 March 1837 Governor Richard Bourke came from Sydney to inspect this 'beautiful and convenient site':

> It does not however promise to afford water, which must be procured (at first at least) entirely from the River. A good <u>Dam</u> will need to be constructed here to keep up the fresh water & to effect its entire separation from the Salt ... Timber is to be had but at a distance of about 8 miles ... the soil in the neighbourhood is generally good, in many spots very rich.[150]

Here was a place for a village, but not a port, and with too little fresh water. Its beauty recommended it. The people who made it so were not there when it was taken, for it was winter, a time safe to be up in Mountain Ash country or to go north to trade for greenstone, perhaps near where Batman met them. They avoided the city area in spring, when taking eggs and young was banned. They came in summer, when yams were dug, fish and mussels got from the river, and land burnt. By then they found strangers plundering their country.

The strangers spread. 'For some miles around Melbourne', Thomas Winter recalled,

> the country bears the same beautiful character—grassy and luxuriant, with trees scattered over it, as in the least woody parts of old forests in England . . . [most] is plain, generally without trees, nearly flat and often stony. Some of these plains are lightly timbered, and are then called forests. The hills vary much, some . . . with . . . short pasturage; others covered with rich, long herbage, and spotted with trees; while others are woody to the top.[151]

Backhouse wrote, 'The country, as far as the eye can reach, has the appearance of a continued series of parks, even to the ascent of the distant hills. In many places, it is clear of trees; the grass is verdant, and pretty thick for a country which has not been subjected to the fostering hand of man.'[152] Charles Griffiths thought the country

> very picturesque . . . a good deal of it . . . is perfectly clear of timber; other parts are wooded about as thickly as the open parts of an English park; while in those most heavily timbered the trees are about ten to thirty yards apart, with grass growing under them, and the ground perfectly free from brushwood of any kind, though flowering shrubs are interspersed here and there.[153]

Swamps grew 'fine grass, fit to mow; not a bush in it', and 'swarmed' with 'swans, geese, ducks, quail and other wild-fowl'. Snipe 'abounded' in Yarra backwaters. On the plains emu were so common and so curious that newcomers shot them from their tents. Other habitats supported kangaroo, wallaby, pademelon, bettong, koala, possum, pygmy possum, sugar glider, wombat, bandicoot, antechinus, dunnart, water rat, quoll, echidna, platypus, bat, quail, parrot, pelican, eel, shellfish, at least 20 fish species, herbs, yam, manna, wattle seed and gum, and more. It was a staggering variety.

It varied locally. At Southern Cross Station stood Batman's Hill, a place of dazzling beauty commanding the country in most directions. John Lancey claimed it for Fawkner, and on 24 August 1835 told the prospective squire,

> Your lordship has been fortunate in the lot I chose for you. A more delightful spot, I think, cannot be. Beautiful grass, a pleasant prospect, a fine fresh-water river, and the vessel lying alongside the bank discharging at musket-shot distance from a pleasant hill where I intend to put your house. The garden will trend to the south by the east side of the hill . . . The west side of the hill is a beautiful prospect. A salt lagoon and piece of marsh will make a beautiful meadow and bounded on the south by the river. The hill is composed of rich, black soil, thinly wooded with honeysuckle and she-oak. Good grass, a quantity of herbage that I cannot name more than three, viz., parsley of good flavour, peppermint, as good as any I ever tasted, and geraniums in abundance.[154]

Sheoak stood along the river and sprinkled the slopes, but after summer fires such as in March 1836 the hill 'looked so green and fresh that . . . I thought it was cultivated ground and that a crop of grain had been sown on it'.[155] Every newcomer admired Batman's Hill.

The hill sloped north down to grassy yam and herb flats and through scattered gum, sheoak, wattle and 'patches of bushes'[156] to Blue Lake and Flagstaff Hill. Beyond, 'as far as the eyes could see' shady trees, commonly Yellow or White Box, dotted 'soft green grass, of a height that if a person rode through it it would reach above the saddle-girths'.[157] At Preston was 'Good cattle pasture'; at Coburg several small plains lay in 'Light forest'. West of Batman's Hill 'a beautiful green lawn' extended for 3–4 miles around a 'small saltwater lake . . . generally covered with swans and wild fowl. On the banks of its margin the sheoak is thinly scattered, giving the whole the appearance of an extensive English park.'[158] This was Melbourne Swamp, fed by Moonee Ponds and smaller creeks, 'a wonderfully abundant resource' now Victoria Dock.

North of Melbourne Swamp, Flemington's hills were 'Well wooded'. West was land

> of the most excellent quality . . . very rich alluvial soil . . . unrivalled for sheep and cattle. A great part of it is plains, some vast in extent,

but few trees. Other parts are highly timbered and bear a strong resemblance to a gentleman's park kept for ornament . . . the land free from underwood, except in small patches near the rivers . . . The grass all through summer has retained its greenness and goodness . . . Fish are plentiful . . . Wild fowl and kangaroo abound.[159]

Wedge reported in August 1835, 'The country between these rivers [Yarra and Maribyrnong] extending to the north forty or fifty miles, and to the east about twenty-five miles . . . is moderately wooded . . . to the north there are open plains.'[160] Bourke wrote, 'The route [west] for the first 4 miles leads through a very pretty country having the appearance of an English Park. Thence over a very arid plain of coarse grass to the Salt River.'[161]

Others located this change on the basalt plains further west:

> The scenery from the Settlement to the Ford on the Saltwater river is most beautiful and some of the spots quite enchanting. The grass had been burnt about a month previously and it was then quite green and beautiful . . . the country completely changed when we crossed the Ford the Land was then quite flat and rather rocky and . . . up to Geelong Harbour consists of open plains with a thin coat of grass and exposed to the cold winds.[162]

From the Saltwater to the lower Werribee the land was 'one-third grass, one-ditto stone, and one-ditto earth, mostly new burnt', 'bleak & herbage coarse, great part lately burnt', but with 'belts' of trees.[163] It was 'exceedingly rich, and beautiful in the extreme', Batman wrote,

> thinly-timbered, richly grassed . . . The soil was of a fine, rich, oily, decomposed whinstone [basalt] . . . The trees were thinly-scattered in a park-like form, averaging five or six to the acre . . . Its general character presents that of cultivated pasture for centuries past; the few trees appear as though they owed their plantation to the hand of man. All the high hills are covered with grass to their summits.[164]

Grass and open forest followed the Saltwater up. It was salt 20 kilometres inland, showing how flat the delta was, and a succession of stone fish traps followed its course.[165] It divided the country: grassy basalt plains beyond its high west bank, grass with scattered blackwood or banksia patches on its low east bank. Kangaroo Grass or in low places Wallaby Grass dominated. Batman thought the 'whole of the land' 'excellent', 'with grass three feet high in places where it had not been burnt by the natives. Where it had been burned by these people, the young blades are from ten to twelve inches high, affording fine feed for kangaroos and other animals.' Then he met an altered landscape:

> an open forest two miles in length, composed of oak, with about ten of those trees to the acre, and the stems or buts [sic] about a foot in circumference . . . all around are rich open plains, with trees, gentle rising hills, and valleys of the best description of soil . . . We again renewed our journey over plains, until reaching a small forest of box gum trees, which formed a belt of about two miles . . . From the box and oak forest we came upon beautiful open plains, with the usual interruptions of gently rising eminences, on which grew oak, black wood, and wattle trees, and grass up to our waists, through which walking was both painful and tedious. We eventually came to a small lovely valley, where, to our great delight, was a dense tea-tree scrub, which we knew to be the surest indication of good water.[166]

Hoddle mapped this country. East of the Saltwater to Moonee Ponds Creek he marked 'Thickly wooded country', but upstream he mapped grass and named Westmeadows and Broadmeadows. West to Tullamarine was a 'Plain, lightly timbered with clumps of She-oak, Banksia, and Blackwood Trees', each of which respond differently to fire. East were plains with 'Honeysuckle, Lightwood and Oaks' enclosing clearings.[167] These are familiar templates: grass on good soil broken by tree belts especially on higher ground, and sheoaks needing a decade to re-seed after fire above Kangaroo Grass burnt every 1–3 years, though as Leichhardt found in Queensland (ch 1), on the Saltwater headwaters the pattern reversed: 'the country . . . [was] covered with timber excepting the tops of the hills. The country was well grassed, and might be called grassy open forest land.'[168]

East of the city, tea-tree and grass alternated up the Yarra until the country became 'rather over thickly wooded, and with a good deal of underwood, which gives a scrubby appearance'.[169] This was relieved by grass and open forest belts: Richmond was a 'grassy hill', Collingwood a 'grassy forest', Kew a 'grassy range', Bulleen 'good grassy hills', Heidelberg 'an ever-varying succession of lightly-timbered hill and dale, well-grassed downs alternated with groups of tall, handsome trees', Doncaster off the river a 'barren forest of dwarf stringy bark', about Lower Plenty 'timber but of indifferent quality . . . Swampy Flat',[170] in the far hills Kangaroo Ground,[171] grass then, forest now.

A few newcomers sensed that this variety was made. Griffiths reflected:

> It is difficult when you see trees intermixed with the most graceful flowering shrubs, grouped with all the effect which a landscape gardener could desire, and growing from a green sward, entirely free from overgrowing weeds or brushwood, not to fancy that the hand of man had been engaged in combining and arranging these elements of natural beauty.[172]

'Where else but in Australia', Richard Howitt asked,

> could I find such a park-like Arcady?—mile after mile of the smoothest greensward, unbroken by any kind of fence; a sweet undulating land of knoll and slope and glen, studded over, not too thickly, but in a most picturesque manner, with she-oaks, trees of the softest and richest character imaginable?[173]

Dozens of sharp-edged templates meshed into a seamless mosaic, a boundless estate, a lesson in beauty and utility.[174]

Adelaide, 28 December 1836

By 1836 the British knew not to be picky in trying to combine a port and fresh water. In South Australia this was just as well. On Kangaroo Island newcomers found a port in July 1836, but not enough fresh water, so most moved to the mainland, there to begin a squabble lasting years, on whether the capital should be at the port or the water.

Settlers first tried Holdfast Bay: Glenelg. 'The country, as far as we could see, was certainly beautiful', Mary Thomas wrote, 'and resembled an English park, with long grass in abundance and fine trees scattered about, but not so many as to make it unpleasant, and no brushwood. We were about a hundred yards from the nearest lagoon.'[175] Being summer the grass was green, on dunes pigface and other flowers mingled with shrubs and 'cranberries' [muntheries?], and wattle and banksia stood with 'tall and stately gum-trees on all sides'. The district was alive with kangaroo, kangaroo rat, 'kangaroo mouse' and possum.[176] Inland, lagoons and the Sturt River, thick with tall reeds, opened to 'level land studded with trees, and every here and there a stretch of rich meadow-land ... the grass in many places three or four feet high, and the whole tract evidently of the most luxurious description'.[177]

Glenelg was no port. For that William Light chose Port Adelaide, swampy, lined with mangroves in smelly mud, little fresh water, but a useful harbour.[178] At its head Light saw 'something like the mouth of a small river, and a country with trees so dispersed as to allow the sight of most luxuriant green underneath'. He probed inland, 'seeing no bounds to a flat of fine rich-looking country with an abundance of fresh-water lagoons, which, if dry in summer, convinced me that one need not dig a deep well to give sufficient supply'. The plain had 'fine soil ... not a rock, tree, or bush in the way for six miles'.[179]

Not 'in the way' perhaps, but there. From the port's 'gloomy swamp', salt land with pigface and saltbush reached past a sheoak bank to 'two level plains, separated by a slight, sandy rise, covered with wood' or 'belts of wood'. Wattle, mallee, sheoak and perhaps pine formed these belts and lightly dotted the plains. Herbs, everlastings and other flowers sprinkled Spear or Wallaby Grass, some 'eaten with avidity by cattle' and therefore by kangaroos.[180] A few miles inland the plains rose gently east, still grassland 'scattered about with noble park-like' eucalypts:[181]

> The rich green plains, not covered by dense forest, but by stately trees, rising here and there from their green foundations in the same way as they do in the noble parks of England, the pretty streams, the broad lakes, margined with beautiful shrubs and flowers, and the gently undulating hills crowned with trees, forms altogether frequent scenes of interest and beauty.[182]

Stately giants survive in Adelaide's eastern suburbs.

The plains ended at Mt Lofty Range, 'covered with fine wood and grass to the very summits. There is little or no brushwood.'[183] Hills parks are now heavily timbered, with thick undergrowth. East lay 'a beautiful, open, undulating country, with grass up to the horses manes; the trees consisting principally of box and blue gum, were of large size',[184] and northeast

> a most beautiful and rich Country. The Ranges ... broken into smooth grassy vallies and the more level country resembled more an English Park than any thing else ... dense brushes ... separate the [grassy] limestone downs of the Murray from the richer country in which we were travelling.[185]

Hill and plain were usually burnt in late summer. In February 1837 the hills were 'a mass of flame ... At the end of summer as this was, the natives had set fire to the long dry grass to enable them more easily to obtain the animals and vermin on which a great part of their living depends.'[186] These were controlled fires (ch 6), lit 'generally ... in January or February'[187] meshing hill and plain into grass-forest templates. The plains were summer country, the time to burn, dig yams, fish in the warm coastal water, gather herbs and thistles, hunt possum and lure kangaroo. The hills were for winter and the hottest summer weather.[188]

The fires varied. Newcomers found pine stands in eucalypt woodland, scrub or tree belts on plains, grass clearings in forest. Just east of the city a 'belt of small' wattles ran 'about half a mile wide',[189] recent regenerators from fire, perhaps the belt Berkeley painted in 1840 (picture 18). A plain lay 'several miles wide ... covered with grass, and intersected with belts of Gum-trees, and a sickle-leaved *Acacia*. Some of the Kangaroo-grass was up to our elbows, and resembled two years' seed meadows, in England, in thickness; in many places, three tons of hay per acre, might be mown off it.'[190] Norwood was 'a magnificent gum forest with an undergrowth of Kangaroo Grass, too high in places for a man to see over. In fact people had lost their way in going from Adelaide to Kensington.' Southeast was a corroboree ground, 'a nice piece of cleared land ... a few acres backed by noble gum trees'.[191] North and south were stringybark belts and other forests. The Peachy Belt reached towards Gawler, about 15 x 5 kilometres of Grey Box, mallee, pine and shrubs thrusting into open country south and east. The Black Forest looped from the Sturt near Marion to the city and east to the hills, dominated by big, 'densely packed' Grey Box–SA Blue Gum over thick undergrowth and clogging debris.[192] Yet it had a 'very few clearings',[193] while irrespective of soil type, forest closed the land here but left it open nearby.

The soft soil plains held plenty of water, shielded by summer flourishing grasses (ch 3). It came from hills creeks and accumulated in swamps behind coastal dunes from south of Glenelg north past Port Adelaide, where it gave way to mangrove and samphire flats. In this vast, rich system people camped and raised mounds, perhaps when unclogging swamp inlets. Edging dunes carried flowers, sheoak and scrub sheltering bilbies, bandicoots and bettongs. *Cowandilla*, the Reedbeds, from the Torrens south, were especially bountiful.

They were fed by the Torrens, shallow, in summer a chain of ponds. A few observers despised it. A 'miserable dribbling current with an occasional waterhole', one called it. 'Any number of fallen trees blocked the bed ... and here and there were patches of ti-tree.'[194] Most admired it. 'A very beautiful stream it then was. The deep banks were covered with underwood and trees of various kinds, while the bed of the stream was covered with a thick, close, and beautiful growth of tea-tree, with a great variety of aromatic flowers and shrubs.'[195] The water was 'fresh, and of excellent quality', even though

> about one foot in depth, and four feet in width; there are numerous pools, of several fathoms deep, in its course, which are not likely to lack water in the driest seasons. In some places there are reedy flats below the [false] banks of the river, which are of red loam, and are ornamented by a variety of shrubs and flowers.[196]

Hawdon, skilled at assessing grass and water, found Adelaide

> laid out on both sides of a very small stream of excellent water . . . In the summer season this stream is found running only for a short distance below the Town, where it disappears beneath its gravelly bed . . . The scenery around is very pleasing. Towards the sea it consists of plains studded and intersected with belts of trees. The Mount Lofty Range distant about two miles to the eastward, presents a beautiful picturesque appearance, with its various and sloping sides variegating by its shadow the luxuriant grass to every shade of green.[197]

George Hamilton, another overlander, wrote,

> The land in the vicinity of this river was timbered with noble trees, and its banks sloped down to the water in gentle undulations thickly clothed with grass. The river itself meandered through a tangle of tea-tree, rushes, reeds, and many flowering weeds, here and there almost hidden by vegetation, but at intervals opening out into pretty ponds or tolerably large waterholes; along its banks grew in profusion the wattle (acacia) with its golden sweet-scented blossoms, as well as the noble eucalyptus, here at that time in great beauty. Towards the sea, to the westward, the land was flat, swampy, and not very picturesque; but towards the hills on the plains, where Norwood and Kensington now stand, wooded glades of great beauty opened out in all directions, extending to the foot of the Mount Lofty Range, the hills of which rose up in graceful gently

swelling acclivities, picturesquely sprinkled with a variety of trees until they joined the forest which crowned the lovely mountain range.[198]

Hamilton caught the Torrens' variety. It quit the hills through tea-tree, gouging 10-metre banks before it steadied on the plain over a shallow bed choked with tea-tree. Its banks were 'closely covered with beautiful shrubs of all sorts; splendid gum trees also . . . small fish were plentiful, and . . . the platypus was occasionally seen'.[199] It then spilled into reedy swamps, and River Red and SA Blue Gum, Drooping Sheoak, tea-tree, wattle and bottlebrush graced its banks and overflows, until above the city it was 'picturesque in the extreme', 'full of shallow places and deep holes . . . a great number of Gum trees lying in the bed . . . apparently washed down by winter floods'.[200] Below the city, wattle and River Reds tracked its sometimes dry course 'across a plain of exceedingly fine land', until it filtered through the Reedbeds to the sea.[201] It was a typical Australian river, spreading and slow, easily forded, rich in swamps and reeds, with deep holes for fish, yabbies and platypus, and lined with possum trees, marsupial grassland, and bird and reptile shelter.[202]

Light put his capital 12 kilometres southeast of his port, where the Torrens curved south between 'two gentle slopes . . . Beautiful grassy plains surround it, with a sufficiency of timber to make it look well.'[203] North, open forest dominated grassy flats and hills, pines upstream, gums at the city and below, including the giant gums of *piltawadli*, possum place, at the golf course.[204] South, a narrow plain rose to a plateau. George Kingston, Light's deputy, put his tent there,[205] and soon Light chose it for his city. It had more trees than the land around: 'the obstructions for this work were greater on this particular spot than any other part of the plain', Light claimed. 'It may be asked then, "Why choose it?" I answer, "Because it was on a beautiful and gently rising ground, and formed altogether a better connection with the river than any other place."'[206] It was Grey Box–SA Blue Gum woodland, north grassy slopes and scrub patches to the river, east open gum forest with some Drooping Sheoak, west mallee, centre and south scrub clumps or belts under tall, spreading eucalypts. Perched above Kangaroo Grass land, it was a summer rest place for kangaroos—*tarndana*, red kangaroo place, with somewhere on it the rock of the Red Kangaroo ancestor.[207] Light designated a park belt round the city; some newcomers thought it already there:

> This park land is a pleasant scene, and has much the appearance of English parks, being adorned in many places by large native trees

growing in clumps, and having the river passing through the grounds for some distance, with handsome trees lining its banks.[208]

Fire made the district's templates. It kept grass dense and water-shielding, touched wetlands rarely but cleared undergrowth, and put trees in belts and clumps. In the city, 'trees are very few and mostly damaged by fire',[209] but by March 1839, with fire banned, wattles were regenerating densely: it 'was easy to lose oneself in the heavily wooded city even in the daytime and at night it was scarcely possible to avoid doing so. The maze-like character of the spot was greatly enhanced by a multitude of wattles, which occupied spaces between gum or she-oak trees.'[210] This is rapid regeneration: perhaps this newcomer was on the city's west, which people were not burning in 1836 because it was *wirranendi*, 'being transformed into a forest'.[211]

Family groups worked fires, neighbours sometimes helping (ch 6). About 20–30 people managed a *yerta*, a range, divided into *pangkarra*, 'a district or tract of country belonging to an individual, which he inherits from his father . . . As each *pankarra* has its peculiar name, many of the owners take that as their proper name, with the addition of the term *burka*.' *Pangkarra* names might identify a dominant totem and template— red gum people, reed people, possum people; personal names might signify a right and a duty to say how a *pangkarra* should be managed, and declare an interest in the well-being of a totem and its habitat.[212]

Few newcomers imagined such discipline. Light thought the country 'looked more like land in the possession of persons of property rather than that left to the course of nature alone', and John Morphett considered it 'very picturesque and generally well timbered, but in the disposition of the trees more like an English park than we would have imagined to be the character of untrodden wilds'.[213] At Adelaide newcomers learnt more about its people than at any other state capital, yet could still think the careful construction around them 'untrodden wilds'. For manager and spoiler alike, the loss was irrecoverable.[214]

Darwin, 5 February 1869

Port Darwin is 'one of the finest harbours in the world, dotted here and there with wooded islands, small bays, and headlands tapering off into the sea, fringed in some places with mangroves, in others with hills and ravines covered with trees of the most beautiful and luxuriant foliage'.[215] Here at last newcomers could put a port right on the coast, though most fresh water came from wells.

The port completed Britain's strategic occupation of Australia. Since 1824 it had tried to establish a northern port west of 135 degrees longitude, the western limit of its 1788 claim.[216] It garrisoned Melville Island in 1824, Raffles Bay in 1826 and Port Essington in 1838. All soon faltered, and none survived more than a dozen years. In 1864 Adelaide attempted a northern settlement at Escape Cliffs, which also failed, so in 1869 it mimicked its own foundation by sending a well-equipped expedition under its surveyor-general, George Goyder, to Port Darwin.

Goyder mapped a harbour mostly mangrove but with openings, and a coast varied by cliffs, rocks, vine forest, sheoak rimmed beaches and small grassy flats.[217] Initially he reported

> thickets of vegetation fringing the rocks of the coast and a few mangroves where the water is shoal, open forest of gum, iron and stringybark, cedar, banyan, and other trees . . . three varieties of palm (fan, corkscrew, and another with leaves resembling long feathers), an endless variety of shrubs, herbs, and grasses; the table land mostly of good rich soil, stony in places, as are the ridges.[218]

Later he described even more intricate plant patterns:

> The cliffs, except at Point Emery and Point Elliot, where the land is more open, are fringed by a dense thicket from five to twenty yards through, of various sized timber, matted together by bamboo, convolvuli, and a variety of other vines and shrubs. The low lands near the sea . . . [are covered] by dense mangroves of two or three varieties; these give place as you go inland and ascend to the higher levels, to paper bark (some of large growth), palms, fan and fern, screw pines, iron bark, gum, stringy bark, fig, cedar, cotton, and a variety of other trees and shrubs forming an open forest. The grass over the whole, or nearly the whole of the surface of the ground, grows luxuriantly, from a rank species resembling holcus [Spear Grass] to the finer varieties.[219]

In short, the further inland the more often the land was burnt. Mangrove, fig, cedar, coastal 'thickets' and some palms were burnt rarely or never, sheoak perhaps every decade, grass and open forest in patches every 1–3 years.

Goyder chose a camp at the 'best landing place', a coastal flat below Fort Point at the harbour's eastern tip.[220] It had

> most luxuriant vegetation—the hibiscus, grevillia, bamboo, ironbark etc giving a delightful shade—most beautiful varieties of convolvulus and hibiscus in bloom—the fan palms and corkscrew palms bending ever so gracefully and twined with creepers in flower to the top. The grass is very long, in some patches it is twelve feet high.[221]

Goyder had rocks and timber cleared, a well deepened in nearby Doctor's Gully, and 'tracks cleared from well to beach'.[222] But the flat was too small, and he moved up to a gully on Fort Hill, levelled in 1965 to make Kitchener Drive. His men spilled onto the tableland, which became Palmerston, renamed Darwin in 1911. It was

> fairly covered with timber & a variety of grasses—mostly coarse & rank—one better variety of which horses & stock are fond [Kangaroo Grass]—herbs abundant . . . several varieties of Eucalypti:— Acacia— pines—Screw & fan palms &c &c too many to name . . . intersected by small water-courses none of which have got water.[223]

Goyder's surveyors described a more subtly varied town area. 'Except in the Open flats', the land ranged from 'thickly' to 'thinly' timbered, the ground was generally 'well grassed' but in places had 'luxuriant undergrowth', fire sensitive and fire tolerant palms each had a place, and creeks had mangroves on one bank but grass on the other.[224]

The newcomers' interest was at first along the coast northeast. Larrakia people had many camps there, and Goyder's men sank the Doctor's Gully well by opening a spring, one of several that people had shielded with a 'dense thicket' of vine, ferns, palms and Green Plum.[225] A thicket strip ran to Point Elliot, where the land opened as far as Point Emery, a big camp. In 1839 James Emery of HMS *Beagle* dug a deep well in a beachside gully just south of the point, and persuaded people to inspect it.

> It was . . . some time before this party could be induced to look down the well. At length by stretching their spare bodies and necks to the utmost, they caught sight of the water in the bottom. The effect upon them was magical, and they stood at first as if electrified. At length their feelings gained vent, and from their lips proceeded an almost mad shout of delight.[226]

They had cause: the well was near a men's ceremonial ground,[227] where important creator ancestors came from the sea, as the well water seemed to.

From Point Emery, Fannie Bay's palm and sheoak was backed by eucalypt-dominated woodland, perhaps thickest at East Point. This gave way to mangrove flats, then returned at Nightcliff to a shore lined by tall sheoak and split by a 'strong' freshwater creek amid 'luxuriant vegetation', including 'native melon, & cape gooseberry'.[228] Here were more camps and a tidal fish trap.[229] Rocks led to Rapid Creek, then sheoak edged the great reach of Casuarina Beach to Lee Point. Behind it ran a familiar 1788 pattern: a 100–200 metre strip of 'open grassed plain' bounded inland by an 'edge of timber' (ch 7; picture 55), which merged with Marrara Swamp at the airport.[230]

Rapid Creek ran out of Marrara Swamp. Swampy near its mouth, inland it was lined with springs and shady trees fronting open forest, good campsites. East of Marrara an 'open forest of ironbark gum stringy bark grevillea and several varieties of Palms' stopped abruptly 60 metres short of Knuckeys Swamp, with 'three varieties of Lillies'. Grass margins ringed it, perhaps marking high water in the Wet, then ironbark country resumed.[231] Southeast, a 'small open plain' lay in 'ironbark, plum, cotton &c' which reached to Packard's Knob, just north of the university's Palmerston campus. East of the Knob two open plains broke the forest, and south lay Elrundie Flat, where a surveying team set up camp and sunk a 2-metre well. The flat merged into a swampy plain now Marlow Lagoon. West and northwest was 'Mostly gum forest, well grassed, with a variety of other timber, herbs, shrubs & grasses, honeysuckles & kangaroo grass'.[232] Extensive mangroves along East Arm and Frances Bay led back below Marrara Swamp to the town.

Marrara's southern reaches carried pandanus and ironbark until it met slightly higher 'clear land' falling south to Ilwaddy Flat, along Tiger Brennan Drive below the airport. The Flat was open stringybark and peppermint forest, swampy in the Wet, with 'plum' and 'fern palm' patches. Green Plum, rich in vitamin C, fruits best under carefully timed fire; fern palm may have been a cycad but seems more like Goyder's palm 'with leaves resembling long feathers'[233]—Darwin Palm, fire sensitive and now endangered. Ilwaddy Flat ran south to coastal mangroves and west to a 'thickly timbered' flat with 'Fan palms & luxuriant undergrowth' about where The Narrows separate Ludmilla and Sadgroves mangrove creeks. Southwest towards the town, 'undulating country', the valleys 'exceedingly well grassed', the ridges 'rough and covered with the usual vegetation', led to open forest dominated by stringybark, wattle and palms. Then 'bare patches destitute of vegetation' jostled with 'Abundance of Kangaroo grass & other grasses', while creeks edged by alternating mangroves and clear land led to wetlands with vine brush patches from the Botanic Gardens towards Mindil Beach. In the town area the timber became 'taller thinner and closer together', with grassy patches.[234]

There were many more plant species than Goyder's surveyors noted. For example they never or rarely named bloodwood, cycads and yams, all certainly there. They mapped in the Dry: most of their flats became swamps in the Wet. But they describe typical Top End grassy forest interspersed with mangroves, wetlands, and vine forest patches. All were rich resources: 38 of the Territory's 51 mangrove species grow around the harbour,[235] and in clear spaces middens and shell mounds marked the feasts of centuries. Goyder mapped a mound in East Arm 4 metres high, and some middens were over 30 metres long.[236]

The land was locally managed. In 1885 a resident reported distinct boundaries between the Darwin people and their neighbours, and stated,

> The land is subdivided among the several families, with territorial rights, and the ownership is a real one . . . on the Lammerru Beach . . . is the camp of the family in whom that part is vested. A half-mile distant, at the head of Smith and Cavenagh streets, is the main camp of the Larrakia, comprising several circles of wurleys.[237]

Families cared for their country, and co-operated with clansmen and neighbours to manage bigger areas. In general they worked with the country, over centuries extending the dominance of fire tolerant species and burning back vine forest. The burning was precise and selective, mosaic burning, deliberately distributing fire tolerant and fire sensitive templates. Most grass was burnt every Dry as it still is (ch 6), yet grass might be open or in woodland, or stop suddenly at 'luxuriant' undergrowth or fire sensitive vine thickets sheltering springs, particularly on the coast and the creeks. Grass on good valley soil alternated with timber on stony ridges; flats and swamps might have grass, forest or mangrove margins; clearings and small plains lay in eucalypts or mangroves. An annual Wet and Dry dictated means unlike those in southern and central Australia, but the ends were the same. The country was made, obeying the Law, associating unlike plant communities, and making resources abundant and convenient. Darwin was part of an Australian estate.[238]

Canberra, 12 March 1913 (1824)

Within months of finding Lake George (picture 51), Europeans reached the Canberra district. In December 1820 Charles Throsby Smith rode from the lake west then southeast to Gundaroo. Farm or forest now, then it was 'a beautiful Clear plain . . . as far as the Eye could reach all round . . . a finest Country as ever was seen'. Smith continued south,

> thro' a fine forest country for 3 miles ascending a Stony Range . . . some beautiful clear plains in sight . . . Descended the Range & into a scrubby Country for about ½ a Mile then into a most beautiful country gentle Hills and Valleys . . . Came on to one of the plains we saw at 11 o'clock—at past 1 came to a very extensive plain Rich Soil and plenty of Grass—Came to a Beautiful River that was running through the plain in a SW direction.[239]

He was on the Molonglo, possibly upstream of the Queanbeyan junction, perhaps near a limestone outcrop at the National Museum.

In 1832–5 Robert Hoddle, soon to survey Melbourne, surveyed between Yass and Michelago, including Canberra and Queanbeyan. 'Open plains' and 'fine open grassy forest' without undergrowth were easily most common, and commonly alternated, sometimes with Hoddle dotting a line to mark their boundary. Kangaroo Grass and Blakely's Red Gum, Ribbon Gum or Apple Box dominated, with Yellow Box on lighter soils, and wattle or casuarina in places. Hoddle marked no dense forest, not even on hills thickly forested now, and only two 'scrubby' places, one on hills south of Lake George, one east of Jerrabombera Creek towards Burra. Another scrub belt, possibly the scrub Smith passed through, bordered the northeast corner of the airport plain.[240] Scrub undergrowth now typifies Australian Capital Territory bush.

Almost all watercourses were 'chains of ponds' with frequent fords and dry crossings. The biggest, the Murrumbidgee, was 'a rapid stream with a Stony bed, difficult to ford in many places, with high rocky banks, and abounds with Fish and wild Fowl'. Its clear 'pebbly' bed was easily forded except after rain. The Queanbeyan River, Ginninderra Creek and Gooramon Ponds were 'incomplete channels', whim choosing their labels. The Molonglo was variously called a 'rivulet', 'a Chain of connected Ponds', and a 'creek' with 'ponds'. In the 1829 winter it was 'only running in some places, but consists large Ponds', in May 1833 and August 1835 it was dry and 'difficult to trace its bed, only a Pond in intervals'. It was a typical inland watercourse, spreading shallowly around small islands, flooding readily into wetlands, with a scatter of reedy pools some more permanent than it, holding fish, eel, platypus and yabbies. On each side were grassy plains. Word spread: in 1820–4 at least six European parties inspected the district, and in 1824 the first landtaker's huts stood on the Molonglo.[241]

One hut was near where Canberry (Sullivan's) Creek joined the river. The creek rose in hills north and trickled shallow and swampy to Turner. Above Barry Drive it spread into a 300–400 metre wetland, narrowed to a small 'spring' or 'pond' at the Australian National University pond, then squeezed between high banks through a kilometre or so of 'open plain' backed by 'grassy open forest'. The right (west) plain tapered to meet open forest at O'Connor Ridge, the forest continuing until the ground fell gently to a narrow reedy flat below Ursula College. The left bank opened to undulating grass plains with tree clumps on rises such as at Manning Clark Theatre, and to a tree-ringed plain towards Civic. The bank continued to a sharp-edged 'grassy open forest' belt. Its outer edge ran from Fellows Road Bridge roughly south to below University House. Its inner edge began on a gravelly rise lower down the creek, circled higher ground across several soil types towards the Menzies Library, then curved back to the creek, making an edge and a tree belt around a grass plain about 600 metres by 400, roughly today's South Oval.

People burnt carefully to make this plain. It associated grass and water with shelter on an enclosing rise, which let people hunt easily. Naturally they usually kept away, harvesting perhaps once a patch-burn, but there were many such plains, each burnt in turn. Downstream the creek widened over a permanent spring, then threaded between ridges at Parkes Way onto grassy flats below Black Mountain spur, where at Springbank another spring never ran dry, and people camped. South Oval paddock was just over the ridge, many plants including Yam Daisy were at hand, and the 'woody' spur was good winter shelter from floods and cold flats. Stone tools and chips lie there. Black Mountain was open lower down, a little thicker higher up. The summit was clear, 'a very high Hill from the Top of which we had an extensive View all round'. Today there are no views, and scrub and debris clog densely regenerating eucalypts, with few pre-1788 trees.[242]

Opposite Black Mountain a 'pebbly ford' spanned the Molonglo. East, the river divided Limestone Plains, 'extensive plains and good grazing country on each side, with a considerable portion of rich meadow land on the banks of the rivers'.[243] Swampy 'alluvial flats' with reed and lignum stretches backed by grassy downs suited emu, plains turkey, yams and native artichoke. North of the river this country continued across the city to below Russell Hill, where the river looped south around an 'open plain', now East Basin, and through rich reedy swamps, perhaps the district's most extensive. Wetlands tracked the river up to Pialligo, where back from the north bank long sandy rises, excellent warm-weather camps, were littered with stone tools. Within a few hundred metres, closer than most supermarkets, swamp, river, plain, hill and forest were handy.

Most forest was on ridges. On Acton Ridge a sharp edge divided an 'open forest' crest from grass slopes below, except for a tree clump at the National Museum. Above Russell Hill ridges came close to the river: Mt Pleasant 'covered slightly with gum trees', from there to Mts Ainslie and Majura 'Open Forest' on a 'Range of Fine Grassy Hills',

Mt Majura 'well timbered'. West and northwest, open plains with reed and bulrush swamps extended to 'a chain of ponds in forest [Ginninderra Creek?] . . . Saw many emu which feed on the plain and retire to the brushy hills'. East, forest skirted Campbell's Hill below Mt Pleasant and above an 'Open Plain' which reached to 'Undulating Open Forest' beyond the airport, and northeast to 'a dense brushwood of White Gum saplings', then 'fine forest country' almost to Lake George. Woolshed Creek threaded the plain. It was more open than Canberry Creek, 'as near a Plain or Plane as any spot of timberless Land I have observed in this Continent', home to emu, plains turkey, quail, shingle-back lizards, tubers and grass orchids.[244]

South from the airport, hills 'quite low, with very few Trees on them, and abounding with beautiful fine Grass'[245] guided the Queanbeyan River and Jerrabombera Creek north to the Molonglo. The river was a 'beautiful range of Ponds', the land on its upper reaches and Burra Creek 'a little scrub and some fine forest country', on its lower reaches grassy.[246] The creek came from thin forest hills into 'level forest', then mostly grass and a few open forest belts to river wetlands now East Basin.[247] West of these streams, 'perfectly dry' in April 1824, was 'a beautiful open flat . . . lying in the midst of lofty mountains'.[248] It ran south past a 'Grassy' Red Hill to 'the finest Plain we ever saw . . . not a Tree . . . The soil on most parts . . . very good and the Herbage excellent',[249] 'quite free from trees', but not naturally treeless (appendix 1). Northeast of the Wanniassa hills the grass gave way to 'fine forest country' including coolamon and canoe trees, which continued south beyond the ACT, with at least one 'beautiful small plain' at Isabella Plains.[250]

The Murrumbidgee's bordering hills were 'rather high, but very thinly wooded and fine Herbage', 'thinly timbered, with a useless Description of Wood quite free from Scrub or Brush Wood', some 'covered with nothing but Honeysuckle'—banksia, a rapid regenerator after occasional fire.[251] From Mt Tennant north Hoddle noted 'grassy hills open forest',[252] and about Lambrigg Allan Cunningham declared, 'we climbed the steep Grassy Hills and pursued our Journey a few miles on their Main Ridge . . . The lofty hills around us . . . were grassy to their Summits & therefore afford no scope for botanical enquiry.'[253] They are thick forest now.

From the Murrumbidgee, Weston Creek led back to the Molonglo, where 'open plain' and 'open forest' alternated, Hoddle dotting lines to mark their boundaries. About Yarralumla a small 'fall' and a ford spanned the river. Both banks carried 'undulating grassy hills' or 'fine grassy open forest', with at least one 'open plain' ringed by 'open forest'. Smith seems to describe this country up to Black Mountain: the banks 'on both sides the whole of the way we went which was a distance near 10 miles is a most beautiful

Forest as far as we could See thinly wooded . . . in the Valleys a fine Rich Soil'.[254] By 1853 the trees were thickening: 'dark forests', a tourist called them. Northeast from Black Mountain, grass plains and slopes alternated with open forest crests to the city. East from City Hill, 'bare of trees', a small creek ran, or didn't run, through an 'open plain'. North, another 'snug plain . . . about one mile in length' reached to Mt Ainslie. A ceremonial ground may have been in forest at one end, at Corroboree Park.

In short, good soil grew grass, and most hills carried grass or scattered trees with little or no undergrowth. This pattern reversed that normal now. To make it required knowledge and skill greater than we have today, and constant work. It was done by people who 'spread themselves over the district in bands of 20 to 30, camping for a week or a month, according to the available food and the season of the year'.[255] Near Tuggeranong Cunningham unwittingly recorded how valuable this mobility was:

> 5 Emus were observed at a short distance from us feeding on the open plain and altho' my Horses were moving about in their presence they manifested not the slightest alarm: a like conscious feeling of [no] danger was exhibited by three fox-colour'd native dogs who not heeding us were howling within view of our Fire—a clear proof of the absence of molestation towards these Animals by the Aborigines.

Next day he saw more emu along Weston Creek.[256] Other newcomers recalled Canberra's plenty: fish and eels in the rivers, birds in the wetlands, emu, brolga, Wonga pigeon and other now vanished animals abundant.[257]

It was done with fire. On 8 December 1820 several fires were burning 'at a distance' from the Molonglo;[258] in February 1822 much country north of the Queanbeyan had been burnt;[259] in February 1824 Weston Creek 'had been burnt in patches about 2 months since, and as the tender blade had sprung up these portions, assuming a most lively verdant cast, form'd a most striking contrast with the deaden'd appearance of the general Surface, still clothed with the vegetation of last Year'.[260] At Woolshed Creek in April 1824 it was 'Evident that these Wandering Beings were at no considerable distance from us, as the Country to the Eastw'd . . . has been in flames all the Day.'[261] In May 1832 Hoddle wrote 'Black Hill' on his sketches of Black Mountain and O'Connor Ridge because both were burnt: for Black Mountain the name stuck.[262] These were summer to early autumn fires, now times too dangerous to burn, but in 1788 best to expose ripe yams, kill saplings, and make grass.

Newcomers were hungry for grass. Late in 1824 Joshua Moore's overseer John

McLaughton built 'Canberry' on Acton Ridge at Old Canberra House, and a shepherd's hut overlooking South Oval. Early in 1825, reputedly guided by an Aboriginal girl, Robert Campbell's stockman James Ainslie located 'Pialligo' at Duntroon House. From flood-free ridges both stations commanded grass—forest templates, springs, swamps, fords, camps and ceremonial grounds. In both senses they overlooked the work of generations. That work dictated where they located, for they took the best places, the most refined and beautiful country. The two biggest runs, Duntroon and Yarralumla, stood on prime sites on each side of Limestone Plains, and when in 1913 Canberra was proclaimed the national capital, they squeezed the new city between them. In this way those unknown and unknowing families whose land they took were the city's founders.[263]

1788's plant patterns were unnatural but universal. How people did this varied from region to region, but everywhere they made similar templates for similar purposes. Different lives, from Spinifex to rainforest, the Wet to the snow, coast to desert, obeyed a strict inheritance, followed the same Law, allied with fire and worked locally to make plants and animals abundant, convenient and predictable. They made a continent a single estate.

10

Farms without fences

People farmed in 1788, but were not farmers. These are not the same: one is an activity, the other a lifestyle. An estate may include a farm, but this does not make an estate manager a farmer. In 1788 similarly, people never depended on farming. Mobility was much more important. It let people tend plants and animals in regions impossible for farmers today, and manage Australia more sustainably than their dispossessors. It was the critical difference between them and farmers.

Being a farmer implies full-time work. No-one did that in 1788, not by farmer notions of work anyway. It also implies treating plants as things, denying them a 'transmigration of souls',[1] an equality of being, because cultivators so obviously control them. In 1788 plants and animals had souls, making ritual more effective than cultivation in managing them. People negotiated as well as tended, offering preferred conditions to persuade, not command (ch 4). After a harvest or hunt they left, but by knowing the cycles and watching the weather knew when to return. With less labour and no guarding, they managed resources as reliably as did fencing.

That should not obscure how much people did farm and how clearly the farmer option confronted them. This is worth exploring because most Europeans think farming explains the lifestyle differences between them and Aborigines. There must be a way to explore those differences and their momentous consequences. There must be a way to say why a white man writes this book in Australia rather than an Aborigine in England. Farming is a place to begin—first animals, then plants.

Kangaroos and cattle have similar preferences. Hence the Cowpastures, the self-concentration of Sydney's escaped herd on a kangaroo ground. Henry Waterhouse wrote in 1804,

> I am at a loss to describe the face of the country otherways than as a beautiful park, totally divested of underwood, interspersed with

> plains, with rich, luxuriant grass; but, for want of feeding off, rank, except where recently burnt. This is the part where the cattle that have strayed have constantly fed—of course, their own selection.[2]

He describes some grass templates dormant and others active, luring and locating grazing animals. After a fire, 'the young herbage that springs up . . . is sure to attract the kangaroos and other game; and the horned cattle are also very fond of feeding upon this *burnt ground*, as it is termed in the Colony'.[3] Without fences, 'burnt ground' concentrated kangaroos and cattle in the same places for the same reasons. No wonder settlers took such country so quickly. Grass templates were farms without fences.

People also reared dingos, possums, emus and cassowaries, penned pelican chicks and let parent birds fatten them, moved rats and caterpillars to new breeding areas, and carried fish and crayfish stock across country.[4] Endless ingenuity worked water. Nets of European quality, mesh and knot varied to suit a prey, were put in or over suitable water, and margin land shaped to match. Duck nets with floats and sinkers spanning inland rivers meant reeds and shallows; fish nets half a mile long circling coasts or tidal flats meant camps and plant food. Coast and inland, thousands of weirs, dams and traps of stone, mud, brush or reeds extended species and harvests. Wicker gates or woven funnels let fish or crayfish upstream on in-tides and trapped them on the ebb. Grass fronds laid over shallow edges gave fish shade and made them vulnerable. Along the Mary east of Darwin,

> Many fish weirs were seen and one could not help being struck with the ingenuity displayed in their construction, on one creek we were surprised to find what looked like the commencement of work for a line of tramway. There were sapling sleepers about eight feet in length and of various thicknesses laid a few feet apart for at least half a mile. The work must have been done by natives but am quite at a loss to understand their motive.[5] [6]

An extensive weir system helped harvest the Darling at Brewarrina. William Mayne saw it in 1848:

> In a broad but shallow part . . . where there are numerous rocks, the Aborigines have formed several enclosures or Pens, if I may use that word, into which the fish are carried, or as it were decoyed by the current, and there retained. To form these must have been the work of

> no trifling labour, and no slight degree of ingenuity and skill must have been exercised in their construction, as I was informed by men who had passed several years in the vicinity, that not even the heaviest floods displace the stones forming these enclosures. The Aborigines catch immense quantities of fish in these and are also enabled to destroy great numbers of fishing Birds of various kinds that are attracted to them by their prey thus imprisoned; and from these two sources the Tribes in that locality derive a considerable portion of their subsistence.[7]

Several hundred successively smaller traps caught 'drayloads' of fish. Mathews noted, 'Each division of the tribe, and the families composing it, had their own allotted portion of the fishing grounds, and every pen or trap had a name by which it was known and spoken of among the people.'[8] [9]

In southwest Victoria people remained 'many months' beside intricate flow systems made to farm eels. With 'some attention to the principles of mechanics', they cut 300-metre canals into bedrock, built 50-metre aqueducts a metre high, and dug kilometres of channels to join and extend eel ranges and abundance. Even in drought or flood the systems regulated flows so that pot traps worked in water coming or going. At Toolondo and Mount William people cut canals across watersheds to let eels into inland waters. This took at least decades, and works were still being extended when Robinson saw them in 1841. As at Brewarrina, traps were owned: 'My native attendants pointed out an extensive weir, 200 feet long and five feet high; they said it was the property of a family, and emphatically remarked, "that white men had stolen it and their country".'[10] [11]

Eel farming showed people promoting a resource, yet they left surplus to rot. 'The Fishing Season had terminated,' Robinson reported. 'Putrid eels, some of them three feet in length, lay in mounds and tainted the air . . . the Lake was indicated to our olfactory senses, by the tainted breeze, when at the distance of at least a couple of miles.'[12] People similarly balanced other templates. Too many plants or animals forced the excess off-template, prompting open season; too few warned people to prohibit and conserve. Temporary bans were declared for scarcity or ceremony. Permanent bans might relate to age, gender or totem. Commonly, women or children could not eat certain foods, nor people kill or eat their totem, though this was not universal. Fire and hunting regimes were adjusted to help species in decline; no plant was cropped out; young, guardian and totem species, sometimes females, and in spring eggs and breeding animals and plants were prohibited. In 1841 Grey reported several bans, including a 'law that no plant bearing seed is to be dug up after it has flowered . . . I have never seen a native violate this rule.'[13] In South Australia the 'wealth and variety' of Ngarrindjeri resources was affirmed by 'the fact that twenty types of food were forbidden to young men, and thirteen types were forbidden to boys... these... were considered relatively easy to obtain, so were reserved for older, less vigorous people'.[14] Carpentaria people could not hunt in the country of someone recently dead. Ronald and Catherine Berndt concluded that conservation

> was much more widespread than is realized. Their intimate knowledge of the growth of various creatures, as well as of the increase of vegetable and other plants and trees, led many of them to realize that conservation was essential even in times of plenty. They could not afford to be careless... there are also cases of Aborigines sprinkling seeds around or preserving certain valuable trees; or saying, for instance, 'The stingray are breeding just now, we won't kill any for food until the new ones have grown.'[15]

No doubt 100-year droughts and rogue fires helped teach this wisdom, but only affluent societies can afford such lavish restraints.

People were so affluent and provident that they could declare fauna sanctuaries. Lindsay remarked of South Alligator (NT) people, 'Portions of the country are conserved for two or three years to allow the game and reptiles to increase. Then, about August, a tribe will visit the spot, and by setting fire to the grass in patches will find abundance of food.'[16] 'For several years before a gathering in mass', Gilmore wrote, 'no kangaroos, possums, or wild fowl were hunted or disturbed round the area devoted to the meeting.'[17] Permanent sanctuaries might be in places difficult to harvest, like gorges, but most were on the best regenerating localities, usually totem sites. Strehlow wrote of Irbmangkara (Running Waters) on the Finke (NT), magnificent wildfowl country, that since the beginning of time no game or fowl could be killed within about two miles of its sacred cave.[18] Helena Spring (WA), in tough desert northwest of Lake Mackay, is the best water for hundreds of miles. Carnegie found it much used by birds and animals, but

> Curiously enough, but few native camps were to be seen, nor is this the first time that I have noticed that the best waters are least used... These desert people... have some provident habits, for first the small native wells are used, and only when these are exhausted are the more permanent waters resorted to.[19]

Latz explained,

> In the desert you've got to have this system because you have really bad droughts and so on. You've got to have a sanctuary from where your animals can expand back out after a drought. Not a single animal was allowed to be killed in this area. Not a single plant was allowed to be picked. These sanctuaries were scattered all over the landscape—wherever there was important Dreaming there was a sanctuary area.[20]

Every year or so Murray and Edward (NSW) people alternated the camping and sanctuary sides of swamps, and Murrumbidgee people

> invariably set aside some parts to remain as breeding-places or animal sanctuaries. Where there were plains by a river, a part was left undisturbed for birds that nested on the ground. They did the same thing with lagoons, rivers, billabongs for water-birds and fish. There once was a great sanctuary for emus at Eunonyhareenyha, near Wagga Wagga. The name means 'The breeding-place of the emus'—the emu's sanctuary . . . The law of sanctuary in regards to large or wide breeding-grounds, such as Ganmain or Deepwater, where once there were miles and miles of swamps . . . was that each year a part of the area could be hunted or fished, but not the same part two seasons in succession.[21]

Such places calibrated abundance.[22]

Bans and sanctuaries uncorked culling. Balance and continuity were reciprocal: no species should threaten or overrun another, and totem guardians were bound to prevent it—hence the putrid eels. Animals forced off their templates intruded onto the templates of others, offending the Law and the land. They were fair game. In central Australia, for

> a few months after a rain a large wandering horde of men, women and children revelled in an abundance of food. Animals were slaughtered ruthlessly, and only the best and fattest parts of the killed game were eaten; every tree was stripped bare of its fruits; and all that was unripe or tasteless were tossed away.[23]

Kimber explained, 'There is a distinct concept of *maintaining* a specific supply, and of *culling* from it, in a *known* area.'[24] Such slaughter was reducing excess, not reducing excessively. It was balance more than waste, and although hunting off-template was less predictable, people may have preferred it, conserving templates for ceremonies or hard times. Abundance indeed, if so much planning and care went into making and rotating templates, only to avoid them.

In good seasons kangaroos breed prolifically. On Eyre Peninsula (SA) people slaughtered excess roos; in the Blue Mountains they drove wallabies over cliffs.[25] This kept roos on their templates. Explorers sought roo meat daily, yet many reported no kangaroos for days, then many, then none. On 19 March 1798 a party southwest of Sydney 'fell in with' kangaroos, on 23 March it 'had no signs of a kangaroo for three days', on 28–9 March it 'saw hundreds'.[26] On 23 June 1817 Oxley saw a 'flock' of kangaroos for 'the first time since we quitted the Lachlan' on 18 May. He reported no more until he found them 'abounding' on 8 August. In 1818 they were 'in very great numbers' on 12 June, in 'hundreds' on 6 August, 'abounding' on 26 August, in 'abundance' on 31 August and 'abounding' on 12 September, but on the other days he reported none even though his party sought them, and he was where later they were common. Finally he declared, 'These animals live in flocks like sheep.'[27] On Cooper's Creek, Burke and Wills, armed and used to shooting roos, saw none and starved, and between 1849 and 1886 Creek settlers saw none or few, though later they were common.[28] On Tasmania's aptly named Forester River, Robinson

> came to a large plain of tolerable good feed; it was of great extent and abounded with kangaroo. I had seen no place like it on this side of the island, and the clumps of trees of various sorts gave it a delightful park-like appearance. I named it kangaroo park. This country had been well burnt off.[29]

On the Yarra, Hoddle 'entered some forest land distant from Melbourne 23 miles called Kangaroo Ground for about 5 miles—then barren scrub. The Kangaroo Ground has excellent soil and appears to extend for several miles to the north-west. It abounds with Kangaroo.'[30] Long after the animals have vanished, Kangaroo Grounds speckle Australia, and Kangaroo Creek, Flat, Ground, Gully, Point and Valley have post codes. Roos were on paddocks without fences.[31]

After 1788 roos multiplied and spread as their preferred habitats degraded. Where they were not seen in 1788 they became plagues. When the Tasmanians were 'removed',

'Opossums and Brush Kangaroos . . . increased in many districts, and are very troublesome'.[32] Three years after Adelaide was settled, Hahn declared,

> It is almost inconceivable that these people used to live solely on kangaroo meat, as the country has never been particularly well supplied with these animals . . . if they were so common, then some . . . would have been encountered on the overland journeys between Adelaide and Sydney . . . Anyway, there are very few now in the surrounding district. It is therefore more likely that the people eat the fish which abound in the rivers.[33]

The Adelaide plain and the overland stock route soon swarmed with kangaroos. In northern New South Wales BE Norton found few early references to them, but 'large-scale slaughter' by the 1880s, 'one property killing 10,000 in 1881 and another destroying 20,000 in four years . . . graziers offered an incentive of 6d a head for kangaroos and 3d for wallabies'.[34] On a Murray station kangaroos cut carrying capacity by over 75 per cent between 1848 and 1862, and in 1878 the station shot 11,000 roos in six months.[35] That year pastoralists petitioned parliament for relief from 'the increase and ravages of marsupials in many parts of the colony . . . a large extent of country . . . [is] virtually useless . . . being wholly overrun with these pests'.[36] In 1881, New South Wales paid a bounty on 581,753 roo scalps—1600 a day—and in 1884 on 260,780 scalps in the Tamworth district alone, but roo plagues continued. In Victoria a station killed 10,000 roos annually for six years without reducing their number, but Curr thought 'the evil . . . much more serious' in Queensland.[37] Central Queensland roos merely in 'goodly number' in 1862 'overwhelmed' the district in 1875–7.[38] As late as 1901–2 in the Centre, where by the 1930s roos were common, Murray several times noted their scarcity, once remarking, 'Saw half a dozen kangaroos here, a large mob for these parts.'[39] Where Canberra grassland carried small mobs in the 1820s, roo numbers today threaten its survival. After 1788 roos ran wild.[40]

In 1788 koalas ranged the southeast and east coasts inland to the edge of the plains, but their locations were distinct, lightly populated, and few. Europeans did not record a koala until 1798 (ch 7), nor get one live until 1803, from Sydney people,[41] yet by the 1900s koalas were common around Sydney. Mt Yarrahapinni (NSW) ('koala falling down') is an ancestral koala place 'densely wooded to the summit, with an almost impenetrable forest of gigantic trees, but its spurs descend in beautiful verdant park-like declivities to the beach, the grass growing luxuriantly' where the koala fell down.[42]

This is rainforest country, but those 'gigantic trees' were eucalypts, feeding koalas and keeping them confined.

Within a few decades koalas were a plague. In 1844 Robinson thought them 'in places abundant' in Gippsland; 30 years later they were a pest there. On the Goulburn (Vic) no-one reported them in the 1840s; by 1870 there were 'thousands'. Around Bega (NSW) they were not noted by the earliest settlers, common by 1860, and in streets and gardens from the 1880s until 1905. At Port Stephens (NSW) no-one thought koalas common until the 1890s. In southeast Queensland early Europeans occasionally noted them; after 1900 millions of skins were sold there, including a million in 1919 and 584,738 in one month in 1927.[43]

Other species multiplied. Crocodiles may have been fewer in 1788 than in 1888 and now. On the Murray in 1856 Gerard Krefft listed all the district's animals and birds, but not wombats, later common there. In 1788 possums were common, in places a staple. 'White fellow shoot 'em like possum', Wiradjuri said in telling Rolf Boldrewood how readily settlers killed their people. Possum numbers exploded after 1788. By the 1870s they were killing forests by eating new leaves, and Riverina station hands could shoot them without leaving camp. Emus range widely and in some parts of the Centre did so in 1788,[44] but in woodland they seem to have been restricted to particular plains, and not numerous there. Rolls pointed out that Leichhardt's hundred or so at Seven Emu River was thought a big mob. By the 1880s New South Wales governments and pastoralists were annually paying bounties on thousands of birds and eggs. Forrest saw only odd birds south of the Murchison (WA) in 1874, but by the 1920s the district carried tens of thousands. Western Australia built over 300 miles of fence, paid a beak bounty, and in the 1930s called in the army with machine-guns to cull the birds, with no success. In the 1880s New South Wales declared noxious kangaroos, wallabies, kangaroo rats, pademelons, wombats, bandicoots, possums, emus, eagles, hawks, crows and dingos. None were thought numerous when settlers arrived.[45]

Why these increases? After 1788 stock shortened the grass, increasing feed for native grazers, but so far the only explanation common to all increases is that until 1788 animal numbers were kept low by human or dingo predation.[46] Yet dingos too were uncommon in 1788 and increased later, including by eating grazers.[47] Only people were fewer, decimated by germs and guns. This mattered, but so did its companion change to settler land management and the collapse of the templates.

People grew crops in 1788. They knew plants intimately. Several languages had five or six words for a leaf's life stages. In 1985 Kakadu (NT) elders named 420 scarp species including several not known to science, and detailed the behaviour of each.[48] People cultivated New Zealand Spinach, Bunya and Queensland Nut (Macadamia), tended vines on forest edges, portulaca on raised mounds, Bush Tomato on burnt ground before rain, Pituri in deep sand. They planted fruit and berries, sometimes backburning or log-fencing them from animals. When young Mary Gilmore spat out a Quandong seed, a woman scolded her and picked it up to plant.[49]

The two main crop groups were tubers, bulbs, roots, rhizomes and shoots (hereafter tubers), and grain. Tubers were easier to gather and better to eat. People grew them where it was wet enough: from most coasts as far inland as water would sustain them, and in wet places elsewhere. Grain, particularly Native Millet, was a supplement or staple in places without enough tubers or other plant food. In general dry places grew grain; elsewhere grew tubers. Either might cover many hectares or be in small niches. Agriculture spread more widely over Australia than now.

Yams such as *warran* and *murnong* declare their farming heritage. Cape York people know that replanting tops not only ensures more yams, but leads to a 'multiple-ended tuber', a 'mother yam, which is especially succulent'.[50] Many accounts mention replanting tops,[51] but people did much more. *Warran* and *murnong* prefer open grassland thinned by fire, and to flourish in the millions they did in 1788 they need soft soil, seasonally dug over. In season women spent hours a day tilling, replanting, transplanting and weeding. In Western Australia they dug *warran* paddocks over many square miles. North of the Hutt in April 1839, Grey found

> a tract of light fertile soil, quite overrun with *warran* plants . . . for three and a half consecutive miles we traversed a fertile piece of land, literally perforated with the holes the natives had made to dig this root; indeed we could with difficulty walk across it on that account, whilst this tract extended east and west as far as we could see . . . more had here been done to secure a provision from the ground by hard manual labour than I could have believed it in the power of uncivilised man to accomplish . . . [The ground was] fuller of holes than a sugar plantation, all of which had been dug by the natives to extract their favourite yams. There were also many large beaten paths, along the sides of which we every here and there found native wells, of a [great] depth and size . . . these circumstances all combined to give the country an appearance of cultivation, and of being densely inhabited, such as I had never before seen.[52]

In 1851 a settler thought *warran* people 'very little addicted to hunting and very few of them are even expert at tracking a kangaroo. This may result from the great variety of edible roots, particularly the A-jack-o or warang, which grows here in great abundance and to a very large size.'[53] People cultivated it on the Swan and in the Kimberley, but as Rupert Gerritsen noted, not continuously down the West Australian coast. It is a tropical plant; how, he asked, did it get south of the break?[54]

In southeast Australia people farmed *murnong*. Varieties grow in dry places, high country, and open forest, but its heartland was the open plains from Melbourne to Mt Gambier (SA). The seed does not last in the soil so crops need continuous mature plants, yet 'millions' grew there, and where women dug them, for mile on mile the ground looked ploughed. 'Today the native women were spread out over the plain as far as I could see them, collecting *punimim, murnong* . . .', Robinson wrote in July 1841. 'They burn the grass the better to see these roots.'[55] Further west Mitchell met 'open grassy country, extending as far as we could see, hills round and smooth as a carpet, meadows broad, and either as green as an emerald, or of a rich golden colour, from the abundance, as we soon afterwards found, of a little ranunculus-like flower . . . we went on our way rejoicing'. His way interrupted a woman digging *murnong*, 'the only visible inhabitant of this splendid valley, resembling a nobleman's park on a gigantic scale'.[56] At Sunbury (Vic) Batey recalled a slope of

> rich basaltic clay, evidently well fitted for the production of myrnongs. On the spot are numerous mounds with short spaces between each, and as all these are at right angles to the ridge's slope, it is conclusive evidence that they were the work of human hands extending over a long series of years. This uprooting of the soil to apply the best term was accidental gardening, still it is reasonable to assume that the Aboriginals were quite aware of the fact that turning the earth over in search of yams instead of diminishing that form of food supply would have a tendency to increase it.[57]

'There is a nutritious root which they eat and are fond of', a settler near Melbourne told a Select Committee in 1845,

> that, I think, has greatly diminished, from the grazing of sheep and cattle over the land, because I have not seen so many of the flowers of it in the spring as I used to see. It bears a beautiful yellow flower. The native name of this root is 'murnong' . . .

> It is rather agreeable to the taste . . . a man named Buckley . . .
> tells me, that a man may live on the root for weeks together.[58] [59]

Other yams were grown. On the Hawkesbury in July 1789 Hunter observed:

> The natives here, appear chiefly to live on the roots which they dig from the ground; for these low banks appear to have been ploughed up, as if a vast herd of swine had been living on them. We put on shore, and examined the places which they had dug, and found the wild yam in considerable quantities, but in general very small, not larger than a walnut [seed yams?]; they appear to be in greatest plenty on the banks of the river; a little way back they are scarce.[60]

On the Arnhem coast,

> the parsnip yam was particularly important. When yams were dug out, the top of the tuber was left still attached to the tendril in the ground so that the yam would grow again. The same practice has been recorded from other parts of Arnhem Land and Cape York. At Lockhart on the east coast of Cape York Peninsula the vines were marked as sign of 'ownership'. Yams were also planted on offshore islands.[61]

Specialising in one variety was not universal. When after seventeen years with Queensland people Jimmy Morrill detailed the many tubers they ate, each had its totem place:

> one of which grows at the tops of the mountains is the best eating called 'moogoondah', it is white, sweet, firm, dry, and grows in red clay soils. There is another, lower down, at the foot of the mountains, in the scrub, called 'mulboon', which is soft and more moist and is very nice eating. There is another root rather of a sticky nature when cooked, grown on the mountains, not in the scrub, but in the grass, and white like a turnip, with a small thin leaf, called 'cornool'. There is another smaller and darker in its colour, but in other respects very much like it, called 'cahnan'. Another, a creeper which grows on the high banks of the fresh water rivers, with a small green leaf, the leaves very thick, called 'booan'. There

is another, similar to a turnip, but smaller, called 'manoon'. There is one
which runs in and out among the grass with a little blue flower, called
'cardoala' or 'cardoabar', and many others more or less like them.[62]

Here is a hint of cropping: Morrill once says 'grown', and some of these tubers need fire to thin competition. There is also a hint of transplanting: might 'manoon' be *murnong*? Like *warran*, did plant and name come from the tropics?[63]

To grow grain, people chose water margins or overflows, in dry places blocked channels to extend them, burnt ground preferably before rain (ch 6), spread seed, watched the season to know when to return, reaped the crop by pulling or stripping with stone knives, dried, threshed and winnowed the grain, and stored it in skin bags or pounded it 'between stones with water, forming a kind of paste or bread'.[64] Augustus Gregory recalled,

> On Cooper's Creek, the natives reap a Panicum grass [millet]. Fields of 1,000 acres are there met with growing this cereal. The natives cut it down by means of stone knives, cutting down the stalk half way, beat out the seed, leaving the straw which is often met with in large heaps; they winnow by tossing seed and husk in the air, the wind carrying away the husks. The grinding into meal is done by means of two stones . . . sometimes dry and at others with water into a meal.[65]

On the Darling Mitchell found Native Millet

> pulled, to a very great extent, and piled in hay-ricks, so that the aspect of the desert was softened into the agreeable semblance of a hay-field. The grass had evidently been thus laid up by the natives, but for what purpose we could not imagine . . . we found the ricks, or hay-cocks, extending for miles . . . All of the grass was of one kind, a new species of *Panicum* . . . not a spike of it was left in the soil, over the whole of the ground.[66]

Millet heads at different times, so people pulled or cut and stacked it when most heads were full but most stalks green. Near Lake Narran (NSW) they

> made a brush-yard and the grass was put in . . . fire was set to
> the grass which was full in the ear yet green. While the fire was

burning the blacks kept turning the grass with sticks all the time to knock the seeds out. When this was done, and the fire burnt out, they gathered up the seed into a big opossum rug.[67]

Elsewhere they spread stalks to dry, threshing when the grain ripened, and piling up straw 'like hay cocks'.[68] On the Narran, Mitchell saw

> Dry heaps of this grass, that had been pulled expressly for the purpose of gathering the seed, lay along our path for many miles. I counted nine miles along the river, in which we rode through this grass only, reaching to our saddle-girths, and the same grass seemed to grow back from the river, at least as far as the eye could reach through a very open forest.[69]

'Through this grass only . . . as far as the eye could reach.' This was no casual sowing. On overflow land, where each flush brings fresh debris, it also suggests weeding. This was a grain template.

Grain was also cropped on floodplains off the rivers. With Sturt west of the Darling, Brock saw a crop, probably millet, 'quite like a harvest field. The seed which supplies the natives with a nutritious food grows here in season in great quantities. In every hollow we found the remains of the natives' labour in the shape of straw, from which they had beaten out the seed.'[70] Sturt too saw 'a boundless stubble the grass being of the kind from which the natives collect seeds'.[71] Even remote claypans might be cropped, and perhaps seeded. In 1857 William Suttor crossed 'the great, almost treeless, level plain' from the lower Lachlan towards the Darling:

> Our camp for the night was on a low sand ridge covered with hopbush scrub. It stands like an island in the level waste and had been visible on the horizon for hours before we reached it. There is a small morass close by where the wild blacks have scooped out a small hole, which was filled with rain water. We were about 100 miles from anywhere. The wild blacks had been here lately, as we learned from the heaps of grass straw scattered about, from which they had thrashed the seeds . . . We pitched our tents and made luxuriant beds of the grass straw.[72]

The New South Wales Government Botanist Fred Turner identified at least four other grains which 'developed very much under cultivation', notably Bull Mitchell Grass, which produced 'ears nearly 6 inches in length, well filled with a clean-looking, firm grain, which separates easily from the chaff, somewhat like wheat'.[73] On Flood's Creek Sturt found that although 'the heat was very great, the cereal grasses had not yet ripened their seed, and several kinds had not even developed the flower... We found there a native wheat, a beautiful oat, and a rye, as well as a variety of grasses.'[74]

For many crops either fire or no fire was essential. Without fire, grass or bracken smothers *murnong*, but cool, well-timed burns extend its range. People burnt ripe tubers about early summer. This timing would destroy grain coming into head: grain-growing people burnt after the late summer harvest, and as seed was sprouting in autumn or winter—timely smoke increases Native Millet germination from about 8 per cent to 63 per cent.[75] 'In all parts of Australia', Eyre wrote of Broadleaf Cumbungi, 'even when other food abounds, the root of this reed is a favourite and staple article of diet.'[76] At the right time people burnt cumbungi to improve its taste and fertilise its beds, then cropped and stored it. Timely fire promoted Pituri, Kangaroo Apple, Coconut and Waterbush, and in cycads and Grass Trees it induced more plants, much better fruiting, and concurrent ripening, letting people congregate. It promoted manna, the sweet secretion lerp insects make under eucalypt leaves. Curr wrote, 'There were bags full of it in almost every camp, and I understood the Blacks to say that they used to set fire to a portion of the mallee every year and gather the manna the next season from the young growth.'[77] Timely fire may also explain the seeming absence in 1788 of the biblical-scale bird, insect and mice plagues farmers periodically suffer today (ch 6).[78]

Like *warran*, species were transplanted. In northern South Australia people distributed vine cuttings, and Carpentaria people moved water lilies, though only within the same clan area, otherwise the lilies would not be kin.[79] In Victoria Cabbage Palm 'is the only Palm found wild... and legend affirms it was even there introduced by Aborigines',[80] and coastal pigface was traded to the Grampians where it still grows in rock shelters.[81] Transplanting is 'a possible explanation for the discontinuous distribution of bunya pine'.[82] At Kungathan on Cape York, 37 edible plant species grew in a 300 x 100 metre patch. It was near camps, distinct from adjacent vegetation, and carefully burnt.[83] In north Australia there is a 'consistent association of edible fruit trees and old camp sites'. People throw tree seeds into litter at camp edges, knowing the compost grows them. 'All the same gardeny', one man said. Rhys Jones observed, 'You can predict a camp by the vegetation... [Native Apple] would be growing north of the central casuarina because that is the shade when the fruit is ripe in January... dry season fruit trees like Pandanus and Terminalia are to the south of it.'[84] Coconuts, figs and shade trees were planted, owned and sometimes protected by clearings.[85]

Seed was easily transplanted and traded (ch 5). Bush Tomato, Desert Raisin and other *Solanums* were traded 'beyond their normal range'.[86] Northeast of Alice Springs, Aruabara

> was not entirely a natural garden. Before the rains came, the local people used fire to promote the growth of some plants. They protected other patches, and seeded the fired patches and some other areas. The seeds, carried in emu feather containers called *apwas*, were exchanged as gifts at major gatherings. They were scattered near soakage waters or other sites favourable to the particular species.[87]

Fiona Walsh argued,

> The introduction of species to sites beyond their 'normal' range or habitat may have been a consequence of trade, exchange and storage. Martu stated that plant foods, particularly seeds and fruits, were exchanged at social events and through trade practices. They dried and preserved a range of fruit species for use in the short-term, and cached large quantities of seed and *Cyperus bulbosus* tubers in anticipation of drought and large meetings.[88] [89]

Many crops were 'cached'. Tubers last only a few months. Dried fruit stores better, nuts better still. Bunya nuts were put in water or buried in bags, cycads sliced, dried, wrapped in paperbark and buried in 7-metre grass-lined trenches, Quandong, plum and fig strung on sticks or made into cakes, waterlily corms dried and stored.[90] Dry seed stores well. Portulaca was wrapped in mud and baked, stored and traded. On the Finke near Mt Charlotte (NT), Christopher Giles

> discovered a native granary. This was a rude platform built in a tree, about 7 or 8 feet from the ground, on this were placed in a heap a number of bags made of close netting. Dismounting, I climbed the tree to examine the bags, and was astonished to find that they contained different kinds of grain, stored up for the winter, or rather the dry season . . . the legs of our [stolen] trousers and the sleeves of our shirts, tied up at each end, [were] filled with seeds.[91]

North of Newcastle Waters (NT) Arthur Ashwin

> chanced upon . . . large wooden dishes . . . filled with grass seed as
> large as rice [Native Rice?] with the husk or the skin on the seed.
> I think it was a species of rice which grows in the flooded country
> 40 or 50 miles in extent and north of Newcastle Waters. There
> must have been about a ton of seed stored there in 17 large dishes,
> full and all covered with paper-bark. The dishes were nearly all
> five feet long and a foot deep, scooped out of solid wood.[92]

On the 'flooded country' Ashwin found six dishes of rice stored in trees and covered with paperbark. He boiled a bagful. It was good: 'pity we did not take more', he wrote.[93] In central New South Wales Charles Coxen

> found a considerable store of grass-seed, gum from the mimosa, and other
> stores, carefully packed up in large bags made from the skin of the kangaroo,
> and covered over with pieces of bark, so as to keep them properly dry.
> The weight of the bags containing the grass-seed and gum was about one
> hundred pounds; the seeds had been carefully dried after being collected.[94]

Near Milparinka (NSW) Sturt pitied people thrashing wattles for seed,[95] and west of the lower Castlereagh he

> found a number of bark troughs, filled with the gum of the mimosa,
> and vast quantities of gum made into cakes upon the ground. From
> this it would appear these unfortunate creatures were reduced
> to the last extremity, and, being unable to procure any other
> nourishment, had been obliged to collect this mucilaginous food.[96]

In time he would suck that gum with relief. Storing was familiar everywhere, not always in response to scarcity. It might be for ceremony, or to stockpile, trade or transplant. On the Carpentaria coast, and as Latz observed of desert people, 'Stored foods were probably mostly used for ceremonial purposes and do not appear to have played a critical role in tiding people over severe droughts.'[97] [98]

Some researchers see nascent farming in these various practices from tilling to trading.[99] Ian Keen suggested that they 'involved a more radical intervention in the ecology than was recognised earlier', and Beth Gott remarked, 'the boundary between foraging and farming is blurred . . . it might be more appropriate to classify Aboriginal subsistence production as that of hunter-gatherer-cultivators'.[100] Kimber thought 'Aborigines had developed a "farming attitude". Their use of "game and vegetable reserves", general concepts of culling and conservation of resources, capture of young animals for "hunter-display" pets, and semi-domestication of the dingo, all suggest moves towards farming people.'[101] In two important theses Daphne Nash put a strong case for farming. In 1984 she listed examples of every farm practice, detailed how Mt Liebig (NT) women moved plants and spread seed to increase their number and range, and concluded, 'it is clear that Aborigines are involved in management regimes which stretch the definition of hunting and gathering to include many techniques more commonly associated with agriculture'. By 1993 her Pintupi friends had taught her even more. She titled her thesis 'Aboriginal Gardening'. For Europeans the difference between a farm and a garden is a matter of scale,[102] but they are vague on where the two meet: is a market garden a garden or a farm? Nash concluded,

> in hunting and gathering trips, as well as in domestic gardening, people dealt with plants and other resources for social and cultural reasons. They were not solely motivated by biological survival . . . In the bush-gardens, people continued to manage their favoured traditional resources. In both locations, culturally significant species were planted, protected and encouraged in ways that are readily recognised by observers as gardening techniques when used by other cultural groups, but rarely recognised as such in Aboriginal Australia.[103]

She supported this with examples of horticulture and agriculture in various parts of Australia, affecting both 'the entire landscape' and individual plants like yams, bulbs, cycads, Pituri and Bush Tomato. Nothing was accidental or incidental: people acted deliberately to improve quality and yield.[104]

Some researchers puzzle at why people did not 'go further', that is, become farmers. Josephine Flood wondered whether people 'were so affluent that they had no need to increase the yield of food plants . . . There would thus have been no stimulus to increase the food supply by developing agriculture.'[105] Harry Allen and Tim Flannery noted that many Australian tubers, seeds, nuts and fruits were 'closely related to plants domesticated elsewhere in the world', and Allen saw that the Darling country where some of these foods grew was 'not more arid or unpredictable than areas where domestication took place'. He thought a 'hunting and gathering economy rather than an agricultural one may have been the most efficient subsistence strategy for the Darling

River Basin, one that enabled them to withstand considerable environmental pressures without any population loss', but concluded that he did not know why people did not become farmers.[106]

Most observers, lay and expert, are adamant that Aborigines were not farmers, and did not farm. Farming peoples attach notions of civilisation, even hierarchies of civilisation, to farming. They think agriculture more civilised and civilising than pastoralism, let alone hunter-gathering. This makes them reluctant to concede that Aborigines farmed. As evidence eroded their initial assumptions and arguments, they put increasingly tougher definition hurdles in the way of what people did in 1788. They began with a simple objection. The land was not disturbed; people had no husbandry and no agriculture. In 1798 Malthus was among the first to sow this seed. Using accounts from New South Wales, he proposed that all populations are limited by their food supply. Hunter-gatherers depend for food on the whims of nature, and this uncertainty deprives them of control over their lives, limits their number, and blocks their road to civilisation. Hunter-gatherers are victims of nature.[107]

This wouldn't do. Clearly people did disturb the land, and did control their food supply, even in Malthus' terms. Farmers raised the bar. Aborigines did till and toil, but did not farm. 'In digging up these yams', AC Gregory observed in 1882, 'they invariably re-insert the head of the yams so as to be sure of a future crop, but beyond this they do absolutely nothing which may be regarded as a tentative in the direction of cultivating plants.'[108] In 1965 Mervyn Hartwig stated of the Arrernte, 'No attempt is made to grow crops or breed animals, ritual and magic being employed to maintain food-supplies.'[109] This assessment reflected the times, but was after Sturt, Eyre, Mitchell and others proved such notions wrong. The prejudice persisted even after Rhys Jones' brilliant insight on firestick farming incinerated it.[110] In 1971 Jones himself wrote,

> Western Desert people do harvest certain staple food-plants, but they do not handle these in a way that closely matches the behaviour of agricultural societies. For example, they possess certain techniques for storing a variety of vegetable foods, but they do not use these techniques to build up surpluses except in times of shortage or extended drought. They do not have any kinds of 'first fruits' ceremonies usually associated with agricultural harvests. They do not practice any form of cultivation. And they do not build dams, terraces, or any constructions which might enhance the growth of their wild food resources. Indeed, fire appears to be their only means of taking what we may regard as direct action to encourage

> the growth of these plants, and present evidence suggests strongly that they are not fully aware of this as an outcome of their burning activity.[111]

All this is now disproved, including by Jones, but the standard it demands, 'the behaviour of agricultural societies', lingers. In 2000 David Horton stated that Australia was 'the only continent in which there was no indigenous agriculture'.[112] This hinges on his definition of indigenous agriculture. In 1998 Jared Diamond wrote of tuber growers, 'All that they would have had to do to meet the definition of farmers was to carry the stems and remaining attached tubers home and similarly replace them in soil at their camp.'[113] Some did, some didn't: were all or none farmers thereby?

The bar went higher. In a thoughtful article in 1995, DE Yen defined farmers not only as managing plants and animals but also as experimenting to improve breeds and strains, thereby excluding Aborigines:

> Had Australian Aborigines invented agriculture independently, the major genetic elements in the systems of the tropical north and its easterly and westerly subtropical coastal extensions might have resembled the taro-yam complex [further north] . . . In over a century of historical observation, ethnography and archaeology, however, there has been no indication of agriculture in the diverse Australian landscapes. That the operational results of foraging techniques can offer striking parallels to agriculture ('the agronomy of hunter-gatherers') is really no argument for Aborigines being on some pathway towards cultivation, for domestication of plant species through control of breeding systems and adaptation through modification of the environment, both artificial processes in the human manipulation of the nature-nurture equation, are missing in Australia.[114]

People did modify plant environments in 1788, by cultivation and selective burning, while 'breeding systems' are not inherent to farming. They simply raise productivity (yield per hectare), usually in response to population increase.

This population–productivity spiral is critical. In time it obliged farmers to stay put, and in more time made bar-raisers think sedentism integral to farming. 'A separate consequence of a settled existence', Diamond declared, 'is that it permits one to store food surpluses, since storage would be pointless if one didn't remain nearby to guard the stored food . . . stored food is essential for feeding non-food-producing specialists.'[115] In 1788 many people stored, none stayed by their stores, and many who did not store specialised in tool, net and hut making, trade and ritual. 'Sedentism as a pre-requisite [to farming]', Yen wrote, 'remained undeveloped in Aboriginal society as did well-developed hierarchical social systems.'[116] About 1822 Berry put both pre-requisites, one directly, the other unconsciously, to a Shoalhaven man:

> I asked him if they could not erect houses for themselves like the men's huts which would afford them better protection from the weather than a sheet of bark. He replied that they no doubt could do so—and that such Huts would afford them better Shelter—but that it would not suit their mode of life—that it was necessary for them constantly to change their place of residence in search of the means of subsistence and that their means of subsistence had become more scanty since the country had been occupied by white men—that the sheep and cattle eat all the grass in consequence of which Kangaroos had become very scarce—and that they now lived chiefly on squirrels and opossums and such small animals.[117]

Berry missed both hints—people did not want to be servants, and they managed kangaroos better than he did. They had no reason to keep within fences.

They ignored not only Europeans. In the north they knew about farmers. Cape York people traded with Torres Strait gardeners, and Arnhem Landers watched Macassans and Baijini from the Indies till land and plant rice, tamarind and Coconuts, build stone houses, wear cloth, make pottery and feed domestic fowls, dogs and cats. Some visited the Indies.[118] None copied either group, instead maintaining typical Australian templates. If anything, people farmed more often beyond the range of these northern groups than within it, and if anything, hunter-gathering can as readily be seen as moving north from Cape York as farming moving south.[119][120]

Many people did live in villages, but most only when harvesting—not, as Berry hoped, to be civilised as cheap labour. The villages best known now were by Victoria's eel farms. Lake Condah's stone houses could hold about 700 people, and near Mt William were 'fixed residences: at one village were thirteen large Huts—they are warm and well constructed . . . One Hut measured 10 feet diameter by five feet high, and sufficiently strong for a man on horseback to ride over.'[121] People elsewhere built stone houses, and villages were on Hutt and Swan *warran* templates.[122] At Westernport 'huts form villages of forty or fifty, and one was seen built . . . with a doorway and two windows'.[123]

In 1845 Sturt found huts

made of strong boughs with a thick coating of clay over leaves and grass. They were impervious to wind and rain, and were really comfortable, being evidently erections of a permanent kind to which the inhabitants frequently returned. Where there were villages these huts were built in rows, the front of one house being at the back of the other, and it appeared to be a singular and universal custom to erect a smaller hut at no great distance from the large ones, but we were unable to detect for what purpose they were made, unless it was to deposit their seeds; as they were too small even for children to inhabit.[124]

Where Ashwin found stored seed, he

chanced upon a native encampment of mia-mias, or wurleys, all fenced in with a brush fence . . . There was one large mia-mia, about seven feet high in the middle, and about 16 feet diameter. It was round and arched off to the ground . . . All around this storeroom there were about 50 small mia-mias, or miahs, or gunyahs, as some tribes call them. The fence enclosing the lot was about 200 yards across, and appeared to be kept in order.[125]

On the Cooper hut-building 'was a specialised activity with good builders being in great demand and borrowed from camp to camp'.[126] To farmers huts mark sedentism, but on the Cooper mobile specialists built them. Neither in Australia's richest nor poorest parts, by European standards, were people tempted to settle. Instead they quit their villages and eels, their crops and stores and templates, to walk their country.[127]

So people burnt, tilled, planted, transplanted, watered, irrigated, weeded, thinned, cropped, stored and traded. On present evidence not all groups did all these, and few Tasmanians may have, but many mainlanders did. What farm process did they miss?

There was one difference. They were mobile. No livestock, no beast of burden, anchored them. They did not stay in their houses or by their crops. Sedentism has been used to disqualify Aborigines as farmers,[128] but sedentism contrasts with mobility rather than hunter-gathering. Thomson noted that north Australian clans spent several months mobile and several months sedentary each year, but each period was equally planned and predictable, 'a regular and *orderly* annual cycle carried out systematically, and with a rhythm parallel to, and in step with, the seasonal changes . . . the nomadic movements of these people can be forecast with accuracy, and . . . their camps . . . foretold with reasonable certainty'.[129] Mobility is an attitude, a habit of mind and body, stirring the same pleasant sensations which cheer bushwalkers, of being your own boss, outside, free of the crowd. In the 1930s an Arnhem woman remarked,

> rather patronizingly, as she watched a Fijian missionary working in his mission garden, anxiously concerned because a few plants had died: 'You people go to all that trouble, working and planting seeds, but we don't have to do that. All these things are there for us, the Ancestral Beings left them for us. In the end, you depend on the sun and the rain just as we do, but the difference is that we just have to go and collect the food when it is ripe. We don't have all this other trouble.'[130]

This was a critical advantage, and not only in drought or crisis. Kaberry thought Kimberley women worked less hard than farmers' wives, yet got food more certainly:

> It is not the steady strenuous labour of the German peasant woman bending from dawn to dusk over her fields, hoeing, weeding, sowing, and reaping. The aboriginal woman has greater freedom of movement and more variety . . . the agriculturalist may be left destitute and almost starving if the [crops] fail or are destroyed by drought, flood, fire, locusts, or grasshoppers, as sometimes happens in China and in Europe. I never saw an aboriginal woman come in empty-handed, though in 1935 there was a drought.[131]

She concluded, 'women's work . . . compares favourably with a European eight-hour day and possibly overtime as well'. Blainey too pointed out that people worked many fewer hours a day to secure food and shelter than farmers anywhere.[132] Perhaps neither counted fire or ritual as work, but only people untroubled about food could have held so many corroborees and ceremonies. Of course there were hungry times, or people would not have managed their resources so carefully, but this is so of farming, and as with farming was not the norm. People were not hinging on uncertainty or toil.

Then why did farmers elsewhere become sedentary? Not by choice, 1788 suggests. Was it a step not towards something better, but away from something worse? Were people forced to stay put to defend crops, stock or stores? Not from climate: Europe's harsh winters and Australia's harsh summers explain why people might store food, but not why they must stay by the stores throughout the year and throughout the years. Not from pests or diseases: concentrated plants and animals are more vulnerable to these, not less. Sedentary villagers are more vulnerable too, until they build up immunity: introduced diseases were catastrophic for people in 1788, whereas no serious disease was native to Aboriginal Australia. To protect stock from large predators like big cats, wolves and bears? Possibly: only in Australia did people not confront these. But the most dangerous predators are humans. Did farmers stay put to defend their property from other people? Did barbarism put them on the road to civilisation?

Or did plenty tempt them into a population–productivity spiral, crowding the land and cramping them into sedentism? Diamond suggested this: not enough wild food led to domesticating plants, then to better farm skills and increased production, then to a merry-go-round of more people, more food, more people and so on.[133] This is a deadly and ultimately futile treadmill, its manifestations now being disputed. Diamond thought southeast people may have been on it: their eel channels, fish traps and nets, and 'winter' villages 'appear to have been evolving on a trajectory that would have eventually led to indigenous food production'.[134] The 'intensification' theory too argues that over the last 3000–4000 years Australia's population increased significantly as people refined resources. Tuber and grain templates did support more people, but mobility limits population. No land was crowded in 1788, no warrior obliged to stay and defend, no-one stopped from managing the far reaches of their country. Living on earth's driest occupied continent may have let people escape a population juggernaut.[135]

Mobility scandalised Europeans. Their road obliged them to fence and guard, to stay put, to make hard work a virtue. This gave great advantages, including the numbers and technology to explain why a white Australian writes this book. It also led them to condemn people who reduced their material wants, sat yarning in daylight, and gave so much time to ceremony and ritual. These were preserves and pursuits of gentry. It did not seem right that Aborigines should be like that. Aborigines were 'shiftless and improvident', uncivilised. The words meant to degrade hunter-gatherers, not to explore how they lived. Is it, for example, uncivilised to protect land and property by religious sanction rather than physical force? The key question is not 'Why weren't Aborigines more like us?', but 'How did people in 1788 manage lives and land so sustainably, for so long?'[136]

Somewhere on mainland Australia people used every farm process. Climate, land, labour, plants and knowledge were there. Example was there, in the north and after 1788. Templates and tending made farms without fences, but nothing made people farmers. They used fire so well that nature ruled their resources less than farmers, not more, because they managed over larger areas. In seasons which suited farming this made resources as predictable as farming, and in drought, flood and fire made them more predictable. People limited population but used all their land, gave all life totem guardians, and even under extreme duress rarely stole. They rejected or avoided the farmers' road, and lived comfortably where white Australians cannot. What they did stands on its own.

Northwest of Birdsville (Qld) Sturt reported,

> The spinifex was close and matted, and the horses were obliged to lift their feet straight up to avoid its sharp points . . . the ridges extended northward in parallel lines beyond the range of vision, and appeared as if interminable. To the eastward and westward they succeeded each other like the waves of the sea. The sand was of a deep red colour . . . [Browne] involuntarily uttered an exclamation of amazement when he first glanced his eye over it. 'Good Heavens', said he, 'did ever man see such a country!'[137]

'Man' made such country home for at least 20,000 years. People civilised all the land, without fences, making farm and wilderness one. In the Great Sandy Desert women replanted yam tops and scattered millet on soft sand, then watched the seasons: millet crops a year after its first rain.[138] This is farming, but not being a farmer. Doing more would have driven them out of the desert. Mobility let them stay. It imposed a strict and rigid society, but it was an immense gain. It gave people abundant food and leisure, and let them live in every climate and terrain. It made possible a universal theology, and it made Australia a single estate. Instead of dividing Aborigines into gentry and peasantry, it made them a free people.

INVASION

11

Becoming Australian

In July 1837 Alexander Mollison, camped with cattle near Barnawartha (Vic), went with 'a native black to examine two plains which he describes as well adapted for a station. This black, Jimmy, came to us at the Murray and has been daily pressing me to make my station on his ground.' They rode to

> a forest plain between three or four miles when Jimmy pointed to the right. We . . . shortly came upon a small open plain of very sound ground, the grass quite young, having been burnt only a month before. Proceeding much in the same direction, about two miles through timber, we came to a creek having very fine large water holes and, ascending a bank on the right, we stood on the edge of a very fine and extensive plain. The grass was too young for immediate pasturage but the ground was very firm and we thought ourselves well repaid for our journey from the camp. Jimmy was delighted to observe that we were pleased and repeatedly reminded me of it, saying, 'Cobawm bimble, Bunderambo', fine ground at Bunderambo, 'Tousand birribi (emu), tousand duck'.

Mollison thought the place too close to the Sydney–Melbourne road for a head-station, but set up a lambing station—proof of its plenty. George Faithfull took it over, then abandoned it because of Aboriginal attacks. This problem overcome, Reverend Joseph Docker took possession.[1]

So the white man came to Bontharambo, a template associating a 'forest plain' with an 'open plain' edged by a creek and circled by forest. To activate it before he began seeking a settler, Jimmy burnt it. He knew what would result: a park abundant with emu, duck and more. He managed his land in every sense, indeed with so much sense that he seems to have thought that the newcomers would manage and share it equally sensibly. He paid fearfully for his mistake. Unknowing how momentous his gift was, unseeing how carefully his land was made, uncaring of his pride, they displaced him, and within months his people were fighting a losing battle to save his country.

Places like Jimmy's, grass and shelter near water, inevitably attracted questing stockmen. Eyre warned, 'The localities selected by Europeans, as best adapted for the purpose of cultivation or grazing, are those that would usually be equally valued above others, by the natives themselves, as places of resort, or districts in which they could most easily procure food.'[2] At Albany (WA) John Wollaston noted, '*Warrung*... flourishes where the best feed for stock is found. Hence the usurpation of the ground and the secret destruction of the aborigines.'[3] 'The very spots most valuable to the aborigines for their productiveness,' Edward Parker declared, 'the creeks, water courses, and rivers—are the first to be occupied.' TS Powlett reported, 'nearly all the Stations are near the very Waters, that the Natives were in the habit of camping at, before the country was settled'.[4] [5]

Naturally people objected. 'Damn your eyes, go to England, this is my land', a man demanded, and a woman, 'You go to England, that your country; this our country.'[6] They 'complained of the white men bringing animals into their country that scare away the kangaroo, and destroy the roots which at certain seasons of the year form part of their sustenance. This... was a very general complaint.'[7] It came too late. Courtesy and curiosity usually welcomed the first strangers. Most soon went away, and when others arrived it took time to learn who meant to stay. Even then landtakers impacted unevenly. A family finding a hut on its land could move without much trouble—there was plenty to spare. Trouble came later, as spreading settlement squeezed families, then clans, then country and religion, until an ancient duty to seasons and totems dissolved. Dispossession crept up on the people of 1788.

Some tried to compromise. After Morrill was rescued in 1863, he warned his tribe that white men would take their country. 'They told me to ask the white men to let them have all the ground to the North of the Burdekin, and to let them fish in the rivers; also the low ground they live on to get the roots—ground which is no good to white people, near the sea-coast and swampy.'[8] Few whites had come, yet people were ready to give them country, for they too were of the Dreaming. When such offers were spurned, some people resisted, destroying stock, killing whites, driving out invaders. Always they came back.

They brought the mind and language of plunderers: profit, property, resource, improve, develop, change. They had no use for people who wanted the world left as it was. The *Sydney Herald* declared,

> this vast country was to them a common . . . their ownership, their right, was nothing more than that of the Emu or Kangaroo. They bestowed no labour upon the land and that—and that only—it is which gives a right of property to it. Where, we ask, is the man endowed with even a modicum of reasoning powers, who will assert that this great continent was ever intended by the Creator to remain an unproductive wilderness?[9]

Darwin called Aborigines 'a set of harmless savages wandering about without knowing where they shall sleep at night, and gaining their livelihood by hunting in the woods'.[10] The people of 1788 spent more time each year managing land than Darwin or the *Herald* editor in a lifetime. They had no hope of countering such myopia.

The most newcomers would do, even at Albany (ch 8), was to urge people to be like them, or more exactly like the poorest of them, the casual worker, the toiling convert, the loyal servant. For as long as they could, people said no. They valued what they had and believed. Cook saw this:

> From what I have said of the Natives of New Holland they may appear to some to be the most wretched people upon Earth; but in reality they are far more happier than we Europeans, being wholly unacquainted not only with the Superfluous, but with the necessary Conveniences so much sought after in Europe; they are happy in not knowing the use of them. They live in a Tranquility which is not disturbed by the Inequality of Condition. The Earth and the Sea of their own accord furnishes them with all things necessary for Life. They covet not Magnificent Houses, Household-stuff etc.; they live in a Warm and fine Climate and enjoy a very wholsome Air, so that they have very little need of Cloathing; and this they seem to be fully sencible of, for many to whom we gave Cloth etc., left it carelessly upon the Sea beach and in the Woods, as a thing they had no manner of use for; in short, they seem'd to set no Value upon anything we gave them, nor would they ever part with anything of their own for any one Article we could offer them. This in my opinion argues that they think themselves provided with all the necessarys of Life, and that they have no Superfluities.[11]

Cook could not know whether Aborigines were 'far more happier' than Europeans, but their demeanour and self-sufficiency strongly suggested it. In 1823 James Ross wrote of Tasmanians near Lake Echo, '[their elegant gait] was quite indicative of persons who had little to do . . . Their air of independence was quite charming . . . I know of no race of people who have greater claims to that property.'[12] South of the Ovens (Vic) in 1824 Hovell decided, 'Those are the people we generally call "miserable wretches", but in my opinion the word is misapplied . . . Their only employment is providing their food. They are happy within themselves; they have their amusements and but little cares; and above all they have their free liberty.'[13] 'From our observation', a New South Wales doctor remarked in 1828, 'the interior tribes consider the whites, as a strange plodding race, for the greater part slaves, obliged to get their living by constant drudgery every day. Whereas, for themselves, their wants being easily supplied, "they toil not, neither do they spin".'[14] In 1839 two Queensland squatters declared, 'they are not labourers at all, and for the same reason that any other gentleman is not, viz. that he can live without labour'.[15] In 1841 a Canberra squatter observed, 'they in general shew a determined dislike to settled habits of any kind . . . they are so wedded to their own habits—supporting themselves with so much ease by the chase—that it can scarcely be expected they should adopt ours'.[16] Matthew Marsh recalled, 'There is a kind of gentlemanlike ease about [their] manners. Not all the drill sergeants in Europe can make a man hold himself as the savage does, who never has stooped to a desk or a plough. There is also a natural grace about their carriage.'[17] In 1844 Simpson stated, 'they are in general a good natured, cheerful race, by no means deficient in intelligence, but having few wants, they consider encreased comforts dearly purchased by encreased toil and the abandonment of that merry reckless life they lead in the wilds of Australia'.[18] In 1845 a New South Wales Select Committee asked Reverend William Schmidt,

> *Were they conscious of inferiority to the whites, or did they fancy their own mode of life the most pleasant and best?* From some of their own expressions, I judged that they considered themselves superior to us.
>
> *Do you mean that they consider themselves superior to the whole of the white race, or to those they saw in the condition of convicts?* To the whole; they preferred their mode of living to ours; when they have accompanied us on some of our journeys, they have expressed the opinion, that they were our masters in the bush, and our servants at the stations; they pitied us that we troubled ourselves with so many things.[19]

Europe's social gradations are not apt to 1788 Australia, but Aborigines were more akin to Europe's gentry than to its peasantry. They commanded no-one, but they had land, sought knowledge, had much time for religion and recreation, and usually lived comfortably in parks they made.

They were therefore unlikely to ask the question Yali asked Jared Diamond in New Guinea: 'Why do you have more than us?'[20] It puzzles PNG villagers that whites so ignorant of plants, so clumsy on a log bridge, so easily tired on the march, so unready to work, should have so much. Something supernatural must explain such unfairness. Aborigines were not puzzled: they had no doubt which lifestyle the Dreaming favoured. Amid the common tumult of humanity, they prospered. Outside cities and towns Australia may have carried more people in 1788 than now. Observers thought so on the Murray, the Murrumbidgee and the Dawson. In 1788 only about 10 per cent of Australia's people lived in its arid third, but only about 3 per cent do now. Gilmore wrote that the 'invader' who lived off the land's 'teeming life' 'never realised that less than fifty years later, with a population much more sparse than that of . . . the aboriginal he displaced, fish were no longer caught in profusion, and meats had to be taken from the farm and the home-paddock'.[21][22]

What people did ask was, 'Why have we been dispossessed? What have we done wrong?' Ahead of advancing Europeans smallpox chastised them (ch 5), and after 1788 disease after disease struck them, unseen and unexpected: measles, venereal, leprosy, smallpox again, flu. A great burden descended, reproaching them for generations, so that they met newcomers militarily and psychologically disabled. Yet no epidemic disease struck the Tasmanians, who suffered as much as mainlanders or worse. Technological differences mattered: the gun, the horse, the poisons. The advantage of muskets over spears is exaggerated, and guns and horses did not save people elsewhere who used them against whites, but it is easy to find examples where they led to successful 'dispersals'. People fought by ambushing isolated whites; whites fought from a base, a refuge, and a store. Storing is an immense military advantage. It releases people from a constant food quest, letting individuals and armies stay in the field. Except in parts of Asia, no people successfully resisted European occupation, but farmers and storers held out longer and won better compromises. People stored in 1788 (ch 10), but not to dependence, perhaps especially after epidemics in effect doubled resources. Many a shepherd survived siege with a hut, gun, powder and flour, whereas time and again Aborigines holding a military advantage over Europeans had to disperse for food. Stores negated mobility. The plodding newcomer might be slow, but sooner or later he got there.

Above all, there were fundamental differences in thinking. In the white world savages had no place, though their souls might; in the Dreaming all things had a place, so newcomers must be accommodated. Even before they quit Britain Europeans intended to possess; in Australia people could not even be certain that the newcomers meant to stay, or if so on what terms. Both could attach to land and devote lives to its care, but in 1788 one saw a landscape rich in lore and Law, while the other saw profit. One defended by religious sanction, the other by force. One cared for a local fragment, the other was a fragment of an export economy, inspired and trammelled from overseas.

The most catastrophic idea was the notion of race. In 1788 Europeans were beginning to assume a hierarchy of races, with themselves at the top. Almost all Australians could have no concept of race until there was more than one, after invasion. The difference crippled all the negotiations people attempted in 1788, rejected their compromises, and mocked what efforts they made to 'be like us'.

Life and land may not have been perfectly balanced in 1788. Near Narrandera grassland may have been expanding at the expense of forest, and as Oxley hinted, plants and seasons don't repeat perfectly:

> clear plains extended to the foot of very lofty forest hills ... their surfaces were slightly broken into gentle eminences with occasional clumps, and lines of timber. Their white appearance was occasioned by the grass having been burnt early in the year, and the young growth killed by the frosts.[23]

Fire in particular exacted a price. It can cause salination and erosion,[24] though probably not under 1788 management. It reduces surface water, kills fire sensitive plants and animals, and impoverishes soil as compost becomes uncommon and ash the readiest nutrient. Latz saw the Simpson as desert man-made by fire, 'the only large area of Australia where Eucalypts are totally absent.'[25] Mitchell noted, 'the trees and shrubs being very inflammable, conflagrations take place so frequently and intensively, in the woods during summer, as to leave very little vegetable matter to return to earth'.[26] Sturt judged:

> The proportion of bad soil to that which is good ... is certainly very great ... the general want of vegetable mould over the colony [is due] chiefly to [fire] ... whereby the growth of underwood, so favourable in other countries to the formation of soil, is wholly prevented ... There is no part of the world in which fires create such havoc ... The climate ... and the wandering habits of the natives ... which induce them to clear the country before them by conflagration, operate equally against the growth of timber and underwood.[27]

Gunn attributed

> the general poverty of the Soil in V.D.L. [Van Diemen's Land] to the habit the Aborigines had of regularly burning the Bush, thereby preventing that accumulation of decayed vegetable matter . . . which would otherwise have necessarily occurred . . . The Natives burned the Country . . . to clear the way & enable them to walk more easily, but also the season after a fire the grass springs up luxuriantly & tender & the kangaroos resort to those places & are therefore more easily killed.[28]

Yet if people did jar the land's regenerative capacity, imbalances were slight and their threat remote. What came after 1788 was much more serious. Damage then was ignorant rather than wilful, but revolutionary. Mitchell depicted how a small local change heralded general destruction. In 1845 he returned to springs he camped at in 1835:

> instead of being limpid and surrounded with verdant grass, as they had been then, they were now trodden by cattle into muddy holes where the poor natives had been endeavouring to protect a small portion from the cattle's feet, and keep it pure, by laying over it trees they had cut down for the purpose. The change produced in the aspect of this formerly happy secluded valley, by the intrusion of cattle and the white man, was by no means favourable, and I could easily conceive how I, had I been an aboriginal native, should have felt and regretted that change.[29]

In 1853 John Robertson perceptively traced how slight changes could accumulate quickly and devastatingly:

> When I arrived [in 1840] . . . I cannot express the joy I felt at seeing such a splendid country . . . The whole of the Wannon [Vic] had been swept by a bushfire in December, and there had been a heavy fall of rain in January (which has happened, less or more, for this last thirteen years), and the grasses were about four inches high, of that lovely dark green; the sheep had no trouble to fill their bellies; all was eatable; nothing had trodden the grass before them . . . I looked amongst the 37 grasses that formed the pasture of my run. There was no silk-grass, which had been destroying our V.D.L. pastures . . . The few sheep at first made little impression on

the face of the country . . . [Then] Many of our herbaceous plants began to disappear from the pasture land; the silk grass began to show itself in the edge of the bush track, and in patches here and there on the hill. The patches have grown larger every year; herbaceous plants and grasses give way for the silk-grass and the little annuals . . . The consequence is that the long deep-rooted grasses that held our strong clay hill together have died out; the ground is now exposed to the sun, and it has cracked in all directions; also the sides of precipitous creeks—long slips, taking trees and all with them. When I first came here, I knew of but two landslips, both of which I went to see; now there are hundreds found within the last three years . . . all the creeks and little watercourses were covered with a large tussocky grass, with other grasses and plants, to the middle of every watercourse but the Glenelg and the Wannon, and in many places of these rivers; now that the soil is getting trodden hard with stock, springs of salt water are bursting out in every hollow or watercourse, and as it trickles down the watercourse in summer, the strong tussocky grasses die before it, with all others. The clay is left perfectly bare in summer. The strong clay cracks; the winter rain washes out the clay; now mostly every little gully has a deep rut; when rains falls it . . . rushes down these ruts . . . carrying earth, trees, and all before it . . . Ruts, seven, eight, and ten feet deep, and as wide, are found for miles, where two years ago it was covered with a tussocky grass like a land marsh.[30]

All pastoralists want good grass, but not all think long term to get it, and an export economy chokes their cash and choice. Early pastoralists mimicked 1788 fire, but without its subtlety and variety. Until fences and haystacks made fire an enemy, they burnt for fresh pick. 'The custom of setting the dry grass on fire is very prevalent throughout the colony, as the young grass shooting up soon after affords fine feeding for cattle, &c', Bennett reported.[31] In 1824 WC Wentworth declared this practice 'necessary and useful'.[32] But almost all pastoralists used clean-up fires, burning large areas rather than templates, and setting cooler autumn fires more pliant than 1788's summer fires. 'In the western desert,' Burrows wrote in 2003,

> there has been a momentous change in the scale and intensity of fires over the last 40 or 50 years, where the Aboriginal people have not been active on the land. Under Aboriginal management we know that

> the mean burnt patch size was up to about 30 hectares, with most
> patches being less than five hectares. Today . . . the mean fire sizes
> are around 34,000 hectares, with the largest fires burning in excess of
> 500,000 hectares . . . My Aboriginal informants tell me that fires on
> this scale are unprecedented and are no good [pictures 29–30].[33]

As a result, in the Centre Spinifex is spreading at the expense of other grasses, and 'savage wildfires' have 'scourged' the Lake Amadeus country, carbonising topsoil, eradicating native plants and animals, and turning pleasant places into 'a wilderness of spinifex'.[34] A west MacDonnells area where Stuart found grass now carries Spinifex,[35] and parts of the Centre full of life then would hardly run a rat to the square mile now. In inland Western Australia, Spinifex has replaced other grasses because pastoralists overgraze and winter-burn.[36] East Gippsland stockowners

> aimed to burn about 1000 acres or so each spring or summer to provide
> feed for the following winter, the main idea being that this would
> confine the cattle to a small area and make for easier musterings.
> A different patch would be fired each year and after a few years
> the original patch would carry enough fuel to be burnt again. They
> would thus work the forest after the style of a rotation. However the
> fires often burnt a larger area than they bargained on, and kept on
> burning until a rain extinguished them. The result was good enough,
> say the old timers, because it kept the forest clean of scrub,

but only for a time.[37] Eventually the scrub thickened (ch 6), the government ordered the cattlemen to stop, and some did.[38]

While this mistake was common, so was its opposite—no fire at all. Converting fire from ally to enemy was most damaging. West of the Glenelg (Vic),

> The country when we took it up was lightly timbered . . . [It] remained
> open until brush fences were started, and the use of wholesale fire
> given up. This gave the timber a chance of going ahead as it liked.
> Something favourable to the honeysuckle started it first on the light
> sandy soil, and it became a dense scrub . . . Then bulloak sprang
> up everywhere, taking possession of the best of the country. Where
> the seed came from is a mystery. Red gum also went ahead.[39]

Rolls reported similar regeneration in northern New South Wales.[40] Regeneration manifests what far-reaching control fire once had. In 1898 Brian and Jenny Wright's 20-acre block north of Brisbane was 'dense vine scrub'. By 1981 it was largely clear and heavily grazed. In 1991 the stock was taken off, and although there were no wattles within 5 kilometres, by 2001 two wattle species were thriving. Their seed lay in the soil, predating the vine scrub. Under the wattle, Red Cedar, Silky Oak, Birds Nest Fern and vines appeared, and Gympie Messmate blew in from a neighbouring state forest.[41] This is climax rainforest country. Twice it was suppressed, once by 1788 fire, once by stock, twice it returned, before 1898 and after 1991.

If the sward was dense or the soil unyielding, scrub and tree regeneration might be slow, but usually was rapid. By edge invasion or from seeded soil, ready opportunists raced to colonise land people denied them in 1788. Breton claimed,

> Land which at my former visit to New South Wales (1830) was entirely clear of wood, is now (1833) thickly covered by trees of some size; and it always happens, that land once cleared and neglected for a year or two, becomes concealed by a forest far more dense than any before seen upon it.[42]

In 1860, less than 30 years after most Tasmanians were 'removed', Gunn wrote,

> my impression is, that nearly all the level land which I saw lower down the Leven must at some time have been open *grassy plains*, as the greater portion of the trees seem to be under that age. A very considerable extent of the Surrey Hills is also becoming rapidly covered with forests of young *Eucalypti*, so as to render it probable that they will also in time become useless for pasture purposes. The want of the usual and regular aboriginal fires to clear the country seems to be the cause.[43]

Mitchell condemned an Imperial order to stop such fires:

> The omission of the annual periodical burning by natives, of the grass and young saplings, has already produced in the open forest lands nearest to Sydney, thick forests of young trees, where, formerly, a man might gallop without impediment, and see whole miles before him. Kangaroos are no longer to be seen there; the grass is choked by underwood; neither are there natives to burn the grass . . . These consequences, although

so little considered by the intruders, must be obvious to the natives, with their usual acuteness, as soon as cattle enter on their territory.[44]

Rolls knew the New South Wales Pilliga as dense forest, but when Oxley saw it in 1818

there was little forest there as the word is used now . . . 'Brush' he called it in small areas, 'a very thick brush of cypress trees and small shrubs'. 'Scrub' he called the stunted growth on the dry ridges, 'mere scrub'. Most of it, about 800,000 hectares, was a 'forest' of huge ironbarks and big white-barked cypress trees, three or four only to the hectare. We would . . . call it open grassland . . . Australia's dense forests are not the remnants of two hundred years of energetic clearing, they are the product of one hundred years of energetic growth.[45]

In western New South Wales Jim Noble found that scrub took over grassland within twenty years of settlement. All the problem seedlings, White Cypress, Budda, Yarran, Bimble Box, were fire sensitive, and all made headway because fire stopped and grazing thinned the perennial grass. Where in 1788 the country was grass with patches of scrub, from these refuges the scrub spread inexorably.[46] High country grass near Jindabyne (NSW) was by 1949 'overgrown with thick scrub',[47] and near Canberra dense forest now covers land where once a horse could gallop.[48]

In Queensland Judith Wright tracked changes to Wadja Plain west of the Dawson. When Leichhardt saw it in 1844 it was open forest, recently burnt; by 1900 it was choked with wattle and scrub; by 1917 it was 'thickly timbered, with much undergrowth', and it was still so in the 1970s.[49] The Longreach district was once so grassy that Europeans thought it could not grow trees, but Aborigines said,

'Look at the trees growin' at Longreach since white man's been there because he wouldn't let the fires go.' You see, that was all plain country, nothing . . . you see old photographs . . . and it's all empty . . . the old Aboriginals will burn the bloody lot and took all the trees out. So they said, 'Black soil won't grow trees' but you go there now . . . and the trees are back.[50]

By 2000 Seven Emu Station on the Gulf (NT) had carried cattle for 80 years, but 'everywhere' grass then was scrub now.[51] In 1903 Alfred Norton recalled that despite grazing, since 1857 'the brigalow has spread very largely on Juandah and Hawkwood [south of Taroom, Qld] ... At that time it was comparatively open and much of the scenery was very beautiful, numbers of bottle trees of great size standing out on the open patches or growing along the edge of the brigalow.'[52] In western Tasmania trees invaded grassland so densely that they made travel difficult and living impossible.[53]

In Western Australia, Henry Bunbury wrote in 1836 of 'bush fires' every 2–3 years by which

> the country is kept comparatively free from under wood and other obstructions, having the character of an open forest through most parts of which one can ride freely; otherwise, in all probability, it would soon become impenetrably thick ... This has already been proved in the case of Van Dieman's Land, where, in consequence of the transportation of the Natives to Great or Flinders Island, and the consequent absence of extensive periodical fires, the bush has grown up thick to a most inconvenient degree ... It is true that we might ourselves burn the bush, but we could never do it with the same judgement and good effect as the Natives, who keep the fire within due bounds, only burning those parts they wish when the scrub becomes too thick or when they have any other object to gain by it.[54]

Go into a native forest, look at trunk size and distribution (ch 3), and widespread regeneration becomes obvious. On this count alone, Australia in 1788 was made, not natural.[55]

The most notorious regenerator was cypress pine in inland eastern Australia. Two species are common: Black Cypress on hills, White Cypress or Murray Pine on sand or loam. In 1788 they grew either as open woodland where people could 'see for miles', or in 'various sizes and dimensions from seedlings, generally growing in clumps, to lofty trees of about 60 feet'.[56] This did not last. Pine is an excellent milling timber, impervious to white ants. Loggers attacked it enthusiastically. It hit back hard. Especially after rain, within weeks of logging millions of seedlings emerged. Squatters employed gangs of 'scrubbers', often Chinese under a contractor, to clear the pine. It came back denser. Scientists were amazed at its speed and extent. One wrote that it took 'possession of thousands of acres of what was, at one time, splendid pastoral country',[57] another that what was mainly eucalypts with a few pines before clearing in the 1860s became by the 1880s pine scrub so thick that it smothered all other trees,[58] a third that in 1863 'there was little or no pine scrub in the Lachlan district' but by 1883 'the pine had taken possession'.[59] He pronounced the pine 'impassable', and his seedling count let Elaine van Kempen calculate a density of 6.35 million per hectare.[60] Stations were abandoned, station owners who fought ruined. 'When my firm first bought the place', the manager of Nymagee (NSW) stated in 1900,

> it was open box country, covered with a waving mass of herbage...
> I thought it was a pastoral paradise. That was before the growth of
> the pine scrub. When I came up in 1885, the pine scrub had started to
> spread to an enormous extent. I scrubbed the place in 1886, again in
> 1890, and later in 1894, and some of it is now nearly as bad as ever.[61]

The pine behaved more like an exotic weed than a native tree.

Why? A few saw biblical retribution, which was no help. Many thought pine spread when bushfires were stopped. 'Young pines are now springing up over large tracts of country so thickly that in a very short time they will form a dense scrub', an official reported in 1880. 'The cause... is ascribed to the discontinuance of bush fires.'[62] In 1887 another told the New South Wales parliament that formerly well grassed, open country was now a 'Great Central Scrub' because pine was no longer 'kept in check by sweeping bushfires'.[63] In 1901 a New South Wales Royal Commission concluded, 'overstocking... coupled with the rabbits, prevented the growth of grass to anything like its former extent, and so caused a cessation of bush fires, which had formerly occurred periodically. This afforded the noxious scrub a chance of making headway.'[64] Yet pine was on the march long before rabbits, and surveyor CF Bolton pointed out that by the 1850s bushfires were being stopped as much as they ever would be, but in the mid 1860s the country was still open. He wrote in 1881, 'extensive tracts of country which fifteen years ago were beautifully grassed open downs are now so overgrown with young pines that sheep can hardly make their way through them, whilst the original grasses have almost entirely disappeared'. He suggested that sheep spread seed during the 1866 drought.[65]

In 1998 Mick Allen, an acute observer, puzzled about bushfires. Newcomers found pine country 'a mosaic of vegetation cover—open plains, brushes and scrubs, open and dense forests, myall plains', but as early as 1848 Ben Boyd stated that Jemelong on the Lachlan had 'pine scrubs... of late years getting nearly impassable, and destroying the pasturage'. 'It stretches the credulity', Allen wrote, 'to believe that the right conditions for widespread dense pine regeneration did not occur over the 100–50 years before European exploration and settlement, and then there were neither rabbits nor sheep!' He blamed fewer fires, and soil compaction which let shallow-rooted annuals replace perennials and herbs, so providing more sub-surface water and letting more pines germinate.[66] Yet by 1848 pine was claiming places with little grazing or compaction, and in general newcomers lit more fires than in 1788, not fewer.[67] Credulity must be stretched: the 'right conditions' for pine regeneration did not occur in the century before Europeans came. The change was man-made, from controlled to random fire.

1788 fire killed most pine seedlings but not most big trees, pine or other. Allen estimated that an 1883 pine count on Mungery West (NSW) indicated a few scattered trees germinating about the 1770s, the 1800s and the 1830s, then numbers increasing soon after Europeans came, thickening to forest by 1883.[68] At Berembed on the Murrumbidgee four pines cut in 1905 are almost a metre wide and hardly lose girth over 13 metres: they must have grown in open country.[69] These examples suggest clean-up fires every 30 years or so, plus cool burns every 1–3 years to kill seedlings. Clearly great care went into managing so ready a regenerator (picture 50).[70]

Newcomers liberated other species. Acacias have gone feral, notably Cootamundra Wattle in southern New South Wales, sometimes transplanted, sometimes spreading from its 1788 habitat. Why didn't it spread earlier, to similar soils and climates? Galahs increased and spread dramatically after 1788, for surprising reasons, as did little corellas, crimson rosellas, crested pigeons, crows, currawongs and white-backed magpies,[71] and even a few animals, notably red kangaroos and euros onto 'marsupial lawns' when stock shortened the grass.[72]

Such changes make 1788 Australia hard to recognise now. It was even a different colour (pictures 10–12). It had more green grass in summer, much less undergrowth, and fewer trees. In 1888 it had more trees than in 1788, deceiving newcomers into thinking that regenerating forest marked virgin land. Today there are fewer trees on farms, swampland, and I suspect arid and semi-arid country, but more in forests, national parks and remote places. Soil and water have changed, species have come, gone or moved (ch 2–3). Australia is a world leader in animal and plant extinctions, reflecting how ancient and vital 1788's unnatural fires were (ch 1).

We know too little about 1788 to measure these changes, and our attempts are disabled by contemporary preferences and assumptions. For example we think trees 'green' and good, so we assume there must once have been more of them. Yet we accept wilderness: typical farming people, not for us the care of every inch. Peter Dwyer compared three New Guinea highlands groups, one gardeners, one largely hunter-gatherers, one both. Mentally and physically, only the gardeners fenced their world. The others had no words for centre and periphery, no sense of being spiritually distinct from the rest of creation, no landform hierarchy. For the gardeners 'wilderness' began just beyond their fences, for the hunter-gatherers it did not exist. Fences on the ground made fences in the mind.[73] Australia had no fences in 1788. Some places were managed more closely than others, but none were beyond the pale.[74]

There is no return to 1788. Non-Aborigines are too many, too centralised, too stratified, too comfortable, too conservative, too successful, too ignorant. We are still newcomers, still in wilderness, still exporting goods and importing people and values. We see extinctions, pollution, erosion, salinity, bushfire and exotic pests and diseases, but argue over who should pay. We use land care merely to mitigate land misuse. We champion sustainability, which evokes merely surviving, whereas in 1788 people assumed abundance, and so did Genesis. We take more and leave the future less. Too few accept that this behaviour cannot survive the population time bomb. When the time comes to choose between parks and people, species and space, food and freedom, 1788's values will be obliterated.

Yet across the shattered centuries 1788 can still teach, and some have begun to learn. Tree corridors replicate belts, wetlands are being restored, reserves and sanctuaries declared. Aborigines sometimes have more say in fire management, and whenever a city burns more people accept control fires, though these remain too few. Peter Andrews and others advocate land care which in part echoes 1788, such as slowing water and making tree–grass mosaics.[75] When Bob Purvis took over Woodgreen Station northeast of Alice Springs in 1958, he faced serious land degradation. The run was 350 square miles, but only 50 square miles was good for stock, and that was eaten bare. Bob bought another 140 square miles of fair country, watched which grasses his cattle preferred, say 6–12 species, tested these for protein content, then adjusted his stocking rate to sustain them. If the grasses spread he increased his herd. More often they declined and he reduced it, until he got a balance at about 1000 head, a third of the 1958 herd. To support it he adjusted his fodder grasses to soil type, introduced a palatable buffel grass, fenced off fattening paddocks, stopped shooting dingos and netted dams in his useless country to keep kangaroos down, and sold or shot most horses.

Bob says he is still learning, but his cattle are prime, and Woodgreen is a grass oasis amid bare scrub. 'Most of central Australia', he says, 'is carrying at least twice or, in some cases, four times what it can actually sustain, and that's why you see bare ground... A lot of what you see is man made drought... When I was a kid, central Australia was regarded as fat cattle country. Today it is regarded as store cattle country.'[76] Before he was a kid it was sheep country. Even Woodgreen is no longer that. Bob evolved his management over decades of trial and error, but it is easy to see 1788 in what he learnt. He uses space, manages locally, favours fodder grasses, concentrates stock on good country, makes templates of fattening paddocks, culls and adjusts to ensure balance and continuity.

On 10 July 1890 Alfred Howitt addressed the Royal Society of Victoria, the same which 30 years before had sent him to find Burke and Wills, on 'The Eucalypts of Gippsland'. His talk was remarkable.

1. He grouped and described 24 species of Gippsland eucalypt, plus numerous forms and local variations. His descriptions were based on up to 26 samples of each species and form taken from scattered Gippsland locations, and showed both typifying characteristics and minute local differences in leaf, bud, flower, fruit and sometimes wood. Dozens of differences were depicted in nine plates drawn by his daughter Annie.
2. He set down where each species and form occurred, whether local or general, on what soils, at what heights, in what terrain. For example he named species which rose from the coast up cool gullies on south facing slopes but gave way to others on warm north facing slopes, or still others in subalpine areas. He argued in detail that it followed that even small climate changes in the past must have affected and in the future would affect eucalypt distribution, perhaps even to extinction. This is accepted today, but on that night in 1890 Ferdinand von Mueller, director of Melbourne's Botanic Gardens and no mug on eucalypts, observed that it was 'work in an entirely new direction'.
3. He discussed the 'Influence of Settlement' on Gippsland's eucalypts. This began 'on the very day when the first hardy pioneers' arrived. They put an end to the 'annual' fires of the Aborigines, letting undergrowth fill open forest and grass revert to bush. Howitt gave examples from all over Gippsland where it was 'difficult to ride over parts which . . . were at one time open grassy country', and concluded that in spite of European clearing, Gippsland's forests were denser and more widespread than in 1788. Howitt's chairman 'confessed' that he 'had never heard or dreamt of' this 're-foresting'.
4. He argued that ending Aboriginal fire let insect populations explode. In the 1870s he saw whole forests dying, and found them infested with myriads of insect larvae. These also made headway because stock hardened the ground, causing water which had once seeped in to run off, so weakening the eucalypts by thirst. Hard ground and increased water flow were also why floods were more catastrophic than before Europeans came.

With breathtaking detail and economy, Howitt illuminated much of what this book labours to cover. He could do this because he thought as an Australian. He understood less than the Aborigines, and he knew it. He acknowledged often what they taught him, and his talk began with a list of eucalypts and their Kurnai names, but he never offered what was common then and now: comparison with Europe. He never said eucalypts were less deciduous, less green, less shady than Europe's trees. He never mentioned England, where he lived his first 21 years. He was not merely describing Australian examples; he was evolving Australian premises.[77][78]

Important books wait on pre-contact management in other lands, but only in Australia did a mobile people organise a continent with such precision. In some past time, probably distant, their focus tipped from land use to land care. They sanctioned key principles: think long term; leave the world as it is; think globally, act locally; ally with fire; control population. They were active, not passive, striving for balance and continuity to make all life abundant, convenient and predictable. They put the mark of humanity firmly on every place. They kept the faith. The land lived. Its face spoke. 'Here are managers', it said, 'caring, provident, hardworking.' This is possession in its most fundamental sense. If *terra nullius* exists anywhere in our country, it was made by Europeans.

This book interrupts Law and country at the moment when *terra nullius* came, and an ancient philosophy was destroyed by the completely unexpected, an invasion of new people and ideas. A majestic achievement ended. Only fragments remain. For the people of 1788 the loss was stupefying. For the newcomers it did not seem great. Until recently few noticed that they had lost anything at all. Knowledge of how to sustain Australia, of how to be Australian, vanished with barely a whisper of regret.

We have a continent to learn. If we are to survive, let alone feel at home, we must begin to understand our country. If we succeed, one day we might become Australian.

APPENDIX 1

Science, history and landscape

In 2008 the Department of Geography and Environmental Studies, University of Tasmania, invited me to talk on 1788 land management when next in Hobart. This is Bill Jackson's old department, among the first and best in studying pre-contact vegetation, and home to many who helped me. I prepared by preferring examples from work by them or their students, some of whom I hoped might hear the talk. I never gave it: the invitation had a time limit I was unaware of. In its focus on work by Tasmanian scientists across Australia, what follows reflects these origins, but questions a more general mindset among scientists who study landscapes in disciplines from anthropology to zoology.

One scientist summarised this mindset as, 'If there is a natural explanation, prefer it', and another emailed, 'You must assume that natural features have natural causes until you can prove otherwise.' For 1788 landscapes this is circular thinking, based on assuming that they were natural. I think they were made. When I say so, many scientists, not all,[1] correct me, as in the email. Usually I let this pass. Life is short, and debating one by one with people so many and so well-resourced is futile. Yet their condescension has forced this book into more detail than a general reader might prefer, perhaps still without satisfying the specialist.

In the physical sciences experiments are repeated and laws established. All science uses this notion of objectivity, and sees history, which admits itself unable to control every variable, as subjective, hence unreliable. Like some historians, scientists form a hypothesis then test it, but unlike historians they seek a measurable outcome. A thing is objectively true if a test can be repeated with the same result. A valid test puts an end to speculation. But, a historian would say, it does not put an end to assumption. Any hypothesis is unavoidably loaded with cultural and personal assumptions, only sometimes apparent, which lie in wait to shape a test's premises and so its results. Objectivity suppresses but does not eradicate this. It produced notions claimed to be scientific such as that the earth is flat or began in 4004 BC, or that malaria is caused by miasmas, or that measuring heads can prove a hierarchy of humanity, or that the atom is the smallest unit of matter, or that bushfires can be prevented. Later disowning these notions as unscientific simply reinforces a dogma of objectivity despite them.

I must not over-generalise. My dad was a botanist, including of natives, and his memory has been close throughout the years of this book. A geographer, Bill Jackson, and an archaeologist, Rhys Jones, pioneered research into 1788 fire. John Banks, Dave Bowman, RC Ellis, Beth Gott, Jamie Kirkpatrick, Peter Latz, Ian Lunt, Henry Nix, Jim Noble, Peter Sutton, Ian Thomas and but two pioneer historians, Sylvia Hallam and Eric Rolls, have illuminated my understanding. Not all accept my claims. Some think rightly that many have not been tested scientifically, and wrongly that many have little or no supporting evidence. More historical evidence exists than most scientists realise, but as well they and I differ in interpreting it. I value it; most of them devalue it, using it as preamble or for want of an alternative. I hope this book shows that I appreciate what scientists do, but have a different mindset.

A habit for natural explanation emerges in scientists who decree against 1788 fire. Some deny it completely, some minimise its impact, some accept it but deny purpose or control. These deniers push their assumptions hard.

Before offering specific examples, I list five common assumptions and my responses.

1. Especially in 'remote' areas such as desert or high country, Aborigines had no reason to touch the landscape, and therefore didn't.
At the risk of their souls, people cared for every inch of their country, even after smallpox halved their numbers and management capacity. When no-one survived to manage a country, some distant connection tried to learn it (ch 4). Care did not always mean action: people might leave land alone for long periods.

2. Most Australian genera adapted to drought and hence to fire long before people arrived.
Of course this is true. Had not so many species adapted to fire there would have been no alliance for people to join. This in no way disproves 1788 fire. One could equally say that mining has not affected the landscape because metals pre-date Europeans. The claim does reveal a mindset.

3. The impact of 1788 fire was slight. Climate, soil, altitude, aspect, nutrients or growth habits suffice to explain Australia's vegetation.
This book shows that people often broke these parameters; they cannot explain all, or even most, 1788 landscapes.

4. Aborigines used fire, but there is no evidence of its conscious use as a fine-grained management tool.
This book has a tsunami of evidence, though perhaps a trickle of what exists. For many scientists the problem is that most of it is historical, and they dismiss history as 'impressionistic'. I once heard a capable scientist, Dave Bowman, say this in a public lecture, misinterpreting what I told him about subjectivity. I said that historians know that history is subjective. People never agree on what evidence to select or emphasise, so no two studies of a subject can be the same. All disciplines, including science and history, persuade not by truth, but by fidelity to evidence and context. Bowman limited what I said to history, then said that this distinguished history from science! One day Bowman's work will become history. I hope future researchers will be more generous to him.

5. Even if people did plan 1788 fire it is unwise to say so, because this would license ill-informed burning and extensive environmental damage.
Subjective, isn't it? Fortunately I encountered it in only one scientist, though I'm told others think it.

Bowman's lecture began, 'It is intuitively obvious that historians should be natural allies of ecologists and land managers'.[2] I agree, but Bowman and I soon part, because he applies disqualifying strictures to history but not to science, whereas I see them as intrinsic to both. His abstract concludes,

> no matter how sociologically or psychologically satisfying a particular environmental historical narrative might be, it must be willing to be superseded with new stories that incorporate the latest research discoveries and that reflect changing social values of nature. It is contrary to a rational and publicly acceptable approach to land management to read a particular story as revealing the absolute truth.[3]

Of course this is true of history, otherwise there would be only one history per topic. Bowman states the obvious because he assumes that it is not so of science, not so of 'objective' research. He made this clear in 2004: 'while "fire-stick farming" is now a generally accepted concept, little effort has ever been made to test it. Indeed, while there is abundant anecdotal evidence of Aboriginal use of fire to attract kangaroos and maintain kangaroo populations, little empirical evidence exists.'[4] Historians would find this laughable.

Bowman lists 'isms' (capitalism, feminism etc) to which history is subject, then quotes Stephen Pyne: 'natural science builds on data banks; the humanities, on values'.[5] What do data banks build on? One might say that they accumulate objectively verifiable answers. But where do the questions come from? They build on values, by what is seen to matter at the time in some social or personal context. Recall the head measurers, and how priorities change in wartime—if values don't build data banks, why did planes progress in six years from barely flying to racing from England to Australia, and in another six from biplanes to rockets? Why didn't the Chinese develop guns once they'd invented gunpowder? Objectivity is a research method, not a philosophy.

'It is unacceptable', Bowman states, 'to make inferences about vegetation based solely on an uncritical acceptance of historical records that have not been checked in the field.'[6] To the extent that is true, so is the reverse. He continues, 'historical records concerning vegetation characteristics may be erroneous',[7] supporting this non-claim by noting that von Mueller's 1867 tallest tree height was disproved in his lifetime. Mueller was a botanist, a scientist reporting contemporary objective data, not a historian using historical records or building on values. Bowman continues that when Mueller was challenged by theodolite and surveyor in about 1889, he 'distanced himself . . . saying that he had had to "trust his memory"'.[8] Mueller's distancing is from a historical record, was subjective, and does not objectively prove him wrong, but Bowman accepts it, thereby crippling his case for the relative value of historical vs scientific research. He may be wrong anyway: in 1874 Mueller took a visiting naturalist to the fallen giant, needing neither theodolite nor surveyor. It measured 146 metres, supporting Mueller's initial claims.[9] A scientist might see objective data verified by repetition in this, even a data bank, but Bowman concludes, 'Obviously there is a need to make objective assessments of landscape change rather than to rely solely on historical records.'[10] Yet he quotes and relies solely on a historian's use of a historical record.[11] Time has made an objective measurement 'anecdotal'.

Bowman cites nine Bradford Hill criteria used to infer causality. Most are sensible and verifiable by analogy or experiment, though one is merely 'logical' and another 'plausible given current knowledge'. 'Very few ecological theories about Australia's environmental history', Bowman writes, 'would pass these exacting criteria unscathed.'[12] That's true—that's why they are theories—but most are proffered by scientists, not historians. Fortunately neither will be deterred from a healthy curiosity about them, or cease to benefit from the stimulus they generate. History makes no bones about this, and put this way I hope that disciplines which produced the *Origin of Species* and the *Theory of Relativity* might agree, even though neither theory now passes those criteria unscathed.

Bowman concludes, 'Practitioners of environmental history must accept that their studies are politically charged and that their findings are bounded by great uncertainty.'[13] The first claim I accept, the second depends on the evidence. I think this obvious of any research; it seems Bowman does not. The history discipline above all others welcomes dabblers, but it is a delusion to think it not a discipline, not capable of refinement by training in skills, methods and values. I can only suggest that scientists wanting to use historical records study history.

Anthropologists apart, scientists rarely take the subjective implications of Aboriginal culture and values into their research. Many admire Aboriginal knowledge and skill, and especially in northern Australia many use it, but they don't seek Aboriginal mindsets which inform what a historical source says, or which integrate land and people in the Aboriginal way. I have not found a single scientist who takes into consideration the fundamental Aboriginal conviction that people risk their souls if they do not manage every inch of ground they are responsible for. How far this conviction impinges on any land at any time is subjective and variable, but decisive. Science rarely admits culture: culture is subjective, which science has made a subjective decision to deny.

Natural factors must be considered, but do not always explain. For example soil type can explain a change in plant species (a change in place), but not why a species grows now where it didn't then (a change in time). Many scientists focus on the first, I on the second. In the best history of its kind I know, Mick Allen writes of state forests in central New South Wales, 'The mosaic of vegetation described by the explorers as they passed through this district quite probably has as much to do with variations in soil type as anything else.' Here a good forester makes an assumption, but it is not proven, and it cannot explain why, as Allen notes, bordering tree species have since invaded grassland the explorers saw.[14]

Ron Vanderwal and David Horton similarly confuse a change in time with a change in place. They state of the southwest Tasmanian coast,

> The current vegetational mosaic . . . reflects the mosaic of generally poor soils which have created relatively static boundaries. Fire plays some role in maintaining this mosaic. Bushfires occur today, but their frequency may have been greater when Aborigines inhabited

the area, a hypothesis that receives some support from the apparent recent incursion of closed forests into grassland areas.[15]

Have those closed forests spread on the same soil or not? Yes or no, why spread now but not then? Perhaps this puzzle led Vanderwal and Horton to mention fire, but they do so very cautiously, suppressing the most sensible possibility, that fires could only have been more frequent then than now if Aborigines lit them (picture 39). Was their vision obscured by a subjective urge towards a natural explanation?

In the north, BA Wilson suggested of Melville Island's boundaries between open forest and 'treeless' plains 'that the deep sandy soils of the plains have been subjected to heavy leaching of nutrients, which is a primary factor associated with changes in vegetation across the forest–plains boundary. Fire is implicated as a secondary agent.'[16] Do the forest–treeless boundaries follow soil boundaries or not? If they do, why is fire an agent at all? If they don't, why is soil mentioned at all? And while strictly the plains Wilson discusses are treeless, they carry acacias, banksias and other shrubs. Why not more? Isn't it possible that Melville Islanders worked with the country, burning more where trees find growing difficult and less where they find it easier, so that without their fires there might have been more trees on one or both sides of a boundary? Cloaking that possibility by vaguely naming 'fire' may be scientific, but a historian would consider human intervention.

Rod Fensham and Jamie Kirkpatrick investigated whether a want of soil moisture or chemicals explains why Melville Island's woodland is so open. They found no universal correlation, instead noting, 'the relative dominance of *Eucalyptus miniata* and *Eucalyptus tetrodonta* is changing in a mixed forest on Melville Island', and concluding, 'The coincidence of random historical events and the phenology and life-stage of the tree species at a site may determine some of the structural and compositional patterns at the local scale in the tropical savannah forest.'[17] Phenology is the 'study of the times of recurring natural phenomena'. Fensham and Kirkpatrick are saying that tree life cycles and chance or randomness explain why this woodland is as it is and was. Tree cycles alone poorly explain a change in species composition, while chance is the last and least useful historical explanation, because in the end it clarifies nothing. To prefer it to possible human intervention carries a liking for natural explanation a long way.

In a thoughtful article, Kevin Mills puzzles at the 'close proximity' of grassy eucalypt forest and rainforest in the Illawarra (NSW). He considers soil, nutrients, rain shadow, wind, frost and aspect, finally offering a tentative explanation in soil and rainfall boundaries. Yet his Yarrawa Brush map shows both eucalypts and rainforest across his key soil boundaries, and of rainfall he concedes, 'The location of the eucalypt—rainforest boundary in the west cannot only be due to a decrease of rainfall. If this were so, the boundary would be located 8 kilometres or so further west.' He does mention 'possibly fire' and 'perhaps' fire, but not as a general cause, and not 1788 fire.[18] I suggest that his well-researched vegetation anomalies show people working with and against the country in 1788.

Even scientists who know the importance of fire might prefer not to mention Aborigines. Jennifer Read found that in Tasmania phosphorus deficient soils retard Native Beech growth and canopy, but that high phosphorus concentrations occur on some Buttongrass plains, heath and eucalypt forest, which therefore should be growing Beech. She concludes, 'the results are consistent with Jackson's (1968, 1983) hypothesis that the absence of rainforest from some low nutrient soils may be influenced more by fire frequency (via the interactions among soil nutrients, vegetation and fire) than directly by soil nutrients'.[19] Does this go far enough? At least on those higher phosphorus soils, how did those other plants dislodge rainforest in the first place? Read doesn't say. She suspects chance fire, but not 1788 fire. Why is chance the better explanation, random as it is and inconsequential as Jackson found it?[20]

Darrell Kraehenbuehl has written a good account of Adelaide's 1788 vegetation, the most detailed for any Australian capital.[21] He recognises that Aboriginal fire 'would inevitably have had an impact upon the ground-storey plant species, even perhaps converting some woodland areas and forest to tall shrubland and grassland'.[22] He then ignores this, even when detailing such vegetation anomalies as the grass around Black Forest and the Peachey Belt. He thus describes what the land might have looked like without 1788 fire, not how it was in 1836.

On the Monaro (NSW) Alec Costin mapped a correlation between basalt soils and treeless plains. He suggested that there was 'insufficient soil moisture' and too much cold air drainage to carry trees.[23] This is the common view. As George Seddon put it, 'most ecologists who have studied the Monaro are convinced that the basaltic soils and cold-air drainage from the surrounding ranges down to the relatively lower plateaux are enough to inhibit natural tree growth without any other agency'.[24] Trees on or beside the Monaro plains, scientists say, are on granite, not basalt.

On the Dawson, rarely frosty, Leichhardt puzzled at why trees grew well on some basalt soils but not at all on others of similar consistency (ch 1). Parallel questions rise about the Monaro. Was there in 1788 a good correlation between treeless basalt and treed granite? Are other valleys of similar size and altitude treeless or frost stricken? Are trees returning naturally to basalt grasslands despite these causes?

Mark Currie first described the Monaro. His account supports Costin. From about

Michelago on 3 June 1823 he went south 'through a forest country, and near several stony ranges, to a rather extensive plain, which proved to be the commencement of a very long chain of down country'. Near Bredbo next day he 'Passed through a chain of clear downs to some very extensive ones, where we met a tribe of natives . . . we learned that the clear country before us was called Monaroo, which they described as very extensive.' Across the Bredbo on 5 June he 'observed a continuation of downs to the southward clear of timber'. On 6 June he rode south 'say forty miles' to about Billilingra Hill or east of it, and saw grass all the way. On a map he marked 'Extensive downs clear of timber'.[25]

Yet not all, and not only, downs were treeless, nor all granite hills treed. In July 1844 Robinson saw plains with trees and hills without:

> The immense Downs with their undulating grassy surface stretched out before me as far as the eye could scan, a Park of great magnitude and beauty studded with copses of Banksia, Casuarinae, Mimosa, Shrubs, and small belts of Eucalyptus with bare and isolated mamillary shaped and flat-top'd hills.[26]

Further, the forests were open, so burnt regularly. Sometimes miles off, Currie saw 'hills for the most part stony', therefore open: before the 2003 fires they were dense forest with few stones visible. On or near Currie's route near Bredbo, Lhotsky 'passed all the way forests of blue and white gum, but remarkably destitute of any underwood',[27] while Bunbury found the district 'covered with fine grass; it is part plain and part fine undulating hills with groups of trees sprinkled all over them in a most picturesque manner . . . it bears a most park-like appearance'.[28] 'The forest ground is thinly timbered with the white gum, and gently undulated', Stewart Ryrie wrote from his Monaro station in 1840. The granite ranges east of Bredbo were 'all bare of timber (except in the gullies), and . . . covered with species of heath and coarse wiry grass', while the country south and west was 'undulated, with rich flats between the hills, some of which are lightly timbered, others perfectly clear'. North of Cooma he 'came to open downs . . . about six or seven miles long by five broad . . . travelled through a mile of open forest and came out upon more open downs called Belaira [Monaro], and travelled across them for some miles to the Murrumbidgee'. West of Cooma he found country 'beautiful in appearance, consisting of open forest ranges, well clothed with grass to the very summit, and large meadows lying between them'.[29] These are familiar patterns, showing 1788 fire on ridges, hills and flats. Why not the rest of the downs?

The patterns were similar from Yass south. The Yass district, which no-one thinks is the treeless Monaro, was 'for the most part open forest, with luxuriant pasturage... The "Plains", or more properly speaking, extensive downs, are destitute of trees.'[30] At Lake George and Canberra the plains were grassy, the hills usually scattered trees and grass (ch 9; pictures 51–2), but in 1954 Lindsay Pryor wrote, 'there is little doubt that the Canberra Plains, Ginninderra and Tuggeranong were treeless and therefore true climax grassland'.[31] These plains carry naturally regenerating trees now. As a result, 'the Monaro' has retreated south. In 1820 it began at Canberra, as a 'beautiful clear plain... very extensive. Rich Soil and plenty of grass.'[32] For Costin in 1954 it began south of Michelago,[33] but today grassland there is intersected by low hills dense with eucalypts, there are patches of natural regeneration, and native tree plantings are flourishing. In short, while Monaro trees may grow more readily on granite than on basalt, there is no evidence of a fixed tree–grass boundary along a basalt–granite divide, and there is evidence of 1788 fire patterns. Ground where trees find it hard to grow is precisely where people working with the country might burn most intensively.

In cold country soil steps back, and treeless valleys become frost hollows. Costin put the prevailing view of their cause:

> The dominance of dry tussock grasslands along many treeless valleys of the Monaro is also related to a high frost incidence determined by cold air drainage. The absence of trees is apparently due to the inhibition of seedling development, since it has been shown that trees can be grown successfully in these areas provided the seedlings are protected from frost during their early life.[34]

Millennia ago the Monaro was not frosty, and presumably trees protected seedlings then. How did it get clear? The question is also pertinent to open high valleys ringed by Snow Gum, Black Sallee and similar eucalypts, whose seedlings survive metres of snow. It is hard to see how frost might kill so completely where frost and snow in turn do not. Equally telling, trees are now returning, edge-invading hollows from forest both higher and lower. Nursery Swamp near Canberra lies in a grassy valley flanked by sheltering hills. Stockmen once used it to nurse calving cows, hence its name. Today tea-tree is capturing the grass: it has spread visibly in recent decades. Not far away, Smokers Flat is described as 'treeless due to cold air drainage from the surrounding slopes'.[35] Tea-tree is reclaiming it too, and eucalypts are invading its edges.

Another 'frost hollow', Orroral Valley, was grass when Europeans came, began reverting to forest soon after, then was cleared by axe. Several portion plans between 1858 and 1870 state, 'good open forest' or 'open undulating forest. Ringbarked.' In 1998 Brian Egloff noted eucalypts 'regenerating on the fringes of the grassland'. Across the river from Orroral homestead, an undulating grass plain is flanked on the east by steep timbered hills and on west by a narrow tree belt along the slope edging the swamp. North a creek blocks it; south, swamps, hills and rocks steadily narrow it until it meets a steep bank which blocks views further south. Just over the bank the ground drops sharply away. This is a wallaby trap, not a frost hollow, burnt from forest but in every direction terminating in obstacles. Prey could be driven to suit the wind, and always be at a disadvantage.[36] Trees are now reclaiming the plain's edges.

John Banks, who had unsurpassed knowledge of Canberra's high country eucalypts, observed that even if frost did inhibit one tree species, this would merely let others in.[37] Further, rarely is a valley floor entirely treeless, but where it is, so are adjacent slopes for a short distance up. This is a classic trap pattern in and out of frost zones. People lived at Nursery Swamp for 'at least' 3700 years before 1788,[38] and as Hovell saw at Micalong swamp, they burnt hollows: 'Here we found some little good grass, as the Natives had burned the old grass, some short time previous.'[39] 'Frost hollow' carries natural explanation an unnaturally long way. 'Fire hollow' is a better term.

Some landscape scientists are interested in forest thickening. In 1991 EH Norris, PB Mitchell and DM Hart used three 1870s small area maps plus sources dated 1914, 1938 and 1970 to test claims about changing tree density in the New South Wales Pilliga.[40] They gave Aborigines short shrift: 'No research has been done on the occupation of the forest area by the Kamilaroi aborigines, but the few sites that have been recorded are only short distances from main creeks and it seems likely that they rarely visited the forest core.'[41] I recall Blainey's observation that most Australian goldfields were found near roads, and Aboriginal Law that people never leave any land long unchecked. Norris et al are venturesome in making their claim simply because they failed to find contrary evidence. Yet the claim lets them dismiss the possibility of human intervention in the forest core, so clearing the way for a natural explanation. They make an unproven and improbable assumption to lay down a supposedly objective baseline.

Among their conclusions in 1991, they report 'evidence which seems to point to a remarkably stable vegetation pattern over the past century'.[42] They go back further, sometimes to the 1830s, more often to the 1870s–1890s, though both at best sketchily, including when criticising Eric Rolls' book on the Pilliga, *A Million Wild Acres*. They say that Rolls 'offers opinion' on the effect of Aboriginal fire on the forest, and that they will 'question the details' of his 'sequence of events', the first of which is the pre-European state of the forest.[43] They do not do this, resting instead on the baseline they set by excluding Aboriginal intervention—and early European intervention, because 'there is little evidence of it'.[44] This brings their baseline closer to the date of their first useful source, 1914. How can they claim to question Rolls' details on the pre- and early post-European Pilliga when their earliest substantial evidence is dated 1914? They don't say, and they don't do it, yet they imply that objective data shows that Rolls is wrong. This sense permeates the paper.

Norris et al write, 'In the 1914 survey, the surveyor recognised areas of thick forest ... While problems arise here with the exact meaning of a "thick forest", these denser areas are not obvious on the air photographs of later years [1938 and 1970]; a reversal of the expected trend if the forest was becoming denser.'[45] Thick forest was there in 1914: a scientist saw it. If Norris et al could not see it in the photos, they might more sensibly, though not objectively, assume that the thick forest has thinned. Yet they state that humans rarely impacted on the forest core between 1914 and 1938.[46] How do they know? Did the forest self-thin? And how does this demonstrate a 'remarkably stable vegetation pattern over the past century'?

The authors then state that dense pine patches in the Pilliga core are evident in three twentieth century records, and take issue with 'the general belief that ... dense shrub cover was virtually unknown at the time of first settlement'.[47] Who had that belief in 1991? Not Rolls. Not any historian or scientist I know of. Aboriginal mosaic burning, including leaving dense scrub, was quite widely accepted by 1991. The authors cite no source to support their claim. Their earliest detailed source is 1914: they seem to think that the 1914 forest is a guide to its condition 80 years before. Perhaps it is as an 'impression', but not in the precise way the authors use. For example they report 1914 mosaics ('areas'[48]): were these survivors of 1788 fire, or favourable regeneration areas, or both, or something else? We don't know. We don't know where the 1914 mosaics were. A better method is to seek this evidence for about 1914 and about the 1830s, and if that fails try a different study area, or try other questions: how did those dense patches get there? If trees were dense there, why not elsewhere?

Scientists (and historians) thirsting to milk the historical record often shackle themselves in this way, confining their sources to a limited study area. This deprives them of sources and context, tempting them to ask and assume more than the sources they do find can sensibly say. Of course all evidence should be probed for what it might say, but that does not justify making it say what it doesn't, or making it say of one time or place what it actually says of another. A better approach is to seek as well sources and context beyond the study area. Context is vital. You must get inside a source's head, steadily building a subjective impression not of what you think was meant, but what he or she thought was meant.

Rod Fensham compares Leichhardt's maps and descriptions of inland Queensland with 1945–78 aerial photographs of the same country.[49] With such work, Fensham says, the 'challenge is to develop more rigorous and explicit ways of interpreting [historical] information'.[50] Like Norris et al he is interested in vegetation thickening, and he too concludes that his comparison 'does not support the hypothesis that vegetation thickening has been extensive or substantial. On the contrary the study suggests that the structure of the vegetation has been relatively stable.'[51]

To establish his baseline—Leichhardt's route—Fensham cites Glen McLaren's *Beyond Leichhardt* to claim that Leichhardt's 'navigation records have proved highly accurate'.[52] McLaren says no such thing, instead writing that Leichhardt's latitudes average 2 kilometres south and his longitudes 34 kilometres east or west of his actual location, and that within three months the loss of his compass rendered his bearings 'frequently somewhat inaccurate'.[53] McLaren could trace Leichhardt's route with 'considerable accuracy' as far as the Mitchell River, that is for about 70 per cent of the country Fensham discusses, but of 309 Leichhardt campsites he could locate only 79 exactly, 35 within about 400 metres, 93 within 400–800 metres, and therefore 102—a third—not at all.[54] Whether this is enough to compare vegetation then and now along Leichhardt's route is difficult to say. My guess is sometimes yes, sometimes no. Fensham always says yes. A good historian would be cautious of investing so much in so little, instead keeping to when vegetation happens to be described near one of those 79 proven campsites—of course assuming McLaren's 'impressions' as a historian are acceptable.

Fensham assumes that Leichhardt uses words consistently to describe country, influenced neither by changing landscapes nor by adjusting usages as he understands the land better. Fensham writes, 'It is clear from Leichhardt's journals and letters that terms describing the structural character of vegetation have specific meaning.'[55] It is not clear. Fensham often quotes Leichhardt qualifying key words for country.[56] No doubt the words are broadly consistent: rainforest could never be called open. But this does not make them 'rigorous and explicit' enough to compare them usefully with 1945–78 aerial photographs across a stretch of inland Queensland.

To tabulate Leichhardt's words, Fensham constricts them. He quotes Governor King's 1805 definition of scrub—'shrubs of low growth'—which he says is 'consistent with Leichhardt'.[57] Yet he quotes Leichhardt's men riding horses through 'scrubs' overtopping them.[58] What then does 'low' mean? He offers another definition: scrub 'includes a very broad range of tall stratum and low stratum structural categories'.[59] Is this 'rigorous and explicit'? Do we know if Leichhardt ever used 'scrub' in this sense, let alone consistently? In 1832 his contemporary Mitchell stated, '"bush" or "scrub" consists of trees and saplings, where little grass is to be found',[60] while in 1834 Breton wrote, '"Open forest" is that description where there is no underwood, and the trees in general are far asunder. "Scrub" is dense forest with much underwood and bad soil.'[61] Fensham compounds the problem by stating that 'brush' is 'virtually synonymous' with scrub.[62] It might be now, it wasn't then. Breton noted,

> 'Vine brush' is almost impenetrable forest, where great numbers of climbers, parasitical plants and underwood, are found: the soil is generally good. 'Brush' is forest with occasional underwood, but not so dense as 'scrub': besides which, the latter may be without large trees: 'brush' is never destitute of such.[63]

'Brush' often meant what we call rainforest. Sometimes Leichhardt seems to use it in that sense ('vines'), sometimes not ('low bushes'). How to be rigorous or consistent about that?

From scrub to dense forest. Fensham claims that Leichhardt 'does not refer to "dense forest"',[64] yet quotes Leichhardt's 'very dense scrubby Ironbark forest'.[65] What did Leichhardt mean? A dense forest can be spaced trees with dense understorey, or close trees with or without understorey, or each in patches, and in time one might or might not become another. To argue for Fensham's 'relatively stable' vegetation structure[66] you need to know which was which in Leichhardt's time. Fensham merely subsumes one alternative under Leichhardt's word 'thicket': 'The term thicket seems [sic] to be applied to forest with dense patches of young trees of species represented as tall stratum dominants.'[67] I suggest that a 'thicket' is confined in area, with an understorey and canopy sometimes of different species. Leichhardt thought so too: he refers to 'Melaleuca and grass (?) thickets'.[68] I can't link this to Fensham's definition. Neither can he: except for cypress pine he later excludes references to 'thicket' as ambiguous.[69] Since his central purpose is to test whether vegetation has thickened, excluding thickening's most likely source is venturesome.

In Leichhardt's time people called 'forest' what we might call woodland, or even grassland. The *Australian National Dictionary* offers: 'Forest *Obs[olete]* A tract of open, well-grassed land, with occasional trees or stands of trees.' It quotes first King in 1805: 'Forest land—is such as abounds with Grass and is the only Ground which is fit to graze; according to the local distinction, the Grass is the discriminating character and not the Trees, for by making use of the Former it is clearly understood as different from Brush or Scrub', and second the American Charles Wilkes in 1844: '"forests" . . . are very different from what we understand by the term, and consist of gum trees . . . so widely scattered that a carriage may be driven rapidly through them without meeting any obstruction'.[70] How did those forests become so? Why aren't they still so, if 'stable', as Fensham claims?

'The term "plain"', Fensham states, 'clearly implies flat country that is either treeless or very thinly timbered.'[71] This is not clear. It nearly matches Mitchell in 1831: 'almost all land free from trees',[72] but not Peter Cunningham in 1828:

> *Plain* is a term of varied meaning throughout the colony, being generally however applied only to spots of land destitute of trees, without reference to the evenness of the surface; a patch of a few acres receiving this appellation equally with an area of many thousands[73]

or David Waugh in 1834: 'by plains in this country is meant not level ground, but ground either wholly or partially clear of timber—they may be real flats, and indeed generally are, but not necessarily so'.[74] In any case Fensham soon confronts Leichhardt's 'scrub plains', which he says 'include patches of scrub within an otherwise treeless area'.[75] These might or might not be today's 'patchy plains',[76] but either way, how does Fensham know? A little historical context should have convinced him that people then used the same word in different ways, just as they do now.[77]

This treatment of Leichhardt's language, making it 'rigorous and explicit' because Fensham needs it so, is alarming. Fensham says Leichhardt's usage is consistent; Leichhardt's text shows it is not. Even had it been, it does not follow that Fensham categorises it accurately or usefully, for he makes unproven assumptions about where Leichhardt was, and what he is saying. In part Fensham recognises these and other imprecisions,[78] but they do not deter him. He points out that he is 'specifically addressing the hypothesis that vegetation thickening has been substantial and extensive over more than 100 years of pastoral management'.[79] 'Substantial' has been claimed. Has 'extensive', in pastoral areas? Fensham's conclusions do focus on forest, but include 'open forest' defined as 5–55 per cent crown cover.[80] Mitchell defined 'forest' as 'an open wood, with grass'.[81] How to get 5–55 per cent from that?

Fensham assumes that early reports can be used as baselines for tracking changes in vegetation density over time. I agree, and as he states he and others have elsewhere found evidence of vegetation thickening since 1788.[82] The changes can be extensive and obvious, suggesting that they began when Aboriginal management ceased: certainly, apart from random fire, no-one has yet proposed an alternative. But changes in time should not be pushed too far. Imprecision in the sources, even by someone as observant as Leichhardt, warns against that. What he and others better tell us is of changes in place. Fensham quotes Leichhardt on one type of vegetation giving way to another: forest to plain, grass to tree belts or clumps, and so on.[83] Where they can be found, such locations are worth checking. They puzzled Leichhardt. Fensham quotes him observing, 'It is a singular character of this remarkable country, that extremes so often meet; the most miserable scrub, with the open plain and fine forest land.'[84] Singular indeed. Why? Leichhardt could see that they did not correlate with soil, salt, altitude or aspect. Instead they point to controlled and repeated burning in 1788. When Fensham suggests reduced fire 'frequency and intensity' in European times,[85] isn't the most puzzling conclusion that the vegetation has remained stable? He suggests that rain and drought regulate woody vegetation fluctuations around a rough equilibrium.[86] How rough, and why over his 100-year span? In short, Fensham employs assumptions about historical sources fully accredited within his discipline, and gets into a tangle as a result.[87]

In 1997 JS Benson and PA Redpath 're-examined' DG Ryan et al's 1995 booklet on early landscapes, and questioned landscape 'hypotheses' by Rolls (1981) and Flannery (1994).[88] They examined three main themes: fire frequency, how much forest was dense and/or with a dense understorey, and how much regrowth occurred because Aborigines ceased burning. On the first, they show that Ryan et al exaggerate in claiming general fires every year or so. The second becomes a quibble on words: if it has substance Benson and Redpath don't show it. On the third they and Ryan et al are both right, depending on how long after 1788 fire ceased their various examples are. Their criticism of Flannery is largely on matters relating to deep time, and of Rolls is ineffectual and based on 'evidence' of the Fensham variety. For example they criticise Rolls' estimate based on historical sources of 3–4 large trees per hectare in the Pilliga. They think 30 more likely.[89] They don't say why.

They begin by noting the presence of history and the absence of science in Ryan et al: 'Ryan et al present one line of evidence in trying to explain pre-European vegetation and overlook the extensive scientific literature on past and present vegetation, and on fire ecology in Australia. By referring to the scientific literature, and by re-examining the same historical sources' they propose to challenge Ryan et al, Rolls, and Flannery.[90]

In fact, where scientific research exists they simply assert its paramountcy. Where science and history clash, they say, science must be right. This leads them to claim, on no scientific basis, that Cook's 'lawns' (ch 1) were heath, seen from out to sea.[91] Cook lived by one of his lawns, Grassy Hill at Cooktown, for seven weeks, and climbed it several times (picture 13). The claim is not objective, and wrong. Similarly, Benson and Redpath merely speculate on alternatives to Ryan et al's sources, and sometimes show little skill in interpreting historical evidence.[92] They write, 'Vegetation types such as rainforest, wet sclerophyll eucalypt forest, alpine shrublands and herbfields, and inland chenopod shrublands, along with a range of plant and animal species, would now be rarer or extinct if they had been burnt every few years.'[93] Some of these types *were* rarer in 1788; in any case no-one suggests that people burnt all Australia with the same fires at the same intervals. Yet Benson and Redpath conclude that climate is 'the main determinant in vegetation change'.[94]

Benson and Redpath concede some regrowth after 1788, but claim that clearing outweighed it.[95] Others argue this,[96] but it is a non-sequitur, and doubtful anyway, especially for hills. Early squatters did not graze hills: they had better grass on flats, so hills thickened. The people who called Black Mountain in Canberra heavily timbered in the 1860s and the 1960s were describing the same burnt woodland Hoddle saw in 1832 (ch 9). More to the point, why did Benson and Redpath's regrowth occur? Why wasn't the vegetation as dense in 1788? The clearing baseline Benson and Redpath use was well after 1788 fire was stopped, so too late. In general only accounts within say 20–40 years of the end of 1788 fire suffice, depending on the country. Later than this, and trees and scrub have got away.

Benson and Redpath use definitions for closed vs open forest and woodland vs open woodland set down by scientists in 1990,[97] echoing assumptions Fensham and others use. This is useless in assessing historical sources, which had no obligation to be consistent even within themselves, let alone across future centuries. People differ, and over years or even days might change thinking, or use the same word to include the very landscapes later researchers are trying to distinguish. Few if any state measurably what they mean, none I know uses defining words consistently, and no definition of vegetation from any single historical source can be converted into a general description of landscape, let alone used as an objective baseline. Yet scientists readily attach meanings to defining words, sometimes even tabulating or quantifying them as percentages, then using these to show some hypothesis or other. Here is a cutting edge between subjective history and objective science: history knows how circumscribed evidence is; science imagines that making a statement stark, or converting it to numbers or tables, makes it objective. This may save space, but gains no precision or clarity, rests on unproven assumptions, and generates venturesome conclusions. I puzzle why any discipline committed to objectivity troubles with attempting to force-fit sources.

These attempts matter both on their own, and because others rely on them, with distracting results. George Seddon, a fine ecologist well aware of the impact of Aboriginal fire, quotes Alfred Howitt on Gippsland forest thickening after 1788 (ch 11). He has 'no doubt' that Howitt's observations 'are essentially correct', but he finds Howitt's explanation, that thickening was because 1788 fire ended, not 'universally applicable'. He offers two proofs: that some forests were 'dense and almost impenetrable at the time of settlement', and, quoting a scientist, that it 'seems that after a fire there is a natural succession from shrub understorey to an open parkland of mature trees and grass, but this takes some 40 years' unless fire interrupts it. He therefore states that 'Aborigines rarely burnt this country', and quotes the scientist that a 'natural succession is now re-asserting itself within the Kosciusko National Park'.[98]

Seddon's first proof has only some forests dense, so some were open. Open forest is the puzzle Howitt addresses: there is no point in discussing what he was not. Neither proof shows that 'Aborigines rarely burnt this country'. Gippsland was patterned with grass, open and dense forest, and clear roads over a great variety of soils and altitudes.[99] People visited Kosciuszko country annually for bogong moth:[100] is it likely that there alone they ignored the Law and did not burn? Historical sources show that they did burn: for example compare Ryrie's 1840 account of Rams Head's grassy range with its dense forest now (picture 5). This is no natural succession, and it questions why a natural explanation is preferred.

By far the most frantic denier is Bill Lines.[101] He claims that there is no evidence for 1788 fire. He writes of Judith Wright and Ted Strehlow, 'In this racial fantasy it is white men, not black, who are barbarous and ignorant. Neither Wright nor Stehlow provided details as to what Aboriginal intimate knowledge of their environment comprised';[102] of Rhys Jones and Sylvia Hallam on firestick farming, 'This assertion quickly became received wisdom but not on the basis of merit or on evidence marshalled on its behalf';[103] of Kath Walker on Aboriginal land ownership, 'While this romantic cant highlighted Aboriginal moral superiority, it bore no resemblance to the manner in which human beings actually live on the planet';[104] of Tim Flannery and Marcia Langton on the absence of wilderness, 'This ill-reasoned, chaotic argument rested on a terrifying ignorance of history, language, biology and ecology',[105] and so on.[106] I hope this book helps.[107]

Few historians ask how Australia became as it was, whereas many scientists do. I urge them to see historical sources not as bones to be picked but as bodies to be studied, and to consider that history's 'impressions' and science's 'objectivity' alike stem from assumptions. Of course sources can be wrong, but to think them inherently wrong brings flat-earthers frighteningly close. I think Bill Jackson knew this. Some of his work may be disproved. I assume he would expect so: it would be catastrophic if knowledge ossified. But he asked questions and offered ideas. These are the great spurs to enquiry, giving future researchers the fire and purpose to seek on. I hope that, even as Jackson's work recedes from objectivity into impression, his successors learn to mine more fully and objectively the rich treasure trove it has joined.

APPENDIX 2

Current botanical names for plants named with capitals in the text

Botanical names are changed frequently.

Acacias *Acacia*

From their DNA some *Acacia* are now classified *Senegalia* or *Vachellia*.

Blackwood *melanoxylon*
Boree, Myall *pendula*
Brigalow *harpophylla*
Cootamundra Wattle *baileyana*
Georgina Gidgee *georginae*
Golden Wattle *pycnantha*
Inland Gidgee *cambagei*

Ironwood *estrophiolata*
Lancewood *shirleyi*
Mimosa Bush *farnesiana*
Mulga *aneura*
Silver Wattle *dealbata*
Witchetty Bush *kempeana*
Yarran *homalophylla*

Eucalypts *Eucalyptus*

From their DNA many northern and some western eucalypts are now classified *Corymbia*.

Alpine Ash *delegatensis*
Apple Box *bridgesiana*
Bangalay *botryoides*
Bimble Box *populifolia*
Black Box *largiflorens*
Blackbutt *pilularis*
Black Peppermint *amygdalina*
Black Sallee *stellulata*
Blakely's Red Gum *blakeyii*
Coastal Moort *platypus*
Coolibah *microtheca*
Darwin Stringybark *tetrodonta*
Darwin Woollybutt *miniata*
Desert Bloodwood *opaca*

Fan-leaved Bloodwood *foelscheana*
Forest Red Gum *tereticornis*
Ghost Gum *papuana*
Grey Box *microcarpa*
Gympie Messmate *cloeziana*
Hill Red Gum *dealbata*
Imlay Mallee *imlayensis*
Inland Bloodwood *terminalis*
Jarrah *marginata*
Karri *diversicolor*
Lemon-flowered Gum *woodwardii*
Mallee Box *porosa*
Marri *calophylla*
Meelup Mallee *phylacis*

Messmate Stringybark *obliqua*
Mongarlowe Mallee *recurva*
Morrisby's Gum *morrisbyi*
Mountain Ash *regnans*
Mugga Ironbark *sideroxylon*
Pink Gum *fasciculosa*
Poplar Gum *platyphylla*
Ramel's Mallee *rameliana*
Red Bloodwood *gummifera*
Ribbon (White, Manna) Gum *viminalis*
Risdon Peppermint *risdonii*
River Red Gum *camaldulensis*
SA Blue Gum *leucoxylon*
Scribbly Gum *haemastoma*
Shining Gum *nitens*
Silver-leaved Gum *pulverulenta*
Smithton Peppermint *nitida*
Snappy Gum *leucophloia*
Snow Gum *pauciflora*
Southern Blue Gum *bicostata*
Spotted Gum *maculata*
Sugar Gum *cladocalyx*
Swamp Gum *ovata; regnans* (Tas)
Swamp Peppermint *rodwayi*
Sydney Blue Gum *saligna*
Sydney Red Gum *Angophera lanceolata*
Tasmanian Blue Gum *globulus*
Tuart *gomphocephala*
Varnished Gum *vernicosa*
White Box *albens*
White Mallee *dumosa*
Yellow Box *melliodora*

Other trees

Belah *Casuarina cristata*
Black Sheoak *Allocasuarina littoralis*
Bottle Tree *Brachychiton* spp
Bunya Pine *Araucaria bidwillii*
Celery-top Pine *Phyllocladus aspleniifolius*
Coral Tree *Erythrina variegata*
Corkwood *Hakea suberea*
Cypress *Callitris*
    Black *endlicheri*
    Blue *intratropica*
    White (Murray Pine) *glaucophylla*
Deciduous Beech *Nothofagus gunnii*
Desert Oak *Allocasuarina decaisneana*
Drooping (Coast) Sheoak *Allocasuarina verticillata*
Fig *Ficus platypoda*
Forest Oak *Allocasuarina torulosa*
Green Plum *Buchanania obovata*
Hoop Pine *Araucaria cunninghamii*
Huon Pine *Lagarostrobos franklinii*
King Billy Pine *Athrotaxis selaginoides*
Kurrajong *Brachychiton populneum*
Lady or Native Apple *Syzygium suborbiculare*
Myrtle or Native Beech *Nothofagus cunninghamii*
Native Cherry *Exocarpus cupressiformis*
Nonda Plum *Parinari nonda*
Ooline *Cadellia pentastylis*
Paperbark *melaleuca* spp
Pencil Pine *Athrotaxis cupressoides*
Quandong or Native Peach *Santalum acuminatum*
Queensland Nut, Macadamia *Macadamia ternifolia*
Red Bauhinia *Bauhinia carronii*
Red Cedar *Toona ciliata* syn *australis*
Red Kapok *Bombax ceiba*
Sandalwood *Eremophila mitchellii*
Sassafras *Atherosperma moschatum*
Silky Oak *Grevillea robusta*
South Esk Pine *Callitris oblonga*
Sweet Pittosporum *Pittosporum undulatum*
Tea-tree (paperbark) *Melaleuca* spp
Tulipwood *Harpullia pendula*
Weeping Pittosporum *Pittosporum phylliraeoides*
Wilga *Geijera parviflora*

Bushes and shrubs

Bluebush, Cottonbush *Kochia* spp
Budda *Eremophila mitchellii*
Bush Plum or Plumbush *Santalum lanceolatum*
Bush Tomato *Solanum chippendalei*

APPENDIX 2

Caley's Grevillea *Grevillea caleyi*
Cassia *Cassia* spp
Desert Raisin *Solanum centrale*
Dogwood *Pomaderris* spp
False Sandalwood *see* Budda
Heath Banksia *Banksia ericifolia*
Hopbush *Dodonea viscosa*

Kangaroo Apple *Solanum rescum*
Mountain Pepper *Tasmannia lanceolata*
Native Gooseberry *Cucumis melo*
Old Man Saltbush *Atriplex nummularia*
Pituri *Nicotiana* spp
Tranquility Mintbush *Prostanthera askania*
Waterbush *Grevillea nematophylla*?

Grass

Blady *Imperata cylindrica*
Blue *Dichanthium sericeum*
Bull Mitchell *Astrebla squarrosa*
Buffel (introduced) *Cenchrus ciliaris*
Bunch Spear *Heteropogon contortus*
Button *Gymnoschoenus sphaerocephalus*
Kangaroo *Themeda triandra*
Mitchell *Astrebla* spp
Native Millet *Panicum decompositum*
Native Rice *Oryza australiensis*

Never-fail *Eragrostis setifolia*
Nut *Cyperis rotundis*
Queensland Blue *Dichanthium sericeum*
Spear *Stipa* spp
Spinifex *Triodia* spp
Tall Oat *Themeda avenacea*
Wallaby *Austrodanthonia caespitosa*
White or Common Tussock *Poa labillardieri*
Wild Oats (introduced) *Avena fatua*
Woollybutt *Eragrostis eriopoda*

Others

Birds Nest Fern *Asplenium nidus*
Bracken *Pteridium esculentum*
Broadleaf Cumbungi *Typha orientalis*
Bush Banana *Marsdenia australis*
Bush Potato *Ipomoea costata; I. polpha*
Cabbage Palm *Livistona australis*
Cape York Lily *Curcuma australasica*
Coconut *Cocos nucifera*
Darwin Palm *Ptychosperma bleeseri*
Grass Tree *Xanthorrhoea* spp

Gymea Lily *Doryanthes excelsa*
Native Truffle *Choiromyces aboriginum* and other spp
New Zealand Spinach *Tetragonia tetragonioides*
Tree Fern *Dicksonia antarctica*
Yam Daisy
    murnong *Microseris scapigera* syn *M. lanceolata*
    warran *Dioscorea hastifolia*
    wukay (parsnip) *Dioscorea transversa*
Zamia *Macrozamia reidlii*

NOTES

Titles or page numbers which follow '&' in any reference denote more evidence on the same point.

Introduction

1. Curr 1883, 189–90.
2. J Banks 1982, 16, 89; Brownlea 147–8; Enright & Thomas 983–4, 988, 1002; Hallam 2002, 177–81.
3. Lightning: Bill Jackson 8 Feb 01; Bowman & Brown 167; JM Gilbert 144; Jackson 1999a, 3; R Jones 1975, 25–8; Kay 2007a; Kirkpatrick 1977, 3; Luke & McArthur 246, 256, 338; National Academies Forum 41–3; J Webster 9; BA Wilson 8.
4. Hallam 1975, 7.
5. Barlow 243–8; RC Ellis 1984, 1985; Frawley & Semple 199–214; Hallam 1975, 1986 116–32, 2002; Jackson 1965, 1968, 1973, 1999a, 1999b; Jones 1968, 1969; Lake 153–65, 270–3; Latz 1995, 2007; Merrilees; Rolls 1984a, 1984b, 1999; I Thomas 1991, 1993, 1994; EK Webb 9.

1 Curious landscapes

1. Parkin 189.
2. Parkin 174, 178.
3. 27 Apr 1770. Parkinson 134.
4. 4 Jun 1770. Parkin 280, & 243.
5. Blackwood 88–9.
6. Parkin 448.
7. 2 Dec 1642. I Thomas 1994, 5, & 298.
8. Hovell 357–9.
9. Nov 1826. R Dawson 103.
10. Eyre vol 1, 156.
11. Sturt 1849 vol 2, 229–30.
12. Mossman & Banister 155, probably from T Walker 18.
13. Grass on good soil: Carron 44, 53; C Griffiths 8–9; Leichhardt 1847a, 31–2; Wilkinson 203.
14. Govett 3–4. Also picture 38; Andrews 1964, 60.
15. 14 Apr 1865. Sholl 211, & 206.
16. Haygarth 136–7.
17. Pendergast 4.
18. 22 May 1837. T Walker 145.
19. Bride 207; Dargavel 232, 240.
20. 8 Feb 1834. Andrews 1979, 81.
21. 10 Sep 1834. D Clark 439. Also Macquarie 152.
22. Govett 21–2, & 23. Also Cunningham J 4 Apr 1824, Reel 46, SRNSW.
23. Perry 14.
24. Sturt 1833 vol 1, xxxii.
25. Byrne 1987, 53.
26. Byrne 1987, 53. Also Birrell 20–30 & map.
27. 6 Nov, 14 Dec 1844. Leichhardt 1847a, 31–2, 73.
28. Eyre vol 1, 35–6. Eyre's examples: vol 1, 34, 149–50, 198, 208–9, 307, vol 2, 4, 7. Also S Hunter 91; Rolls 1999; Stuart 1865, 39.
29. Bischoff 165.
30. Gilmore 1934, 139–43. Tree bridges: Binks 93, 118–19, 126; Brodribb 23; Burn 14; Carron 117; Cross 4, 28, 148, 187, 202; Franklin 19; B Hiatt 193; Hovell 338, 350–1; HRNSW vol 5, 495; J Kelly et al 32; Lee 193, 281; J Ross 53; Shellam 34; Vallance et al 508, 555.
31. Henderson 1832, 145; HF Thomas 109.
32. Angas 1847a vol 1, 220.
33. 16 Feb 1827. F Ellis 29.
34. Jackson 1965, 30; Jackson 1999a, 1.

35 R Jones 1975, 26.
36 Jackson 1999a, 7.
37 Barlow 243. Also Flood 1989, 223; Reid 10; I Thomas 1991, 286–95.
38 9 Jul 1827. Dargavel et al 2002, 152–3.
39 10 Nov 1827. Dargavel et al 2002, 148.
40 Bowman & Jackson; Gunn J 30 Jan 1833, A316, 15–16, ML; Plomley 1966, 371.
41 25 Oct 1880. Savage 81–2, & 225. Also Horsfall 1991, 42.
42 Lake 2006, 153–65, 270–3.
43 BG; Barker 1990, 117–20; Cary et al 6; Griffiths 2001a, 8–9; Latz 1995, 38–9; Low 2002, 250; K Mills 232.
44 Noble 1997, 72.
45 Bowman 1998, 395; Kirkpatrick 1994, 69; Marsden-Smedley 1998a, 25.
46 BG; Bowman & Panton; Bowman 1995, 8–11; Bowman 1998, 392–3; Haynes 1985, 212–13; Norton 1903, 153; Price & Bowman.
47 Ward 2000b, 14.
48 Dovers 40–1.
49 Jurskis 2005, 257.
50 BG; Gott 2005; Kohen 1995, 108–9; Lunt & Morgan 84; JW Morgan.
51 Latz 1995, 19–22; Rose & Clarke 78.
52 Latz 1995, ix.
53 Nov 1826. R Dawson 108–9, & 52, 114.
54 Ellen & Fukui 157–86.
55 J Hunter 403.
56 18 Oct 1820. Macquarie 146, & 148.
57 11 Jun 1818, 8 Sep 1820. J Oxley 219, 291.
58 Ebsworth L 1826, B852, ML.
59 4 Nov 1830. SA Perry J c~ Eric Rolls & Elaine van Kempen.
60 Cross 16.
61 Haydon 25–6.
62 Mossman & Banister 62.
63 Giblin vol 2, 306.
64 Frankland 1997, 31.
65 Mitchell 1848, 137, & 261.
66 Bowen 209.
67 Rolls 2002, 171–2.
68 James 269.
69 Moon 45.
70 Buchanan 76.
71 8 Dec 1830. GF Moore 1884, 33.
72 12 Jun 1831. Greig 1927, 24.
73 Barrow 5.
74 1 Nov 1845. Leichhardt 1847a, 463–4.
75 Brock 22.
76 Sturt 1849 vol 1, 286–7.
77 Eyre vol 1, 190.
78 Warburton 1875, 148.
79 Giles 1889, 176.
80 Lewis J 17 Feb 1875, SAPP 19/1876.
81 Parks: Angas 1847b, pl.1 & 20; Bennett 1834, 137; Boyce 156; Breton 1834, 91–3; Clark 1998 vol 1, 179; Cross 16–17; P Cunningham vol 1, 118; Darwin 441; R Dawson 48; Eyre vol 1, 190, vol 2, 43; Govett 21; T Griffiths 2002, 380; R Howitt 87, 108; Mackaness 1942, 327; Marsh 55, 74; K Mills 235; Mitchell 1839 vol 1, 328, vol 2, 168, 248; BE Norton 3; Plomley 1966, 385; Robinson J 1845, Ar4, 4, ML; Rosenman 66–7; J Ross 58; Sorell J 17 Dec 1821, HRA 3, vol 2, 644; Statham 27; Stokes vol 1, 287, vol 2, 231; Stuart SAPP 21/1863, 22; Sturt 1838, 19; Sturt 1849 vol 1, 94–5; Tietkins SAPP 1890/111, 6; T Walker 18; Warburton 1875, 148.
82 P Andrews 2006, 2008; Ratcliff 1936, 1948.
83 Extinctions: H Allen 1983, 15–22, 30–42; R Baker 50; Flannery 1994, 223–4, 237–8; Frawley & Semple 147–8; Garnett & Crowley; Latz 1995, 32; Lunney 2001; Olsen; Stanbury 18; EK Webb 9–10.

2 Canvas of a continent

1 Jeanette Hoorn 20 Dec 02; Ryan 2005, 2007; D Smyth.
2 Youl 85–6.
3 PIC T65 NK12/27, NLA.
4 D Smyth 9. Also Kolenberg 8, 12; Ryan 2005, 40; B Smith 262, 268.
5 I Thomas 1991, 1.
6 Dexter 168, 185; Hoddle FB375 sketch 50, 2/5000, SRNSW.
7 Fred Duncan 19 Feb 03.
8 Giblin vol 2, 306.

NOTES

9. Fred Duncan 31 Jan 03.
10. Kirkpatrick et al 24–30; Marsden-Smedley 1998a; I Thomas 1991, 313–16.
11. Phillips 5–8.
12. 15 Feb 1840, & 14 Feb, 3, 5, 18 Mar 1840. Roll CY2715, ML.
13. Feb 1846. WB Clarke 228.
14. Argue 30–5; Flood 1980, 92–6, 285; Good 149, 276–9.
15. D Clark 279–80. Also AG Hamilton 188.
16. John McEntee 16–18 Aug 07.
17. Aurousseau vol 2, 719.
18. Curr 1883, 185. Also Ratcliffe 1936, 20–1.
19. Arch Cruttenden Aug 07. Also Rolls 1999, 211.
20. Parkin 331, 363.
21. Cook 638–9.
22. BG; K Mills 234; S Hunter 91.
23. Jan 1804. Collins R, HRNSW vol 5, 306. Also J Oxley HRA 3, vol 1, 760–1.
24. B Smith 260.
25. AG3318 sketches 1–11, 99–105, TMAG c~ David Hansen.
26. Hansen; B Smith 258–68.
27. Glover 6 c~ Tim Bonyhady.
28. Glover 7, 9.
29. House of Commons 1812/341, app 78–9.
30. AH Campbell 1987, 25–63.
31. Glover 4–5.
32. Map, Kraehenbuehl et al 2001.
33. Stokes vol 2, 402.
34. 26 Nov 1836. Linn 1991, 18. Also Twidale et al, 99.
35. 14 Feb 1850. T Griffiths 1988, 78.
36. Angas 1847b, pl.33.
37. Angas 1847b, pl.29, 39.
38. Kraehenbuehl 1996, Kraehenbuehl et al, map 2000.
39. Moon 45.
40. 12 Dec 1837. Backhouse 519.
41. Angas 1847b, pl.10, 53, 58; EC Frome, *Adelaide and St Vincent's Gulf from Glen Osmond road*, 1845 (AGSA); von Guerard, *Fall of the first creek near Glen Osmond*, 1855 (NLA).
42. T Griffiths 1988, 69.
43. 24 Jan 1839. Hahn 120–1, & 126 vs Buchhorn 67.
44. Sturt 1849 vol 2, 224. Also Chapman & Read 78.
45. Franklin D Dec 1840, MS114, NLA; Sturt 1838, 21.
46. Hoddle FB 377 sketch 61, 5 Dec 1832, 2/5002, SRNSW.
47. Hoddle FB 375 sketch 70, 5 May 1832, 2/5000, SRNSW.
48. Colville ff160; vn3289506, NLA.
49. J Oxley 174–5.
50. PICs 9027/3–4, NLA; Presland 2008, 86.
51. Colville 177–9.
52. 6 Apr 1839. MS114, 14, NLA; P Russell 31.
53. Tietkins J 9 Jul 1889, SAPP 1890/111, 22; scrapbook, PICACC 450, SLNSW; L *SMH* 26 Dec 1922.
54. Friedl et al attachment 13, 8–9.
55. B Hill 203–4.
56. 2 Jul 1902, SAPP 43/1904.
57. Friedl et al 13.
58. Friedl et al n2.
59. Spencer & Gillen 114, 121.
60. 8–9 Aug 1873 & map. Gosse 11.
61. 4 Jul 1902, SAPP 43/1904.
62. Frank Young 24 Aug 02.
63. 16 Oct 1873. Gosse 16.
64. Mountford 1953, 93.
65. Mountford Coll 1170, MSA.
66. Friedl et al attachment 4, 3.
67. Kimber 1983, 39–40.
68. Burrows et al 2000, 2006; D Carnegie 209–10. Also Nodvin & Waldrop 297–305.
69. Burrows et al 2000, 2006.
70. Burrows et al 2000, 7.
71. Frank Young 24 Aug 02; BG 25 Aug 02.
72. Kimber 39.
73. BG 11 May 05.
74. Hoorn 1986, 1990 1–3; McPhee 22–3, 203; J Turner 103–5.
75. BG 7 Mar 08; Thompson 123–4.
76. c1819. Rolls 2002, 72.
77. 6 May 1817. J Oxley 21–2, 26.
78. BG 1 Nov 07.

349

79 Plomley 1966, 260–1.
80 I Thomas 1994, 70.
81 D Smyth 22.
82 ML DGD24, SLNSW.
83 Tipping 44.
84 31 Mar 1842. CCL Portland Bay L, A1426, ML.
85 Darke map 821.123, SLV; Smyth 108–9; Townsend VPRS 19 40/1075A, 21 Oct 1840; von Guerard.
86 5 Dec 1813. Mackaness 1965, 23–4.
87 Morton 197.
88 15–16 Feb 1856. AC & FT Gregory 131.
89 J Oxley 300.
90 Mittagong 1:25,000 8929–11-S, 506812; Wild R 17 Jan 1824, Col Sec Index reel 6031, 4/7082C, 17, SRNSW; Weatherburn.
91 2 Aug 1845. Leichhardt 1847a, 354–5.
92 Apr 1820. Meehan FB reel 2624 (SZ 750/161), SRNSW.
93 18 Oct 1820. Macquarie 146.
94 Macquarie map.
95 Statham-Drew 74, opp 80; BG & Arch Cruttenden 4 Jan 08.
96 13–14 Mar 1827. HRA 3, vol 6, 560. Stirling missed 12 Mar.
97 Hallam 1975, 58; Hallam 1986, 122.
98 19 Jan 1838. Backhouse 538.
99 Steele 1972, 246.
100 Steele 1972, 263.
101 Map MT55, ERM.
102 Steele 1972, 249.
103 9–10 Aug 1828. Fraser D, OM 87–25, JOL.
104 M Cameron 19; Smith & Banks 103.
105 MH Walker 111, 115.
106 photo H89.265/80, SLV.
107 Cosgrove et al.
108 Brown & Podger 1982b.
109 B Hiatt 121.
110 Gee & Fenton 17–21; Sim & West; Vanderwal & Horton 38.
111 3–4 Mar 1772. Duyker 1992, 29–30, 45.
112 10 Mar 1773. I Thomas 1991, 44–5.
113 Jan 1799. D Collins vol 2, 130.
114 14 Dec 1815. Boyce 92. Southwest coast: I Thomas 1991, 96, 134 & 1993, 3, 8.
115 Sib Corbett Feb 02; Flanagan 6–13; Marsden-Smedley 1998a, 17; Marsden-Smedley & Kirkpatrick; I Thomas 1994.
116 Gee & Fenton 263.
117 Fensham & Fairfax 1995, 7.
118 18–19 Mar 1843. P & G Ford 299. Also Aurousseau vol 2, 708; Birrell 20–30, 47; Herbert 145; LJ Webb 160.
119 23–8 Mar 1843. P & G Ford 300–1.
120 Anon 1854?, 59.
121 Herbert.
122 Herbert 145. Also LJ Webb 161.
123 Fensham & Fairfax 1995, 1996a, 1996b, 519.
124 Boyd et al; Stubbs.
125 BG 11 Apr 01.
126 17 Dec 1813. HRA 1, vol 8, 173.
127 Grey vol 2, 271.
128 Coutts 4; RG Gunn et al 10–13, 22–3; Russell & Isbell 123–5.
129 PWS Tas 13.
130 PWS Tas 24–6.
131 Hurley PIC FH/1834, NLA; PWS Tas 24–6; Tas Field Nat Club 6, 9.
132 BG 21 Feb 03.
133 Fensham 1985, 102–3.
134 Plomley 1966, 398.
135 29 May 1890. SUR/A 91/5517, QSA.
136 Hill et al 2004, 77.
137 Mac Core 6 Oct 02, OHU; Hill et al 2000, 142; Jack vol 1, 211; vol 2, 479–80, 536–43, 547–8, 555, 587; Jack R 1881 vol 2, 230–1, 255, 257, QPP; Savage 73, 78, 81–2, 85, 100, 171.
138 26 Oct 1886. Savage 229–30.
139 Milman 29 Jul 1890. SUR/A 91/5517, QSA.
140 29 May 1890. SUR/A 91/5517, QSA.
141 27 Apr 1891. SUR/A 91/5517, QSA.
142 Helenvale 7966 run 14, 19 Oct 1994; Mossman 7965 run 1, 1 Oct 1991.
143 Hill et al 2004, 49.
144 Cubit.
145 12 Jun 1834. Plomley 1966, 884.
146 BG 14 Feb 02.

147 Bill Tewson Feb 02; Binks 63–4; Plomley 1966, 884.
148 16 Feb 1827. F Ellis 30.
149 R Jones 1975, 27.
150 Gilfedder 2.
151 BG 14 Feb 02; Gilfedder 25–30, 43.
152 12 Jul 1831. Plomley 1966, 376.
153 6–7 Mar 1841. PIC T3386, NLA; Hodgkinson 37–40; Ryan et al 10.
154 Giles 1889, 20–2.
155 Griffin & McCaskill 14–15.
156 Eyre vol 1, 35–6.
157 M Williams 126–7.
158 AC & FT Gregory xiii.
159 Rothery 36.
160 Rothery xii, xxi, 37.
161 RE Oxley esp 24–5, 31–2, 35–7.
162 Macquarie 157–9 & map.
163 28 Aug 1820. MS351, NLA.
164 Breton 1834, 53–6, 235; Cambage 1921, 259–60; Cunningham 7 Apr 1824, reel 46, SRNSW; Field 372; Gibbney 3; Jervis 261; C Throsby Smith J 3 Dec 1820, MS689, NLA; T Walker 8.
165 Govett 22–3.
166 15 Dec 1831. Colville 148.
167 FBs 376 Jun 1832, 23–30, & 377 20 May 1833, 158, 2/5001–2, SRNSW.
168 BG 2000–9.
169 Hoorn 1986, 1990.
170 Mathew 1910, 87, & 53–4. Also Byrne 1987, 26–30, 43–4; Curr 1887, 174.
171 BG 9 Oct 08.
172 Vallance et al 542.
173 PIC T693 nk762/22, NLA.
174 Wedge 5.
175 Flannery 1994, 221.
176 14 Jul 1850. T Griffiths 1988, 128.
177 Parkin 448.
178 Ryan 2007, 80–1.
179 14 Aug 1841. PL Brown 1952–71 vol 3, 79.
180 10 Nov 1835. GF Moore 2001 unpub c~ Jim Cameron.
181 Ward et al.
182 Rosenman 44.
183 Dale 11.
184 Dale 5.
185 30 Jun 1828. HRA 3, vol 6, 540.
186 Feb 1836. Darwin 449–50.
187 Burrows and Abbott 120.
188 12 Sep 1820. PP King 404.
189 12 Mar 1865. Richardson 51.
190 Nunn 1981, 1989.
191 P Andrews 2006, 2008.
192 *Canberra Times* 22 Aug 03.

3 The Nature of Australia

1 Mitchell 1839 vol 1, 238.
2 de Satge 147.
3 Field 374.
4 Frankel 44.
5 Turner 1891, ix–x.
6 G Martin 1.
7 Soil: BG; MR Allen 118; Barr & Cary 16–18; Brock 33, 198; S Clarke 102; Dixson 204; Gammage 1986, 224; Gott 1983, 12; Gott 2005; Hahn 120; Mitchell 1839 vol 1, 135–6, 214; Mitchell 1848, 266; Norton 1903, 156; Ratcliffe 1936, 21, 23, 64 c~ Jan Cooper; GH Reid 5; Rolls 1984a, 246; Seddon 1994, 41–2; Youl 30–1.
8 1 Jun 1832. Mitchell 1839 vol 1, 222.
9 Anon 1854?, 33–4.
10 13 Jan 1839. Waterhouse 181.
11 1–2, 5 Jul 1817. J Oxley 92–5, 100.
12 P Andrews 163–4; Ratcliffe 1936, 23, 64.
13 Howitt 1891, 129.
14 S Clarke 100, 102.
15 11 May 1889. Donovan 93.
16 B Finlayson 215–16, 221.
17 Reid & Mongan 61–7.
18 Gammage 1986, 5.
19 Water: Abbott 1890, 41–59; P Andrews 2006, 51–4, 173–5, 182–3; Arthur 10, 23, 31; Barr & Cary 16–18; Bland 47, 82; Brock 33; Darwin 443; Franklin D Dec 1840 & 10, 27 Apr 1843, MS114, NLA; Gammage 1986, 4–5, 11, 223; Hancock 107–9; Hawdon 38; Hood 170, 205; R Howitt 154; Mitchell 1839 vol 1, 237, vol 2, 311; Norton 1903, 157; Peters 25; Randell 1, 5, 7; Ratcliffe 1936, 22–3, 64; Robinson

R May 1846, Governor's Des ZA7081, 38, ML; Scott vol 2, 60; T Walker 17; Waterhouse 178.
20 5 Aug 1818. J Oxley 256–7.
21 Donovan 15.
22 Hawdon 19–25.
23 Gott 1991.
24 17 Oct 1845. Sturt 1849 vol 2, 38–9.
25 DI Smith 106.
26 McMaster 645.
27 Morton 1859, 197.
28 Curr 1883, 185.
29 BE Norton 4–6.
30 TM Perry 14.
31 JC Hamilton 37.
32 H Allen 1983, 23–30.
33 26 May 1827. Lee 558.
34 24 Jan 1839. Buchhorn 66.
35 Mitchell 1848, 43–79.
36 Sturt 1849 vol 1, 205.
37 Grass: H Allen 1983, 9–14; JM Black; Curr 1883, 186; Lunt et al 1998b, 32; A Mitchell 137; RM Moore; Rolls 1984a, 111–14; Rolls 1999; Stuwe 93–4; F Turner 1891; Ward 2001.
38 5–6 April 1839. P Russell 31.
39 Fortey R 5 Aug 1875, AA Co P 1/256/3 (WP-F1a), 3–4, Noel Butlin Archives, ANU c~ Jim Noble.
40 Andrews 2006, 11–13, 70–87; Rozycki; DI Smith 42–61; ME White 222; Youl 57.
41 Gammage 1986, 31–2, 51.
42 Donovan 15.
43 BG; Andrews 2006, 166; Lunt et al 1998b, 9.
44 BG; Christine Jones Sep 04; C Jones 2001, 2002.
45 Hallam 1975, 6.
46 Keast vol 1, 163–297; Kirkpatrick 1994, 3.
47 BG Feb 02; Brad Potts 17 Mar 08.
48 I Thomas 1994, 12.
49 Moulds & Hutton 6.
50 Constraints: BG; Anderson & Ladiges; Ashton 397; Foreman & Walsh 159–94; Gee & Fenton 98–101; RS Hill 1994, 380; S Kelly et al vol 1, 12; Kirk 7; Kirkpatrick 1977, 10, 47; Kirkpatrick 1994, 3, 12–17, 60; TM Perry 96; Presland 2008, 109–53.
51 Breton 1834, 261.
52 Gillen & Drewien 18.
53 Kirk 7.
54 Barney Foran 12 Apr 02; Leigh & Noble 5 map, 12–15, 21; RM Moore 250.
55 Henry Nix 21 Jun 02.
56 Mullette 9.
57 Anderson & Ladiges; J Read.
58 Gammage 1986, 6.
59 17 Oct 1845. Sturt 1849 vol 2, 38.
60 Sturt 1833 vol 1, xxxi–iii, xlii. Also Rolls 1984a, 260.
61 Noble et al.
62 Acacias: RS Hill 1994, 122; Isaacs 1987, 114; Keast et al 6; Latz 1995, 13; Riley; Simmons 7–9, 70, 110, 128–32, 164, 232, 248, 266, 314; Urban 78–85; van Oosterzee 1995, 131; ME White 190, 207–12.
63 CJ Lacey 29.
64 Barker & Greenslade 153.
65 Nutrient mobility: Attiwill et al; J Banks 1982, 211–12; Crane; Pyne 1991, 17–18.
66 Kelly et al vol 1, 34.
67 Grimwade 43.
68 Rare eucalypts: BG; M Cameron 98; Duncan 1990, 157; Grimwade 25; Haw & Munro 303–4; S Kelly et al vol 1, 77, vol 2, 50, 68; Mullette 9; Rossetto et al.
69 Keast vol 1, 510–18.
70 BG; Grimwade 9, 17; S Kelly et al vol 1, 60.
71 Eagle 82.
72 Eucalypts: BG; J Banks 1982, v, 35, 208, 211; Cary et al 6; Gammage 1986, 5–6; Gill et al 24, 362; Good 146–9; Griffiths 2001a, 14–23, 158; Grimwade; Haynes 1977, 6; Haynes et al 54; RS Hill 1994, 410–13; Keast vol 1, 499–536; Keast et al 2; Kelly et al vol 1, 4–5, 49; Kirkpatrick 1994, 40, 56–7; MacPherson 1939; Pate & McComb 149–53, 161, 173–5; Pyne 1991, 17–28; Seddon 2005, 179, 185–6; Seddon 1972, 99–100, 111; ME White 190.
73 Fire and plants: Clarke & Knox; Gee & Fenton 94; Gill et al 412–14; Kirkpatrick

1977, 5–10; Latz 1995, 6; Lines 1991, 7–8; Lunt et al 1998b, 13; A Mitchell 137; Pate & McComb 77–8; Pyne 1991, 31; J Read; Seddon 1972, 100–1; JMB Smith 142–3; Smith & Banks 101–2; Ward 2000b, 10; ME White 223.
74 Acacias and fire: BG; Henry Nix 21 Jun 02; Bradstock et al; Clarke & Knox; Duncan 1985, 32–3; Fensham 1985, 47; Flannery 1994, 227; Foreman & Walsh 212–26; Gill et al; Keast vol 1; Kirkpatrick 1977, 1994; Latz 1995; Lunt et al 1998b; A Mitchell 137; Noble 1997; Pyne 1991, 29, 38–41; Seddon 1972; JMB Smith; A Stewart 22; Ward 2000a, 2000b.
75 Breton 1834, 248.
76 Eucalypts and fire: eucalypt notes; BG; H Allen 1983, 23–35; J Banks ii-v, 19, 75, 81–90, 96, 136, 144, 206; Blainey 81–2; Gill 362; Good 143–68; Griffiths 2001a, 7; Haynes et al 54; Jackson 1968, 3, 9–16; Jurskis 2002, 689–90; A Keast et al 2–3; SGM & DJ Kerr 122; Kirkpatrick 1994, 56–7; Latz 1995, 6; Pate & McComb 77–81, 169; Phillips 5–8; Seddon 2005, 179–81; Ward 2000b, 14; ME White 190, 222.
77 Tierney.
78 Stuwe 1994.
79 Gill et al 412–13; Kirkpatrick 1977, 3, 8–10.
80 JMB Smith 142.
81 Managed fire: Clarke & Knox; Duncan 1985, 32–3; Fensham 1985, 47; Foreman & Walsh 212–26; Lonsdale & Braithwaite; Pate & McComb 81; Tierney.
82 TM Perry 28.
83 Noble 1996, 62–3; Norris et al 91, 216.

4 Heaven on earth

1   Berndt 1970, 132. Also Myers 52–3.
2   Cawthorne n, A1447, ML.
3   Teichelmann 13.
4   R Jones 1975, 28; Keen 236–40, 392; Lee & Daly 319.
5   Plomley 1966, 369, 376–7, & 186, 498.
6   Tasmanian Dreaming: Backhouse 82, 181–2, 557; G Calder 19–35, 69, 118; J Clark 28; McFarlane 2002, 29–34, 39; McFarlane 2010, 112–14; Stokes vol 2, 451.
7   Strehlow 1971, 284–6. Quoted c~ Strehlow Research Centre, Alice Springs.
8   Strehlow 1971, 666. Quoted c~ Strehlow Research Centre, Alice Springs.
9   R & C Berndt 1965, 128, & 133.
10 Lumholtz 172.
11 Songlines: Stuart Cooke 20 Jun 09; Dick Kimber 2 Aug 09; Berndt 1970, 94–5; C Ellis 17–93; de Graaf 15–16; Eyre vol 2, 229; Grey vol 2, 303–4; Elkin 1935, 171–4; B Hill 236; Kassler & Stubington 149–53; McBryde 2000, 157–8; Meggitt 60–61; Morphy 1991, 100–03; W Roth 117; Strehlow 1971; Sutton 1998a vol 2 bk 3, 360–1.
12 21 Feb 1838. Hawdon D, A1493, ML.
13 Soul: John Bradley 11 Jul 01; Murray Garde 1 Jul 05; Bulmer P box 9, F1 XM 900–10, MV; Corris 34; Gammage 1986, 12–13; Keen 145; McCourt & Mincham 62–3; Rose 1992, 82–3, 100; Rose 2000, 291.
14 R & C Berndt 1978, 19; Cawthorne n, A1447, ML; Home 10; Stanner 1976, 25–32.
15 de Graaf 34.
16 John Bradley 11 Jul 01.
17 Words and music Ted Egan, c~ Ted Egan.
18 Bride 426–7.
19 de Graaf 103.
20 Rubuntja & Green 16.
21 J Hunter 150; Kohen 1995, 108; Kohen 1996, 24; Powell & Hesline 134–7.
22 Yates 49–50.
23 Berndt 1970, 102–3.
24 Shaw 1986, 33–4.
25 Totem: East 572.993E, 4–5, ML; Grey vol 2, 84; Hale & Tindale 1933–4, 107–8; Howitt 1889, 103–4; Mitchell 1839 vol 2, 29, 346–7; Pepper 1–4; Spencer & Gillen 1899, 9–11, 34; Worgan L 12 Jun 1788, B1463, ML.

26 McBryde 2000, 156.
27 Strehlow 1947, 30–31.
28 Religion, soul, totem: LA Allen 3, 16–17, 20–3, 44, 54, 62, 196–9; Berndt 1970, 92–140; R & C Berndt 1978, 63–71; R & C Berndt 1993, 81, 112; R & C Berndt 1996, 137–8, 232–8; Bride 421–2; Cameron 1904, 91; Caruana & Lendon 22; Cawthorne n, A1447, ML; Charlesworth et al 145–66; Clarke 1994, 125–6, 349; Clarke 1997, 1999; Corris 40–1; Davis & Prescott 40–2; de Graaf 9–10; Elkin 1931, 1935, 174–9; Fison & Howitt 246; Gammage 1986, 12–17; Greenway n 1873, 13, 4/788.2, SRNSW; Grey vol 2, 228; Gunther c1843, B505, ML; Gunther ms 536–8, 541, COD 294B no 81, SCMC, SRNSW; Hartwig 67–8; Hetzel & Frith 78; Horton 2000, 142; Howitt 1889, 98–100; Howitt 1904, 144–51; Kaberry 1938, 266–74; Kassler & Stubington 109–10; Keen 145; Krefft 1862, 1; Krichauff 11–12; Latz 1995, 17, 69; Love 83–4; McKaige et al 1997, 75–9; Meggitt 59–66, 251–2, 317; Mulvaney 23; Myers 52–4; Parker R 1 Jan 1845, app 8, CSC 4/7153, SRNSW; KL Parker 15–20; Pepper 1–4; Pink 176–8; Rose 1992, 44, 54–5; Rose 1996, 28; Rose 2000, 289; Rose & Clarke 142–51; RSC 1860/165 vol 2 pt 2, Qs 1270, 1403, 2069, SAPP; Shaw 1981, 31–2, 119–20; Shaw 1986, 51, 83–6, 124–5, 183; Spencer & Gillen 1999, 112–13, 119–27, 138, 167–8, 207; Stanner 1976, 1979, 23–5, 34; Strehlow 1947, 16–17, 25–6; Strehlow 1971, 181; Strehlow 1978, 35–6; P Sutton 1989, 13–19; TM Sutton 17; Swain 16–19, 41–3; Threlkeld R 21 Jun 1826, Bonwick Box 53, Missionary vol 5, 1643, ML; Unaipon chap 2 1–5, chap 3 2–3, chap 18 1–3, chap 26 1–5, A1930, ML; Woods 1–2, 63–4.
29 HL Roth 1886.
30 Fraser D 26 Jul 1828, OM 87–25, JOL.
31 Sturt 1849 vol 2, 138.
32 Meggitt 246.
33 29 Sep 1836. Backhouse 431.
34 Haynes 1997, 11; R Jones 1975, 25.
35 Isaacs 1987, 46, 93. Also Nash 1984, vi, 8–10, 34–5.
36 Curr 1886 vol 2, 450; Morrill chap 3.
37 BG; Charlesworth et al 14–17, 32; Gammage 1993; Strehlow 1947, 5.
38 Mathews 1904, 209–10. Also Rose 2000.
39 Gammage 1986, 15–17.
40 Robinson R Apr–Oct 1844, VPRS 4414 unit 1; Thomas R Sep 1849, VPRS 10 unit 11, 5, 19–20, 41.
41 P Sutton 1978, 80.
42 No empty land: John Bradley 11 Jul 2001; S Anderson 116; Chapman & Read 85–7; Clarke 1994, 141–2; Davis & Prescott 70–9, 93; Langton 20; Meggitt 35–46; Parkhouse 638; Spencer & Gillen 1899, 152–4; P Sutton 1978, 69–83; Sutton & Rigsby 158–61; Unaipon chap 18, 3, A1930, ML.
43 Newsome 1980. Also Elkin 1933, 281; Morphy 1996, 192–3; Radcliffe-Brown 1929, 408–11; Sherratt et al 34–5, 39–40; M Thomas 91–2.
44 Songline as map, signal: Frost 28; Griffiths 2001a, 58–9; Isaacs 1987, 13; McBryde 2000; McFarlane 2008, 37; Shellam 41; Spencer & Gillen 1899, 447–9; Walsh 1990, 30–2; EK Webb 5, 36–40.
45 John McEntee 16 Aug 07.
46 Merlan 20, 22; van Oosterzee 1995, 145.
47 Unaipon chap 6, A1930, ML.
48 Ecological inspiration: John Bradley 11 Jul 01; Davis & Prescott 107; Flannery 1994, 284; Haynes 1985, 210; LR Hiatt 284–6; Hill et al 1999, 215–16; TN Howard 225; Isaacs 1987, 49; R Lawrence 217–23; McComb 92; McKaige et al 1997, 75–9; Presland 2008, 204–5.
49 10 Oct–3 Nov 1830. Plomley 1966, 245–66, 438–9 ns44, 51.

5 Country

1 25 May 1817. J Oxley 46.
2 Rose 1996, 38.

NOTES

3 Stormon 130–1.
4 Gillen & Drewien 16.
5 Mob, clan, tribe: Backhouse 542; Cane 54–6, 127; Clark 1998 vol 6, 5; J Clark 24; Clarke 2003, 36–8; CCL Geelong (Addis) R 28 Dec 1841, A1227, ML; CCL Moreton Bay (Simpson) R 1 Jan 1844, A1233, 1129, ML; Davis & Prescott 39; Dredge R 1839–40, VPRS 4410 unit 2 no 47; Hallam 1975, 15; Myers 95; Penney 23–4; Peterson & Long 63; Shellam 32; Stanner 1965, 2; Twidale et al 115; Wettenhall 22.
6 J Dawson 7.
7 HL Roth 1886, 132.
8 c1836. Browne 256.
9 W Roth 1903, 50, & 55.
10 Eyre vol 2, 297, & 298–300.
11 Powell & Hesline.
12 Hood 158.
13 GF Moore L c~ Jim Cameron, 347.
14 Boundaries, 'no': Anderson et al 67–8; R Baker 50; Curr 1886 vol 3, 363; Davis & Prescott 33, 54; J Dawson 7; T Donaldson 25–9; Gammage 1986, 12, 17; Green 85; Grey vol 2, 232–3, 273; Gunson 1974 vol 2, 186; Hallam 1975, 42; Jackson-Nakano 2001, xxiii; Latz 1995, 26; Meggitt 69–70; Mulvaney & Green 382–3; Myers 54–7, 98–100, 156–7; Peterson 1976; Peterson & Long 63; Powell & Hesline 131, 134; Rose 1996, 12–13, 38, 44–5; Rose & Clarke 30; RSC Aborigines 1845, 27 (Docker), NSWLC; Shellam 32; P Sutton 1978, 69; P Sutton 1998a; Tindale 1940, 142; J Wright 14; Wyndham 36–7.
15 McFarlane 2002, 43–4.
16 Gammage 1986, 19–20, 28.
17 Nelson 1965, 63.
18 Gould 1977, 182, & 175, 180. Also R & C Berndt 1965, 127; R Lawrence 60; MA Smith 1986, 29.
19 Country and family: Bates 1985, 49; Bonwick Box 52, Missionary vol 4, 968–9, ML; W Bradley 76; Browne 256–60; Chapman 96; Clark 1998 vol 1, 182, vol 2, 15, 337; CSC 4/1146.4, Wright 20 Feb 1851, SRNSW; CSC 4/7153, Durbin 9 Jan, Manning 26 Mar 1852, SRNSW; D Collins vol 1 app 1, 544–5; Dale 1834, 7; J Dawson 7; R Dawson 63; Ebsworth L 1826, B852, ML; Gunson 1974 vol 2, 334, 341, 351; Hallam 1975, 42–3, 65; Hanna 4–5; Hassell 681; Hodgkinson 222; Horton 2000, 57–8; AW Howitt 1889, 101–2; HRA 1, vol 22, 174, vol 23, 486, 589; Kaberry 1938, 271; Langton 1; R Lawrence 224–6; Meggitt 49–50; A Mitchell 123; GF Moore L c~ Jim Cameron, 347; Munster 46; Myers 100; Newland 1888, 3, 31; J Oxley 117; Parker R 1839–40, VPRS 4410 unit 2 no 52; Parkin 202, 448; Radcliffe-Brown 1930, 34–5, 63; Reynolds 1987, 140; Reynolds 1992, 65–73; Rose 1992, 65, 106–7; Spencer & Gillen 1899, 8–9, 16; P Sutton 1978, 56; Twidale et al 115; Wettenhall 26.
20 PL Brown 1989, 59.
21 A Atkinson 208.
22 12 Jun 1839. Schurmann L, Anon newspaper R, OM 90–6/6, JOL.
23 1841. Chapman 96.
24 1876. RB Smyth 41.
25 Stanner 1969, 44–5.
26 'Owners': Curr 1883, 174–5, 243–4; J Dawson 7; Eyre vol 2, 299; Grey vol 2, 234–5; Haddon 338; Parker R 1839–40, VPRS 4410 unit 2 no 52; Reynolds 1987, 140; Shellam 27–9; P Sutton 1978, 57.
27 Eyre vol 1, 351.
28 Eyre vol 2, 244.
29 1841–2. RD Murray 241. Also Wettenhall 22–5.
30 29 Nov 1824. Hovell 347.
31 Bowdler 1981; Scougall 83–7, 109–13; Seddon 1994, 114–15; Mulvaney & White 125.
32 Eyre vol 2, 317.
33 I & T Donaldson 198–9.
34 Thomson 1949, 6–7.
35 Hanna 9.
36 Rumsey & Weiner 107.
37 Eyre vol 2, 247–8.

38 R & C Berndt 1965, 126.
39 1849. Therry 289–90.
40 PL Brown 1986, 176.
41 c1841. Steele 1983, 100–1. Also Backhouse 431; Petrie 70–1.
42 Isaacs 1987, 16.
43 Kaberry 1939, 17.
44 Local knowledge: Blainey 171–84, 190–3; Cane 208–12; Foreman & Walsh 195–211; Gammage 1986, 13–14; Grey vol 2, 262–3; Haynes 1977; Rose 1996, 7–12, 32.
45 Councils: Browne 259–60; Dredge R 1839–40, VPRS 4410 unit 2 no 47; Gammage 1986, 15; Gunther n, B505, ML; Jenkin 13; Spencer & Gillen 1899, 11.
46 Blay 2005, 14.
47 Eyre vol 1, 279–81.
48 27 Sep 1844. Finnis 30.
49 Beveridge 1889, 165–7; J Morgan 78.
50 Nobbs 136.
51 GF Moore L c~ Jim Cameron, 360.
52 Travel, geography: M Bennett 39, 62; Bland 79–80; Blay 2005, 2008; Browne 260–1; G Calder 24–35; Cambage 261, 285; Howitt 1904, 262–3; Jetson 13, 31, 40; McFarlane 2002, 59; McKenna 17–20; TM Perry 99; Roxburgh 288, 291; L Ryan 19, 23–5, 29–37, 41–3; Sullivan 25–6; Twidale et al 117.
53 McBryde 2000, 158.
54 C Giles 7.
55 McBryde 2000; Mulvaney & White 94, 224.
56 RSC Aborigines 1845, 20, NSWLC.
57 W Roth 1897, 117.
58 Eyre vol 2, 229.
59 Robinson R 25 Apr 1846, Governor's Des ZA7081, ML.
60 Lee & Daly 319. Also R Lawrence 229; compare Ebsworth L 1826, B852, ML, with Egan 1996, 5, 114–15.
61 Trade, songs: Tom Gara 8 Sep 02, 1 Feb 05; Peter Gifford 6 Sep 02; R & C Berndt 1993, 117; Blainey 203–16; Brine 1983; D Carnegie 243–4, 395; J Clark 30–31; Clarke 2003, 107–11; Dingle 1988, 18; Enright 323; Flood 1989, 247, 250; C Giles 7; Gillen & Drewien 16; JW Gregory 139, 217–8; Hardy 4–6; B Hill 236; Kerwin 84–120; D Lawrence 264–6, 339; Lee & Daly 319; Low 1987b, 258–9; Lumholtz 172; McBryde 1984, 2000; McCarthy; Mulvaney 114; Mulvaney & Kamminga 93–101; Mulvaney & White 92–4, 224, 231, 253–73; Munster 2; Rose 1992, 54–5; AGL Shaw 29; Shaw 1986, 150; Spencer & Gillen 1899, 12–14; Tindale 1974, 75–88; Walsh 1990, 32; Wettenhall 31–2; Wyndham 41.
62 R Jones 1975, 28.
63 Davis & Prescott 40, 111–12; Gammage 1986, 17; Jackson-Nakano 2001, 19, 31; Meggitt 1, 35–46.
64 Gammage 1986, 18–19; Haw & Munro 6; J Wright 20.
65 Blainey 273; Curr 1883, 259–60.
66 Gillen & Drewien 16–17; Hetzel & Frith 78; Latz 1995, 22.
67 Allen 1972, 93. Also Allen 1974, 313; Griffiths & Robin 55.
68 Hardwicke R 1823, VDL Co P 20/222, MM 71/5, AOT.
69 15 Feb 1827. F Ellis 29.
70 Govett 28–9.
71 Gammage 1986, 11, & 19.
72 Gilmore 1934, 117.
73 Le Soeuf Rem 34–6, A2762, ML.
74 15 Jan 1840. Mackay 87.
75 Grey vol 2, 262–3.
76 Fitzhardinge 274.
77 Steele 1972, 331.
78 Corris 2.
79 Oct 1896. D Carnegie 283.
80 25 Jul, 6, 8 Aug 1901, 43/1904, SAPP.
81 Eyre vol 2, 206–7.
82 3 Nov 1845. Sturt 1849 vol 2, 77, & 111.
83 2, 4 Jan 1816. J Kelly 165–6.
84 Physique, abundance: Angas 1847a vol 1, 787–9; Attenbrow 40–3, 62–84; R Baker 57; Berndt 1970, 96; R & C Berndt 1996, 109; Beveridge 1883, 36, 47–9; Billot 1979, 100; Blainey 157, 162–3, 167, 200,

218–28; Bland 38; Bonwick 1870, 141–9; Bossence 9; Boyce 112–18; W Bradley 132–3; Bride 273; PL Brown 1986, 230; Butlin 1983, 157–8, 167–75; Byrne 1983, 35–6, 43–51, 80; D Carnegie 283; Corris 2; P Cunningham vol 1, 310–11; Curr 1883, 255–60; Dargavel 177–8; Dingle 1988, 12; Evans J 6, 10 Dec 1813, HRA 1, vol 8, 170–1; Eyre vol 2, 206–7, 250–4; Gammage 1986, 11, 32; Gammage 2005a; Garnsey vol 1, 6–9, B1055, ML; Gillen & Drewien 16–18; Giles 1889, 60, 176; Grey vol 2, 259; Hallam 1975, 36, 39, 64; Hetzel & Frith 30; Hodgkinson 222–7; Horton 2000, 54–5; Hume J Nov 1821, Berry P MSS 315/44/3, ML; W Jones 131–3; Kirby 28; Kirk 77–8; Krefft 1865, 359; 'A Lady' 215; Latz 1995, 22–5; Leichhardt 1847a, 8, 184; Lewis R, 3, 114/1875, SAPP; Lindsay 1888, 15; Lines 1991, 105; Mathews 1897a, 112; McKinlay 35–6; Mitchell 1839 vol 2, 36; Morgan 43; Mulvaney & Green 260, 273n35; Mulvaney & White 124–5; J Oxley 219, 291–2; ES Parker 8; Petrie 13; Rose 1992, 99; Savage 181–6, 208, 221, 225; Steele 1972, 147, 331; PM Stevenson 310; Stirling to Darling, HRA 6, vol 3, 556–8; E Stockton 92; Stokes vol 2, 81; Stuart 1863, 11, 62, 70, 115; Sullivan 8–10; Therry 296; Tietkins 1961, 31 Aug 1879; Waterhouse 178; Worgan L, B1463, ML; J Wright 14, 20, 23.
85 Morgan 46, & 47, 54, 62–7, 74.
86 J Clark 19.
87 Butlin 1983, 160.
88 Fitzhardinge 146n.
89 Smallpox: Angas 1847a vol 1, 123, vol 2, 226; Beveridge 1883, 40; Bonwick 1883, 15, 28; Brayshaw 49; Butlin 1983; AH Campbell 75; J Campbell 1985, 2002; M Carnegie 107, 110; Cosby 205–7; Curr 1883, 236–9; Curr 1886 vol 1, 208–27, 252, vol 2, 73; Fitzhardinge 146–9; Foelsche 7–8; Gammage 1986, 25; Gason 28; Giles 1875, 133; Grant 119; AC & FT Gregory 210; JC Hamilton 100; Hartwig 30–2; Jenkin 29–30; Kerwin 26–34; Kimber 1988; Linn 1997, 6–9; Linn 1999, 39–40; Mear; EW Mills 15; Mitchell 1839 vol 1, 218, 261, 307; Mulvaney & White 343; E Richards 283–4; AGL Shaw 19–20; RB Smyth 253–6; E Stockton 102; Sturt 1833 vol 1, 93, 105; Tietkins 1881–2, 112; Warren; Woods 44–5, 283; J Wright 55.

6 The closest ally

1 *Canberra Times* 18–24 Jan 03.
2 Latz 1995, 29.
3 1882. HL Roth 1886, 133.
4 23 Dec 1831. Mitchell 1839 vol 1, 53.
5 Jul 1838. Sturt 1838, 37.
6 Clean-up fires: JR Ford 17; Fox 16; Haynes et al 64; Keast et al 42; Rosenman 44.
7 J Ross 28–9, 50–1.
8 Dec 1819. Mackaness 1965, 95.
9 Burrows & Abbott 130.
10 25 Jan 1802. Cornell 2006, 194; Peron 191–2, & 187.
11 I Thomas 1991, 64–5.
12 28–9 Dec 1815. J Kelly 163.
13 3–4 Jan 1814. Evans J, HRA 1, vol 8, 176.
14 5 May 1832. Mitchell 1839 vol 1, 198.
15 Finlayson 1046/2, MSA; M Thomas 1925, 123 both c~ Tom Gara.
16 Angas 1847a vol 1, 43.
17 *Register* 27 Mar 1841, 4 c~ Tom Gara.
18 Hallam 2002, 181.
19 25 Nov, 2 Dec 1824. Hovell 343, 349.
20 Breton 1834, 248.
21 Cool fire: Burrows & Abbott 126–8, 133–4; Hallam 2002, 181–8; I Thomas 1991, 25–7, 304; I Thomas 1994, 9–12.
22 JR Reid 95.
23 Newland 1921, 3–4. Also L Baker 49–50; Latz 1995, 31.
24 John Bradley 11 Jul 01; R Baker 50; Horsfall 1991, 42; McKaige et al 1999, 79.
25 G Kelly 11.
26 Rumsey & Weiner 109.
27 Leichhardt 1847a, 355.
28 Fire and Law: RB Bird et al; J Bradley

1–4; Gould 1971, 18; Hill et al 1999, 210; TN Howard 225; Langton 1; Mulvaney & White 131; Rose & Clarke 28–9; Russell-Smith et al 174; Shellam 40–1; Yibarbuk et al 340–1.
29 RD Murray 199–201.
30 *Cassell's Illustrated Family Paper* 4 Feb 1854, 46 c~ John Blay.
31 J White 129; Mitchell 1839 vol 2, 328; Giles 1889 vol 2, 318.
32 8 Oct 1872. Giles 1889, 42. Also JR Ford 15–17; Hallam 1975, 75; Vigilante 152; Warburton 1875, 194–6.
33 Vallance et al 142, & 146.
34 7 Jul 1829. Steele 1972, 330.
35 Hetzel & Frith 78–9.
36 Thomson 1949, 7.
37 22 Sep 1891. Lindsay 1893 vol 1, 106.
38 Hill et al 1999, 211–12.
39 23 Sep 1872. Giles 1875, 31.
40 Latz 1995, 30. Also Burrows & Abbott 129–33.
41 Latz 2007, 31–46.
42 Hill et al 1999, 214.
43 1826–9. Nind 28.
44 Gilmore 1934, 152–3.
45 1802. Gott 2005.
46 16–17 Sep 1819. PP King vol 1, 289–91.
47 Flood 1989, 225.
48 Kimber 1983, 38. Also N Williams 94.
49 Frequency: Burrows 18; Burrows & Abbott 119, 165; Cary et al 8; Costin 130; Frawley & Semple 149; Gill et al 427; Gould 1971, 22; I Thomas 1994; Ward 2001b, 1; Ward & Sneeuwjagt 6; Ward & van Didden 16–20; Ward et al 323.
50 Max Lines 4 Apr 05, OHU.
51 Hill et al 1999, 213–14. Also Cary et al 178.
52 Nov 1840. Stokes vol 2, 228.
53 Ward 2000b, 11.
54 Frawley & Semple 147. Also Gott 2005; Hallam 1975, 45–6; Sneeuwjagt 28; I Thomas 1994.
55 McLoughlin 1998, 393–6; Veitch 1985, 4.
56 PR Williams.
57 C Jones 2002, 7.
58 Latz 2007, 15, 31–3, 47–9, 84–97.
59 EK Webb 9.
60 L Baker 50.
61 Bradstock et al.
62 Kohen 1995, 130–4.
63 Burrows 24.
64 B Hill 189. Also JRW Reid 96.
65 Bradstock et al 412. Also Benson & Redpath 296–7; Frawley & Semple 147–8; Garnett & Crowley.
66 25 May, 19 Jun, 16 Aug 1817. J Oxley 45, 72, 179.
67 18 May 1846. Mitchell 1848, 170, & 296, 299.
68 25 Jun 1838. Angas P, PRG 175, 419–22, MSA c~ Bernie O'Neil.
69 Murray 14 Jun 1901, SAPP 43/1904.
70 Bolton & Latz.
71 Giles 1875, 44–5; Lindsay 1893 vol 1, 169; Stuart 1865, 159.
72 1826. J Atkinson 21.
73 Lindsay 1893 vol 1, 64.
74 7 Mar 1846. Ward 1998, 11–12.
75 Timing: H Allen 1983, 23–35; Burrows 18; Burrows & Abbott 119–46; Enright & Thomas 988; JR Ford 17; Gammage 2009; Hallam 1975, 35–6; Marsden-Smedley 1998a, 19; Nash 1993, 96–8; J Stockton 1982b, 65; Vallance et al 108–99.
76 Burrows & Abbott 134–5.
77 Feb 1832. I Thomas 1991, 93–4.
78 27 Sep 1861. AC & FT Gregory 207.
79 Dec 1827. Crawford et al 40; I Thomas 1991, 23.
80 17–19 Jun 1817. Lee 234–5.
81 1862. de Satge 142.
82 Jack vol 2, 485–7.
83 Mitchell 1839 vol 1, 32.
84 Friedl et al, attachment 4, 9 Oct 1995; Gould 1971, 22; C Walker D 3 May 1913 c~ Tom Gara; EK Webb 10.
85 Mulvaney & White 221–3.
86 Fire before rain: Brodribb 24; G Calder 64; Donovan 12; McLoughlin 1998, 394; Stokes vol 1, 105–6.
87 Wakefield. Also Burrows & Abbott 137–40;

NOTES

    Hancock 26; Seddon 1994, 297–300.
88 27 Apr 1844. Clark 1998 vol 4, 49.
89 Cary et al 8.
90 J Banks 1997, 12.
91 J Banks 1982, iv, 81–4, 89–93, 209; J Banks 1997; Good 274; J Stockton 1982b, 66.
92 Haynes 1985, 210; Haynes et al 64, 69.
93 Waterhouse 148–9.
94 19 Sep 1879. Jack vol 2, 510, & 480–98. Also Carron 53.
95 Top End fire: Bowman et al 2004, 2007; Cary et al 199; JR Ford 23–5; Gill 69; Hallam 2002, 180; Haynes 1977, 6–14; Haynes 1985; Haynes et al 66–9; R Jones 1975, 25; R Jones 1980a, 14; R Jones 1980b, 124; Langton 3; Love 14; Rose 1995, 16; Rose & Clarke 132–3; Russell-Smith 81–5; Russell-Smith et al 159, 174–6; Stocker 225–7; Thomson 1949, 6–8; Vigilante 143–4.
96 16–17, 26 Sep 1891. Lindsay 1893 vol 1, 103, 111.
97 25 Aug 1845. Leichhardt 1847a, 376.
98 4 Jun 1889. Tietkins J, SAPP 1890/111, 14–15.
99 Centre fire: L Baker 49–51; Basedow 1913, 167–9; Cane 205–7; Cary et al 193–4; Fox 16; Kimber 1983; Latz 1995, 34; Tonkinson 51.
100 Ward 2000b, 4.
101 2 Mar 1846. Ward 1998, 4–5.
102 WA fire: David Ward 23 Apr 01; Enright et al; JR Ford 15–17; Hallam 1975, 35–9, 114–26; Hallam 2002, 178–84; Stormon 164; Ward 1998, 2, 17; Ward 2000a, 1, 5; Ward 2000b, 1; Ward & van Didden 19–20.
103 4 Apr 1842. Burn 15–16.
104 Tasmanian fire: Crawford 5; I Thomas 1991, 37, 91, 100–3, 257, 313–16; I Thomas 1994, 9–12, 91.
105 Yibarbuk et al, 325–6.
106 Bunbury & Morrell 106.
107 Boyce 194–5; Krichauff 49, 51; BE Norton 7.
108 Eyre vol 2, 357. Also Latz 1995, 30.
109 19 Nov, & 5, 11–12 Dec 1824. Bland 42, 57, 63–4.
110 12 Oct 1845. Sturt 1849 vol 2, 28–9.
111 1840s. Marsh 41–2.
112 Fire for grass: Angas 1847a vol 1, 48; Backhouse 541; Carron 44, 50, 53; JR Ford 17; Giles 1889, 45; J Hunter 61; Leichhardt 1847a, 347; Lindsay 1893 vol 1, 105, 169; Menge to Angas 14 Aug 1840, Angas P, PRG 175, 551–5, MSA c~ Bernie O'Neil; Stuart 23, SAPP 21/1863; Mulvaney & Green 215; Murray 19 Aug 1902, SAPP 43/1904; Rose 1996, 67; Vancouver vol 1, 177–8.
113 Lunt et al 1998b, 19.
114 Latz 1995, 19–22, 30. Also Gould 1971, 22; Rose 1995, 79; EK Webb 9.
115 Jul 1788. J Hunter 81.
116 Fire for food: Burrows & Abbott 130; Cross 187; Gould 1971, 22–3; Hallam 1975, 45; AG Hamilton 200–1; Hetzel & Frith 78; Kirby 28; Lourandos 1997, 68; Mitchell 1848, 296; O'Connell et al 99; Penney 28–9; Sturt 1833 vol 1, 111–13; Vigilante 144; Waterhouse 181; EK Webb 9–10.
117 13 Sep 1846. Mitchell 1848, 306.
118 12 Jan 1829. Sturt 1833 vol 1, 58.
119 Bennett 1834, 290.
120 Cunningham J 19 Apr 1824, Reel 46, SRNSW.
121 2 March 1846. Ward 1998, 5.
122 P Cunningham vol 1, 197–8.
123 Fire for pick: Anderson et al 61–78; Aurousseau vol 2, 680; Brayshaw 21; Cary et al 200; Chapman 98; R Dawson 218; Eyre vol 2, 299; JR Ford 17; Freycinet 173–4; Gould 1971, 19; Govett 23; Hallam 1975, 42; AG Hamilton 200; Haydon 26; Latz 1995, 29; Murphy & Bowman; BE Norton 7; O'Connell et al 99; Rose 1996, 66.
124 Eyre vol 2, 299; Mulvaney & Green 382–3.
125 Burrows 2000, 5.
126 Hassell 698, 700.
127 1834. Meagher 33.

128 Love 85.
129 Thomson 1949, 7.
130 J Hunter 61.
131 HRNSW vol 5, 751n.
132 HH Finlayson 66–7.
133 Traps: Austin 18; Basedow 1913, 82; Beveridge 1883, 44–7; Blainey 139–42, 151–3; Eyre vol 2, 283; Giles 1889, 43; Hall Rem, DOC1784, ML; Lumholtz 103; B McDonald 114; Morrill chap 3 np; Steele 1983, 6.
134 Fire to drive or flush game: Tom Gara May 08; Buchhorn 117; W Finlayson 40–1; Fox 16; Hallam 1975, 32, 42; Hill et al 1999, 212; Kaberry 1939, 18; Latz 1995, 29; Love 15; Morgan 2002, 120; Mulvaney & White 131; Nash 1984, 28; Nind 28; O'Connell et al 99; JRW Reid 95–7; Schurmann 42; M Thomas 1925, 123.
135 Murray 11 Aug 1902, SAPP 43/1904; Plomley 1966, 54; Sturt 1838, 34–6.
136 Bunbury & Morrell 95; ch 8.
137 J Hunter 61.
138 L Ryan 22–3, 39.
139 1841–2. Bride 272.
140 Hill et al 1999, 213–14.
141 John Blay May 06; Blay 2005, 2008.
142 20 Jun 1817. J Oxley 73.
143 18 Jun 1836. Mitchell 1839 vol 2, 134–5. Also Kirby 28.
144 Jul 1838. Sturt 1838, 34–6.
145 10 Mar 1832. J Kelly et al 32–3, & 22.
146 Roads: BG; Binks 22–3; Bonwick 1883, 8–13; G Calder 24–35; Flood 1980, 116; JR Ford 17; AC & FT Gregory 207; Grey vol 2, 8–12; Hallam 1975, 47, 68–71; Hardwicke R 1823, VDL Co P 20/222, MM71/5, AOT; Hunt 15–38, 59; Latz 1995, 30; Love 14–15; McBryde 1974, 163–6; Mackaness 1965, 18; Marsden-Smedley 1998a, 17–19; Plomley 1966, 376, 601, 616; Reynolds 1980, 220–1; Reynolds 2000, 23–5; Rose 1995, 13.
147 Fox 16.
148 Gould 1971, 21.
149 Barrallier J 8 Nov, 15 Dec 1802, HRNSW 5, 1, 757, 819.
150 B Hill 87, & 188. Also Fox 16–17; Gould 1971, 20; Latz 1995, 30; Mulvaney & Green 248.
151 Peron 331.
152 27 Nov 1826. Rosenman 66.
153 Oct 1826. Rosenman 48.
154 *Register* 26 Jun 1841, 3 c~ Tom Gara.
155 Oct 1872. Giles 1889, 36.
156 Curr 1883, 188–90.
157 P Cunningham vol 1, 321–35.
158 18–19 Jan 1829. Sturt 1833 vol 1, 71–2.
159 Sturt 1849 vol 1, 254–5, 278.
160 1827. P Cunningham vol 1, 321–2.
161 P Cunningham vol 1, 331–5; TM Perry 27–32, 127–8.
162 T Griffiths 2001a, 40.
163 GF Moore 1884, 36.
164 Wilkinson 240.
165 Gunn J 25 Jan 1833, 1313/1 AOT or A316 ML, 1.
166 Low 2002, 244.
167 Insects: Barr & Cary 75; Boyce 208–9; Burn 11–12; Curr 1883, 185–7; Eagle 68; Gammage 2002; Gould 1971, 17; Griffiths 2001a, 168–9; Gunn J 25–6 Jan 1833, A316 ML or 1313/1 AOT, 1–2; AG Hamilton 202–3; Haynes 1985, 210; Howitt 1890–1, 109–13; Jones 1980b, 124; Jurskis 2005; Lunt et al 1999; Marsh & Adams; Mitchell 1839 vol 1, 135; Norton 1887, 16–17; Plomley 1966, 840.
168 McKaige et al 1999, 79.
169 P Sutton 1978, 49.
170 Head 1994, 176.
171 McKaige et al 1999, 77.
172 JRW Ford 25–6; Fox 16.
173 Langton 1.
174 Rose 1995, 26.
175 Allen 1972, 97.
176 Rose 1995, 27.
177 Russell-Smith 82; Russell-Smith et al 174.
178 RB Bird et al 14796.
179 EK Webb 39–40.
180 GF Moore 1884, 12, 45, 60, 81.
181 GF Moore 1884, 39.

182 Fire names: Clarke 2003, 115; Hercus 2002, 261–3; B Hill 186–9; JRW Reid 86–9.
183 Curr 1883, 188–9.
184 Mitchell 1848, 412–13. Also Leichhardt 1847a, 355.

7 Associations

1. Vancouver vol 1, 355.
2. Enright & Thomas 980–1; Kay 2007b; Lewis & Ferguson; Stewart 2002.
3. Sturt 1833 vol 2, 35.
4. Worgan J 21–8 Apr 1788, B1463, ML. Also Flannery 1998, 73.
5. 1847. H Turnbull 45.
6. T Walker 44, & 25.
7. Evans J 30 Nov, 6, 9–10 Dec 1813, HRA 1, vol 8, 168, 170–1.
8. 5 Nov 1819. Campbell 1928, 239.
9. 8 Jul 1836. Mitchell 1839 vol 2, 167.
10. Hodgkinson 61.
11. 18 Jan 1839. Grey vol 1, 321–2.
12. 10 Jun 1815. J Oxley 365. The same words are in Macquarie to Bathurst, 24 Jun 1815, HRA 1, vol 8, 575.
13. J Atkinson 18.
14. Jan 1833. Gunn J 3–4, & 13–14, A316 ML or NS 1313/1, AOT. Soil: Spanswick & Zund.
15. 7 May 1823. Brayshaw 31.
16. P Cunningham vol 1, 150.
17. 20 Jun 1817. J Oxley 73.
18. Giles 1875, 104.
19. 21 Apr 1862. Landsborough 101. Also pictures 50–1; Sturt 1833 vol 1, 46.
20. 19 Jan 1836. Darwin 441.
21. 24 Apr, 12 Aug 1817. Lee 189, 281.
22. June 1839. PL Brown 1986, 190.
23. 10 Nov 1831. Plomley 1966, 512.
24. 16 Feb 1827. F Ellis 30.
25. 7–23 Nov 1828. Hellyer R, VDL Co P, MM71/5/20, 238, AOT.
26. Grass, open forest. *NSW*: Anon 1854?, 21; Aurousseau vol 2, 632; Bennett 1834, 167–8, 280; Bland 10–11; Breton 1834, 53–4, 92–3; Cambage 1921, 246; Cornell 2006, 317; P Cunningham vol 1, 43, 117–18, 146–9; R Dawson 103–4, 111, 138, 171, 204; Donovan 18; Field 145, 166, 172; Forbes D 1 Jul 1830, Mfm M1172, NLA; Franklin D 24 Apr 1839, MS114, NLA; Govett 22; Grant 110; Hodgkinson 19; Hovell J 23 Oct 1824, Safe 1/32b, ML; King to Hobart 1 Mar 1804, HRNSW 5, 319; Kirkpatrick 1994, 42; Kohen 1995, 41; Lee 206, 288, 557; Macquarie 96, 103, 149, 152; Mitchell 1839 vol 1, 58, 70, vol 2, 336; J Oxley 21–7, 132, 163, 279, 327; Paterson J, HRA 1, vol 3, 175, 179; Paterson to King 15 Jun 1801, HRNSW 4, 415, 448, 452; JA Richards 71–4, 110; Robinson R 25 May 1846, Governor's Des ZA7081, 40–1, ML; Rolls 1999, 199–200, 209; Starr 15; Sturt 1833 vol 2, 17; T Walker 16; Waterhouse 62–3; G Wilson 106. *Vic*: Bland 49; PL Brown 1989, 103; Clark 1998 vol 1, 167, 173, vol 2, 119; Colville 239; Curr 1883, 420; Franklin D 12 Apr 1839, MS114, NLA; Hawdon 1952, 7; Hovell 359; Mitchell 1839 vol 2, 207, 275, 280, 331; Mossman & Banister 62; Munster 27; Randell 29; Robinson R March–May 1845, Ar4, 8–9, ML; Stuwe 93–5. *Tas*: Bischoff 116–17; *Coventry Herald* 17 Jan 1834 c~ Andrew Gregg; Hardwicke R 1823, VDL Co P 20/222, MM71/5, AOT; R Jones 1975, 26; Paterson J 1 Dec 1804, HRNSW 5, 495–6 or HRA 3, vol 1, 614–17; Plomley 1966, 250, 384–5, 601, 893; Scott vol 2, 14; Sorell J 18 Dec 1821, HRA 3, vol 2, 644. *Qld*: Aurousseau vol 2, 652; Landsborough 87; Leichhardt 1847a, 76–7, 339; Mitchell 1848, 127, 136, 158; Richardson 47; Steele 1972, 210–12, 263. *WA*: Austin 8, 10; Cross 161; AC & FT Gregory 27; Hallam 1975, 22, 46–8, 53, 59–62, 68–9. *SA*: Angas 1847a, vol 1, 149; Arthur 35; Clark 1998, vol 4, 290; Robinson R Mar–May 1845, Ar4, 16, ML.
27. 30 May 1835. Billot 1979, 88–9. Also Gellibrand 75.
28. 1841–2. RD Murray 135.
29. 30 Jul 1839. EM Christie 47, & 45, 49–50.

30 Evans J 28 May 1815, HRA 1, vol 8, 615.
31 19 Dec 1828. Sturt 1833 vol 1, 23–4.
32 Brayshaw 33. Also Leichhardt 1847a, 8; Stuart 1863, 55.
33 Jul 1829. Steele 1972, 325.
34 Mossman & Banister 152.
35 Sturt 1849 vol 2, 209–10.
36 27 Aug 1873. Giles 1889, 86–7, & 114.
37 Grass & forest on water: Brodribb 23; Byerley 9; Fensham 1985, ff 87; Giles 1875, 81–2, 106–7; Landsborough 91; Lee 575; Lindsay 1893 vol 1, 68–9; Rolls 2002, 78–9; Sturt 1838, 15.
38 17 Mar 1845. Leichhardt 1847a, 184–5, & 216.
39 Domin 65–73. Original italics.
40 Sturt 1833 vol 1, xlvii–iii.
41 1824. Hovell 341–59. Also Bland 59.
42 May 1862. Stuart 1863, 18–25, & map 1863/21 vol 2, SAPP. Also Stuart 1865, 38–9, 140, 299, 304–9. For help I thank Peter Sutton, Nugget Collins, David Nash & Chris Materne.
43 Fortey R 5 Aug 1875, AA Co P, 1/256/3 (WP-F1a), 3–4, Noel Butlin Archives, ANU c~ Jim Noble; Noble 1997, 63–4.
44 I Thomas 1991, 91, 257.
45 Plomley 1966, 367–8, & 384.
46 Eyre vol 1, 351, & vol 2, 246.
47 Angas 1847a vol 1, 150; Beck & Balme; Benson & Redpath 296–7; Byrne 1987, 25–7, 43–4, 51–2; Chisholm 1955b, 84.
48 1–2 Oct 1818. J Oxley 317–19.
49 Hodgkinson R 25 Apr 1841, 3, Reel 3070, SRNSW; Hodgkinson 89, 222–6.
50 Birrell 20–30.
51 17 Mar 1829. Bischoff 127.
52 7 Sep 1886. Savage 213.
53 8 Aug 1828. Steele 1972, 270–1.
54 Wilson: ADB 2, 610; Cambage 1920; Chisholm 1955a; HRNSW 3, 820–3.
55 9 Jul 1834. Plomley 1966, 898.
56 27–30 Nov 1821. Berry P, MSS 315/44, item 3, ML; RH Webster 42–4.
57 21 Oct 1851. WB Clarke 25. Also Anon 1918, 160; Cambage 1921, 246; Gibbney 1978, 6–7.
58 Grass and/or dense forest or scrub. *NSW*: Aurousseau vol 2, 632; P Cunningham vol 1, 113–14; R Dawson 167–8; Freycinet 82; Govett 21; PP King vol 1, 175; Lee 407; Mitchell 1839 vol 1, 32, 46, 59, 64; J Oxley 61–3, 315–17; TM Perry 96; Scott vol 2, 60–3. *Vic*: Thomas R Jan 1850, VPRS 10 Unit 11, 1850/55. *Qld*: Chisholm 1955b, 84; Steele 1972, 312, 318. *WA*: Burrows & Abbott 130–2; Chapman 52. *SA*: Angas 1847a vol 1, 150. *Centre*: D Carnegie 228; Giles 1889, 264–5, 271–3; Lindsay 1893 vol 1, 107–8, 172–3.
59 Latz 1995, 23.
60 5 May 1844. Angas 1847a vol 1, 166.
61 Edges: Henry Nix 21 Jun 02; Evans J 4 Dec 1813, HRA 1, 8, 169; Gammage 2009, 282; Griffiths 2001a, 8; A Mitchell 133; Reid et al 88–95.
62 Oct 1860. Warburton 1918, 112.
63 Jan 1844. Angas 1847a vol 1, 49.
64 GF Moore 1884, 14.
65 Nov 1840. Eyre vol 1, 307.
66 25 Jun 1903. Basedow 1913, 151.
67 c1853–5. Bulmer P, F1 XM915, box 9, MV.
68 6 Dec 1811. Macquarie 65–6.
69 17 Feb 1827. Bischoff 170.
70 P Cunningham vol 1, 149.
71 9 May 1817. J Oxley 26.
72 9 Mar 1829. Sturt 1833 vol 1, 118, & 63, 99, 158.
73 15 Dec 1831, 21 Jan 1832, 6 May 1836. Mitchell 1839 vol 1, 41, 90, vol 2, 64.
74 22 Jul 1836. Mitchell 1839 vol 2, 188, & 274–7, 280.
75 30 Jan 1838. Hawdon 1984, 19.
76 *Port Phillip Gazette* 1 Dec 1849 c~ Leith MacGillivray.
77 8 Feb 1838. Waterhouse 127, & 157.
78 14 Dec 1824. Hovell 362.
79 24 Jan 1840. Clark 1998 vol 1, 136–7.
80 22 Jan 1840. Bride 207.
81 Brodribb 24.
82 12 Dec 1829. Steele 1972, 323–4.

83 Sep, 30 Dec 1844, 26–7 Jun, 5 Jul 1845. Leichhardt 1847a, 88, 304, 317.
84 H Turnbull 48.
85 29 Apr 1862. Landsborough 105.
86 Belts. *Vic*: PL Brown 1989, 40–1; Clark 1998 vol 4, 68; Haw & Munro 268–9; Hawdon 1984, 1; Mackay 87. *NSW*: MR Allen 32, 68, 176–7; Donovan 18; Evans J 6, 9–10 Dec 1813, HRA 1, 8, 170–1; Mackaness 1965, 23; Sturt 1838, 34. *Qld*: Mitchell 1848, 105, 107, 261. *WA*: Cross 24; Grey vol 2, 53; Hallam 1975, 153. *SA*: Campbell et al 492–3; Goyder FB 15, 20, 22, 27 Jul 1862, GRG 35/256, SRSA.
87 3 Apr 1829. Plomley 1966, 54, & 148.
88 3 Dec 1830, 23 Jul 1831. Plomley 1966, 285, 385.
89 Flinders 1965, 14–15.
90 5 Apr 1842. Burn 19.
91 Breton 1834, 305.
92 1838. JG Johnston 17.
93 22 Dec 1824. Bland 73.
94 26 Feb 1840. Clark 1998 vol 1, 179.
95 17 Jan 1832. Mitchell 1839 vol 1, 87, & 66, 70.
96 25 Sep 1844. Sturt 1849 vol 1, 108.
97 25 Aug 1828. Steele 1972, 288.
98 5 Oct 1844. Leichhardt 1847a, 7–8.
99 11 Nov 1844. Chisholm 1955b, 100.
100 20 Aug 1843. Henderson 1925, 124.
101 10 Jul 1854. Austin 6.
102 21 Apr 1865. Sholl 218, & 208.
103 11 Mar 1838. Stokes vol 1, 151.
104 Hann 25.
105 Clumps. *General*: Gill 69; Haynes 1977, 11; R Jones 1975, 25. *Vic*: Andrews 1986, 122; Clark 1998 vol 2, 122; Hawdon 1952, 27; Hovell 363; Mitchell 1839 vol 2, 150, 193; Morcom & Westbrooke 280. *NSW*: MR Allen 116–17; Bennett 1834, 122, 145; Bland 6; Breton 1834, 92; R Dawson 208–9; Gilmore P, 91, MSS806, NLA; Jervis 225; J Oxley 275; Waugh 22. *Qld*: Aurousseau vol 3, 1012; Mitchell 1848, 266. *SA*: Eyre vol 2, 43. *WA*: Chapman 45; Harris & Hillman 143.
106 1913. Cambage 1915, 394.
107 22 Dec 1884. Savage 171.
108 Jan 1864. Bowen 205.
109 Mathews 1896, 295–9, 318.
110 24, 28 Mar 1825. Crawford 13–14.
111 2 Oct 1827. Curr R, VDL Co P 20/231, MM71/5, AOT.
112 2 Apr 1829, 9 Jul 1834. Plomley 1966, 54, 898.
113 Nov 1838. JMR Cameron 1999, 22–3.
114 21 May 1817. J Oxley 41–2.
115 A Andrews 1964, 70; Mackaness 1965, 6, 27. Also JA Richards 74.
116 1840. Hodgkinson 3.
117 Anon 1854?, 60.
118 A Harris 30.
119 BG 7–9 Jul 06; Bass J 7 Dec 1797, HRNSW 3, 314; M Bennett 65–6; Berry Rem 1838, COD 294B, 573–4, SCMC, SRNSW; Field 466; Mossman & Banister 276.
120 *Port Phillip Gazette* 1 Dec 1849 c~ Leith MacGillivray.
121 Curr 1883, 170–2.
122 9, 21 Aug 1843. Henderson 1925, 118, 125.
123 20 Jun 1839. Waterhouse 209, & 160.
124 GF Moore 1884, 33.
125 JR Ford 14.
126 31 Mar 1875. Giles 1889, 229, & 227.
127 10–11 Jun 1889. Tietkins J, SAPP 1890/111, 16–17, & 12–13.
128 Warburton 1918, 112.
129 8–9 Jun 1870. Forrest 100–1, & 111, 209.
130 6–7 Apr 1838. Waterhouse 140–1; CR Harris 2–3, 6.
131 Clearings: *Tas*: Louise Gilfedder 13 Feb 04; D Collins vol 2, 130–1; J Kelly et al 22, 24. *Vic*: Colville 249 sketch; Curr 1883, map; Daley 43; Griffiths 2001a, 25; Haw & Munro 117, 268–9; Shire of Korumburra 33; Tuckey 1805, 200; T Walker 29. *NSW*: Andrews 1964, 70, 79–80; Andrews 1979, 94, 124; Barrallier J, HRNSW 5, 757; Birrell 46–7; Buchanan 65; Dargavel et al 263; Evans J, HRA 1, vol 8, 167–8; Field 150–1, 178, 180; Gibbney 5–7; Gresser

234–5; Hood 143; S Hunter 12–20; Kirby 33; Lee 238, 247, 264, 275–9, 416; K Mills 230–1; A Mitchell 95, 130; Mitchell 1839 vol 1, 94; Ogilvie 18, 22; J Oxley 7–8, 21–7, 41–2, 53–5, 151; Rolls 1999, 209; Rosenman 67; Scott vol 2, 61. *Qld*: Aurousseau vol 2, 708; Boyd et al; Carron 28; Curr 1886 vol 2, 450; Dargavel 174; Jack vol 1, 211, vol 2, 479–80, 536–43, 547–8, 555, 587; Jack R, QPP 1881 vol 2, 230–1, 255–7; Keast et al 43; Lumholtz 98–102; McKinlay 102; Steele 1972, 221, 242, 283; Stubbs. *WA*: D Carnegie 422; AC & FT Gregory 18. *SA*: Goyder FB 16, 19, 27 Jul 1862, GRG 35/256, SRSA. *Centre (desert)*: Forrest 191, 199; Gosse 11, 16; Lindsay 1893 vol 1, 100–5, 111–15, 120–22, 132, 169, 172, 179; Murray 20 Aug 1902, SAPP 43/1904; Tietkins 1961, 23 Aug 1879; Walsh 1990, 31. *Top*: Stuart 1863, 48.
132 Feb 1864. Bowen 208.
133 *Sydney Mail* 10 Jul 1880, 56 c~ Leith MacGillivray.
134 22 Oct 1886. Savage 225, & 73, 78, 85, 100, 171, 229–30.

8 Templates

1   Latz 1995, 190.
2   Aug 1831. Plomley 1966, 398.
3   4 Jun 1801. Cornell 1974, 174.
4   26 May 1848. Carron 8–9, & 27.
5   Research VPRS and SLV c~ Lawrence Niewojt, May 09.
6   J Morgan 43.
7   21 May 1846. Colville 229.
8   27 Jun 1840. Eyre vol 1, 42.
9   Grey vol 2, 8–13.
10 Mitchell 1839 vol 2, 211–12.
11 14 Feb 1840. Clark 1998 vol 1, 170.
12 21 Oct 1830. Plomley 1966, 255.
13 Wheelwright 8–9.
14 F Ellis 30.
15 Gresty 63.
16 Backhouse 112.
17 1882. Lumholtz 99–100.
18 Grey vol 2, 297.
19 29 May 1835. Munster 16–17.
20 13 Sep 1846. Mitchell 1848, 305–6.
21 10 Aug 1817. Lee 280.
22 McBryde 1978, 263.
23 Kangaroos: BG; Mac Core 6 Oct 02, OHU; Dick Kimber 3 Feb 05; Eric Rolls 1 Sep 02; Barker & Greenslade 181–2; Bryce 1992, 34; Ealey 41; Frith & Calaby; Gould 1971; McAlpine et al 104, 123; Murphy & Bowman; Newsome 1975, 404, 407; Robinson et al 209; Rolls 1984b, 488–93, 505; Wheelwright 33.
24 Ivor Thomas & BG 7 Oct 06.
25 1840. Strzelecki 242.
26 17, 21 Jan 1832. Mitchell 1839 vol 1, 85, 90.
27 26 May 1837. T Walker 40–1, & 36–7, 42.
28 G Lacey 56–9.
29 Hawdon 1984, 1; Mitchell 1839 vol 2, 282–3.
30 P Andrews 2006, 30, & 153.
31 Bradstock et al; Hallam 1975, 6; Hallam 2002, 178; Robin 105.
32 Bill Mollison 12 Feb 02.
33 Frawley & Semple 211. The sequence at Paradise Plains was disturbed but not disguised by post-contact fires, notably in 1908. RC Ellis 1985, 305.
34 4, 7 Jul 1831. Plomley 1966, 371–2.
35 Hunt et al.
36 Curr R 2 Oct 1827, VDL Co P 20/231, MM71/5, AOT.
37 Templates moved: BG; Boyd et al 335; Colhoun 4; Craven 12; RC Ellis 1984, 1985; Frawley & Semple 202–5; Lake 2006, 153–65, 270–3; Lehman ms 9 c~ Greg Lehman; I Thomas 1991, 1993, 1994.
38 17 Apr 1846. Mitchell 1848, 127.
39 4 May 1862. McKinlay 88.
40 24 Nov 1863. Henry P, Anon newspaper R OM90–18, 2–3, JOL.
41 28 Jul 1828. Steele 1972, 258–9. Also Fraser D 27–31 Jul 1828, OM87–25, JOL.
42 23, 28 Apr 1823. Field 140, 142.
43 c1832. Rolls 2002, 117–18.
44 15 Dec 1828. VDL Co P, MM71/5,

NOTES

45 20/232, AOT. Also Bischoff 127–8.
45 1840. Hodgkinson 14, & 40, 98.
46 2–3 Mar 1880. Jack vol 2, 582–3, & 493, 537, 580, 607, 623.
47 11–12 Aug 1836. Andrews 1986, 160–1.
48 Haydon 25–6.
49 28 Aug 1839. PL Brown 1952–71, vol 2, 244–5.
50 14 Jul 1863. J Martin 255.
51 13 Apr 1845. Leichhardt 1847a, 216.
52 Gammage 1986, 20–1.
53 Gilmore 1934, 134–43; Gunson 1968, xviii.
54 Gunn 1908, 209. Also Flood 1989, 241; Merlan 56–7.
55 A Campbell 1965, 206–7.
56 Gammage 1986, 20–1.
57 *Port Phillip Gazette* 29 Nov 1849 c~ Leith MacGillivray.
58 10 May 1841. Clark 1998 vol 2, 197, & 202.
59 11–14 Sep 1872. Giles 1889, 21–3 & 1875, 21.
60 Swamps: Hope & Coutts 105; Paterson J 5 Jul 1801, HRNSW 4, 451 or HRA 1, vol 3, 179; E Stockton 99–100.
61 5 Jan 1798. HRNSW 3, 324.
62 17 Nov 1826. Rosenman 56, 59.
63 27 Dec 1826, 14 Jan 1827, HRA 3, vol 5, 832, 839, & 835–8.
64 30 Nov, 2? Dec 1826. Hovell J, Safe 1/32c, ML.
65 20 May 1826. P Cunningham vol 1, 123.
66 Stokes vol 1, 287.
67 Niel Gunson 3 Dec 09.
68 Westernport: Flinders 1946, 34; Grant J 1–2 Apr 1801, HRNSW 4, 484–5; G Lacey 87–211; Shire of the Korumburra 33.
69 Hill, Anon newspaper, OM90–6/3, JOL.
70 Blainey 196; Rowlands.
71 26 Mar 1875. Giles 1889, 225–6 & 1880, 14.
72 WR Murray 1901, 34.
73 3 Sep 1875. Giles 1889, 271–3.
74 26 Sep 1875. Giles 1876/22, 8, SAPP.
75 Dams: Blainey 196; Kimber 1984, 19; Murray R 27 May 1901, 43/1904, SAPP; MA Smith 1986, 30.
76 Daly 165–6; Hallam 1986, 118.
77 28 Aug 1845. Sturt 1849 vol 1, 386–7.
78 Worsnop 106–7.
79 7 Nov 1840. Eyre vol 1, 208.
80 22 Sep 1845. Sturt 1849 vol 2, 8–9.
81 12 Sep 1873. Giles 1875, 94. Also Hardy 7; Waterhouse 199.
82 Wells: Tom Gara 7 May 01; D Carnegie 215–16, 228, 236, 263–4; Chapman 52; Davidson 1905/27, 22, SAPP; Eyre vol 1, 192, 219; Gara 6–7; Hercus & Clarke; W Jones 140–1; Lindsay 1888, 4; Spencer & Gillen 1912, 107, 111; Worsnop.
83 Colville 144–5.
84 Mar 1818. Roxburgh 291.
85 K Mills 233–5.
86 Wilson Plan S112–3, ERM.
87 Wilson R, 6 Sep 1864, 2372–64, & 4 Apr 1865, 1342–65, ERM.
88 Hynes & Chase 41.
89 1 Sep 1874. Moseley 352.
90 9 Mar 1865. Richardson 50.
91 D Walker 387–8.
92 Jardine 79.
93 S Anderson 98–9, 103–7; GBRMPA (Chase); Rigsby 3.
94 Cooktown 59–2, run 19, photo 3, 19 Jun 1992.
95 Hynes & Chase 41.
96 Somerset: Byerley 73, 79–80, 87; Chester L in Jardine Letterbook 1, CYPOS 725, ML; Crowley & Garnett 1998, 134, 138–9; Haddon 307–9; Harris & Hillman 42–54; DR Harris et al 433, 437; Hynes & Chase 39–44; Jack vol 2, 623; DR Moore 18–19; Rigsby 4; D Walker 330, 387–9.
97 Evans Bay: Allen & Corris 159; JMR Cameron 163; Jukes 138, 145, 307; J MacGillivray vol 1, 121–2, 127–8, 132, 316–8; DR Moore 21, 50, 114, 118.
98 DR Moore 127.
99 Simpson R, 1868/519–23 & 525–6, QPP.
100 12 Dec 1801. PI Edwards 47.
101 17 Dec 1801. Vallance et al 99.
102 7 Oct 1791. Hallam 1975, 17.

103 Sep–Oct 1791. Vancouver vol 1, 56, 336.
104 Nind 28.
105 Nind 28.
106 Nind 28.
107 30 Jun 1828. HRA 3, vol 6, 520.
108 Albany summer fire: Mulvaney & Green 382; Rosenman 47; Vallance et al 89.
109 Dale 7.
110 22 Dec 1838. Backhouse 532.
111 Nind 28.
112 13 Jan 1831. Mulvaney & Green 382–3, & 260, 295.
113 Mulvaney & White 131.
114 Albany: Browne; Cornell 2003, 119–20; Ferguson 82–9, 109; Hallam 1975, 17; & 2002, 10; PP King vol 1, 16; Mulvaney & Green 249–64, 377–86; Mulvaney & White 121–45; Rosenman 36; Shellam; Vancouver vol 1, 339–40.
115 Hallam 2002, 177, & 180–4.
116 Jan 1864. Bowen 204–5.
117 Other templates: Angas 1847a vol 1, 150, 155–6; Cross 67; P Cunningham vol 1, 145–8; Harris & Hillman 140, 143; Heathcote 94; Lee 554 (map), 556; Mackaness 1965, 22; Macknight 94–5; Marsh 55; A Mitchell 132; Westgarth 25–8; Wills 199.

9 A capital tour

1 Tamsin Donaldson 26 Mar 03; Melinda Hinkson 18 Dec 09; Meehan, Plan of Sydney 31 Oct 1807, HRNSW 6, opp 366.
2 Tank Stream: Aplin 22; Campbell 1921, 65–9; Hinkson 3; Houison 6; Low 1987a, 292; Mulvaney & White 413; Nagle 94; TM Perry 19; Selfe 1901, 55.
3 Fidlon & Ryan 1979, 65.
4 W Bradley 69.
5 Phillip 59.
6 Phillip 122–3.
7 Sydney: Aplin 20, 55–7; Blackburn L 12 Jul 1788, Ab163, ML; W Bradley chart 7; Camm & McQuilton 48; D Collins vol 1, 4–7; Fitzhardinge 38–9; HRA 1, vol 1, 23–4; Kartzoff 11–15; McGuanne 73; Nagle 95, 98, 104; Phillip 59; J White 113.
8 Fidlon & Ryan 1979, 72; HRA 1, vol 1, 31; Phillip 104.
9 Kangaroo Ground: Campbell 1930, 274; D Collins vol 1, 266; Fitzhardinge 261; J White 27.
10 Fidlon & Ryan 1981, 263.
11 HRNSW vol 1(2), 300.
12 28 May 1788. Worgan J B1463, ML.
13 Cobley 250.
14 25–6 Apr 1788. J White 129–30.
15 Fire and plants: Benson & Howell 1995, 15; Clark & McLoughlin; Kartzoff 15.
16 HRNSW vol 1(2), 124.
17 D Collins vol 1, 563–4; Hinkson 10; McGuanne 73.
18 Phillip 63–4.
19 J Hunter 77.
20 Fidlon & Ryan 1979, 63; HRNSW vol 2, 392.
21 Worgan 9.
22 27 Jul 1790. HRNSW vol 2, 716.
23 Phillip 63.
24 W Bradley 143.
25 Worgan L 12 Jun 1788, B1463, ML.
26 Irvine 66.
27 Napier 260.
28 14 May 1788. Worgan 45.
29 HRA 1, vol 1, 76; Phillip 133.
30 Mar 1788. J Hunter 77.
31 T Saunders 2.
32 Peron 280.
33 W Bradley 143, 132.
34 Parramatta: W Bradley 83; HRA 1, vol 1, 29–30; J Hunter 403; McLoughlin 2000, 585.
35 J Hunter 202.
36 Mulvaney & White 360.
37 23–7 Apr 1788. Fitzhardinge 58; HRNSW vol 1(2), 133–5; Irvine 79; Phillip 100; Worgan 43.
38 Worgan L 12 Jun 1788, B1463, ML.
39 HRNSW vol 2, 510.
40 HRA 1, vol 1, 20, 31, 156.
41 Harbour land: Benson & Howell 1990, 115; Fidlon & Ryan 1982, 266–7; Fitzhardinge

NOTES

65; HRNSW vol 2, 743, 807; Kartzoff 11–15; Mulvaney & White 413–44; Saunders et al 115–19; B Smith 133–4.
42 Franklin L 18 Oct 1802, C231, ML; Irvine 85–6; Phillip 135.
43 Feb 1788. Fitzhardinge 48.
44 Blackburn L 12 Jul 1788, Ab163, ML.
45 Harbour: Helen Gammage 9 Dec 1998; Aplin 1998, 22; W Bradley 79–80, chart 7; Campbell 1921, 69; D Collins vol 1, 544, 599; Hinkson 2001; McGuanne 10–11; McLoughlin 2000, 186, 579; Mulvaney & White 343–65, 413; Napier 1928, 261; Phillip 125; Selfe 58; KV Smith 2001, vii–ix.
46 15 May 1788. HRNSW vol 1(2), 122; HRA 1, vol 1, 18–19.
47 HRA 1, vol 1, 25; Phillip 47–8.
48 21 Jan 1788. W Bradley 59; Worgan 8.
49 2 Dec 1642. Kenny 34.
50 Jan 1799. D Collins vol 2, 132.
51 Camm & McQuilton 49; Darwin 446.
52 22 Feb 1792. I Thomas 1994, 14.
53 19 Jan 1802. Peron 187.
54 4 Mar 1804. HRA 3, vol 1, 489–90; Vallance et al 487.
55 D Collins vol 2, 133–4.
56 G Calder 298.
57 Risdon: BG 17 Feb 02; G Calder 124–5, 296–312; HRA 3, vol 1, 197; HRNSW 5, sketch opp 226.
58 HRNSW 5, 312–13; Humphrey 98; Vallance et al 487.
59 JB Walker 1889b, 226–8.
60 Bolger 3; Tardif 108.
61 17 Feb 1804. Nicholls 43.
62 25 Jan 1804. Tardif 107.
63 24 Jan 1802. Plomley 1983, 27.
64 Humphrey 105.
65 7 Aug 1804. Hamilton-Arnold 66.
66 Mt Wellington: D Collins vol 2, 132; de Quincey 12–14; Flinders 1965, 9; Humphrey 103, 105; Peron 193.
67 Giblin vol 1, 143.
68 Breton 1834, 313. Also Vallance et al 491.
69 Tardif 110.
70 HRA 3, vol 2, 644; JB Walker 1889b, 240.
71 J Ross 35, 41–2, 56, 60.
72 Lycett 1825, pl.17.
73 Hamilton-Arnold 61; Tardif 107.
74 HRA 3, vol 1, 197–8.
75 D Collins vol 2, 134.
76 Tardif 82.
77 Feb 1804. Hamilton-Arnold 61.
78 24 Jan 1802. Peron 189.
79 Dixon map 1839, M1076.1, ERM.
80 Wade map 1844, MT12, ERM.
81 16 Sep 1824. Steele 1972, 150.
82 Wade map 1844, MT12, ERM.
83 Warner map 1841, M1172.3–7, ERM.
84 2 Dec 1823. Steele 1972, 111.
85 Steele 1972, 186, 233.
86 Steele 1972, 233.
87 Fraser D 6 Jul 1828, JOL.
88 Steele 1972, 255.
89 Fraser D 25 Jul 1828, JOL.
90 Camm & McQuilton 49.
91 HRA 1, vol 11, 219–23; Steele 1972, 154–5.
92 11–15 Sep 1825. HS Russell 589–92.
93 Fraser D 11 Jul 1828, JOL.
94 2 Oct 1825. HS Russell 598.
95 Oxley map Bremer's River 1824, ERM.
96 16 Sep 1825. Steele 1972, 191.
97 Map MT55 1829, ERM; Steele 1972, 346.
98 Steele 1975, 28–9.
99 20 Oct 1825. Steele 1975, 40.
100 Hodgkinson 105.
101 HRA 1, XI, 219–23; Steele 1972, 106, 111, 120.
102 Brisbane: ERM maps c~ Bill Kitson: Dixon 1839, M1076.1; MT55 1829; Oxley 1824, Bremer's River; Wade 1844, MT12; Warner 1841, M1172.3–7. *Brisbane Retrospect* (Steele), 3–4; Camm & McQuilton 49; Fraser D, OM 87–25, JOL; HRA 1, XI, 219–23; HS Russell 589–601; Steele 1972, 106, 111, 120, 150–5, 186, 231–3, 255; Steele 1975, 28–9; Steele 1983, 122.
103 Playford 18–42.
104 Jan 1832. Stannage 1979, 30.
105 HRA 3, vol 6, 556–8.

106 Camm & McQuilton 49.
107 10 Mar 1827. HRA 3, vol 6, 556–8.
108 11 Mar 1827. HRA 3, vol 6, 556–8.
109 11 Mar 1827. HRA 3, vol 6, 556–8.
110 10 Mar 1827. HRA 3, vol 6, 581.
111 12 Mar 1830. Hasluck 77.
112 1 Jan 1838. Backhouse 532.
113 1830. Breton 1834, 19–20.
114 Breton 1834, 21.
115 Landor 98.
116 Breton 1834, 16–17.
117 Bates 1992, 1, 4, 49; Green 173.
118 O'Connor et al 14, 23.
119 Hallam 1986, 128.
120 HRA 3, vol 6, 558.
121 Perth: Bekle & Gentilli 442–3; Camm & McQuilton 49; Green 173; O'Connor et al 14, 21–3, 33–5; Seddon 1972, 174, 230, 238–40; Stannage 1979.
122 2 May 1802. Flinders 1966 vol 1, 218.
123 30 Apr 1802. PI Edwards 77.
124 HRA 3, vol 1, 116.
125 Oct 1803. Currey 1987, 71.
126 8 Nov 1803. HRNSW 5, 255–6.
127 27, 29 Sep 1836. Cannon vol 1, 65.
128 Backhouse 503; Curr 1883, 1–2; Russell map 1837, 821.02 A1837, SLV.
129 4 Jun 1835. Harcourt 154.
130 Bonwick 1883, 16.
131 Nov 1839. Were 255.
132 Greig 1928, 113.
133 Bonwick 1883, 297.
134 Finn vol 1, 4.
135 Eidelson 6; Presland 1994, 35, 47.
136 Finn vol 1, 21; Presland 1994, 17.
137 Nicholls 39.
138 Hobson D 3–7 Apr 1839, MS8457 box 865/1C, SLV.
139 Jan 1803. Vallance et al 191.
140 27 Apr 1802. PI Edwards 75. Also Bonwick 1883, 8.
141 Backhouse 500; Bride 393; Stokes vol 1, 283.
142 Howard 1917, 47.
143 McCrae 1912, 118.
144 PL Brown 1938, 131.
145 Labilliere vol 2, 98.
146 Finn vol 1, 4.
147 Bunce 63.
148 PL Brown 1938, 80.
149 McCrae 1912, 133.
150 Boys 63–4.
151 Bride 394.
152 Backhouse 505.
153 C Griffiths 7.
154 Greig 1928, 114.
155 PL Brown 1938, 80.
156 McCrae 1912, 118.
157 Finn vol 1, 4.
158 1 Jan 1838. Hawdon D, A1493, ML; Hawdon 1952, 4.
159 Harcourt 81.
160 Labilliere vol 2, 52.
161 9 Mar 1837. Cannon vol 1, 102.
162 2 Feb 1836. Bride 18.
163 11 Feb 1803, 10–11 Mar 1837, 5 Sep 1835. Bonwick 1883, 13, 261–2; Boys 66.
164 30 May 1835. Batman 12–13.
165 Billot 91.
166 4–5 Jun 1835. Batman 18–19.
167 Hoddle plan 1837, SLV; picture 20.
168 Mar–Apr 1836. PL Brown 1938, 113.
169 6 Jun 1837. T Walker 51.
170 JH Kerr 10; Hoddle plan 1837, SLV.
171 Colville 241.
172 1845. C Griffiths 8.
173 May 1840. R Howitt 87.
174 Melbourne: SLV maps 821.02 A1837 Russell 1837; 821.02 BJF1837 Hoddle 25 Mar 1837; 821.1 Roll 104 Hoddle plan 1837; Roll 112 Hoddle Nov 1842; CS113 Tuckey Oct 1804. Backhouse 500–3; Bonwick 1883, 11, 259, 297, 355; Bride 393; PL Brown 1938, 80; Bunce 63; Camm & McQuilton 48; Cannon vol 5, 22–7; Cannon & Macfarlane 4; Colville 178; Curr 1883, 1–2; J Dawson 19; Finn vol 1, 3–4, vol 2, 497; Howard 1912, 33–4; R Howitt 165; McCrae 1912, 114–19, 133; Presland 1994, 2008; AGL Shaw 84; Stokes vol 1, 283; T Walker 47; Waterhouse 109, 113.
175 16 Nov 1836. Rolls 2002, 139–40.

176 Backhouse 509; Mantegani 70–2.
177 31 Dec 1836. G Stevenson 55.
178 12, 22 Nov 1836. Elder 77, 80.
179 1, 4 Oct, 12 Nov 1836, 18 Jan 1837. Elder 69–70, 77, 99.
180 Backhouse 510; Sturt 1849 vol 2, 189–90.
181 Angas 1847b, pl.1.
182 Moon 45.
183 31 Dec 1836. G Stevenson 55.
184 24 Jan 1838. James 230.
185 Aug 1838. Sturt 1838, 19.
186 Feb 1837. W Finlayson 41.
187 Twidale et al 113.
188 Twidale et al 116; V Campbell 1988, 226–40.
189 Moon 57.
190 1 Dec 1837. Backhouse 511.
191 c1839. Stephens 484, 494–5; RSC 165/1860, 7, 55, SAPP.
192 Kraehenbuehl 1996, 1–10, 63, 150–1.
193 Daniels & Tait 99.
194 Oct 1838. Hawker 7.
195 Feb 1837. W Finlayson 42.
196 1 Dec 1837. Backhouse 511.
197 Apr 1838. Hawdon 1952, 61.
198 1839. G Hamilton 67.
199 cNov 1836. Mantegani 74.
200 25, 29 Dec 1849. T Griffiths 1988, 60–1.
201 24 Nov 1836. Hawker 23.
202 Torrens: Arthur 31; S Clarke 11, 20; Franklin P Dec 1840, MS114, NLA; Peters 25.
203 June 1837. Everard 77–8.
204 S Clarke 11, 52–3; Hercus et al 262.
205 24 Dec 1836. Elder 90.
206 12 Jan 1837. Elder 95.
207 Chapman & Read 77.
208 1840s. Wilkinson 45.
209 20 Jan 1837. G Stevenson 65.
210 Peters 12.
211 Hercus et al 263.
212 BG; Chapman & Read 78; Twidale et al 115.
213 Moon 45, 47.
214 Adelaide: BG; Tom Gara 7 May 01; Angas 1847a vol 1, 208; Chapman & Read 75; S Clarke; Daniels & Tait; Elder; W Finlayson 43–4; Hawker 9–10; Hercus et al 255–76; Howchin 9–10; JG Johnston 46; Kraehenbuehl 1996, 1, 168, 171, 177; Kraehenbuehl 2000, 2001; Sturt 1833 vol 2, 190; Twidale et al 113–4; Wilkinson 44–5.
215 24 Feb 1869. Lockwood 34.
216 HRA 1, vol 1, 1; 3, vol 5, 780.
217 Goyder map 1869, B1/2, NT Lib.
218 2 Mar 1869. R 31/1869–70, 2, SAPP.
219 R 157/1869–70, 3–4, SAPP.
220 D 6 Feb 1869, SRSA.
221 Daly L 23 Feb 1869, MSA.
222 D 6–8 Feb 1869, SRSA.
223 Goyder FB 12 Feb 1869, SRSA; D 6, 26 Feb 1869, SRSA.
224 FB 1869, LPE: 1A p10 Mar (Woods); L Feb–May (Knuckey); U p3 16 Feb (King); X Apr (Smith); Harvey R May 1869, GRG 35/8, SRSA (c~ Samantha Wells).
225 Bauman 32, 46, 50; FB U p5 16 Feb 1869 (King), LPE; Hoare D 23 Feb 1869, MSA.
226 24 Sep 1839. Stokes vol 2, 19–20.
227 Bauman 87.
228 Goyder D 3 Apr 1869, SRSA.
229 Bauman 122–3.
230 Diagram Book vol 1, plan 5, 30 Apr 1869 (Woods), LPE; Sections 1–299, Hundred of Bagot, 32/1870–1, SAPP.
231 Goyder D 6 Apr 1869, SRSA.
232 Goyder D 21 Mar 1869, SRSA.
233 Goyder R, 31/1869–70, 2, SAPP.
234 Bauman map 17–18, 124; FB 1A pp16–7 Mar 1869 (Woods), LPE; Diagram Book vol 1 30 Apr 1869, plans 6 (Woods) & 10 (Mitchell), LPE; Goyder D 9–13, 21 Apr 1869, SRSA.
235 Bauman 109.
236 Bauman 9–10; Goyder Traverse on East Arm, LPE.
237 Parkhouse 638–9.
238 Darwin: Goyder 1869: D, GRG 35/655, SRSA; FB, GRG 35/256, SRSA; Map B1/2, NT Lib; R, 31 & 157/1869–70, SAPP; Traverse on East Arm, LPE. Bauman; Daly L 23 Feb 1869, D6993(L),

MSA; Deane L 8 Feb 1869, D2785(L), MSA; FB 1869, LPE; Harvey R May 1869, GRG 35/8, SRSA c~ Samantha Wells; Hoare D 1869, PRG 294/2 vol 1, MSA; Wells 1995, 2001.

239 7 Dec 1820. CT Smith J, MS689, NLA.

240 Colville 161; Cunningham J 8 Apr 1824, reel 46, SRNSW; Hoddle FB377, 5, 8 Dec 1832, 2/5002, SRNSW.

241 Watercourses: picture 19; Andrews 1979, 61, 64; Colville 156; Cunningham J 17–18 Apr 1824, reel 46, SRNSW; Dixon L 6 Jun 1829, reel 3063, SRNSW; Gibbney 3–4; Hoddle FB377, 61, 66, 141–56, 2/5002 & FB433, 125, 2/5063, SRNSW.

242 Canberry Creek, Black Mountain: Avery 12–13; Bluett 1; Dexter 22, 163–8, 183; Dixon map 1987, NLA; Federal Territory map sheet 4, NLA; Gillespie 1979, 21; Hoddle FB375, 52–3, 16 May 1832, 2/5000, SRNSW; Jackson-Nakano 2001, 86, 89, 189; Scrivener sheet 4, NLA; CT Smith J 8 Dec 1820, MS689, NLA.

243 10 May 1821. Cambage 1921, 278.

244 Cunningham J 8, 19 Apr 1824, reel 46, SRNSW; Field 380.

245 1, 4 Feb 1822. Gibbney 3–4.

246 31 May, 9 Jun 1823. Field 374, 379.

247 Hoddle FB377, 55, 3 Dec 1832, 2/5002, SRNSW; Starr 14, 19.

248 Cunningham J 15 Apr 1824, reel 46, SRNSW; Jervis 262.

249 Dixon map 3643 1829, SRNSW; Gibbney 4.

250 1–2 Jun 1823. Field 374.

251 Dixon L 6 Jun 1829 & Docker L 6 Jul 1829, reel 3063, SRNSW; Gibbney 4.

252 FB375, 70, 21 May 1832, 2/5000, SRNSW.

253 Cunningham J 16 Apr 1824, reel 46, SRNSW.

254 CT Smith J 8 Dec 1820, MS689, NLA.

255 Jackson-Nakano 2001, 85.

256 Cunningham J 17–18 Apr 1824, reel 46, SRNSW.

257 Bluett 1954, 6; Jackson-Nakano 2001, 85; Jervis 263.

258 CT Smith J, MS689, NLA.

259 Gibbney 3–4.

260 Cunningham J 18 Apr 1824, reel 46, SRNSW.

261 Cunningham J 8 Apr 1824, reel 46, SRNSW.

262 Hoddle FB375, 52–3, 16 May 1832, 2/5000, SRNSW.

263 Canberra: General: NLA maps G8981. G46 1832 (HOD) Hoddle 1911; G8981. G46 Federal Territory 1915?; G8984.C3 Scrivener 1910; G8984.C3S1 Dixon [1829], 1987. SRNSW map M595.2 FB7, Dixon 3643, May 1829. Avery; Bluett 1927, 1954; Cunningham J 1822–31, reel 46, SRNSW (summary in Havard); Dexter; Dixon L 6 Jun & Docker L 6 Jul 1829, reel 3063, SRNSW; Gibbney; Gillespie 1979, 1984, 1991; Hoddle FB 1832–5, 2/5000–2, 5063, SRNSW; Jackson-Nakano 2001, 2002; FW Robinson; P Saunders; Selkirk; CT Smith J Dec 1820, 9/2733 fiche 3271, SRNSW (extracts MS689 NLA & Dexter 17–18).

Molonglo: Andrews 1979, 61–2; Bluett 1954, 6; Cunningham J 18 Apr 1824; Hoddle FB375, 44–60, 15–31 May 1832, 2/5000, SRNSW.

City region: Andrews 1979, 59, 65; Avery 12–13; Cunningham J 8, 17–19 Apr 1824; Dexter 197; Hoddle FB375, 49, 54–60, 16–18? May 1832, 2/5000; Mossman & Banister 168, 176; FW Robinson 38; P Saunders 20–2, 27, 84; Starr 19.

Settlers: Andrews 1979, 70; Bluett 1954, 1; Dexter 18–19, 173; Gillespie 1991, 9–10, 18; Hoddle FB375, 50, 16 May 1832, 2/5000; Jackson-Nakano 2001, 38–46; FW Robinson 7n; P Saunders 20–2, 27, 84; G Wilson 44–5. In 1831 Ainslie got 50 acres at Bong Bong, portion 32, parish unnamed, which he sold when he returned to Scotland in 1835 (Hoddle FB377, 32, Nov 1832, 2/5002; *Sydney Gazette* 5 Oct 1836).

10 Farms without fences

1. Haddon 318.
2. 12 Mar 1804. HRNSW 5, 359.
3. 1826. J Atkinson 21.
4. Dovers 27–8; Gilmore 1932, 168–9; Keen 95; E Williams 1998, 78, 93.
5. Sep 1881. GB McMinn R 1883/131, A1640, NAA.
6. Nets: H Allen 1974, 312; Beveridge 1883, 45; Bride 271; Eyre vol 2, 259–61; Gerritsen 2008, 14–15, 43–5; Lewis J 10 Mar 1875, 19/1876, SAPP; Mitchell 1839 vol 2, 153; Newland 1888, 22–3; Norton 1907, 116; Steele 1983, 6.
   Traps: Tom Gara 7 May 01; Attenbrow & Steele 49; Baudin 178; V Campbell 1969, 58; Clarke 1994, 167; Gerritsen 2008, 107; Gilmore 1934, 134–43, 1935, v–vi; Godwin 50–3; Hale & Tindale 1933–4; Hardy 8; McBryde 1978, 121–34; Mulvaney & Kamminga 34–5; Penney 48–62; Robinson R 1846, Governor's Des ZA7081, 46, ML; Stockton 1982b, app 3.
   Weirs: Batman 15; Blainey 139–42, 151–3; Byerley 4–5, 35; Clarke 2003, 62–3; GH Dawson Rem, A1805, 61, ML; Gerritsen 2008, 12–13; Hovell 333; Kirby 35; Leichhardt 1847a, 396–8, 402; Lewis J 16 Jan 1875, 19/1876, SAPP; Merlan 79; Mountford 1939b, 197; Mulvaney 19–21; Robinson R March–May 1845, Ar4, 10, ML; Savage 220; Sturt 1833 vol 1, 41; & 1849 vol 1, 105; Wills 195; Worsnop 101–7.
7. 1 Jun 1848. HRA 1, vol 26, 635.
8. Mathews 1903, 151.
9. Brewarrina: L Black; Dargin; Hardy 8–9; Mathews 1903; Norton 1907, 102.
10. Robinson R 1842, in P & G Ford, 241.
11. Eels: BG; A Campbell 1965, 206–7; Clark 1998 vol 2, 162–3, 196–7, 307–8; Coutts et al; Dingle 1998, 15; Dovers 27; Flood 1989, 215–18; Gammage 2005a, 18–19; Gerritsen 2008, 107; Hemming 2–6; La Trobe Des 13 Nov 1842, COD 294B, 82, SRNSW; Lourandos 1980, 1997; Mulvaney & White 293–307; Robinson J 1841, Governor's Des 1842, A1230, 927, ML; AGL Shaw 25.
12. Robinson P vol 59, 16 Apr 1841, ZA7080, ML.
13. Grey vol 1, 228, 231, vol 2, 292.
14. Jenkin 13–14.
15. R & C Berndt 1996, 108–9.
16. Lindsay 1888, 14.
17. Gilmore 1934, 138.
18. Strehlow 1978, 34–5.
19. 5–10 Oct 1896. D Carnegie 274.
20. Rose & Clarke 82–3, & 30.
21. Gilmore 1934, 118.
22. Bans & sanctuaries: Dick Kimber 1 Jul 1999; R Baker 48–50; Bates 1985, 240; R & C Berndt 1965, 139, 143–4, 1979, 74; Gammage 1986, 20; Gilmore 1932, 168–9, 1935, viii, 117; Hetzel & Frith 79; Kohen 1995, 66; Latz 1995, 22, 25–6, 2007, 137–8; A Mitchell 160; Newsome 1980; Rose 1992, 100, 1995, 30; Spencer & Gillen 1889, 134; Sutton 1998b, at n38; E Williams 1998, 78.
23. Strehlow 1947, 49. Also Foran & Walker 1986, 2.4.
24. Kimber 1976, 144.
25. Kohen 1995, 41; Tindale 1936, 57, 60.
26. HRNSW 3, 826–8.
27. J Oxley 78–329.
28. W Jones 44–6.
29. 23 Jul 1831. Plomley 1966, 385, & 198.
30. 15 Feb 1838. Colville 241.
31. Kangaroos: Caughley et al 1; Flannery 2004, 212–15, 227–8; Mitchell 1839 vol 1, 291; Rolls 1984b, 484–5.
32. Backhouse 476.
33. Jan 1839. Buchhorn 116.
34. BE Norton 5.
35. Penney 278–9.
36. B McDonald 118.
37. Curr 1883, 85, 184–5.
38. de Satge 142.
39. Murray D 26 Jul 1901, 16, 19 Jul 1902, 43/1904, SAPP.
40. Kangaroo numbers: H Allen 1972, 82; H Allen 1983, 31–3; Babbage R

371

Mar–Nov 1858, 151/1858, 10, SAPP; Boldrewood 1866, 736; Flannery 1994, 212–15; Gammage 1986, 20; Low 2002, 231; Mitchell 1839 vol 1, 308; Morton & Mulvaney 287, 294–7; Penney 283.
41 *Sydney Gazette* 24 Aug 1803.
42 Hodgkinson 3. Also Janet Fingleton 23 Jun 02; Lane 1.14, 11.3.
43 Koalas: Brodribb 26; Henderson 1851–4 vol 2, 174; Knott et al; Lee & Martin 82–4; Low 2002, 238–9; Lunney & Leary 69–72; Moyal 6–9, 81, 124–8.
44 Babbage R Mar-Nov 1858, 151/1858, 10, SAPP.
45 Species increases: KH Bennett 453; Gammage 1986, 35, 222, 226–7; Gilmore 1932, 168–9; Gilmore 1935, 117; 'A Lady' 208; Low 2002, 242; J Oxley 275; Penney 39, 281–3; Rolls 1984b, 485; I White 54.
46 Blainey 95; Gammage 2009, 291–2; B McDonald 122–3; RM Moore 78; Penney 281; Robinson et al 209.
47 Gammage 1986, 226–7.
48 Home 7.
49 Crops: H Allen 1974, 313; Butlin 1983, 158–9; Campbell 1965, 209; Dix & Lofgren 74; Flood 1989, 210–45; Gammage 1986, 20, 2005a, 2005b, 2009, 282–7; Gerritsen 2008, 19–25, 41–3; Gilmore P, MS806, 91, NLA; Gilmore 1932, 168–9, 1934, 134–43, 196, 208, 222, 1935, 231–2; Hallam 1975, 12–15; Harris & Hillman 99–100; Jones 1975, 21–8; Keen 95; Kerwin 20–43; Lourandos 1997, 48–58; Mitchell 1839 vol 1, 238, 1848, 98; Pilling & Waterman 278–9; Tonkinson 52; Veth & Walsh 21; Walsh 1990, 34; E Williams 1998, 78.
50 Hynes & Chase 40.
51 Replanting tops: Dick Kimber 1 Jul 1999; Anderson et al 63–5; R & C Berndt 1993, 109–10, 1996, 108–9; Campbell 1965, 208–9; Gerritsen 1994, 84; Hale & Tindale 1933–4, 113; Harris & Hillman 59–60; Keast vol 3, 1833; Keen 95; Russell-Smith et al 25, 167–8; Sutton 1998b, at n38; Tonkinson 51; N Williams 93.
52 Grey vol 2, 8–12, 20.
53 Gerritsen 1994, 85–6.
54 *Warran*: Bates 1985, 261; Chapman 44; Gerritsen 1994, 82–7, 92–102, 2000, 2002, 3–4, 2008, 33–5; Green 116, 121, 138, 198–9; Grey vol 2, 8–20; Hallam 1975, 12–15; Harris & Hillman 136–9, 146; GF Moore 1884, 74, 81; HL Roth 1886, 131; Saunders 34–5; Seddon 2005, 71.
55 Lourandos 1997, 68.
56 10 Aug 1836. Mitchell 1839 vol 2, 211–12, & 271–2.
57 Frankel 44.
58 Malcolm, NSWLC RSC on Aborigines, 1845, 13.
59 *Murnong*: Angas 1847a vol 1, 89; Beilby, *Port Phillip Gazette* 29 Nov 1849; R & C Berndt 1993, 108–9; Beveridge 1883; Campbell 1965, 208–9; Chapman 44; CCL Lower Darling R 14 Jan 1852, 4/7153, COD 294B, SCMC, SRNSW; Clark 1998 vol 2, 196; J Dawson 19–20; Flood 1989, 213, 236; Foreman & Walsh 1, 195–211; Gerritsen 1994, 87–8, 2008, 112–13; Gott 1982, 1983, 2005; Grey vol 2, 8–12, 20; Harris & Hillman 42–54, 59–60; Hawdon 41; Hynes & Chase 40; Karskens 13–14; Keast vol 3, 1833; Keen 95; Lourandos 1980, 245–64, 1997; Lunt 1996; Lunt et al 1998b, 19–20; Mathew 1910, 92; Penney 36; Plomley 1966, 255; Randell 27.
60 J Hunter 150.
61 Flood 1989, 236. Also R Jones 1975, 23.
62 Morrill chap 3, np.
63 Other yams: Chisholm 1955b, 221; Clarke 1985b, 4–6, 9; Gammage 2005a, 2009, 286; Gott 1993, 196; Harris & Hillman 42–60, 136–9; Nash 1993, 95, 128–34; Veth & Walsh 22; Walsh 1990, 29, 34; N Williams 93.
64 15 Feb 1846. Mitchell 1848, 60.
65 1882. HL Roth 1886, 132.
66 19 Jun 1835. Mitchell 1839 vol 1, 237–8, & 290–1.
67 Allen 1972, 76–7.

68 Sturt 1849 vol 1, 294, & 285. Also Flood 1989, 237–8; Finnis 39; W Jones 112–3, 144–9; Tolcher 46.
69 9 Mar 1846. Mitchell 1848, 89–90.
70 13 Mar 1845. Brock 133.
71 Sturt 1849 vol 1, 294.
72 Gresser 233, & 234. Also Noble 1997, 71.
73 Turner 1891, xvi.
74 9 Nov 1844. Sturt 1849 vol 1, 205.
75 Gammage 2009, 286; Read & Bellairs.
76 Eyre vol 2, 62.
77 Curr 1883, 430. Also Beveridge 1883, 63; Campbell et al 486; Haw & Munro 53–4; S Kelly et al vol 1, 26; R Lawrence 54–5; Le Soeuf Rem 34–6, A2762, ML; Penney 35; Robinson R, Ar4, 5, ML.
78 Fire for crops: Jim Noble 31 Aug 05; Beaton 52–4; Cary et al 178; Flood 1989, 211–13; Frawley & Semple 161; Gammage 2009; Gott 1999, 33–42; Green 138; Lamont in Lunt et al 1999; Lindsay 1893 vol 1, 66–9; Lourandos 1997, 48–58; Lunt et al 1999, 5; GF Moore 1884, 81; Penney 28–9, 36.
79 John Bradley 11 Jul 01; E Williams 1998, 78.
80 Lord 29.
81 Wettenhall 31.
82 Frawley & Semple 157.
83 Hynes & Chase 41.
84 Frawley & Semple 155; R Jones 1975, 24–5.
85 Transplanting: Gerritsen 2008, 19–25; Gott 1982, 65; Grey 266; Hynes & Chase 40–4; Lee 371; Penney 36; PM Stevenson 313.
86 Tonkinson 52.
87 Mulvaney & White 233. Also MA Smith 1986, 30.
88 Walsh 1990, 35.
89 Grain: H Allen 1974, 313–14; Gammage 2009, 282–9; Gerritsen 2008, 41–3, 58–62, 84; Gilmore 1934, 153–4; Kirk 75; 'A Lady' 215; Latz 1995, 55; Nash 1984, 128–34, 1993, 95; MA Smith 1986, 30; Sturt 1849 vol 1, 294–6, vol 2, 140; Tindale 102; Veth & Walsh 20–2; Walsh 1990, 28–9; E Williams 1998, 78; RVS Wright 347.
90 Blainey 195; Flood 1989, 240; Pilling & Waterman 280.
91 1870. C Giles 7.
92 Mar 1871. Ashwin 64.
93 Ashwin 66.
94 1836. RB Smyth 143n.
95 30 Dec 1844. Sturt 1849 vol 1, 226–7, & 296.
96 9 Mar 1829. Sturt 1833 vol 1, 118–19.
97 Harvey 191; Latz 1995, 27–8.
98 Storing: H Allen 1972, 78–9; & 1974; R Baker 47; R & C Berndt 1979, 74–5, 1993, 79–81, 109–10, 1996, 114; Blainey 194–6; Clarke 2003, 63; Dovers 27–8; Flood 1989, 210, 240–2; Gerritsen 2008, 55–8, 122; Gillen & Drewien 16; Gould 1971, 23; Harris & Hillman 104; Harvey 191–2; Hetzel & Frith 27; Horne & Aiston 7; Isaacs 1987, 62, 79; Kimber 1984, 19; Latz 1995, 46–8, 55; Lourandos 1997, 56–7; Mathew 1910, 92–3; Mitchell 1839 vol 1, 237; Newland 1921, 13–14; Penney 37; Robinson R 1846, Governor's Des ZA7081, 9, ML; RB Smyth 302; Sweeney 290–2; Tunbridge 1985, 10–15; Veth & Walsh 20–2; Williams 1998, 78; Withnell 9; RVS Wright 346–7.
99 Gerritsen 2008.
100 Keen 96.
101 Kimber 1976, 149–50, & 144–5.
102 Gammage 2005b.
103 Nash 1993, ix, & 8–18.
104 Nash 1984, 72–7, 128–34; & 1993, 4, 18–24, 95–8, 120–34, 149–54, 237. Also H Allen 1983, 53–8.
105 Flood 1989, 239.
106 H Allen 1972, 96; & 1974, 316–18; Flannery 1994, 281.
107 Malthus.
108 HL Roth 1886, 131.
109 Hartwig 64.
110 R Jones 1969.
111 Gould 1971, 23.
112 Horton 2000, 58–9.
113 Diamond 107.

114 Yen 844, & 831–47.
115 Diamond 89.
116 Yen 844.
117 Berry Rem 1838, COD 294B, 558–9, SCMC, SRNSW.
118 Macknight 1976.
119 DR Moore, 301–3.
120 Cape York, Macassans: Byerley 79–80; Flood 1989, 233–4; Jukes 138–9, 145, 307; D Lawrence 264–6, 339; DR Moore 160, 203, 211, 279–80, 301–3; Mulvaney & Kamminga 407–19; D Walker 387–8.
121 Robinson J 1841, Governor's Des 1842, A1230, 927, ML.
122 Grey vol 2, 20; Harris & Hillman 137.
123 1825–6. P Cunningham vol 1, 124.
124 Sturt 1849 vol 2, 139. Also Finnis 40.
125 Ashwin 64.
126 Gillen & Drewien 17.
127 Houses, villages: Braim n, A614, ML; G Calder 34, 85; Clark 1998 vol 2, 196; J Clark 25; J Dawson 10; Flood 1989, 216; Gerritsen 1994, 87–92, 2002, 1–3, 21, 2008, 46–8, 99–112; Grey vol 2, 20; Harris & Hillman 137–9, 146; Keen 99; Kerwin 15–18; La Trobe Des 13 Nov 1842, COD 294B, SRNSW; Memmott 189–205; Mitchell 1839 vol 1, 240; Mulvaney 49; Mulvaney & White 298; Robinson R 1842, in P & G Ford, 241; Robinson R 1845, Ar4, 6, 16, ML; Sturt 1849 vol 1, 380, vol 2, 61, 73–4, 139; E Williams 1984, 1987, 1998, 77; Worsnop 103.
128 Diamond 89; Yen 844.
129 D Thomson 1939, 209, 211–12.
130 R & C Berndt 1996, 108.
131 Kaberry 20.
132 Blainey 162–3, 167; Kaberry 23.
133 Diamond 110–12, 308.
134 Diamond 155.
135 Intensification: Diamond 155; Gerritsen 1994, 86–7; Head 1989; R Lawrence 92; Lourandos 1980, 1983, 1997; Sturt 1833 vol 2, 39, 50, 81, 124; RVS Wright 345.
136 Gammage 2005a; Thomson 1949, 7.
137 7 Sep 1845. Sturt 1849 vol 1, 405–6.
138 Laurent Doussot 18 Jun 04.

11 Becoming Australian

1 Angus & Forster 11–13; Randell 17–18, 40.
2 Waterhouse 168.
3 Hallam 1975, 72.
4 Parker R 1839–40, VPRS 4410 unit 2, 52; Powlett R 1843/22, VPRS 10 unit 5, 31 Dec 1842.
5 Best places: P Cunningham vol 1, 146; Forbes D 1 Jul 1830, Mfm M1172, NLA; Hallam 1975, 25, 41, 47, 63–4, 72–7; T Walker 16.
6 Pedler 65; Reynolds 1992, 78.
7 2 Jan 1839. Stokes vol 1, 289.
8 Morrill ch 2, np.
9 7 Nov 1838. Rowley 37.
10 16 Jan 1836. Darwin 434.
11 23 Aug 1770. Parkin 453–4.
12 J Ross 33.
13 29 Nov 1824. Hovell 347.
14 Gunson 1974 vol 2, 354.
15 J Wright 55.
16 Avery 16.
17 Marsh 68.
18 Simpson R 1 Jan 1844, Governor's Des, A1223, 1137, ML or HRA 1, vol 23, 487.
19 LC RSC on Aborigines, NSWPP 1845, 18.
20 Diamond 14.
21 Rose 1996, 76.
22 More people in 1788: Gammage 1986, 18–19; Gerritsen 2008, 49–55; Haw & Munro 6; Kerwin 57–9; Lee & Daly 319; Penney 30; J Wright 20.
23 26 Aug 1818. J Oxley 275–7.
24 Hallam 1975, 6; Kohen 1995, 98–100.
25 Latz 1997, 3.
26 3 Nov 1836. Mitchell 1839 vol 2, 328.
27 Sturt 1833 vol 1, xxviii–ix.
28 28 Jan 1833. Gunn J, 6–7, A316 ML or 1313/1 AOT.
29 20 Dec 1845. Mitchell 1848, 14.
30 Bride 167–9.
31 28 Sep 1832. Bennett 1834, 132–3.
32 Gilbert 1971 vol 1, 214.
33 Cary et al 208. Also Low 2002, 252–3.

34. Latz 1997, 3–4, 2007, 47–8, 84–97, 105–20, 131–43; Rothwell, *Aust Mag* 5–6 Apr 03, 28–30, & 177–8.
35. 15 Apr 1860. Stuart 1865, 159.
36. Ealey 17; Newsome 1975, 389, 392, 413.
37. Seddon 1994, 42, 273.
38. T Griffiths 2001a, 43–4, 140.
39. JC Hamilton 38.
40. Dovers 42–4; Rolls 1999.
41. Brian & Jenny Wright 11 Jul 01; Plan M371268, parish Woodum, 21 Nov 1898 c~ Brian & Jenny Wright.
42. Breton 1834, 252.
43. F Ellis 23.
44. Mitchell 1848, 413.
45. Rolls 1984a, 1, & 70, 182–6, 245–6.
46. Noble 1996, 62–3.
47. M Young 58.
48. John Banks Nov 02.
49. J Wright 277–9.
50. Max Lines 4 Apr 05, OHU.
51. Clarrie Shadforth & Ted Firkin 18 Jul 00.
52. Norton 1903, 153.
53. Barlow 244; Davies 30, 33; Pyne 1991, 128–9.
54. Bunbury & Morrell 105–6.
55. Scrub and tree regeneration: H Allen 1972, 97; Anon 1918, 160; Bossence 7–9; Bowman et al 2001; Bride 324; WB Clarke 25; Dovers 42–4; Flannery 1994, 218–22; Gammage 1986, 223; Gilbert 1971 vol 1, 47; JC Hamilton 38; Lunt 1998a, 649, 1998c; Mulvaney & Kamminga 59–60; L Murray 59–63, 70, 153–9; Noble 1997, iv, 8–12; Pendergast 4–5; Penney 29–30; Ranken 369–70; Rolls 1999, 200–1; RB Smyth 32; Starr 69; Stephens 494; van Kempen 37.
56. 30 Apr 1817. MR Allen 114.
57. Turner 1890, 588.
58. AG Hamilton 188.
59. van Lendenfeld 721.
60. van Kempen 40, & 50–2.
61. Barnard 438.
62. Rolls 1999, 205.
63. 23 Jul 1887. Allen 1972, 16.
64. Noble 1997, iv.
65. Rolls 1999, 206.
66. MR Allen 118–20.
67. J Banks 1982, 1997.
68. MR Allen 68.
69. Gammage 1986, 10.
70. Pine: MR Allen 3, 18–19, 90, 114, 117–20; Clark 1998 vol 4, 49; Dixson 200; Dovers 42–4; Gammage 1986, 233; AG Hamilton 188; Noble 1997, 8–12; Ranken 369–70; Rolls 1984a, 182–6, 245–6, 1999, 204–6; F Turner 1890, 588; van Lendenfeld.
71. BG; Gammage 2009; Low 2002, 7–21, 60–71, 125–32; Lunt et al 1998b, 18.
72. Marsupial lawns: Lunt et al 1998b, 29; RM Moore 78; Morton & Mulvaney 287; Newsome 1975, 297, 389, 394, 410, 420; Noble 1997, 54–5; Penney 241, 281; Rolls 1984b, 488–93.
73. Ellen & Fukui 177–81.
74. Wilderness: T Griffiths 1996, 14–15, 259–65.
75. Andrews 2006, 2008; picture 59.
76. Bob Purvis 5 Apr 05, OHU.
77. Howitt 1890, 1891.
78. Support for Howitt: ch 6; KH Bennett 453; Burn 11–12; Gunn J 25–6 Jan 1833, 1313/1 AOT or A316 ML, 1–2; R Mackay 88; Seddon 1994, 41–2, 297–300.

Appendix 1

1. See Gott 2005.
2. Bowman 2001, 549.
3. Bowman 2001, 549.
4. Bowman & Prior; Murphy & Bowman 238.
5. Bowman 2001, 551.
6. Bowman 2001, 551.
7. Bowman 2001, 552.
8. Bowman 2001, 552.
9. Moseley 260–1.
10. Bowman 2001, 552.
11. T Griffiths 2001a, 16–22.
12. Bowman 2001, 556–7.
13. Bowman 2001, 559.
14. MR Allen 123, & 136.
15. Vanderwal & Horton 5.

16 BA Wilson ii–iii.
17 Fensham & Kirkpatrick 1992a, 329.
18 K Mills 236–7.
19 J Read.
20 Bill Jackson 8 Feb 01; Jackson 1965, 1999a.
21 Kraehenbuehl 1996, maps 2000, 2001.
22 Kraehenbuehl 1996, 1.
23 Costin 1954, 181 & map.
24 Seddon 1994, 296–7. Also Lunt et al 1998b, 26.
25 B Field 375–7.
26 Mackaness 1942, 327.
27 8 Feb 1834. Andrews 1979, 85.
28 Mar 1835. Bunbury 14.
29 Ryrie J 19 Feb, 3, 5, 18 Mar 1840, Roll CY2715, ML. Also Andrews 1998, 156; Starr 18.
30 3 Oct 1832. Bennett 1834, 167–8.
31 HL White 165.
32 Smith J 7 Dec 1820, MS689, NLA; ch 9.
33 Costin 3 & map.
34 Costin 183.
35 T Thomas 37.
36 BG 22 Sep 07; Egloff.
37 John Banks Nov 02.
38 Rosenfeld & Winston-Gregson.
39 31 Oct 1824. Hovell J, Safe 1/32b, ML.
40 Norris et al.
41 Norris et al 213.
42 Norris et al 217.
43 Norris et al 209, 211.
44 Norris et al 213.
45 Norris et al 213–16.
46 Norris et al 213–15.
47 Norris et al 217.
48 Norris et al 213.
49 Fensham 2008.
50 Fensham 2008, 143.
51 Fensham 2008, 141.
52 Fensham 2008, 144.
53 McLaren 188, 199.
54 McLaren 200.
55 Fensham 2008, 145.
56 Fensham 2008, 147–8.
57 Fensham 2008, 146.
58 Fensham 2008, 147.
59 Fensham 2008, 146.
60 8 Jan 1832. Mitchell 1839 vol 1, 71n.
61 Breton 1834, 52n.
62 Fensham 2008, 146.
63 Breton 1834, 52n.
64 Fensham 2008, 146.
65 Fensham 2008, figure 2.
66 Fensham 2008, 141.
67 Fensham 2008, 146.
68 Fensham 2008, figure 2.
69 Fensham 2008, 148.
70 Ransom 257.
71 Fensham 2008, 146.
72 Mitchell 1839 vol 1, 41.
73 P Cunningham vol 1, 147.
74 Waugh 22.
75 Fensham 2008, 146.
76 Henry Nix 4 Aug 2010.
77 J Atkinson 6; Macknight 1998, 52; Rolls 2002, 64.
78 For example Fensham 2008, 152.
79 Fensham 2008, 146.
80 Fensham 2008, 151.
81 Mitchell 1839 vol 1, 71n.
82 Fensham 2008, 142.
83 Fensham 2008, 145–50, figure 4.
84 Fensham 2008, 145.
85 Fensham 2008, 142.
86 Fensham 2008, 154.
87 Also Fensham & Holman vs Lunt 1998a.
88 Benson & Redpath.
89 Benson & Redpath, 314–16.
90 Benson & Redpath, 285.
91 Benson & Redpath, 299.
92 Benson & Redpath, 288–98.
93 Benson & Redpath, 286.
94 Benson & Redpath, 286.
95 Benson & Redpath, 311–13.
96 Jurskis 2002, 689.
97 Benson & Redpath, 288.
98 Seddon 1994, 298–300.
99 ch 6; Blay; McMillan.
100 Flood 1980.
101 Lines 2006.
102 Lines 2006, 49.
103 Lines 2006, 166.

NOTES

104 Lines 2006, 243.
105 Lines 2006, 336.
106 Lines 2006, 15–16, 154–5, 166–9, 244–5, 293, 353–4.
107 Other deniers: RL Clark; P Collins; Horton 1982, 2000, 2002, 2008; G Lacey; Lunt 1997a,b,c, 1998, 2002; PB Mitchell; Walker in Gill et al; Witt et al.

BIBLIOGRAPHY

1 Unpublished documents

Aboriginal Affairs, Dept of Natural Resources, Melbourne
1621 RG Gunn et al, *Mudgegonga Aboriginal Art-Site Complex*, Melbourne 2000

Archives Office of Tasmania, Hobart
Colonial Secretary's Office
CSO 1/95/2276 J Rolland N 1823–4
CSO 1/317–18 GA Robinson R 1830s
Lands and Survey Department
LSD 355/1–10 FB 1803–34
MM 71/5/20 VDL Co P:
222 CB Hardwicke 1823; 227 C Lorymer Jan–Feb 1827; 228 J Garth & A McGeary Mar–Apr 1827; 229 J Fossey Apr–May 1827; 230 A Goldie Aug 1826; 231 E Curr Sep–Oct 1827; 232 H Hellyer 12–24 Dec 1828; 233 J Fossey Dec 1828; 236 H Hellyer 4–26 Jan 1829; 237 A Goldie Mar 1829; 238 H Hellyer 7–23 Nov 1828; 240 Hellyer to Curr Oct 1828; 241 H Hellyer Oct 1828
MM109 RC Gunn, 'Journal of a visit to southern Victoria', Mar 1836
NS1313/1 RC Gunn, 'Account of a journey inland from Launceston to Deloraine', Jan 1833 [is also ML A316]

Canberra and District Historical Society
'Charles Throsby', Canberra district 1820s, ms from ML

Clarence River Historical Society, Grafton
C53 J Warner, 'Plan of the Big River from an eye survey by Mr Butcher', Dec 1838

Fryer Library, University of Queensland, Brisbane
MSS5/486 RA Johnstone, 'Reminiscences of the Habits and Manners of the Aborigines of Queensland', c1880

John Oxley Library, State Library of Queensland, Brisbane
OM67–20 J Oxley, Moreton Bay FB 1823, 4, 5 & 8; OM74–8 SE Pearson, 'The Prospector of Argylla' nd; OM79–17/1 C Archer, Durundur D 16 Apr 1843–20 Feb 1844; OM80–10 Archer family L 1838–55; OM87–25 C Fraser D 'Residence on the Banks of the Brisbane and Logan Rivers', 30 Jun–6 Sep[=11 Aug] 1828; OM90–6 'Extracts relating to Aborigines 1839–1905'; OM90–18 E Henry P 24 Nov 1863–1919

La Trobe Library, State Library of Victoria, Melbourne
MF235 F Tuckfield J 1837–41
MS8457 box 865/1C EC Hobson, 'Diary of a Journey with Lady Franklin's Party', 1839
MS9356 AW Howitt P
MSM534 J Dredge J 1839–40
Maps
821.02 A1837 R Russell, 'Map shewing the site of Melbourne... in 1837', 1837
821.02 BJF1837 R Hoddle, 'Town of Melbourne', 25 Mar 1837
821.1 R Hoddle, 'Plan of the Surveyed Lands to the Northward of Melbourne', 1837 (Roll Plan 104)
821.123 WW Darke, 'Survey of part of the River Werribee', 1839–40
CS26(1) copy C Grimes, 'Port Phillip', 1803
CS113 copy J Tuckey, 'Survey of Port Phillip', Oct 1804
Roll Plan 104A copy Draft of Roll Plan 104
Roll Plan 112 copy R Hoddle & WW Darke, 'Plan of North and South Melbourne', Nov 1842

Land Titles Office, Adelaide
Section survey plans, Hundreds of Burra, Kadina, Lincoln and Minnipa

Lands Museum, Dept of Environment & Resource Management, Brisbane
JJ Cobon, Survey and R, C153.301–2, Parish Tribulation
[A Cunningham et al], 'A Geographical Sketch . . . [west of] Moreton Bay', 1829, Map MT55
R Dixon, 'Plan of the Brisbane River', 26 Jul 1839, Plan M1076.1
J Oxley, 'An Outline of the Bremer's River', 1824
H Wade, 'Map of the Environs of Brisbane Town', 1844, Map MT12
J Warner, Cancelled plans M1172.3–7 (Brisbane area), Sep–Nov 1841
WNB Wilson, 'Plan of the Town of Somerset' 1865 (S112–3), & R 6 Sep 1864 (2372–64), & 4 Apr 1865 (1342–65)

Mitchell Library, State Library of New South Wales, Sydney
572.993E JJ East, 'The Aborigines of South and Central Australia', 1889
A316 RC Gunn J Jan 1833; 597 JE Calder P; 610 P re Tas Aborigines; 614 T Braim n 1830s; 1206 vol 17 267–82 J Darling Des 17 Feb 1830; 1227, 1230, 1233, 1236, 1240, 1246, 1267/23 NSW Governor's Des 1842–8 incl CCL & mission R 1841–3, Robinson J 1841, 1843; 1426 CJ Tyers L 1855–63; 1447 WA Cawthorne n c1855; 1450 J Gunther D 1836–65 & n; 1493 J Hawdon D 1838 & G Langhorne statement 1838; 1531/3 G Macleay L 3 Jan 1830; Deas Thomson P vol 3, 63–7; 1579 H Stockdale P 1850–1900; 1805 GH Dawson Rem 1834–90; 1930 D Unaipon 'Legends' 1924–5; 2053 S Marshall L 1842; 2535–7 G Aiston L 1920–40; 2645 CP Wilton, 'The Native Black of the Past' 1848–50; 2762 A Le Soeuf Rem 1840–53; 4360 pt 10, 923–7 Macarthur P; 7022–93 GA Robinson P & guide
Ab163 D Blackburn L 12 Jul 1788
Ar4 GA Robinson J 1845
B505 J Gunther Lecture c1843; 748 EJ Eyre; 756 W Scott P 1850–73; 852/2 41–62 HT Ebsworth L; 1055 EJ Garnsey, 'History of Dubbo' vol 1; 1463 GB Worgan J & L
Bonwick Transcripts Boxes 51–4, Missionary vols 3–6
C213 A Phillip L 2 Jul 1788, 26 Jul 1790; 231 J Franklin L 15 Oct 1802; 339 W Thomas J c1849
CY2715 S Ryrie, 'Journal of a tour in the Southern Mountains', 1840
CYPOS 725 HM Chester L extracts 28 Jul 1869–1 Dec 1871 in FL Jardine Letterbook 1, Somerset
DGD E von Guerard sketches & n
DOC1784 T Hall Rem c1903
MSS130/2 HM Eastman Rem; 214 W Thomas P box 2; 259 F Bonney Rem; 315/44 Berry P incl H Hume, 'Journal of a journey made from Lake Bathurst to Pigeon House Mountain and North to the Shoalhaven'; 610 W Thomas P; 672 RJE Gormly P; 1007 Wall J 1844; 1192 J Russell P 1832–77 pt b; 1822 'Remarks on the Aborigines of NSW' c1820–30; 1863 C Henderson Rem; 2137 p549 A Carroll P
PICACC 450 WH Tietkins *Scrapbook*, Ayers Rock photo, Jul 1889
Q572.991/B M Bundock, 'Richmond River Blacks'
Safe 1/32a–d WH Hovell J & n on journeys 1824, 1826–7
ZA2188 G Arthur P re Aborigines; 7080–1 GA Robinson P vols 59–60, 1841–7 journeys
ZB505 J Gunther lecture c1843

Mortlock Library, State Library of South Australia, Adelaide
1046/2 W Finlayson Rem (c~ Tom Gara)
1170 CP Mountford collection
D2875 (L) G Deane D 1869
D6993 (L) D Daly D 1869

BIBLIOGRAPHY

PRG 175 419–22, 551–5 Angas P, J Menge L (c~ Bernie O'Neil)

PRG 294/2 WW Hoare D, n & photographs 1869–70

Museum of Victoria, Melbourne
J Bulmer P
AW Howitt P

National Archives of Australia, Canberra
A1640 1883/131 GB McMinn, 'Report on Exploration on Mary River', 26 Jan 1862

National Library of Australia, Canberra
Mfm M1172 JD Forbes D Jun–Jul 1830, Apr–May 1832
MS114 Franklin P, visits to NSW 1839, SA 1840–1; 351 AR Jones, 'Lake George' 1952 (for J Wild to C Throsby 28 Aug 1820); 689 C Throsby Smith J extracts Dec 1820; 727, 806 Gilmore P; 1217 Gould P, Elsey to Gould, 29 Sep 1857
Maps
G8981.G46 1832 (HOD) R Hoddle, 'Survey of Limestone Plains' [1832], 1911
G8981.G46 'Federal Territory Feature Map', 1915?
G8984.C3 CR Scrivener, 'Contour Survey for ... the Federal Capital', 1910
G8984.C3S1 R Dixon, 'Canberra: Molonglo' [1829], 1987
Oral History Unit
B Simpson & B Gammage, Drovers' Oral History Project interviews: M Core, Mt Fullstop Station, Cape York, 6 Oct 02; M Lines, Aileron Station, Alice Springs, 4 Apr 05; R Purvis, Woodgreen Station, central Australia, 5 Apr 05

Noel Butlin Archives, Australian National University, Canberra
1/256/3 (WP–F1a) AA Co P, G Fortey, R on Dunlop and Toorale back blocks, 5/8/1875 (c~ Jim Noble)

Northern Territory Archives, Darwin
F515 Exploration maps and plans of the NT 1860–1911, folders 18, 23

NTRS541/Pt1, PC5, WB Douglas D 1/1–31/12/1872

Northern Territory Library, Darwin
GW Goyder D 5/2–1/3/1869
DB Wiltshire D 1865
Map B1/2 Port Darwin 1869

Place Names Unit, Dept of Lands, Planning and Environment, Darwin
Diagram Book vol 1 1869, 5 Woods; 6 Woods; 10 Mitchell
FB 1869, 1A Woods; 4A Smith; 5A Harvey & King; L Knuckey; N Woods; P Woods; Q Aldridge; U King; X Smith; Woods 18 Mar 1869
FB 26 Mar 1869, Goyder (c~ Samantha Wells)
GW Goyder, 'Traverse on East Arm', 26 Mar 1869

Private possession
J Glover, *Catalogue of 68 Pictures ... of VDL*, London 1836 (Tim Bonyhady)
Letters and Journals of GF Moore (WA), ms 2001 (Jim Cameron)
'Lyndhurst' farm records, Kangaroo Island, 1951–84 (Ron & Jean Nunn)
SA Perry's Journal at Port Macquarie, 3 Nov 1830–9 Feb 1831 (Jillian Oppenheimer, Eric Rolls & Elaine van Kempen)
J von Sturmer, 'Aborigines and their environment ...', ms 1973?

Public Record Office of Victoria, Melbourne
VPRS 10 CCL R on Aborigines 3/1841/2032 Airey; 3/1841/2040 Addis; 4/1842/2357 Airey; 4/1842/2373 Addis; 5/1843/22 Powlett; 9/1848/2172 Thomas; 9/1848/2173 Parker; 11/1850/55 Thomas
VPRS 11 CCL R on Aborigines 4/147 Parker 1840; 7/292 Thomas 1840
VPRS 19 40/1075A T Townsend, 'Survey of the proposed line of road leading from Geelong towards Boninyon', 21 Oct 1840
VPRS 1189 CCL R on Aborigines 1/53 (1853–5)

VPRS 2891, 2893, 2894 Weekly R on Aborigines: Thomas 1856–60, 1850–1, 1856
VPRS 4410 R on Aborigines 2/47 Dredge 1839–40; 2/52–65 Parker 1839–50 & J; 3/66–112 Thomas 1839–48 & J
VPRS 4414 GA Robinson, 'Report on a journey . . . April–Oct 1844'

Queensland State Archives, Brisbane
SUR/A 91/5517 L re Cape York survey C153.301–2, 1890–1

South Australian Museum, Adelaide
M572.1 JF Forgeur, 'Aboriginal words, Woradgery tribe', nd, Tindale Collection (ref c~ Philip Clarke)

State Records of New South Wales, Sydney
Map 3643 (M595.2) R Dixon Molonglo River, May 1829
2/5000–2, 5063 R Hoddle FB 375–7, 443 1832–3, 1835
4/713.2 CCL R 1853; 719.2 Native Police 1840s–50s; 788.2 Ridley P 1871–5; Greenway 1873; 1141.2 Reserves for Aborigines 1848–9; 1146.4 CCL R 1851; 2219.1 Aborigines 1833–5; 2302.1 Aborigines 1836; 2433.1 Aborigines 1839; 2479.1 Aborigines 1840; 2831.1 Aborigines 1849; 7153 Robinson R 1842; Parker R 1845; Thomas J to Feb 1845; CCL R 1852; 8020.4 Aboriginal outrages 1830–1
COD 294A & B Supreme Court Miscellaneous Correspondence
Fiche 3271 C Throsby Smith J Dec 1820
Reels 46 A Cunningham J 1822–31; 3063 R Dixon L 1829, R Docker L 1829; 2624 FB J Meehan, J Oxley, W Harper; 3070 R Hoddle L 1828, C Hodgkinson R Apr 1841

State Records of South Australia, Adelaide
GRG 35/: 8 NT Survey Expedition Monthly R 1868–70 (c~ Samantha Wells); 256 GW Goyder FB 1862, 1869; 256 vol 2, JWO Bennett Plan, Escape Cliff to Anson Bay, 1865–9 (c~ Samantha Wells); 655 GW Goyder D 1869

Tasmanian Museum and Art Gallery, Hobart
AG3318 J Glover Sketch Book 97, 1832+ (c~ David Hansen)

2 Newspapers, Parliamentary Papers and published maps

Maps
T Ham, *A Map of Australia Felix*, Melbourne 1847
D Kraehenbuehl et al, *Forests & Woodlands of the Adelaide Plains in 1836*, Adelaide 2000
——, *Woodlands & Shrublands of the Southern Adelaide Region in 1836*, Adelaide 2001

Newspapers
Argus, 6 Feb 1861 (Macpherson)
Bendigo Advertiser, 7 Mar 1861 (Macpherson)
Port Phillip Gazette, 29 Nov, 1 Dec 1849 (Beilby) (c~ Leith MacGillivray)
Sydney Gazette, 24 Aug 1803, 5 Oct 1836
Sydney Mail, 10 Jul 1880 p 56 (Leycester)
SMH, 6 p4 & 10 pp4–5 Jan 1862 (c~ Leith MacGillivray)
Sydney Truth Jun–Jul 1927 (Govett)

Parliamentary Papers
Great Britain, House of Commons
Aborigines 1839/34; 1844/34
Transportation 1812/341

NSW
1845 *RSC on the Aborigines*

Queensland
1868/519–23 HG Simpson, *General R on the settlement of Somerset*
1868/525–6 —— *Further paper respecting the General R on the settlement of Somerset*
1881 2/229–74 RL Jack, *R on explorations in Cape York Peninsula 1879–80*

South Australia
156/1857–8 S Hack, *Explorations* 1857
25&151/1858 BH Babbage & PE Warburton, *Northern Explorations* 1858

165/1860 *RSC on the Aborigines*
219/1862 JM Stuart, *J* 4 Nov—18 Dec 1859
21/1863 JM Stuart, *J* 20 Dec 1861—10 Dec 1862 & map
31, 157, 161, 204/1869–70 GW Goyder, *R & map Port Darwin and vicinity*
32/1870–1 *Northern Territory Survey, Surveyors' Descriptions*
67/1875 *Mr J Ross's Explorations, 1874*
114/1875 JW Lewis, *R on Lake Eyre Expedition 1874–5*
19/1876 *J of Mr Lewis's Lake Eyre Expedition 1874–5*
22/1876 *Giles's Explorations 1875*
111/1890 WH Tietkins, *J of the Central Australian Exploring Expedition*
43/1904 WR Murray, *R etc re exploration trip of RT Maurice from Fowler's Bay to Rawlinson Ranges and from Fowler's Bay to Cambridge Gulf*, 1901 and 1902
54/1904 LA Wells & FR George, *R on prospecting . . . in the Musgrave, Mann and Tomkinson Ranges*
27/1905 AA Davidson, *J of explorations in Central Australia*

Victoria
LC 1858–9 *RSC on the Aborigines*

Western Australia
2/1902 FS Brockman, *R on Exploration of the North-West Kimberley 1901*

3 Published sources and theses

Abbott, WE, *Essays: Political and scientific*, Sydney 1890
——, 'Notes of a journey on the Darling', *JRSNSW* 15, 1881, 81–109
Allen, H, '19th c. faunal change in western N.S.W. and N-W Victoria', Auckland Uni Anthrop working P 64, Apr 1983
——, 'The Bagundji of the Darling Basin: Cereal gatherers in an uncertain environment', *World Arch* 5, 1974, 309–22
——, 'Where the Crow Flies Backwards: Man and Land in the Darling Basin', ANU Anth PhD 1972
Allen, J et al (eds), *Sunda and Sahul*, London 1977
Allen, J & Corris, P (eds), *The Journal of John Sweatman*, St Lucia 1977
Allen, LA, *Time Before Morning*, New York 1975
Allen, MR, *Case Studies of . . . Back Yamma, Euglo South and Strahorn State Forests*, State Forests of NSW 1998
Amadio, N & Kimber, R, *Wildbird Dreaming*, Melbourne 1988
Anderson, A et al (eds), *Histories of Old Ages: Essays in honour of Rhys Jones*, Canberra 2001
Anderson, CA & Ladiges, PY, 'A comparison of three populations of *Eucalyptus obliqua* . . . growing on acid and calcareous soils in southern Victoria', *AJBot* 26, 1978, 93–109
Anderson, H, 'The place for a township: John Helder Wedge at Port Phillip in 1835', *Vic Hist Mag* 41, 1970, 351–9
Anderson, S, *Pelletier*, Melbourne 2009
Andrews, AEJ, *A Journey from Sydney to the Australian Alps by Dr John Lhotsky*, Hobart 1979
——, *Earliest Monaro and Burragorang*, Canberra 1998
——, *Kosciusko: The mountain in history*, Canberra 1991
——, *Stapylton with Major Mitchell's Australia Felix Expedition 1836*, Hobart 1986
—— (ed), *The Devil's Wilderness: George Caley's Journey to Mt Banks 1804*, Hobart 1964
——, 'The three land excursions of Governor Phillip', *JRAHS* 85, 1999, 148–70
Andrews, P, *Back from the Brink*, Sydney 2006
——, *Beyond the Brink*, Sydney 2008
Anell, B, 'Hunting and trapping methods in Australia and Oceania', *Studia Ethnographica Upsaliensa* 18, 1960, 1–23
Angas, GF, *Savage Life and Scenes in Australia and NZ* [1847a], New York 1968
——, *South Australia Illustrated*, London 1847b
Angus, JC & Forster, HW, *The Ovens Valley*, Melbourne 1970

Anon, *Australia: Its scenery, natural history and resources*, London 1854?
Anon, 'Darke's Peak', *PRGSA SA* 19, 1918, 154–62
Aplin, G (ed), *A Difficult Infant: Sydney before Macquarie*, Sydney 1988
Argue, D, 'Aboriginal occupation of the Southern Highlands: Was it really seasonal?', *Aust Arch* 41, 1995, 30–36
Armstrong, PH, 'The Aboriginal practice of firing the bush', *Early Days (JRWAHS)* 8, 1978, 31–4
Armstrong, REM, *The Kalkadoons*, Brisbane nd
Arthur, E, *A Journal of Events* [c1844], Hobart 1975
Ashton, DH, 'The development of even-aged stands of *Eucalyptus regnans*...', *AJBot* 24, 1976, 397–414
Ashwin, AC, 'From South Australia to Port Darwin with sheep and horses in 1870–71', *JRGSA SA* 32, 1930–31, 47–93
Atahan, P et al, 'A fine-resolution Pliocene pollen and charcoal record from Yallalie, south-western Australia', *J Biogeog* 31, 2004, 199–205
Atkinson, A, *Camden*, Melbourne 1988
Atkinson, J, *An Account of the State of Agriculture and Grazing in NSW* [1826], Sydney 1975
Attenbrow, V, *Sydney's Aboriginal Past*, Sydney 2002
—— & Steele, D, 'Fishing in Port Jackson', *Antiquity* 69, 1995, 47–60
Attiwill, PM et al, 'Nutrient cycling in a *Eucalyptus obliqua*... forest', *AJBot* 26, 1978, 79–91
Aurousseau, M, *The Letters of F.W. Ludwig Leichhardt*, vols 2–3, Hakluyt Society 134–5, Cambridge 1968
Austin, R, *Journal of Assistant Surveyor R. Austin*, Perth 1855
Australian Dictionary of Biography [ADB], Canberra
Avery, S, 'Aboriginal and European encounters in the Canberra region', ANU Arch BA Hons 1994

Backhouse, J, *A Narrative of a Visit to the Australian Colonies* [1843], New York 1967
Baker, D, *The Civilised Surveyor. Thomas Mitchell and the Australian Aborigines*, Melbourne 1997
Baker, L (comp), *Mingkiri*, Alice Springs 1996
Baker, R, *Land is Life... The Story of the Yanyuwa People*, Sydney 1999
Balmer, J, 'Two moorland boundaries', *Tasforests* 2, 1990, 133–41
Banks, JCG, 'The use of dendrochronology in the interpretation of the dynamics of the Snow Gum forest', ANU Forestry PhD 1982
——, 'Trees: the silent fire historians', *Bogong* 18, 1997, 9–12
Banks, MR (ed), *The Lake Country of Tasmania*, Hobart 1973
—— & Kirkpatrick, JB (eds), *Landscape and Man*, Hobart 1977
Barker, M, 'Effects of fire on the floristic composition, structure and flammability of rainforest vegetation', *Tasforests* 2, 1990, 117–20
——, *The Effect of Fire on West Coast Lowland Rainforest*, Hobart 1991
Barker, WR & Greenslade, PJM (eds), *Evolution of the Flora and Fauna of Arid Australia*, Adelaide 1982
Barlow, BA (ed), *Flora and Fauna of Alpine Australasia*, Melbourne 1986
Barnard, A (ed), *The Simple Fleece*, Melbourne 1962
Barr, N & Cary, J, *Greening a Brown Land: the Australian Search for Sustainable Land Use*, Melbourne 1992
Barrow, J, 'State of the Colony of Swan River, 1 Jan 1830', *JRGS* 1, 1831, 1–16
Basedow, H, 'Journal of the Government North-West Expedition... 1903', *JRGSA SA* 15, 1913, 57–242
——, 'Narrative of an expedition of exploration in north western Australia', *JRGSA SA* 18, 1916, 105–295
Bates, D, *Aboriginal Perth*, Perth 1992
——, *The Native Tribes of Western Australia*, Canberra 1985

Batman, J, *The Settlement of Port Phillip* [1856], Melbourne 1985
Bauman, T, *Aboriginal Darwin*, Canberra 2006
Bayly, I, *Rock of Ages*, Perth 1999
Beaglehole, JC (ed), *The Journals of Captain James Cook*, Cambridge 1961
Beard, JS, *The Vegetation of the Perth Area*, Perth 1979
Beaton, JM, 'Fire and water: aspects of Australian Aboriginal management of cycads', *Arch in Oceania* 17, 1982, 51–6
Beck, W & Balme, J, 'Dry rainforests: a productive habitat for Australian hunter-gatherers', *Aust Ab Stud* 2003/2, 4–20
Beckler, H, *Journey to Cooper's Creek*, Melbourne 1993
Bekle, H & Gentilli, J, 'History of the Perth lakes', *Early Days (JRWAHS)* 10, 1993, 442–60
Bellwood, P, *First Farmers*, Melbourne 2005
Bennett, G, *Gatherings of a Naturalist*, London 1860
——, *Wanderings in New South Wales* [1834], Adelaide 1967
Bennett, G, *The Port Stephens Blacks*, Dungog 1934
Bennett, KH, 'Remarks on the decay of certain species of Eucalypt', *Proc Linn Soc NSW* (2nd series), 1885, 453–4
Bennett, M, 'For a labourer worthy of his hire: Aboriginal economic responses ... in the Shoalhaven and Illawarra, 1770–1900', U Can Hist PhD 2003
Benson, DH & Howell, J, 'Sydney's vegetation 1788–1988', *Proc Ecol Soc Aust* 16, 1990, 115–27
——, *Taken for Granted*, Sydney 1995
Benson, JS & Redpath, PA, 'The nature of pre-European native vegetation in south-eastern Australia', *Cunninghamia* 5, 1997, 285–328
Bern, J & Larbalestier, J, 'Rival constructions of traditional Aboriginal ownership in the Limmen Bight land claim', *Oceania* 56, 1985, 56–76

Berndt, RM, *Aboriginal Sites, Rights and Resource Development*, Perth 1982
—— (ed), *Australian Aboriginal Anthropology*, Perth 1970
Berndt, RM & CH (eds), *Aboriginal Man in Australia*, Sydney 1965
——, *Aborigines of the West*, Perth 1979
——, *Arnhem Land: Its History and People*, Melbourne 1954
——, *A World That Was*, Melbourne 1993
——, *Pioneers and Settlers. The Aboriginal Australians*, Melbourne 1978
——, *The Speaking Land: Myth and Story in Aboriginal Australia*, Penguin 1989
——, *The World of the First Australians*, Canberra 1996
Berry, SL & Roderick, ML, 'CO_2 and land-use effects on Australian vegetation over the last two centuries', *AJBot* 50, 2002, 511–31
Bethell, LS, *The Story of Port Dalrymple*, Hobart 1980
Beveridge, P, 'Of the Aborigines inhabiting the great lacustrine and riverine depression of the lower Murray, lower Murrumbidgee, lower Lachlan, and lower Darling', *JRSNSW* 17, 1883, 19–74
——, *The Aborigines of Victoria and Riverina*, Melbourne 1889
Bickford, S & Mackey, B, 'Reconstructing pre-impact vegetation cover in modified landscapes ... in the Fleurieu Peninsula, SA', *J Biogeog* 31, 2004, 787–806
Billis, RV & Kenyon, AS, *Pastures New*, Melbourne 1930
Billot, CP, *John Batman*, Melbourne 1979
——, *John Pascoe Fawkner*, Melbourne 1985
—— (ed), *Melbourne's Missing Chronicle*, Melbourne 1982
Binks, CJ, *Explorers of Western Tasmania*, Launceston 1989
Bird, DW et al, 'Aboriginal burning regimes and hunting strategies in Australia's western desert', *Human Ecol* 33, 2005, 443–64
Bird, RB et al, 'The 'fire stick farming' hypothesis...', *PNAS* 105(39), 2008, 14796–14801

Birrell, WK, *The Manning Valley. Landscape and Settlement 1824–1900*, Brisbane 1987

Bischoff, J, *Sketch of the History of VDL* [1832], Adelaide 1967

Black, JM, *Flora of South Australia*, Adelaide 1922

Black, L, 'Aboriginal fisheries of Brewarrina', *Wild Life*, April 1944, 105–7

Black, MP & Mooney, SD, 'The response of Aboriginal burning practices to population levels... Sydney Basin', *Aust Geog* 38, 2007, 37–52

Blackburn, D, 'Letters of David Blackburn', *JRAHS* 20, 1934–5, 318–34

Blackwood, R, *The Whitsunday Islands*, Rockhampton 1997

Blainey, G, *Triumph of the Nomads*, Melbourne 1975

Bland, W (ed), *Journey of Discovery to Port Phillip... in 1824 and 1825* [1831], Adelaide 1965

Blandowski, W, 'Recent discoveries in natural history on the Lower Murray', *Trans Phil Inst Vic* 2, Jan–Dec 1857, 124–37

Blaskett, BA, 'The Aboriginal response to white settlement in the Port Phillip District 1835–1850', UMelb Hist MA 1979

Blay, J, *Bega Valley Region Old Path Ways Mapping Project*, Bega 2005

——, 'Pathways of the ancestors', *Aust Geographic* 92, 2008, 44–5

Bluett, WP, 'Canberra's Blacks in early settlement days', *SMH* 21 May, 2 Jun 1927

——, 'The Aborigines of the Canberra district at the arrival of the white man', *Canberra Hist Soc*, 29 May 1954

Bolam, AG, *The Trans-Australian Wonderland*, Melbourne 1923

Boldrewood, R [TA Browne], 'A Kangaroo Drive', *Cornhill Mag* 14, 1866, 735–46

——, *Old Melbourne Memories* [1884], Melbourne 1969

Bolger, P, *Hobart Town*, Canberra 1973

Bolton, BL & Latz, P, 'The Western Hare-wallaby... in the Tanami Desert', *Aust Wildlife Res* 5, 1978, 285–93

Bonney, F, 'On some customs of the Aborigines of the River Darling, New South Wales', *JRAI* 13, 1883, 122–37

Bonwick, J, *Daily Life and Origin of the Tasmanians*, London 1870

——, *Discovery and Settlement of Port Phillip*, Melbourne 1856

——, *Port Phillip Settlement*, London 1883

Bonyhady, T, *The Colonial Earth*, Melbourne 2000

—— & Griffiths, T (eds), *Prehistory to Politics*, Melbourne 1996

——, *Words for Country*, Sydney 2002

Booth, EC, *Australia in the 1870s*, Melbourne 1875?

Border, A & Rowland, MJ, *The Mitchell Grass Downs*, Brisbane 1990

Borschmann, G (ed), *The People's Forest*, Blackheath 1999

Bossence, WH, *Numurkah*, Melbourne 1979

Bottoms, T, *Djabugay Country*, Sydney 1999

Bowdler, S, 'Hunters and farmers in the Hunter Islands', *Rec QV Mus Launceston* 70, 1980, 1–17

——, 'Hunters in the highlands: Aboriginal adaptations in the eastern Australian uplands', *Arch in Oceania* 16, 1981, 99–111

Bowen, GF, 'On the new settlement in Rockingham Bay', *JRGS* 35, 1865, 191–212

Bowman, DMJS, *Australian Rainforests*, Cambridge 2000a

——, 'Evidence for gradual retreat of dry monsoon forests under a regime of Aboriginal burning, Karslake Peninsula, Melville Island, northern Australia', *ProcRSQld* 102, 1992, 25–30

——, 'Future eating and country keeping: what role has environmental history in the management of biodiversity?', *J Biogeog* 28, 2001, 549–64

——, 'Rainforests and flame forests', *Aust Geog Stud* 38, 2000b, 327–31

——, 'The impact of Aboriginal landscape burning on the Australian biota', *New Phytol* 140, 1998, 385–410

——, 'Two examples of the role of ecological biogeography in Australian prehistory', *Aust Arch* 41, 1995, 8–11

—— & Brown, MJ, 'Bushfires in Tasmania: a botanical approach to anthropological questions', *Arch in Oceania* 21, 1986, 166–71

——, & Jackson, WD, 'Vegetation succession in south-west Tasmania', *Search* 12, 1981, 358–62

——, & Panton, WJ, 'Decline of *Callitris intratropica*... in the Northern Territory', *J Biogeog* 20, 1993, 373–81

—— & Prior, LD, 'Impact of Aboriginal landscape burning on woody vegetation... in Arnhem Land', *J Biogeog* 31, 2004, 807–17

—— et al, 'Forest expansion and grassland contraction within a Eucalyptus savanna matrix... in the Australian monsoon tropics', *Global Ecol & Biogeog* 10, 2001, 535–48

——, 'Landscape analysis of Aboriginal fire management in Central Arnhem Land', *J Biogeog* 31, 2004, 207–23

——, 'Seasonal patterns in biomass smoke pollution... in northern Australia', *Global Ecol and Biogeog* 16, 2007, 246–56

Boyce, J, *Van Diemen's Land*, Melbourne 2008

Boyd, WE et al, 'The "Grasses" of the Big Scrub District, North-eastern NSW', *Aust Geog* 30, 1999, 331–6

Boys, RD, *First Years at Port Phillip*, Melbourne 1935

Bradley, J, '"Same time poison, same time good tucker...": a discussion of the social, economic and historical importance of the cycad palm in the south west Gulf of Carpentaria', ms, Brisbane 2001

Bradley, W, *A Voyage to New South Wales*, Sydney 1969

Bradstock, RA et al (eds), *Flammable Australia*, Cambridge 2002

——, 'Which mosaic?', *Wildlife Research* 32, 2005, 409–23

Braithwaite, RW, 'Aboriginal fire regimes of monsoonal Australia in the 19th century', *Search* 22, 1991, 247–9

Bray, J, 'Tribal districts and customs', *Science of Man* 4, 1901, 9–10

Brayshaw, H, *Aborigines of the Hunter Valley*, Scone 1986

Brennan, M, *Australian Reminiscences*, Sydney 1907

Breton, WH, 'Excursion to the Western Range, Tasmania', *Tas J Nat Sci* 2, 1844, 121–141

——, *Excursions in NSW, WA & VDL 1830–33*, London 1834

Bride, TF (ed), *Letters from Victorian Pioneers* [1898], Melbourne 1983

Brine, M, 'Aboriginal long-distance trading: an economic analysis centred on South Australia', Adel Hist Hons 1983

Brisbane Retrospect: Eight Aspects of Brisbane History, Brisbane 1978

Brock, DG, *To the Desert with Sturt*, Adelaide 1975

Brodribb, WA, *Recollections of an Australian Squatter* [1883], Melbourne 1976

Brody, H, *The Other Side of Eden*, London 2001

Brooker, I & Kleinig, D, *Eucalyptus*, Sydney 1999

Broome, R, *The Victorians, Arriving*, Sydney 1984

Brown, MJ, 'The distribution and conservation of King Billy Pine', Hobart, 1998

—— & Podger, FD, 'Floristics and fire regimes of a vegetation sequence from sedgeland-heath to rainforest at Bathurst Harbour, Tasmania', *AJBot* 30, 1982a, 659–76

——, 'On the apparent anomaly between observed and predicted percentages of vegetation types in South West Tasmania', *AJEcol* 7, 1982b, 203–5

——, et al, 'Vascular plants of the Denison Range and Vale of Rasselas', *Tas Naturalist* Nov 1982, 2–6

Brown, PL (ed), *Clyde Company Papers*, Oxford 1952–71

——, *Memoirs... by Foster Fyans*, Geelong 1986

——, *Narrative of George Russell*, London 1938

——, *The Todd Journal*, Geelong 1989

Brown, R, 'General view of the botany of the vicinity of Swan River', *JRGS* 1, 1830–1, 17–21

Browne, J, 'The Aborigines of Australia', *Canadian Mag* 3, 1856, 251–71

Brownlea, SJ, 'The Pre-European Vegetation of the Ulverstone Region', Tas Geog Hons 1999

Bryce, S, *Women's Gathering and Hunting in the Pitjantjatjara Homelands*, Alice Springs 1992

Buchanan, A, 'Diary of a journey overland', *PRGSA SA* 24, 1922, 51–76

Buchhorn, M, *Emigrants to Hahndorf*, Adelaide 1989

Bulmer, J, 'Some account of the Aborigines', *Trans RGSVic* 5(1), 1887, 15–43

Bunbury, WS & Morrell, WP (eds), *Early Days in Western Australia*, London 1930

Bunce, D, *Twenty-three Years' Wanderings in the Australias and Tasmania*, Geelong 1857

Burbidge, AA et al, 'Aboriginal knowledge of the mammals of the central deserts of Australia', *Aust Wildlife Res* 15, 1988, 9–39

——, 'Vanishing desert mammals', *Landscape* 2, 1987, 7–12

Burbidge, NT, 'Ecological succession observed during regeneration of Triodia pungens, R.Br. after burning', *JRSWA* 28, 1943, 149–56

Burn, D, *Narrative of the Overland Journey of Sir John and Lady Franklin . . .* [1842], Sydney 1955

Burns, TE & Skemp, JR, 'VDL correspondents', *Rec QV Mus Launceston* 14NS, 1961

Burrell, JP, 'Vegetation of the Sydney area: 1788 and 1961', *Proc Ecol Soc Aust* 7, 1972, 71–8

Burrows, ND, 'A fire for all reasons' and 'Seasoned with fire', in D Gough (ed), *Fire. The Force of Life*, Perth 2000, 14–26

—— & Abbott, I (eds), *Fire in South-Western Australian Ecosystems*, Leiden 2003

——, et al, 'Evidence of altered fire regimes in the Western Desert region of Australia', *Conservation Science WA* 5, 2006, 272–84

——, 'Nyaruninpa: Pintupi burning in the Australian Western Desert', *Native Solutions Symposium*, Hobart 2000, 1–7

Butlin, NG, *Economics and the Dreamtime*, Cambridge 1993

——, 'Macassans and Aboriginal smallpox', *Hist Stud* 84, 1985, 315–35

——, *Our Original Aggression*, Sydney 1983

Byerley, FJ (ed), *Narrative of the Overland Expedition of the Messrs Jardine from Rockhampton to Cape York* [1867], Bundaberg 1995

Byrne, DR, *The Aboriginal and Archaeological Significance of the NSW Rainforests*, Sydney 1987

—— (ed), *The Five Forests*, Sydney 1983

——, *The Mountains Call Me Back*, Sydney 1984

Calder, G, 'Levee, Line and Martial Law', Tas Hist PhD 2009

Calder, JE, 'Some account of the country lying between Lake St Clair and Macquarie Harbour', *Tas J Nat Sci* 3, 1849, 415–29

Calder, WB, 'A history of the Mornington Peninsula as it relates to vegetation', *Vic Hist J* 45, 1974, 5–29

Cambage, RH, *Captain Cook's Pigeon House and Early South Coast Exploration*, Sydney 1916

——, 'Exploration between the Wingecarribee, Shoalhaven, Macquarie and Murrumbidgee Rivers', *JRAHS* 7, 1921, 217–88

——, 'Exploration beyond the Upper Nepean in 1798', *JRAHS* 6, 1920, 1–36

——, 'Notes on the native flora of NSW. Part VII. Eastern Monaro', *Proc Linn Soc NSW* 34, 1909, 310–339

——, 'Notes on the native flora of NSW. Part X. The Federal Capital Territory', *Proc Linn Soc NSW* 43, 1918, 673–711

——, 'Notes on the native flora of tropical Queensland', *JRSNSW* 49, 1915, 389–447

Cameron, ALP, 'Notes on some tribes of NSW', *JRAI* 14, 1885, 344–70

——, 'Notes on a tribe speaking the "Boontha-Mura" language', *Science of Man* 7, 1904, 91–2

Cameron, JMR, *Ambition's Fire*, Perth 1981

—— (ed), *Letters from Port Essington 1838–1845*, Darwin 1999
Cameron, M, *Guide to Flowers and Plants of Tasmania*, Sydney 1994
Camm, JCR & McQuilton, J (eds), *Australians: A historical atlas*, Sydney 1987
Campbell, AH, 'Discovering Batman's Port Phillip exploration', *Vic Hist J* 62, 1991, 98–106
——, 'Elementary food production by the Australian Aborigines', *Mankind* 6, 1965, 206–11, 288
——, *John Batman and the Aborigines*, Melbourne 1987
Campbell, J, *The Early Settlement of Queensland*, Ipswich 1875
Campbell, J, *Invisible Invaders*, Melbourne 2002
——, 'Smallpox in Aboriginal Australia', *Hist Stud* 84, 1985, 336–58
Campbell, JF, 'Historical notes on Government House Domain, Sydney', *JRAHS* 17, 1931, 111–26.
——, 'John Howe's exploratory journey from Windsor to the Hunter River in 1819', *JRAHS* 14, 1928, 232–41
——, 'The early history of Sydney University grounds', *JRAHS* 16, 1930, 274–92
——, 'The valley of the Tank Stream', *JRAHS* 10, 1921, 63–103
Campbell, TD et al, 'The Aborigines of the lower south-east of South Australia', *Rec SA Mus* 8, 1946, 445–501
Campbell, V, 'A field study of shell middens of the lower Macleay Valley', UNE Hist Hons, 1969
——, 'The coastal archaeology of the Fleurieu Peninsula', Flinders Arch MA, 1988
Cane, S, *Pila Nguru: The Spinifex People*, Fremantle 2002
Cannon, M (ed), *Historical Records of Victoria*, Melbourne. Vol 1 (P Jones, ed, 1981); 2A (I Macfarlane, ed, 1982); 2B (I Macfarlane, ed, 1983); 3 (M Cannon & I Macfarlane, eds, 1984); 5 (M Cannon & I Macfarlane, eds, 1988)

Carnegie, D, *Spinifex and Sand* [1898], Melbourne 1973
Carnegie, M, *Friday Mount*, Melbourne 1973
Carr, DJ & SGM (eds), *People and Plants in Australia*, Sydney 1981
Carr, SGM & DJ, 'Oil glands in the bark of Victorian eucalypts', *Vic Nat* 87, 1970, 120–6
Carron, W, *Narrative of an Expedition under . . . Kennedy* [1849], Adelaide 1965
Caruana, W & Lendon, N (eds), *The Painters of the Wagilag Sisters Story 1937–97*, Canberra 1997
Cary, G et al, *Australia Burning*, Canberra 2003
Caughley, G et al, 'Does dingo predation control the densities of kangaroos and emus?', *Aust Wildlife Res* 7, 1980, 1–12
Cawood, M, 'Unconventional water management that really works', *Aust Farm J*, Sept 1994, 74–7
Cawthorne, WA, 'Rough notes on the manners and customs of the natives', *JRGSA SA* 27, 1926, 47–77
Chapman, HS, *The New Settlement of Australind*, London 1841
Chapman, V & Read, P (eds), *Terrible Hard Biscuits*, Sydney 1996
Charlesworth, M et al, *Ancestor Spirits*, Geelong 1990
Chatwin, B, *The Songlines*, London 1987
Chisholm, AH, 'How and when the lyrebird was discovered', *Emu* 55, 1955a, 1–15
——, *Strange New World*, Sydney 1955b
Christie, EM (ed), 'The discovery of the Adelaide River', *JRGSA SA* 47, 1945, 44–53
Christie, MF, *Aborigines in Colonial Victoria*, Sydney 1979
Clancy, R, *The Mapping of Terra Australis*, Sydney 1995
Clark, D (ed), *Charles von Hugel: New Holland Journal 1833–4*, Melbourne 1994
Clark, I (ed), *Aboriginal Languages and Clans . . . Western and Central Victoria*, Monash Pubs in Geog 37, 1990

——, *The Journals of George Augustus Robinson*, Melbourne 1998
Clark, J, *The Aboriginal People of Tasmania*, Hobart 1986
Clark, RL, 'Pollen and charcoal evidence for the effects of Aboriginal burning on the vegetation of Australia', *Arch in Oceania* 18, 1983, 32–7
Clark, SS & McLoughlin, LC, 'Historical and biological evidence for fire regimes in the Sydney region', *Aust Geog* 17, 1986, 101–12
Clarke, PA, 'Aboriginal use of plant exudates', *J Anth Soc SA* 24/3, 1986a, 3–18
——, 'Aboriginal uses of plants as medicines', *J Anth Soc SA* 25/5, 1987, 3–23
——, 'Adelaide Aboriginal cosmology', *J Anth Soc SA* 28/1, 1990, 1–10
——, 'Contact, conflict, and regeneration: Aboriginal cultural geography of the Lower Murray, South Australia', Adelaide Geog & Anth PhD 1994
——, 'Fruits and seeds as food for South Australian Aborigines', *J Anth Soc SA* 23/9, 1985a, 9–22
——, 'Spirit beings and the Aboriginal landscape of the Lower Murray', *Rec SA Mus* 31, 1999, 149–63
——, 'The Aboriginal cosmic landscape of southern South Australia', *Rec SA Mus* 29, 1997, 125–45
——, 'The importance of roots and tubers as a food source for southern South Australian Aborigines', *J Anth Soc SA* 23/7, 1985b, 2–14
——, 'The study of ethnobotany in southern South Australia', *Aust Ab Stud* 1986b/2, 40–47
——, *Where the Ancestors Walked*, Sydney 2003
Clarke, PJ & Knox, KJE, 'Post-fire response of shrubs in the tablelands of eastern Australia', *AJBot* 50, 2002, 53–62
Clarke, S, 'The Creation of the Torrens: A History of Adelaide's River to 1881', Adel Hist MA 2004
Clarke, WB, *Researches in the Southern Gold Fields of NSW*, Sydney 1860

Cleland, JB, 'Some aspects of the ecology of the Aboriginal inhabitants of Tasmania and southern Australia', *Tas J Nat Sci* 74, 1939, 1–18
—— & Johnston, TH, 'Notes on native names and uses of plants in the Musgrave Ranges region', *Oceania* 8, 1937, 208–15; 8, 1938, 328–42
Clendinnen, I, *Dancing with Strangers*, Melbourne 2003
Cobley, J, *Sydney Cove 1791–1792*, Sydney 1965
Colhoun, EA, 'Field problems of radiocarbon dating in Tasmania', *PPRSTas* 120, 1986, 1–6
Collett, B, *Wednesdays Closest to the Full Moon: A History of South Gippsland*, Melbourne 1994
Collins, D, *An Account of the English Colony in New South Wales* [1798], Sydney 1975
Collins, P, *Burn: The epic story of bushfire in Australia*, Sydney 2006
Colville, BH, *Robert Hoddle, Pioneer Surveyor*, Melbourne 2004
Cook, J, *An Account of a Voyage Round the World . . .* [1773], Brisbane 1969
Cornell, C (trans), *The Journal of Post Captain Nicholas Baudin*, Adelaide 1974
——, *Voyage of Discovery to the Southern Lands*, 2 vols, Adelaide 2006 & 2003
Corris, P, *Aborigines and Europeans in Western Victoria*, Canberra 1968
Cosgrove, R, *The Archaeological Resources of Tasmanian Forests: Aboriginal Use . . .*, Hobart 1990
—— et al, 'Late Pleistocene human occupation in Tasmania: a reply to Thomas', *Aust Arch* 38, 1994, 28–35
Costin, AB, *A Study of the Ecosystems of the Monaro Region*, Sydney 1954
Cottesloe, L (ed), *Diary and Letters of Admiral C.H. Fremantle* [1928], Fremantle 1979
Coutts, PJF, 'The Victorian Archaeological Survey Activities Report 1977/78', *Rec Vic Arch Survey* 8, July 1978, 1–23
—— et al, 'Aboriginal engineers of the Western District, Victoria', *Rec Vic Arch Survey* 7, 1978, 1–47

BIBLIOGRAPHY

Cox, K, *Angus McMillan, Pathfinder* [1973], Melbourne 1984
Crane, WJB, 'Nutrient mobility and leaching in forest soils' in CSIRO, *Nutrient Cycling in Indigenous Forest Systems*, Perth 1977, 87–93
Craven, B, 'The Subalpine Grasslands of Paradise Plains, Northeast Tasmania', Tas Geog BA Hons 1997
Crawford, G et al, *The Diaries of John Helder Wedge*, Hobart 1962
Crosby, AW, *Ecological Imperialism*, Cambridge 1991
Cross, J (ed), *Journals of Several Expeditions Made in Western Australia* [1833], Perth 1980
Crowley, GM & Garnett, ST, 'Changing fire management in the pastoral lands of Cape York...', *Aust Geog Stud* 38, 2000, 10–26
——, 'Vegetation change in the grasslands and grassy woodlands of east-central Cape York Peninsula, Australia', *Pacific Conservation Biology* 4, 1998, 132–48
Cubit, S, '"Burning back with the snow": traditional approaches to grassland management in Tasmania', *Aust Geog Stud* 34, 1996, 216–24
Cunningham, P, *Two Years in New South Wales*, 2 vols, London 1827
Curr, EM, *Recollections of Squatting in Victoria* [1883], Adelaide 1968
—— (ed), *The Australian Race*, 4 vols, Melbourne 1886
Currey, JEB (ed), *George Caley: Reflections on the Colony of NSW*, Melbourne 1966
——, *Memoir of a Chart of Port Philip*, Melbourne 1987
Dale, R, *Descriptive Account of the Panoramic View of King George's Sound*, London 1834
Daley, C, 'Count Paul Edmund Strzelecki', *Vic Hist Mag* 19, 1941, 41–53
Daly, TJ, 'Elements of the Past. An Environmental History of the Blue Mountains, Australia', Sydney Hist PhD 2000
Daniels, C & Tait, C (eds), *Adelaide: Nature of a City*, Adelaide 2006

Dargavel, J (ed), *Australia's Everchanging Forests 3*, Canberra 1997
——, & Feary, S (eds), *Australia's Everchanging Forests 2*, Canberra 1993
——, et al (eds), *Australia's Ever-changing Forests V*, Canberra 2002
——, et al (eds), *Perfumed Pineries*, Canberra 2001
Dargin, P, *Aboriginal Fisheries of the Darling–Barwon Rivers*, Brewarrina 1976
Darwin, C, *The Voyage of the Beagle* [1845], London 1968
Davidson, DS, 'The family hunting territory in Australia', *Am Anth* 30, 1928, 614–31
Davies, CL et al, *Perennial grain crops for high water use*, RIRDC 05/024, Canberra 2005
Davis, SL & Prescott, JRV, *Aboriginal Frontiers and Boundaries in Australia*, Melbourne 1992
Dawson, J, *Australian Aborigines* [1881], Canberra 1981
Dawson, R, *The Present State of Australia* [1830], Alburgh UK 1987
de Graaf, M, 'Nintirringu: the role of knowledge in traditional Aboriginal Australia', ms 1984
De La Rue, K, 'An Historical Geography of Darwin to 1874', NTU Hist Grad D 1999
——, *An Historical Geography of Darwin*, Darwin 1988
de Quincey, E, *The History of Mount Wellington*, Hobart 1987
de Satge, O, *Pages from the Journal of a Queensland Squatter*, London 1901
de Vries-Evans, S, *Historic Sydney*, Sydney 1987
Denny, MJS, 'Historical and ecological study of the effects of European settlement on inland NSW', *Report* to Heritage Council of NSW [1987], Sydney 1992
Devereux, MG, 'A Growing Understanding of Van Diemen's Land', Tas CAE Hist BEd 1979
Devitt, J, 'Fraser Island: Aboriginal resources and settlement pattern', UQ Anth Hons 1979
Dexter, D, *The ANU Campus*, Canberra 1991
Diamond, J, *Guns, Germs and Steel*, London 1998

Dickey, B & Howell, P (eds), *South Australia's Foundation: Select Documents*, Adelaide 1986
Dingle, T, *Aboriginal Economy*, Melbourne 1988
——, *The Victorians, Settling*, Sydney 1984
Dix, WC & Lofgren, ME, 'Kurumi: Possible Aboriginal incipient agriculture associated with a stone arrangement', *Rec WA Mus* 3, 1974, 73–7
Dixon, RMW et al, *Australian Aboriginal Words in English*, Oxford 1992
Dixson, S, 'The effects of settlement and pastoral occupation in Australia upon the indigenous vegetation', *TransRSSA* 15, 1892, 195–206
Dodson, J (ed), *The Naïve Lands*, Melbourne 1992
Domin, K, 'Queensland plant associations', *ProcRSQld* 23, 1911, 57–74
Donaldson, I & T (eds), *Seeing the First Australians*, Sydney 1985
Donaldson, M & Elliot, I (eds), *Do Not Yield to Despair: the 1895–1908 Exploration Diaries of Frank Hugh Hann*, Perth 1998
Donaldson, T, 'What's in a name?', *Aboriginal Hist* 8, 1984, 21–44
Donovan, P, *A History of the Millewa Group of River Red Gum Forests*, State Forests of NSW 1997
Dortch, CE, 'Past Aboriginal hunter-gatherer economy and territorial organisation in coastal districts of Western Australia's lower South-west', UWA Arch PhD 2000
Dove, T, 'Moral and social characteristics of the Aborigines of Tasmania', *Tas J Nat Sci* 1, 1843, 247–54
Dovers, S (ed), *Still Settling Australia*, Melbourne 2000
Duncan, F, 'Eucalypts in Tasmania's changing landscape', *Tasforests* 2, 1990, 151–65
——, 'Tasmania's Vegetation and its Response to Forest Operations', EIS/Woodchip Paper 6, Hobart 1985
—— & Brown, MJ, *Dry Sclerophyll Vegetation in Tasmania*, NPWS report 85/1, Hobart 1985
Dutton, G, *Founder of a City*, London 1960
Duyker, E, *An Officer of the Blue*, Melbourne 1994
——, 'Land use and ecological change in central NSW', *Hist Stud* 69, 1983, 120–32
——, *Citizen Labillardiere*, Melbourne 2003
——, *The Discovery of Tasmania*, Hobart 1992
Duyker, E & M (eds), *Bruny d'Entrecasteaux: Voyage to Australia and the Pacific 1791–1793*, Melbourne 2001
Eagle, C, *House of Trees* [1971], Penguin 1987
Ealey, EHM, 'Ecology of the euro... in north-western Australia', *CSIRO Wildlife Res* 12, 1967, 9–80
Easty, J, *Memorandum of... Botany Bay*, Sydney 1965
Eccleston, GC, *Major Mitchell's 1836 'Australia Felix' Expedition*, Monash Pubs in Geog 39, 1992
Edwards, PI, 'The journal of Peter Good', *Bull Brit Mus (Nat Hist), Hist Series* 9, 1981, 1–213
Egan, T, *Justice All Their Own*, Melbourne 1996
——, *Sitdown Up North*, Sydney 1997
——, *The Aboriginals Songbook*, Melbourne 1987
Egloff, B, *Ororral Valley Heritage Conservation Plan*, Canberra 1988
Eidelson, M, *The Melbourne Dreaming*, Canberra 1977
Elder, D (ed), *William Light's Brief Journal*, Adelaide 1984
Elkin, AP, 'Cult-totemism and mythology in northern South Australia', *Oceania* 5, 1935, 171–92
——, 'Notes on the social organization of the Worimi, a Kattang-speaking people', *Oceania* 2, 1932, 359–63
——, 'Reaction and interaction: a food gathering people and European settlement in Australia', *Am Anth* 53, 1951, 164–86
——, *The Australian Aborigines*, Sydney 1964
——, 'The social organization of South Australian tribes', *Oceania* 2, 1931, 44–73
——, 'Totemism in north-western Australia', *Oceania* 2, 1932, 296–333; 3, 1933, 257–96, 435–81; 4, 1933, 54–64
Ellen, R & Fukui, K (eds), *Redefining Nature*, Oxford 1996

Ellis, C, *Aboriginal Music*, Brisbane 1985
Ellis, F (ed), *Venturing Westward*, Hobart 1987
Ellis, RC, 'Aboriginal influences on vegetation in the northeast highlands', *Tas Naturalist* 76, Jan 1984, 7–8
——, 'The relationships among eucalypt forest, grassland and rainforest in a highland area in north-eastern Tasmania', *AJEcol* 10, 1985, 297–314
Enright, NJ & Thomas, I, 'Pre-European fire regimes in Australian ecosystems', *Geog Compass* 2, 2008, 979–1011
Enright, NJ et al, 'Anomalies in grasstree fire history reconstructions for south-western Australian vegetation', *Austral Ecology* 30, 2005, 668–73
Enright, WJ, 'Notes on Aborigines of the north coast of NSW', *Mankind* 2, 1940, 321–4
Eseli, P et al, *Eseli's Notebook*, St Lucia 1998
Everard, Dr, 'Early reminiscences of South Australia,' *RGSA SA* 5, 1901, 77–9
Eyre, EJ, *Journals of Expeditions of Discovery into Central Australia and Overland from Adelaide to King George's Sound* [1845], 2 vols, Adelaide 1964
Facey, AB, *A Fortunate Life*, Fremantle 1981
Fels, M, 'Culture contact in the County of Buckingham', *TasHRAPP* 29, 1982, 47–9
Fensham, RJ, 'Aboriginal fire regimes in Queensland, Australia', *J Biogeog* 24, 1997a, 11–22
——, 'Leichhardt's maps: 100 years of change in vegetation structure in inland Queensland', *J Biogeog* 35, 2008, 141–56
——, 'The pre-European vegetation of the Midlands in Tasmania', Tas Geog Hons 1985
——, 'The pre-European vegetation of the Midlands, Tasmania', *J Biogeog* 16, 1989, 29–45
—— & Fairfax, RJ, *Final Report* on the conservation of grassy vegetation on the Darling Downs, Australian Heritage Commission, Canberra 1995
——, 'The disappearing grassy balds of the Bunya Mountains, south-eastern Queensland', *AJBot* 44, 1996a, 543–58
——, 'The grassy balds on the Bunya Mountains, south-eastern Queensland', *Cunninghamia* 4, 1996b, 511–23
——, 'The use of the land survey record to reconstruct pre-European vegetation patterns in the Darling Downs', *J Biogeog* 24, 1997b, 827–36
—— & Holman, JE, 'The use of the land survey to assess changes in vegetation structure ... the Darling Downs', *Rangeland J* 20, 1998, 132–42
—— & Kirkpatrick, JB, 'Soil characteristics and tree species distribution ... Melville Island', *AJBot* 40, 1992a, 311–33
——, 'The eucalypt forest-grassland/grassy woodland boundary in central Tasmania', *AJBot* 40, 1992b, 123–38
Ferguson, WC, 'A mid-Holocene depopulation of the Australian southwest', ANU Prehist PhD 1985
Fidlon, PG & Ryan, RJ (eds), *The Journal and Letters of Lt Ralph Clark 1787–1792*, Sydney 1981
——, *The Journal of Arthur Bowes Smyth*, Sydney 1979
Field, B, *Geographical Memoirs of New South Wales*, London 1825
Finlayson, B, 'Sir Thomas Mitchell and Lake Salvator ...', *Hist Stud* 21, 1984, 212–28
Finlayson, HH, *The Red Centre*, Sydney 1936
Finlayson, W, 'Reminiscences by Pastor Finlayson', *PRGSA SA* 6, 1903, 39–55
Finn, E, *The Chronicles of Early Melbourne*, Melbourne 1888
Finney, C, *Paradise Revealed. Natural History in Nineteenth-century Australia*, Melbourne 1993
Finnis, HJ (ed), 'Dr John Harris Browne's journal of the Sturt Expedition 1844–1845', *South Australiana* 5, 1966, 23–54
Fison, L & Howitt, AW, *Kamilaroi and Kurnai*, Melbourne 1880
Fitzhardinge, LF (ed), *Sydney's First Four Years*, Sydney 1961
Flanagan, R, *A Terrible Beauty ... the Gordon River Country*, Melbourne 1985

Flannery, T, 'Beautiful lies: population and environment in Australia', *Quarterly Essay* 9, 2003a, 1–73
——, *Country*, Melbourne 2004
——, *The Birth of Sydney*, London 2003b
——, *The Explorers*, Sydney 1998
——, *The Future Eaters*, Sydney 1994
—— (ed), *The Birth of Melbourne*, Melbourne 2002
Flinders, M, *Narrative of his Voyage in . . . 1798*, London 1946
——, *Observations on the Coasts of VDL* [1801], Adelaide 1965
——, *Voyage to Terra Australis* [1814], Adelaide 1966
Flood, JM, *Archaeology of the Dreamtime*, Sydney 1989
——, 'Fire as an agent of change: Aboriginal use of fire in NSW', *Forest and Timber* 22, 1986, 15–18
——, *The Moth Hunters*, Canberra 1980
Foelsche, P, 'Notes on the Aborigines of north Australia', *TransRSSA* 5, 1881, 1–18
Foott, J, *Sketches of Life in the Bush*, Sydney 1872
Foran, B & Walker, B (eds), *Science and Technology for Aboriginal Development*, Melbourne 1986
Ford, J & Sedgwick, EH, 'Bird distribution in the Nullarbor Plain and Great Victoria Desert region', *Emu* 67, 1967, 99–124
Ford, JR (ed), *Fire Ecology and Management in WA Ecosystems*, Perth 1985
Ford, P & G (eds), *British Parliamentary Papers: Australia 8*, Shannon 1969
Foreman, DB & Walsh, NG (eds), *Flora of Victoria*, Sydney 1993
Fornaserio, J et al, *Encountering Terra Australis*, Adelaide 2010
Forrest, J, *Explorations in Australia* [1875], London 1969
Fox, RE (ed), *Report on the Use of Fire in National Parks and Reserves*, Darwin 1976
Frankel, D, 'An account of Aboriginal use of the yam-daisy', *Artefact* 7, 1982, 43–5
Frankland, G, *A Narrative of an Expedition to the Head of the Derwent*, Hobart 1983

——, *Five Letters from George Frankland*, Adelaide 1997
Franks, SM, 'Land exploration in Tasmania 1824–1842', Tas Hist MA 1958 (AOTas)
Frawley, K & Semple, N (eds), *Australia's Ever Changing Forests*, Canberra 1988
Freycinet, L, *Reflections on NSW 1788–1839* [1839], Sydney 2001
Friedl, M et al, 'Impact of tourist infrastructure on environmental processes at Uluru', National Ecotourism Program report, CSIRO 1996
Frith, HJ & Calaby, JH, *Kangaroo*, Canberra 1969
Frost, A, *East Coast Country*, Melbourne 1996
Fyans, F, *Memoirs*, Geelong 1986
Gale, J, *Canberra History and Legends*, Queanbeyan 1927
Gallagher, W, 'Land use and land degradation in the catchment of Burrinjuck Dam since European settlement', UMCCC Report, Wagga 1989
Gamble, C, 'The artificial wilderness', *New Scientist* 10/4/1986, 50–54
Gammage, B, *Australia under Aboriginal Management*, Canberra 2003
——, 'Becoming Australian', unpub Canberra 2002
——, '"Far more happier than we Europeans": Aborigines and farmers', *London Papers in Aust Stud* 12, London 2005a
——, 'Fire in 1788: The closest ally', First Eric Rolls memorial lecture, 20 October 2010 (in press)
——, 'Galahs', *Hist Stud* 40, 2009, 275–93
——, 'Gardens without Fences? Landscape in Aboriginal Australia', *Aust Humanities Review* 36, July 2005b, np
——, *Man and Land*, Adelaide 1978
——, *Narrandera Shire*, Adelaide 1986
——, 'Plain facts: Tasmania under Aboriginal management', *Landscape Research* (UK) 33, 2008, 241–54
——, *The Achievement of the Australian Aborigines*, Hawaii 1993
——, 'Victorian landscapes in 1788' (in press)

Gara, T, 'Aboriginal techniques for obtaining water in South Australia', *J Anth Soc SA* 23/2, 1985, 6–11

Garnett, S & Crowley, G, 'Burn-out threatens parrots' paradise', *Geo* 20/1, 1998, 72–6

Gason, S, *The Dieyerie Tribe*, Adelaide 1874

GBRMPA (ed), *Workshop on the Northern Sector of the Great Barrier Reef*, Townsville 1978

Gee, H & Fenton, J (eds), *The South West Book*, Melbourne 1979

Gell, PA & Stuart, I, *Human Settlement History and Environmental Impact. The Delegate River catchment*, Monash Pubs in Geog 36, 1989

Gellibrand, JT, 'Memoranda of a trip to Port Phillip in 1836', *Trans Phil Inst Vic* 3, 1858, 63–85

Gerritsen, R, *And Their Ghosts May be Heard*, Fremantle 1994

——, *Australia and the Origins of Agriculture*, Oxford 2008

——, *Nhanda Villages of the Victoria District, WA*, Canberra 2002

——, *The Traditional Settlement Pattern in Southwest Victoria Reconsidered*, Canberra 2000

Gibbney, J, 'Currency walkabout of 1822', *Canberra Hist J* 2, 1978, 1–8

Giblin, RW, *The Early History of Tasmania*, 2 vols, London 1928, Melbourne 1939

Gilbert, JM, 'Forest succession in the Florentine Valley, Tasmania', *PPRSTas* 93, 1959, 129–51

Gilbert, LA, 'Botanical Investigation of NSW 1811–1880', UNE PhD 1971

——, 'Botanical Investigation of the Eastern Seaboard of Australia, 1788–1810', UNE BA Hons 1962

——, 'The bush and the search for a staple in NSW, 1788–1810', *Rec Aust Academy Sci* 1, Dec 1966, 6–17

Giles, C, 'The Adelaide and Port Darwin Telegraph Line', *J SA Electrical Soc* 1–2, Feb–Nov 1888

Giles, E, *Australia Twice Traversed* [1889], Perth 1995

——, *Geographic Travels in Central Australia* [1875], Bundaberg 1993

——, *The Journal of a Forgotten Expedition* [1880], Adelaide 1979

Gilfedder, L, *Montane Grasslands of North-Western Tasmania*, Hobart 1995

—— & Kirkpatrick, JB, 'Culturally induced rarity? The past and present distributions of *Leucochrysum albicans* in Tasmania', *AJBot* 42, 1994, 405–16

Gill, AM et al (eds), *Fire and the Australian Biota*, Canberra 1981

Gillen, JS et al (eds), *Biodiversity and the Reintroduction of Native Fauna at Uluru-Kata Tjuta*, Canberra 2000

Gillen, JS & Drewien, GN, *A Vegetation Survey of the Kanowna Wetlands, Cooper Creek SA* (Report to Aust Nature Conservation Agency), Adelaide 1993

Gillespie, L, 'Aborigines of Canberra...', *Can Hist J* 4, 1979, 19–25

——, *Aborigines of the Canberra Region*, Canberra 1984

——, *Canberra 1820–1913*, Canberra 1991

Gilmore, M, *More Recollections*, Sydney 1935

——, *Old Days: Old Ways*, Sydney 1934

——, *Under the Wilgas*, Melbourne 1932

Goddard, C & Kalotas, A (eds), *Punu: Yankunytjatjara Plant Use*, Sydney 1985

Godwin, L, 'Around the traps: a reappraisal of stone fishing weirs in northern New South Wales', *Arch in Oceania* 23, 1988, 49–59

Good, R (ed), *The Scientific Significance of the Australian Alps*, Canberra 1989

Gosse, WC, *Gosse's Explorations* [1874], Adelaide 1973

Gott, B, 'Aboriginal fire management in south-eastern Australia—aims and frequency', *J Biogeog* 32, 2005, 1203–8

——, 'Australia Felix and Major Mitchell', Monash Uni Botany paper, 1986

——, 'Cumbungi, *Typha* species: a staple Aboriginal food in southern Australia', *Aust Ab Stud*, 1999/1, 33–50

——, 'Ecology of root use by the Aborigines

of southern Australia', *Arch in Oceania* 17, 1982, 59–67
——, 'Murnong—*Microseris scapigera*: a study of a staple food of Victorian Aborigines', *Aust Ab Stud*, 1983/2, 2–18
——, 'Use of Victorian plants by Koories' in DB Foreman & NG Walsh (eds), *Flora of Victoria*, Melbourne 1993, vol 1, 195–211
Gough, D (ed), *Fire. The Force of Life*, Landscope Magazine, Perth 2000
Gould, RA, *Puntutjarpa Rockshelter and the Australian Desert Culture*, New York 1977
——, 'Uses and effects of fire among the Western Desert Aborigines of Australia', *Mankind* 8, 1971, 14–24
Govett, WR, *Sketches of NSW*, Melbourne 1977
Grant, J, *The Narrative of a Voyage . . . in the Lady Nelson* [1803], Adelaide 1973
Green, N, *Nyungar—The People*, Perth 1979
Greenway, CC, 'The Borah, Boohra, or Boorbung', *Science of Man* 4, 1901, 117–18
—— et al, 'Australian languages and traditions', *JRAI* 7, 1877, 232–76
Gregory, AC, 'Memoranda on the Aborigines of Australia', *JRAI* 16, 1887, 131–3
Gregory, AC & FT, *Journals of Australian Explorations* [1884], Adelaide 1969
Gregory, JW, *The Dead Heart of Australia*, London 1909
Greig, AW, 'Letters from Australian pioneers', *Vic Hist Mag* 12, 1927, 21–108
——, 'Some new documentary evidence concerning the foundation of Melbourne', *Vic Hist Mag* 12, 1928, 109–17
Gresser, PG, 'Small camp-sites of the Aborigines—central western NSW', *Vic Naturalist* 82, 1965, 233–6
Gresty, JA, 'The Numinbah Valley', *Qld Geog J* 51, 1946–7, 57–72
Grey, G, *Journals of Two Expeditions of Discovery* [1841], Adelaide 1964
Gribble, JB, *Black but Comely*, London 1884
Griffin, G & Allan, G, 'Fire and the management of Aboriginal owned lands in Central Australia' in BD Foran & BW Walker (eds), *Science and Technology for Aboriginal Development*, Alice Springs 1985, section 2.6
Griffin, T & McCaskill, M, *Atlas of South Australia*, Adelaide 1986
Griffiths, C, *The Present State and Prospects of the Port Phillip District of NSW*, Dublin 1845
Griffiths, T, *Forests of Ash*, Melbourne 2001a
——, 'How many trees make a forest? Cultural debates about vegetation change in Australia', *AJBot* 50, 2002, 375–89
——, *Hunters and Collectors*, Cambridge 1996
——, 'One hundred years of environmental crisis', *Rangeland J* 23, 2001b, 5–14
—— (ed), *The Life and Adventures of Edward Snell*, Sydney 1988
—— & Robin, L (eds), *Ecology and Empire*, Melbourne 1997
Grimwade, R, *An Anthography of the Eucalypts*, Sydney 1930
Gunn, J, *The Little Black Princess* [1905], Melbourne 1958
—— *We of the Never-Never* [1908], London 1964
Gunn, RC, 'On the heaps of recent shells which exist along the shores of Tasmania', *Tas J Nat Sci* 2, 1845, 332–6
Gunson, N, *The Good Country. Cranbourne Shire*, Canberra 1968
—— (ed), *Australian Reminiscences and Papers of L.E. Threlkeld*, 2 vols, Canberra 1974
Haddon, AC, 'Ethnography of the western tribes of Torres Straits', *JRAI* 19, 1890, 297–440
Hahn, DM, 'Extracts from Reminiscences . . .', *South Australiana* 3, 1964, 119–34
Hale, HM & Tindale, NB, 'Aborigines of Princess Charlotte Bay, north Queensland', *Rec SA Mus* 5, 1933–34, 63–172
——, 'Observations on Aborigines of the Flinders Ranges', *Rec SA Mus* 3, 1925, 45–60
Hale, P & Lamb, D, *Conservation outside Nature Reserves*, Brisbane 1997
Hallam, SJ, *Fire and Hearth*, Canberra 1975
——, 'Peopled landscapes in south-western Australia in the early 1800s . . .', *Early Days (JRWAHS)* 12, 2002, 177–91

———, 'Yams, alluvium and "villages" on the west coastal plain' in GK Ward (ed), *Archaeology at ANZAAS*, Canberra 1986, 116–32

Hamilton, AG, 'On the effect which settlement in Australia has produced upon the indigenous vegetation', *JRSNSW* 26, 1892, 178–239

Hamilton, G, *A Journey from Port Phillip to South Australia in 1839* [1880], Adelaide 1974

Hamilton, JC, *Pioneering Days in Western Victoria*, Melbourne 1913

Hamilton-Arnold, B (ed), *Letters and Papers of G.P. Harris*, Sorrento 1994

Hancock, WK, *Discovering Monaro*, Cambridge 1972

Hann, F, 'Exploration in Western Australia', *ProcRSQld* 16, 1901, 9–34

Hanna, C et al, *Corartwalla . . . Penola*, Adelaide 2001

Hansen, D, 'Not in an English Country Garden', ms, Hobart 2002

Harcourt, R, *Southern Invasion Northern Conquest*, Melbourne 2001

Hardy, B, *Lament for the Barkindji*, Adelaide 1976

Harris, A, *Settlers and Convicts* [1847], Melbourne 1969

Harris, CR, 'Mantung—a man–land study in the Murray Valley of South Australia', *JRGSA SA* 71, 1970, 1–25

Harris, DR, 'Subsistence strategies across Torres Strait' in J Allen et al (eds), *Sunda and Sahul*, London 1977, 420–63

——— & Hillman, GC (eds), *Foraging and Farming*, London 1989

Hartwig, MC, 'The progress of white settlement in the Alice Springs district . . . 1870–94', Adel Hist PhD 1965

Harvey, A, 'Food preservation in Australian tribes', *Mankind* 3, 1945, 191–2

Hasluck, A, *Georgiana Molloy* [1955], Fremantle 2002

Hassell, E, 'Notes on the ethnology of the Wheelman tribe of southwestern Australia', *Anthropos* 31, 1936, 679–711

Havard, WL (ed), 'Alan Cunningham's journal of a tour into Argyle, March–April 1824', *Canberra Hist Soc*, 1956

Haw, P & Munro, M, *Footprints across the Loddon Plains*, Boort Vic, 2010

Hawdon, J, *Journal of a Journey from New South Wales to Adelaide*, Adelaide 1952

———, *Journal of a Journey from Port Phillip to Adelaide*, Adelaide 1984

Hawker, JC, *Early Experiences in South Australia* [1899], Adelaide 1975

Hawkesworth, J, *An Account of the Voyages . . .*, London 1773

Haydon, GH, *Five Years' Experience in Australia Felix* [1846], Melbourne 1983

Haygarth, HW, *Recollections of Bush Life in Australia*, London 1848

Haynes, CD, 'Fire in the mind: Aboriginal cognizance of fire-use in north central Arnhem Land', ms 1977

———, 'The pattern and ecology of munwag: traditional Aboriginal fire regimes in north-central Arnhemland', *Proc Ecol Soc Aust* 13, 1985, 203–14

——— et al (eds), *Monsoonal Australia*, Rotterdam 1991

Hayward, JF, 'Reminiscences', *JRGSA SA* 29, 1927–8, 79–176

Head, L, 'Environment as artefact', *AJEcol* 13, 1988, 21–49

———, 'Environment as artefact: a geographic perspective on the Holocene occupation of southwestern Victoria', *Arch in Oceania* 18, 1983, 73–80

———, 'Landscapes socialised by fire', *Arch in Oceania* 29, 1994, 172–81

———, 'Prehistoric Aboriginal impacts', *Aust Geog* 20, 1989, 36–47

———, *Second Nature: the History and Implications of Australia as Aboriginal Landscape*, Syracuse 1999

Heathcote, RL, *Back of Bourke*, Melbourne 1965

Helms, R, 'Anthropological Notes', *Proc Linn Soc NSW* 20, 1895, 387–408

Hemming, S, 'An Aboriginal fish trap from Lake

Condah, Victoria', *J Anth Soc SA* 23/4, 1985, 2–6
Henderson, J, *Excursions and Adventures in NSW*, 2 vols, London 1851, 1854
——, 'Narrative of an expedition to Lake Frome in 1843', *JRGSA SA* 26, 1925, 85–128
——, *Observations on the Colonies of New South Wales and Van Diemen's Land* [1832], Adelaide 1965
Herbert, DA, 'The upland savannahs of the Bunya Mountains, south Queensland', *ProcRSQld* 49, 1937, 145–9
Hercus, L, 'Leaving the Simpson Desert', *Ab Hist* 9, 1985, 22–43
—— & Clarke, P, 'Nine Simpson Desert wells', *Arch in Oceania* 21, 1986, 51–62
—— et al, *The Land is a Map*, Canberra 2002
Hetzel, BS & Frith, HJ (eds), *The Nutrition of Aborigines in . . . Central Australia*, Melbourne 1978
Hiatt, B, 'The food quest and the economy of the Tasmanian Aborigines', *Oceania* 38, 1967–8, 91–133, 190–219
Hiatt, LR, 'Local organization among the Australian Aborigines', *Oceania* 32, 1961–2, 267–86
Hill, B, *The Rock. Travelling to Uluru*, Sydney 1994
Hill, R et al, 'Aborigines and fire in the wet tropics of Queensland', *Soc and Natural Res* 12, 1999, 205–23
——, 'Rainforests, agriculture and Aboriginal fire-regimes in wet tropical Queensland', *Aust Geog Stud* 38, 2000, 138–57
——, *Yalanji-Warranga Kaban*, Cairns 2004
Hill, RS, 'Attempting to define the impossible', *Aust Geog Stud* 38, 2000, 320–6
—— (ed), *History of the Australian Vegetation*, Cambridge 1994
Hinkson, M, *Aboriginal Sydney*, Canberra 2001
Hodgkinson, C, *Australia from Port Macquarie to Moreton Bay*, London 1845
Home, RW (ed), *Australian Science in the Making*, Cambridge 1988, 1–22
Hood, J, *Australia and the East*, London 1843

Hoorn, J, 'Joseph Lycett: the pastoral landscape in early colonial Australia', *Art Bulletin Vic* 26, 1986, 4–14
—— (ed), *The Lycett Album*, Canberra 1990
Hope, G, 'Vegetation and fire response to late Holocene human occupation in island and mainland north-west Tasmania', *Quaternary Internat* 59, 1999, 47–60
—— & PJF Coutts, 'Past and present Aboriginal food resources at Wilson's Promontory, Victoria', *Mankind* 8, 1971, 104–14
Horne, G & Aiston, G, *Savage Life in Central Australia*, London 1924
Horsfall, N, 'Aboriginal cultural issues in the Wet Tropics of northern Qld' in NJ Goudberg et al (eds), *Tropical Rainforest in Australia*, Townsville 1991
—— 'Living in rainforest: the prehistoric occupation of North Queensland's humid tropics', JCU Behavioural Sci PhD 1987
Horton, DR, 'Burning of the bush', *Canberra Times* L, 19 Apr 08
——, 'Fire and Australian Society', unpub 2002
——, 'Tasmanian adaptation', *Mankind* 12, 1979, 28–34
——, 'The burning question: Aborigines, fire and Australian ecosystems', *Mankind* 13, 1982, 237–51
——, *The Pure State of Nature*, Sydney 2000
—— (ed), *Encyclopedia of Aboriginal Australia*, Canberra 1994
Houison, A, 'The Tank Stream', *JRAHS* 1, 1901, 5–7
Hovell, WH, 'Journal kept on the journey from Lake George to Port Phillip, 1824–1825,' *JRAHS* 7, 1921, 307–78
Howard, ECO, 'Batman's Hill', *Vic Hist Mag* 2, 1912, 33–4
——, 'The Flag Staff Hill', *Vic Hist Mag* 6, 1917, 43–8
Howard, TN, 'Australian Aboriginal burning, mishaps and conflict: implications for ethnobiology', *J Ethnobiology* 16, 1996, 224–33

Howchin, W, *The Stone Implements of the Adelaide Tribe*, Adelaide 1934
Howitt, AW, 'On some Australian beliefs', *JRAI* 13, 1883, 185–98
——, 'On the organisation of Australian tribes', *TransRSVic* (2), 1889, 96–137
——, 'The eucalypts of Gippsland', *TransRSVic* 2, 1890, 81–120; discussion *ProcRSVic* 3, 1891, 124–9
——, *The Native Tribes of South East Australia*, London 1904
Howitt, R, *Impressions of Australia Felix*, London 1845
[HRA], F Watson (ed), *Historical Records of Australia*, 33 vols, Sydney 1914–22; P Chapman (ed), *HRA Resumed Series*, 2 vols, Melbourne 1997–2003
[HRNSW], FM Bladen (ed), *Historical Records of NSW*, 7 vols, Sydney 1892–1901
Humphrey, AWH, *Voyage to Port Phillip and VDL*, Melbourne 1984
Hunt, MA et al, 'Ecophysiology of the Soft Tree Fern', *Austral Ecology* 27, 2002, 360–8
Hunt, P, 'Movement and Landscape', ANU Arch Hons 1992
Hunter, J, *An Historical Journal of the Transactions at Port Jackson and Norfolk Island* [1793], Adelaide 1968
Hunter, S, 'From rainforest to grassland... Jamberoo area, NSW', Sydney Geog Hons 1974
Hynes, RA & Chase, AK, 'Plants, sites and domiculture: Aboriginal influence upon plant communities in Cape York Peninsula', *Arch in Oceania* 17, 1982, 38–50
Ingles, A, 'Fire', EIS/Woodchip Paper 6, Hobart 1985
Irvine, N (ed), *The Sirius Letters*, Sydney 1988
Isaacs, J (ed), *Australian Dreaming*, Sydney 1980
——, *Bush Food*, Sydney 1987
Jack, RL, *Northmost Australia*, London 1921
Jackson, WD, 'Fire, air, water and earth—an elemental ecology of Tasmania', *Proc Ecol Soc Aust* 3, 1968, 9–16
——, 'Nutrient stocks in Tasmanian vegetation and approximate losses due to fire', *PPRSTas* 134, 2000, 1–18
——, 'The Tasmanian legacy of man and fire', *PPRSTas* 133, 1999a, 1–14
——, 'Vegetation' in JL Davies (ed), *Atlas of Tasmania*, Hobart 1965, 30–35
——, 'Vegetation of the Central Plateau' in MR Banks (ed), *The Lake Country of Tasmania*, Hobart 1973, 61–86
——, 'Vegetation types' in JB Reid et al, *The Vegetation of Tasmania*, Hobart 1999b, 1–10
Jackson-Nakano, A, *The Kamberri*, Abor Hist Monograph 8, Canberra 2001
——, *The Pajong and Wallabalooa*, Abor Hist Monograph 9, Canberra 2002
Jacobs, MR, 'Forests and forestry in the ACT', *Canberra Hist Soc Papers*, 1963
James, TH, *South Australia* [1838], Adelaide 1962
Jardine, J, 'Description of the neighbourhood of Somerset, Cape York, Australia', *JRGS* 35, 1866, 76–85
Jenkin, G, *Conquest of the Ngarrindjeri*, Adelaide 1979
Jervis, J, 'The journals of William Edward Riley', *JRAHS* 32, 1946, 217–68
Jetson, T, 'The Roof of Tasmania—the History of the Central Plateau', Tas Hist MA 1987
Johnston, JG (ed), *The Truth*, Edinburgh 1839
Johnston, TH, 'Aboriginal names... in the Eyrean region', *TransRSSA* 67, 1943, 244–311
Jones, C, *Recognise, Relate, Innovate* (Rangelands Project R), Armidale 2002
——, 'The Great Salinity Debate', *Aust Farm J*, Oct 2000, 90–92, Jan 2001, 58–61, + a longer ms c~ Christine Jones
Jones, R, 'Archaeological fieldwork in Tasmania', *Antiquity* 38, 1964, 305–6
——, 'A speculative archaeological sequence for north-west Tasmania', *Rec QV Mus Launceston* 25, 1966, 1–12
——, 'Cleaning the country: the Gidjingali and their environment', *BHPJ*, 1, 1980a, 10–15
——, 'Fire-stick farming', *Aust Natural Hist* 16, 1969, 224–8

——, 'Hunters in the Australian coastal savanna' in DR Harris (ed), *Human Ecology in Savanna Environments*, London 1980b, 107–46
——, 'Landscapes of the mind' in DJ Mulvaney (ed), *The Humanities and the Australian Environment*, Canberra 1991, 21–48
——, 'The geographical background to the arrival of man in Australia and Tasmania', *Arch in Oceania* 3, 1968, 186–215
——, 'The Neolithic, Paleolithic and the hunting gardeners' in RP Suggate & MM Creswell (eds), *Quaternary Studies*, Wellington 1975, 21–34
—— (ed), *Northern Australia: Options and Implications*, Canberra 1980c
Jones, W, 'Up the Creek: hunter-gatherers in the Cooper Basin', UNE Arch Hons 1979
Joyce, B, 'Reading the Land' (review), *Aust Geologist* Mar 2010, 34
Jukes, JB, *Narrative of the Surveying Voyages of HMS Fly and Bramble . . . 1842–6*, London 1847
Jurskis, V, 'Decline of eucalypt forests as a consequence of unnatural fire regimes', *Aust Forestry* 68, 2005, 257–62
——, 'Restoring the prepastoral condition', *Aust Ecol* 27, 2002, 689–90
——, 'Vegetation changes since European settlement', *Aust Forestry* 63, 2000, 166–73
Kaberry, PM, *Aboriginal Women: Sacred and Profane*, London 1939
——, 'Totemism in east and north Kimberley, north-west Australia', *Oceania* 8, 1938, 265–88
Karskens, G, *Holroyd. A Social History of Western Sydney*, Sydney 1991
Kartzoff, M, *Nature and a City*, Sydney 1969
Kassler, J & Stubington, J (eds), *Problems and Solutions*, Sydney 1984
Kay, CE, 'Are lightning fires unnatural? . . .', *Tall Timbers Fire Ecology Conf* 23, 2007a, 16–28

——, 'Were native people keystone predators? . . .', *Canadian Field-Naturalist* 121, 2007b, 1–16
Keast, A (ed), *Ecological Biogeography of Australia*, 3 vols, The Hague 1981
—— et al (eds), *Biogeography and Ecology in Australia*, The Hague 1959
Keen, I, *Aboriginal Economy and Society*, Oxford 2004
Kelly, G, 'Karla Wongi—Fire Talk', in D Gough (ed), *Fire. The Force of Life*, Perth 2000, 9–13
Kelly, J, 'First discovery of Port Davey and Macquarie Harbour', *PPRSTas*, 1920, 160–81
Kelly, J et al, *Log of the Circumnavigation of VDL*, Hobart 1986
Kelly, S et al, *Eucalypts*, 2 vols, Melbourne 1983
Kennedy, EB, *Extracts from the Journal of an Exploring Expedition into Central Australia*, London 1852
Kenny, J, *Before the First Fleet*, Kenthurst 1995
Kenyon, AS, 'Camping places of the Aborigines of South-East Australia', *Vic Hist Mag* 2, 1912, 97–110
[Kerr, JH], *Glimpses of Life in Victoria* [1872], Melbourne 1996
Kerr, MG, *The Surveyors*, Adelaide 1971
Kershaw, AP, 'Climatic change and Aboriginal burning in north-east Australia', *Nature* 322, July 1986, 47–9
Kerwin, D, *Aboriginal Dreaming Paths and Trading Routes*, Eastbourne UK 2010
Kimber, RG, 'Beginnings of farming? Some man-plant-animal relationships in central Australia', *Mankind* 10, 1976, 142–50
——, 'Black lightning: Aborigines and fire in central Australia and the Western Desert', *Arch in Oceania* 18, 1983, 38–45
——, 'Resource use and management in central Australia', *Aust Ab Stud* 1984/2, 12–23
——, 'Smallpox in central Australia', *Aust Arch* 27, 1988, 63–8
——, 'The end of the bad old days: European settlement in central Australia 1871–1894', SLNT Occasional Paper 25, Darwin 1991

King, J, *The First Settlement*, Sydney 1984
King, PP, *Narrative of a Survey of the Intertropical and Western Coasts of Australia* [1827], Adelaide 1969
Kirby, J, *Old Times in the Bush of Australia*, Ballarat 1895?
Kirk, RL, *Aboriginal Man Adapting*, Oxford 1981
Kirkpatrick, JB, *A Continent Transformed*, Melbourne 1994
——, *The Disappearing Heath*, Hobart 1977
—— et al, *City Parks and Cemeteries*, Hobart 1988
Knott, T et al, 'An ecological history of koala habitat in Port Stephens Shire and the lower Hunter... 1801–1998', *Pac Cons Biol* 4, 1998, 354–68
Kohen, JL, *Aboriginal Environmental Impacts*, Sydney 1995
——, 'Aboriginal use of fire in southeastern Australia', *Proc Linn Soc NSW* 116, 1996, 19–26
——, *The Aborigines of Western Sydney*, Blacktown 1983
——, *The Darug and their Neighbours*, Sydney 1993
Kolenberg, H, 'Hobart's 1832 Glover sketchbook', *Art Bull Tas*, Hobart 1984
Kraehenbuehl, D, *Pre-European Vegetation of Adelaide*, Adelaide 1996
Krefft, G, 'On the manners and customs of the Aborigines of the Lower Murray and Darling', *Trans Phil Soc NSW* 1, 1865, 357–74
——, 'On the vertebrated animals of the Lower Murray and Darling', *Trans Phil Soc NSW* 1, 1862, 1–33
Krichauff, S, 'The Narungga and Europeans: Cross-cultural relations on Yorke Peninsula in the nineteenth century', Adel Hist MA, 2008
Labillardiere, M, *Voyage in Search of La Perouse* [1800], Amsterdam 1971
Labilliere, P, *Early History of Melbourne*, London 1878
Lacey, CJ, 'Rhizomes in tropical eucalypts and their role in recovery from fire damage', *AJBot* 22, 1974, 29–38
Lacey, G, *Reading the Land*, Melbourne 2008
'A Lady' [E Macpherson], *My Experiences in Australia*, London 1860
Lake, M (ed), *Memory, Monuments and Museums*, Canberra 2006
Landor, EW, *The Bushman* [1847], Twickenham 1998
Landsborough, W, *Journal* [1862], Adelaide 1971
Lane, K, 'The Nambucca Aborigines at the time of the first white settlement', UNE Hist Hons 1970
Langton, M, *Burning Questions*, Darwin 1998
Latz, P, 'Burnt stumps everywhere—fire in northern and central Australia' in BJ McKaige et al, *Bushfire '97. Proc Aust Bushfire Conf*, Darwin 1997
——, *Bushfires and Bushtucker*, Alice Springs 1995
——, *The Flaming Desert*, Alice Springs 2007
—— & Johnson, K, 'Nature conservation on Aboriginal land' in BD Foran & BW Walker (eds), *Science and Technology for Aboriginal Development*, Alice Springs 1985, section 2.4
Lawrence, D, 'Customary exchange across Torres Strait', *Memoirs Qld Mus* 34, 1994, 241–446
Lawrence, R, 'Aboriginal habitat and economy', ANU Geog MA 1968
Layton, R, 'Relating to the country in the Western Desert' in E Hirsch & M O'Hanlon (eds), *The Anthropology of Landscape*, Oxford 1996, 210–31
——, *Uluru: An Aboriginal History*, Canberra 1989
Lee, A & Martin, R, *The Koala: a Natural History*, Sydney 1996
Lee, I, *Early Explorers in Australia*, London 1925
Lee, RB & Daly, RH, *Cambridge Encyclopedia of Hunters and Gatherers*, New York 1999
Lehman, G, 'Turning Back the Clock: Fire, Biodiversity and Indigenous Community Development in Tasmania' in X Jianchu

(ed), *Links between Cultures and Biodiversity*, Kunming 2000

Leichhardt, L, *Journal of an Overland Expedition in Australia* [1847a], Adelaide 1964

——, 'Lectures on the Geology, Botany, Natural History... between Moreton Bay and Port Essington', *Tas J Nat Sci* 3, 1847b, 81–113

Leigh, JH & Noble, JC, *Riverine Plain of NSW*, Canberra 1972

Lendon, AA, 'Dr Alexander Imlay', *JRAHS* 17, 1931, 206–8

Lewis, HT, 'Burning the "Top End": kangaroos and cattle' in JR Ford (ed), *Fire Ecology and Management in Western Australian Ecosystems*, Perth 1985, 21–31

—— & Ferguson, TM, 'Yards, corridors and mosaics: how to burn a boreal forest', *Human Ecol* 16, 1988, 57–77

Lindsay, D, 'Explorations in the Northern Territory of South Australia', *JRGSA SA*, 1/3, 1888, 1–16

——, *Journal of the Elder Scientific Expedition 1891–2*, Adelaide 1893

Lines, WJ, *An All Consuming Passion*, Sydney 1994

——, *Patriots: Defending Australia's Natural Heritage*, Brisbane 2006

——, *Taming the Great South Land*, Sydney 1991

Linn, R, *Battling the Land*, Sydney 1999

——, *Cradle of Adversity... Willunga District*, Adelaide 1991

——, *The River Flows... Mannum*, Adelaide 1997

—— & F Hawker, *Bungaree*, Adelaide 1992

Lloyd, CJ, *Either Drought or Plenty*, Parramatta 1988

Lockwood, D, *The Front Door. Darwin 1869–1969*, Adelaide 1974

Long, CR, 'Who founded Melbourne?', *JRAHS* 19, 1933, 67–72

Lonsdale, WM & Braithwaite, RW, 'Assessing the effects of fire on vegetation in tropical savannas', *AJEcol* 16, 1991, 363–74

Lord, EE, *Shrubs and Trees for Australian Gardens*, Melbourne 1960

Lourandos, H, 'Change or stability?: hydraulics, hunter-gatherers and population in temperate Australia', *World Arch* 11, 1980, 245–64

——, *Continent of Hunter-Gatherers*, Cambridge 1997

——, 'Dispersal of activities—the East Tasmanian Aboriginal sites', *PPRSTas* 102, 1968, 41–6

——, 'Intensification: a late Pleistocene–Holocene archaeological sequence from southwestern Victoria, Australia', *Arch in Oceania* 18, 1983, 81–94

Love, JRB, *Stone Age Bushmen of Today*, London 1936

Low, T, 'Foods of the First Fleet', *Aust Nat Hist* 22, 1987a, 292–7

——, 'Pituri: tracing the trade routes of an indigenous intoxicant', *Aust Nat Hist* 22, 1987b, 257–60

——, *The New Nature*, Melbourne 2002

Luke, RH & McArthur, AG, *Bushfires in Australia*, Canberra 1978

Lumholtz, C, *Among Cannibals* [1889], Canberra 1980

Lunney, D, 'Causes of the extinction of native mammals of the Western Division of New South Wales', *Rangeland J* 23, 2001, 44–70

—— & Leary, T, 'The impact on native mammals of land-use changes and exotic species in the Bega district, NSW', *AJEcol* 13, 1988, 67–92

—— et al (eds), *Future of the Fauna of Western NSW*, Mosman 1994

Lunt, ID, 'Allocasuarina invasion of an unburnt coastal woodland at Ocean Grove, Victoria: structural change 1971–1996', *AJBot* 46, 1998a, 649–56

——, 'A transient soil seed bank for the yam daisy', *Vic Nat* 113, 1996, 16–19

——, 'Effects of long-term vegetation management on remnant grassy forests and anthropogenic grassland in south-eastern Australia', *Biological Cons* 81, 1997a, 287–97

——, 'European management of remnant grassy forests and woodlands in south-eastern Australia', *Vic Nat* 112, 1995, 239–49

——, 'Grazed, burnt and cleared: how ecologists have studied century-scale vegetation changes in Australia', *AJBot* 50, 2002, 391–407

——, 'The distribution and environmental relationships of native grasslands on the lowland Gippsland Plain . . .', *Aust Geog Stud* 35, 1997b, 140–52

——, 'Tree densities last century on the lowland Gippsland Plain, Victoria', *Aust Geog Stud* 35, 1997c, 345–57

——, 'Two hundred years of land use and vegetation change in a remnant coastal woodland in southern Australia', *AJBot* 46, 1998, 629–47

—— & Morgan, J, 'Effect of fire frequency on plant composition at . . . Laverton North', *Vic Nat* 116, 1999, 84–9

—— et al, 'Effects of European colonization on indigenous ecosystems . . .', *J Biogeog* 33, 2006, 1102–15

——, *Plains Wandering*, Melbourne 1998b

—— et al (eds), *Bushfire '99*, Albury 1999

Lycett, J, *Drawings of the Natives and Scenery of Van Diemens Land*, London 1830

——, *Views of Australia*, London 1825

McAlpine, CA et al, 'Influence of landscape structure on kangaroo abundance in a disturbed semi-arid woodland of Queensland', *Rangeland J* 21, 1999, 104–34

McArthur, AG, 'Fire as an ecological tool', *Riverina Conf Papers* 2, Wagga 1969

——, 'The historical place of fire in the Australian environment' in Monash University (ed), *Papers of the Second Fire Ecology Symposium*, 1970, 1–22

McBryde, I, *Aboriginal Prehistory in New England*, Sydney 1974

——, 'Exchange in south eastern Australia', *Ab Hist* 8, 1984, 132–53

——, 'Subsistence patterns in New England prehistory' in PK Lauer (ed), *Occasional Papers in Anthropology* 6, Brisbane 1976, 48–68

——, 'Travellers in storied landscapes', *Ab Hist* 24, 2000, 152–74

—— (ed), *Records of Times Past*, Canberra 1978

McCarthy, FD, '"Trade" in Aboriginal Australia, and "trade" relationships with Torres Strait, New Guinea and Malaya', *Oceania* 9, 1939, 405–38; 10, 1939–40, 80–104, 171–95

McComb, HS, 'Surveyor Hoddle's field books of Melbourne', *Vic Hist Mag* 16, 1937, 77–101 & 17, 1938, 20–40

McConnel, U, 'The Wik-Munkan tribe of Cape York Peninsula', *Oceania* 1, 1930, 97–104, 181–205

McCormick, T et al, *First Views of Australia 1788–1825*, Sydney 1987

McCourt, T & Mincham, H (eds), *Two Notable South Australians*, Beachport 1977

McCrae, GG, *Recollections of Melbourne*, Adelaide 1987

——, 'Some recollections of Melbourne in the "Forties"', *Vic Hist Mag* 7, 1912, 114–36

——, 'The early settlement of the eastern shores of Port Phillip Bay', *Vic Hist Mag* 1, 1911, 17–26

McDonald, B, 'Some account of kangaroo hunting on the northern tablelands of NSW', *Aust Folklore* 10, 1995, 108–32

McDonald, J, *Dreamtime Superhighway* (*Terra Australis* 27), Canberra 2008

McEntee, JC, 'Lake Frome . . . Aboriginal trails', *TransRSSA* 115, 1991, 199–205

McFarlane, I, 'Aboriginal Society in North West Tasmania: Dispossession and Genocide', Tas Hist PhD 2002

——, 'Adolphus Schayer . . .', *THRA PP* 57, 2010, 115–18

——, *Beyond Awakening. The Aboriginal Tribes of North West Tasmania*, Hobart 2008

MacGillivray, J, *Narrative of the Voyage of HMS Rattlesnake* [1852], Adelaide 1967

MacGillivray, LG, 'Land and People . . . south-east SA 1840–1940', Adel Hist PhD 1982

McGuanne, JP, 'Bennilong Point and Fort Macquarie', *JRAHS* 1, 1901a, 9–13

——, 'Old Government House, Sydney', *JRAHS* 1, 1901b, 73–82
McIver, G, *A Drover's Odyssey*, Sydney 1935
McKaige, BJ et al, *Bushfire '97. Proc Aust Bushfire Conf*, Darwin 1997
—— et al, *Bushfire '99. Proc Aust Bushfire Conf*, Albury 1999
Mackaness, G (ed), *Bligh's Discoveries . . . in Van Diemen's Land*, Dubbo 1976
——, *Fourteen Journeys Over the Blue Mountains of NSW*, Sydney 1965
——, 'George Augustus Robinson's journey into south-eastern Australia, 1844', *JRAHS* 27, 1942, 318–49
Mackay, R, *Recollections of Early Gippsland Goldfields* [1916], Ringwood 1977
McKenna, M, *Looking for Blackfella's Point*, Sydney 2002
McKinlay, J, *Journal of Exploration* [1862?], Adelaide 1962
Macknight, CC, *Low Head to Launceston*, Launceston 1998
——, *The Voyage to Marege'*, Melbourne 1976
McLaren, G, *Beyond Leichhardt*, Fremantle 1996
McLoughlin, L, 'Estuarine wetlands distribution along the Parramatta River, Sydney', *Cunninghamia* 6, 2000a, 579–610
——, 'Season of burning in the Sydney region', *AJEcol* 23, 1998, 393–404
——, 'Shaping Sydney Harbour . . . 1788–1990s', *Aust Geog* 31, 2000b, 183–208
[McMaster, F], 'The evils of overstocking', *Pastoral Review* June 1938, 645–6
McMillan, JM, *The Two Lives of Joseph Docker*, Melbourne 1994
McPhee, J (ed), *Joseph Lycett: Convict Artist*, Sydney 2006
MacPherson, JA, 'Aboriginal fish and emu poisons', *Mankind* 1, 1933, 157–61
——, 'John MacPherson, First resident landowner at Canberra', *JRAHS* 20, 1934–5, 99–113
——, 'The Eucalyptus in the daily life and medical practice of the Australian Aborigines', *Mankind* 2, 1939, 175–80

Macquarie, L, *Journals of his Tours in NSW and VDL 1810–22*, Sydney 1956
Maiden, JH, 'History of the Sydney Botanic Gardens', *JRAHS* 14, 1928, 1–42
Malthus, T, *An Essay on the Principle of Population* [1798], London 1803
Mann, JF, 'Notes on the Aborigines of Australia', *JRGSA SA* 1, 1883, 27–63
Mantegani, H, 'Recollections of the early days of SA from 1836', *RGSA SA* 5, 1901, 70–6
Marsden-Smedley, JB, 'Changes in southwestern Tasmanian fire regimes since the early 1800s', *PPRSTas* 132, 1998a, 15–29
——, 'Fire and fuel in Tasmanian buttongrass moorlands', Tas Geog PhD 1998b
—— & Kirkpatrick, J, 'Fire management in Tasmania's Wilderness World Heritage Area: ecosystem restoration using indigenous-style fire regimes?', *Ecol Management & Restoration* 1, 2000, 195–203
Marsh, MH, *Overland from Southampton to Queensland*, London 1867
Marsh, NR & Adams, MA, 'Decline of *Eucalyptus tereticornis* near Bairnsdale . . .', *AJBot* 43, 1995, 39–50
Martin, G, 'The role of small native mammals in soil building and water balance', *Aust Farm J*, May 2001 (ms c~ Christine Jones)
Martin, J, 'Explorations in North-Western Australia', *JRGS* 35, 1865, 237–89
Mathew, J, 'The Australian Aborigines', *JRSNSW* 23, 1889, 335–449
——, 'The origin, distribution, and social organization of the inhabitants of Victoria before the advent of Europeans', *Vic Hist Mag* 1, 1911, 79–89
——, *Two Representative Tribes of Queensland*, London 1910
Mathews, RH, 'Ethnological notes on the Aboriginal Tribes of NSW and Victoria', *JRSNSW* 38, 1904, 203–381
——, 'The Aboriginal fisheries at Brewarrina', *JRSNSW* 37, 1903, 146–56

——, 'The Burbung of the Wiradthuri Tribes', *JRAI* 25, 1896, 295–318; 26, 1897, 272–85
——, 'The Burbung of the Wiradthuri Tribes', *ProcRSQld* 16, 1901, 35–8
——, 'The Burbung, or initiation ceremonies of the Murrumbidgee tribes', *JRSNSW* 31, 1897a, 111–53
——, 'The totemic divisions of Australian tribes', *JRSNSW* 31, 1897b, 154–76
May, P & Fullagar, RLK, 'Aboriginal exploitation of the southern mallee', *Rec Vic Arch Survey* 10, June 1980, 152–74
Meagher, SJ, 'The food resources of the Aborigines of the south-west of Western Australia', *Rec WA Mus* 3, 1974, 14–65
Mear, C, 'The origin of the smallpox outbreak in Sydney in 1789', *JRAHS* 94, 2008, 1–22
Meehan, B, *Shell Bed to Shell Midden*, Canberra 1982
Meggitt, MJ, *Desert People*, Chicago 1965
Memmott, P, *Gunyah, Goondie + Wurley*, Brisbane 2007
Meredith, LA, *Notes and Sketches of NSW* [1844], Melbourne 1998
Merlan, F (comp), *Big River Country*, Alice Springs 1996
Merrilees, D, 'Man the destroyer: late Quaternary changes in the Australian marsupial fauna', *JRSWA* 51, 1968, 1–24
Mills, EW, *W. Whitfield Mills: Experiences with the Darwin Survey*, Adelaide 1993
Mills, K, 'The clearing of the Illawarra rainforests', *Aust Geog* 19, 1988, 230–40
Mitchell, A, 'Traditional economy of the Aborigines of the Richmond River NSW', UQ Anth Hons 1978
Mitchell, PB, 'Historical perspectives on some vegetation and soil changes in semi-arid NSW', *Vegetatio* 91, 1991, 169–82
Mitchell, TL, *Journal of an Expedition into . . . Tropical Australia*, London 1848
——, *Three Expeditions into the Interior of Eastern Australia* [1839], 2 vols, Adelaide 1965

Moon, K, 'Perception and appraisal of the South Australian landscape 1836–1850', *JRGSA SA* 70, 1969, 41–64
Moore, B, *Cotter Country*, Canberra 1999
Moore, CWE, 'The vegetation of the southeast Riverina NSW', *AJBot* 1, 1953, 485–568
Moore, DR, *Islanders and Aborigines at Cape York*, Canberra 1979
Moore, DT, 'Some aspects of the work of the botanist Robert Brown . . . in Tasmania', *Tasforests* 12, 2000, 123–46
Moore, GF, *A Diary of Ten Years of an Early Settler in Western Australia* and *Descriptive Vocabulary*, London 1884
Moore, RM (ed), *Australian Grasslands*, Canberra 1970
Morcom, LA & Westbrooke, ME, 'The pre-settlement vegetation of the Western and Central Wimmera Plains', *Aust Geog Stud* 36, 1998, 273–88
Morgan, J, *Life and Adventures of William Buckley* [1852], Melbourne 1967 (also intro T Flannery, Melbourne 2002)
Morgan, JW, 'Importance of canopy gaps for recruitment of some forbs in *Themeda triandra* dominated grasslands', *AJBot* 46, 1998, 609–27
Morphy, H, *Ancestral Connections*, Chicago 1991
——, 'Landscape and reproduction of the ancestral past' in E Hirsch & M O'Hanlon (eds), *The Anthropology of Landscape*, Oxford 1996, 184–209
Morrill, J, *The Story of James Morrill* [1863], Bowen 1965
Morrison, E, *Early Days in the Loddon Valley*, Daylesford 1967a
——, *Frontier Life in the Loddon Protectorate*, Daylesford 1967b
Morton, SR & Mulvaney, DJ (eds), *Exploring Central Australia*, Sydney 1996
Morton, WL, 'Notes of . . . the unoccupied Northern District of Queensland', *Trans Phil Inst Vic* 4, 1859, 188–99
Moseley, HN, *Notes by [a] Naturalist on the Challenger* [1879], London 1944

Mossman, S & Banister, T, *Australia Visited and Revisited*, London 1853

Moulds, FR & Hutton, HB, *The Macedon Ranges*, Mt Macedon 1994

Mountford, CP, 'Aboriginal crayon drawings, Warburton Ranges, Western Australia', *Oceania* 10, 1939a, 73–9

——, 'Aboriginal methods of fishing and cooking as used on the southern coast of Eyre's Peninsula, South Australia', *Mankind* 2, 1939b, 196–200

——, *Brown Men and Red Sand*, Melbourne 1953

—— (ed), *Records of the American–Australian Scientific Expedition to Arnhem Land*, vol 2, Melbourne 1960

Moyal, A, *Koala*, Melbourne 2008

Mullette, KJ, 'Studies of the lignotubers of *Eucalyptus gummifera*', *AJBot* 26, 1978, 9–13

Mullins, S, *Torres Strait*, Rockhampton 1995

Mulvaney, DJ, *Encounters in Place*, St Lucia 1989

—— & Golson, J (eds), *Aboriginal Man and Environment in Australia*, Canberra 1971

—— & Green, N (eds), *Commandant of Solitude. The Journals of Captain Collett Barker 1828–1831*, Melbourne 1992

—— & Kamminga, J, *Prehistory of Australia*, Sydney 1999

—— & White, JP (eds), *Australians to 1788*, Sydney 1987

Munster, PM, *Putting Batman and Buckley on the Map of St Leonards*, St Leonards 2004

Murphy, BP & Bowman, DMJS, 'The interdependence of fire, grass, kangaroos and Australian Aborigines . . . Arnhem Land', *J Biogeog* 34, 2006, 237–50

Murray, L, *A Working Forest: Selected Prose*, Sydney 1997

Murray, RD, *A Summer at Port Phillip*, Edinburgh 1843

Murray, WR, 'Mr RT Maurice's expedition north of Fowler's Bay', *JRGSA SA* 5, 1901, 33–39

Murrells, J, *Sketch of a Residence . . .* , Brisbane 1863

Myers, B et al, *Fire Management in the Rangelands*, Darwin 2004

Myers, F, *Pintubi Country, Pintubi Self*, Canberra 1986

Nagle, J, *The Nagle Journal . . .* , New York 1988

Napier, SE, 'Balmain: The man and the suburb', *JRAHS* 14, 1928, 245–81

Nash, D, 'Aboriginal gardening: Plant resource management in three Central Australian communities', ANU Anth MA 1993

——, 'An ethnobotanical study of women's plant use at Mt Liebig', ANU Human Sci BLitt 1984

National Academies Forum, *Fire! The Australian Experience*, Canberra 2000

Nelson, A, 'Aboriginal practices in East Gippsland forests precontact' in J Dargavel & B Libbis (eds), *Australia's Ever-changing Forests IV*, Canberra 1999, 5–16

Nelson, HN, 'Early attempts to civilize the Aborigines of the Port Phillip District', UMelb MEd 1967

——, 'The missionaries and the Aborigines in the Port Phillip District', *Hist Stud* 45, 1965, 57–67

Newland, S, 'Annual address', *JRGSA SA* 22, 1921, 1–64

——, *The Parkengees . . . on the Darling River*, Adelaide 1889

——, 'The Parkengees, or Aboriginal tribes on the Darling River', *JRGSA SA* 3, 1888, 20–33

Newsome, AE, 'An ecological comparison of the two arid-zone kangaroos in Australia', *Quarterly Review of Biology* 50, 1975, 389–424

——, 'The eco-mythology of the red kangaroo in central Australia', *Mankind* 12, 1980, 327–33

Nicholls, M (ed), *The Diary of the Reverend Robert Knopwood*, Hobart 1977

Nicholson, A & Cane, S, 'Pre-European coastal settlement and use of the sea', *Aust Arch* 39, 1994, 108–17

Nind, IS, 'Description of the natives of King George's Sound', *JRGS* 1, 1830–1, 21–51

Nobbs, CW, 'The inhabitants of Cooper Creek', *Rec SA Mus* 26, 1993, 129–38

Noble, JC, 'Shrub population regulation in semi-arid woodlands before and after European settlement' in LP Hunt & R Sinclair (eds), *Proceedings of the 9th Biennial Australian Rangeland Conference*, Canberra 1996, 62–5

——, *The Delicate and Noxious Scrub*, Canberra 1997

——, & Kimber, RG, 'On the ethno-ecology of mallee root-water', *Ab Hist* 21, 1997, 170–202

——, et al, 'Landscape ecology and the burrowing bettong', *Austral Ecology* 32, 2007, 326–37

Nodvin, SC & Waldrop, TA (eds), *Ecological and Cultural Perspectives*, South Carolina 1990

Norris, EH et al, 'Vegetation changes in the Pilliga forests', *Vegetatio* 91, 1991, 209–18

Norton, A, 'Notes of travel 1859–60', *ProcRSQld* 18, 1904, 81–107

——, 'On the decadence of Australian forests', *ProcRSQld* 3, 1887, 15–22

——, 'Settling in Queensland', *ProcRSQld* 17, 1903, 147–60

——, 'Stray notes about our Aborigines', *Science of Man* 9, 1907–8, nos 5–8.

Norton, BE, 'Grasslands of the New England tableland in the nineteenth century', *Armidale & D HSJP* 15, 1971, 1–13

Nunn, J, *Soldier Settlers*, Adelaide 1981

——, *This Southern Land*, Adelaide 1989

O'Connell, JF et al, 'Traditional and modern plant use among the Alyawarra of central Australia', *Economic Bot* 37, 1983, 80–109

O'Connor, R et al, *Report on . . . Aboriginal Significance of Wetlands and Rivers in the Perth–Bunbury Region*, Perth 1989

Ogilvie, E, *Diary of Travels in Three Quarters of the Globe*, London 1856

Oliver, I et al, 'Pre-1750 vegetation, naturalness and vegetation condition', *Ecol Management and Restoration* 3, 2002, 176–8

Olsen, P, *Glimpses of Paradise*, Canberra 2007

Osterstock, A (ed), *South Australia*, Adelaide 1979?

Oxley, J, *Journals of Two Expeditions into the Interior of New South Wales* [1820], Adelaide 1964

Oxley, RE, 'Analysis of historical records of a grazing property in south-western Queensland', *Aust Rangeland J* 9, 1987, 21–38

Palmer, K & Williams, N, 'Aboriginal relationships to land in . . . East Kimberley' in RA Dixon & MC Dillon, *Aborigines and Diamond Mining*, Perth 1990, 5–28

Parker, ES, *The Aborigines of Australia*, Melbourne 1854

Parker, KL, *The Euahlayhi Tribe*, London 1905

Parkhouse, TA, 'Native tribes of Port Darwin and its neighbourhood', *ProcAAS* 6, 1895, 638–47

Parkin, R, *HM Bark Endeavour*, 2 vols, Melbourne 1997

Parkinson, S, *A Journal of a Voyage to the South Seas* [1784], London 1984

Parks and Wildlife, 2(5), Sydney 1979?

Pate, JS & Dixon, KW, *Tuberous, Cormous and Bulbous Plants*, Perth 1982

—— & Beard, JS (eds), *Kwongan. Plant Life of the Sandplain*, Perth 1984

—— & McComb, AJ (eds), *The Biology of Australian Plants*, Nedlands 1981

Pearson, M, 'Seen through different eyes . . . the upper Macquarie river region . . .', ANU Prehist PhD 1981

Pedler, W, 'Recollections of early days', *RGSA SA* 6, 1903, 63–5

Pendergast, JV, *Pioneers of the Omeo District*, Melbourne 1968

Penney, J, 'Encounters on the river: Aborigines and Europeans in the Murray Valley 1820–1920', La Trobe Hist PhD 1989

Pepper, P & De Araugo, T, *The Kurnai of Gippsland*, Melbourne 1985

——, *You Are What You Make Yourself To Be*, Melbourne 1980

Peron, F, *A Voyage of Discovery to the Southern Hemisphere* [1809], Melbourne 1975

Perry, TM, *Australia's First Frontier. The Spread of Rural Settlement in NSW*, Melbourne 1963

Peters, AL (ed), *Recollections. Nathaniel Hailes' Adventurous Life in SA*, Adelaide 1998
Peterson, N, 'Totemism yesterday: sentiment and local organization among the Australian Aborigines', *Man* 7, 1972, 12–32
——, *Tribes and Boundaries in Australia*, Canberra 1976
—— & J Long, *Australian Territorial Organisation*, Sydney 1986
Petrie, CC, *Tom Petrie's Reminiscences of Early Queensland*, Brisbane 1932
Phillip, A, *The Voyage of Governor Phillip* [1789], Adelaide 1968
Phillips, M, 'A study of isozyme variation . . . in Eucalyptus pauciflora', ANU Botany BSc Hons 1975
Piddington, R, 'Totemic system of the Karadjeri tribe', *Oceania* 2, 1932, 371–400
Piguenit, WC, 'Among the western highlands of Tasmania', *ProcAAAS* 4, Hobart 1892, 787–94
Pilling, AR & Waterman, RA (eds), *Diprotodon to Detribalization*, Michigan 1970
Pink, O, 'Spirit ancestors in a northern Aranda horde country', *Oceania* 4, 1933, 176–86
Playford, P, *Voyage of Discovery to Terra Australis by Willem de Vlamingh in 1696–97*, Canberra 1998
Plomley, NJB, *Friendly Mission*, Hobart 1966
——, *Weep in Silence*, Hobart 1987
—— (ed), *The Baudin Expedition and the Tasmanian Aborigines 1802*, Hobart 1983
Powell, M & Hesline, R, 'Making tribes? . . .', *JRAHS* 96, 2010, 115–48
Preece, N, 'Aboriginal fires in monsoonal Australia from historical accounts', *J Biogeog* 29, 2002, 321–36
Presland, G, *Aboriginal Melbourne*, Melbourne 1994
——, *The Place for a Village*, Melbourne 2008
Price, O & Bowman, DMJS, 'Fire-stick forestry', *J Biogeog* 21, 1994, 573–80
[PWS] Parks and Wildlife Service, Tasmania, *Freycinet National Park Management Plan*, Hobart 1995

Pyke, WT, *Thirty Years among the Blacks of Australia*, London 1904
Pyne, SJ, *Burning Bush*, New York 1991
——, *The Still-Burning Bush*, Melbourne 2006
Quinn, MJ, 'Knowing the rangelands of western NSW: the past in the changing present', *Rangeland J* 19, 1996, 70–9
Radcliffe-Brown, AR, 'Notes on totemism in eastern Australia', *JRAI* 59, 1929, 399–415
——, 'The social organization of Australian tribes', *Oceania* 1, 1930, 34–63, 206–46, 322–41, 426–56
Ramson, WS (ed), *The Australian National Dictionary*, Canberra 1988
Randell, JO (ed), [AF Mollison's] *An Overlanding Diary* [1837], Melbourne 1980
Ranken, G, 'The crisis in the land question', *Sydney Quarterly Mag*, Dec 1887, 368–78
Ratcliffe, FN, *Flying Fox and Drifting Sand*, Sydney 1948
——, *Soil Drift in the Arid Pastoral Areas of SA* (CSIR Pamphlet 64), Melbourne 1936, c~ Jan Cooper
Rattray, A, 'Notes on the physical geography, climate, and capabilities of Somerset, and the Cape York Peninsula, Australia', London 1868
Read, J, 'Soil and rainforest composition in Tasmania . . .', *AJBot* 49, 2001, 121–35
Read, P, 'Being is a transitive verb: four views of a life site in southern NSW', *Landscape Research* 19, 1994, 58–67
Read, TR & Bellairs, SM, 'Smoke affects the germination of native grasses of NSW', *AJBot* 47, 1999, 563–76
Reid, GH, *An Essay on New South Wales*, Sydney 1876
Reid, JB et al, *The Vegetation of Tasmania*, Hobart 1999
Reid, JRW et al, *Kowari 4: Uluru Fauna*, Canberra 1993
Reid, R & Mongan, C, *A Decent Set of Girls*, Yass 1996
Reynolds, H, *Black Pioneers*, Melbourne 2000
——, *Frontier: Aborigines, Settlers and Land*, Sydney 1987

BIBLIOGRAPHY

——, *Law of the Land*, Penguin 1992
——, 'The land, the explorers and the Aborigines', *Hist Stud* 19, 1980, 213–26, & ns c~ Henry Reynolds
Richards, C, 'Wirra Athooree [Wiradjuri]', *Science of Man* 5, 1902, 98–102
Richards, E (ed), *Flinders History of South Australia*, 2 vols, Adelaide 1986
Richards, JA (ed), *Blaxland–Lawson–Wentworth 1813*, Hobart 1979
Richardson, –, 'An overland expedition from Port Denison to Cape York', *JRGS* 36, 1866, 19–51
Rigsby, B, 'Aboriginal people, land rights and wilderness on Cape York Peninsula', *ProcRSQld* 92, 1981, 1–10
Riley, K, 'Pilbara project goes for gold', *Aust Geographic* 95, 2009, 44
Robin, L, *How a Continent Created a Nation*, Sydney 2007
Robinson, AC et al (eds), *A Biological Survey of the Anangu Pitjantjatjara Lands South Australia*, Adelaide 2003
Robinson, FW, *Canberra's First Hundred Years and After*, Sydney 1927
Rolls, E, *A Million Wild Acres*, Melbourne 1984a
——, 'Land of grass: the loss of Australia's grasslands', *Aust Geog Stud* 37, 1999, 197–213
——, *They All Ran Wild*, Sydney 1984b
——, *Visions of Australia*, Melbourne 2002
Rose, DB, *Dingo Makes Us Human*, Cambridge 1992
——, *Nourishing Terrains*, Canberra 1996
——, *Preliminary Report: Ethnobotany in the Bungles*, EKIAP Paper 5, Canberra 1984
——, 'To dance with time: a Victoria River Aboriginal study', *AJAnth* 11, 2000, 287–96
—— (ed), *Country in Flames*, Canberra 1995
—— & A Clarke (eds), *Tracking Knowledge in North Australian Landscapes*, Darwin 1997
Rosenfeld, A & Winston-Gregson, J, 'Excavations at Nursery Swamp 2', *Aust Arch* 17, 1983, 48–58
Rosenman, H (ed), *Two Voyages to the South Seas* [d'Urville], Melbourne 1987

Ross, A, 'Holocene environments and prehistoric site patterning in the Victorian Mallee', *Arch in Oceania* 16, 1981, 145–54
Ross, J, *Dr Ross's Recollections of a Short Excursion to Lake Echo* [1823], Adelaide 1992
Rossetto, M et al, 'Conservation genetics and clonality in two critically endangered eucalypts', *Biological Conservation* 88, 1999, 321–31
Roth, HL, 'On the origin of agriculture', *JRAI* 16, 1886, 102–36
——, *The Aborigines of Tasmania*, Hobart 1983
Roth, W, *Ethnological Studies among the North-West-Central Queensland Aborigines*, Brisbane 1897
——, 'Notes of savage life in the early days of WA settlement', *ProcRSQld* 17, 1903, 45–69
Rothery, FM, *Atlas of Bundaleer Plains and Tatala*, Canberra 1970
Rothwell, N, 'Heart of grass', *Weekend Aust Mag* 5–6 Apr 2003, 28–30
——, *The Red Highway*, Melbourne 2009
Rowlands, RJ & JM, 'An Aboriginal dam in northwestern NSW', *Mankind* 7, 1969, 132–6
Rowley, C, *The Destruction of Aboriginal Society*, Melbourne 1972
Roxburgh, R, 'The Meryla Pass', *JRAHS* 66, 1981, 287–92
Rozycki, J, 'Poor fellow my country', *Aust Geographic* 72, 2003, 36–51
Rubuntja, W & Green, J, *The Town Grew Up Dancing*, Alice Springs 2002
Rumsey, A & Weiner, J (eds), *Emplaced Myth*, Honolulu 2001
Russell, HS, *The Genesis of Queensland*, Sydney 1888
Russell, JS & Isbell, R (eds), *Australian Soils: The Human Impact*, Brisbane 1986
Russell, P, *This Errant Lady*, Canberra 2002
Russell-Smith, J, 'The relevance of indigenous fire practice for contemporary land practice: an example from western Arnhem Land' in BJ McKaige et al, *Bushfire '97. Proc Aust Bushfire Conf*, Darwin 1997, 81–5

—— et al, 'Aboriginal resource utilisation and fire management practice in Western Arnhem Land', *Human Ecol* 25, 1997, 159–95

Ryan, DG et al, *The Australian Landscape: Observations of Explorers and Early Settlers*, Wagga 1995

Ryan, JS (ed), *The Land of Ulitarra*, Grafton 1964

Ryan, L, *The Aboriginal Tasmanians*, Brisbane 1981

Ryan, MF, 'Colonial art work as an indicator of the nature and structure of the pre-European forests . . .', *Proc Inst Foresters Biennial Conf*, Mt Gambier 2005, 35–60

——, 'Does early Colonial Art provide an accurate guide to the nature and structure of the pre-European forests . . . ?', ANU M Forestry 2007

Ryan, S, *The Cartographic Eye. How Explorers Saw Australia*, Cambridge 1996

Sahlins, M, *Stone Age Economics*, New York 1972

Saunders, DA et al (eds), *Australian Ecosystems (Proc Ecol Soc Aust 16)*, Sydney 1990

Saunders, P, 'Confounded by carrots . . . Pialligo, ACT', ANU Arch Hons 1989

Saunders, T, 'Parrots of the Sydney Region', *CBOC Newsletter* 27 (3), 2005, 2–4

Savage, P (BJ Dalton, ed), *Christie Palmerston, Explorer*, Townsville 1992

Scarlett, NH, *A Preliminary Account of the Ethnobotany of the Kija People of Bungle Bungle Outcamp*, EKIAP Paper 6, Canberra 1985

Scott, E (ed), *Australian Discovery, By Land*, London 1929

Scougall, B (ed), *Cultural Heritage of the Australian Alps*, Canberra 1992

Seddon, G, *Searching for the Snowy*, Sydney 1994

——, *Sense of Place*, Perth 1972

——, *The Old Country*, Cambridge 2005

Selfe, N, 'A century of Sydney Cove', *JRAHS* 1, 1901, 55–68

Selkirk, H, 'The origins of Canberra', *JRAHS* 9, 1923, 49–78

Shaw, AGL, *A History of the Port Phillip District*, Melbourne 1996

Shaw, B (ed), *Countrymen*, Canberra 1986

——, *My Country of the Pelican Dreaming*, Canberra 1981

Shellam, T, *Shaking Hands on the Fringe*, Perth 2009

Shephard, M, *The Great Victoria Desert*, Sydney 1995

——, *The Simpson Desert*, Adelaide 1992

Sherratt, T et al, *A Change in the Weather*, Canberra 2005

Shillinglaw, J (ed), *Historical Records of Port Phillip*, Melbourne 1879

Shire of Korumburra, *The Land of the Lyre Bird*, [1920] Melbourne 1966

Sholl, RJ, 'Journal of an expedition . . . in North-Western Australia', *JRGS* 36, 1866, 203–27

Sim, R & West, D, *Archaeological Project Report . . . Southwest Tasmanian Hinterland*, Hobart 1993

Simmons, MH, *Acacias of Australia*, Melbourne 1981

Simpson, B, *Packhorse Drover*, Sydney 1996

Smith, B, *European Vision and the South Pacific*, Sydney 1960

Smith, DI, *Water in Australia*, Oxford 1998

Smith, DL, 'The pre-settlement hydrology and vegetation of the Northern Adelaide Plains', *Aust Geog* 19, 1988, 242–58

Smith, J, *Aborigines of the Goulburn District*, Goulburn 1992

Smith, J, *The Booandik Tribe of South Australian Aborigines* [1880], Adelaide 1965

Smith, JMB (ed), *A History of Australasian Vegetation*, Sydney 1982

Smith, KV, *Bennelong*, Sydney 2001

——, *King Bungaree*, Sydney 1992

Smith, MA, 'Biogeography, Human Ecology and Prehistory in the Sandridge Deserts', *Aust Arch* 37, 1993, 35–50

——, *Peopling the Cleland Hills* (*Ab Hist* Monograph 12), Canberra 2005

——, 'The antiquity of seedgrinding in arid Australia', *Arch in Oceania* 21, 1986, 29–39
Smith, SJ & Banks, MR, *Tasmanian Wilderness—World Heritage Values*, Hobart 1993
Smyth, D, *Views of Victoria in the Steps of von Guerard*, Melbourne 1984
Smyth, RB, *The Aborigines of Victoria* [1876], Melbourne 1972
Sneeuwjagt, R, 'Fighting fire with fire', in D Gough (ed), *Fire. The Force of Life (Landscape)*, Perth 2000, 27–30
Spanswick, S & Zund, P, *Quamby Soil Report, Reconnaissance Soil Map Series of Tasmania*, Hobart 1999
Specht, RL & Mountford, CP (eds), *Records of the American–Australian Scientific Expedition to Arnhem Land* 3, Melbourne 1958
Spencer, RJ & Baxter, GS, 'Effects of fire on . . . open eucalyptus forests', *Austral Ecol* 31, 2006, 638ff
Spencer, WB, *Native Tribes of the Northern Territory of Australia*, London 1914
—— (ed), *Report on . . . the Horn Expedition* 1, London 1896
—— & Gillen, FJ, *Across Australia*, London 1912
—— *The Native Tribes of Central Australia* [1899], New York 1968
Stanbridge, WE, 'On the astronomy and mythology of the Aborigines of Victoria', *Trans Phil Inst Vic* 2, Jan–Dec 1857, 137–40
Stanbury, PJ (ed), *Bushfires: Their Effect on Australian Life and Landscape*, Sydney 1981
Stannage, CT (ed), *A New History of Western Australia*, Perth 1981
——, *The People of Perth*, Perth 1979
Stanner, WEH, 'Aboriginal territorial organization: estate, range, domain and regime', *Oceania* 36, 1965, 1–31
——, *After the Dreaming*, Sydney 1969
——, 'Religion, Totemism and Symbolism' in M Charlesworth et al (eds), *Religion in Aboriginal Australia*, Brisbane 1984, 137–72

——, 'Some aspects of Aboriginal religion', *Colloquium* 9, 1976, 19–35
——, *White Man Got No Dreaming*, Canberra 1979
Starr, BJ, *Soil Erosion, Phosphorus & Dryland Salinity in the Upper Murrumbidgee*, Wagga 1999
Statham, P (ed), *The Origins of Australia's Capital Cities*, Melbourne 1989
——, *The Tanner Letters*, Perth 1981
Statham-Drew, P, *James Stirling*, Perth 2003
Steele, JG, *Aboriginal Pathways in Southeast Queensland and the Richmond River*, Brisbane 1983
——, *Brisbane Town in Convict Days 1824–1842*, Brisbane 1975
——, *The Explorers of the Moreton Bay District 1770–1830*, Brisbane 1972
Stelling, F (ed), *South West Slopes Revegetation Guide*, Wagga 1998
Stephens, E, 'The Aborigines of Australia', *JRSNSW* 23, 1889, 476–503
Stevenson, G, 'Extracts from . . . journals', *RGSA SA* 30, 1928, 21–73
Stevenson, PM, 'Traditional Aboriginal resource management in the wet-dry tropics: a Tiwi case study', *Proc Ecol Soc Aust* 13, 1985, 309–15
Stewart, A, *Gardening on the Wild Side*, Sydney 1999
Stewart, OC (HT Lewis & MK Anderson, eds), *Forgotten Fires*, Oklahoma 2002
Stirling, AW, *The Never Never Land . . . North Queensland*, London 1884
Stirling, J, 'Private letter . . . to Mr Barrow', *JRGS* 1, 1830–1, 255–7
Stocker, GC, 'Effects of fires on vegetation in the Northern Territory', *Aust Forestry* 30, 1966, 223–30
Stockton, E (ed), *Blue Mountains Dreaming*, Winmalee 1993
Stockton, J, 'Fires by the seaside: historic vegetation changes in northwestern Tasmania', *PPRSTas* 116, 1982a, 53–66
——, 'The Prehistoric Geography of northwest Tasmania', ANU Prehist PhD 1982b

—— & Waterman, P, 'Anthropological, Archaeological and Historic Information for South West Tasmania', *South West Tas Resources Survey* 7, Hobart 1977

Stokes, JL, *Discoveries in Australia* [1846], 2 vols, Adelaide 1969

Stone, AC, 'The Aborigines of Lake Boga, Victoria', *ProcRSVic* 23NS, 1911, 433–68

Stormon, EJ (ed), *The Salvado Memoirs*, Perth 1977

Strehlow, TGH, *Aranda Traditions*, Melbourne 1947

——, *Journey to Horseshoe Bend*, Adelaide 1978

——, *Songs of Central Australia*, Sydney 1971

Strzelecki, PE, *Physical Description of NSW and VDL* [1845], Adelaide 1967

Stuart, JM, *J McDouall Stuart's Explorations* [1863], Adelaide 1963

——, *The Journals of John McDouall Stuart* [1865], Adelaide 1975

Stubbs, BJ, 'The "grasses" of the Big Scrub district, north-eastern NSW', *Aust Geog* 32, 2001, 295–319

Sturt, C, *An Account of a Journey to South Australia* [1838], Adelaide 1990

——, *Narrative of an Expedition into Central Australia* [1849], 2 vols, Adelaide 1965

——, *The Mount Bryan Expedition 1839*, Adelaide 1982

——, *Two Expeditions into . . . Southern Australia* [1833], 2 vols, Adelaide 1963

Stuwe, J, 'The role of fire in ground flora ecology', *Vic Nat* 111, 1994, 93–5

Sullivan, S, 'The material culture of the Aborigines of the Richmond and Tweed Rivers . . .', UNE Hist BA Hons 1964

Sutton, P, *Country: Aboriginal Boundaries and Land Ownership in Australia*, Canberra 1995

——, 'Icons of Country: Topographic representations in classical Aboriginal traditions' and 'Aboriginal maps and plans' in D Woodward & GM Lewis (eds), *The History of Cartography*, Chicago 1998a, vol 2 bk 3, 353–416

——, 'New Age spirituality and the Simpson Desert (Wangkangurru) Land Claim', ms 1998b c~ Peter Sutton

——, 'The pulsating heart: large scale cultural and demographic processes in Aboriginal Australia' in B Meehan & N White, *Hunter-gatherer Demography*, Sydney 1990, 71–80

——, 'Wik', UQ Anth PhD 1978

——, *Wik-Ngathan Dictionary*, Adelaide 1995

—— (ed), *Dreamings: The art of Aboriginal Australia*, Melbourne 1989

—— & Rigsby, B, 'People with "Politicks" . . . Cape York' in N Williams & ES Hunn (eds), *Resource Managers*, Colorado 1982, 155–71

Sutton, TM, 'The Adjahdurah tribe of Aborigines on Yorke's Peninsula: some of their early customs and traditions', *JRGSA SA* 1, 1888, 17–19

Swain, T, *A Place for Strangers*, Cambridge 1993

Sweeney, G, 'Food supplies of a desert tribe', *Oceania* 17, 1947, 289–99

Tardif, P, *John Bowen's Hobart*, Hobart 2004

Tas Field Naturalists' Club, *Easter Camp-Out, 1909, to Wineglass Bay, Freycinet Peninsula*, Hobart 1909

Taylor, JA, *A Study of Palawa . . . Place Names*, Launceston 2006

Teichelmann, CG, *Aborigines of South Australia* [1841], Adelaide 1962

Therry, R, *Reminiscences of Thirty Years* [1863], Sydney 1974

Thomas, DA, 'Studies on leaf characteristics of a cline of *Eucalyptus urnigera* from Mount Wellington, Tasmania', *AJBot* 22, 1974, 501–12, 701–7

Thomas, HF, 'A possible Aboriginal ceremonial ground at Lake Gol Gol, NSW', *Mankind* 6, 1964, 105–20

Thomas, I, 'Ethnohistoric sources for the use of fire by Tasmanian Aborigines', UMelb Occ Ppr 2, 1994

——, 'Late Pleistocene environments and Aboriginal settlement patterns in Tasmania', *Aust Arch* 36, 1993, 1–11

BIBLIOGRAPHY

——, 'The Holocene Archaeology and Palaeoecology of Northeastern Tasmania, Australia', Tas Geog PhD 1991

Thomas, M, *The Artificial Horizon. Imagining the Blue Mountains*, Melbourne 2003

Thomas, M, *The Diaries and Letters of Mary Thomas*, Adelaide 1925

Thomas, T, *70 Walks in Southern NSW and the ACT*, Melbourne 1998

Thomson, DF, 'Arnhem Land: explorations among an unknown people', *Geog J* 112, 1948, 146–64; 113, 1949, 1–8, 53–67

——, 'The seasonal factor in human culture', *Proc Prehist Soc* 5, 1939, 209–221

Thompson, J, *A Road in Van Diemen's Land*, Hobart 2004

Tierney, DA, 'The effect of fire-related germination cues on the germination of a declining forest understorey species', *AJBot* 54, 2006, 297–303

Tietkins, WH, *Diary of Exploration in South Australia*, Adelaide 1961

——, 'Smallpox and Australian Aborigines', *JRGSA SA* 5, 1881–2, 112–13

Tindale, NB, *Aboriginal Tribes of Australia*, California 1974

——, 'Distribution of Australian Aboriginal Tribes', *TransRSSA* 64, 1940, 140–55

——, 'Notes on the natives of the southern portion of Yorke Peninsula', *TransRSSA* 60, 1936, 55–70 c~ Tom Gara

Tipping, M, *Eugene von Guerard's Australian Landscapes*, Melbourne 1975

Tolcher, HM, *Conrick of Nappa Merrie*, Adelaide 1997

Tonkinson, R, *The Mardu Aborigines*, Sydney 1991

Tuckey, J, *Account of a Voyage to . . . Port Phillip*, London 1805

Tunbridge, D, *Flinders Ranges Dreaming*, Canberra 1988

——, 'Language as heritage', *J Anth Soc SA* 23(7), 1985, 10–15; 23(8), 1985, 3–15

Turbet, P, *The Aborigines of the Sydney District before 1788*, Sydney 1989

Turnbull, H, *Leichhardt's Second Journey*, Sydney 1983

Turnbull, LH, *Sydney*, Sydney 1999

Turner, F, 'Fodder plants and grasses of Australia', *ProcAAS* 2, 1890, 586–96

——, *The Forage Plants of Australia*, Sydney 1891

Turner, J, *Joseph Lycett*, Newcastle 1997

Twidale, CR et al (eds), *Natural History of the Adelaide Region*, Adelaide 1976

Urban, A, *Wildflowers and Plants of Central Australia*, Melbourne 1990

Vaarzon-Morel, P (ed), *Warlpiri Women's Voices*, Alice Springs 1995

Vallance, TG et al, *Nature's Investigator*, Canberra 2001

Vancouver, G, *A Voyage of Discovery . . . 1791–1795* [1801], 4 vols, London 1984

Vanderwal, R & Horton, DR, *Coastal Southwest Tasmania (Terra Australis 9)*, Canberra 1984

van Kempen, E, *A History of the Pilliga Cypress Pine Forests*, Sydney 2007

van Lendenfeld, R, 'Recent changes in the forest-flora of the interior of NSW', *Proc Linn Soc NSW* (2nd series), 1885, 721–2

van Oosterzee, P, *A Field Guide to Central Australia*, Sydney 1995

——, *The Centre*, Sydney 1991

Veitch, B, 'Burning Bracken Fern', UNE Prehist BA Hons 1985

——, 'What happened in the mid-Holocene?', UWA Arch PhD 1999

Veth, PM & Walsh, FJ, 'The concept of "staple" plant foods in the Western Desert region of Western Australia', *Aust Ab Stud* 1988/2, 19–25

Vigilante, T, 'Analysis of explorers' records of Aboriginal landscape burning in the Kimberley', *Aust Geog Stud* 39, 2001, 135–55

von Guerard, E, *Australian Landscapes*, Melbourne 1867

Wakefield, NA, 'Bushfire frequency and vegetational change in south-eastern Australian forests', *Vic Nat* 87, 1970, 152–8

Walker, D (ed), *Bridge and Barrier*, Canberra 1972

Walker, F, 'Some notes on the history of Tasmania', *JRAHS* 6, 1920, 245–62

Walker, G (ed), *The Aboriginal Photographs of Baldwin Spencer*, Melbourne 1987
Walker, JB, *Early Tasmania*, Hobart 1950
Walker, JB, 'The English at the Derwent...', *PPRSTas*, 1889a, 65–90
——, 'The founding of Hobart', *PPRSTas*, 1889b, 223–48
Walker, K et al, *Bidgee Bush*, Canberra 2001
Walker, MH, *Come Wind, Come Weather*, Melbourne 1971
[Walker, T], *A Month in the Bush of Australia* [1838], Adelaide 1965
Walpole, B et al, *Geology of the Katherine–Darwin Region*, Canberra 1968
Walsh, FJ, 'An ecological study of traditional Aboriginal use of "country": Martu in the Great and Little Sandy Deserts, WA' in DA Saunders et al (eds), *Australian Ecosystems (Proc Ecol Soc Aust 16)*, Sydney 1990, 23–37
——, 'Interactions between land management agencies and Australian Aboriginal people' in DA Saunders et al (eds), *Nature Conservation 4: The Role of Networks*, Sydney 1995, 84–106
Warburton, PE, 'Explorations by Major Egerton Warburton', *RGSA SA* 19, 1918, 109–18
——, *Journey Across the Western Interior of Australia* [1875], Adelaide 1968
Ward, D, 'Balga, boodja and measles', Native Solutions Conf, Hobart, July 2000a
——, 'Fire, flogging, measles and grass', CALM, Perth 1998
——, 'Trouble in the tuart', CALM, Perth 2000b
—— (comp), 'References to the grass *Themeda triandra* in S. Africa, India and Australia', ms, Perth 2001
—— & Sneeuwjagt, R, 'Believing the Balga', in D Gough (ed), *Fire. The Force of Life*, Perth 2000, 3–8
—— & van Didden, G, 'Reconstructing the fire history of the jarrah forest of south-western Australia', *Report to Environment Aust*, Perth 1997
—— et al, 'Grasstrees reveal contrasting fire regimes', *Forest Ecol and Management* 150, 2001, 323–9

Warren, C, 'Could First Fleet smallpox infect Aborigines?', *Ab Hist* 31, 2007, 152–63
Waterfield, JH, 'Extracts from the diary of Rev William Waterfield... Port Phillip, 1838–43', *Vic Hist Mag* 3, 1914, 105–27
Waterhouse, J (ed), *Edward Eyre's Autobiographical Narrative 1832–1839*, London 1984
Watts, D, *Tasmanian Mammals*, Hobart 1987
Waugh, D, *Three Years' Practical Experience... in NSW*, Edinburgh 1838
Weatherburn, AK, 'The exploration and surveys of James Meehan...', *JRAHS* 64, 1978, 167–81
Weatherstone, J, 'Lyndfield Park', Canberra 2003
Webb, EK, *Windows on Meteorology*, Canberra 1997
Webb, LJ, 'An historical interpretation of the grass balds of the Bunya Mountains, South Queensland', *Ecology* 45, 1964, 159–62
Webb, S, 'Intensification, population and social change in southeastern Australia: the skeletal evidence', *Ab Hist* 8, 1984, 154–72
Webster, J, *The Complete Bushfire Safety Book*, Sydney 2000
Webster, RH, *Currency Lad... Hamilton Hume*, Sydney 1982
Wells, FH, 'The habits, customs and ceremonies of the Aboriginals on the Diamentina, Herbert and Eleanor Rivers', *ProcAASS* 5, 1893, 515–22
Wells, SJ, 'Land and meaning', draft PhD chapter, Darwin 2001 c~ Sam Wells
——, *Town Camp or Homeland?*, Canberra 1995
Were, JB, *A Voyage from Plymouth to Melbourne in 1839*, Melbourne 1964
West, J, *The History of Tasmania* [1852], Adelaide 1966
Westgarth, W, *Australia Felix*, London 1848
Wettenhall, G, *The People of Gariwerd*, Melbourne 1999
[Wheelwright, HL], *Bush Wanderings of a Naturalist*, London 1864
White, HL, *Canberra, a Nation's Capital*, Sydney 1954

White, I, 'Dimensions of the Wiradjuri', ANU Prehist Bach L 1986
White, J, *Journal of a Voyage to NSW* [1790], Sydney 1962
White, ME, *After the Greening*, Sydney 1997
White, SA, 'The country traversed by the scientific expedition of Professor Edgeworth David to the Finke River', *RGSA SA* 24, 1923, 43–50
Widowson, H, *The Present State of VDL*, London 1829
Wilkinson, GB, *South Australia* [1848], Adelaide 1983
Willey, K, *When the Sky Fell Down*, Collins 1979
Williams, E, 'Complex hunter-gatherers: a view from Australia', *Antiquity* 61, 1987, 310–21
——, 'Documentation and archaeological investigation of an Aboriginal 'village' site in south western Victoria', *Ab Hist* 8, 1984, 21–44
——, 'The archaeology of lake systems in the middle Cooper Basin, north-eastern SA', *Rec SA Mus* 30, 1998, 69–91
Williams, M, *The Making of the South Australian Landscape*, London 1974
Williams, N, *The Yolngu and their Land*, Stanford 1986
—— & Baines, G, *Traditional Ecological Knowledge*, Canberra 1993
Williams, PR, 'The effect of fire regime on tropical savannahs of north-eastern Australia', JCU Env Sci PhD, 2002
Wills, W, *A Successful Exploration*, London 1863
Wilson, BA, 'The Open-Forest—"Treeless" Plains Boundary on Melville Island, Northern Territory', Tas Geog MSc 1991
Wilson, G, *Murray of Yarralumla*, Canberra 2001
Withnell, JG, *The Customs and Traditions of the Aboriginal Natives of North Western Australia* [1901], Adelaide 1965
Witt, GB et al, 'Is "vegetation thickening" occurring in Queensland's mulga lands', *AJBot* 57, 2009, 572–82
Wood, GA, 'Explorations under Governor Phillip', *JRAHS* 12, 1926, 1–26
Wood, P & Philpott, M (eds), *Brisbane and its River*, ANZAAS, Brisbane 1971
Woods, JD (ed), *The Native Tribes of South Australia*, Adelaide 1998
Woolmington, J, *Aborigines in Colonial Society*, Melbourne 1973
Worgan, GB, *Journal of a First Fleet Surgeon*, Sydney 1978
Worsley, PM, 'Totemism in a changing society', *Am Anth* 57, 1955, 851–61
Worsnop, T, *The Prehistoric Arts . . . of the Aborigines of Australia*, Adelaide 1897
Wright, J, *The Cry for the Dead*, Melbourne 1981
Wright, RVS (ed), *Stone Tools as Cultural Markers*, Canberra 1977
Wright, WD, *Canberra*, Sydney 1923
Wyndham, WT, 'The Aborigines of Australia', *JRSNSW* 23, 1889, 36–42
Yates, P, 'The Bush Foods Industry . . .', *Dialogue* 28 (2), 2009, 47–56
Yen, DE, 'Sahul agriculture and Australia', *Antiquity* 69, 1995, 831–47
Yibarbuk, D, 'Notes on traditional use of fire on upper Cadell River' in M Langton, *Burning Questions*, Darwin 1998, 1–6
—— et al, 'Fire ecology and Aboriginal land management in central Arnhem Land', *J Biogeog* 28, 2001, 325–43
Youl, R (ed), *Landcare in Victoria*, Melbourne 2006
Young, J, *Recent Journey of Exploration . . .* [1878], Melbourne 1978
Young, M (comp), *The Aboriginal People of the Monaro*, Sydney 2000

INDEX

Page references in *italics* are to illustrations.

'1788' 321
  definition xviii

Abbott, J 65
Aboriginal groups; *see also* place names
  Adnamatana 136
  Anungu 48, 50, 160, 168, 185
  Arrernte 170, 298
  Bagundji 150
  Cannemegal 244
  Dieri 149
  Guueu Yimithirr 36
  Kamilaroi 334
  Kurnai 323
  Larrakia 153, 273–5
  Martu 185, 295
  Ngarrindjeri 284
  Pintupi 54–6, 146, 178, 297
  Pitjantjatjara 160
  Tiwi 151
  Walpiri 150, 185
  Wiradjuri 136, 150, 228, 288
  Yanyuwa 184
Aborigines
  attitudes to
    country 139–54, 184–5, 216, 234–8 *passim*, 308, 326
    creation 123, 126–35, 145, 150, 211, 216, 281–2, 323
    Europeans 35, 124, 129–31, 246–7, 283, 300, 307–13
    land 71, 125–54 *passim*, 184–5, 196–8, 234–5, 238, 275, 288–97
    property 131–3, 142–3, 205, 209–10, 234–8, 246, 275, 283, 291, 294, 309

ceremonies 11, 124–61 *passim*, 178, 205–6, 234–79 *passim*, 295–8
knowledge 43, 55, 126–7, 133, 140, 153
  geographic 146–50, 236
  local 3–4, 48, 54–6, 135–7, 144–7, 198, 201, 263, 275, 288–92
  value of 132, 147–8, 201
land management 1–4, 27, 35–99, 114–38 *passim*, 147–50, 161–296 *passim*, 307–23 *passim*; *see also* associations; belts; clearings; clumps; crops; edges; farming; fire; grain; grazing; local moderators; parks; plants; mosaics; religion; storing; templates; totems; traps; tubers; yams
  influences city layout 239–40, 249, 280
  influences run selection 278–80, 307–8
mobility 152–3, 213, 236, 247, 279–81, 300–4, 310–11, 323
'no' principle 140–1
physique 152–3, 310
society xviii, 71, 124, 130–4, 150–1, 300–4, 310–11; *see also* families
  & ecology 133–4, 144–6
Tasmanian & mainland 20, 125, 212, 250
villages 194, 219, 253, 300–1
water management 106–7, 212–13, 226–32, 246, 282–3; *see also* dams; water; wells
words for fire 184–5
abundance 4, 38, 43, 59, 79, 88–9, 138, 151–3, 167, 188, 208, 213–15, 226–62 *passim*, 276–87 *passim*, 304–11 *passim*, 321
'abundant, convenient, predictable' 3–4, 75, 87, 146, 218, 275, 303–4, 323
acacia 13, 27–9, 39–40, 59, 75, 85–9, 114–15, 119–20, 169–94 *passim*, 208–26 *passim*, 240,

417

249–76 passim, 296, 316–17, 320, 332, 343; see also brigalow; gidgee; mulga
Adelaide district 41–2, 109, 112, 124, 135, 142, 159–60, 182–3, 239, 266–72, 287, 331
Adelaide River 193
Ainslie, J 280, 370
Albany 126, 140, 165, 178, 182, 235–8, 308–9
Albany Island 98–9, 233–4
Albury 41, 144, 148
Aldinga 41
Alice Springs district 56, 166; see also Centre
Allen, H 297
Allen, MR 319–20, 329
Alpha 194
Amata 56
Amity Point 255
Andrews, P 100, 220, 321
Angas, GF 41, 159, 199–200
Angaston 194
animals
 introduced 54, 126–7, 177, 218, 246, 256–67 passim, 281–300 passim, 308–17 passim
 native 80–1, 95, 100, 114, 147, 151, 167–8, 196–9, 211–18 passim, 262, 266–8, 285–8; see also bettongs; birds; dingos; extinctions; increases; kangaroos; koalas; possums; wallabies; wombats
aridity 112, 152
Armidale (NSW) 108
Arnhem Land 13, 16, 136, 144–5, 150, 161–5, 171–2, 175, 179, 207, 291, 300–2
art see paintings
Arthur's Seat 260
artists, accuracy 18–19, 39, 90
Aruabara 295
Ashwin, AC 295–6, 301
associations (plant) 11, 27, 35–87 passim, 113–14, 121–2, 181–213 passim, 226–80 passim, 341; see also templates
 definition xviii
Atkinson, J 169, 190
Austin, R 205
Australia
 character & dimensions 1, 320–1
 colour 34, 111, 320

one estate 1–2, 20, 124, 162, 275, 280, 304, 323; see also estate
Avon River 255
Ayers Range 194
Ayers Rock see Uluru

Backhouse, J 42, 65, 216, 236, 256–7, 262
Baijini 300
Bairnsdale 151
balds see clearings
Balonne River 222
Bangus Station 106
Banks, John 172, 326, 334
Banks, Joseph 5
banksia 7, 12, 29, 119, 122, 183, 208, 214, 217, 240, 251–78 passim, 315, 332
bans 131, 135–7, 211, 262, 283–4; see also sanctuaries
Barcoo River 191
Barellan 113
Bargo Brush 62
Barker, C 178, 237
Barnawartha 307
Barnett River 205
Barrallier, F 179, 181
Barrengarry Creek 232
Barrow, J 16
Barwon River 94–5, 148
Basedow, H 200
Bass, G 69, 227–8
Bateman's Bay 13
Bates, D 257
Batey, I 103, 290
Bathurst 188, 191, 201
Bathurst Falls 62
Bathurst Island 133
Batman, J 40, 192, 217, 259–65 passim
Batman's Hill 45, 263
Baudin, N 213
Beattie, JW 75
Beaufort 204
Bedwell, EP 18, 98–9
Bega 288
Beilby, BL 201, 226
Bellarine Peninsula 192
Bellenden Ker 205

INDEX

Bellingen 189
belts (tree) 47, 50, 57–9, 66, 80–7 *passim*, 94–7, 100, 199–203, 217, 223–5, 233–5, 254–78 *passim*
Ben Lomond 39
Bennett, G 177
Bennett, JF 16
Benson, JS & Redpath, PA 339–40
Berembed Station 320
Berkeley, M 41–2, 268
Berndt, R & C 284
Berridale 31–2
Berrima 62, 144, 197
Berry, A 132, 207, 300
bettongs 114, 262, 268
Big Heathy Swamp 221
Billilingra Hill 332
birds 17, 88–9, 125–6, 136, 151, 168, 178, 182–3, 196–214 *passim*, 226–7, 244–64 *passim*, 276–94 *passim*, 307, 320; *see also* emu; extinctions; galahs; increases
Birdsville 304
Birrell, WK 196–7
Black Gins' Lookout 94
Black Mountain (ACT) 277–9, 340
Black, N 183
Blackall 203
blady grass 35, 119, 167, 224, 233
Blainey, G 150, 302, 334
Blaxland, G 108
Blay, J 180
Bligh, W 112, 247
Blue Mountains 7, 72, 114, 117, 158–9, 188, 197, 207, 230, 286
Blue Tier 12, 67
Bogan River 44, 148, 159, 182
'Boldrewood, R' 288
Bolton, CF 319
Bong Bong 15, 62
Bontharambo Station 307
Boonah 66
Boort 189
bora grounds *see* ceremonies
Botany Bay 188, 241–6 *passim*
Boundary Dam 230
Bourke 104, 195

Bourke, R 261
Bowes, A *see* Smythe, AB
Bowman, D 170–1, 326–9
Boyd, B 319
bracken 119, 294
Bradley, W 240, 244–6
Brady's Sugarloaf 192
Branxholm 75–7, 84, 87
Bredbo 332
Bremer River 66
Breton, WH 88, 112, 121, 160, 316, 337
Brewarrina 282–3
brigalow 85–7, 113–14, 119, 204, 318
Brisbane district 72, 131–2, 152–3, 239, 250–5, 316
Brock, D 16–17, 293
Brodribb, W 202
Broken Hill 109
Broome 7
Browne, J 140
Browne, JH 231, 304
Bruny Island 117, 203, 206
brush *see* rainforest; scrub
Buchanan, A 16
Buckley, W 153, 214, 291
budda 87, 119, 122, 206, 317
buffel grass *see* plants, introduced
bulbs *see* tubers
Bulli Pass 117
Bulloo River 229
Bulmer, J 200
Bunbury 16, 140, 178
Bunbury, H 318, 332
Bundal 142
Bundaleer Station 85–7
Bundock, M 218
Bungin 181
bunya *see* pine
Bunya Mountains 9, 12, 70–2
Burdekin River 308
Burke & Wills 152, 286, 322
Burnie *see* Emu Bay
Burra (NSW) 276
Burra Creek 278
Burrows, N 54, 314–15
Burt Well 128–9

'bush' 14
bush tomato 129, 289, 295–7
bushfire 2–3, 17, 23–9, 48, 70, 99, 122, 157–65 *passim*, 242, 247, 319–20, 329–30
    definition xviii
Bussell, JC 11
Busselton 213
buttongrass 6, 13, 67–70, 119, 174, 331

Cairns 126, 166
callistemon 113, 270
Calvert's Plains 9
Cambridge Gulf 165
Cameron, P 58
Campaspe River 188
Campbell, R 280
Campbell, T 147
Camperdown (Vic) 191–2
Canambaigle 181
Canberra district 22–33 *passim*, 43–4, 117, 136, 157, 172, 275–80, 287, 310, 317, 333, 340
Canning River 257
Cape Byron 1
Cape Jervis 16
Cape Otway 213–14
Cape Tribulation 78
Cape York 1, 12, 78–80, 87, 98–9, 135, 153, 166, 170, 173, 184, 224, 232–5, 289–91, 300
Cardwell 238
Cardwell Range 209
Carnegie, D 54, 152, 284–5
Carrickalinga 41
Carron, W 94
Casterton 225
Castlereagh River 201, 296
casuarina 13, 29, 40–59 *passim*, 120, 163–8 *passim*, 192–201 *passim*, 213–19 *passim*, 227–9, 247–76 *passim*, 315, 332; *see also* drooping sheoak
cattle *see* animals
Cazneaux, H 30
central Australia *see* Centre
Centre 14, 17, 48–56, 83, 110, 122–35 *passim*, 151–76 *passim*, 191, 211, 285–8, 315, 321–2
ceremonies *see* Aborigines, ceremonies
Chapman, H 30, 142

Chauncey, PLS 65
Circular Head 197
Clark, R 241
Clarke, WB 198
Clause, F 64
clearings 5, 10–12, 36, 57, 68–99 *passim*, 133, 193, 205–77 *passim*, 224–77, 294; *see also* plains; plants, mosaics
Clermont 103, 170, 202
clumps 44, 58–67 *passim*, 76–97 *passim*, 193–229 *passim*, 259–77 *passim*, 286, 312, 318, 332
Cluny 18
coasts *see* water
Cobar 104
Cobon, JJ 78–80
Collins, D 241, 247–8, 258–9
Collins, W 38
Constitution Hill 57
Cook, J 5, 35–6, 94, 309, 339–40
Cooktown 5, 35–6, 340
Coolangatta 207
Coolbun 237
Cooma 332
Cooper's Creek 106, 112–13, 148, 152–3, 175, 286, 292, 301
copses *see* clumps
Costin, A 331–3
Cotton, J 104
Cowie Point 78–80
Cowpastures 142, 198, 225, 281
Coxen, C 296
Coxes Bight 125
Crook, WP 258
crops 288–98
Crystal Brook 214
Cudgegong River 223
culling 283–8, 322
cumbungi see reeds
Cunningham, A 18, 65–6, 88, 109, 152, 170, 177, 191, 197, 202–4, 218, 223, 251, 278–9
Cunningham, P 182, 338
Cunningham's Gap 204
Curr, E (Tas) 12, 206, 221–2
Curr, EM (Vic) 2, 12, 34, 108, 182–5, 207–8, 287, 294
Currie, M 103, 331–2

INDEX

Currockbilly 198
cycads 119, 131, 140, 161, 275, 294–7
cypress *see* pine

Daby 223
Daintree River 12
Dale, R 96–7
Dalrymple, JE 16, 205, 209, 238
Daly River 148–9
dams 160, 226–30 *passim*, 249, 282–3; *see also* Boundary Dam; wells
dances *see* ceremonies
Darke, WW 59
Darling Downs 202
Darling River 104, 110, 134, 137, 148–50, 204, 282–3, 292–3, 297–8
Darling Scarp 174
Darwin, C 97, 191, 247, 309
Darwin district 153, 239, 271–5
Davis, J 71
Dawson, J 140
Dawson, R 6, 14
Dawson River 9, 204, 311, 317, 331
Daylesford 215
de Wesselow, S 95
Deadman's Bay 69–70
Deddington 39
Deering Creek 227
Deloraine 75, 190
Deniliquin 105
Depot Glen 183
Derby (Tas) 203
Derby (WA) 56, 225
Derwent River 247–50
desert 152, 169, 173, 284, 296–9, 312; *see also* aridity; Great Sandy Desert
desert raisin 14, 122, 295
Diamantina River 230
Diamond, J 299, 303, 311
Diddleum Plain 221
dingos 182, 212, 282, 288, 297, 321
disease 150, 302–3, 311; *see also* smallpox
Docker, J 307
Dr Uredale 237
Domin, K 194
Donavon, D 78–80

Dongai Creek 224
Dorrigo 9
Dreaming xviii–xix, 56, 123–53 *passim*, 168, 172, 239, 273, 308, 311
 & ecology 132–7, 238, 255, 285–7, 302
Dredge, J 142
drooping sheoak 38, 41, 213–14, 270
drought 48–50, 107–15 *passim*, 150–2, 164, 285, 295, 298, 302
Drysdale, A 95
Dufresne, M 69
Dunkeld 227
Duntroon Station 280
D'Urville, D 182, 228
Dwyer, P 320–1

Earle, A 18, 68
Ebsworth, HT 15
Echuca 201
edges (plant) 9–12, 21, 35, 41–4, 54–67, 74–6, 91–4, 194–206 *passim*, 216, 250–2, 261, 275–8, 287, 318, 330–1, 339
Edward River 105, 285
eels 52, 131, 140, 198, 246, 257, 262, 276–85 *passim*, 300
Egan, T 128
Egloff, B 334
Ellen Brook 64–5, 256
Ellesmere Station 23–4
Ellis, RC 3, 12, 220–1, 326
Emerald 187
Emery, J 273
emu 83, 151, 168, 171, 191–227 *passim*, 249–50, 262, 277–88 *passim*, 307
Emu Bay 12, 82, 90, 206
Emu River 10
Encounter Bay 43
Endeavour River 35–6
Erldunda 208
Erudina Station 29–30
Escape Cliffs 272
estate, definition xix; *see also* Australia
eucalypts 12–40 *passim*, 48, 58–70 *passim*, 82, 112–21, 165, 171–2, 183, 190, 197–8, 203, 213–77 *passim*, 312–23 *passim*, 330–4, 343–4; *see also* eucalypt names

overtop rainforest 12–13, 65, 70, 80–3, 206, 221, 232
responses to
drought 29–30, 115–17
fire 21–31 *passim*, 115, 119–21
light 21–5, 118, 242, 249
Eungai Creek 82–3
Eunonyhareenya Station 285
Europeans
arrive 98, 152, 233–80 *passim*
attitudes to
Aborigines 2, 17, 40, 71, 97, 128–53 *passim*, 173–81 *passim*, 197–8, 235–55 *passim*, 271, 276, 281, 303–12 *passim*
farming 296–304, 320–1; *see also* storing
fire 3, 17, 31–2, 36, 48, 87, 108, 120–22, 157–77 *passim*, 187, 279, 294, 314–23 *passim*
land 4, 17–19, 44–50 *passim*, 80–5 *passim*, 95, 99–100, 188–9, 196–201, 208, 219–77 *passim*, 282, 297, 304–23 *passim*; *see also* grazing
'natural' landscape 2–3, 10, 27, 72, 137, 212, 228, 250–71 *passim*, 325–42
land management 54, 85–7, 99–122 *passim*, 218, 288, 313–23
Evans Bay 235
Evans, G 57–9, 62, 72, 90, 159, 188
Everett, J 108
extinctions 17, 56, 103, 111, 320; *see also* increases
Eyre, EJ 6, 10, 17, 82–5, 104–6, 141–52 *passim*, 172, 175–7, 196–215 *passim*, 231, 294, 298, 308
Eyre Peninsula 17, 286

Fairfax, R 72
Faithfull, G 307
families 71, 139–44, 150, 236–61 *passim*, 271, 275, 283, 308; *see also* Aborigines, land management; Aborigines, society
farming
Aboriginal 212–17 *passim*, 234, 281–304; *see also* Aborigines, land management; crops; fire, firestick farming; grain; tubers
non-Aboriginal 80, 98–100, 111, 129–30, 218, 242, 245, 281–2, 296–304, 311, 320–1

Fawkner, JP 259–60, 263
Fensham, R 72, 330, 336–40
Ferguson, WC 237–8
ferns 75, 207, 221–2, 227, 245, 252; *see also* bracken
Finke River 149, 284, 295
fire (1788) 10, 56, 89, 118–21, 137–8, 157–86, 203, 226–55, 271, 298–9, 312–13, 333; *see also* Aborigines, land management; bushfire; edges; lightning
as ally 2, 36, 119–22, 157, 161, 178, 184–6, 303, 326
as totem 128, 160–1
before rain, damp 46, 56–8, 157, 169–72, 176–8, 261, 295, 313
control 1–3, 11–13, 21–99, 109, 121–2, 133, 158–92 *passim*, 203, 211–21, 247, 268, 273, 295, 320
cool & hot *see* intensity
effect on
animals 1, 17, 56, 68, 76, 79, 167–79 *passim*, 192, 215–18, 282, 286, 312
plants 1–3, 11–14, 21–99, 109, 118–22, 157–76 *passim*, 194–5, 203, 213–35 *passim*, 247–58 *passim*, 273–94 *passim*, 312–19 *passim*
firestick farming 65, 83, 92–3, 163–85 *passim*, 203–22 *passim*, 260–1, 298, 327–8, 341
frequency 32–41 *passim*, 54, 79, 161–76 *passim*, 213–14, 235–42, 272, 275, 329–31, 339
intensity 13, 27, 52, 90, 122, 158–78 *passim*, 203, 216, 240, 314–15, 320
local 38, 48–62 *passim*, 82, 92, 97, 121–2, 164–75 *passim*, 232–8, 242, 275
mosaics, patches, patterns *see* plants, mosaics
purposes 2–4, 35, 54–99 *passim*, 161–212 *passim*, 234–6, 254–68 *passim*, 279, 313
timing 27, 52, 56, 70, 82, 92, 121–2, 162–79 *passim*, 208, 216, 247, 294, 320
in summer 160–78 *passim*, 236, 254, 260, 268, 279
fish 59, 79, 94, 106, 136, 151–2, 188–9, 212–14, 226–85 *passim*
Fish River (NSW) 59

INDEX

Fitzroy Falls (NSW) 232
Fitzroy River 205
Flannery, T 297, 339–41
Flemming, J 259
Flinders, M 69, 203, 247
Flinders Peak 46
Flinders River 222
Flood, J 297
floods 105–6, 112, 118, 150, 270, 322
Flood's Creek 109, 294
Forbes 57, 201
fords 62, 76, 106, 250–64 *passim*, 276–8
forest 13, 333–8 *passim*; *see also* trees
    closed, dense 6–8, 13, 43, 59–66 *passim*, 121, 171, 189–209 *passim*, 219, 240–4, 249, 261–87 *passim*, 315–20, 334–41
    definitions 337–8, 340
    on poor soil 6–8, 277–8
    open, grassy 5–23 *passim*, 39–48 *passim*, 59, 62–3, 78–88 *passim*, 121, 158–180 *passim*, 186–209 *passim*, 219–82 *passim*, 312–20 *passim*, 332–7 *passim*; *see also* belts; clumps; grass; parks
Forester River 286
Forrest, J 209, 288
Fort Point 272–3
Fortey, G 110, 195
Fowler's Bay 148, 199–200
Frankland, G 16
Franklin, J 43, 46, 110
Fraser, C 66, 131–2, 256
Fremantle 255
Frenchman's Cap 174, 203
Freycinet Peninsula 74
frost hollows 331–4
Furneaux, T 69
Fyans, F 147

galahs 199, 320
Gammage, JW 326
Ganmain 285
gardening *see* farming
Garling, F 44
Gatcomb Plain 80–4, 87, 220
Gawler 268
Geelong 95, 264

Gellibrand River 214
Georges River 129
Gerritsen, R 290
gidgee 85–7, 114, 122, 191, 195, 203
Gilbert, J 204
Giles, C 149, 295
Giles, E 17, 83, 100, 162–4, 169, 182, 194, 227–32
Gilmore, M 11, 284, 289, 311
Ginninderra Creek 43, 276–8
Gippsland 8, 112, 171–2, 180, 183, 226, 288, 315, 322–3, 341
Glen Helen 17
Glenelg 266–8
Glenelg River (Vic) 180, 207, 225, 314–15
Glenelg River (WA) 7
Glenorchy 249
Glover, J 18–19, 39–40
Goderich Plain 80
Gogy 181
Good, P 258
Goondal 181
Gooramon Ponds 276
Goorooyaroo 25
Gordon River 10, 180
Gosse, W 50–2
Gosse's Bluff 56
Gott, B 296–7, 326
Goulburn 151, 197
Goulburn Plain 8–9
Goulburn River (NSW) 10, 190
Goulburn River (Vic) 195, 284
Gould, R 142, 171–2
Govett, W 7–9, 68, 89, 151
Goyder, G 272–3
grain 289, 292–6, 304
Grampian Ranges 180, 294
grass *see also* clearings; fire; grass names; plains
    introduced 32–4, 50, 108–9, 313–14
    native 6–8, 14, 19, 32–5, 43, 57, 72, 84–5, 88, 107–11, 121–2, 167–229 *passim*, 247–78 *passim*, 313–20 *passim*, 332–3
    beside water 59–85 *passim*, 188–95 *passim*, 222–4, 232, 253–78 *passim*, 345
    corridors 91–5, 180, 199, 214; *see also* belts; paths

on good soil 6–9, 43–8 *passim*, 58–9, 65, 78, 97, 187–94, 201, 204, 215, 223–5, 241–3, 253–8, 275–9, 333
grass tree *see* xanthorrhoea
Grassy Hill 36, 340
Grassy Island 5
grazing 1, 17–19, 32–4, 54–6, 87, 103–19 *passim*, 316–17, 340; *see also* Aborigines, land management; Cowpastures
Great Australian Bight 200, 209
Great Lake 206
Great Sandy Desert 54–5, 149, 152, 304
Gregory, A 59, 131, 158, 292, 298
Gregory, F 170
grevillea 168, 274
Grey, G 73, 151, 177, 189–90, 214–17, 283–4, 289
Griffiths, C 262, 266
Grose Valley 207
Gulf of Carpentaria 161, 284, 294–6
Gundagai 7, 106
Gundaroo 8, 275
Gunn, R 183, 190, 313, 316
Gunning 100
Gurra 131
Gurrmanamana, F 144–5
Gwydir River 201, 204, 218–19

Hahn, D 43, 109, 287
Hall, C 180
Hallam, S 3, 65, 160, 173–4, 238, 326, 341
Hamilton, G 269–70
Hampshire Hills 16, 201, 221–2
Hann, F 205
Hardwicke, C 93, 151
Hardy, WM 84–5
Harris, G 249–50
Hartwig, M 298
Hastings River 15, 196
Hawdon, J 126–7, 201, 219, 269
Hawkesbury River 129–30, 245, 291
Hawkwood Station 318
Haydon, G 15, 225
Haygarth, H 7
Hazards Beach 74–5
heath 17, 75, 80–3, 93–4, 119, 168, 189–96 *passim*, 207, 213–14, 224–8, 241–3, 260, 331–2
Helena River 255
Helena Spring 284
Hellyer, H 11–12, 82, 151, 192, 201, 206, 223–4
Henderson, J 205, 208
Henry, E 222–3
Hepburn, J 215
Herbert, DA 71–2
Herbert River 126, 216
Herberton 205
herbs 9, 32, 59, 82, 109–11, 167, 170, 188, 215–17, 220, 240, 253–74 *passim*, 319–20
historians *see* Europeans
HMS *Beagle* 273
HMS *Endeavour* 5, 35
HMS *Fly* 235
HMS *Rattlesnake* 235
Hobart district 112, 117, 158, 218, 247–52
Hoddle, R 18, 22, 43–6, 89, 213–14, 232, 265, 276–9
Hodgkinson, C 82–3, 189, 196, 224, 254
honeysuckle *see* banksia
Hooker Creek 59
hopbush 13, 293
Horton, D 299, 329–30
Hovell, W 6, 148, 160, 175, 195, 202–4, 228, 310, 334
Howe, J 188
Howitt, Alfred 68, 105, 183, 206, 322–3, 341
Howitt, Annie 322
Howitt, R 266
Howitt, W 161–2
Hudspeth, J 16
Huggins, WJ 64
Hughenden 222
Hume, H 148, 195, 198, 204
hunter-gatherers 152–3, 218, 296–304, 320–1
Hunter, J 15, 129, 176, 179–80, 197, 244, 291
Hunter River 150, 188, 193, 201, 223
Hurley, F 75
husbandry *see* Aborigines, land management
Hutt River 214, 230, 289, 300

Ilbalintja 131
Illawarra 207, 330–1

INDEX

increases (animal, plant) 103, 183, 286–8, 315–22
Inkadunna Soak 231–2
Innisfail 197
insects 115, 136, 177, 181–3, 200, 211, 255–6, 294, 322, 346; *see also* increases
Ipswich 254
Irbmangkara 284
Isaacs, J 147–8

Jack, RL 170, 173, 224
Jackson, W 3, 11, 325–6, 331, 342
Jacottet, LJ 97
Jardine, J 233–4
Jeffreys, C 57
Jemelong Station 319
Jericho (Qld) 194
Jericho (Tas) 16, 23–4
Jerrabombera Creek 276–8
Jerry's Plains 188
Jervis Bay 182
Jimmy 307–8
Jindabyne 317
Jingo, J 54
Jones, R 3, 11, 294, 298–9, 326, 341
Juandah Station 318
Jugiong 106
Julia Creek 222

Kaberry, P 148, 302
Kadina (Hundred) 84–7
Kakadu 288–9
Kalgan River 97, 235–6
kangaroo grass 32–3, 108–13 *passim*, 121, 165–6, 191–2, 205, 215, 253–76 *passim*
Kangaroo Ground(s) 241, 266, 286
Kangaroo Island 13, 99–100, 266
Kangaroo Valley (NSW) 232
kangaroos 58, 73–94 *passim*, 135, 151, 177–9, 198, 203, 211–19, 227, 241–70 *passim*, 281–8 *passim*, 300–21 *passim*
Kantju 48–50
Katajuta 50–4, 231
Katoomba 207
Keen, I 296
Kelly, J 70, 153, 159

Kennedy, EB 213
Kerry, A 80
Kiama 17
Kimber, R 165, 167, 170, 286, 297
Kimberley 126, 140, 148–9, 178, 184, 193, 290, 302
King George Sound 96–7, 149, 187, 235–8
King George's Plains 249
King Parrot Creek 195
King, PG 336–8
King, PP 98, 165
King River (WA) 235
Kingston, G 270
Kintore 208
Kirkpatrick, J 326, 330
koalas 47, 128, 148, 197–9, 211, 260–2, 287–8
Kooweerup Swamp 227
Kosciuszko National Park 119, 341
Kraehenbuehl, D 331
Krefft, G 288
Kungathan 294
Kununurra 130
kurrajong 13, 113, 200

La Trobe, CJ 214
La Trobe River 202
Lachlan River 10, 104, 149, 168–70, 180, 191–3, 293, 318–20
Lake Amadeus 315
Lake Bathurst 103, 198
Lake Bronto 233
Lake Clarendon 202
Lake Condah 300
Lake Echo 309–10
Lake Eyre 17, 130, 149
Lake George 88–90, 103, 148, 275–8, 333
Lake Hindmarsh 201
Lake Mackay 284
Lake Narran 292–3
Lake Salvator 105
Lake Torrens 230–1
Lake Victoria (NSW) 17
Lake Waljeers 201
Lake Wicheura 233
Lambrigg Station 278
Lancey, J 263

land management *see* Aborigines; Europeans
Landsborough, W 203
Lang, JD 177, 223
Langton, M 341
Latz, P 3, 14, 157, 164, 176, 285, 296, 312, 326
Launceston district 37–8, 203
Law 2, 123–5, 131–5, 142, 154, 162, 285, 334
'lawns' *see* clearings
Lawson Plains 67
Le Soeuf, AH 151
Leichhardt, L 3, 9, 16, 32, 62, 106, 161, 173, 194, 202, 226, 265, 288, 317, 331, 336–9
Leigh River 225
Leigh, WH 16
Leven River 316
Lewes, H 106, 110
Lewin, J 37–8
Lewis, JW 17
Lewis, T 58
Leycester, A 209
Lhotsky, J 8, 332
Light, W 41, 267, 270–1
lightning 2, 13, 69–70
Lilitjukurba 146
Limestone Plains (ACT) 277
Lindsay, D 169, 173, 284
Lines, M 166
Lines, W 341
Lively's Bog 58
Liverpool Plains 190–1
'local moderators' 112, 169, 327–33, 339; *see also* rain; soil
Lockhart River 291
Lockyer, E 251–2, 255
Lockyer's Creek 193, 254
Loddon River 201–2
Logan, P 65, 132
Logan River 223
Longreach 317
Lord, E 39
Lord Howe Island 152
Louisa Bay 69
Love, JRB 178
Lumholtz, C 126, 216

Lunt, I 326
Lycett, J 18–19, 57, 62–3, 88–94, 243, 250
Lyndhurst (SA) 99–100

Maatsuyker Islands 69
Macarthur, E 245
Macarthur, J 122, 206
Macarthur, W 28
Macarthur's Crossing 62
Macassans 300
McBryde, I 130–1
McCubbin, F 19
McDermott family 218
MacDonnell Ranges 163, 182, 227, 315
McEntee, J & S 29–30, 136
Macintyre River 109
Mackenzie River 59
McKinlay, J 222
Maclaine Plains 201
McLaren, G 326
McLaughton, J 280
Macleay River 207, 224
McMillan, A 151
McPherson Range 12
Macquarie Harbour 159
Macquarie, L 15, 18, 57, 62–3, 88–90, 201
Macquarie Plains 201, 249
Macquarie River 109, 177, 191–3, 205
McRae River 205
Maffra 202
Maiden, J 9
Major's Line 103
mallee 10, 26, 82–5, 113–20 *passim*, 163, 180, 191–209 *passim*, 226–31 *passim*, 267–70 *passim*, 294
Malthus, TR 152, 298
Mandi 130
mangroves 78, 240, 246, 259–75 *passim*
Manilla 201
manna 200, 261, 294
Mannalargenna 58, 137–8, 216
Manning River 197
Mannum 208
Maragnan 237
Maranoa River 168
Maribyrnong River 110, 259, 264–5

INDEX

Marks, G 9
Marrngawi, D 184
Marsh, M 310
Martin, J 225
Mary River (NT) 282
Mary River (Qld) 70
Mathew, J 92
Mathews, RH 205–6, 283
Mathinna 220
Maurice, R 152
Mayne, WC 282–3
Meehan, J 62, 249
Meggitt, M 132
melaleuca 119, 168, 189, 202, 210, 226–43 *passim*, 259–72 *passim*, 333
Melbourne district 45–6, 135, 150, 153, 239, 258–66, 290
Melville Island 272, 330
Menge, J 168, 182
Merrewah 205
Merrilees, D 3
Mew River 235
Micalong Swamp 334
Michelago 8, 276, 332–3
Midgegooroo 141
Mildura 11
Milkshake Hills 67
Mills, K 330–1
Milner Point 94
Milparinka 296
Mitchell River 336
Mitchell, TL 3, 16, 103–5, 109, 148, 158–9, 168–89 *passim*, 215–25 *passim*, 290–3, 298, 312–13, 316, 337–8
Mittagong 63
Moama 106
Moira Station 110
Mokare 237–8
Mollison, A 307
Mollison, W 220
Molonga *see* ceremonies
Molonglo River 276–9
Monaro 148, 331–3
Moorabool River 59
Moore, G 16, 96, 141–2, 148–9, 208
Moore, JJ 279

Moree 218–19
Moreton Bay 66, 92–3, 147, 152, 250
Morphett, J 16, 271
Morrill, J 291–2, 308
Mortlock River 110
Morton, WL 59, 107–8
mosaics *see* plants, mosaics
Mt Abrupt 59
Mt Ainslie 277–9
Mt Alexander 15, 202, 219
Mt Barker (SA) 16
Mt Barney 65–6
Mt Barren 198
Mt Bryan 117, 205, 208
Mt Charlotte 295
Mt Clarence 96
Mt Conner 54
Mt Eccles 46–7
Mt Field National Park 12, 67
Mt Gambier 290
Mt Gosse 152
Mt King William 174
Mt Kintore 173, 200
Mt Kosciuszko 119, 341
Mt Leura 192
Mt Liebig 297
Mt Lindesay 65–6
Mt Lofty 41–3, 267–70
Mt Macedon 45–6, 110–12, 219
Mt Majura 277–8
Mt Maurice 221
Mt Mowbullan 70–2
Mt Pleasant 277–8
Mt Rumney 247
Mt Serle 208
Mt Tennant 43–4, 278
Mt Terrible 43
Mt Townsend 18
Mt Towrang 197
Mt Warning 209
Mt Wellington 247–9
Mt William (Tas) 203
Mt William (Vic) 283, 300
Mt Yarrahapinni 287
mountain ash 21–2, 115–20 *passim*, 165–6, 180, 262

mountain pepper 29
Mountford, C 52–4
Mowle Plains 223
Mudgeegonga 72–3
mulga 50–6, 85–7, 112–22 *passim*, 136, 164–5, 194, 200, 208, 230
Mungery West Station 320
Murchison River 230, 288
murnong see yams
Murray, RD 161
Murray River 2, 10–11, 16, 104–10 *passim*, 126, 148–50, 158, 195, 209, 267, 285–8, 311
Murray, WR 48, 51, 152, 168, 287
Murrumbidgee River 8–10, 106, 118, 148, 151, 180, 193–4, 226, 276–8, 285, 311, 320, 332
Musgrave Ranges 52
music *see* ceremonies
Mutitjulu 48
Mypunga (Myponga) 43

Nagle, J 240
Nakinah 237
Nambucca R 196
Namoi River 158
nardoo 226
Nares, GS 5
Narragan 223
Narran River 109, 293
Narrandera 106, 135, 165, 226, 132
Nash, D 297
Natimuk 201
nets 132, 179, 282
nettles 75
New England 141, 175–6
New Norcia 140
New Norfolk 249
New South Wales 10, 15, 106–17 *passim*, 132–53 *passim*, 177, 201–7 *passim*, 218, 287–8, 296–8, 310, 316–20, 329; *see also* place names; New England; Riverina
Newcastle 91–3
Newcastle Waters 195, 295–6
Newsome, A 135
newspapers, quoted 159–60, 308–9
Nind, IS 165, 236–7
Ninganga, I 184

Nix, H 326
Noble, J 114, 317, 326
Nogoa River 105
non-Aborigines *see* Europeans
Norris, EH et al 334–6
Northam 205
Northern Territory 144–6, 257; *see also* Arnhem Land; Centre; place names; Top End
Norton, A 317–18
Norton, BE 287
Nullarbor Plain 149
Nullinan 198
Nunn, J & R 99–100
Nursery Swamp 333–4
Nymagee Station 319

O'Connor Ridge 277–9
Olga Ranges *see* Katajuta
Omeo 7–8, 148
One Tree Hill (Brisbane) 72
Onkaparinga district 40–3
Ooldea 168, 208, 229–30
Oranmeir 198
Orroral Valley 29–30, 333–4
Ouse River 206
Ovens River 195, 310
Oxley, J 15, 44, 57, 62–3, 88, 104–6, 139, 168, 180, 190–1, 196, 207, 251–5 *passim*, 286, 312, 317
Oyster Bay 96, 125

Page, E 103
paintings 18–20, 73, 138; *see also* artists; artist names
A break away! 34
A panoramic view of King George's Sound 96, 95–7
A view of the Endeavour River 35, 35–6
A view of the Snowy Bluff 68, 68
Aborigines hunting kangaroos 91, 91
Aborigines spearing fish 93, 93–4
Aborigines using fire 92, 92–3
Adelaide and St Vincent's Gulf 349
Batman's Lookout 40
Bulli from the Coal Cliffs 93
Captain Stirling's exploring party 64, 64–5

INDEX

Crater of Mt Eccles 47, 46–7
Down on his luck 19
Encampment at the head of the river 64
Entrance to the gorge of Yankalillah 41
Fall of the first creek near Glen Osmond 349
Ginninginderry Plains 44, 43–4
Golden Summer 34, 33–4
Govett's Leap 68
Halt near a fern tree scrub 83
King George's Sound, view from Peak Head 97
Mills' Plains 19, 39, 39–40
Mount Lindesay 66, 65–6
Mount Lofty 42
Mount Lofty from the Terrace 42, 41–3
My harvest home 39
Near Heidelberg 34
North-east view from the top of Mt Kosciusko 18
Onkaparinga 40, 40–1
Somerset 97, 97–8
Spring in the valley of the Mitta Mitta 59
Sydney Heads 243
The cataract near Launceston 38
The River Barwon 94, 94–5
The River Derwent and Hobart Town 19
The second cataract on the North Esk 37, 37–8
The sources of the River Wannon 60, 59–62
The Table Mountain 250
View at Yankalillah 41
View from Batman's Hill 46
View from Melbourne 45, 45–6
View from near the top of Constitution Hill 57, 57
View from the bald hills 46
View in the Kangaroo Valley 232
View of Lake George 18–19, 88, 88–90
View of Moroit or Tower Hill 18
View of Tasman's Peak 57
View of the Heads 243
View on Lake Patterson 62
View on the Glenelg Plains 42
View on the Wingecarrabee River 63, 62–3
Vue de Port du Roi Georges 97
Waterfall in Australia 68

Palmerston, C 12, 79–80, 197, 205
palms 111, 196, 207–9, 224–40 *passim*, 252, 272–4, 294
Papua New Guinea 149, 234, 311, 320–1
Parachilna 149
Paradise Plains 220, 364
Parish, S 74–5
Parker, E 308
Parkinson, S 5, 35–6
parks 5–18 *passim*, 39–46 *passim*, 59, 62, 95, 113, 137, 161–71 *passim*, 188–204 *passim*, 215–90 *passim*, 307–8, 332
Parramatta 15, 181–3, 244–5
patches *see* clearings; clumps; plants, mosaics; templates
Paterson, W 38
paths 180–1, 198–214 *passim*, 224, 228, 238, 244, 251, 289, 341
patterns *see* plants, mosaics
Patterson, JH 59
Peak Hill 44
Peel's Range 180
Pemulwuy 129
Peron, F 158–9, 181–2, 244, 247–50
Perry, SA 15
Perry, TM 9
Perth district 16, 141, 148–9, 185, 200, 208, 236, 239, 255–8
Peter, J 110
Petermann Ranges 17
Peterson, N 150
Phillip, A 129, 187, 241–4
photographs 21–89 *passim*, 99–100
Pialligo 277
Pigeon House Mountain 198
Pilbara 114
Pilliga 317, 334–5, 339
pine 38, 119, 205–9 *passim*, 225–6, 267–8, 273
    araucaria, bunya 66, 70–1, 140, 251–5, 289, 295
    cypress 13, 85–7, 122, 317–20, 335–7
plains 8–10, 15, 43–6, 57–85 *passim*, 93–6, 174–5, 187–235 *passim*, 249–79 *passim*, 312, 331–3, 338; *see also* clearings
    definitions 338

plants
 introduced 32–4, 50, 111, 114, 321
 native 111–12, 167, 288, 343–5; *see also*
  associations; belts; clearings; clumps; crops;
  fire; forest; grain; grass; local moderators;
  plant & genus names; rainforest; templates;
  trees; tubers
  as historians 19–31, 118
  mosaics 2–14 *passim*, 35–100, 160–85
   passim, 205–38 *passim*, 250–80
   passim, 314–15, 319, 329–35; *see also*
   associations; templates
  similar across Australia 172–5
  regeneration 315–22, 333–4; *see also*
   trees
platypus 80, 136–7, 262, 270, 276
Point Brown 231
Point Elliot 272–3
Point Emery 272–4
Polo Creek 233
Poor feller my country 128
population
 Aboriginal 150–1, 288–9, 298, 303–4, 311
 non-Aboriginal 107, 299, 303, 311, 321
porpoises 132, 147
Port Adelaide 267–8
Port Augusta 126
Port Essington 207, 272
Port Hedland 170
Port Jackson 241–4
Port Lincoln 163
Port Noarlunga South 40
Port Phillip *see* Melbourne
Port Stephens 6, 14–15, 288
possums 95–100 *passim*, 151, 167–8, 175, 183,
 196–9, 211, 215, 224, 260–70 *passim*, 284,
 287–8, 300
Powell, M xix
Powlett, TS 308
Precipitous Bluff 69–70
predators 1, 56, 212, 303
Price, J 197
Prion Bay 69
prohibitions *see* bans
Prout, JS 94–5
Pryor, L 333

Puntutjarpa 142
Purrar Point 69
Purula, WS 170
Purvis, R 321–2
Pylebung 229
Pyne, S 328

Queanbeyan 276, 291–2
Queanbeyan River 276–9
Queensland 10, 16, 133, 141, 163, 166–7, 180,
 194–210 *passim*, 287–92 *passim*, 310, 336–9;
 see also place names
Quorn 114
Quoy, J 158, 182

Raffles Bay 272
rain 1, 48–54 *passim*, 104–12 *passim*, 175,
 330–1; *see also* fire, before rain
rainforest 6, 11–13, 58–83 *passim*, 98–9, 121,
 174–5, 189, 197–7, 209–10, 220–35 *passim*,
 249–55, 272–5, 288, 316, 331, 337
Rams Head Range 27, 341
Rapid Bay 41
Read, J 331
Redhead Bluff 93
Reedbeds (Adelaide) 268–70
reeds 106, 176, 180, 208, 215, 228, 261–77
 passim, 294
regeneration *see under* plants; trees
religion (1788) 4, 123–38, 148–53, 207, 212,
 281, 298–312 *passim; see also* ceremonies;
 Dreaming; knowledge; Law; songlines; soul;
 totems
 & ecology 132–7, 145–6, 302
reptiles 56, 168, 174, 182, 196, 211, 236, 257,
 278, 288
researchers *see* Europeans
Richardson, – 99
Riche, C 158
Richmond (NSW) 209
Riley, WE 88
Ringarooma River 75–7, 221
Risdon 248–50, 257
ritual *see* Aborigines, ceremonies; religion
river red gum 29–30, 113, 116–17, 270
Riverina 111, 226, 288

INDEX

rivers *see* river names
    shallow 43, 104–6, 198, 239, 250, 257–8, 268–70, 276–9; *see also* fords
roads *see* paths
Roberts, T 34
Robertson, J 313–14
Robinson, GA 58, 76, 80–2, 125, 137–49 *passim*, 171, 192–227 *passim*, 283–90 *passim*, 332
Rockhampton 59, 126
Rockingham Bay 213
Roe, – 197
Rogers, JC 171–2
Rolls, E 3, 288, 316–17, 326, 334–5, 339
Roper River 136, 226
Rose, D 145–6
'Rose Hillers' 244
Ross, J 158, 250, 309–10
Roth, W 149
Rothery, FM 85–7
Rubuntja, W 128–9
Russell, G 191–2
Russell, W 225
Ryan, DG et al 339–40
Rylstone 223
Ryrie, S 27, 332, 341

St George 16
St Helens 58
St Leonards 142
St Valentine's Peak 151
salt 110–11, 255, 314
saltbush 85–7, 103–4, 110–11, 267
Salt River *see* Mortlock River
Saltwater River *see* Maribyrnong River
sanctuaries 89, 151, 200, 211, 283–5; *see also* bans
Schmidt, W 310
Schurmann, C 142
scientists *see* Europeans
Scott, J 75–7
Scott, JR 75
Scott, L 166–7
Scott, Theodore 41
Scott, Thomas 75
Scott, W 75

Scottsdale 21–2
scrub 9–10, 43–66 *passim*, 85–7, 120–2, 146, 171–214 *passim*, 224–40 *passim*, 249, 259, 276, 315–17, 336–7; *see also* Pilliga
    definitions 336–7
sea *see* water
Seddon, G 331, 341
sedentism 153, 299–304; *see also* Aborigines, mobility
Serra Range 59
Seven Emu River 288
Seven Emu Station 317
Shannon River 158
Shark Bay 1
Sharland, W 169–70, 180–1
Shaw, B 130
Shaw, W 16
sheep *see* animals
Shelford 225
shellfish *see* fish
sheoak *see* casuarina
Shoalhaven River 148, 198, 207, 300
Sholl, RJ 7, 205
shrubs *see* scrub
Simpson, S 70–1, 310
Singleton, FC 169
Skipper, JM 40–2
smallpox 153–4, 311, 326
Smith, CT 275–9
Smokers Flat 333
Smyth, AB 240–2
Smyth, D 18
Smyth, RB 143
Smythe, GD 213
Snell, E 41, 94
snow gum 26–7
Snowy Bluff 68
Snowy Mountains 27, 180
Snowy Range (Tas) 117
Snowy River 105
soil 9, 47–72 *passim*, 84–7, 103–16 *passim*, 183, 214, 219–20, 257, 264, 268, 312–31 *passim*
Somerset 98–9, 148–9, 232–5
songlines 125–6, 135–6
songs *see* ceremonies

431

soul 125–38 *passim*, 146, 281
South Alligator River 284
South Australia 16, 82, 85, 153, 168, 199–200, 205, 231, 257; *see also* Centre; place names
South Esk River 38
Southeast Cape 1
Southwell, D 243
Spencer, B 48–52
spinifex 14, 48–56 *passim*, 115–22 *passim*, 163, 167–9, 185, 200, 222
SS *Llewellyn* 98
Staaten River 202
Stanner, W 143
Stapylton, G 225
Stirling, J 64–5, 255–7
Stokes, JL 166, 205, 229
storing 153, 246–7, 295–302, 311
Storm Bay 248
Strawberry Hill (WA) 96
Streaky Bay 231
Streeton, A 33–4
Strehlow, TGH 123–5, 131, 146, 284, 341
Strutt, C 106
Stuart, JM 169, 195
Sturt, C 7–9, 17, 43, 106–13 *passim*, 148, 152–3, 158, 180–3, 194, 230–1, 293–304 *passim*, 312, 315
Sturt, EPS 151
Styx River 12, 67
Success Hill 257
Sugarloaf 198
Sullivan's Creek 276–8
Sunbury 290
Surrey Hills (Tas) 80, 82, 201
survey plans 19, 76, 78, 79, 84, 86, 75–87 *passim*, 196
Sutton, P 135, 195, 326
Suttor, WH 293
swamp gum *see* mountain ash
swamps 76–8, 206, 215, 224–77 *passim*, 285
Swan Bay (Vic) 217
Swan Hill (Vic) 151
Swan Island (Tas) 137
Swan River 64–5, 255–7, 290, 300
Swans Hill (Tas) 57
sweet pittosporum 112, 120

Sydney district 45, 113, 122, 129, 141–2, 152, 167–87 *passim*, 239–47, 250, 286–7, 316–17

Talbragar River 15
Tallarook 204
Tam O'Shanter Point 94
Tambo 217
Tamworth (NSW) 287
Tank Stream 239–40, 249, 252
Tarkine 12
Tasman, A 6, 247
Tasmania 10–11, 16, 40, 67–94 *passim*, 112–25 *passim*, 135–58 *passim*, 169–222 *passim*, 259, 301–31 *passim*; *see also* place names
Taylor, J 57, 62
tea-tree *see* melaleuca
templates 35–8, 47, 58–99 *passim*, 198, 210–93 *passim*, 300, 307–8, 321–2, 334; *see also* associations
  definition xix, 211
  moved 220–2
Tench, W 153, 241, 245
terra nullius see wilderness
Therry, R 147
Thomas, I 3, 20, 159, 220–1, 326
Thomas, JA 42
Thomas, M 266
Thomas, W 128
Thomson, D 179, 301
Thredbo 26–7
Throsby, C 232
Throsby Park 15
Tibooburra 229
Tietkins, WH 48, 173, 208
Tomghin 148–9
Tooalla 210
Toolondo 283
Toonda 148
'Toongabie' 245
Top End 153, 171–3
Torrens River 105, 268–71
Torres Strait 98, 149, 300
totems 125–39 *passim*, 150, 212, 257, 270–1, 281–4, 294, 303–4
Tower Hill 18

INDEX

Townsend, T 27, 59, 106
tracks *see* paths
trade 129, 149–50, 180, 257, 262, 295–6, 300
traps 38, 47, 58, 72–92 *passim*, 110–11, 179, 218, 233, 243–64 *passim*, 274, 282–3, 334; *see also* dams; nets
trees 5–10 *passim*, 39, 62–86 *passim*, 183, 187, 242, 320, 328, 344; *see also* belts; clumps; forest; plants; tree & genus names
    bridges 10–11
    invade grass after 1788 5–12 *passim*, 23–7, 36–72 *passim*, 80–99 *passim*, 118, 181, 191–224 *passim*, 234–5, 247, 266–79 *passim*, 315–41 *passim*; *see also* plants, regeneration
    lanes, lines 11, 35, 41–7 *passim*, 65; *see also* belts
    on poor soil 190–3, 273–5
tubers 14, 90, 119–21, 167–9, 176, 220, 232, 257, 278, 289–99 *passim*, 308
Tuckey, J 258
Tumut 148
Turnbull, H 187, 202
Turner, F 293–4
Turner, J 256
tussock grass 6, 22–4, 32–4, 82, 107–19 *passim*, 216–18, 257–68 *passim*, 314, 317, 333; *see also* kangaroo grass
Twofold Bay 148, 180
Tyers, CJ 59

Udaaduck 198
Uluru 48–54, 126
Unaipon, D 137
undergrowth *see* forest

Valley of Lagoons 16
van Kempen, E 319
Vancouver, G 187
Vanderwal, R 329–30
Vasse River 213
VDL Coy 80, 142, 313–14
vegetation *see* fire; forest; grass; heath; mangroves; plants; plant & genus names; rainforest; reeds; scrub; trees
Venus Bay 171

Victoria 10, 15, 68–73 *passim*, 103, 108, 140–214 *passim*, 226–9, 283–94 *passim*, 308; *see also* place names
vine brush *see* rainforest; scrub
Vlamingh, W 255
von Guerard, E 18, 46–8, 59–61, 68, 243
von Hugel, C 8, 28
von Mueller, F 322, 328

Wade, H 251
Wadja Plain 317
Wagga Wagga 10, 136, 285
Wagin 207
Wakefield, J 97
Walcha 15
Walker, K 341
Walker, T 8, 188, 219
wallabies 58, 72–82 *passim*, 157–78 *passim*, 199–217 *passim*, 236–8, 248, 288; *see also* kangaroos
Wallajar 80
Wallan 202
Wallanippie 200
Wallis, J 18, 91
Walsh, F 295
Wandle River 80
Wannon River 59–61, 180, 313–14
Warburton 142
Warburton, PE 17, 209
Ward, D 174
Warman Rocks 208
warran see yams
Warrego River 85
water 103–11 *passim*, 147, 208, 222–45 *passim*, 266, 322; *see also* creek, lake, river names; floods; rain; rivers; swamps
    changes since 1788 104–7; *see also* rivers
Waterhouse, H 281–2
wattle *see* acacia
Waugh, D 338
Wearyann River 161
Weatherstone, J 100
Wedge, J 142, 170, 206, 264
weirs *see* dams
Weld 67
wells 199–201, 208, 214, 226–35, 255, 284, 289

433

Wells, L 163, 169
Wentworth Falls 68
Wentworth, WC 314
Werribee River 59
Westall, W 97
Western Australia 10, 16, 73, 97, 142, 158–90 *passim*, 205, 288, 315, 318; *see also* Kimberley; place names
Westernport 128, 165, 227–9, 300
Westmacott, RM 93, 232
Weston Creek 278–9
Wetherall, FA 228
White, E 248
white grass *see* tussock grass
Whitsunday Islands 5
Wild, J 18, 88–90
wilderness 2, 15, 130–1, 143–4, 162, 184–5, 197, 234–5, 309, 320–3, 341
wildfire *see* bushfire
Wilkes, C 338
Williams, M 85
Willunga 41
Wilpena Creek 29–30
Wilson, BA 330
Wilson, JB 15
Wilson, John 197–8
Wilson, WCB 232–4
Wineglass Bay 74–5
Wingecarribee River 62–3, 197
Winter, T 262
Wollaston, J 308
Wollongong 207

wombats 197–9, 206, 212, 260–2, 288
Wonnangatta River 68
Woodgreen Station 331–2
Woolshed Creek (ACT) 278–9
Worgan, G 241–6
Worsnop, T 230–1
Wright, B & J 316
Wright, J 317, 341
wukay see yams
Wynbring 7, 208

xanthorrhoea 90, 96–7, 119, 132, 243, 253, 257, 294

Yagan 141–2
Yali 311
yams 65, 90, 98, 109, 129, 133, 163, 166, 202, 234, 245–304 *passim*
    murnong 46, 111, 119, 214–15, 260–1, 277, 290–1, 294
    warran 214–15, 289–90, 300, 308
    wukay 80, 291
Yarralumla Station 278–80
Yarra River 116, 258–66 *passim*, 286
Yarrawa Brush 330–1
Yass 276, 333
Yelvertoft Station 31
Yen, DE 299–300
Yibarbuk, D 175, 184
Yorke Peninsula 84–5
Young, F 56

Other books by Bill Gammage

The Broken Years: Australian Soldiers in the Great War
An Australian in World War I
Narrandera Shire
The Sky Travellers: Journeys in New Guinea 1938–1939

Co-authored:

The Story of Gallipoli

Co-edited:

Australians 1938
Crown or Country: The Traditions of Australian Republicanism
Hail and Farewell: Letters from Two Brothers Killed in France in 1916
Six Bob a Day Tourist